PP&L

75 YEARS OF POWERING THE FUTURE

An Illustrated History of Pennsylvania Power & Light Co.

by Bill Beck

FIRST EDITION

Published by Pennsylvania Power and Light Co.
Copyright © 1995 by Pennsylvania Power and Light Co.
Design and Production by
Westmoreland Larson Webster Inc., Duluth, MN 55802
Cover Illustration by Jim Butcher, Bel Air, MD 21015

Library of Congress Catalog Card
95-67810

International Standard Book Number
Hardcover 0-9645915-0-2
Softcover 0-9645915-1-0

Printed in the United States of America by
Viking Press Inc., Eden Prairie, Minnesota

Foreword

In the midst of the most extensive restructuring we have ever undergone at PP&L, it is somehow fitting that we take a moment in our 75th year of operations to pay tribute to those who have faced the immense changes of the past.

PP&L: 75 Years of Powering the Future is a record of the tremendous change that our company has dealt with in the three-quarters of a century since a group of shareholders, entrepreneurs and investors sat down at a board table here in Allentown on a hot June day in 1920 and set Pennsylvania Power & Light Co. into motion as a modern corporation.

It is an exciting story, replete with examples of how our predecessors built the company from the ground up out of a diversified group of small-town utilities in the 1920s. Those who went before us kept the lights shining for central eastern Pennsylvania through the breakup of the holding companies and the Great Depression of the 1930s; through the supply and manpower shortages of World War II; through the dramatic postwar construction boom in the 1950s and 1960s; through the energy crisis of the 1970s; through the struggle to get our Susquehanna nuclear plant completed and in commercial operation in the 1970s and 1980s; and through the immense changes posed by deregulation and competition in the 1990s.

It is first and foremost a story of people, with a heavy emphasis on the de facto leadership provided to this organization by the middle-level people and the workers at all levels of the company. That de facto leadership brought us through all kinds of crises during the past 75 years, whether it involved the flood of 1936, the ice storm of 1948, the 1967 blackout, Tropical Storm Agnes, Three Mile Island and its aftermath, or the brutal winter of 1994.

You'll find their stories in this book. You won't find a litany of how this company merged with that company or a litany of the oil paintings on the wall of some former board chairman. You'll read about some of the legendary people of PP&L, from Edward Kimball Hall to John S. Wise Jr. to Chas. E. Oakes to Jack Busby, Bob Campbell and John Kauffman and the challenges they faced that seemed equally as daunting then as the challenges we face today.

One of the things that I like to do is go around to our various field locations and shoot the breeze with the people. I'll typically talk to 40 or 50 people, and I like to have a roundtable discussion at lunch. I try to be there around 3 p.m. when the linemen are coming in off their shift.

Recently, one lineman at our West Shore crew quarters was talking with me about some of the changes being brought about as a result of the National Energy Policy Act of 1992. He told me that he'd "had enough of this woe is me." And I thought, "You're absolutely right. I've had enough of this woe is me myself."

There in a nutshell is the real benefit of this history of PP&L. It gives all of us at PP&L a standard of personal excellence that those who have gone before us have lived up to in the past.

William F. Hecht
Allentown, Pennsylvania
February 20, 1995

Acknowledgments

As a writer for more than two decades now, I'm rarely accused of being at a loss for words. However, completion of a project like *PP&L: 75 Years of Powering the Future* is always a time for personal reflection on just how insignificant my role is in such an undertaking.

It was nearly three years ago when Jim Marsh of the PP&L Corporate Communications Department called and asked if I could meet with the company's 75th Anniversary Steering Committee. Nearly a thousand days later, a manuscript of more than 750 typewritten pages goes to the printer. Along the way, a cast of hundreds contributed to the innumerable details that made this book a reality.

Support for the project came right from the top. Bill Hecht had a vision encompassing the lessons history can teach us about the past, the present and the future. At a time when PP&L was undergoing the most extensive restructuring in its history, Hecht gave unstintingly of his valuable time for lengthy interviews. His clear, concise explanations of PP&L's more recent history contributed immeasurably to my understanding of the complex events of the past five years.

John Kauffman, Hecht's predecessor, and the person who first proposed this history book, sat in on my initial meeting with the 75th Anniversary Steering Committee almost three years ago. His presence was an indication of the importance that top management ascribed to the project. His willingness to sit down in front of a tape recorder was invaluable to a clear understanding of how PP&L has transformed itself in the 45 years he has been associated with the company and its predecessors.

Jack Busby is unquestionably one of the more intriguing personalities of the American electric utility industry's past half-century. Busby's insights about the electric utility industry today are as valid as when he joined PP&L as an attorney almost 50 years ago. Jack Busby opened his North Carolina home for two days in the fall of 1992 and held forth on the history of the electric utility industry in Pennsylvania, the Mid-Atlantic states and the nation. My only regret was that I couldn't take him up on his offer to play the courses of his beloved Pinehurst.

LoisAnn Oakes has kept the memory of her father, Chas. E. Oakes, alive and vibrant. During several lengthy interviews, she was able to provide both memories and mementos of PP&L's third president. She was instrumental in explaining the critical period in which PP&L was spun out from the Electric Bond and Share Co. and embarked upon its ambitious—and successful—postwar construction program.

For three years, LoisAnn has served on the company's 75th Anniversary Steering Committee. The committee is an indication of just how thoroughly PP&L approaches all its projects. The suggestions and recommendations of committee members were always welcomed. John Biggar, Dorothy Eyer, Roger Gilbert, Robert Gombos, Jim Marsh, LoisAnn Oakes, Janice Osborne, Donald Simmons, Bernie Steber and John Trimble gave freely of their time to review chapters and give their input about PP&L's corporate culture and history.

Roger Gilbert shared his collection of electric railway materials. Janice Osborne facilitated the search for historical materials in the Robert Campbell and John Kauffman files. Bernie Steber, who wrote much of the first rough draft of PP&L's history with his articles in the *PP&L Reporter* and *PP&L Today*, made sure that many of the important materials he cleaned out of his desk upon retirement made their way to the PP&L history files.

Without Jim Marsh, the project would never have happened. Jim shepherded the history through the innumerable hoops that a project of this magnitude inevitably entails. Jim provided support, encouragement, invaluable suggestions and attended to the host of administrative details that freed me up for the task of researching and writing the manuscript.

Bob Compton of the Corporate Communications Department was amanuensis and friend. During his 21 years with PP&L, Bob has made friends with just about everybody in the company. He used those friendships to provide me with introductions to dozens of people. He interviewed dozens of people himself, and proved to be a boon traveling companion during our jaunts to every corner of the PP&L system. In many ways, this is as much Bob's book as it is mine.

People in the PP&L's Corporate Communications Department were consistently friendly, helpful, cheerful, courteous, kind, etc. Justine Nagle spent hours at the copier, copying one-of-a-kind files and reports that couldn't leave the premises. Chris Eckhart and Nancy Minnich spent countless hours keeping Jim Marsh straight in what turned out to be several filing drawers of text, photos and proof pages. Paul Wirth shared his knowledge of the Lehigh Valley's steel industry, and David Osterhout—since departed to follow a dream in Europe—spent hours discussing the PP&L corporate culture. Don Cunningham shared his research on 1930s power politics in Bethlehem.

Brent Schaefer, an employee of the Power Systems Support Department, and an accomplished self-taught artist, developed a number of pen-and-ink sketches that provided a whole new perspective for a number of PP&L facilities.

Many outside the company also made major contributions to the success of this project. Frank Whelan of *The Allentown Morning Call*, an accomplished researcher and historian in his own right, spent long hours explaining the historical context of economic development in the Lehigh Valley and the anthracite regions. It was through Frank's dogged efforts that many of the illustrations in this book were first brought to light. Frank also provided a valuable introduction to Lance E. Metz and his competent staff at the Hugh Moore Historical Park and Museum in Easton.

During the bicentennial year in 1976, PP&L donated more than 20 tons of records of its predecessor companies to the Hagley Museum and Libraries in Wilmington, Del. Michael Nash and his staff consistently went above and beyond the call of duty in locating obscure documents relating to the company's history during my half-dozen research visits to their facilities. Mary Ann Hellrigel of Cleveland, Ohio, allowed me to consult her thesis on Thomas Edison and the Edison Construction Company, which was extremely valuable for providing insight on the spread of Edison's three-wire system in Pennsylvania in the 1880s.

On the production side of the ledger, a project of this size involves dozens of people. Jeanne Lamb at Westmoreland Larson Webster Inc., my Minnesota publisher, has developed a talent for tracking down historical photographs and illustrations that would be the envy of most doctoral candidates. Jeanne also serves in the absolutely essential role of author's nag, an indispensable task where deadlines and 44 chapters of text are involved. "A chapter a day keeps Jeanne away" became my mantra in the latter stages of the project.

Once again, I am blown away by the talent of Bonnie Wenborg, the WLW staff designer who has now collaborated with me on two of our longer history projects. Bonnie has an eye for pictorial elements that continues to astound me, especially given the fact that I've known since the second grade that I can neither cut, paste nor draw a straight line—even with a computer. Loralee Olson capably handled the electronic transfer of several megabytes of copy and—with the assistance of Carol Leger and Sara Dougherty—was responsible for proofing and reproofing that copy before it went to Allentown.

Harold Webster, my partner in this historical endeavor for the past seven years and twice that many books now, was always ready to talk over problems and concerns. Donn Larson, the senior partner in Westmoreland Larson Webster Inc., remains an inspiration.

Closer to home, Eric Mappes made the complexities of organization far less complex with his computerization of the PP&L history database. Sharon Richardson of our Indianapolis office handled the ongoing retrieval of the nearly 200 PP&L history files with aplomb and good humor.

As Lara and Jenny, our children, have left for college and lives of their own, my wife and business partner, Betty, has tacked on the added duties of research assistant to her job title. Living with a writer has to be a monumental task in itself.

Break it all down, and writing is a solitary task, albeit with a support tail about a mile long. But the solitary nature of the craft comes from the realization that all those errors and omissions that invariably creep into the text can't be blamed on staff help. I take responsibility for those all by myself.

Bill Beck
Indianapolis, Indiana
February 1995

Contents

PP&L

75 YEARS OF POWERING THE FUTURE

An Illustrated History of Pennsylvania Power & Light Co.

At the Beginning

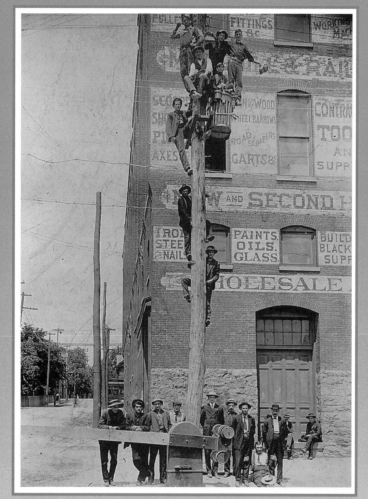

For fun and a photo opportunity, these linemen from one of PP&L's predecessors, Consumers Electric Light & Power Co. of Hazleton, crowd around and on a utility pole. Years later, their grandchildren would try to see how many people they could cram into a telephone booth. *circa 1907*

The birth of Pennsylvania Power & Light Co. can be reliably dated to June 4, 1920. On that late spring day in the Lehigh Valley, eight utilities serving central eastern Pennsylvania were merged into a single corporate entity that has continued under the same name to this day. The documents incorporating Pennsylvania Power & Light Co. that day were signed in New York City, the home of the utility holding company that organized the new Pennsylvania utility.

Eight days later, the directors of Pennsylvania Power & Light Co. met for the first time in Allentown, the Lehigh Valley community chosen to serve as headquarters for the new company. "At 9 o'clock that morning," wrote Richard Lichtenwalner of the company's advertising and marketing department some 45 years later, "the directors gathered at the company's offices then in the Buckley Building on the southwest corner of Eighth and Hamilton streets in Allentown. Early morning temperatures already promised another humid 90-degree day."

One Saturday morning in 1920, Brig. Gen. Harry C. Trexler and four other directors met for the first of many PP&L board meetings.

Outside, Lichtenwalner reported, "vendors hawked their morning papers, which headlined news that the Republican Convention in Chicago that Harding was gaining steadily on Lowden for the presidential nomination." The genial Ohio newspaper publisher would go on to win the Republican nomination later that day and the presidency in November. Elsewhere in the world that week, the U.S. Supreme Court unanimously upheld the 18th Amendment to the Constitution, the Volstead Act that had ushered in Prohibition at the first of the year. On Thursday of that week, the Republican Convention had endorsed women's suffrage, and the U.S. Census Bureau had reported that nearby New York City, with a population of 5.6 million, was the nation's largest city.

Pennsylvania Power & Light Co.—known to generations of residents of central eastern Pennsylvania as PP&L—came into being at a time of critical importance to the American electric utility industry. From a patchwork quilt of isolated, privately owned municipal lighting plants that had grown up in the

wake of Thomas Edison's discovery of the feasibility of incandescent electric lighting systems in the 1880s, the industry evolved into a streamlined network of electric power plants and transmission lines during the 1910s and 1920s. Indeed, just three years before PP&L was formed in 1920, the region of central and eastern Pennsylvania was served by more than 70 electric companies.

The consolidation of PP&L was a model for much of what would happen to the nation's electric utility industry during the 1920s. "The history of PP&L serves well as an example of the widespread and long-term process of organizational merger and consolidation that has characterized the history of electricity supply in the United States," noted Thomas Parke Hughes, the dean of American electric utility historians, in his landmark 1983 work, *Networks of Power.* "As in the case of many other U.S. regional utilities, PP&L's business history culminated in the 1920s with the consolidation of the merger movement, the formation of a holding company pyramid embracing the company, its predecessor companies, and other large regional systems."

In a larger sense, however, the history of Pennsylvania Power & Light Co. coincides with the industrial, economic, political and social history of Pennsylvania for much of the 20th century. And although the year 1920 is separated from us by little more than the typical lifespan of a 20th-century American, it is in many ways a world apart.

THE YEAR 1920

In early June 1920, World War I was barely over. "The War to end all Wars," as it was then known, had ended in November 1918, just a year-and-a-half before. Pennsylvanians had taken quiet pride in the fact that more than a third of a million young men had joined the armed forces, even though the state's German roots went deep. The 28th Division had been composed almost entirely of native sons;

its exploits in the Forest of St. Mihiel and the 1918 offensive in the Argonne had been widely followed by the state's press. Pennsylvanians Tasker H. Bliss and William S. Sims had acquitted themselves with particular honor during the war. Bliss, a native of Lewisburg, had been appointed chief of staff of the U.S. Army in 1917; Sims, a graduate of the U.S. Naval Academy, had been in charge of American naval operations during the war.

The more than 300,000 returning veterans found ample opportunities for employment, particularly in central and eastern Pennsylvania. The region's economy at the end of the war was dominated by several large industries, including iron and steel, anthracite coal mining, textiles, and foundries and machine shops. The war had been especially kind to Charles S. Schwab and the Bethlehem Steel Co. Formed in 1905, Bethlehem Steel Co. became the largest munitions manufacturer in the world. Located on 600 acres in South Bethlehem along the banks of the Lehigh River, the blast furnaces, coke ovens and rolling mills of Bethlehem Steel Co. became the arsenal of democracy during World War I. Some 25,000 employees manufactured 750,000 shells a month to supply the allied armies on the Western Front.

At the end of 1916, *Iron Age*, the journal of the U.S. iron and steel industry, had noted that "when Mr. Schwab came to Bethlehem, the town had 13,000 inhabitants. Today, the employees of Bethlehem Steel Co. are sufficient to make a city of 150,000 people. Ten years ago the annual sales of Bethlehem were $10 million. Last year, they were $230 million." Bethlehem Steel's importance to the Lehigh Valley would hardly be diminished by the coming of peace in 1918. As

the 1920s opened, the building industry would require millions of tons of steel beams for the skyscrapers then on the drawing boards for urban America. Similarly, more millions of tons of sheet steel would be required for the American automobile industry, then gearing up in Detroit for peacetime production.

Already by 1920, 2.2 million automobiles were rolling off the nation's assembly lines, four times as many automobiles as had been produced in 1914, the year that Henry Ford, a former electrical engineer at the Detroit Edison Co., began producing Model-T Fords on the line at River Rouge, Mich.

Bethlehem Steel Co.'s labor needs would increase all through the 1920s as the Bethlehem-based company absorbed the 1916 acquisition of Pennsylvania Steel Co. and its mills at Steelton and Sparrows Point, Md., and the acquisition the next year of the Lebanon and Reading plants of the American Iron and Steel Manufacturing Co. Two years after the formation of PP&L, Bethlehem Steel Co. expanded further, acquiring the Lackawanna Iron

Downtown Allentown, around 1925, at the intersection that would later become the site of PP&L's General Office.

The more than 300,000 returning veterans found ample opportunities for employment, particularly in central and eastern Pennsylvania.

3

Allentown companies B and D of the Pennsylvania National Guard were given a royal send-off on Sept. 10, 1917.

Shown here in his captain uniform, William S. Sims became vice-admiral for the U.S. Navy during World War I.

(photo courtesy of the Military History Institute)

Tasker H. Bliss, a native of Lewisburg, was appointed chief of staff of the U.S. Army during World War I.

(photo courtesy of the Military History Institute)

The Lehigh Valley provided employment opportunities for women in the early 1900s. As men went to the coal mines and off to war, their wives, sisters and daughters went to work.

(photo courtesy of Hugh Moore Historical Park and Museums, Inc.)

and Steel Co. of Lackawanna, N.Y.; in 1923, Bethlehem Steel Co. bought the Cambria Plant of Midvale Steel and Ordnance Co. at Johnstown.

Anthracite coal mining was another mainstay of the region's economy. As World War I ground to a halt, Pennsylvania was producing virtually all of the nation's anthracite coal and 32 percent of U.S. bituminous coal needs. The hills and valleys of northeastern Pennsylvania were underlaid with anthracite, an exceptionally hard, high-Btu (British thermal unit) coal, and miners had begun digging anthracite from pits located near Wilkes-Barre as early as 1762. By 1820, the Lehigh Coal and Navigation Co. was shipping 365 tons of anthracite down the Lehigh and Delaware rivers to Philadelphia. The strategic nature of the four anthracite fields in eastern Pennsylvania was a function of their market location.

The hard coal fields were only 90 miles from Philadelphia, 140 miles from New York City, 265 miles from Buffalo and 250 miles from Pittsburgh. The high-Btu content and relatively clean-burning nature of anthracite made it particularly suitable for use in manufacturing operations and for home heating applications. For much of its history, PP&L burned anthracite in its power plants to generate electricity.

Anthracite reached its peak during World War I. From 1917 to 1921, between 90 million and 100 million tons of anthracite were produced by Pennsylvania collieries each year. During the war, more than 100,000 residents of mining villages and towns in the anthracite area, places like Mahanoy City, Shenandoah, Tamaqua, St. Clair, Mauch Chunk, Hazleton and Pottsville, were employed in the anthracite industry. Another 45,000 residents of northeastern Pennsylvania were employed in the retail end of the business, handling the sale and delivery of anthracite to the end-use consumer. Thousands more of Pennsylvanians were employed in transporting anthracite to market. In 1919, the year prior to the incorporation of PP&L, 254 anthracite mines and collieries accounted for $364 million of revenues, slightly more than the revenues posted by the state's 1,938 bituminous mines.

Unlike many U.S. communities of the time, the Lehigh Valley boasted ample employment opportunities for its female residents. By the second decade of the 20th century, the Lehigh Valley was the second

Thirteenth Street in Harrisburg is a busy thoroughfare today; but, as these photos show, the corner of Paxton Street and Thirteenth Street was just a muddy,

largest silk manufacturing region in the country, behind nearby Paterson, N.J. Silk in 135-pound bales imported from Japan was shipped to the mills in the Valley and processed into the fashionable silk shirts and blouses of the day. Allentown had 16 mills employing more than 5,000 workers, and by the early 1920s, Bethlehem boasted 13 mills. All told, there were 136 companies in the Valley in 1919 either manufacturing or dyeing silk. Hazleton, which figures prominently in PP&L's 75-year history, housed the Duplan silk mill, once the largest factory in the world under one roof.

The wives, sisters and daughters of the anthracite coal miners of the Wyoming Valley found employment in the lace mills at Wilkes-Barre. All told, more than 56,000 people worked in the lace and silk mills of the Wyoming and Lehigh valleys in 1919. The 330,000 Pennsylvania veterans who had served in World War I wore the Victory Medal issued by a grateful government in 1918; the rainbow-hued ribbon from which the medal hung had been manufactured in Allentown's Adelaide Ribbon Mill.

Returning central eastern Pennsylvania veterans could also find work in the region's booming machine shop and foundry industry. By 1919, Pennsylvanians made many of the tools and components that drove American industry. Machine shops and foundries were getting larger, with an average-sized workforce of 68 highly skilled, well-paid employees. In Williamsport, the Lycoming Motors Corp. turned out engines for such manufacturers as Cord, Auburn, Duesenberg, Yellow and Checker Cabs, International Harvester and John Deere.

The extractive industries of the region weren't just limited to anthracite coal. Central eastern Pennsylvania had thriving slate and zinc industries by the

end of World War I. Slate from quarries in Lehigh and Northampton counties roofed houses all up and down the East Coast, and produced school blackboards and billiard tables for national consumption. At the turn of the century, the Lehigh Valley was already the greatest cement-producing region on earth, accounting for nearly 75 percent of U.S. production. Lehigh Portland Cement was the

---

As World War I ground to a halt, Pennsylvania was producing virtually all of the nation's anthracite coal and 32 percent of U.S. bituminous coal needs.

---

standard by which all other cement was judged, and mills dotted the Valley, providing the mainstay of the economy for communities like Martins Creek, Nazareth, Fogelsville, Coplay and Stockertown. Although other regions had caught up with cement-producing capability by 1920, the Valley still

rutted streak across the countryside when the first transmission lines began to carry electricity through the area around the turn of the century.

accounted for more than a quarter of U.S. production.

Finally, returning veterans could find work back on the farms they left in 1917 and 1918. Pennsylvania was still very much an agricultural state, and the rich bottomlands of the Lehigh, Susquehanna and Delaware river systems supported a wide variety of crop production. Central eastern Pennsylvania farmers produced small grains like winter wheat and corn, abundant truck gardens and fruit from well-tended orchards.

mented and not entirely reliable.

The five men who gathered in the Buckley Building that Saturday morning intended to rectify that situation. The first directors of PP&L were all veterans of either the electric utility industry nationwide or the industrial development of central eastern Pennsylvania. Their charge was to consolidate the isolated electric utilities of the area into a modern regional utility capable of serving as a catalyst for further economic and industrial development in the region. Chief among them

Spreading the Risk

Key to the continued development of central eastern Pennsylvania's industrial vitality in 1920 was the generation, transmission and distribution of electric power. The technology was already approaching its 40th anniversary in central eastern Pennsylvania when the directors of PP&L met for the first time in Allentown in 1920; but for much of its history, the industry had been frag-

was Sidney Zollicoffer Mitchell, first chairman of PP&L and president of the new utility's major predecessor, the Lehigh Power Securities Corp. An Alabamian, Mitchell had been associated with General Electric Co. even before the turn of the century; and in 1905, he had organized Electric Bond and Share Co. to hold the stock of operating electric utilities that had purchased generating equipment from General Electric Co.

Mitchell's southern roots were commented upon by another of the first directors, Gen. Harry Clay Trexler, the organizer of the Lehigh Portland Cement Co. and the father of Allentown's park system. "Mr. Mitchell, I assume your middle initial stands for Zollicoffer and you no doubt are named after General Zollicoffer, a famous confederate officer," Trexler noted upon being introduced to the new PP&L chairman. Mitchell, who had been named for confederate generals Albert Sidney Johnston and Felix Kirk Zollicoffer, was momentarily taken aback. "General, you are the first northerner I ever met that

of Mitchell. A Harvard-educated lawyer from Illinois, Hall had worked with Electric Bond and Share and Lehigh Power Securities Corp. from 1917 to 1919 in New York to set up PP&L. After 1919, Hall took a job as vice president of American Telephone & Telegraph Co. in New York City, but Mitchell prevailed upon him to serve as PP&L's first president; AT&T allowed Hall to ride down to Allentown from New York on the train several times a month to look after PP&L business.

made that observation," he replied.

Paul Backus Sawyer was a utility executive of longstanding experience. A native Hoosier, he had spent 12 years with Iowa utilities following his graduation from Purdue University before joining Utah Power & Light Co. as vice president and general manager in 1914. Utah Power & Light was affiliated with Electric Bond and Share Co.; and in 1917, Mitchell brought him to New York to help with the formation of Pennsylvania Power & Light Co.

Edward Kimball Hall was another ally

The final initial director was Charles M. Walter, a respected local utility veteran who had been involved on the financial side of PP&L predecessors from before the turn of the century. A West Virginia native, Walter had moved to Allentown in 1894 to serve as the auditor of the Allentown & Bethlehem Rapid Transit Co. Walter would serve as secretary and treasurer of PP&L until his death in December 1946.

The system that Mitchell and his fellow board directors formed in June 1920 was organized around a philosophy

In 1905, Bethlehem Steel Co. was the largest munitions manufacturer in the world. *(photo courtesy of Hugh Moore Historical Park and Museums, Inc.)*

Pennsylvanians began mining anthracite coal as early as 1762. By World War I, coal mining in the region had reached peak production. These photos from the 1920s show undercutting, fire boss testing for gas and the typical miner's uniform for the time.

(photos courtesy of Hugh Moore Historical Park and Museums, Inc.)

of "spreading the risk." Mitchell had borrowed the concept from the insurance industry, and in essence it meant that a consolidated utility had the resources to withstand financial hardship. Mitchell had gotten involved in central eastern Pennsylvania three years earlier when Electric Bond and Share Co. had acquired a controlling interest in the Lehigh Navigation Electric Co. Two years later, Bond and Share purchased the Lehigh Valley Light & Power Co., and merged it with Lehigh Navigation Electric Co. under the ownership of a subholding company, the Lehigh Power Securities Corp. Soon after, Lehigh Power Securities Corp. gained a controlling interest in the Columbia and Montour Electric Co., which provided service to Danville, Bloomsburg and Berwick; Northumberland County Gas & Electric Co., which provided gas and electric service to Sunbury and electric service to Milton; Northern Central Gas Co., which supplied gas in Williamsport and Milton; and Lehigh Valley Transit Co., which operated urban and interurban street railways connecting Allentown, Bethlehem, Easton and Philadelphia.

Lehigh Power Securities Corp. had also gained control of the Harwood Electric Co. and the Schuylkill Gas & Electric Co. through investments made as early as 1913 by the Lehigh Navigation Electric Co. By 1917, the six operating companies under Lehigh Power Securities Corp. provided service to 370 Pennsylvania communities with a population of more than 1.417 million. A measure of the development work that needed to be done was the fact that only about one in 12 of the residents of those 370 communities was

served with electric power in 1917; the six operating companies had only 3,500 miles of distribution line energized at the time.

The acquisition of Pennsylvania Lighting Co. in April 1920 set the stage for formation of PP&L two months later. Pennsylvania Lighting Co., which was owned by the investment banking firm of Chandler and Co. in Philadelphia, provided electric and gas service to the coal region communities of Shamokin and Mount Carmel. Pennsylvania Power & Light Co. was a non-operating company, selected solely in order to preserve the name for use of the new utility.

At its inception in June 1920, PP&L had acquired 62 steam electric and hydroelectric generating plants. All were small, with the exception of Harwood Electric Co.'s Harwood Steam Electric Station near Hazleton and Lehigh Navigation Electric Co.'s Hauto Steam Electric Station near Lansford. With the exception of isolated systems in Shamokin and Mount Carmel, the PP&L system was tied together by 416 miles of high-voltage transmission lines.

The system that Sidney Z. Mitchell formed in the late spring of 1920 was uniquely situated to serve the needs of post-World War I central eastern Pennsylvania. It would grow exponentially during the coming decade and become an engine for the area's continuing economic growth. In many ways, however, and not always successfully, its component parts had already been serving those needs since well back into the previous century.

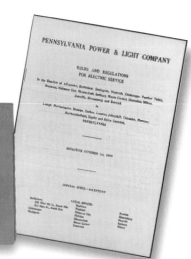

Only four months from its inception, rules and regulations were formalized and distributed to all offices.

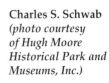

Charles S. Schwab *(photo courtesy of Hugh Moore Historical Park and Museums, Inc.)*

Birth of the FPC

Just six days after Pennsylvania Power & Light Co. received its official incorporation papers, and two days before the company's first meeting of its board of directors in the Buckley Building in Allentown, the U.S. Congress passed a Federal Water Power Act, setting up the Federal Power Commission. The FPC, the federal regulatory agency with oversight authority for the nation's electric and gas utilities, continues in existence today as the Federal Energy Regulatory Commission (FERC). For the entire 75 years of its corporate history, Pennsylvania Power & Light Co.'s destiny has been intertwined with that of the Federal Power Commission, and its successor, the FERC.

Gifford Pinchot spearheaded the move to regulate hydroelectric power and was later elected governor of Pennsylvania.

suspicious of monopolies. Writing to William Jennings Bryan in 1908, Pinchot offered the opinion that "the General Electric Co. and the Westinghouse Co. are securing control of water and power development over very extensive areas of the country."

Spearheaded by Pinchot's efforts, Congress passed waterpower acts in 1901 and 1910. The Town Sites and Power Act of 1906 established a precedent for leasing waterpower privileges, albeit only for projects associated with irrigation sites. From 1905-1911, the U.S. Reclamation Service built Roosevelt Dam on the Salt River near Phoenix; in a precedent-setting move, surplus electric power from the federal dam project was sold to the city of Phoenix.

Hydroelectric power production in the United States is well over a century old. In the summer of 1882, a year before he installed the first three-wire incandescent lighting system in America at Sunbury, Pa., Thomas Edison licensed three Appleton, Wis., businessmen to operate a generating system in the Fox River Valley. On September 30, the three entrepreneurs started up the world's first hydroelectric station on the Fox River in downtown Appleton.

During the next 20 years, regulation of hydroelectric generation was almost nonexistent. But following Theodore Roosevelt's elevation to the White House in 1901, the federal government took a much more serious interest in hydroelectric development. The creation of the U.S. Reclamation Service in 1902—later the Bureau of Reclamation—got the federal government involved in dam building in a big way and set the stage for half-a-century of conflict between the proponents and opponents of public power.

The sparkplug behind the move to regulate hydroelectric sites was Gifford Pinchot, a Pennsylvania politician whom Pennsylvania Power & Light Co. clashed with repeatedly during the 1920s and 1930s. Pinchot, a forester who headed Roosevelt's U.S. Forest Service, was even then

The struggle to regulate hydroelectric power came to a head during World War I. The National Defense Act of 1916 authorized the government to construct hydroelectric facilities and associated chemical plants for the production of strategic nitrates, particularly on the Tennessee River at Muscle Shoals, Ala. The investor-owned electric utility industry argued that federal entry into the hydroelectric power business and overzealous regulation by the 1910 Water Power Act put it at a competitive disadvantage.

The compromise was the Federal Water Power Act of 1920, enacted June 10, 1920. The Act created the Federal Power Commission, which was initially made up of the Secretaries of War, Interior and Agriculture, and gave the new Commission authority to regulate nonfederal hydroelectric projects on the nation's navigable waterways. Key to the Commission's powers was the authority to issue 50-year licenses for hydroelectric power developments.

For the next 75 years, Pennsylvania Power & Light Co., and every other utility in the United States for that matter, would become very familiar with the workings of the Federal Power Commission and its successor, the FERC.

2

Roots in Gas and Water

In the late 1800s, manufactured gas was used primarily to provide street, commercial and residential lighting in Pennsylvania's urban areas. *(photo courtesy of the Lehigh County Historical Society)*

In actuality, the roots of Pennsylvania Power & Light Co. go deep into the 19th century, but those earliest predecessors were organized to sell Pennsylvanians artificial gas and water power from primitive dams laid across the state's rivers and streams. Thomas Edison didn't invent his incandescent lighting system until the fall of 1879, and it was nearly four years later before Edison and his associates installed the first three-wire lighting system in what was then the bustling little Susquehanna River town of Sunbury, Pa.

Two decades prior to the advent of incandescent lighting, PP&L predecessors in places like Carlisle, Mauch Chunk, Milton, Sunbury and Williamsport provided streetlighting services by burning the state's abundant coal resources to make a low-Btu artificial gas. Some of those early gas companies would still be making gas from Pennsylvania coal as much as a century

The Susquehanna Boom Co.'s first office was the Herdic House, also known as the Park Hotel, on the corner of West Fourth and Campbell streets. circa 1900. *(photo courtesy of the James V. Brown Library)*

later. At the time of the Civil War, as Pennsylvania troops defended their native soil at the crossroads town of Gettysburg, other Pennsylvanians were busy driving logs down the Susquehanna River. In the years before the war, the logging companies cutting in the hills above the Susquehanna and its tributaries banded together to form the Susquehanna Boom Co.

The boom, a series of piers across the river, held millions of logs and provided sawtimber for some 30 sawmills in the Williamsport area from 1846 until the turn of the century. The boom company was sold to the Lycoming Improvement Co. in 1908, which was subsequently acquired by the Lehigh Power Securities

Corp.—the parent holding company for PP&L—and thus, PP&L's oldest predecessor.

The Town Gas Era

Artificial gas, or "town gas," as it was known to many 19th century Pennsylvanians, was introduced first in Europe and came to the United States in 1816. As early as 1802, a public display of gas lighting was given at Soho in London, and four years later, Frederick Albert Winsor, a German, built the first gas mains ever laid in a public street from Haymarket to St. James Street in the commercial section of London. The mains in that London street were made of lead, and in 1807, Winsor turned on gas streetlights in London's Pall Mall neighborhood, the first commercial use of gas streetlighting in the world.

Manufactured gas technology leapfrogged the Atlantic in 1812 when David Melville of Newport, R.I., installed a gas retort in his home and successfully lighted his house and the street in front of it. The next year, Melville contracted to light cotton mills at Watertown, Mass., and Providence, R.I., with gas lights.

Rembrandt Peale, an artist and business executive in Baltimore, took gas technology the next step in 1817 when he convinced four other Baltimore businessmen to assist him in chartering the Gas Light Co. of Baltimore. Peale had installed gas lights in his Baltimore salon the previous year, and his new company installed the first gas streetlight in the United States at the intersection of Market and Lemon streets—now the corner of Baltimore and Holliday streets—on Feb. 7, 1817. Manufactured gas technology was quick to disperse to the other urban communities along the East Coast. Boston got gas in 1822, and the New York Gas Light Co. was organized in 1823; within five years, New York Gas Light Co. had installed gas lamps all up and down Broadway, leading to the coinage of the descriptive "Great White Way."

*Booms, which held millions of logs and sawtimber for Williamsport sawmills, stretched across the
Susquehanna River from 1846 until the turn of the century.*
(photos courtesy of the James V. Brown Library)

Philadelphia received its first gas service in 1836, the same year that Americans back East were reading in their newspapers of the fate of the defenders of the Alamo in far-off Texas. Those early gas companies heated coal in the absence of oxygen to manufacture a low-Btu lighting gas. The methane/hydrogen gas produced in primitive retorts generated 400-550 Btu of heating content and was typically rated at between 17 and 19 candlepower.

After experimentation with lead early in the 19th century, gas companies by mid-century typically used wood for gas mains. Logs were hollowed out and tapered at one end, and the sections of gas main were tapped into each other. Sometimes the joints were soldered with lead or reinforced with iron couplings. Service extensions into businesses or homes were usually constructed of copper tubing or even old musket barrels, especially in the years following the Civil War.

PP&L's oldest utility predecessor is the Carlisle Gas and Water Co. Carlisle was occupied by Lt. Gen. Richard S. Ewell's Second Army Corps in 1863 during one of the Civil War's most important battles. (photo courtesy of the Military History Institute)

Early Gas Companies in Central Eastern Pennsylvania

Manufactured gas made its presence felt in central eastern Pennsylvania in the 1850s. Like its use elsewhere in America during the latter half of the 19th century, manufactured gas was used primarily to provide street, commercial and residential lighting in the state's urban areas. Street-lighting was extremely important to the development of America's cities, and with the exception of a few oil lamps, which often lighted the way to taverns, was generally not available in the U.S. prior to the development of coal gas.

When London's Pall Mall was lit by gas streetlights in 1807, the *Monthly Magazine* noted that "the effect is beyond all dispute superior to the old method of lighting our streets. One branch of the lamps illuminated with gas affords a

greater intensity of light than 20 common lamps lighted with oil. The light is beautifully white and brilliant." Gas also was frequently used for indoor lighting, at first in commercial establishments, and later in homes. Gas lamps replaced whale oil lamps in mid-century. They were cleaner to use, burned with little or no odor, and were easy to use.

Several predecessors of Pennsylvania Power & Light Co. can lay claim to being the first organized utilities in the company's service territory. Gas companies in Mauch Chunk, Carlisle, Williamsport, Wilkes-Barre and Milton all were in operation in the decade before the Civil War broke out. PP&L's oldest utility predecessor is the Carlisle Gas and Water Co. The Cumberland County firm was organized in 1853 under the terms of a special charter granted by the Pennsylvania legislature "for the purpose of making, raising and introducing into the Borough of Carlisle a sufficient supply of gas and pure water." Soon after, the New York Gas & Water Co. constructed a gas plant and gas distribution system to serve the bustling little community located just south and west of the state capitol at Harrisburg. One of the company's earliest customers was the Carlisle barracks of the U.S. Army.

In 1855, the company supplied the town water from a waterworks that had been constructed along the Conodoguinet Creek north of Carlisle. The pumping was done by hydraulic power furnished by a dam built across the creek at the waterworks. Carlisle Gas and Water Co. financed construction of the waterworks with a stock subscription, which it had been authorized to do in its original

> *"The effect is beyond all dispute superior to the old method of lighting our streets. One branch of the lamps illuminated with gas affords a greater intensity of light than 20 common lamps lighted with oil. The light is beautifully white and brilliant."*
> —Monthly Magazine, *1807*

state incorporation. The Borough of Carlisle early on became a significant owner of stock in the new company, even securing representation on the board of managers.

The borough's investment in the gas and water company must have seemed less than astute at the beginning. During the first 10 years of the company's existence, it paid no dividends whatsoever. Part of the reason for the financial rocky start was the fact that Carlisle found itself in the middle of one of the Civil War's most important battles.

In the summer of 1863, Robert E. Lee's Army of Northern Virginia struck its colors and marched north into southeastern Pennsylvania. By the last week of June, Carlisle found itself occupied by Lt. Gen. Richard S. Ewell's Second Army Corps. The hungry Confederates were under strict orders not to burn the town or loot the civilian population. Lee had even ordered Ewell not to burn the Carlisle barracks, hastily abandoned by retreating federal troops.

But Ewell did requisition more than $50,000 worth of medicines and other provisions, and the Confederate troops destroyed the bridge and 600-foot trestle of the Cumberland Valley Railroad outside of town. Rails were warped by heating them in the fires of burning railroad ties, and telegraph poles from Hagerstown, Md., to Harrisburg were chopped down for firewood for the advancing Army of Northern Virginia. Area farmers were paid in next to worthless Confederate scrip for their livestock and supplies; some enterprising farmers later sold the Confederate scrip to soldiers of the Army of the Potomac as souvenirs of the Gettysburg campaign.

It took years for the citizens of Carlisle and the surrounding countryside to recover from the unwitting part they played in one of the Civil War's most momentous battles. The Carlisle Gas and Water Co. "was put to considerable expense during the invasion of Southern

James L. Blakslee organized the Mauch Chunk Gas Co. in 1856.

Pennsylvania by the Confederate Army in 1863," a later historian laconically reported.

Carlisle wasn't the only central eastern Pennsylvania community to get gas service in the mid-1850s. Far to the northeast of Carlisle, the Mauch Chunk Gas Co. was incorporated in early March 1854, also under the terms of a special act of the Pennsylvania Legislature. Located on the headwaters of the Lehigh River and named for a conical formation overlooking the town that local native Americans called Bear Mountain, Mauch Chunk was already a thriving coal-mining community by 1850.

Initially known as Coalville, Mauch Chunk had been designated the county seat of Carbon County in 1843 and was incorporated as a borough early in 1850. Mauch Chunk was one of the gateways to Pennsylvania's anthracite regions; and as early as the 1840s, coal cars were emptied into chutes at Mauch Chunk for shipment in canal boats operated by the Lehigh Coal and Navigation Co.

By 1850, Mauch Chunk was the commercial center for the Upper Lehigh Valley. The community had a population of more than 2,500, and although Mauch Chunk was ravaged by a cholera epidemic in the summer of 1854, the borough prided itself on its modern amenities. Using the special charter provided by the Pennsylvania Legislature, James L. Blakslee organized the Mauch Chunk Gas Co. in 1856 with an initial capitalization of $15,000.

Blakslee built a gas plant along the Lehigh River inside the borough, and the Mauch Chunk Gas Co. originally attempted to make gas from the abundant wood supply on the surrounding hillsides. However, Mauch Chunk Gas Co. was soon making gas from coal.

Like Carlisle Gas and Water Co., the Mauch Chunk Gas Co. had a rocky financial start. Six years after its gas plant was up and running, the company was devastated financially by a flood on the Lehigh River. The June 1862 flood carried away a major portion of the gasworks, destroyed the Mauch Chunk-White Haven

Floods like this one in 1889 plagued the Susquehanna Boom Co. (photos courtesy of the James V. Brown Library)

Canal and destroyed about half of the buildings on the lower portion of Susquehanna Street. Blakslee rebuilt the gasworks, which were partially destroyed by fire in 1881 and flooded out again in 1905.

Fire also was the bane of the Milton Gas Co. in Northumberland County. Organized in 1856, the company took four years to line up the financing for construction of a gas plant. In 1860, Milton Gas Co. contracted with William Helm, a local builder, to build a gas plant together with a gas distribution system. The terms of the $15,500 contract called for payment of $7,000 in cash, $4,500 in

bonds and the issuance of $4,000 in common stock. The Milton gas plant was in operation for 20 years. When it burned in 1880, it was rebuilt almost immediately.

The Williamsport Gas Co., which in later years would be merged into the Northern Central Gas Co., began supplying Williamsport and surrounding areas of Lycoming County with manufactured gas shortly after it was organized in 1856. By 1875, it was strong enough financially to lease the gasworks and distribution system of its chief rival, the Lycoming Gas & Water Co.

One of the more successful of the manufactured gas predecessors of PP&L

was the Wilkes-Barre Gas Co. A trio of local entrepreneurs, Oliver P. Hillard, George P. Steele and Harrison Wright, organized the company in 1854 and entered into a contract with S.R. Dickson to build a gas plant. Dickson charged $45,000 for the job and was paid with 900 shares of stock, valued at $50 per share.

Wilkes-Barre's gas plant started out with one bench in 1856 and was expanded with the construction of additional benches in 1858. Benches were essentially brick-lined hearths upon which the coal was burned. In 1869, the company's gas business had grown so sharply that Wilkes-Barre Gas Co. added a fourth bench and a new purifier set to its gasworks.

The Conversion to Water Gas

The organizers of the Wilkes-Barre Gas Co. were quick to convert to the new water gas process when it was introduced in the mid-1870s. All of the Pennsylvania gas utilities made use of the coal carbonization process that had been brought to the United States from Europe prior to 1820. Coal carbonization involved the distillation of coal in the absence of air, which in essence drove off approximately 30 percent of the coal by weight as gas and residual chemicals. Early coal gas plants first used water to quench the burning coal and then purified the resulting gas to remove sulfide, cyanide and ammonia. Much of the residue consisted of coke–an almost pure form of carbon–which the utility then sold to foundries to be used in the making of iron and steel, and for home heating.

The coal gas process was simple to use, and it produced manufactured gas inexpensively. But the gas produced was low-Btu, and even lower in candlepower. That problem was resolved by Thaddeus S.C. Lowe. Born and raised on a New Hampshire farm, Thaddeus Sobieski Coulincourt Lowe spent most of his life tinkering with chemistry and gases. During the Civil War, President Abraham Lincoln named Lowe chief of the Union Army's Corps of Aeronautics. His observation balloons flew over the war's battlefields; Lowe and his cohorts reported back to the federal Army of the Potomac on the disposition of the confederate troops spread out below them.

In 1872, Lowe experimented with the manufactured gas processes of the day. According to the history of UGI Corp., which later patented the talented inventor's process, "Lowe exposed water gas vapors to a thin stream of petroleum naphtha, enriching the gas with hydrocarbons from the oil. The enriched, or carburetted, water gas burned with a far brighter flame than coal gas."

Not only was the flame brighter, the process was actually cheaper than coal carbonization. In 1874, Lowe helped build the first carburetted gas plant at Phoenixville, northwest of Valley Forge. Lowe's process boosted the concentration of hydrogen and carbon monoxide in the gas, thereby enriching it and making it more suitable for illumination. By the turn of the century, water gas was well on its way to becoming the predominant gas manufacturing process in America.

In Carlisle, the directors of the Carlisle Gas and Water Co. converted to water gas in 1878. Wilkes-Barre Gas Co. officials also followed the news of the new process with much interest. In 1879, the company converted its coal carbonization equipment to the water gas process, adding two Lowe water gas sets in the plant. Six years later, in 1885, the company added a third Lowe water gas set.

The manufactured gas utility predecessors of Pennsylvania Power & Light Co. were true utility companies. They generated and distributed a primary energy product, negotiated franchises, metered the sale of their product and set rates for different classes of customers. But by the late 1870s, manufactured gas was facing

Natural Gas Lamp.
circa 1880s.

competition on several different fronts. In western Pennsylvania, oil had been discovered in the summer of 1859. Although it would be decades before oil could be efficiently distributed to end-use consumers, its very existence cast a pall over the future of the manufactured gas industry.

Further west, in northern Ohio and north central Indiana, the first commercial discovery of natural gas was in the process of being exploited as the decade of the 1870s drew to a close. And all over America, tinkerers and inventors were experimenting with a technology that promised to replace manufactured gas in the field of streetlighting. The era of electric arc lighting would bring sweeping technological change to Pennsylvania and the nation.

Pennsylvania state seal.

The Susquehanna Boom Company

In 1937, Pennsylvania Power & Light Co. acquired the stock of the Susquehanna Boom Co. at Williamsport. Included in the purchase was a dam across the Susquehanna, which had been acquired by the Lycoming Edison Co. when it built the Williamsport Steam Electric Station. Lycoming Edison Co. had acquired the dam as a source of condensing water for the steam electric station.

The origin of the dam on the Susquehanna at Williamsport went back to the middle of the 19th century, some 40 years before entrepreneurs began utilizing Thomas Edison's invention of an electric system, powered by hydroelectricity from the nation's rivers. At the time the Susquehanna Boom Co. was formed in 1846, rivers in Pennsylvania were dammed up to concentrate sawtimber floating down the rivers to sawmills. Log rafting on the Susquehanna began in 1795, and by the middle of

Log rafting on the Susquehanna River began in the late 1700s.

the 19th century, the West Branch of the Susquehanna was the most important rafting stream in the state; Williamsport's concentration of sawmills made it one of the most important lumber centers in 19th century America. Logs were rolled into the river at a landing and then lashed side by side for their trip down the Susquehanna.

The pine and hemlock floating in rafts down the Susquehanna and its tributaries had to be collected and sorted for the Williamsport sawmills, some of which were cutting as many as 130,000 feet of timber daily. Floods and thefts caused havoc in the industry, and tim-

ber company executives searched for a solution to the problem. According to Thomas T. Taber III, the historian of the Susquehanna lumber industry, "the key to making Williamsport the lumber city was the boom." As early as 1836, lumber executives in Williamsport examined the idea of building a boom—or series of piers—in the river at Williamsport to collect and sort the lumber rafted from upstream.

In 1845, James H. Perkins, a New Englander who had made a fortune in the calico business in Philadelphia, visited Williamsport. Early the next year, Perkins incorporated the Susquehanna Boom Co. with John DuBois as president. It was another six years, however, before the boom was actually built. A six-mile-long series of piers built into the river at Williamsport, the boom allowed the local sawmills to collect and store logs during the annual spring log rafting drives along the Susquehanna. The cribbed log piers were anchored by stone and connected by iron chains stretched diagonally across the Susquehanna. The boom cost $1.5 million to build, an astronomical sum at the time.

Some 20 Williamsport sawmills depended upon the boom for logs, and the boom handled an immense amount of sawtimber. In 1873, some 300 million board feet of timber came down the Susquehanna for storage in the boom. The boom company, which employed an average of 150 workers a year between 1862 and 1891, charged mill operators a dollar per thousand feet for logs rafted out of the boom.

The above photo shows logs stored on the Susquehanna Boom. *(photo courtesy of the James V. Brown Library)*

Williamsport's Market Square during the flood of 1889. *(photo courtesy of the James V. Brown Library)*

Throughout its history, the Susquehanna Boom Co. was plagued by floods along the turbulent river. The boom broke during floods in both 1860 and 1861, sending some 50 million board feet of lumber each year downriver on the flood crest. Cribs of heavier construction were built during the Civil War years, and the boom held until the disastrous spring flood of June 1889. Taber notes that 200 million board feet of logs washed down river that year, many of which reached the Chesapeake Bay and were never recovered. Another flood in 1894 washed an equal number of logs downriver.

With the turn of the century, the logging industry along the Susquehanna was already in a state of decline. Williamsport's peak year of production had occurred in 1885, and Pennsylvania's rank as a timber-producing state had fallen to fourth in the U.S.; lumber barons like John DuBois had already been drawn west in the 1890s by the virgin stands of white pine in the lake states forests of Michigan and Minnesota.

The Susquehanna Boom Co. continued in business during the early part of the 20th century, but the volume of lumber rafted downriver to Williamsport steadily dwindled. By 1907, the boom handled only slightly more than 20 million tons of lumber. Just three years before, the Lake Superior port city of Duluth, Minn., had shipped close to 475 million board feet of lumber down the Great Lakes to Chicago and Erie and Buffalo.

The Susquehanna Boom Co. suspended operations in 1909, although the company itself wasn't officially dissolved until after its 1937 acquisition by Pennsylvania Power & Light Co.

The Arc Light Revolution

The Thomson-Houston System.

DYNAMO MACHINES,	HALF-ARC LAMPS,	AUTOMATIC CUT-OUTS,
AUTOMATIC REGULATORS,	INCANDESCENT LAMPS,	ABSOLUTE CUT-OUTS,
REGULATOR MAGNETS,	DISTRIBUTION SWITCHES,	DUPLEX ARC LAMPS,
SINGLE ARC LAMPS,	ELECTRIC MOTORS,	FOCUSING ARC LAMPS,

ORNAMENTAL LAMPS, SWITCH-BOARDS,
ARC LAMPS FEEDING CARBON PENCIL DIRECT,
ARC LIGHTS RUNNING IN MULTIPLE SERIES,
INCANDESCENT LIGHTS ON ARC LIGHT CIRCUIT,
LILIPUTIAN WORKING PLANT SHOWING SYSTEM COMPLETE.

YOU CANNOT AFFORD to BUY or USE ANY OTHER SYSTEM of ELECTRIC LIGHTING.

CARDS, ILLUSTRATED PAMPHLETS, ETC., TO BE HAD IN THE EXHIBITION.

ADDRESS OF PARENT COMPANY:

THE THOMSON-HOUSTON ELECTRIC CO.

131 DEVONSHIRE STREET, BOSTON, MASS.

circa 1882. (courtesy of The Franklin Institute in Philadelphia)

Gas lamps lit the streets of Pennsylvania and the world for much of the 19th century. However, in the last quarter of the century, a revolution in lighting technology swept across Europe and America. Between 1876 and 1900, the new science of electricity—championed by inventors/entrepreneurs like Thomas Edison, Elihu Thomson and Charles F. Brush—advanced across America from east to west, transforming industry and society in the process.

Edison's invention of the incandescent electric light bulb in New York City in 1879 and his construction of a generation and distribution system at Pearl Street Station in New York City three years later are generally considered by historians to be the events signaling the dawn of the electrical age. But Edison's incandescent

Volta, generated a continuous current with the first crude battery at the turn of the nineteenth century. Early in the century, Sir Humphrey Davy, a chemist and member of the prestigious Royal Society in London, built a 2,000-cell battery to pass current across a silver and copper wire. When the wire heated up

Many of PP&L's predecessors started out in the early 1880s by supplying arc light services to the communities of central eastern Pennsylvania.
(photo courtesy of the Lehigh County Historical Society)

system was preceded in general use in the United States and Europe by arc lighting systems. Many of the predecessors of Pennsylvania Power & Light Co. got their start in the early 1880s by supplying arc lighting services to the communities of central eastern Pennsylvania.

The idea of electricity had been around since late in the previous century. Philadelphian Benjamin Franklin's experiments with kites and lightning, familiar to generations of schoolchildren, had sparked interest in the phenomenon of electricity, both here and abroad. In the 1780s, Luigi Galvani, an Italian anatomist, discovered the concept of the electric current, and another Italian, Allesandro

and began to glow, Davy inserted two pieces of charcoal into the wire circuit and then began to pull them apart. An electric arc leaped across the gap between the two pieces of charcoal. When Davy adjusted the gap between the two pieces of charcoal, he created a continuous spark, or arc.

In 1820, Danish scientist Hans Christian Orsted sent electricity from a battery through a wire surrounded by a magnetic field to demonstrate the relationship between magnetism and electricity. Orsted's work was picked up by the Frenchman Andre Marie Ampere and the German Georg Simon Ohm, and by mid-century, the concept of electromagnetism was beginning to be well understood on both sides of the Atlantic.

Davy's one-time assistant, Michael Faraday, discovered in the 1830s that by shaping a copper wire into a coil, he was able to increase the electricity generated when he moved a bar magnet into the coil. Faraday's discovery was the essential building block for the concept of an electrical generator, which in its simplest form consists of a strong magnet, a rotating copper coil, and a power source to spin the coil.

Arc Lights Take the World by Storm

When the citizens of Philadelphia trooped by the thousands down to the Belmont Avenue entrance of Fairmount Park to attend the Centennial Exposition in the spring of 1876, electricity was still basically a scientific curiosity. Six years before, the Belgian Zenobe Theophile Gramme had devised the first workable alternating current generator, but there was as yet no application for the invention. Elihu Thomson, then a young high school teacher living in Philadelphia, noted that the Centennial Exposition in his hometown couldn't really showcase electricity because arc lights, incandescent lighting, alternating current transformers and practical storage batteries were all then unknown.

Although Alexander Graham Bell used a weak electric current from primitive batteries to demonstrate his invention of the telephone at the Exposition, historian David Nye points out that "the Philadelphia Centennial Exposition of 1876 was the last great exposition based on steam power, and its central symbol was the huge Corliss steam engine." Indeed, fair-goers rode horse-drawn streetcars to the exposition grounds, and the Exposition was shut down each night for want of sufficient lighting.

Two years later, in 1878, Paul Jablochkoff, a Russian inventor who had resigned his position as director of

Telegraph Service between Moscow and Kursk in 1875 to attend the Philadelphia Centennial Exposition, demonstrated his Jablochkoff Candles at the Paris Exposition at the Champs de Mars. Essentially two parallel carbon rods separated by layers of plaster of Paris or clay, the candles were powered by the Gramme generator and were the first working arc lights. In a typical Jablochkoff set-up, 16 lamps of approximately 700 candlepower each—far brighter than the gaslights then in use—were connected in series supplied by a single generator. The introduction of the Jablochkoff Candle in Europe set off a frenzy of activity in this country. Inventors here had been closely following events in Europe, and arc light systems were soon in operation in the United States.

Charles F. Brush, a British citizen then living in Ohio, had perfected a dynamo-driven arc light system in 1878. In the spring of 1879, Brush's Telegraph Supply Co. demonstrated its arc lamp lighting system for the citizens of Cleveland, Ohio. The Brush lamps lit up the town square along the Lake Erie shorefront as thousands of Clevelanders cheered.

Telegraph Supply Co. soon after changed its name to the Brush Electric Co. of Cleveland and began manufacturing arc lighting systems for customers in the Midwest. In March 1880, Brush

Charles F. Brush perfected a dynamo-driven arc light system in 1878. By the early 1880s, his company, The Brush Electric Light Co., was selling arc lighting systems to entrepreneurs all over the United States. *(photo courtesy of Houston Lighting & Power Company)*

installed one of his machines in the courthouse of the farm community of Wabash, Ind. The generator ran one bright arc light atop the courthouse, the glow of which could be seen for miles. At the time, Brush sold his dynamos for $2,250, a steep price, but not at all unreasonable given the Brush company's claims that arc lighting cost half the price of gas streetlighting.

Charles Brush sold his arc lighting system to entrepreneurs located as far away as Texas, but the Cleveland-based inventor soon had competition. In New York, Hiram Maxim, the chief engineer of the United States Electric Lighting Co., invented the Maxim arc light and sold systems to customers up and down the East Coast. A showcase for USELCO was the franchise it granted to several Washington, D.C., investors in the fall of 1882 "to supply electricity for all purposes, whether for lighting, motors, storage or other purposes for which it may be used in the city of Washington." Maxim's light was a common fixture in U.S. arc lighting systems in the late 19th century, but the inventor is more widely known for another of his creations. Following the establishment of USELCO, Maxim went to England and designed the World War I machine gun that bears his name.

Closer to home, Philadelphia became a beacon for arc lighting technology, as both Brush and Maxim set up competing systems in the City of Brotherly Love. A young Philadelphia high school teacher, Elihu Thomson, in collaboration with Edwin Houston, had already designed and built an alternating current arc light system in the fall of 1878. In tests at the Franklin Institute, however, the balky alternating current system failed to perform well. Thomson and Houston left the field of teaching to design a workable direct current arc light system. Thomson eventually wound up in Lynn, Mass., where his Thomson-Houston Electric Light Co. became a major force in the manufacture of electrical equipment.

Electric arc lighting had become so commonplace in Philadelphia by

The International Electrical Exhibition of 1884 displayed more than 1,500 electrical exhibits, all of them listed in the official catalogue. (courtesy of The Franklin Institute in Philadephia)

This shows the exhibit of the Thomson-Houston Electric Light Co. of Boston from the October 18, 1884 issue of the New York Daily Graphic. (courtesy of The Franklin Institute in Philadelphia)

September 1884 that the Franklin Institute recognized the new technology with an International Electrical Exhibition. The Exhibition building at 32nd Street and Lancaster Avenue could accommodate 5,000 visitors at a time, and contained more than 1,500 electrical exhibits. It was a far cry from the Centennial Exposition of just eight years before, when evidence of electrical technology was in scant supply. And by 1884, arc light systems had taken a firm hold in the communities of central eastern Pennsylvania.

The 'New Thing' Was a Great Success

"Our people can take just pride in Allentown being the first city in Eastern Pennsylvania, outside of Philadelphia, to adopt the electric light for illuminating hotels and business places," *The Daily Chronicle* reported in its editions of Dec. 4, 1882, "and the success attending the first public exhibition of the light on Saturday night was so decided that the general adoption by businessmen of the new method will very likely follow." *The Daily Chronicle* was saluting the efforts of William H. Roney, who operated a shoe factory on the north side of Hamilton Street between 8th and 9th streets. Roney, who had opened his tanning and manu- facturing plant to make girls' and women's shoes in 1843, had already installed primitive generators in his factory to power the shoe-making equipment. He reasoned that as long as he had the machinery, he might as well operate a dynamo dedicated to providing electrical current for night lighting.

In the fall of 1882, he purchased a 10-arc light dynamo using the Maxim system from the United States Electric Lighting Co. in Philadelphia. Installed in the basement of Roney's shoe factory, the dynamo was tested during the fall of 1882. Contemporary newspaper accounts noted that light blazed forth from the three-story building, a light that flickered considerably, but one "that shone like the sun compared with the gas lamps in front of his building."

Skeptics questioned the safety of the new lighting system. "If Billy Roney wants to make electricity," they said, "attract all the lightning for 20 miles and shock himself to death, that's his busi- ness." Roney ignored the criticisms and set about signing up other Allentown businesses for the new lights. The Allen House; New York Savings Store; Bittner and Hunsicker; Hergesheimer's Restau- rant; Schnureman, Roth and Co.; Koch and Shankweiler; H.M. Leh and Co.; and W.R. Lawfer and Co. were some of the local merchants who signed up for the new lights. Because of their brightness, arc lights were particularly suited for streetlighting and for lighting the interior of commercial establish- ments. "To say that the light proved satisfactory is stating the case but mildly," *The Daily Chronicle* reported. "The result was far beyond the anticipation, and those wiseacres who shook their heads in a knowing sort of way and predicted the failure of the enterprise were forced to admit that the 'new thing' was a great success."

The lighting of the Hamilton Street commercial center was the second technological marvel introduced to Allentown in less than two years. In 1880, Samuel Cortright had started the city's first telephone exchange in the Ruhe Building at 6th and Hamilton. In short order, the Pennsylvania Telephone Co. had signed up 50 subscribers, mostly merchants doing business along Hamilton Street. Roney's success in signing up merchants along Hamilton Street for his arc lighting services con- vinced him to take the next step. In March 1883, Roney incorporated the Allentown Electric Light and Power Co. to supply electricity in the city of Allentown.

Roney moved the dynamos from the basement of his shoe factory to the Seagraves Stable Building at the southwest corner of Penn and Maple

> Skeptics questioned the safety of the new lighting system. "If Billy Roney wants to make electricity," they said, "attract all the lightning for 20 miles and shock himself to death, that's his business."

streets. Allentown Electric Light and Power Co. had a contract to furnish electricity to 150 arc light streetlamps along Hamilton Street, and the original power plant generated electricity during the day and then stored it in large batteries for the streetlighting operation.

Bob Dornblaser, who started with the company in its earlier days and retired in the 1920s as PP&L's Allentown line superintendent, recalled that the personnel of the plant included an engineer, a fireman and two light-men, whose duties included turning the lights on and off each night and morning and trimming the carbons during the day. Alexander

HEY! WHAT'S THE IDEA TAKING THAT ADDING MACHINE?

WE'VE BEEN ADDING UP THE LIST OF PROF. THOMSON'S INVENTIONS, AND IT'S GOT THE LOCAL MATHEMATICIANS EXHAUSTED

Bowman was the first plant superintendent. When Bowman died in the early 1890s, he was succeeded by Uriah Wieand.

Dornblaser told reporters in 1928 that Allentown Electric Light and Power Co. induced the city's merchants to install arc lighting in their stores by offering to wire the stores free of charge. By the late 1880s, "practically every store from the terminal station to Ninth Street had taken advantage of the offer." In addition, Allentown Electric Light and Power Co. boasted one of the first successful farm electrification programs in the nation. Jeremiah Roth, then president of the Allentown Fair, had his farm at 19th and Hamilton wired for electricity; people came from miles around to gape at the brightly lit farm.

In the mid-1880s, the Grand Central Hotel, located on the site later occupied by Hess Brothers Store, installed an electric motor in the basement of the building for running the hotel's elevators. Allentown Electric Light and Power Co. charged its customers for lighting service rather than electricity itself. The price was 50 cents or 65 cents per light per night, depending upon whether the light was in

service from dusk until 9 p.m. or dusk until 11 p.m.

Roney traded in his original Maxim equipment in 1885 and purchased a Schyler dynamo and 30 more pull-arc lamps to supply additional load. By 1887, the plant at Penn and Maple was being powered by one 30-light and six 10-light dynamos.

The Belt Ran for 12 Minutes

In the early 1880s, arc lighting spread across central eastern Pennsylvania, from the anthracite region to the state capital of Harrisburg in the Susquehanna River Valley. Residents of the anthracite region had first been introduced to arc lighting on the evening of Oct. 30, 1880. Republican presidential candidate James Garfield was in Wilkes-Barre that evening, and the local campaign committee installed four electric arc lights on the square for Garfield's parade that night. However, it would be two more years, before arc lights were more than a political curiosity.

On the night of Dec. 14, 1882, just 10 days after William Roney lit his Allentown shoe factory, a group of Wilkes-Barre entrepreneurs previewed the electric era for the citizens of the northeastern Pennsylvania city. The 7 p.m. test was less than a resounding success. A 15-light dynamo was installed in the foundry room of the Dixon Works on North Pennsylvania Avenue. The dynamo was belted to a counter shaft, which during the day drove the blower in the foundry. Just 12 minutes into the lighting test, the belt broke. It was soon repaired, but the new belt kept stretching, and the lights kept going out. Finally, the engineers belted the dynamo directly to the engine, weighing the dynamo down with "several pounds of pig iron" to provide a stable platform for the contraption.

The incorporators of the Wilkes-Barre Electric Light Co. nevertheless signed a contract with the city for furnishing electricity to 20-30 arc lights. Work was

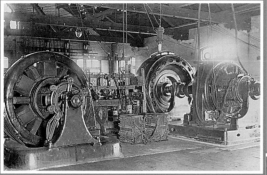

Views of the equipment at the Ninth Street Station. (Top clockwise): 300 and 500 kwh motor generators; arc machines; steam turbine; standard engine; old pump pit.

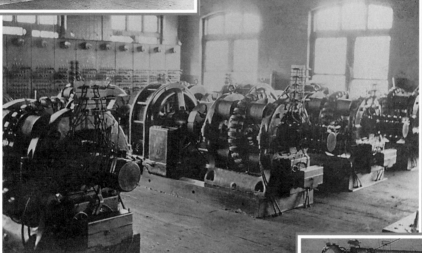

Harrisburg's Ninth Street Station in the 1890s. By this time, it was becoming apparent that the arc light had serious limitations. Note how open and unprotected the equipment is; safety and environmental standards weren't quite like they are today.

soon begun on a small generating plant in the city's Butler Alley. Two European systems, the Arnoux and Hochhausen arc lighting machines, were installed. As in Allentown, merchants in the downtown section signed up for arc lights, and the new company also supplied steam heating to several customers located in the immediate vicinity of the plant.

Another Pennsylvania community that experienced a less than successful introduction to arc lighting was the state capitol of Harrisburg. In the spring of 1883, a syndicate of local investors floated a $50,000 stock issue for the incorporation of the Pennsylvania Electric Co. They secured a site at the Novelty Works, located at the foot of Third Street along the Pennsylvania Railroad tracks, and ordered equipment. "This plant," wrote W. Maxwell Mailey, long-time superintendent of the service and complaint department of the Harrisburg Light and Power Co., "which consisted of a Westinghouse Engine and Dynamo, was not a success. The experts who installed (them) misrepresented things and were unable to operate the machine (thought to be a Brush), the lights flickering out as often as three times in one night."

Mailey reported that "the owners became disgusted and sold out to the newly organized Harrisburg Electric Light Co." Harrisburg Electric Light Co. soon became interested in expanding into incandescent lighting and signed a franchise agreement with the Edison operating department in New York City. The general manager of the Harrisburg company was John I. Beggs, a native Vermonter who left Harrisburg in the spring of 1887 to take over superintendency of Edison Illuminating Co.'s flagship generating plant in New York City. In later years, Beggs would migrate west to Wisconsin, where his Milwaukee Electric Railway and Light Co. became one of the nation's premier electric street railway companies and the chief operating utility of the North American Cos., a major utility holding company of the 1920s and 1930s.

Harrisburg Electric Light Co.'s concen-tration on wiring homes and businesses for incandescent lighting spurred competition for the city's arc lighting business. Early in 1887, the Excelsior Electric Co. was formed for the express purpose of lighting the streets of Harrisburg. Excelsior Electric Co., which had secured a franchise from a Brooklyn, N.Y., manufacturer of arc lighting equipment, got a contract from the Harrisburg City Council to light the streets of Harrisburg in March 1887.

Harrisburg Electric Light Co. responded by signing a contract with the Thomson-Houston Electric Co. for the installation of a 50-light machine belted to an Ide Engine. Harrisburg Electric Light Co. fixed its charges for arc lighting at $9 per month per light, used until midnight.

Five years later, Harrisburg Electric Light Co. and the Excelsior Electric Co. were merged, retaining the name of the Harrisburg Electric Light Co. By that time, Thomson-Houston Electric Co. had acquired a controlling interest in the arc lighting business of the Excelsior Electric Co.'s parent firm. Edgar Z. Wallower, the president of the merged Harrisburg Electric Light Co., engaged in an extended correspondence with Thomson-Houston Electric Co. officials during 1891 to establish a purchase price of $262,200 for the Excelsior Electric Co.'s interests and franchises in Harrisburg.

Between 1887 and 1892, Harrisburg Electric Light Co. concentrated on selling arc lighting service to commercial accounts. The Excelsior Electric Co. had the lucrative streetlighting contract, and incandescent lamps did not yet furnish sufficient illumination for interior store lighting. But by the dawn of the 1890s, it was already becoming apparent to electric utility entrepreneurs in Pennsylvania and across the nation that the arc light had serious limitations. Even though arc-lit streetlights were common on the streets of Pennsylvania's cities for much of the late 19th and early 20th centuries, the future of the industry lay in the incandescent systems being sold by Thomas Edison's sales force in New York City.

Trimming the Lamps

rc lights had several drawbacks, although none of them were particularly fatal where business was concerned. They also had one major advantage over gas and incandescent lighting, their major competitors; arc lights cast a far more brilliant light than either gas or incandescent bulbs. At a time when incandescent bulbs rarely exceeded 32 candlepower, arc lights as bright as 2,000 candlepower were installed in the streets of Pennsylvania cities and on the merchandise floors of stores and shops.

The disadvantages, however, outweighed the advantages. Arc lights did have to be trimmed on a regular schedule, and arc lighting for stores and shops was a tricky proposition in the early days, primarily because early arc lights for street lamps were all in a series; when one lamp was shut off, all the lamps on the circuit went out. The very brilliance of arc lighting made it unsuitable for home use, and the adaptation of arc lighting to nighttime use meant that most of the capital investment of the utility was tied up in machinery that only ran several hours each evening.

Gas lamps in America's cities required the services of a lamplighter, a person who went out at dusk each evening and lit the gas in each bulb with a long taper. Arc lights continued this tradition, although the lights themselves did not have to be physically lit each evening. Instead, the carbon rods in the arc light had to be trimmed periodically. As the carbon rods burned away, the gap between them lengthened, which caused the spark to leap an ever greater distance. Carbon rods lasted eight to ten hours if uncased, and considerably longer if enclosed in a glass bulb. The arc lamp trimmer made his rounds each day, trimming the carbon rods or replacing them altogether.

Most streetlights of the day were sus-

Gas lamps were lit by lamplighters, like this one, who made their rounds each night at dusk. Arc lights required the employment of arc lamp trimmers whose responsibilities were to trim the carbon rods in the arc light on a more periodic basis.

pended over the thoroughfare, and could be lowered by rope and pulley to chest level so the trimmer could adjust the rods. In commercial establishments, the lamp trimmer lowered the arc light and then stood on a wooden stool, its legs enclosed in glass to prevent the current from going to ground. Although the electric current was normally off during the daylight hours, the arc lamp trimmer took no chances; most wore heavy gloves and rubber boots should a worker at the power plant suddenly throw the wrong switch.

Most of the early electric utility employees were jacks-of-all-trades, familiar with all tasks of the business, so that trimming lamps was an accepted part of the job. Maxwell Mailey, who closed out his career with the Harrisburg division of PP&L in the late 1920s, wrote in 1922 of his years with the company's Harrisburg predecessors that "there were no specialists in electrical work. Men were expected to be able to do whatever they were told to do. They were all-around men—wiring, troubleshooting, line work—all went within a day's work."

During Mailey's forty-some years in the electric utility industry, he worked as a bill passer and collector, "a meter reader, tester and repairman, Excelsior Arc and slattery induction armature winder, wireman, arc lamp inspector and repairman, not mentioning complaints and troubleshooting, and in his spare time, he dug holes and piked poles. Outside of this, he had nothing to do but occasionally trim a street circuit on Sunday when a trimmer failed to show up."

Engineers at Mailey's first employer, the Harrisburg Electric Light Co., helped solve the problem of multiple arc lamps on the same circuit. In 1888, they converted the Thomson-Houston series arc lamp for use on the company's 110-volt direct current (DC) multiple circuit. The conversion was made by taking the regular Thomson-Houston series arc lamp and adding a

33

70-foot coil of #10 German silver wire as a resistor. An electrician then cut out the shunt magnet of the lamp by opening the magnet and wedging an insulator between the open jaws of the magnet.

Care had to be taken in the final step of the process, when the positive and negative wires were applied to the correct binding posts of the lamp. If the electrician was dealing with a concealed wiring job, the circuit had to be tested. Typically, the electrician wet a white blotter with potassium iodide and brushed both wires with the dampened blotter. The positive wire left a black mark.

Arc lighting lit the streets of Allentown. *(photo courtesy of the Lehigh County Historical Society)*

Until early 1892, when the Thomson-Houston Electric Co. introduced a commercially produced arc lamp operating on a two-wire, 110-volt DC circuit, the multiple arc lamp rigged up by the Harrisburg Electric Light Co. was copied all over America.

Carbon arc lights were never able to overcome the problem of their brilliance and were replaced quickly with incandescent bulbs for home and office use in the 1890s. Still, arc lights illuminated many city streets through the 1930s, and even today, arc lights are still in use for outdoor spotlights and some motion picture projection equipment.

The Life and Times of Elihu Thomson

Although Thomas Edison's name is forever associated with the birth of the American electric utility industry, the "Wizard of Menlo Park" must share credit with a host of other late nineteenth century inventors/entrepreneurs. The names of George Westinghouse, Nikola Tesla, Charles F. Brush and Frank Sprague come readily to mind, but relatively few Americans could identify the contributions of Elihu Thomson to the development of the industry. Yet in the 1890s, Thomson rivalled Edison as an inventor, and his company was merged with Edison's in 1892 to form General Electric Co. Without Thomson's contributions, the electrification of America would likely have proceeded much more slowly than it did.

Born in Manchester, England, in 1853, Thomson moved to the United States with his parents at an early age. The family settled in Philadelphia, and young Thomson entered the public schools of Philadelphia at the age of six. Five years later, he was scholastically ready for admission to the Boys' Central High School, the city's most prestigious high school, but his age delayed his entry.

Central High concentrated its curriculum on the sciences, and Thomson took courses in everything offered: physics, chemistry, mathematics and astronomy. Following his graduation in 1870, he spent six months in a Philadelphia laboratory, testing iron ore samples for the area's numerous foundries. By the time classes began in the fall of 1870, Thomson was back at his alma mater, this time as an adjunct to the Department of Chemistry at an annual salary of $500.

While back at Boys' Central High School, Thomson became reacquainted with Edwin J. Houston, one of his former teachers. The two teachers were both fascinated with the emerging science of electricity, and collaborated throughout the 1870s on numerous experiments, many of which they published in the *Journal of the Franklin Institute.*

In 1879, Thomson and Houston built a dynamo with

Elihu Thomson was recognized for his valuable services at the 1901 Pan-American Exposition.

three-phase winding, which they patented the next year. The Thomson-Houston dynamo, which is today on display at the Smithsonian Institution, was the basis for an entire arc lighting system invented by the two Philadelphians. "Arc lighting has largely been superseded by later forms of electrical illumination," Dugald C. Jackson wrote in 1939, "but I am personally inclined to put forward this invention of the automatically regulated dynamo for arc lighting service as one of Thomson's most important, on account of its influence on his own work and the development of his opportunities."

Thomson quit Boys' Central High in 1880 and went to work for the American Electric Co. of New Britain, Conn. Three years later, Thomson moved to Lynn, Mass., and formed the Thomson-Houston Electric Co. with the help of Charles A. Coffin, a Boston shoe manufacturer. During the next decade, Thomson-Houston Electric Co. became one of the major electric equipment manufacturers, providing arc lighting and incandescent lighting systems to electric utilities in Pennsylvania and nationwide. Thomson's invention of electric resistance welding contributed to the rapid spread of electrification of the nation's factories and shops.

In 1892, Coffin engineered the merger of Thomson-Houston Electric Co. and its chief rival, the Edison General Electric Co. The resulting General Electric Corp. was one of the largest corporations of late 19th-century America, and Thomson became the new company's chief technical and scientific advisor.

Thomson averaged 21 patents a year from 1880 to 1885, and doubled that output during the next five years. He worked from a private workshop at Thomson-Houston Electric Co.'s Lynn, Mass., factory that he termed the "model room," supervising a handful of machinists and technicians. Always content to leave the business decisions in Coffin's hands, Thomson even refused to become a director of GE after its formation in 1892, noting that his value to the corporation was as an inventor and not a manager.

Thomson became a lecturer in the Department of Electrical Engineering at the Massachusetts Institute of Technology in 1894 and served as acting president of MIT from 1920 to 1923. For many years, he also lectured in the electrical engineering department at Harvard University. In the half-century from 1872 to 1932, Thomson held more than 700 patents for electrical equipment. "Scientific facts are of little value in themselves," he told the American Association for the Advancement of Science in 1899. "Their significance has a bearing upon other facts, enabling us to generalize and to discover principles, just as the accurate measurements of the position of a star may be without value in itself, but in relation to other similar measurements of other stars may become the means of discovering their proper motion."

Thomson died in 1937 at the age of 84, but not before the former high school teacher had borne witness to the principles that had laid the foundation for the creation of America's electric utility industry.

4

Mr. Edison's Magic Lantern

The incandescent light bulb revolutionized the electric power industry.

For all its achievement in lighting the streets of America's cities and towns, arc lighting was essentially a bridge technology. True, arc lighting cast a more brilliant illumination than the gas streetlights in common use at the time. But the very intensity of the light and the hazard of burning carbon rods precluded the use of arc lighting for anything other than streetlighting or large commercial facilities.

Simultaneously with the development of commercially available arc light systems in the late 1870s and early 1880s, work was moving ahead on the creation of an incandescent lighting system. The difference between arc lighting and incandescent lighting is simple. In an arc light system, a spark jumps across a pair of parallel carbon rods, creating a brilliant, harsh white light. In an incandescent system, a filament inside a glass bulb is heated until it glows, throwing off a diffused light. For society at large, the difference was simple, yet profound.

Thomas Edison and his associates invented the incandescent light bulb in 1879.

A Wire in a Glass Bulb

"Fundamentally, an incandescent lamp is a simple thing," General Electric noted in a press release in 1954 celebrating the 75th anniversary of the first incandescent light bulb, "just a wire sealed in a glass bulb, with a few supplementary parts. The power required to force electric current through the current wire heats it to incandescence, and light is produced."

Pioneering work by scientists like Ohm, Faraday, Volta and others led to a laboratory in the rural countryside of New Jersey. In 1879, in a warren of buildings, Thomas Alva Edison and his associates found a simple but eloquent solution to the perplexing problem of designing an incandescent electric lamp. In experiments that stretched over much of the year 1879, the Menlo Park team tested material after material for a filament that would conduct electricity to the proper incandescence without bursting into flame. "Edison then tried numerous other experiments with all manner of materials, even using human hair taken from the red whiskers of a visitor," Francis Jehl, a longtime associate recalled in 1924. "He tried all kinds of vegetable fibers, paper and threads, many of his experiments giving promising results. It was while using different kinds of silk and cotton threads that the thought struck him that perhaps the Clark thread mills at Newark might furnish him with a special brand that would give better results. This was in October 1879, and a few days afterwards, he procured a package from the Clark mills containing a pound of white thread."

Finally, in late October, Edison tried the carbonized cotton sewing thread from the Clark mills as a potential filament for his incandescent light. On Oct. 20-21, 1879, Edison's first incandescent bulb burned for a total of 40 hours before the inventor began adjusting the voltage upwards and burned up the carbonized cotton filament. Edison next turned to carbonized cardboard for his new incandescent lamp, and he eventually settled on a carbonized bamboo grown in Japan for the filament of what became known as the Edison Mazda Lamp, the standard in the industry for the first decade or so of its history until 1911, when the bamboo filament was replaced with a long-lasting tungsten filament. Edison's discovery of the efficiency of bamboo filaments was a mark of the man's single-minded pursuit of research; at his winter estate on the banks of the Caloosahatchee River near Ft. Myers, Fla., he grew hundreds of species of exotic plants in search of a suitable candidate for the elusive filament.

Edison's 1879 announcement of the discovery of the incandescent bulb was front-page news across the country. Under a Dec. 21, 1879, headline that trumpeted "The Great Inventor's Triumph in Electric Illumination," *The New York Herald* noted that "the near approach of the first public exhibition of Edison's long-looked-for electric light, announced to take place on New Year's Eve at Menlo Park, on which occasion that place will be illuminated with the new light, has

EDISON'S LIGHT.

The Great Inventor's Triumph in Electric Illumination.

A SCRAP OF PAPER.

It Makes a Light, Without Gas or Flame, Cheaper Than Oil.

TRANSFORMED IN THE FURNACE.

Complete Details of the Perfected Carbon Lamp.

FIFTEEN MONTHS OF TOIL.

Story of His Tireless Experiments with Lamps, Burners and Generators.

SUCCESS IN A COTTON THREAD.

The Wizard's Byplay, with Bodily Pain and Gold "Tailings."

HISTORY OF ELECTRIC LIGHTING.

The Wizard of Menlo Park

At the time of his discovery of the incandescent bulb, Edison was already one of the best-known inventors in the country. Born in Milan, Ohio, on Feb. 11, 1847, Edison left home at the age of 12 to become a newsboy and candy salesman on railroad trains running between Detroit and Port Huron. His lifelong fascination with news led him to become a telegraph operator; and he was 22 years old in 1869 when he made his first commercial invention, an automatic stock ticker.

Edison took the $40,000 he received from inventing the stock ticker and invested it in the establishment of his first laboratory and manufacturing facility at Newark. In 1876, he moved to his newly constructed laboratory at Menlo Park and began a whirlwind of inventive activity. He applied early in 1877 for a patent on a carbon telephone transmitter, which made the telephone—exhibited nine months before at the Philadelphia Centennial Exhibition—commercially feasible and also served as the basis for the microphone. Later in the year, after a frenzy of more than 60 hours without sleep, Edison invented the world's first commercially feasible phonograph.

Edison's work habits were legendary. He and his assistants would burst forth with a frenzy of activity when they got close to one of Edison's numerous inventions. At other times, Edison would lie down on a table in the laboratory and take a cat-nap. "For myself, I never found need of more than four or five hours' sleep in the 24," Edison told reporters in 1921. "I never dream. It's real sleep. When by chance I have taken more, I wake dull and indolent. We are always hearing people talk about 'loss of sleep' as a calamity. They better call it loss of time, vitality and opportunities...."

Largely self-educated, Edison claimed

Edison's 1879 announcement of the discovery of the incandescent bulb was front-page news across the country.

revived public interest in the great inventor's work, and throughout the civilized world, scientists and people generally are anxiously awaiting the results."

When Edison bedecked the Menlo Park property with 60 incandescent bulbs on New Year's Eve 1879, all lit simultaneously by a switch in the inventor's laboratory, more than 3,000 spectators showed up to witness the sight. "Well, it's a pretty fair sight," one old farmer observed, "but danged if I can see how you got the red-hot hairpin in the bottle." That "red-hot hairpin in the bottle" would transform the world in short order.

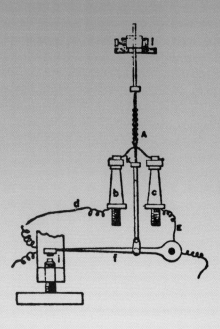

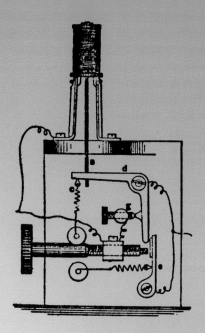

These illustrations show the progression of Edison's great invention. Clockwise from top left: the first light; the bobbin lamp; the reflector lamp; the first platinum vacuum lamp; and the perfected lamp.

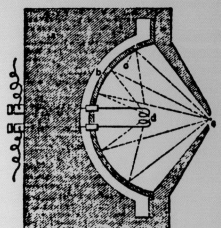

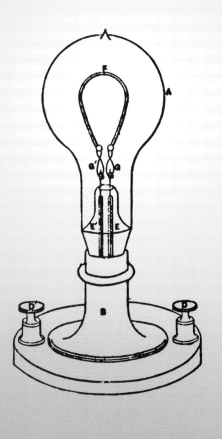

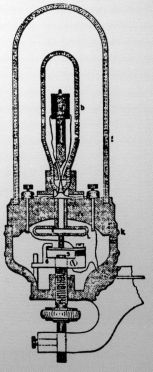

that the vast majority of his inventions were the result of hard work, common sense and an almost unlimited curiosity. "Genius is one percent inspiration and 99 percent perspiration" was one of his favorite sayings, and in an 1890 interview, he explained the role that curiosity plays in invention. "In 1877," Edison recalled, "I finally succeeded in perfecting an instrument which recorded telegrams by indenting a strip of paper with dots and dashes, and also repeated a message any number of times and at any rate of speed desired. Now, as a logical sequence, it occurred to me that if the repeater would again give forth the click of the telegraph instrument, the vibrations of a diaphragm should also be susceptible to similar record and reproduction, and I at once began the series of experiments which led to the phonograph."

Edison and his associates would need all the curiosity and common sense they could muster to get the incandescent electric light into commercial production.

Inventing— And Selling— An Incandescent System

Robert B. Van Atta of the Public Information Department of West Penn Power Co. was a longtime student of the development of electric power systems in Pennsylvania. He noted that Edison faced a number of challenges when he invented his first incandescent light in October 1879. "To serve his purpose, Edison had to do six things," Van Atta wrote. "An economical generator was needed to manufacture a steady flow of current. A system of conductors to carry electricity into individual homes had to be devised. A method of maintaining constant voltage, no matter how many lamps were used, was another need. A lamp had to be invented which gave better, less expensive light than gas jets. Edison also had to

develop a way of feeding current into a multiple circuit that would permit operation of any number of light bulbs, and a meter to measure and record individual customer use of electricity."

Thomas Parke Hughes, the dean of American science and technology historians, calls Edison "a hedgehog," a person "who relates everything to a single central vision, one system less or more coherent or articulate." Hughes wrote that "Edison invented systems, including an electric light system that took form as the Pearl Street Generating Station and distribution network of the Edison Electric Illuminating Co. of New York."

That Edison was able to invent the system and place it into commercial operation in Pennsylvania and elsewhere across the country in the short space of less than four years can be attributed to several factors. Edison's single-minded pursuit of his research goals was buttressed by financial backing of unprecedented scope and by the devotion of his talented staff of scientific assistants.

For all his reputation as a rough-around-the-edges, eccentric scientist, Edison was a shrewd inventor/entrepreneur whose efforts led to the creation of the prototype of the modern industrial research and development laboratory. Asked by a reporter in 1927 on the occasion of his 80th birthday what his greatest invention was, Edison answered without hesitation, the "research laboratory."

Setting up a full-scale research laboratory from scratch required money, and lots of it. A full year before the announcement of Edison's invention of the incandescent light bulb, Wall Street investors put up $300,000 to incorporate the Edison Electric Light Co. Pearl Street station; for Edison, money was the mother's milk of invention, not politics. Months after the formation of the new company, Edison

> *"Genius is one percent inspiration and 99 percent perspiration."*
> – *Thomas Edison*

received $30,000 to pursue his invention of the incandescent light, with $20,000 in installments promised later.

Edison's success with Wall Street stemmed from several different sources. Although post-Civil War capitalism was inherently conservative, Wall Street tycoons like J. Pierpont Morgan, the Vanderbilts and Henry Villard invested in Edison because he had a track record of inventing useful things. Investment capital tends to flow to those who have already demonstrated success. Then, too, Edison had the knack of knowing how to promote his inventions. He had gotten familiar with the newspaper fraternity during his days as a railroad telegrapher, and he

Largely self-educated, Edison claimed that the vast majority of his inventions were the result of hard work, common sense and an almost unlimited curiosity.

had no fear of discussing his inventions with the gentlemen of the press. "Most of the stock components of the Edison myth have their origin in the lore of the Menlo Park years, largely the creation of the numerous newspapermen from nearby New York who frequented the laboratory," historian Wym Wachhorst wrote in 1981. "Always on jovial terms with reporters, the Barnumizing Edison seldom failed to cook up a good story—an exaggerated claim about the imminent success of some project, a sensational prediction, a colorful opinion."

Edison's wooing of Wall Street financiers like Morgan and Jay Gould was reciprocated by the tycoons. If the rumpled inventor from Menlo Park could create an incandescent electric lighting system to rival the monopoly then enjoyed by gas companies, the opportunities for getting in on the ground floor of the new technology promised to be very profitable indeed, although the Morgan interests, in particular, were nervous that too quick a success by Edison would depress the value of their gas company portfolios. Edison vowed to design a central station electric plant that would

drive the gas companies from the illuminating business.

Edison was also blessed by the associates he surrounded himself with at Menlo Park. Edison's "boys," who called their boss "the old man," were innovators in their own right, working alongside the inventor for days at a time without a break. Charles Batchelor and John Kreusi, master mechanics, had been with Edison for years. Francis Jehl had been the office boy of Grosvenor Lowrey, Edison's New York counsel and business and financial advisor; Jehl came to Menlo Park shortly after the incorporation of the first Edison Electric Light Co. in 1878 and stayed with Edison for half-a-century. Lowrey also recommended that Edison hire Francis Upton in 1878. A mathematician and physicist, Upton had been educated at Bowdoin College, Princeton University and Berlin University.

Samuel Insull, a British immigrant, was Edison's secretary, constantly at the side of the inventor. Charles Clarke, an engineering classmate of Upton at Princeton, became Edison's chief engineer in 1882. The next year, Clarke would supervise the engineering work on Edison's first three-wire central station plant at Sunbury, Pa. Assisting Clarke at Sunbury was Frank J. Sprague, a brilliant Naval Academy graduate who resigned his commission to go to work for Edison. Sprague went on to design the first practical electric streetcar system at Richmond, Va., in 1887-1888.

Numerous others worked with Edison at Menlo Park during the pioneer days of electricity from 1878 to 1892. Sigmund Bergmann went on to become president of the Bergmann Electrical works in Berlin. Louis Rau ended his career with the French Edison Co. in Paris; and Emil Rathenau died in 1915 as his Allgemeine Elektrizitats-Gesellschaft—the successor to the original German Edison company—was being municipalized by the City of Berlin. In this country, John W. Lieb became vice president of the New York Edison Co., and Charles L. Edgar ended his career as the president of the Edison Illuminating Co. of Boston.

Pearl Street
and the Jumbo

Edison knew that his 1879 invention of the incandescent electric light was useless without the corresponding development of a system to generate, transmit and distribute electric power. For three years, from 1879 to 1882, Edison and his associates worked feverishly to devise a system with commercial applications. Along the way, they tested hundreds of devices, had constant run-ins with the financial backers of the project, and got by on four or five hours of sleep a night.

Edison had already patented a working generator, even before the announcement of the first incandescent light, but the generator would have to be increased in both capacity and efficiency to handle the duties at a central station plant. There were a myriad of other details to attend to also. "Every detail from the burning of coal to the flipping of the customer's switch had to be thought through, planned and designed; every switch, connector, insulator, conductor, socket and lamp had to be designed to mesh with the overall system," one writer described those three years of frenetic activity. "The generating plant had to be built and the wires laid in city streets; private homes and office buildings had to be wired for power and motors installed or adapted to mesh with the system."

In December 1880, Edison established the Edison Electric Illuminating Co. of New York as a corporate vehicle to build his first big-city central station plant. By then, Edison had moved the offices of the original Edison Electric Light Co. to 65 Fifth Ave. in New York City. The Menlo Park facilities had already been given over to the production of light bulbs and other electrical equipment.

Early in 1881, Edison shipped his "Jumbo" dynamo to Paris for the international exposition that would take place in the French capital that spring. The Jumbo, named after a popular circus elephant of the time, was aptly named. With its driving engine, it weighed 27 tons; the armature alone weighed six tons. The huge new generator was capable of providing electricity for 1,000 of the standard Edison lamps of the day.

Edison scouted around New York City for a suitable site for his proposed central generating station. The inventor, who admitted he "had no real estate, and from lack of experience had very little knowledge of its cost in New York," was soon shocked at the prices commanded by property on Manhattan Island. He eventually settled on a dilapidated building at 255-257 Pearl St., sitting on a 50- by 100-foot lot, which he purchased and began renovating for his four-story central station.

For his central station test, Edison planned to provide electricity to an area one-sixth of a square mile, bounded by Wall, Spruce, Ferry and Nassau streets and the East River. The area was selected for its proximity to Wall Street, where Edison hoped to attract the investment capital all over the remainder of New York City and the nation. Obstacles remained. New York City aldermen demanded $1,000 per mile for the right to lay cable in the streets, plus three percent of the gross receipts of the new lighting company.

Morgan, Edison's financial backer, showed tangible support for his protege's project. The Wall Street financier sold his house on East 40th Street in 1882 and purchased the Manhattan brownstone of copper baron Isaac Phelps at 219 Madison Ave. Morgan installed an Edison dynamo in the basement of the Murray Hill mansion overlooking the East River and boasted the first electrically lighted

The Edison Electric Illuminating Co.

TAMAQUA, PA.,

M

Meters were invented to measure and record individual customer use of electricity. This 1901 contract sought the permission of Edison Electric customers to install Thomson Recording Watt Meters.

private residence in New York City. Unfortunately, Morgan's neighbors complained incessantly about the noise the generator made, proving Edison's point that the future of electric power lay in central station generation.

Throughout 1882, the Edison team readied Pearl Street for its impending debut. In May, three of the Jumbos were delivered to Pearl Street, and on July 5, the first of them was put into test operation. According to Pearl Street employee Thomas Martin, the steam plant was already installed, "consisting of four Babcock & Wilcox boilers, rated at 240 horsepower each, with cast iron headers,

Asked by a reporter in 1927 on the occasion of his 80th birthday what his greatest invention was, Edison answered without hesitation, the "research laboratory."

injectors, and a steam pump with connections to each unit, the water circulating through exhaust heaters at the rear of the building."

A vault under the front sidewalk and the basement contained machinery for coal and ash handling. A multipurpose, counter-shafted 20 horsepower engine in the basement drove machinery delivering coal to the furnaces, machinery taking the ashes from the grates and a fan blower for forced furnace draft. A system of blast pipes provided cooling air to the armatures of the generators.

By summer, Edison was nearly prepared for his demonstration. On July 8, current was switched into a bank of 1,000 lamps upstairs, capacity for each of the Jumbo generators. But when a second generator was started up, all hell broke loose. The problem was in the governors, which would not allow the generators to synchronize. It would not be until early 1883 that Edison licked the

problem with the governors. Still, the system showed promise, and Edison itched to demonstrate his success to the outside world.

At 3 p.m. on Monday, Sept. 4, 1882, Edison threw the knife-style switch on a single dynamo. A total of 800 lamps in the district flickered into light. It was no coincidence that two of the 85 customers wired for electric service were the Drexel-Morgan Building on Wall Street and the offices of *The New York Times*. Only 800 lamps were wired to that first dynamo, and Edison had spent nearly half a million dollars on Pearl Street, three times his original estimate. And because a workable electric meter was still some months in the future, those first customers of Pearl Street got their electric power for free.

But the thing worked, and Edison pronounced himself satisfied. The next day, some 30,000 workers took to the streets and marched through New York's Union Square to demonstrate labor's solidarity to Wall Street. It is ironic that the first Labor Day should come on the heels of the successful demonstration of central station generation, for the successors of Pearl Street would indelibly transform labor in the generations to come.

For Thomas Edison, the successful demonstration of central station generation at Pearl Street was an affirmation and a beginning; he could duplicate the results of Pearl Street anywhere in the country. Now that the world knew the system worked, it had to be convinced of the cost benefits of installing the system. Edison looked to the small cities of the Mid-Atlantic states as the most likely candidates for purchase of an Edison Electric Illuminating Co. franchise. The most likely candidates for central station generation were located in nearby central eastern Pennsylvania.

The Enigmatic Mr. Insull

Few residents would have recognized the young man who accompanied the great inventor, Thomas Edison, when he checked into the City Hotel, in Sunbury, Pa., on the afternoon of July 3, 1883. Edison was instantly recognizable from the photos and etchings that had appeared in the nation's newspapers for years, but the slightly nondescript young man wearing pince-nez glasses and a straw boater at Edison's side would hardly have merited a second glance.

As Edison's private secretary from 1881 to 1892, Samuel L. Insull was used to that kind of anonymity. Ironically, Insull's name, if not his face, would become almost as familiar to another generation of Americans as Edison himself. But by then, the sense of wonder and awe surrounding electric power had dissipated; Insull's name would become synonymous with abuses in the electric utility industry.

Born in London on Nov. 11, 1859, Insull came to the United States in 1881 to be Edison's confidential private secretary. He'd been recommended for the position by Colonel Gourand, Edison's London representative, and for the next decade, Insull was in Edison's company almost constantly. He served as Edison's financial consultant and liaison with all the Edison organizations, and he had the great inventor's power of attorney. Convinced that the central station business and not the manufacturing segment was the future of the electric power industry, and itching to run his own operation, Insull left the Edison General Electric Co. at the time of its merger with Thomson-Houston Electric Co. in 1892. He took a $24,000-a-year pay cut to join the Chicago Edison Co. as its president.

Insull arrived in Chicago at a time when both the city and the electric utility industry were poised on the brink of a tremendous growth spurt. Chicago hosted the World's Columbian Exposition in 1893, the year after Insull arrived, and the year-long fair introduced elec-

Samuel Insull late in his career.
(photo courtesy of Commonwealth Edison Co., Chicago)

tric lighting to America. General Electric and Westinghouse, the two major electrical equipment manufacturers in the U.S., installed some 66,000 incandescent lights and more than 500 arc lamps on the grounds of the fair at Jackson Park; by the time it completed its run in 1894, the Columbian Exposition grounds had more electric lighting than any city in the country and 11 times the light that had been displayed at the Paris Exposition of 1889.

For the residents of Chicago, however, electric lighting was mostly unaffordable in 1893. More than one million people lived in Chicago at the time, but only 5,000 of them had electric lighting in their homes. Insull's Chicago Edison Co. had $1 million invested in 2,800 kilowatts of capacity. Since the plant only operated at about 17 percent capacity, fixed costs were somewhere between 12 and 15 cents per kwh.

Electricity in the 1890s was only for the rich, and Insull reasoned that the future of the business lay in reducing the price per kwh so that electricity was affordable by the common people. With Frederick Sargent, another Englishman, who was coincidentally born on the same day as his boss, Insull built some of the largest coal-fired generating stations on the continent between 1895 and 1915. Insull's philosophy of economy of scale stressed building load and building even bigger power plants. By the time Chicago Edison Co. and Commonwealth Electric merged to form Commonwealth Edison in 1907, the company was 60 times larger than when Insull had taken over the Chicago operations in 1892.

Insull pioneered the concept of customer relations, setting up an advertising and marketing department early in the century. He introduced demand metering to the United States; and in the early 1920s, he began selling shares of common stock in his companies direct to the public. Insull revolutionized employee relations, establishing a partnership with the International Brotherhood of Electrical Workers and publishing the first employee magazine in the electric utility industry.

In the years before World War I, Insull theorized that what he had accomplished in Chicago could be duplicated across the United States. He bought electric street railways in Indiana, small-town utilities in South Dakota, hydroelectric dams in Wisconsin, and utility properties across the nation.

By 1930, Insull's Middlewest Utilities served 6.3 million customers spread out from North Dakota to Texas, from Maine to Florida. The utility holding company generated more than four billion kwh and piled up gross earnings of $162 million. But by 1930, the Insull empire, weakened by the collapse of stock prices on Wall Street, was hopelessly overextended. In the spring of 1932, just months after Insull's old boss, Thomas Edison, died, Middlewest Utilities became the largest bankruptcy in American history up to that time. Insull was pilloried in the press, and condemned by Presidential candidate Franklin Delano Roosevelt. For a generation of Americans, the name Insull was synonymous with fraud, greed, and the abuse of corporate power.

Insull had gone into self-imposed European exile following the collapse of his empire, but he was extradited to stand trial for fraud in 1934. In a series of highly publicized trials, he was exonerated by both federal and state juries. "If two men had walked down Fifth Avenue a year ago," he explained to his State Department guard on the boat taking him back to America for trial, "and one of them had a pint of whiskey in his pocket and the other had a hundred dollars in gold coin, the one with the whiskey would have been called a criminal, and the one with the gold an honest citizen. If these two men had, like Rip Van Winkle, slept for a year and again walked down Fifth Avenue, the man with the whiskey would be called an honest citizen and the one with gold coin a criminal. I find myself somewhat in this sort of situation. What I did, when I did it, was honest; now, through changed conditions, what I did may or may not be called honest. Politics demand, therefore, that I be brought to trial; but what is really being brought to trial is the system I represented."

Samuel Insull returned to Europe following his trials. In July 1938, he collapsed and died of a heart attack while walking down a stairwell to board a Paris subway train. He was 78, more than a half-a-century removed from the events of July 1883 in the little Susquehanna River town of Sunbury, Pa.; and his life had spanned the history of the electric utility industry, from the Pearl Street station to the Public Utilities Holding Company Act.

Newspaper clipping of Nov. 25, 1934. (courtesy of The Morning Call, Allentown)

5

Midwife to an Industry

Edison's Sunbury station was the world's first three-wire electric plant. Built in 1883, it stood only three miles from today's Sunbury Steam Electric Station.

In 1922, Thomas Edison returned to Sunbury, Pa. It was the community's sesquicentennial, and the city fathers intended to honor the Wizard of Menlo Park with an official ceremony to mark the 40th anniversary of the establishment of the Edison Electric Illuminating Co. of Sunbury. Edison was introduced to the respectful crowd by Joseph Cummings, by then the sole remaining member of the original Edison company in Sunbury. As part of the festivities, the community dedicated a plaque at the front entrance of the Edison Hotel on the Market Street side of the building.

It had been 39 years since Thomas Edison set foot in what was then known as the City Hotel to help install the first three-wire system for commercial direct current lighting in the world. In those four decades, electrification had transformed society. Large regional utilities like Pennsylvania Power & Light Co., which had been providing electricity for two years to Sunbury in 1922, were the successors to the original small Edison illuminating companies. Giant coal-fired power plants like the Hauto and Harwood stations were the outgrowth of what Edison had envisioned as central station generating plants. Electric motors and appliances had supplemented manyfold the lighting markets that Edison had hoped to exploit.

The Three-Wire System

"Every man his own electric lighter." One of Edison's ideas was to have every household manufacture their own light. This illustration shows an attempt at developing such a system.

As 1882 turned into 1883, Thomas Edison was disappointed by the results of the Pearl Street Generating Station. The comparatively small size of the generators, and Edison's reliance on direct current for his system, meant that hundreds of central stations would have to be built to serve the residents of a city like New York. Bankers were nervous about financing the expansion of the system because of the high cost of building Pearl Street. They worried that residential electric service would never be able to compete with gas, and as 1883 dawned, only New York and Milan, Italy, were even partially wired for incandescent electric lighting systems.

Edison thought he had a solution for the higher-than-anticipated costs of building and operating Pearl Street. The systems already up and running in 1882—including Pearl Street, the Italian operation and a dynamo at an exhibition

in London—were what were called "two-wire" systems. Edison designed, built and hooked up two bipolar, direct current, two-wire 110-volt dynamos and belted them to a steam engine. "The dynamos were alike in voltage and capacity and connected electrically in series, which doubled the electromotive force of the dynamos," explained Harry L. Keefer in a 1946 speech to the Northumberland County Historical Society. "In the first experiment, only two conductors were used and it was a two-wire, 220 volt," Keefer continued. "The lamps were placed in series in two across the conductors, but he found this not practical for ordinary purposes, for the reason that it would always require a third or neutral conductor between the present two conductors, connected with its point in the circuit between the two dynamos, in order to avoid the difficulty of the lamps and be able to have the two dynamos operate in series, having a voltage of 220 volts between outside conductors and 110 volts between either outside wire and the neutral wire. The lamps were conducted between either outside wire and the neutral wire."

In other words, the three-wire system increased the efficiency of the two parallel generators and allowed the lamps to work in series. One lamp could be switched on or off without affecting the operation of the other lamps. With the three-wire system, the voltage could be raised to 220 volts, but could be supplied to end-use customers at 110 volts. More importantly, the conductors of the three-wire system could operate with one-half the cross-section area of the two-wire system, and the system required only three-fourths as many conductors as the two-wire system.

The significance of the introduction of the three-wire system was its effect on cost reduction for central station generation. One of the biggest costs that Edison faced in getting his stations up and running was the price of copper used in the conductors. At the time Pearl Street went into operation, most U.S. copper came from the deep-shaft mines of the

Calumet & Hecla Consolidated Copper Co. in Michigan's isolated Upper Peninsula. U.S. copper prices averaged 20.1 cents per pound in 1880, falling to just under 16 cents per pound by 1883, the year that the Sunbury station was put into operation.

Edison's three-wire system essentially reduced the amount of copper needed in the conductors by about two-thirds, a major help in slashing the cost of setting up a central station. As it was, new copper mines in Montana were brought into production in the early 1880s, and the Calumet & Hecla responded by increasing production. The resulting price war in the copper markets cut the price of the red metal to 11 cents a pound by 1886, an external economic phenomenon that considerably brightened the prospects of the Edison illuminating companies.

Edison wasn't the only inventor working on the three-wire system. In London, John Hopkinson, a noted British inventor, scientist and professor of engineering at King's College, patented a three-wire system in the summer of 1882, several months before Edison's discovery. In Germany, Wilhelm von Siemens' patent for the three-wire system occurred almost simultaneously with those of Hopkinson and Edison.

The Old Gas-House Plant

With the three-wire system perfected, Edison began searching for small communities suitable for erecting central station plants. The inventor had become convinced that the best chance for making a profit on his system involved selling, equipping and setting up central stations in moderate-sized towns that were served by a gas plant. Edison called these plants "village stations." Accordingly, he formed a construction department of the Edison

Electric Light Co. in May 1883 to oversee installation and operation of Edison central stations. Samuel Insull, his private secretary, was put in charge of the new venture.

Edison's agent in Pennsylvania, Phillip B. Shaw, was asked to suggest local candidates for a central station to be built by the construction department. Shaw, a Williamsport manufacturer, surveyed the field in eastern Pennsylvania and informed Edison and Insull that Sunbury seemed to be the logical place to start. Shaw noted that Sunbury was located near Pennsylvania's anthracite coal fields, which meant that a plentiful supply of fuel for the power company's boilers would be at hand. Gas prices in the community were high, averaging $10 per thousand cubic feet. Finally, the city was conveniently located for Shaw, who lived just upriver in Williamsport.

The Edison construction department crew moved into Sunbury in the spring of 1883. Shaw had already organized electric lighting companies at Sunbury, Williamsport, Shamokin, Mount Carmel and Hazleton, and had raised money through stock sales to finance the installation of

Businesses like this one were wired for new incandescent lighting during the 1880s. Edison, with the help of P.B. Shaw and others, targeted small communities across Pennsylvania building central station plants for delivery of electricity to homes and businesses. (*photo courtesy of the Lehigh County Historical Society*)

Phillip B. Shaw remained close to Thomas Edison even after he left the Edison Electric Light Co. in 1897.

P. B. SHAW
WILLIAMSPORT PA.

May 28th, 1910.

Shaw — When you propose Coming telegraph or Telephone to be sure I will be at home — Edison

Mr. Thos. A. Edison,

    Llewellyn Park,

      Orange, N.J.

My Dear Mr. Edison:-

      On my return home to-day I find your letter of May 23rd, and have noted the contents.

      Replying to the suggestion that I might be too old to take up such a subject, I have only to say that if an old fellow like you can invent or produce a battery, I guess I would be in the running if I undertook to sell it. However, I would be barred from attempting to become interested in it, since I am already very largely interested in the best lead battery ever made, and it is my purpose to give the energy necessary to make this a success before I would tackle any new proposition.

      Do you remember in one of our talks in the long ago at old 65 Fifth Avenue, when I asked you your opinion of the storage battery you replied that you did not know much about it, but that you never had "much luck with wet electricity". That suggestion had the effect to keep me out of wet electricity for a great many years, but now that I am in it and from your letter I find that you, too, are dabbling in "wet" electricity, the incident struck me as a little funny.

      I am going to accept your invitation to come over and look at your battery and have you, personally, tell me the story of its possibilities, but the real purpose of my visit will be to see and talk with you. Do you expect to be at the works for any length of time, or will you be scurrying away to some seashore or mountain resort? I am going to make this trip over there very soon, that is, within the next two or three weeks, and if you are not going to be on the job yourself, advise me, and I will postpone the trip until such time as I will be sure to meet you.

      Hoping that your health and behavior are as good as that of myself, I remain,

      Very truly yours,

P. B. SHAW
PENNSYLVANIA BUILDING
PHILADELPHIA, PA.

MEADOWCROFT.

Confidential.

November 9th, 1912.

Friend Shaw — It is certainly very Curious that only 10 minutes before I opened your letter I closed a deal for $850,000, to go into the battery

Mr. Thomas A. Edison,

    Edison Laboratories,

      Orange, N. J.

Dear Mr. Edison:-

      Remembering our conversation when I was over to see you some months ago, relating to storage batteries, I beg to say I have a party with One Million Dollars REAL MONEY, who I know will consider favorably any proposition I may submit looking to its investment. *So I can't take advantage of the offer made by*

      Why not put him into Edison Storage Batteries?

      If this suggestion strikes you favorably, advise me promptly and I will go over to the Laboratory to talk the matter over with you. *You I have another thing Coming along which*

      In the meantime, please consider the subject strictly personal and confidential.

      Very truly yours

will Shaw if ye March or april — that your party might like to look at

S-H.

the central station at Sunbury. He also negotiated the exchange of cash and stock in the Sunbury and other local companies for an Edison license, and for generating and other equipment from the Edison Electric Light Co.

Shaw had incorporated the Edison Electric Illuminating Co. of Shamokin on Nov. 29, 1882, followed by the incorporation of the Edison Electric Illuminating Co. of Sunbury on April 30, 1883. The Edison company at Mount Carmel was incorporated in November 1883, following the successful start-up of the Sunbury central station. The first board of directors of the Sunbury company included Edison in New York; Shaw, Dr. T.C. Detwiler, S.T. McCormick and F.H. McCormick, all of Williamsport; Lewis Dewart of Sunbury; and Frank S. Marr of Lewisburg.

Heading the construction department crew in Sunbury were Frank Sprague and W.S. Andrews, already an accomplished Edison electrician. Sprague, who had resigned his commission in the U.S. Navy to join the Edison company, was already quite familiar with the three-wire system.

Sprague had been in London during the fall of 1882 reviewing the electrical equipment at the Crystal Palace Exhibition and had become familiar with the three-wire system patented by the British inventor Hopkinson.

Shaw had erected a building at Sunbury's old gas plant site, located at the northeast corner of Fourth and Vine streets, for installation of the Sunbury village station. The one-story wooden structure was painted red. Its 2,400 square feet of space were partitioned into three rooms—a boiler room, an engine and dynamo room and an office and meter room. "The boiler was of the Babcock & Wilcox type and the generating plant consisted of two 'L' dynamos belted to a high-speed Armington and Sims Engine, the total capacity being about 650 10-candle-power incandescent lamps,"

P.B. Shaw incorporated the Edison Electric Illuminating Co. of Shamokin on Nov. 29, 1882. The photo below shows the Shamokin Steam Electric Station in 1921. It was built in 1900 and shut down 22 years later when its load was transferred to less expensive sources of power in PP&L's newly integrated system.

(certificate courtesy of Hagley Museum and Library)

Andrews recalled in 1910. "The 'bus-bars' were made by straightening out some No. 000 copper wire, left over from the line construction, and those wires were fastened to the wooden sheathing on the station walls with iron staples without any attempt at insulation and with the fond idea that this was exactly the right thing to do!"

Andrews continued, recalling that "the switchboard instruments consisted of two voltage indicators which were connected by 'pressure wires' to the end of the three-wire 'feeder' where it joined the 'mains' at the center of electrical distribution, also one ammeter which was interpolated in the 'neutral bus' to show how the system 'balanced'. All these indicators were of crude construction and very doubtful accuracy." Still, Andrews went on, the equipment was "the best that could be procured in those days," and installed "according to designs laid out by Mr. Chas. L. Clarke," the Edison Co.'s chief electrician.

W.S. Andrews noted that the interior wiring of the Sunbury central station, including labor and materials for running feeders the entire length of the building and for wiring up dynamos, switchboard and instruments, amounted to $90. "The writer received a rather sharp letter from the New York Office, expostulating on this 'extravagant expenditure', and stating that greater economy must be observed in the future," Andrews recalled more than a quarter-century later.

A line of three overhead wires was strung from the plant along the Spring Run to Woodlawn Avenue, out Woodlawn to Fourth Street and then down Fourth to Market. A local resident was hired to wire houses and businesses for the new incandescent lights.

Thomas Edison left the installation in

Since the grand start-up of Edison's plant in 1883, there have been many exciting moments in Sunbury, including this one in 1953. School children were among the first community residents to get a peek at the new Sunbury Steam Electric Station's 100,000-kilowatt Unit 3 when it went on line.

the hands of Frank Sprague and Andrews but evidently popped in occasionally during the spring of 1883 to check the progress of the work. "I remember Mr. Edison very well," recalled longtime Sunbury resident Frank Neff in 1968. "We lived immediately across the street from the station where Edison was experimenting, and my mother put me at the front window so I could watch him."

Then seven years old, Neff remembered that "Mr. Edison was hard of hearing. He wore a stiff derby and a Prince Albert coat. He was small but well-built, and he went along and never spoke to anyone. Once, he said that because he was hard of hearing, it helped him to concentrate."

That concentration became legendary later in the summer when a group of Sunbury youths were playing baseball in the vacant lot adjoining the plant. One of the batters sent a high-fly ball soaring toward the building, and the players scattered as the baseball crashed through the exposed window of the plant. Gathering their courage, several of the youths crept up to the building to retrieve their ball. "To say I was surprised when I saw the ball reposing on the floor where Mr. Edison was working would be putting it rather mildly," one of the baseball players later told Harry Keefer. "But having come this far, I wasn't going to back water. So I went over and pocketed the innocent cause of all the trouble and beat it out. Apparently Mr. Edison had never noticed that anything unusual had taken place."

'Radiant With the New Light'

Edison arrived in Sunbury on July 3, 1883, in preparation for the inauguration of his new central station. The construction department had promised the residents that the lights would be turned on for the July 4th celebration, and all was in readiness for the start-up. However, snags threatened to delay Edison and his crew. A test of the dynamos on the night of July 3 ended when bearings melted for lack of lubricating oil.

The bearings were replaced, and with a supply of lubricating oil on hand, the crew began preparing for start-up about 5 p.m. on July 4, but the dynamos refused to pick up the load. "There must be a loose connection somewhere," Edison observed, but all the equipment in the station was in good running order.

Thomas Edison then suggested that there must be an open-circuit along the "gut," the once-open sewer that ran through the middle of the city. Edison and the gang left Andrews behind in charge of the city, and headed out on a tour of the lines, loosely strung from chestnut poles. In short order, two of the feeders were discovered to be crossed and were soon straightened out. "Fortune now smiled on us," Andrews noted, "the outside lines were again connected, the lamps in the station came steadily up to candle power and a general rush was made 'down town' by all hands that could be spared. The 'City Hotel' was the largest 'wiring job', and we found it radiant with the new light. Expectant excitement had given place to loud expression of wonder and delight among the townspeople who thronged the Hotel, and thus was the first Edison three-wire Central Station started up on the 4th of July 1883, amid the firing of cannon crackers and other pyrotechnical displays common to the day."

'The Light was Very Brilliant'

"The electric light was put in operation in the Central and City Hotels and at the works on the night of the Fourth," *The Northumberland County Democrat* editorialized on July 6, 1883. "It worked satisfactorily. The light in the hotels were 12-candlepower lamps, while at the works there was one lamp of 100. The light was very brilliant."

The start-up of the three-wire system at Sunbury didn't garner anywhere the

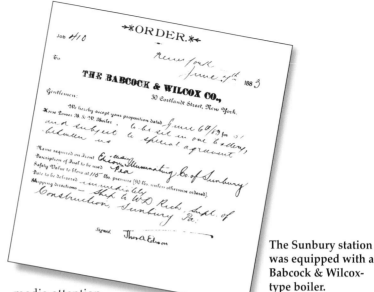

The Sunbury station was equipped with a Babcock & Wilcox-type boiler.

media attention that the opening of the Brooklyn Bridge had just six weeks before. Sunbury was too far off the beaten path for the New York reporters to follow up on the story, and besides, it was really old news in the wake of what had happened at Pearl Street the previous autumn. Edison remained in Sunbury for about a week following the successful start-up of his first village station. W.S. Andrews, who would go on to a long career with General Electric Co., and a small crew from the construction department stayed behind for much of the summer, attending to the mop-up and training duties necessary to turn the station over to the local Edison Electric Illuminating Co. of Sunbury.

The start-up of the three-wire system at Sunbury didn't garner anywhere the media attention that the opening of the Brooklyn Bridge had just six weeks before.

There were still more than enough glitches with this newfangled science of electricity. For one thing, there were no insulators in 1883. It was common practice to fasten the electric wires to the outside of the gas fixtures with tape or string. The wires would then be connected to the lamp sockets, which were screwed to attachments held in place under the gas burners. W.S. Andrews noted that "rubber insulated wire was unknown, cotton covered wire soaked in paraffin or coated with white lead paint being all that was available. The latter was commonly termed 'underwriters' wire', although it was occasionally called 'undertakers' wire' by would-be humorists."

The Sunbury gas company took a rather dim view of its competition, especially of the practice of hanging wire off gas fixtures. Frequently, the gas company filed injunctions against the Edison company, enjoining it from erecting new distribution poles. On several occasions, gas company crews were suspected of throwing logging chains over the wires, shorting out the system.

The inadequate wiring caused a scare in early August. During a heavy evening thunderstorm, a messenger from downtown arrived at the plant with the news that the City Hotel was on fire. Andrews rushed downtown to discover the hotel's proprietor and guests standing outside in the pouring rain, afraid to go back into the hotel and be burned up by electricity.

Upon closer investigation, Andrews discovered that bright blue sparks were snapping between the electric wires and the gas fixtures. "One or two 'short circuits' at weak spots had 'blown' a few fuses," Andrews reported, "but the points of low insulation being thus eliminated, no further damage was done, and the snappy sparks were harmless."

Having assessed the situation, Andrews went out and assured the shaken proprietor and guests that there was no danger from the sparks. Some of

ELECTRIC LIGHT.

Notice!

NOTICE is hereby given to the citizens of Lancaster, Pa., that the Edison Electric Illuminating Co., lawfully operating in the City of Lancaster by permission and license of the Edison Electric Light Co. of New York, is alone authorized to furnish Electric Light and power in the City of Lancaster under the Edison patents, including THE EDISON LAMP PATENT: No. 223,898, No. 266,447, No. 230,255, No. 251,540, No. 265,777, No. 227,229, No. 264,698, No. 223,898, No. 264,737, No. 251,554, No. 265,311, No 317,631, etc. The Edison Feeder and Main Patents. The Edison Three Wire Patents and many others.

Every CONSUMER of Electric Light or Power using any of the Edison Patents, except by permission of the undersigned, is liable in damages and will be prosecuted.

The Edison Electric Illuminating Company.

the bolder guests ventured back into the hotel, but the bulk of the crowd demanded more explanation. Thinking fast on his feet, Andrews rose to the occasion. "Some explanations were requested," the Edison electrician reminisced, "and in order to restore a measure of public confidence in the electric wiring, which was naturally blamed for the scare, the writer had to strain his conscience to some extent in stating that the hotel had certainly been struck by the lightning, and that in all probability it would have been burnt to the ground if it had not been protected by the electric wires, which provided an easy passage for the lightning to the ground."

Andrews later relayed the story to Edison, who assigned the problem to his colleague, Luther Stieringer, a noted gaslight engineer of the day, who designed an insulating joint to prevent the leakage of electricity from fixtures.

Such small setbacks aside, the significance of Sunbury is that the system worked. The Edison equipment would be much improved in subsequent years, but it proved itself at Sunbury capable of powering an incandescent lighting system for an entire community. The dynamos, in particular, were a pleasant surprise. They ran continuously for 20 years, and upon their retirement were shipped to the St. Louis Exposition of 1904 as the centerpiece of an exhibit of early Edison generating equipment; Phillip B. Shaw eventually donated the original dynamos and steam engines at Sunbury to the Franklin Institute in Philadelphia. The little anthracite community of Sunbury, Pa., had served as midwife to an industry.

The Elusive Mr. Shaw

Thomas Edison's incandescent lighting systems wouldn't have been able to spread throughout the Mid-Atlantic states in 1883-1884, and throughout America in the years following, had it not been for the efforts of sales personnel like P.B. Shaw.

Phillip B. Shaw was a Williamsport manufacturer and financier who first contacted Edison in May 1882 after reading of the inventor's intentions to set up village stations in the small communities of the Mid-Atlantic states. Edison asked Shaw to survey communities in the anthracite region of Pennsylvania that might be candidates for the location of a village station, and the inventor appointed the Pennsylvanian as his agent for the Keystone State that summer.

For much of the next 20 years, Shaw served Edison in a number of capacities in Pennsylvania, recommending local communities for establishment of village stations, finding the funding for local Edison Electric Illuminating companies in Sunbury, Shamokin, Hazleton, Mount Carmel and Williamsport, and actually engaging in the management of Edison village stations in Sunbury and Williamsport. "He was very active in setting up the central stations in Pennsylvania," said Doug Tarr, archivist for the Edison National Historic Site in West Orange, N.J. However, Tarr noted that what little is known about Shaw is contained in the correspondence he exchanged with Edison, Samuel Insull and others at the Edison Electric Light Co. in New York between 1882 and 1896. "He proved rather elusive," Tarr said.

For all intents and purposes, Shaw severed his relationship with Edison following the Edison Electric Light Co.'s 1897 decision not to renew his contract as the manager of the Williamsport village station. However, Shaw retained his interest in electrification. He was an early investor in the Northumberland Electric Railway, which completed a streetcar line between Sunbury and Northumberland in 1890.

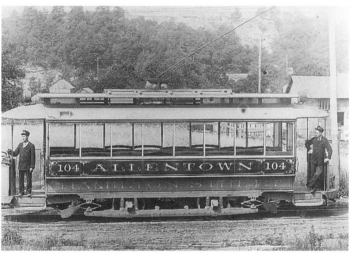

Trolley wheels allowed the wooden pole atop a streetcar to be affixed to an overhead conductor. *(photo courtesy of Lehigh County Historical Society)*

Shaw is credited with the invention of an early trolley wheel, which allowed the wooden pole atop a streetcar—called a "troller" in the early days—to be affixed to an overhead conductor. In 1905, Shaw, then one of the stockholders in the Northumberland Railway and Light Co., was involved in the purchase of the three electric companies then operating in Sunbury.

At the same time, Shaw, who told a reporter "that it is not always wise to have too many things printed about business affairs," claimed to have an interest in gas and electric holdings in Williamstown, Tower City and Lykens, and was planning an interurban electric railroad to link Philadelphia and Atlantic City, N.J.

Shaw was also interested in the gas business. During the 1890s, he served as part-time general manager for his friend, Q.S. Backus, at the Backus Manufacturing Co. in Williamsport. In 1891, the Backus firm employed some 60 workers engaged in "the sole manufacture for the U.S. of the Backus Portable Steam Radiator for Gaseous Fuel." The Williamsport firm also made gas radiating mantles, fireplaces and logs. During his years in Williamsport—which at one time during the 1870s lumber boom had more millionaires than any other community of similar size in the country—Shaw lived in a magnificent estate at Poco Farm in the northeastern part of the city.

Following retirement from active pursuit of his business interests about 1920, Shaw sold his Poco Farm estate and moved to Philadelphia. In September 1936, at the age of 89, Phillip B. Shaw donated the original Edison engine and dynamos at the Sunbury station to the Franklin Institute in Philadelphia, which honored the Williamsport entrepreneur for his "pioneering part in the development of electric lighting and other uses of electricity."

By then living in the Drake

We hardly mourn his inevitable going so much as we rejoice in pleasant memory at having been associated with him in a great work for all peoples under a great man.

P. B. SHAW

On January 31, 1937, at the Hotel Drake, Philadelphia, Pa.

Mr. Shaw entered the employ of the Edison Electric Light Company in 1883 as its Manager for the State of Pennsylvania. He was instrumental in organizing Edison Illuminating Companies at Williamsport, Sunbury, Bellefonte, Shamokin, Mount Carmel and Hazleton, and assisted in the financing of these various companies. The first State charter was issued to the Williamsport Company and the second to the Sunbury Company, each of which had secured licenses from the Edison Electric Light Company for Central Stations under Mr. Edison's patents. The Sunbury installation was the first to be completed, and on July 4, 1883, Mr. Edison closed the switch by which service was started. Following commencement of operation of these various plants in Pennsylvania, Mr. Shaw went to Ohio, where he successfully financed and installed other Edison central stations which, with his pioneer efforts, were among the earliest central stations in the incandescent lighting industry. Mr. Shaw continued to direct the operations of the Sunbury station for a period of over twenty years.

Funeral services were held on February 2nd at the Oliver H. Baer Funeral Parlors, 1820 Chestnut Street, Philadelphia.

He is survived by his widow, Mrs. Sarah Decker Shaw.

Mr. Shaw was an esteemed Member of

EDISON PIONEERS.

40 West 40th Street,
New York, N. Y.

Hotel with his wife, Shaw took ill in January 1937. He died at St. Luke's Hospital in the City of Brotherly Love on Jan. 31, 1937. His hometown *Williamsport Gazette & Bulletin* eulogized Shaw as one of the city's "most prominent and influential men. Mr. Shaw, who had earlier industrial collections in Williamsport before he saw the possibilities of Mr. Thomas Edison's electrical inventions and became interested in introducing them into general use, had a prominent part in bringing the benefit of these inventions to Williamsport."

6

Battle of the Systems

The Hotel Allen in the late 1800s. A typical light bill for a hotel like this in the early 1880s was around $15. *(photo courtesy of the Lehigh County Historical Society)*

William L. Dewart, publisher of *The Northumberland County Democrat*, was impressed enough by Edison's "brilliant light" in the summer of 1883 to see to it that his house on Sunbury Square was the first private residence in the community to be wired for incandescent electric lighting. Necessity is the mother of all invention, and Edison's associates learned things at Sunbury that they put into practice at all their subsequent installations. Luther Stieringer's invention of insulation joints to reduce the leakage of electricity from early fixtures was a direct result of the thunderstorm that scared the residents of the City Hotel in August 1883.

There were other such innovations that took place that first year at Sunbury. At Mr. Dewart's home, for example, a complaint led to the installation of the first wall switch. "The electric lights in the old house were suspended from the ceiling and had switches only at the lights," Heber G. Gearhart reported to the Northumberland County Historical Society in 1936. "As Mrs. Dewart was a woman of short stature, she could not reach the switches without standing on a chair. In order to overcome this difficulty, Sidney Bateman, one of Edison's employees, contrived to make a crude sort of wall switch, by which means the estimable lady was enabled to turn the lights off and on easily. This was the first wall switch to be used anywhere, and it was later improved by Edison...."

The Edison Electric Illuminating Co. of Sunbury also pioneered the first use of meters for a village station. These meters consisted of two zinc plates. Current passing over one of the zinc plates caused a corresponding loss of weight by electrolytic action. To use the meter correctly, it was necessary to weigh the electrodes at the beginning and end of the billing period. By weighing the electrolyzed zinc plate at the end of the billing period and comparing it to the other plate, a fair estimate of the current used could be calculated.

In the 1940s, H.W. Renn, district manager for Pennsylvania Power & Light Co., discovered the original and first billing ledger for the Edison Electric Illuminating Co. of Sunbury in the loft of the company's building at South Fourth Street. The ledgers revealed that the first account listed in the book was the City Hotel, which had been given meter No. 1. The hotel's electric bill for the first month, Aug. 1-Sept. 1, 1883, was $12.42.

The hotel added more lights in the second month, and its bill climbed to $20.41, although by April 1884, the hotel was paying $15 a month after dropping several ceiling fixtures, then called electroliers. The Central Hotel, the second account in the book, paid $14 a month throughout 1883, before adding another light bulb and increasing its bill to $15 by the following spring. "Most of the bills thus made out came very close to the estimated figures," W.S. Andrews recalled of the early electrolytic meter at Sunbury, "but a meter in a large clothing store indicated that about $200 worth of current had been used. As this was an impossible amount, a bill based on a

moderate estimate was sent in. The meter man spent several anxious days and nights trying to figure out where the mistake had occurred, for Mr. Edison had firmly imbued him with the belief that the meter was infallible!

"At length, it suddenly dawned upon him that he had weighed the meter plates to a tenth of a milligram at the station, but on arrival at the clothing store he found that the copper wires connected to the zinc plates were too long to go into the meter case, so, without giving any thought as to the consequences, he just clipt (sic) off an inch or two of copper wire, which represented about $150 worth of electricity, when measured by loss of weight. Moreover, he found the piece of copper wire that he had cut off, and on weighing them up and making proper allowance, the 'faked' bill that had been presented was discovered to be about right."

Another first happened in the spring of 1885. The opening of the new passenger depot of the Philadelphia and Reading Railroad marked the first time in America that a railroad station had been lighted with incandescent bulbs. The station, which looked like a Swiss chalet, was built with wiring already installed, and the first bill for $14.25 was sent to J.H. Olhausen, the Palo Alto-based manager of the Mahanoy and Susquehanna division of the Reading.

Despite its initial difficulties, the Sunbury property of the Edison Electric Illuminating Co. continued to flourish. In 1885, Frank H. McCormick, the first president of the company, resigned and P.B. Shaw and George W. Heim of Williamsport bought control of the company. The new owners abandoned the original plant at Fourth and Vine streets and built a new brick powerhouse on Fourth Street near the tracks of the Shamokin Railroad. Several new dynamos were added, increasing generation capacity to 50 kilowatts.

The Edison Electric Light Co.'s construction department supervised the installation of the new equipment and received in payment 25 percent of the stocks and bonds of the company, suggesting that the Sunbury utility was having difficulty in raising the capital investment needed to keep up with the growth of electric power demand. As early as September 1883, the directors of the company had difficulty dealing with the capital-intensive nature of the electric utility business in Sunbury, and prevailed upon Edison to take some $6,000 of his

Meters, like this Westinghouse Polyphase Wattmeter, were used in the early 1900s.

One could follow the spread of electric power by the transmission poles that sprung up along Pennsylvania's roadways. Using only brute strength and pike poles, crews like these in Harrisburg set 65-foot poles for the main power transmission line at the intersection of Cameron and Cedar streets in the 1890s.

franchise fee in the form of common stock.

Still, by the end of April 1888, Edison Electric Illuminating Co. of Sunbury was serving 128 customers, whose combined load amounted to 13,656 candlepower. By the end of the year, the company reported that there were 1,257 lamps connected to the system, with a total of 18,090 candlepower, more than two-and-one-half times the original installation of 500 lamps less than five years before.

An abundant supply of coal literally generated the growth of Pennsylvania's electric utility industry as early as the 1880s. This photo shows a coal miner pitch mining in the early 1900s. *(photo courtesy of the Hugh Moore Historical Park and Museum)*

Expansion in the Anthracite Region

P.B. Shaw's success in setting up an Edison village station at Sunbury was duplicated in other communities of Pennsylvania's anthracite region between 1883 and 1885. Besides Sunbury, Shaw also obtained local funding for the organization of incandescent electric lighting companies in Williamsport, Shamokin, Mount Carmel, Hazleton and Bellefonte. Except for the stations at

Williamsport and Bellefonte, all the stations were located in the state's anthracite coal fields between the Susquehanna and Lehigh rivers, an area which Thomas P. Hughes, Edison-era historian and University of Pennsylvania professor of the history of technology, likens to the Ruhr Valley of Germany.

The Edison Electric Illuminating Co. of Williamsport, the first such firm to sign a franchise agreement with the Edison Electric Light Co. in 1882, and the second company to start an Edison central station in the fall of 1883, operated a test plant of 1,200 16-candlepower lights. "Our plant has been pronounced by all who have examined it, including a number of experts connected with the Edison Installation Service, as in all respects complete, and the most substantial and perfect one ever yet installed anywhere in this country or in the world," the secretary of the company noted in 1884.

The first power plant at Williamsport consisted of two 200-light machines and two 400-light machines. In 1887, the company got into the arc light business when it installed two 50-arc light dynamos. By that time, P.B. Shaw had taken over management of the company, agreeing to pay all plant expenses and to pay the treasury sufficient money to declare a six percent dividend in 1885, a seven percent dividend in 1886, and an eight percent dividend in 1887. That year, Shaw's original contract with the Edison Electric Light Co. expired. He signed a 10-year extension, in which he agreed to pay a seven percent dividend on the common stock, to pay all interest on the bonded indebtedness and to return to the company 50 percent of all earnings in excess of $12,000 a year.

Both the Edison Electric Illuminating

companies of Mount Carmel and Shamokin started in 1884 after incorporation in 1883. The Mount Carmel company increased the capacity of its plant in 1885 and again in 1888; two years later, the company also got into the arc lighting business when it installed a 50-light dynamo. Street-lights in Mount Carmel were operated on a moonlight schedule until 1898, after which they were lit all night long.

The equipment in the plant of the Edison Electric Illuminating Co. of Shamokin consisted of five 75-light dynamos following start-up in 1884, and the original incandescent plant was in operation until the turn of the century. In a replay of what had happened elsewhere in the anthracite region, the Edison interests organized the Shamokin Arc Light Co. in 1887 to provide arc lighting to streetlight customers in the Borough of Shamokin.

The Markle family, independent coal operators in Luzerne County surrounding Hazleton, were approached by P.B. Shaw in 1883 to invest in the Edison Electric Illuminating Co. of Hazleton. They put up the money to build a generating station at the corner of North Wyoming and Green streets. The original plant had a capacity of 1,000 16-candlepower lights, and that capacity was doubled in 1888. Unlike other companies in the anthracite region, the Hazleton company contracted with the municipality for the installation of incandescent streetlights to replace the gas lamps then in operation.

The 16-candlepower lights "are to burn

Most of the early electric companies used coal to fuel their boilers.

every night when the moon does not shine," an early company proposal noted, "or when the moon is hidden by clouds or night is dark by reason of storms." Later, the company turned on the streetlights one-half hour before sunset in clear weather. On cloudy days, the time the lights were turned on was left to the discretion of the company's engineer. The company assured the community that "the 16-candlepower lamps will be equal to, if not better than, the gas light per post that you have received in the past."

The Edison Electric Illuminating Co. of Hazleton charged its customers 1.25 cents per 10-candlepower lamp; later, the company changed to a flat rate of $1.00 per month per lamp. In 1890, the company built a new plant in Hazleton and installed an arc lighting dynamo of 50-light capacity, after the 16-candlepower incandescent lamps proved unequal to the task of lighting the city's streets.

Shaw wasn't the only person hawking Edison's electric light system in Pennsylvania. Paul D. Dyer, another Edison representative, was active in locating potential lighting customers in communities across New York, western Pennsylvania and Ohio. In the summer of 1883, Dyer was prospecting in Erie, Renovo, Bellefonte and Lock Haven. "This place is truly wonderful," Dyer wrote Samuel Insull, Edison's secretary, from Bellefonte in July 1883. "There are comparatively few houses that are no good considered from a lighting standpoint. Two electric light companies have been formed here, and both applied for a charter the same day."

Occasionally, Shaw and Dyer ran into unexpected objections to electric lighting in Pennsylvania. A woman identifying herself as "Aunt Bessie" voiced her opinion on the newfangled invention in a letter to the editor of the weekly *Bellefonte Watchman.* "When they come to lite up all outdoors with it and make it take the place of the heavenly bodies," Aunt Bessie observed, "that's what I call impious. Nothing more or less than trying to outdo the Creator. When the moon and stars don't shine, let folks walk in the dark or carry a lantern."

Electric power came to Scranton in the northern anthracite fields at a comparatively early date. As early as 1880, the annual "Author's Carnival" played host to a demonstration of a flickering electric arc light, and W.W. Scranton, then head of the Scranton Gas and Water Co., built an arc light plant along the banks of the

Lackawanna River shortly after. Scranton's industrial complex led the way in converting to electric power. The Dickson Locomotive shops, commonly referred to as the Cliff Works, built an isolated electric plant in December 1880. The city's steel mills electrified in February 1881, and the Dickson Works on Penn Avenue followed in October 1882. All were isolated light plants and served no retail or commercial customers.

The Scranton Electric Light and Heat Co. was organized in 1883 to provide streetlighting and home lighting for residents of "the Friendly City." Unlike other cities in the anthracite region, Scranton was characterized by the creation of numerous neighborhood electric companies. Between 1883 and 1907, a total of 19 companies furnished electricity to Scranton residents. Most of the neighborhood companies served areas in the immediate vicinity of the small generating stations, which rarely had a capacity of more than 200 kilowatts.

The Excelsior Electric Co. in Harrisburg operated a 500-light, 110-volt direct current generator; a 500-horsepower Couty Steam Engine; and three 100-horsepower water turbines. This illustration shows the 60 x 100-foot dynamo room in 1890.

Early Electric Operations

The electric companies of central and eastern Pennsylvania were shoestring operations in the 1880s and early 1890s, running small coal-fired boilers to serve parallel arc and incandescent lighting systems. Capital was tight, and breakdowns were frequent. Competition with the local gaslighting companies was always fierce, and disputes with local city councils over franchises were frequent.

Electrical work was often dangerous. In the summer of 1889, John Schmidt, an employee of the Excelsior Electric Co. in Harrisburg, was killed when he got tangled up in one of the machines in the company's powerhouse. Excelsior operated a 500-light, 110-volt direct current generator, which the crew called "the Black Maria"; a 500-horsepower Couty Steam Engine dubbed "the Old Hog"; and three 100-horsepower water turbines.

The water turbines were governed by a belt from the generator shaft, although at night the belt was thrown off and the turbines were governed directly by the "Old Hog." Schmidt was in the process of throwing off the belt when it looped around his heel and drew him up into the shaft. The hapless operator was whirled around until he was pounded to death on the brick floor of the boiler room. His injuries were so extensive that the funeral

home had to insist on closing the casket for the services.

Another time, one of the plant engineers was caught on a projecting bolt and drawn into the shaft, much the same as Schmidt had been. But the engineer had the presence of mind to throw his arms around the shaft and hold on for dear life until the device could be stopped. With the exception of bruised feet, the engineer survived the frightening experience.

A second employee of the plant was killed in 1890 when the armature on one of the arc light machines ran backward, and the brush holder caught in the commutator segment and broke the slate base of the machine into fragments. A piece of slate ricocheting around the boiler room bashed in the skull of the plant engineer, running to shut off the machine. He died the next day.

The vast majority of the early electric companies derived the fuel for their boilers from Pennsylvania's ample supplies of coal. At Honesdale, the Honesdale Consolidated Power & Light Co. built its plant adjacent to lower Ridge Street at the entrance to Gravity Park. The plant burned culm from the local culm banks, which was mixed with soft coal brought in by the D&H Railroad to a spur

To provide water power, the Excelsior Electric Co. built a waterway in the heart of Harrisburg. In 1888, the 10½-foot-diameter steel pipe was laid more than 200 feet through the city.

next to the plant. In the 1890s, Austin Gill, a local resident, used a team of horses and wagons to deliver the culm to the plant; during the winter months, Gill used horses pulling a sleigh to deliver the culm.

The operation of the coal-fired boilers didn't always sit well with the neighbors of the steam plant. In Honesdale, the residents of lower Ridge Street frequently complained that washing set out on clotheslines to dry was often soiled by soot from the plant's stacks.

Introduction of meters vastly improved the cash flow of the infant electric companies. Edison's early chemical meters were inaccurate at best, and many customers of the early electric companies were billed on a flat rate. Inventors like Elihu Thomson, Thomas Duncan and Oliver B. Shallengerger marketed new watt-hour and ampere-hour mechanical meters between 1888 and 1899; for the first time, electricity could be measured accurately.

Honesdale Consolidated Power & Light Co. used a mix of culm and soft coal to generate electricity for the residents and businesses of Honesdale.

Not that the introduction of meters was greeted enthusiastically by customers of the early electric companies. Maxwell Mailey, the first meter reader for the Harrisburg Electric Light Co., recalled in 1922 that there was "a vast difference of opinion regarding this mysterious thing. To the consumer it was considered a device direct from the infernal regions, sent by his Satanic Majesty himself, to torture those who had been persuaded to accept a new commodity which no one could describe and no one knew anything about, except the effect it produced, and it was sometime accompanied by a humming noise as if it was continually reminding the customer that it was just as busy as the bee it seemed to imitate in automatically measuring the dollars out of his pockets into the treasury of the company."

Customers of the Harrisburg Light & Power Co., accustomed as they were to the inadequacies of flat-rate billing, coined a distinctive acronym for the newfangled device:

Made
Expressly
To
Earn
Revenue for the Electric Company.

Mailey and his colleagues in the meter reading department were expressly instructed not to joke about meters with the customers. To the company, however, the mechanical meter was a real breakthrough. "It meant to them increased plant facilities without adding more equipment," Mailey said. "It meant a saving in the coal bill as well as in lamp renewals. It meant, in fact, a fair revenue with a minimum waste."

Meter installers in the 1880s and 1890s operated from the assumption that electricity would not flow upward, since any fool could see that lightning shot down from the heavens above. Consequently, standard operating procedure was to install the meter as high as possible, in the attic, in the upstairs bedrooms, or high up in closets.

Bob Hoy, an installer for Harrisburg Electric Light Co., installed the company's first meter in the store of H. Marks and Son at Fourth and Market streets. Hoy put the meter in the attic just below the roofline. When he came back the next month to read the meter, he discovered that he had hooked it up wrong, that the meter had run backwards for the entire month, and the company owed Marks and Son money for the month. Fortunately, the Harrisburg merchants were understanding about the mix-up and willingly settled the bill.

Not all the customers of Harrisburg Electric Light Co. were as understanding as Mr. Marks and his son. In fact, tampering with meters dated to shortly after the introduction of the meters themselves. While reading meters one day in 1890, the company's meter reader discovered that the disc of the meter at the Antlers Hotel on Strawberry Street had been plugged with paper. When confronted with the evidence, the proprietor admitted that "a bum came in one day and told him that if he gave him a square meal, he would fix his meter so he would get cheap light."

The same hotel proprietor was known to partake of alcoholic beverages during working hours. One day several months later, Mailey was called to the hotel by the meter tester, who had discovered that by removing a fuse, he could get his lights for next to nothing. While Mailey and the meter tester were trying to pry the fuse out of the box, the owner came in—obviously inebriated—and inquired what the two men were doing. "Just trying to get the fuse out," Mailey and his partner said, to which the proprietor suggested that they take a screwdriver and pry it out the way he did.

"He then went out of the room," Mailey recalled, "and while we were testing the meter, we heard a crash, and running out quickly found him hanging down through a sky light. We helped him out of his predicament and then found that he had a fan on the third floor and had run the cord out the window and connected it on the service ahead of the meter. In trying to remove it to avoid detection, he made a misstep and went through the skylight, but with the

proverbial luck of a drunken man, he was not injured, the only damage being done to the skylight."

Another customer, a jeweler on West Third Street, was only using about $2.50 worth of electricity each month. Mailey and a colleague installed a test meter across the street and discovered that the bill should have been $15-$18 per month. The meter department finally figured out that the jeweler had loosened the small frame around the window of the meter with jeweler's tools and set the hands inside to the lower reading.

High bill complaints were another fact of life for the early electric companies. Years later, Mailey told the story of how an increase of the flat rate for hotel fans from $2.50 to $3.50 per month led to the creation of the Steelton Light Heat and Power Co. in the steel mill suburb adjacent to Harrisburg. Mailey, who also doubled as the bill collector for Harrisburg Electric Light Co., presented the company's bill early in 1892 to Samuel Couffer, owner of the Couffer House.

When Couffer saw the bill and asked the reason for the change in rate, "he took exception to it and emphatically and profanely refused to pay the bill presented," Mailey noted. "He immediately went out and in two hours had raised $10,000 with which to build a plant in Steelton." The Steelton Light, Heat and Power Co. was incorporated in August 1892 and soon signed up the Pennsylvania Steel Co., the largest customer for power in Dauphin County. The incorporators were soon a competitive threat to Harrisburg Electric Light Co.

The early electric light companies in Pennsylvania struggled to harness the new technology of arc and incandescent lighting. Along the way, they created the foundation for an industry.

The Harrisburg Light and Power Station in 1890 used the combination of steam and water power.

Edison and Westinghouse at War

For the first decade of incandescent three-wire electric lighting, Thomas A. Edison essentially had the field to himself. There were competitors for incandescent lighting systems between 1883 and 1892, but for the most part, the Brush and Thomson-Houston interests continued to focus on the arc lighting business. Elihu Thomson, however, was already investigating alternating current by the mid-1880s. But it was a Pittsburgh businessman whose name would forever be linked with alternating current, and who would do battle with Thomas Edison in a "battle of the power kings" that would fascinate the American public in the late 1880s and early 1890s.

George Westinghouse was born in a small town in rural New York in October 1846. He served in the Union Army during the Civil War and returned home to work in his father's agricultural implement factory. Westinghouse applied for and received the first of his 400 patents in 1865, the year that the Civil War ended. Four years later, Westinghouse organized the Westinghouse Air Brake Co. in Pittsburgh to make and sell his most famous early invention, an air brake for railroad cars.

The air brake made it possible for the engineer to brake an entire trainload of cars at once. Prior to that time, the brake on each individual car had to be hand-set. Westinghouse became interested in the potential of alternating current transmission of electricity in the mid-

Ames station began producing hydroelectric power in June 1891.

1880s. Most original arc lighting systems and Edison's incandescent lighting system were designed to use direct current. In a direct current generator, the one-way current flow is produced by a commutator, a split metal cylinder with each half of the cylinder attached to one leg of the rotating coil. Stationary contacts, which early engineers called "brushes," capture the current and send it into the electrical circuit.

The direct current system had the advantage of simplicity. But direct current had one major drawback. The line loss of current increased exponentially the further one was removed from the generator. Edison didn't particularly think that was a problem. From the start, he envisioned a series of small generating plants that would serve small towns or neighborhoods in larger cities. Some direct current proponents thought that the transmission problem could be solved by installing storage batteries on the system.

In the mid-1880s, inventors in the United States and abroad began experimenting with alternating current. In an alternating current generator, the commutator is eliminated, and current flows briefly in one direction, and then briefly in the other, all the time in synchronization with the rotating coil. Early experiments in alternating current used generators run at 25 cycles per second; later, a 60-cycle standard was established for lighting, residential and commercial purposes, although 25-cycle generation survived well into the 20th century for customers using industrial power.

The great advantage to alternating current was the fact that it could be transmitted great distances with minimal line loss. Through use of a transformer, the current could be stepped up at the generating station for transmission, then stepped down on the other end for distribution to residential and commercial customers. Alternating current made it possible to build large central electric generating stations at some distance from the urban areas they served. Alternating current was made possible by a mercurial South Slav immigrant who worked briefly for Edison in the early 1880s before quitting the great inventor in a dispute over money. Nikola Tesla was born in Serbian Bosnia in 1857, in what was then the Austro-Hungarian Empire. Tesla studied engineering in Austria, Prague and Budapest before emigrating to the United States in 1884.

Tesla left the Edison Works in 1887 to set up his own company. The young Serb inventor had already applied for patents on alternating currents and generators, and his work soon came to the attention of Westinghouse, whose research department was hard at work perfecting the new electro-technology. In 1888, Westinghouse signed an agreement with the Tesla Electric Co. assigning the Tesla generating and transformer patents to the Pittsburgh manufacturer.

Edison, who genuinely believed that direct current was the only safe way to transmit and distribute electricity, went on the attack against Westinghouse and Tesla. Edison thought that alternating current generators were "unnecessary as they are dangerous. I can therefore see no justification for introduction of a system which has no element of permanency and every element of danger to life and property."

In the late 1880s, residents of West Orange, N.J., began to notice that the community's population of stray dogs and cats was declining rapidly. Edison and his assistants were paying children to trap the animals, which were then electrocuted by experiments with alternating current in Edison's laboratories. "Westinghoused," the great inventor called electrocution.

Edison cranked up his publicity machine to convince America of what he considered the inherent dangers of alternating current. Edison's associates went on the road, electrocuting large dogs and calves in front of public audiences. In 1890, Edison convinced the authorities at Sing Sing Prison in Ossining, N.Y., to change the method of executing prisoners—from hanging to alternating current. The Edison laboratories fashioned a crude electric chair, and on Aug. 6, 1890, a death-row convict by the name of William Kemmler became the first American to die in the electric chair.

Westinghouse worked equally hard to convince Americans that the built-in safeguards of alternating current made it no more hazardous to use than direct current. In 1893, Westinghouse won the contract to light the Chicago Exposition at Jackson Park. The exposition site was several miles from the nearest generating facility of the Chicago Edison Co.—a direct current generator—and Westinghouse reaped the benefits of worldwide publicity for the alternating current system.

Two years before, Westinghouse and Tesla had proved the feasibility of alternating current at a hydroelectric facility high in the mountains of southwestern Colorado. The Gold King Mine in Colorado's Telluride mining district wanted to electrify its workings, but wood fuel was scarce in the 12,000-foot-high mining district, and coal cost too much to ship to the isolated mining camp. Engineers built a small hydroelectric facility at the confluence of two forks of the San Miguel River 2,000 feet below the mine site. The Ames station, which used Westinghouse equipment, began producing hydroelectric power in June 1891, transmitting electric power three miles to the mine site with less than a five percent line loss.

In August 1895, Westinghouse won the battle of the systems when the first power was generated at Niagara Falls. J.P. Morgan had incorporated the Cataract Construction Co. in 1889 to develop the hydroelectric potential of the falls and transmit the power to nearby Buffalo; Westinghouse was awarded the contract for the first two generators, the switchgear and the auxiliary power equipment. Transmission began in 1896, and Westinghouse's alternating current system thus established the standard by which all U.S. transmission would be modeled in the early 20th century.

Following the 1892 merger of Edison General Electric Co. and Thomson-Houston Co. into the General Electric Co., Thomas Edison lost interest in the incandescent electric lighting business. For much of the 1890s, the Wizard of Menlo Park retreated to the wilds of New Jersey's Wachtung Hills, where he spent much of his fortune in trying to develop a commercial version of an electromagnetic iron ore separator. George Westinghouse and alternating current had won the war of the power kings, and the U.S. electric utility industry, including Pennsylvania Power & Light Co., would feel the impact of that victory.

One of George Westinghouse's most famous inventions was an air brake for railroad cars.

Mr. Holt and Mr. Wood

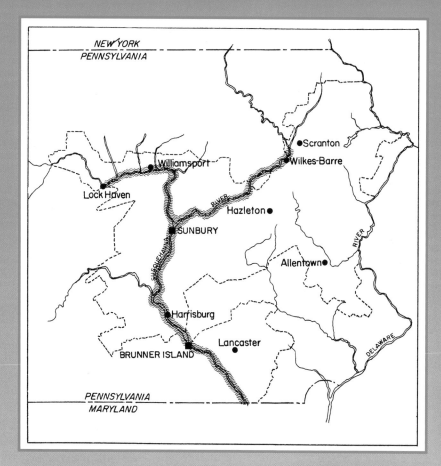

The Susquehanna is the longest non-navigable river in North America.

The Susquehanna River bisects Pennsylvania, draining 27,500 square miles of the state, an area that is larger than Massachusetts, New Jersey, Vermont and Delaware combined. The Susquehanna is shaped like a Y, with a West Branch rising in Pennsylvania and a North Branch rising to the north in New York state. The two branches come together at Northumberland in the center of the state, and the conjoined river then flows south and east to the Chesapeake Bay. It is the longest non-navigable river in North America, a lesson that was painfully learned by several generations of Pennsylvania's pioneers.

White Oil

Hydroelectric power took the nation by storm during the last two decades of the 19th century. The application of electrical generating technology to existing waterpower sites began in late 1881 when a Brush dynamo—belted to a turbine in the basement of a Niagara Falls, N.Y., flour mill—was used to generate power for a bank of arc lamps in the city. The next year, the Minneapolis Brush Electric Co. installed a hydroelectric central electric power station at St. Anthony Falls on the Mississippi River; the plant provided arc streetlighting along Washington Avenue in Minneapolis, Minn.

In the fall of 1882, the Vulcan Street plant went on line in Appleton, Wis., just three days after the start-up of Edison's Pearl Street station. Vulcan Street powered incandescent lighting for the Appleton Pulp and Paper Co. The Wisconsin hydroelectric facility was the first to power incandescent lighting in the United States. By 1886, *Electrical World* noted that nearly 50 electric light plants in the U.S. were "largely or wholly dependent on water power."

The origins of hydropower in Pennsylvania go back to colonial times. In the 18th century and through much of the 19th century, dams were built across Pennsylvania creeks and rivers to power flour mills and sawmills and other industrial applications. The machinery in the mills was run by a complicated series of leather belts powered by waterwheels at the damsite. One such industrial site was the Charming Forge, begun in 1747 by John Nikoll and Michael Miller on the Tulpehocken Creek; in 1777, the owner of the dam across the Tulpehocken Creek purchased the services of 34 Hessian prisoners of war to cut a channel through a bed of rock to supply water to a slitting mill at Charming Forge.

Hydroelectric power came to the Susquehanna River valley shortly after the turn of the 20th century. As early as 1797, a consortium of Philadelphia

McCall's Ferry Bridge was built in 1815 by pioneer bridge builder Theodore Burr. At the time, it was the longest single-span bridge ever built stretching 360 feet across the 100-foot deep channel. Unfortunately, the bridge was destroyed by an ice jam in 1817.

Still, the river was a valuable contributor to the economic life of Pennsylvania, transporting settlers and agricultural goods and anthracite coal to and from the interior in the colonial era and carrying huge rafts of sawtimber to the sawmills of Wilkes-Barre in the 19th century. Below Harrisburg the Susquehanna broadens and increases its volume as it is joined by numerous tributaries, including the Juniata, just north of the city. "A mile wide and a foot deep" is how river biographer Susan Q. Stranahan characterizes the lower reaches of the Susquehanna, which is marred by potholes and deeps—spoon shaped depressions in the riverbed—on its last 75 miles before emptying into Chesapeake Bay.

"A mile wide and a foot deep" – Susan Q. Stranahan

As the river rushes through the Susquehanna Gorge on the Pennsylvania-Maryland border, it takes on a wild and untamed character, crashing over house-sized boulders set between steeply pitched, wooded hills. If the Susquehanna wasn't suitable for navigation, it was eminently suitable for hydroelectric generation.

investors spent $100,000 to build a canal around Conewago Falls on the Susquehanna River, which dropped 19 feet in little more than one-quarter of a mile. In 1904, the York Haven Water and Power Co. completed a dam across the river at the Conewago Falls and installed a turbine. The Dauphin County site south of Harrisburg was the first hydroelectric facility on the Susquehanna.

The 22-foot head at the falls allowed for the generation of just under 20,000 kilowatts of electricity, enough to light the nearby community of York Haven and to generate power for a riverside pulp and paper mill. York Haven Water and Power Co. solved the problem of getting power from one side of the river to the other by burying high-voltage transmission cables in the bed of the Susquehanna.

McCall Ferry Power Company

The success of the York Haven Water and Power Co. led to other proposed hydroelectric developments on the Susquehanna. On April 14, 1905, a New York engineer by the name of Cary T. Hutchinson incorporated the McCall Ferry Power Co. for the purpose of building a dam 2,530 feet long across the Susquehanna about a mile downstream from where the descendants of Samuel McCall operated a ferry across the river.

McCall Ferry Power Co.'s board of directors was made up of people very familiar with the emerging technology of electric power production. Chief among them was Charles A. Coffin, General Electric's first president. A native of Maine, Coffin founded shoe manufacturing firms in Lynn, Mass. In 1883, he took over the business management of Elihu Thomson's electrical manufacturing business, which moved to Lynn that year. Just under a decade later, Coffin engineered the merger of Thomson's business with the Edison General Electric Co. and was named president of General Electric, the new company. In 1905, Coffin was

busy setting up the Electric Bond and Share Co. to hold General Electric's utility investments.

The New York investment community was represented on the board of directors of the McCall Ferry Power Co. by Rodman E. Griscom and Samuel R.

As early as 1797, a consortium of Philadelphia investors spent $100,000 to build a canal around Conewago Falls on the Susquehanna River.

Bertron of Bertron, Griscom & Co. Bertron, Griscom & Co. was one of the most active utility investment firms in New York early in the century, controlling electric utility interests in New Orleans, La.; Birmingham, Ala.; Houston, Texas; and the United Gas and Electric holding company. Bertron, Griscom & Co. partner Samuel R. Bertron later went on to a long career as president and chief executive officer of Houston Lighting & Power Co.

McCall Ferry Power Co. initially held its board meetings at 62 Cedar St. in New York City. The New York address was that of Phillip J. Bartlett, counsel for the company, and a senior partner in the law firm of Simpson, Thacher and Bartlett. In later years, Simpson, Thacher and Bartlett would represent Pennsylvania Power & Light Co. In the fall of 1905, the new company closed the purchase of land along either side of the river at McCall Ferry from Robert T. Fry for what was then the immense sum of $28,000. The company relocated 13 miles of the Columbia and Port Deposit Branch of the Pennsylvania Railroad, opened up bank deposits in Lancaster, Pa., and Port Deposit, Md., and began buying compressors, switching engines and steam excavation machinery.

McCall Ferry Power Co. secured a first mortgage on the property from the Knickerbocker Trust of New York City, a selection that put the project in jeopardy just two years later. "The dam will be so

As a partner in one of the most active investment firms of the time, Samuel R. Bertron represented the New York investment community on the McCall Ferry Power Co.'s board of directors. He later went on to a long career as president and CEO of Houston Lighting & Power Co. *(photo courtesy of Houston Lighting & Power Co.)*

This picture taken in the early 1900s shows the placement of the rotor in Holtwood hydroelectric station's Unit 1 generator. Like the construction of the Holtwood Dam, reinforced steel bars were not used in the construction of the concrete powerhouse.

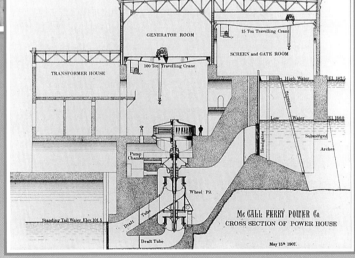

On Aug. 8, 1910, the first of five initial units at Holtwood were operational.

stupendous that it will rival the marvel on the Nile River at Assouan (Aswan)," *The Lancaster New Era* reported on July 27, 1905. "It is of such a tremendous nature—so vast in extent—that the layman can only wonder helplessly how the building proper will be begun."

The plans drawn up by Hutchinson, and approved by the executive committee, were indeed breathtaking. Hutchinson envisioned a dam 55 feet high stretching for nearly half a mile across the Susquehanna. The dam would create a 3.75-square-mile lake, backed up nearly eight miles from the impoundment. Also proposed was a second dam and hydroelectric facility to be built at a future time downstream from McCall Ferry, close to Port Deposit, Md. McCall Ferry Power Co. wouldn't get the chance to build that second dam, but when it was built—by the Philadelphia Electric Co. in 1928—the Conowingo Dam would be the second largest hydroelectric facility in the United States, after Niagara Falls.

Hugh L. Cooper, the consulting engineer for the dam at McCall Ferry, built the world's largest concrete plant to supply the crews building the dam across the Susquehanna. Cooper was able to draw upon the Portland cement industry of the Lehigh Valley for supplies of concrete, but the dam engineer decided not to use reinforced concrete for the massive dam across the Susquehanna. Reinforcing concrete with embedded iron bars was just then coming into vogue for U.S. construction projects, but Cooper elected to build the dam of solid concrete blocks.

McCall Ferry Power Co. broke ground for the dam and power plant on Oct. 24, 1905, and crews began diverting the flow of the river for construction of the dam in January 1906. By the summer of 1906, more than 1,000 men were working on construction of the dam, and newspapers reported in July that the workforce would more than double in the fall of 1906. By the time construction hit its peak in late 1906, more than 2,500 men were working around the clock to complete the hydroelectric facility on the Susquehanna.

The Panic of 1907

The first decade of the 20th century had been a period of frenetic growth in American industry. Industrialization picked up steam dramatically following the turn of the century. In November 1900, some 8,000 New Yorkers toured the New York Auto Show to kick tires of the newfangled horseless carriages. Early the next year, Texas wildcatters brought in the first oil well at the Spindletop Field on the Gulf Coast south of Beaumont. That same year, J.P. Morgan and Andrew Carnegie pooled forces to create United States Steel, the first of the great American 20th-century industrial combinations.

In the summer of 1902, Morgan helped arrange the merger of McCormick Harvesting Machine Co., Deering Harvester Co. and three smaller farm implement manufacturers. The International Harvester Co. controlled 85 percent of the farm implement market and established American dominance in another field of industrial endeavor. Late in 1903, a pair of Dayton, Ohio, brothers ushered in the age of powered flight over the desolate dunes of Kitty Hawk, N.C.

America's rise to industrial prominence didn't come without an accompanying price. In many ways, the early 1900s were analogous to the 1980s. Financiers and arbitrageurs controlled

"The year 1907 began in prosperity and ended in depression." – The Commercial & Financial Chronicle

Wall Street, and the era was characterized by a wave of corporate mergers and acquisitions. But the corporate skein began to unravel in the spring of 1907.

In March, stock prices dropped sharply, led by the railroads, which were still the backbone of the American economy. Even the strongest railroads, including the Reading, Great Northern, Northern Pacific and Union Pacific, were forced to go to the short-term money markets for cash, since the nation's banks were themselves short of cash. "As the year progressed it became more and more difficult to raise money," the reporter for *The Commercial & Financial Chronicle* reported in a year-end wrap-up, "even on the basis of short-term obligations, one reason being that the continued shrinkage in security values was so greatly impairing the resources and the strength of financial institutions and capitalists and men of means, that it was not possible for these to extend assistance in the way so frequently done in the past, even if they had desired."

Matters came to a head on Wall Street in late October. Ironically, the culprit was copper, the metal that had enjoyed a quarter-century rise in price and popu-

larity following the electrification of urban America. F. August Heinze, a copper speculator, had spent much of the summer of 1907 trying to corner the market in copper. By October, investors began selling off copper stocks in fears of a glut of the red metal on the market. Copper shares plummeted, precipitating a general sell-off on Wall Street.

Heinze had enlisted Charles T. Barney, the president of New York's Knickerbocker Trust, in his scheme to corner the copper market. Word quickly spread that the venerable Knickerbocker Trust was in trouble, and on Tuesday morning, Oct. 22, 1907, depositors began lining up outside the Knickerbocker Trust's offices at Thirty-Fourth Street and Fifth Avenue overlooking the Waldorf Astoria in New York City. The bank failed that Tuesday afternoon, and Barney shot himself several weeks later.

In the weeks to come, J. Pierpont Morgan and George Cortelyou, President Theodore Roosevelt's Secretary of the Treasury, rallied Wall Street and kept the panic from spreading. Still, as the reporter for *The Commercial & Financial Chronicle* put it, "The year 1907 began in prosperity and ended in depression."

For McCall Ferry Power Co., the October 1907 failure of the Knickerbocker Trust was an unmitigated disaster. Work stopped on the dam and powerhouse,

McCall's Ferry, the village and the project, was renamed Holtwood, a combination of two Canadian bankers' last names. Sir Herbert Holt and E.R. Wood financed nearly half of the McCall Ferry Power Co. after it had gone into receivership in the spring of 1909.

which were 80 percent complete. The company attempted to raise additional financing, to no avail. On Dec. 15, 1908, McCall Ferry Power Co. defaulted on its bond interest.

McCall Ferry Power Co. wasn't the only major hydroelectric project to be affected by the failure of the Knickerbocker Trust. In far-off northern Minnesota, the Great Northern Power Co. had a $1.7 million line of credit with the Knickerbocker Trust in 1907. But the Great Northern Power Co. was fortunate enough to finish its Thomson hydroelectric project on the St. Louis River in September 1907, just weeks before the collapse of the Knickerbocker Trust. The company was able to begin generating revenues to pay off its bank and bond debt.

The bankruptcy trustees for the McCall Ferry Power Co. began seeking a new management team for the completion of the Susquehanna River dam and powerhouse. John E. Aldred, president of the Shawinigan Falls Power Co. in Canada, submitted a plan to the bondholders of the bankrupt company in the spring of 1909. That August, Aldred was appointed receiver of the McCall Ferry Power Co. Aldred lined up nearly half the financing from two Canadian bankers, Sir Herbert S. Holt of Montreal and E.R. Wood of Toronto. In return for their financial backing, the project and the village of McCall Ferry were named Holtwood by Aldred, a combination of the Canadian bankers' last names.

Aldred reorganized McCall Ferry Power Co. as the Pennsylvania Water & Power Co. (Penn Water) in January 1910; and Hutchinson, the original incorporator of the McCall Ferry Power Co., was forced out. To replace Hutchinson and Cooper at Holtwood, Aldred brought in one of his own engineers from Shawinigan. John Abbett Walls was a member of a prominent family from Lewisburg, Pa. He attended Bucknell University in Lewisburg and then went

on to complete his civil and electrical engineering degree with the class of 1899 at the Massachusetts Institute of Technology.

Shortly after graduation, Walls joined the engineering consulting firm owned by Wallace C. Johnson, who was then engineering the hydroelectric system for the Niagara Falls Hydraulic and Manufacturing Co. Walls worked for Johnson for several years before joining Shawinigan in Canada. In 1910, Aldred brought Walls to Holtwood as chief engineer. Also coming from Shawinigan were F.A. Allner and James L. Rintoul. Allner, an engineer, and Rintoul, an accountant, were part of a multinational contingent that would make Holtwood unique in its early days. Allner, a native of Czechoslovakia, and Rintoul, a Scotsman, were joined on the staff by Edwin Hanson, a Swede; Bill Ballantyne, another Scot; Axel Bang and Axel Benzon, both Danes; and Hugo Lowy, an Austrian.

Old-timers joked that the new plant also had a Cannon, a Bang and a Gunn on staff when the project celebrated its 1910 opening. Rintoul, a native of Glasgow, was associated with Aldred in New York, at Shawinigan and Holtwood, retiring from Pennsylvania Water & Power Co. in 1947 as executive vice president and treasurer.

Sir Herbert S. Holt of Montreal (left) and E.R. Wood of Toronto.

In 1910, John Abbett Walls left the Shawinigan Falls Water Power Co. in Canada to become chief engineer at Holtwood.

Frederick A. Allner, a native Czechoslovakian from Shawinigan Falls Water Power Co., was part of the multinational contingent to join Holtwood in its early days.

Walls telegraphed Aldred on Aug. 8, 1910, that the first of five initial units at Holtwood had gone operational that afternoon. "Big Number One Unit started successfully at 2:16 today," Walls wrote Aldred in New York.

That first unit went into commercial operation in October 1910, and by the following July, the first five units were installed and operational. Holtwood would reach its original design capacity of 100 megawatts in 10 units by 1923. At 55 feet high and 2,398 feet long, the dam across the Susquehanna was the longest in North America in 1910, and the second longest in the world at the time, exceeded in length only by the first Aswan Dam in Egypt. The entire project was in 1910 the largest low-head, run-of-river hydroelectric plant in the nation.

The McCall Ferry Power Co. was reorganized as the Pennsylvania Water & Power Co. in January 1910.

Some 500 feet long and located at the east end of the dam, the powerhouse was also built of the same material as the dam. The first five waterwheels installed in the powerhouse were vertical types, rated at 15,300 horsepower apiece. A design change allowed an increase to 18,000 horsepower on the next five units. The waterwheels turned at 94 revolutions per minute under 53 feet of head and an 80 percent gate opening. "These are unusually large units for hydroelectric work," federal inspectors reported in 1912. The original generators were three-phase, 25-cycle, 11,000-volt units having a capacity of 12,000 kilowatts apiece.

The completion of the Holtwood project was only the first step in bringing Susquehanna River power to commercial use. As far back as 1905, S. Davies Warfield of the United Electric Light & Power Co. and the United Railways Co. of Baltimore had outbid Philadelphia interests for the rights to hydroelectric power from the McCall Ferry Power Co. The collapse of the Knickerbocker Trust and the receivership of the power company following 1907 had negated those contracts, but Warfield established relations with Aldred and renegotiated the contract with Pennsylvania Water & Power Co.

Upon Warfield's recommendation, Aldred was named a vice president of the Consolidated Gas, Electric, Light and Power Co. of Baltimore. When General Ferdinand C. Latrobe retired as president of the company in 1910, the Boston banker who had completed Holtwood was selected to replace him; Aldred served as president of the Baltimore Gas & Electric predecessor until 1915.

Pennsylvania Water & Power Co. completed a 40-mile high-voltage transmission line from Holtwood to Baltimore in 1910. The 100-foot right-of-way contained 500 steel towers varying in height from 58 to 120 feet. The initial line carried two 70,000-volt circuits each consisting of three aluminum cables. Soon after it was completed, company crews installed "the Holtwood Howler," a single-line telephone circuit along the right-of-way of the Holtwood to Baltimore line. Longtime employees recalled being exposed to the hum of the 66,000 volts of 25-cycle power coursing through the conductors above the Howler.

Charlie Street, who retired from Pennsylvania Water & Power Co. in 1953 following 42 years with the company, helped build the Holtwood-Baltimore line in 1910. Street lived on a farm near the right-of-way and frequently had to employ local farmers on a contract basis to assist on the project, particularly in hauling steel to the tower sites.

In October 1912, Pennsylvania Water & Power Co. contracted to supply service to the Lancaster Edison and Conestoga Traction companies in nearby Lancaster. The two companies formed the Conestoga Transmission Co. to acquire the right-of-way and to build a two-circuit transmission line from the dam to Lancaster. Load growth in Lancaster dictated completion of the project as soon as possible, but the transmission company soon ran into trouble, especially in dealing with the equipment and steel manufacturers.

Pennsylvania Water & Power Co. was asked to step in and take over the project. W.D. Abbott, Penn Water's transmission construction engineer, and Sam Gibason, veteran rigging boss, soon had towers springing out of the ground at the rate of six per day. "In those days," recalled longtime chief load dispatcher Reuel D. Shaub, "towers were erected by horses pulling towers to their upright position by means of block and tackle. As the construction crew neared Holtwood, work was continued at night; light was furnished by a search light, then located on the roof of the power house." Lancaster got its first low-tension voltage from Holtwood on June 26, 1913. By November of that year, the entire Lancaster load was being carried by the Holtwood station.

Shaub, who first came to Holtwood in November 1913 as a generator cleaner, recalled being skeptical about his ability to last at what was then the brand new hydroelectric station. "Why, do you know, when I got off the train at Holtwood that November day I looked around in the darkness and said to myself, 'Shaub, if you stick this out six days, much less six months, you're a good man,'" the chief load dispatcher recalled in 1954 at his retirement.

Part of the skepticism was due to the work. Shaub worked from 11 at night to noon the next day for $50 a month; the generator cleaners got off one day a month. A second reason for the skepticism was the isolation of the plant. Those with automobiles, Shaub recalled, put them in storage over the winter months. The red clay roads of the Susquehanna Valley turned into quagmires when wetted by winter snow or spring rain. The company built a village on the hills overlooking the dam to house workers for the hydroelectric project. By the time

Holtwood Village contained a church, a store, a two-room school, a post office and a clubhouse. Housing was provided by Pennsylvania Water & Power Co.

Shaub arrived at Holtwood, the village contained about 500 residents living in the frame housing provided by Penn Water. Holtwood Village also contained a church, a store, a two-room school, a post office and a clubhouse.

Residents of the village could get into Lancaster by taking the train to Pequea, then going by streetcar through Millersville to Lancaster, Shaub recalled. They could also go by train to Columbia and transfer to Lancaster. But "during a good part of the year, Holtwood residents made up their own amusements," Shaub said. A good part of those amusements

were sponsored by the Holtwood Club, organized as the Holtwood Athletic Association by Johnny Riff, Jimmy Stewart, Charley Cannon, Guy Parker, Ward Wells and Ralph Strickler on Nov. 21, 1911. In the early days, meetings were held in the Church Hall, but they were moved to the Club House when it was built in the winter of 1913-1914. The renamed Holtwood Club was still in operation some 40 years later when Pennsylvania Power & Light Co. acquired Penn Water.

The completion of the Holtwood project was a prime example of the industrial development of America in the first decade of the 20th century. Using manual labor, engineers constructed a massive impoundment of the Susquehanna River and brought about the electrification of Baltimore, one of America's great cities. Significantly, much of the electric power generated by Holtwood went to the electric street railway lines serving Baltimore and its suburbs. The electrification of the street railway industry was transforming American society at the turn of the century, and nowhere was that social phenomenon more pronounced than in the cities and communities of central and eastern Pennsylvania.

The Kingsbury Thrust Bearing

One of the problems that the engineers of the Holtwood project encountered was how to keep the massive turbines spinning. In 1910, Holtwood's turbines and generators were some of the largest ever designed, but they had an Achille's heel. The roller bearings wore out at an unacceptably high rate because the vertical shaft of the turbine bore all the weight of the turbine-generator sets. More than 200 tons of dead weight exerted tremendous pressure on the roller bearings, and crews in the early days frequently had to tear down the turbine-generator sets to replace the roller bearings.

John Abbett Walls, Frederick A. Allner, and the engineers at Holtwood experimented with several solutions to the problem. In 1911, Pennsylvania Water & Power Co. tried using a water-lubricated thrust bearing on Unit 2. On paper, it seemed to offer a solution; in practice, the water-lubricated bearing failed within two months.

Allner, who was convinced that a thrust bearing could take the weight and pounding of the turbine-generator sets, introduced Walls to the work of Albert Kingsbury, a college professor and engineering consultant who had recently patented an oil-filled thrust bearing. A native of Illinois, Kingsbury had specialized in the study of friction and the properties of lubricants during his academic career. At Cornell University in the 1880s, he had designed half-journal bearings for the Pennsylvania Railroad that showed no detectable wear after months of continuous use.

In 1910, Kingsbury was a consultant to the East Pittsburgh works of the Westinghouse Electric & Manufacturing Co. That year, he had received a patent for an oil-filled thrust bearing, and he contacted Penn Water to see if it would be interested in installing one of the

Frederick A. Allner and Professor Albert Kingsbury pose for a photo at the 25th anniversary of the Kingsbury Bearing in Unit No. 5 in 1937.

experimental bearings on a turbine-generator set. When Allner and Walls indicated their interest, Kingsbury cashed in an insurance policy and paid Westinghouse to fabricate a prototype bearing.

Kingsbury came to Holtwood in the spring of 1912 and supervised the installation of his bearing on the No. 5 unit of the hydroelectric station. At first glance, the experiment looked like a failure. The oil overheated, and the unit was shut off. Kingsbury told Allner that the problem was easily fixed. He had to scrape metal from the lower bearing shoes so they would be as flat as possible. He returned to Holtwood in June, and the bearing was installed with a new set of shoes. The unit started up at 1:25 p.m. with no sign of overheating. At 4:59 p.m., Unit 5 went on line with a full load. The bearing performed flawlessly.

Kingsbury designed the thrust bearing for Unit 5 at Holtwood to support a 400,000-pound load in continuous operation by a 12,000-kilowatt generator, driven by a waterwheel and operating between 94 and 116 revolutions per minute. A high-grade engine oil then known as "Renown Engine Oil" served as a lubricant, and oil was to be supplied at 17.5 gallons per minute at not more than 40 degrees Centigrade.

With a diameter of 48 inches, a height of 24 inches and a weight of two-and-a-half tons, the Kingsbury Bearing is carried by a wedge-shaped oil film six-thousandths of an inch thick which is formed between the shaft thrust-collar and a series of stationary pivoted pads or segments. Kingsbury designed the six lower shoes of the bearing to be slightly loose so they could slip sideways a negligible amount. The minute twisting motion of the steel ring squeezed oil between the collar and the shoes, allowing the oil to support the entire weight of the shaft. Kingsbury noted that the faster the shaft turned, the more weight it would carry. Because the shoes were always bathed in oil, in theory they would never wear out.

Kingsbury's prediction has been borne out over the years. In September 1912, the unit was pulled apart and the bearing was found to be in near perfect condition. Penn Water engineers estimated at the time that the bearing should last 330 years before the shoes were even half worn away and recommended that Kingsbury Thrust Bearings be installed in all 10 of the first units at Holtwood.

Kingsbury's risk in gambling his insurance money to get the prototype built paid dividends. The oil thrust bearing made it possible for hydroelectric engineers to design much larger projects than Holtwood, and in the years to come, Kingsbury bearings were installed by engineers for Hoover Dam, the Tennessee Valley Authority, Bonneville Power Authority and the Grand Coulee Dam.

Following American entry into World War I, the Kingsbury bearing was used extensively in marine propulsion, for the propellor shafts of capital ships of the U.S. Navy. In the years after World War II, U.S. Navy engineers installed Kingsbury bearings on America's nuclear submarine fleet. On June 27, 1987, the 75th anniversary of the installation of Albert Kingsbury's first bearing at Holtwood, the American Society of Mechanical Engineers designated the Kingsbury bearing an International Historical Mechanical Engineering Landmark. The Kingsbury bearing was still turning its 94 to 116 revolutions per minute, and the estimate of its half-life wear had been updated over the decades to more than 1,000 years.

The Kingsbury Thrust Bearing was developed in 1912.

Margaretta Clulow, Kingsbury's granddaughter and chairman of Kingsbury Inc., accepted the International Historical Mechanical Engineering Landmark award from ASME at ceremonies held at Holtwood. "Having been asked on behalf of the Kingsbury family and company to acknowledge the amazing honor done us here today," she told the crowd, "one thought kept coming to me, how in so many ways that this occasion represents the spirit of pioneering that's been so much a part of American life.

"I think of the pioneering spirit in the Pennsylvania Water & Power Co. that led them to install the historic bearings upon which my grandfather worked with his own hands to get right, and which, 75 years later, as we meet now, are working as effectively as in 1912. I don't have the words to tell you how touched and moved and grateful that Albert Kingsbury would be by your honoring his achievement with this award, and his family and his company thank you with all our hearts."

'Too Stupendous for Oratory'

Local newspapers in the Susquehanna Valley followed the progress of construction at Holtwood with great interest and even more enthusiasm. On Saturday, Oct. 15, 1910, *The Daily New Era* of nearby Lancaster reported on the official commercial turn-on of the big hydroelectric plant south of the city. "Great Power Plant Sends Forth Electric Current," read the headline, written by a copy editor turned local booster. "Great Undertaking at M'Call's Ferry Now a Realization," read the subhead.

The front-page story shared space with an account of Walter Wellman's ultimately unsuccessful attempt to reach Europe from Atlantic City, N.J., in a hot-air balloon. In York, the newspaper reported on the 20th anniversary founding of the Pennsylvania German Society at a banquet Friday evening. From Conway, Mo., a report noted that Stanley Ketchel, the nation's middleweight boxing champion, had been fatally wounded in a shooting at a ranch where he was training. Theodore Roosevelt, who was campaigning for Republican congressional candidates, had bypassed Lancaster on a swing through Pennsylvania and New York, and the newspaper reported that the Lancaster County Fish Protectionists had held a meeting the previous evening to protest the legislature's attempt to approve fishing on Sunday.

But the big news in the newspaper that afternoon was the report from Holtwood. "The big Susquehanna River is now working for Baltimore, so here's to the Pennsyl-

vania Water & Power Co.; may it live long and prosper!" the lead story on the front page reported. "With these words, Mayor J. Barry Mahool, of Baltimore, turned 70,000 volts of electric current in to Baltimore from the great plant at McCall's Ferry at 11:36 o'clock Friday morning. There was a little click and a flash as the thrill of the water-made power danced along the lines to Baltimore and back, completing the circuit, thus making a new epoch in the industrial activity of the Monumental City.

"The central figure of the 200 or more men gathered in the great concrete electrical plant was that of J.E. Aldred, who is called the 'wonder man,' and as Mayor Mahool turned on the current he started the applause which was quickly taken up and echoed through the great concrete structure with a tremendous cheer.

"Thus far, the only purchaser of current is the Consolidated Gas, Electric, Light and Power Co. of the Maryland metropolis, but ultimately the waters of Pennsylvania's great stream will light the streets, drive the trolley cars and run the wheels of many mills in 200 towns and cities within a radius of 45 miles of the river. For, if this venture is commercially successful, two more dams below McCall's Ferry will be built; and three times will the same water be made to churn out power. There was no speechmaking. The occasion was too stupendous for oratory."

The reporter described "two immense generators,

carefully incased, and which looked not unlike monster coffee mills…. Each was producing 13,500 volts, which by a magical process that makes the electrician the wizard of the age, were 'stepped up' to 70,000 volts in the transformers, from which the cables received their current.

"Beneath the floor two turbines, linked tandem on the same shaft, drove each generator. Some distance away two smaller generators, known technically as 'exciters,' spun in measured cadence. Their mission was to magnetize the large generators. The turbines in operation produced a combined propulsive force of 35,000 horsepower, yet they made so little noise that a visitor might have passed through the room without noticing that the machinery was in motion."

The Time of the Trolley in the Lehigh Valley

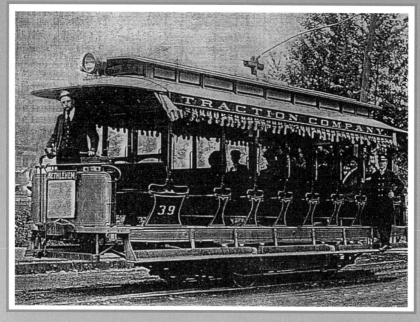

The interurban electric railways connected cities across America. *(photo courtesy of the Lehigh County Historical Society)*

Horse-drawn street railways employed 35,000 people and carried more than 1.2 billion passengers.

At the turn of the century, the United States in general, and Pennsylvania in particular, enjoyed a cheap, efficient method of public transportation that was never equalled before or since. In the years before Henry Ford revolutionized the production of automobiles at his River Rouge plant outside Detroit in 1913, Americans by the millions rode the streetcar to work and back, to shop downtown, and even to their own funerals.

Suburbs grew up around streetcar stops, and the ubiquitous trolley was as familiar a sight to residents of Allentown or Lancaster or Williamsport in 1910 as an interstate highway is to the residents of those same communities today. Lehigh Valley residents could board a streetcar in Allentown or Bethlehem or Easton and ride to Philadelphia to spend the day shopping. The interurban electric railways connected cities across America, and in the Midwest, where the interurban network was strongest, it was possible to board a streetcar in Indianapolis and ride 200-300 miles in any direction.

"The electric railway has become the most potent factor in our modern life," noted Frank Sprague in 1904. Sprague was the U.S. Navy officer who had resigned his commission to design the first electric street railway system in Richmond, Va. In the third of a century between the time that Sprague electrified Richmond's street railway system in the late 1880s and 1920, the trolley became the primary method of transportation for an entire generation of Americans. By the 1920s, the industry was past its peak but still an important factor in American

---

More than 1,900 companies nationwide operated 45,000 miles of electrified track, and ridership totalled 16 billion Americans in 1921.

---

transportation. More than 1,900 companies nationwide operated 45,000 miles of electrified track, and ridership totalled 16 billion Americans in 1921, almost double the ridership of nine billion Americans in 1907. About 50 million Americans had access to local trolley service, and electric street railway service extended to about half of America's cities and towns.

The automobile assembly line and the Good Roads movement made individual ownership of automobiles a reality after the mid-1920s and sounded the death-knell for the electric street railway industry. But even today, advocates of light rail transit, the latest trend in public

transportation, are harking back to an earlier day when trolleys were king in America's cities.

In the Beginning

In the earliest days of the street railway industry, street railway cars were pulled by mules and horses. Allentown had a horse-car system, the Allentown Passenger Railway Co., as early as the 1860s; the company was chartered on March 1, 1865, as the Army of the Potomac under Gen. Ulysses S. Grant closed in on Gen. Robert E. Lee's forces around Richmond. The Passenger Railway Co. began public railway service three years later and operated with five cars and 12 horses. The terminus for the system was just behind the Black Bear Hotel on the northeast corner of Ninth and Hamilton streets, and the original network consisted of about three-and-a-half miles of track.

The original trackage of the Allentown Passenger Railway Co. followed Hamilton Street east to Second Street but skirted the Hamilton Street Hill by detouring to South Fifth, Walnut and South Fourth streets. The tracks crossed the Lehigh River and terminated at the Lehigh and Susquehanna Railway passenger station; another branch terminated at the Reading passenger station and steam engine terminal at East Penn Junction. Branches also went north to the Sixth Ward and were extended throughout the city during the 1870s and 1880s.

Bethlehem and Easton were similarly served by horsecar lines at the same time. Horse cars were small four-wheeled closed cars with open platforms. Some

(courtesy of Trexler Funeral Home, Allentown)

cars were equipped with small coal stoves for heat, but customers were more than likely to travel in unheated cars during the winter; more frequently, the driver just scattered clean straw over the floor of the car so that patrons could at least warm their feet. From his position on the open platform, the driver was totally exposed to the elements. Sometimes, the weather halted operations of the horse

cars for days at a time. The great blizzard that swept the Lehigh Valley in the second week of March 1888 kept horse cars off the streets for more than a week.

By the early 1880s, horse-drawn street railways like that operated by the Allentown Passenger Railway Co. were a fixture in America's cities. There were some 415 street railways in operation nationwide, using 18,000 horse cars and 100,000 horses. The equine motive power consumed 150,000 tons of hay and 11 million bushels of grain each year, and they operated on more than 3,000 miles of

In the early 1900s, streetcars were as familiar a sight as interstate highways are today. *(photo courtesy of the Lehigh County Historical Society)*

The equine motive power consumed 150,000 tons of hay and 11 million bushels of grain each year, and they operated on more than 3,000 miles of track.

track. All told, the nation's street railways in the era just prior to electrification employed 35,000 people and carried more than 1.2 billion passengers. Total investment in the system was more than $150 million.

(*Above*) **This open electric car of the Lehigh Valley Traction Co. is traveling on the Guaffs Hill line to South Bethlehem.** *circa early 1900s*

(*Right*) **A typical horse-drawn railcar near Centre Square in Easton in 1885.** *(photos courtesy of the Howard P. Sell Collection—Railways to Yesterday)*

driving axle of the streetcar, thereby lessening the vibration problem that had defeated other inventors, including Edison. Sprague improved the overhead pick-up system first designed by the Belgian inventor Charles Van DePoele and solved the all important problem of current pick-up. The pole that connected the streetcar to the overhead lines was known as a "troller," and the cars soon became known as trolleys.

The success of the Richmond streetcar system in 1888 and 1889 proved a boon to Sprague. The start-up company soon had close to 200 contracts to electrify street railways in America's cities. William D. Middleton, author of *The Time of the Trolley*, which is one of the standard works on the history of the industry, dedicates the book to Sprague, "Naval officer, engineer and inventor, whose ingenuity and tireless effort, more than those of any other man, made possible the age of electric traction."

But as the 1880s drew to a close, a new technology was poised to transform the street railway industry. By the late 1880s, research and development into the electrification of urban street railways was turning into practical application. As early as 1880, Thomas Edison had built an experimental electric railroad at his Menlo Park, N.J., estate. One of Edison's research assistants, Frank Julian Sprague, established a company to manufacture electric traction motors. A graduate of the U.S. Naval Academy, Sprague had attended the electrical exhibitions at Paris and London in 1881 and 1882 and had written reports for the Navy. He resigned his commission in the early 1880s, worked for Edison and then struck out on his own.

In 1887, Sprague was hired to electrify the streetcar system in Richmond, Va. Sprague's traction motors were the key to the implementation of the successful Richmond system. The Naval Academy graduate fitted his compact motor to the

The Electrification of Pennsylvania Street Railways

Within months of Sprague's successful demonstration of his Richmond electric street railway system, Pennsylvanians began clamoring for the new service. As early as 1885, the Northumberland Electric Railway was granted a charter to build a 3.2-mile electric street railway between Northumberland and Sunbury. The company jumped the gun both technologically and politically, and its charter was called into question by the Pennsylvania Supreme Court. In 1889, the Pennsylvania Legislature passed an act relating to the incorporation and regulation of street railways, and Northumberland Electric Railway, which received its letters of patent on May 20, 1889, began construction of the roadbed in July.

The president of Northumberland Electric Railway was Leffert H. Kase, and Simon P. Wolverton was treasurer of the company. Both men were from Sunbury, but the principal investor in the project was P.B. Shaw of Williamsport, the Thomas Edison associate who had built the first three-wire incandescent electric generating station in Sunbury back in 1883. The new company had budgeted $120,000 to get the project off the ground, but when only $95,000 could be raised in Sunbury and Northumberland, Shaw raised the final $25,000 from investors in Williamsport.

The Northumberland Electric Railway did not contract with Frank Sprague for the electrification of its system. Instead, the company selected the Daft Electric Co. of New York City, a smaller firm but nevertheless a respected name in incandescent and railway electrification. Daft agreed to build the line within 90 days, and the company took delivery of 4,000 railroad ties and 328 poles.

As it was, construction took considerably longer than three months. The first car wasn't delivered until April 1890, and it was July before the line was open to the public. Testing of the system revealed problems in the current pick-up from the overhead two-wire hook-up, and Shaw is reputed to have solved the problem by suggesting the installation of a small wheel and pulley arrangement at the end of the troller pole; for the next half-century, streetcars made use of the wheel and pulley supposedly designed by Shaw.

Business was good at first. Some 800 passengers a day rode the streetcars between Northumberland and Sunbury for the balance of 1890. Fares were six cents; riders could purchase a book of 20 coupons for $1.00. During heavy traffic periods, the two Daft cars operated on a 15-minute schedule. On weekends and late in the day, the cars operated on a 30-minute schedule.

Things soon deteriorated for the fledgling electric street railway when the two-wire overhead system proved unequal to the task of powering the streetcars. Ridership fell off dramatically, and the company was reorganized in 1892 as the Sunbury and Northumberland Electric Railway Co. Among the new directors of the reorganized company were Pierre S. Du Pont and John J. Raskob. Du Pont was president of the Wilmington, Del., chemical and gunpowder manufacturing firm that bore his name, and Raskob was Du Pont's treasurer in the 1890s. In later years, the two men gained control of General Motors.

An electric trolley in South Bethlehem.

The Boston Connection

The problems that plagued the Sunbury-Northumberland line were duplicated in the Lehigh Valley. In January 1888, the Pennsylvania Motor Co. had experimented in Easton with an electrified street railway line, converting a horse car to shuttle between Third and Buckhill streets to the College Hill residential district in the northeast quadrant of the city. In later years, a bronze tablet on the Third Street Bridge over Bushkill Creek called attention to the event: "The Third Electric Railway in the United States, First in Easton, Pa., Built for regular passenger service. Began operation from this point, Jan. 14, 1888,

pulp and paper mill a mile away.

Webster evidently handled the Maine power plant installation, as Stone oversaw electrification of the Allentown property. Stone & Webster would go on to become one of the most prominent firms operating and managing electric street railways. By 1919, the Boston engineering firm would manage nearly 60 electric railway, electric lighting, gas and water-power properties nationwide, including the Beaumont (Texas) Traction Co., the Everett (Washington) Railway and Electric Co., the Galveston-Houston Electric Co., the Houghton County (Michigan) Traction Co., the Keokuk (Iowa) Electric Railway and Power Co., the Northern Texas Traction Co., the Pacific Northwest Traction Co., the Puget Sound Electric Railway, the Savannah, Thunderbolt and Isle of Hope Railway, the Seattle Railway Co., the Tacoma Railway and Power Co. and the Whatcom County (Washington) Railway and Light Co. Stone cut his teeth on engineering the electrification of the street railway system of Allentown and Bethlehem. The lessons he learned in the Lehigh Valley would help him in building a street railway empire in the early 20th century.

Great Public Interest

Charles A. Stone (left) and Edwin Webster. By 1919, Stone & Webster managed nearly 60 electric railway, lighting, gas and water power properties nationwide. *(photo courtesy of Stone & Webster)*

over the line of the Lafayette Traction Co., now the Pennsylvania Motor Co."

In 1891, the Allentown Passenger Railway Co. passed into the hands of a group of Boston investors, including Col. George H. Campbell, Alfred Glacier and Charles A. Stone. The engineering genius of the consortium was Stone. An 1888 engineering graduate of the Massachusetts Institute of Technology, Stone had formed a partnership with a classmate, Edwin S. Webster, in December 1889. Early in 1890, the Stone & Webster firm signed a contract with the S.D. Warren Co. of Cumberland Mills, Maine, to design and build a direct current generating plant on the Presumpscot River and a transmission line to the firm's

The local newspapers followed the electrification work with great interest. On June 22, 1891, the *Allentown Chronicle and News* reported that Stone and his fellow investors had selected the Reed & McKibbin engineering firm of New York for the overhead wiring work, and that the firm had "finished their work in Allentown and will probably begin the wiring of the line from this city to Bethlehem this week. During the course of their operations in Allentown the firm employed about 30 hands and the complicated work was completed in a creditable manner. About 50 men will be employed by the firm in the wiring of the line along the turnpike."

The Allentown newspaper went on to

report that Reed & McKibbin had been engaged in electrical engineering work for eight years, and that the firm had wired the electric street railway in Camden, N.J., the previous year. Reed, who had worked on designing the electrification of the Lafayette Traction Co. in Easton several years before, told the newspaper that his firm had recently signed a contract to electrify 18 miles of street railway in Mobile, Ala.

The work of electrifying Allentown's street railway was sometimes hazardous. On June 29, James Smith, a Reed & McKibbin employee, was injured when fixing the wires in the vicinity of 12th and Hamilton streets. "Smith was driving the wagon on which the trestling used by the men in reaching the wires is mounted," the *Chronicle and News* reported. "For some reason the horse started to back and before Smith could get off the wagon, it upset and fell on him. It is a wonder he was not killed."

On July 1, 1891, readers of the *Chronicle and News* were greeted with the news that the first electric car was run through the city the previous evening. "The 25 people who occupied the car," the newspaper reported, "most of them enjoying their first electric ride, had an air of importance about them as they contemplated the honor of a trip on the first electric car through Allentown."

Hundreds of local residents watched the newfangled trolley car with a mixture of awe and amazement. "Car No. 1 left the depot at Madison and Gordon streets," the report noted. "Hundreds of people stood along Hamilton Street and as the car with electric current flashing like lightning from the wheels and trolley wheel passed along the thoroughfare, many looked on in amazement."

Like their counterparts at Sunbury just eight years ago, the editorial writers at the *Chronicle and News* took considerable civic pride in the new streetcar system. "July 1, 1891, marks an important era in the history of Allentown and the future historian will refer to the day as a red-letter occasion in the city's life," the newspaper concluded.

The trolley was an immediate sensation in Allentown and Bethlehem. By September, the Allentown & Bethlehem Rapid Transit Co. was running 15 cars, three of them the newest enclosed type. Work was begun on the company's new central generating station on Front Street in Allentown, and an extension was pushed out to the Bethlehem Fair Grounds in time for the County Fair in mid-September. The company announced that it was repainting some of the older horse cars, which were to be used as

Also enjoying many narrow escapes were the schoolchildren of the First Ward "who persist on jumping off and on the cars, standing on the track and waiting to see how near the car will approach them before jumping aside." —Chronicle and News

trailers during the expected rush of traffic during fair week. In August, more than 500 people a night had taken the trolley to a religious revival meeting at Rittersville.

The streetcars did cause some consternation during their shakedown runs in the summer and early fall of 1891. In late July, one of the Reed & McKibbin workers was stringing wire at the corner of Court and North Church streets when he reached over to push the wire out of the way. The wire was energized, and the poor worker was wrenched from his perch on a crossbar. He hung suspended some 40 feet above the ground, gripping the wire and the guy rope as an estimated 1,000 volts of electricity surged through his body. "His screams of agony attracted immediate attention," the newspaper reported, "but everybody was powerless to help him. He hung there for about three minutes suffering indescribable agony as the powerful electric current shot through him." The hapless worker finally tore his hand loose from the wire and fell to the street. He bruised his hip and back, and his hand was moderately burned, but he was otherwise miraculously unhurt.

Horses were a constant problem in the

early days of the line's operation. Stephen Rex of North Whitehall, a renowned local cigar maker, had a mishap in front of the Lehigh Trust and Safe Deposit Co. when his team dumped his wagon after being spooked by the passage of a trolley. A goat that roamed Hamilton Street somehow escaped unscathed through the summer of 1891. "Cats, dogs, chickens, ducks and geese have already yielded up to the grinding wheels of the electric car," the *Chronicle and News* reported in September, "but the imperturbable nanny goat has passed unscratched through it all though he has had many narrow escapes."

Also enjoying many narrow escapes were the schoolchildren of the First Ward "who persist on jumping off and on the cars, standing on the track and waiting to see how near the car will approach them before jumping aside," the newspaper reported in the first of a series of warnings that would become familiar to several generations of local parents. "It is only owing to the extra care exercised by the motormen that no accidents have occurred, but the pitcher will go into the well once too often, and then the usual diatribes against the recklessness of the motorman will be indulged in. If parents would exercise more care over their children and instruct them thoroughly on how to behave in going to and from school, they would not be so often called on to stand besides their encoffined remains or see them go crippled and maimed through life." It wasn't too long before Allentown's schoolchildren discovered one of the great Halloween tricks of the trolley age—placing wicker porch furniture or outhouses on the tracks around a blind curve and watching as the streetcar reduced them to kindling.

The initial wave of enthusiasm that greeted the inauguration of streetcar service in the Lehigh Valley evaporated quickly. During the decade between 1891 and 1901, the industry was characterized

> *During the decade between 1891 and 1901, the [streetcar service] industry was characterized by cutthroat competition.*

by cutthroat competition, abysmal relations with local government bodies and even worse relations with the newspapers in Allentown and Bethlehem.

Albert Johnson and the Lehigh Valley Traction Company

The first direct competition for Colonel Campbell and the Boston organizers of the Allentown and Bethlehem Rapid Transit Co. came early in 1893 when the Allentown and Lehigh Valley Transit Co. announced plans to run a streetcar line from Catasauqua through Allentown and into South Bethlehem. Like its Allentown and Bethlehem Rapid Transit Co. predecessors, the management of the new line was composed of out-of-towners.

Tom Loftin Johnson and his brother Albert came from Cleveland, and they were veterans of the street railway business. Born in Kentucky before the Civil War, the Johnson brothers had been raised in Staunton, Va. Tom had gone to work in 1869 for the Louisville (Kentucky) Street Railroad, a horsecar line, and had invented a farebox for coins. With the help of the Du Pont family, which owned the Louisville railroad, Tom bought the Indianapolis Street Railroad and moved to Cleveland in the 1880s where he bought a Cleveland street railway.

By 1883, Tom Johnson was serving his second term in Congress as a Democrat from northern Ohio, and he would serve three terms as the mayor of Cleveland after 1901. Tom was a major investor in the Allentown street railway, and his brother Albert was president of the company and general manager of the line. By October 1893, the new line was in operation, and when the Boston backers approached the Johnsons about buying the new line early in 1894, the Cleveland group made a counter offer to buy Allentown and Bethlehem Rapid Transit

Co. The two lines were merged under the Johnsons' ownership in February 1894, and the name was changed to the Lehigh Valley Traction Co. The sale also included all the assets of the Allentown Electric Light Co., which had been acquired by Allentown and Bethlehem Rapid Transit Co. in 1892 when the light company had been unable to build a new power station on Front Street and had instead sold out to the transit company.

The 1890s were a time of ferment in the electric street railway industry of Pennsylvania and the nation. "The possibilities of electric transportation were considerably magnified at that time," a history of electric street railway development in the Lehigh Valley noted laconically. "Promoters were seeking franchises everywhere; rivalry was very keen and the sky seemed to be the limit of franchise commitments and obligations, in the way of street paving, free electric power and light for all municipal buildings and free transportation for all municipal, township and county officials."

There was a virtual explosion of new lines in the Valley during the 1890s. In Mauch Chunk, Philadelphia investors incorporated the Carbon County Electric Railway Co. in February 1892 to build a railway north from Mauch Chunk to the resort community of Glen Onoko. The

Dorney Park Line, as it was known to Allentown residents, was chartered as the Allentown and Kutztown Traction Co. in 1895. But it was 1902 before a successor company actually reached Kutztown with streetcar service.

Another company that served the Lehigh Valley was the Northampton Transit Co., organized in 1900 as the Easton and Nazareth Street Railway Co. The Slate Belt Electric Railway Co. originally served the slate quarry communities of the valley outside of Easton; in January 1901, the line became a wholly owned subsidiary of the Lehigh Valley Traction Co. The Bangor and Portland Traction Co., a subsidiary of the Delaware, Lackawanna and Western Railroad, was a competing line that succeeded several other street railways in 1904 in Bangor, East Bangor and Portland.

Hugh Crilley, a well-known Allentown

Tom Loftin Johnson began his career in the railway industry at the Louisville Street Railroad in 1869. In the 1880s, he moved to Cleveland, bought a street railway and later went on to serve three terms as mayor of the city. Shown here as mayor, Johnson marches down the trolley tracks of Cleveland during some official parade.

Tom Johnson, pictured left, and his brother, Albert, bought Allentown and Bethlehem Rapid Transit Co. in February 1894. The lines were merged and named Lehigh Valley Traction Co. (photos courtesy of the Cleveland Public Library)

capitalist and local politician, took over the three-year-old South Bethlehem and Saucon Street Railway Co. in the first week of January 1903. Crilley built the system from South Bethlehem to Center Valley via Seidersville, Colesville and Friedensville.

None of the short trolley lines ever equalled the route system of the Lehigh Valley Traction Co., and most were either eventually merged into the larger system or were subsidiaries of other railroads. But the competition that ensued made it all the more difficult for the Lehigh Valley Traction Co. to dominate street railway operation in the Valley.

Albert Johnson had his hands full dealing with local government officials, particularly in Bethlehem. The city council complained that the Lehigh's buff and cream single-end closed cars were tearing through Bethlehem at the unheard of speed of 15 mph, and Bethlehem theater patrons complained at New Year's 1895 that it took three hours for the after-theater car to return from Allentown. Nobody in Bethlehem was particularly happy about the lithographed posters on the side of the streetcars proclaiming that the company was domiciled at "Central Park, Allentown," and Bethlehem merchants complained that Lehigh Valley Traction Co. compelled its motormen to buy their uniforms at Breinig and Bachman's in Allentown for $13 apiece when everybody knew that the same uniforms could be bought on the other side of the river for $5 less.

Lehigh Valley Traction Co. was also involved in a running feud through much of the mid-1890s with the Borough of South Bethlehem, primarily over extension of service to the community and the borough's rights to levy a ridership tax on the traction company. Albert Johnson

> *The [Bethlehem] city council complained that the Lehigh's buff and cream single-end closed cars were tearing through Bethlehem at the unheard of speed of 15 mph.*

appeared before the borough council in the fall of 1895, and broke up the meeting when he stormed out of the room after calling the council members "a damn set of block heads." Still, Lehigh Valley Traction Co. continued to grow and expand its service during the latter half of the 1890s. Johnson reorganized his electric railway holdings in November 1899 and took over a number of other area street railways in the following two years, including the Bethlehem and Nazareth Street Railway Co., the Easton Consolidated Electric Co., the Lafayette Traction Co., and the Slate Belt Electric Railway Co.

Johnson had ambitious plans to connect Allentown with both Philadelphia and New York via interurban street railways. But when Johnson died suddenly in early July 1901 before the age of 40, Lehigh Valley Traction Co. wound up in the hands of Allentown attorney Robert E. Wright. By that time, the interurban project had overextended the company, and Wright was forced to begin selling off rolling stock. When the company defaulted on bond payments in May 1903, Lehigh Valley Traction Co. was forced into receivership.

The Traction Co.—along with the interurban railway to Philadelphia, the Allentown and Slatington Street Railway and the Coplay, Egypt and Ironton Street Railway—was sold on the Lehigh County Courthouse steps on June 20, 1905. The total purchase price was $3,275,000, and the reorganization committee members formed a board of directors to oversee the new organization. In November, the group received a charter to operate as the Lehigh Valley Transit Co.

Gen. Harry C. Trexler was among the members of the new board of directors. The Allentown resident would play an increasingly prominent role in the development of electric utilities in central and eastern Pennsylvania during the next three decades.

The Liberty Bell Line

One of the wonders of early 20th century travel in the United States was the fact that residents of dozens of cities on the East Coast and the Midwest could travel hundreds of miles from home via the long-distance electric street railways of the day. Called interurbans, the big electric cars whisked passengers through the country-side almost noiselessly at unheard of speeds approaching 50 mph and more.

In 1904, Clinton and Louisa Lucas celebrated their marriage by taking a 500-mile wedding trip from Delaware to Maine almost entirely by interurban electric railways. Armed with luggage, schedules, a tube of nickels and a Kodak camera, the young couple sped through Pennsylvania, New York, New Jersey and Connecticut on their way north. The book they wrote describing their adventures—*A Trolley Honeymoon*—was an immediate bestseller.

Part of the route traversed by Mr. and Mrs. Lucas was familiar to residents of the Lehigh Valley. In the late 1890s, Albert L. Johnson had acquired a number of companies south of Allentown and merged them into a company called the Philadelphia and Lehigh Valley Traction Co. By early 1901, Philadelphia and Lehigh Valley Traction Co. had put together a 50-mile through line from Allentown to Chestnut Hill in Philadelphia.

A.L. Johnson died in the summer of 1901, and his ambitious plans for an interurban street railway from Philadelphia to New York died with him. Johnson and his brother Tom had acquired several properties in and around Trenton, N.J. The purchase of the New Jersey properties had been financed with internal company funds, and the acquisition overextended Lehigh Valley Traction Co., throwing it into the hands of receivers. The reorganization of the company as Lehigh Valley Transit Co. in 1905 laid the groundwork for inauguration of improved Allentown-Philadelphia interurban service. Residents of the Lehigh Valley could leave the carbarn in Allentown on an hourly basis for Chestnut Hill station in Philadelphia between 6 a.m. and 11 p.m. and return to Allentown the same day. For the first time, residents of the Lehigh Valley could travel to Philadelphia, shop at Wanamakers, have dinner downtown, see Connie Mack's Athletics play a baseball game and return to Allentown, all without staying overnight.

The route to Chestnut Hill, especially between Erdenheim and Quakertown, paralleled the Bethlehem Pike. Along that Pike, patriots had spirited the Liberty Bell out of Philadelphia in 1777 ahead of the advancing British and hid the famous symbol of America's freedom in the Zion's Reformed Church of Allentown.

The route taken by patriots with the Liberty Bell from Philadelphia to Allentown in 1777 became one of the first interurban street railway routes in Pennsylvania more than a century later. *(courtesy of Trexler Funeral Home, Allentown)*

Lehigh Valley Transit Co. accordingly dubbed its line "The Liberty Bell Route."

Lehigh Valley Traction Co. inaugurated summer service from Chestnut Hill to the Delaware Water Gap in 1908, and the popular summertime excursions also included dinner arrangements with hotels in Rittersville, Allentown, Bethlehem and Nazareth. A $5 million improvement program from 1911 to 1913 preceded the inauguration of new high-speed service to Philadelphia through Norristown. The high-speed interurban service eliminated the change-over at Chestnut Hill and reduced the trip between Allentown and Philadelphia to about one hour.

The Liberty Bell Route continued to prosper through the late 1920s, when automobile traffic

began to cut into the line's passenger traffic. But freight traffic on the Liberty Bell Route continued through World War II into the early 1950s. And older residents of the Lehigh Valley still talk nostalgically about the genteel, fast, efficient way to get to Philadelphia and back on the big St. Louis interurban cars of the Liberty Bell Route.

Allentown's Zion Reformed Church was the hiding place of the Liberty Bell in 1777. *(courtesy of Trexler Funeral Home, Allentown)*

Mr. Crilley and Attorney Wright

Two names linked to the history of electric street railways in the Lehigh River Valley are Hugh Crilley and Robert E. Wright. The two men were as different in background as it was possible to be, one the son of poor immigrants and the other the son of a prominent local attorney. They shared only the fact that they both grew up in the Allentown area, but it was through their efforts that the traction system in Allentown, Bethlehem and Easton became one of the most admired street railway networks on the East Coast of the U.S.

The son of poor Irish immigrants, Hugh E. Crilley was born in County Armagh, Ireland, on Aug. 18, 1852. He came with his parents to America soon after his birth, and grew up in Catasauqua and Allentown. At the age of 17, Crilley went into the rolling mills of the Lehigh Valley, working as a finisher until he joined his father and brother in a general contracting business in 1879. "Bridges, railroads and trolley lines have claimed the greater part of his time," a 1914 biography claimed, "but he has also been connected with contract work in other directions."

Crilley constructed the first electric railway in Allentown for the Allentown & Bethlehem Rapid Transit Co. in 1891; and in later years, he built electric street railways all over the Lehigh Valley, from Allentown to South Bethlehem to Slatington to Mauch Chunk to Philadelphia and points beyond. Crilley at one time reorganized and held a controlling interest in the Lancaster Railway Construction Co., which built the street railway from Lancaster to Lititz and New Holland. In 1896, Crilley's firm rebuilt the trolley system in Reading; that same year, he bid on and won the contract to build an electric street railway from Wilmington to New Castle, Del.

Robert E. Wright was instrumental in getting Allentown Passenger Railway Co. its franchises and rights-of-way. *(courtesy of Lehigh County Historical Society)*

Crilley was a power in democratic politics in Allentown for many years, serving as Sixth Ward Councilman for six years late in the 19th century and as a member of the board of education in Allentown from 1880 to 1911. He built the Bellevue Hotel, and his mansion at the corner of Ridge Avenue and Liberty Street was one of the city's finest residences in the early 20th century. Crilley died in 1921.

Robert Emmet Wright Jr. the other local electric street railway entrepreneur, was a native of Allentown. Born on Feb. 15, 1847, he was the son of a prominent local attorney. Wright followed his father into the practice of law, and his clients included most of the railroad companies serving eastern Pennsylvania and New Jersey, along with some of the more prominent iron and steel companies of the Lehigh Valley. Wright was named president of the Allentown National Bank in 1888. A "gold-standard" Democrat, he served as State Democratic Chairman in 1895-1896, resigning the post when the "free silver" Democrats captured the 1896 presidential nomination for William Jennings Bryan of Nebraska. "Mr. Wright was a leading factor in the development of the great trolley system in the Lehigh Valley," the *Allentown Morning Call* eulogized on his death in 1912, "which now extends, with Allentown as its centre, to Philadelphia on the south, Slatington on the north and Easton and Nazareth on the east."

When Boston capitalists bought the Allentown Passenger Railway Co. in 1891, Wright was selected to be the group's attorney. Wright also was a large stockholder in the firm and served on the company's board of directors. The Allentown attorney was instrumental in getting the electrified line its franchises and rights-of-way from the Allentown, Bethlehem and Catasauqua city councils. The purchase of the company two years later by Tom and Albert Johnson of Cleveland did not sever Wright's connection with the street railway. Instead, the Johnsons kept Wright in his old position, and when Albert Johnson died in the summer of 1901, Wright was named to succeed him as president of Lehigh Valley Transit Co.

Wright presided over the company until it went into receivership in 1903. Even then, he maintained his connections with the company when he was appointed one of the receivers by the United States District Court in Philadelphia. Only when

Wright's longtime friend and associate, Gen. Harry Trexler, was named to head the reorganized Lehigh Valley Traction Co. in 1905 did Wright finally step down from the helm of the street railway.

Robert E. Wright died in Allentown on April 15, 1912. Ironically, news of his death was squeezed off the front page by one of the most momentous transportation stories of the young century: the sinking of the White Star Line's Titanic in the North Atlantic Ocean.

HON. HUGH E. CRILLY PASSES AWAY; ONE OF CITY'S LEADING CITIZENS

Pioneer Electric Railway Builder and General Contractor, and Always Took An Active Part in School and Other Public Affairs For Many Years—Was Born in Ireland on August 18, 1852.

Hon. Hugh E. Crilly died last evening at 7 o'clock in the Sacred Heart hospital.

Although Mr. Crilly had been ailing for some time, his death came as somewhat of a shock to his relatives and friends. Up to Saturday a week ago he was attending to his business as usual. On that day he was stricken and was compelled to take to his bed. Last Saturday his physicians advised his removal to the hospital in order to administer special treatment. Heroic efforts were made to prolong his life, but all were in vain. At the time of his passing away all the members of his family were at his bedside.

Hugh E. Crilly was one of the most well known men in the state and one of his city's most prominent citizens. He had legions of friends, all of whom respected him for his fine personality and clean character.

Mr. Crilly had a most eventful life, being what could be rightly termed a self-made man. He was born in County Armagh, Ireland, August 18, 1852, the son of the late James and Mary (McDonald) Crilly. At the time of his death he was 69 years, 3 months and 25 days of age. James Crilly, his father, born in Ireland, came to this

HON. HUGH E. CRILLY.

country in early manhood, bringing his wife and children with him. Hugh first saw three years of age. The family settled in Lawrence, Mass., where they moved to Phillipsburg, N. J., later to Catasauqua, and then to this city. Hugh received his early education in the public schools of Catasauqua, which he attended until the family came to this city in August, 1865. He worked in the rolling mill for a time and then became associated with his father and brother, James H. Crilly. A large number of most important improvements made in this city and adjoining

(Continued from Page Twenty.)

Dec. 13, 1921. (*courtesy of the* **Morning Call**)

9
King Coal

"Anthracite King" is the name of this dragline shovel that has been digging coal since the early 1960s. As this book went to print, Anthracite King was at work at Jeddo in Luzerne County.

ennsylvania is coal country. From the bituminous beds that cover much of the western half of the state to the anthracite valleys of central and eastern Pennsylvania, coal has provided the underpinnings of Pennsylvania's industrial development since colonial days. The bituminous coal of western Pennsylvania powered the industries of Pittsburgh and Johnstown and Erie. High-grade bituminous metallurgical coal made possible the location of the steel industry in the Monongahela Valley in the 1880s and 1890s, and coal stoked the boilers of the Pennsylvania Railroad.

Pennsylvania's anthracite fields are found in the state's northeastern quadrant, shown here as PP&L's "Core East" service area.

Coal once reigned supreme in north-eastern Pennsylvania. But the coal of the hardscrabble hills and valleys of the northeast wasn't the soft, bituminous coal of the Allegheny Plateau in western Pennsylvania. It was anthracite—hard

The development of a Pennsylvania anthracite industry eliminated America's dependence upon foreign coal and fueled the industrial revolution on the East Coast of the United States.

coal—that was found in a 1,400-square-mile area of northeastern Pennsylvania. Difficult to ignite, but exceptionally clean-burning, anthracite became known as "black diamonds" in the 19th century. The development of a Pennsylvania anthracite industry eliminated America's dependence upon foreign coal and fueled the industrial revolution on the East Coast of the United States. Without anthracite, Philadelphia might never have become the center of commerce that it did, and the Lehigh Valley would most likely have had a much more agrarian and rural character than it does today.

In 1811, at the ripe old age of 16, William Henry began manufacturing muskets with a work force of about 20 men. By the 1840s, Henry had built an anthracite furnace and began smelting iron. *(photo courtesy of the Hugh Moore Park Canal Museum)*

The Anthracite Fields

Pennsylvania's anthracite coal is contained in four separate fields or basins trending southwest to northeast across the rugged terrain of the state's north-eastern quadrant. "The Northern field, shaped like a long canoe, stretches from Forest City on the Lackawanna to Shickshinny on the Susquehanna," wrote Donald L. Miller and Richard E. Sharpless in their definitive *The Kingdom of Coal.* "In the other three anthracite fields, the coal lies in sharply pitched veins and is heavily faulted, making mining extremely difficult and hazardous. But the sub-surface coal beds in the Wyoming Valley lie almost horizontally until they pitch upward to outcrop halfway up the mountains that rim the valley. These

flat-lying beds are easier to mine than beds to the south."

The Northern field was the last of the Pennsylvania anthracite beds to be developed, partly because of its distance from Philadelphia and the lack of river transportation. But the Northern field is the deepest bed in Pennsylvania and its carbon content is the highest; by the late 19th century, half of Pennsylvania's anthracite was mined and shipped from the Northern field, making nearby Scranton and Wilkes-Barre two of the wealthiest cities in the United States during the Gilded Age of the late 19th century.

The Eastern Middle, or Lehigh field, sits 15 miles south of the Northern field. The smallest of the four fields, the Lehigh was bordered by Spring and Green mountains. Blessed with excellent river connections to Philadelphia, the Lehigh and its chief community of Hazleton were home to the Pardee family, the premier group of anthracite entrepreneurs in 19th-century Pennsylvania.

"Southwest of Hazleton is the Western Middle field, located between the Susquehanna and Little Schuylkill rivers; and just south of this field is the long Schuylkill basin, stretching from the town of Jim Thorpe (Mauch Chunk) on the Lehigh River southwestward for 70 miles almost to the Susquehanna River in Dauphin County," Miller and Sharpless wrote. "It is an area of narrow valleys and steep jagged mountains, and it is drained by the Schuylkill River, which flows southward through Pottsville, the Gibbsville of John O'Hara's fiction, to Reading and Philadelphia. During the development of the coal trade, the four fields were reclassified as three: the Northern became the Wyoming-Lackawanna; the Eastern Middle, the Lehigh; and the Western Middle and Southern were joined to become the Schuylkill field."

By the 1840s, the Schuylkill field had become the center of a thriving anthracite-based iron smelting business. William Henry built an anthracite furnace in the Lackawanna Valley north of Pottsville and began smelting iron; the nearby Lackawanna Iron Works began manufacturing T-shaped iron rail for the railroads and weaned U.S. roads away from dependence on British iron rail. Philadelphian Nicholas Biddle called anthracite-based domestic rail production "the second Declaration of Independence."

Almost overnight, Pottsville and the Schuylkill field became the center of a manufacturing revolution. Local boosters noted in 1847 that there were more steam engines in Schuylkill County than in the entire nation of France in 1845. From 1840 to the end of the Civil War in 1866, more than 800 engines totalling 40,000 horsepower were put into operation in the Schuylkill field.

The Lehigh Canal

From the beginning of the anthracite industry in Pennsylvania, the key to developing the industry was the construction of a transportation network to get the coal to market—primarily to Philadelphia, Allentown and Bethlehem. The isolated valleys of the anthracite region were cut off from the rest of the state, and without a secure method of transportation, the industry would eventually wither and die.

Early in the 1800s, Josiah White and Erskine Hazard—who were then in the wire manufacturing business—secured control of the Lehigh Coal Mine Co. in the Panther Valley Region. In 1818, White, who is often referred to as the Father of Pennsylvania Anthracite, merged the coal company with the Lehigh Navigation Co. White's ambitious plan for the Lehigh Coal and Navigation Co. was the construction of a canal along the Lehigh River to bring Pennsylvania anthracite to market.

Lehigh Valley historian Lance Metz notes that "the construction of the Lehigh Navigation Co. brought about the rapid economic transformation of the

Lehigh Valley into one of America's most industrialized regions, the locus of more furnaces, producing more iron, than any other during the early years of the American Industrial Revolution. The Lehigh Navigation also provided the first commercially effective transportation link between the Delaware, Lehigh and Wyoming valleys, and served as the catalyst for the construction of the Delaware and Morris canals."

Josiah White and Erskine Hazard of the Lehigh Coal and Navigation Co. *(photo courtesy of the Hugh Moore Park Canal Museum)*

The Lehigh Navigation Canal was essentially a series of eight timber and rock-crib dams that converted the Lehigh River into a series of slackwater pools suitable for barge traffic. Canals 60 feet wide and dug to a depth of five feet connected the pools on the river, and there were 48 locks that negated the 355-foot drop in elevation between Mauch Chunk and Easton. Mule-drawn barges could haul a total of 200 tons of anthracite apiece.

The success of the Lehigh Navigation Canal spawned other canals from the anthracite region. By the 1830s, anthracite coal from the Northern field was being transported on barges along the Delaware and Hudson Canal to the Hudson River, where it was shipped to New York City, Albany and New England. Lehigh Navigation Co. coal reached Philadelphia by the Delaware Canal, and reached New York by both the Morris and Delaware and Raritan canals, and coal from the Wyoming Valley floated along the North Branch of the Susquehanna and a series of connecting canals to Baltimore.

By 1860, 176 firms engaged in anthracite mining in Pennsylvania. The capitalization the last year before the outbreak of the Civil War totalled almost $13.9 million, and more than $11.8 million worth of anthracite was produced in that year. More than 25,000 workers toiled in the pits and breakers of the anthracite region in 1860. The maturing anthracite industry helped make Pennsylvania "the keystone in the arch of the post-Civil War economy" in the United States.

When PP&L was founded, anthracite—or hard coal— was the primary fuel. Back in the 1800s, mule-drawn boats hauled as much as 200 tons of anthracite a load.
(photo courtesy of the Hugh Moore Park Canal Museum)

Pennsylvania's anthracite industry employed more than 25,000 in 1860.

By 1880, the industry was producing 28 million long tons a year, double its production of just 10 years before, and the work force had increased to 73,000 employees, many of them recent immigrants to the state. Production doubled again between 1880 and 1900, reaching 57 million long tons at the turn of the century; employment also doubled during that period, to 143,000 workers.

The industry reached 100 million tons—its all-time peak—in 1917, the year the United States entered World War I. But by that time, anthracite was a mature industry and fighting to retain many of its traditional markets. Employment increased minimally between 1900 and 1917, even though production had nearly doubled again during the period; electrification of the mines and breakers was increasing productivity in the industry and reducing the need for labor.

Anthracite's markets had changed dramatically from the 1830s. In the 1880s and the 1890s, the iron and steel industry began to rely on metallurgical coking coal for its blast furnaces rather than anthracite. The mills that Edgar Thomson, Andrew Carnegie and Henry Frick built along the banks of the Monongahela River south of Pittsburgh relied on Pennsylvania bituminous for coke for the blast furnaces.

The lost market for blast furnace fuel was largely made up during the latter part of the 19th century by two new markets: home heating fuel and the manufacture of coal gas. The Anthracite Institute noted in the 1930s that the blast furnace market was made up "by the use of anthracite, in the manufacture of water gas which, during several decades, was an active rival of coal gas made from the distillation of bituminous coal." By that time, the canals had been largely supplanted by rail transportation, but millions of homeowners along the Eastern Seaboard used anthracite to heat their homes. Increasingly, anthracite was used as a boiler fuel in Pennsylvania power plant generation in the early 20th century.

Above: Andrew Carnegie, and Henry Clay Frick, as a young man *(courtesy of the Hugh Moore Park Canal Museum)*

Anthracite as Boiler Fuel

The rise of Edison Electric Illuminating Co. stations in eastern Pennsylvania created a ready-made market for anthracite. When P.B. Shaw sold the Edison licenses for Edison incandescent lighting systems in the anthracite country of Pennsylvania in 1883, 1884 and 1885, it was natural that the new companies would turn to anthracite for boiler fuel. The first incandescent three-wire lighting system in the U.S.—the Edison Electric Illuminating Co. of Sunbury—purchased soft coal in 1883 from the Berwind-White Coal Mining Co., a noted bituminous producer of the era.

The Edison Electric Illuminating Co. of Williamsport was also an early consumer of soft coal, purchasing from Donaldson & Thomas Coal Co. as early as 1885. So also did the Consumers Gas Co. of Danville and the Thomson-Houston Electric Co. of Milton. But further east and north, the isolated electric plants established by P.B. Shaw turned to anthracite to fire their boilers.

In 1884, the Edison Electric Illuminating Co. of Hazleton in the Lehigh field purchased anthracite for its boilers from the Highland Coal Co.; well-known local coal baron G.B. Markle Jr. served on the electric company's coal committee. In Mount Carmel, the Edison Electric Illuminating Co. purchased anthracite in 1885 and 1886 from the Bickel Coal Co. and the Hurlow Coal Co. Records indicate that the Edison Electric Illuminating Co. of Ashland bought anthracite coal from the William Penn Coal Co. in 1885.

Other companies that weren't affiliated with the Edison system in the 1880s also purchased anthracite as boiler fuel. The Wilkes-Barre Electric Light Co., in the heart of the Northern field, used anthracite as early as 1885. That year, the company accepted the bid of the Hillman Vein Coal Co. to provide buckwheat anthracite for the price of 90 cents a ton for 1886.

The existence of the riverine transportation network made anthracite available to Pennsylvania electric companies as far from the anthracite fields as the Lehigh Valley and Harrisburg. In Honesdale, northeast of Scranton, the directors of the Honesdale Electric Light, Heat and Power Co. purchased anthracite from the Northern field. In March 1888, the company paid the Delaware and Hudson Canal Co. for transporting 25 tons of pea coal to Honesdale at 10 cents per ton.

Already by 1888, the Allentown Electric Light & Power Co. was purchasing anthracite from the Lehigh Valley Coal Co., and the nearby Bethlehem Electric Light Co. got its anthracite supply from the Lehigh Coal and Navigation Co., delivered in bargeloads via the canal. In the 1890s, the Catasauqua Electric Light and Power Co. bought 21 cars of buckwheat coal from the Davies & Thomas Iron Co., located on the Lehigh Navigation Canal.

Well down the Susquehanna River, the Harrisburg Electric Light Co. was buying pea coal for its arc light plant in May 1885. The company later bought screenings and river coal washed down from the anthracite fields for its boilers. Utilities in Lancaster and Columbia were also purchasing anthracite from dealers doing business on the docks in Columbia.

The Lehigh Navigation Canal consisted of a series of eight timber and rock-crib dams. Top: Coal being loaded onto boats on the Lehigh Canal. Bottom: Weighing the canal boats in the weigh lock on the Lehigh Canal. (woodcuts courtesy of the Hugh Moore Park Canal Museum)

The Pardee family, from Hazleton, were the premier group of anthracite entrepreneurs in the 1800s. Here Gen. Ario Pardee sits with Aunt Mary Allison Pardee. *(photo courtesy of the Hugh Moore Park Canal Museum)*

Harwood Plant and the Pardee Family

The increasing mechanization of the coal industry in the anthracite fields of eastern Pennsylvania spurred a greater use of anthracite as a boiler fuel. Appropriately, the coal companies themselves pioneered the construction and operation of anthracite mine-mouth plants to serve the residents of eastern Pennsylvania.

Initially, the plans called for serving only the mines of the anthracite region. Only certain sizes of anthracite were thought to have commercial possibilities, and large banks of coal that didn't meet those commercial grades—pea, egg, stove, nut and buckwheat coal—dotted

the anthracite fields by the turn of the century. Calvin Pardee, one of the pioneering developers of the fields in Luzerne County, came up with the idea of burning the waste coal, commonly known as culm, to produce electric power for the collieries and breakers in and around Hazleton.

In 1907, Pardee organized the Harwood Electric Power Co. to build an experimental power plant near one of his larger collieries at Harwood Mines in Hazle Township. The plant, which was the first mine-mouth generating station in the western hemisphere, had an initial capacity of 1,100 kilowatts.

Besides supplying power to the Harwood Mines, the new plant also began serving customers in the local area. Harwood Electric Power Co. constructed a transmission line to the city of Hazleton to furnish electricity for the Consumers Electric Light & Power Co., which was also owned by the Pardee family. Harwood Electric also extended its transmission to the village of Lattimer to serve other Pardee coal properties and to the Borough of McAdoo, where the power was distributed by another Pardee company, the McAdoo Electric Co.

The Pardees hired a brilliant young engineer to build and operate their growing electric system. John Shreve Wise was born in July 1877, two years before Thomas Edison introduced incandescent lighting to the world. He grew up in comfort in Philadelphia, summering at the family's country home at Longport on New Jersey's Egg Harbor Bay. Wise graduated from the University of Pennsylvania in 1898 with a degree in what was then the comparatively new field of electrical engineering.

After gaining experience with a predecessor of Philadelphia Electric Co., Wise went through the General Electric Training School at Lynn, Mass. He worked for a short while at the Electric Co. of America at its Atlantic City, N.J., subsidiary before spending five years as the superintendent of the Auburn, N.Y., electric utility.

In the summer of 1906, Alfred Pardee

and A.W. Drake asked Wise to come to Philadelphia. They wanted to discuss their idea of building a generating station to utilize the culm and waste anthracite around their mines in Lattimer. Wise found the concept fascinating and agreed to join Harwood Electric Co. as its general manager in Lattimer; within days of John Wise's arrival at Harwood, he was directing crews in the completion of the new plant.

It took crews of the Schofield Engineering Co. nearly two years to build the plant and the five-mile, double-pole line to Hazleton, but the inauguration of service on March 12, 1907, ushered in a new era for the utility business in eastern Pennsylvania. "The plant Wise designed and built at Harwood," Wise's biographer wrote in a PP&L internal document in 1960, "and manned with men he trained, was the first public utility power installation in the United States to take coal at the mouth of the mine and transform it into the kind of energy that could be transmitted across miles of high tension wires."

One of the keys to the success of the Harwood plant was the design of a traveling grate that allowed the boilers to burn powdered anthracite. "Those culm banks were the size of mountains," Wise recalled in an interview years later. "A lot of good coal went to waste. Eckley B. Coxe designed a traveling grate, and it burned coal all right. But he died before he finished the design.

"I was in the boiler room one day and saw that the tops of the grate had burned off. I decided that was wrong, that the grates were getting too hot." Working with William Lloyd, superintendent of the Drifton Shops of the Lehigh Coal Co., Wise redesigned the traveling grates so the amount of air going through them was increased five-fold. "The redesigned Coxe Traveling Grate made it possible to burn anthracite as fine as granulated sugar," Wise recalled years later.

The Harwood plant began generating electric power with two 300-kilowatt horizontal turbines and a 500-kilowatt vertical turbine. The anthracite was fed into two Maxim boilers that were not yet equipped with superheaters for the most efficient combustion of the fuel; in later years, the original boilers were replaced and shipped to the Pardee colliery at Lattimer.

In 1908, Wise organized the McAdoo Electric Co. for the Pardees in order to lease that community's municipal power plant. Shortly after, he consolidated the Harwood Electric Power Co., the McAdoo company and nine non-operating companies into the Harwood Electric Co. Harwood Electric Co. increased the capacity of its mine-mouth plant to 7,000 kilowatts in 1910, and Wise built transmission lines to expand the rapidly growing company's service territory. Wise constructed a 25,000-volt transmission line that crossed the Susquehanna River at Berwick in a single 2,200-foot span, then one of the longest such river-crossings in the world.

> *It took crews of the Schofield Engineering Co. nearly two years to build the plant and the five-mile, double-pole line to Hazleton, but the inauguration of service on March 12, 1907, ushered in a new era for the utility business in eastern Pennsylvania.*

Hauto Plant and Lehigh Navigation Electric

The success that Pardee and Wise enjoyed with the construction of the Harwood plant did not pass without notice in the anthracite region. In 1911, W.A. Lathrop, the president of the Lehigh Coal and Navigation Co., convinced his board to incorporate an electric power subsidiary. Like Harwood Electric Co., the Lehigh Navigation Electric Co. was set up to provide electric power to the mines and collieries of the parent company; any electricity left over would be provided to residential and commercial customers in surrounding Carbon County.

Lehigh Coal and Navigation Co.'s Early Executives

**W.A. Lathrop—
1907 to 1912**

**S.D. Warriner—
1912 to 1937**

J.B. Warriner—1930

**J.H. Nuelle—
1937 to 1938**

R.V. White—1938

(photos courtesy of the Hugh Moore Park Canal Museum)

Lathrop, a native of Springville and a civil engineering graduate of Lehigh University, had been involved with Pennsylvania coal mining interests since his graduation from Lehigh. In 1907, the year that Wise and Pardee completed the Harwood plant, he was named president of the Lehigh Coal and Navigation Co. in Philadelphia. Lathrop had followed Wise's work in Hazleton with much interest, and his plans called for a significantly larger generating station than the Harwood plant. But Lathrop never saw the plant he envisioned in actual operation; the coal company executive died of an attack of appendicitis in a Wilkes-Barre hospital on the morning of April 13, 1912.

S.D. Warriner, Lathrop's successor as president of Lehigh Coal and Navigation Co., pushed forward the plans for construction of an anthracite-fueled generating station in the village of Hauto in Carbon County. Named for George F.A. Hauto—the 19th century entrepreneur and associate of Lehigh Coal and Navigation Co. founders Josiah White and Erskine Hazard—Hauto plant was built in 1912 and 1913 at the foot of a hill in Carbon County between Hometown and Nesquehoning. L.B. Stilwell, a New York-based consulting engineer, was awarded the contract to build the 20,000-kilowatt plant, and he sited it at the foot of the hill just west of the entrance to the Lansford Tunnel to take advantage of the laws of gravity.

On the hill above the plant, a spur of the Lehigh and New England Railroad allowed rail cars to empty coal by gravity into the plant's bunkers. The anthracite could then go by conveyor to Hauto's stokers and boilers, and the ash remaining after the coal was burned was dropped into pockets at the bottom of the hill. The Hauto plant was well situated with regard to Lehigh Coal and Navigation Co.'s anthracite facilities. To the east were the Lansford and Nesquehoning collieries; south was the Coaldale colliery; and west was the Tamaqua colliery. Executives of Lehigh Navigation Electric Co. planned to supply electricity to the parent company's mines, collieries and breakers, and hoped eventually to transmit electricity to the Portland cement and steel industries of the nearby Lehigh Valley.

By the spring of 1913, the parent Lehigh Coal and Navigation Co. was reporting that "the construction of the Lehigh Navigation Electric Co.'s power plant at Hauto, Pa., has been practically completed, and it is now in partial operation. Full operation will be inaugurated as soon as connections are made with prospective customers, with whom contracts have been made for the sale of a substantial amount of the power to be produced; and it is hoped that negotiations will soon be completed which will provide a satisfactory market for the entire estimated production of the present installation."

By 1913, electrical power for the mines of the Nesquehoning Valley was already being supplied by the Hauto plant, allowing Lehigh Coal and Navigation Co. to shut down and write off a small electric power plant at the Lansford colliery. Company representatives were negotiating to sell Hauto power to the Eastern Pennsylvania Railways Co. and the Panther Valley Electric Light, Heat and Power Co.

The Hauto plant went into full production on May 1, 1914, although initial sales did not meet expectations; Hauto operated at only half-capacity for much of 1914. But the plentiful electric power from the Hauto plant proved to be a boon for Lehigh Coal and Navigation Co.'s mining engineers. Cost-savings for the year attributed to the new power plant totalled $33,000, second only to the savings the company reported with new methods of timbering its mine shafts. "Upon final connection with the Hauto power plant of the Lehigh Navigation Electric Co. in March 1914, electrification work at the various mines was pushed as rapidly as possible, special attention being given to the steam plants, where the cost of steam was excessive, due to long pipe lines and other causes."

In November 1914, the steam hoist at Lehigh Coal's Number 5 shaft was replaced with an electric hoist, "and was the first hoist of this type in the anthracite region," the company told its shareholders in the spring of 1915. Driven by a 750-horsepower alternating current General Electric motor of 2,200 volts, the hoist lifted coal from both the 500- and 250-foot levels at the rate of 80 cars an hour. Installation of a second electric hoist followed within days at the company's Rahn shaft. "The hoist has fulfilled the guarantees of the manufacturers," Lehigh Coal's 1914 annual report noted, "as to both speed and economy, and in addition is equipped with better safety devices for preventing overwinding or any possible mistake of the hoisting engineer, than can be arranged on any steam hoist. Since its installation, this hoist has been operated without stoppage of any cause."

The company's annual report for 1914 also noted that "one great advantage in the use of electric power is the ability to locate fans where ventilation is most needed, instead of being obliged to keep them in proximity to the boiler houses. This has been worked out at Lansford colliery, where one electric fan was built on the western edge of the workings and another is being erected on the eastern edge, so that the haulage gangways can be maintained as intake airways, and the gases and bad air thrown out at the extreme ends of the workings."

Crews from Lehigh Navigation Electric Co. and the Mechanical Department of Lehigh Coal and Navigation Co. spent much of 1914 expanding the system, building substations at Nesquehoning, Lansford and the Number 10 colliery. Rotary converters for the Eastern Pennsylvania Railway Co. were installed at the Lansford substation. Although the street railway system was switched over to power from Hauto in November 1914, a severe sleet storm on Dec. 7, 1914, crippled the electric company's service and disrupted power for several weeks.

By the spring of 1913, the parent Lehigh Coal and Navigation Co. was reporting that "the construction of the Lehigh Navigation Electric Co.'s power plant at Hauto, Pa., has been practically completed, and it is now in partial operation."

By the end of 1915, the Hauto plant was paying its own way. The load factor had increased to 80 percent, and the plant had consumed 172,313 tons of waste anthracite. Hauto reported sales of nearly 95 million kwh, an average of 258,292 kwh each day. "The development of the business of the Lehigh Navigation Electric Co. has made satisfactory progress during the year," the directors reported early in 1916, "and the earnings were sufficient to pay all fixed charges and leave a small surplus."

Lehigh Navigation Electric Co., fueled by the output of the Hauto plant, continued to expand its business in 1916. Sales jumped to 112 million kwh, and the plant on the Nesquehoning Valley hillside consumed 213,000 tons of Lehigh Coal

and Navigation Co.'s waste anthracite. Lehigh Navigation Electric Co. reported revenues for the year of $828,000 and operating expenses of $478,000. Net income, after deducting taxes, interest and fixed charges, was slightly more than $75,000.

What's more, the company's business, aside from supplying power to the parent firm's mines and breakers, was growing rapidly. "At the end of the year," the company reported early in 1917, "the number of customers taking current from the Hauto plant was 112, an increase of 37 as compared with the number at the close of 1915. Among these customers are five cement companies, which used 63 percent of the power sold, and nine public service companies."

Installed capacity of the plant at Hauto in early 1917 was 30,000 kilowatts, consisting of three 10,000-kilowatt turbo-generators, a 50 percent increase over the inauguration of service four years earlier. The rated capacity of the boiler plant was 8,320 horsepower, consisting of eight boilers of 1,040 horsepower apiece. Power was generated at 11,000 volts, which was stepped up to 110,000 volts for transmission purposes.

"The load on this plant has steadily increased during the year," the directors noted in the 1916 annual report, "and the plant is now being operated at the capacity of the units already installed. Your company is therefore now realizing the primary objectives for which this plant was designed, viz.: a supply of electric power for its mining operations and a market for its surplus fine sizes of coal. Attention is now being given by your management to the problem of adequately meeting the growing demands for electric power in the territory served by your electric interests."

Lehigh Coal and Navigation Co. and the Pardee interests at Harwood had both proved between 1907 and 1917 the feasibility of burning Pennsylvania anthracite in utility steam boilers to generate electric power. In a sense, they had been too successful in their endeavors. The two companies had created a growing market demand for electric power outside their core coal business, and by 1917 were wrestling with the dilemma of whether they could continue to run electric companies as subsidiaries of the coal business.

The solution involved a 1917 pooling of interests of the two coal companies' utility subsidiaries, and the resulting wave of consolidation in the utility business in eastern Pennsylvania led to the formation of Pennsylvania Power & Light Co. three years later.

Lines Across the Land

Both Harwood Electric Co. and Lehigh Navigation Electric Co. pioneered the construction of high-voltage transmission lines across the anthracite region and the Lehigh Valley during the years prior to World War I. The reason was simple. Both the Harwood plant and the Hauto plant were mine-mouth generating stations, assured of a secure supply of fuel and dwarfing anything in eastern Pennsylvania other than the Holtwood hydroelectric station on the Susquehanna River.

By the end of 1910, the Harwood Electric Co. had completed the installation of 7,000 kilowatts of generation at its Harwood plant, and another 5,000-kilowatt unit was under construction. Under the supervision of John Wise, the company had already completed transmission lines to supply the villages of Yorktown, Tresckow (near Hazleton), Jeanesville and the township of Bucks in Carbon County. In 1909, Harwood Electric Co. built a 22,000-volt transmission line to Berwick on the Susquehanna to make power available to the Columbia and Montour Electric Co.

Following the merger of a number of nonoperating companies with Harwood Electric Co. in 1912, Wise

Harwood Steam Electric Station (SES) helped make PP&L the world's largest single user of anthracite. The turbine/generator located in the center of this photo provided electricity to mines, collieries and local residents with a transmission line delivering electricity to the city of Hazleton. This photo was taken in 1939, 32 years after Calvin Pardee organized the company.

directed crews in building transmission lines across the hills and valleys of the anthracite region. The Harwood plant added another 5,000 kilowatts of generating capacity in 1913, and tripled the size of the plant with the addition of two 12,000-kilowatt units between 1917 and 1919. A transmission line 12 miles long was built in 1912 to connect Harwood with Mahanoy City in the Schuylkill fields.

The sleet and ice storm that hammered eastern Pennsylvania on Dec. 7, 1914, carried with it the threat of crippling Harwood Electric Co.'s growing transmission system. Wise instructed the operators of the Harwood plant to increase the electric current on the transmission system; the resulting surge of power melted much of the ice accumulated on the lines and became a standard operating procedure for electric utility transmission systems.

At the Hauto plant of the Lehigh Navigation Electric Co., the transmission story was much the same. Hauto was built some six years after the first units at Harwood went on line, but the 30,000-kilowatt plant in the Nesquehoning Valley was substantially larger than its sister plant at Harwood, at least until the 1917-1919 expansion. By 1916, Lehigh Navigation Electric Co. had built a huge substation at Siegfried—with a capacity of 20,100 kilovolt-amperes—and two smaller substations at Pen Argyl and Bethlehem.

The Hauto and Harwood plants were tied together in 1915 by a 10-mile, 66,000-volt transmission line across Broad Mountain. Lehigh Navigation Electric Co. installed a 7,500-kilovolt-ampere frequency changer at Hauto so that 25-cycle current generated at Hauto could be changed to 60-cycle current for transmission to Harwood, and vice versa. The transmission network connected a total of 65,000 kilowatts of generating capacity by the time World War I was over.

Lehigh Navigation Electric Co. built a single-circuit, 110,000-volt transmission line between Siegfried substation and the Quarry substation of Bethlehem Steel Co. in 1917 to augment the 22,000-volt tie that had been established between the two companies in 1915. Also, Lehigh Navigation Electric Co. already had a 22,000-volt line from North Bethlehem substation to Guerber Engineering in West Bethlehem.

In December 1916, Lehigh Valley Transit Co.'s Allentown plant was put out of service when a main steam header in the plant exploded. Although Lehigh Valley Transit Co. and Lehigh Navigation Electric Co. were competitors for wholesale contracts in the Lehigh Valley area, Lehigh Navigation Electric Co. marshalled crews north of Siegfried and began installing a 22,000-volt line to the Allentown plant. Line was strung along the wooden poles of the Transit Co. from Bethlehem to Allentown, and within one day, 25-cycle power from Hauto was routed into the Allentown plant.

After this first interconnection between the two systems, the tie was strengthened in 1918 when Lehigh Navigation Electric Co. built a 22,000-volt line from Siegfried to the Transit Co.'s Catasauqua substation. Later, a 66,000-volt, double-circuit, 60-cycle steel tower transmission line was built to strengthen the ties between the two systems.

Relations were less sanguine with other area power suppliers. Throughout much of the decade following 1910, Lehigh Navigation Electric Co. attempted to extend its lines to cement companies located north of Bethlehem. The Easton subsidiary of what was to become Metropolitan Edison Co. contested the extensions. When Lehigh Navigation Electric Co. tried to extend its 22,000-volt line to Martins Creek to serve the Atlas Portland Cement Co., vandalism became endemic. Lines that were built during the day would often be on the ground by the next morning; several instances of insulators damaged by shotgun blasts were reported by Lehigh Navigation Electric Co.

The successors to the two combatants, Pennsylvania Power & Light Co. and Metropolitan Edison Co., worked out their differences in the 1920s. But by that time, eastern Pennsylvania was linked together with an electric transmission system that was perhaps unsurpassed anywhere east of the Rocky Mountains.

10

The Merger

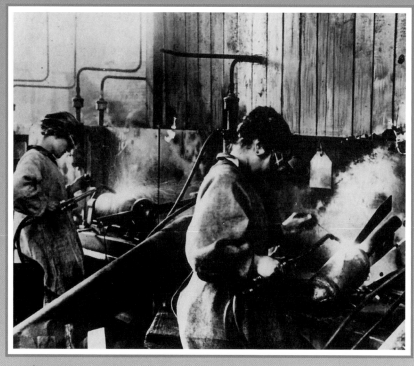

World War I increased demand for electrification. This photo shows women welding fins on bombs. *(photo courtesy of the Hugh Moore Historical Park and Museums, Inc.)*

As America was drawn into World War I after 1914, utility companies in eastern Pennsylvania found them-selves confronting several difficult problems. The industrialization of Pennsylvania, which had begun with the advent of the ironmaking industry in the colonial era, was picking up steam. And as industrialization increased, the man-agers of the anthracite mines and steel mills and cement facto-ries increasingly looked to electrification as a way to reduce labor costs and improve efficiency.

The growth of industrial electrification in Pennsylvania and the rest of America during the years between the turn of the century and World War I created a demand for electric power unprecedented in the industry's history. In 1900, electric motors provided less than five percent of industrial power in America's mines,

mills and factories. By 1910, corporations had increased their electric motor capacity more than 500 percent, buying 250,000 new electric motors in 1909 alone.

The introduction of electric mining locomotives in the anthracite coal industry in the 1890s created a quantum leap in productivity. The New York and Scranton Coal Co. shaved five to six cents off the cost of extracting a ton of coal; three men and an electric-driven locomotive replaced seven boys and 14 mules in the shafts of the Pennsylvania anthracite producer.

Henry Ford—who had started his career in Detroit as an engineer working

Pennsylvania's anthracite mines fueled the state's factories. *circa 1920s (photo courtesy of Hugh Moore Historical Park and Museums, Inc.)*

for Alex Dow, the founder of the Detroit Edison Co.—understood the revolution in manufacturing technology that electric power offered the American factory owner. Ford, who wintered near Thomas Edison's vacation home on the banks of the Caloosahatchee River near Fort Myers, Fla., had an instinctive understanding of the role that electric power would play on the factory floor. "The provision of a whole new system of electric generation emancipated industry from the leather belt and line shaft, for it eventually became possible to provide each tool with its own electric motor," Ford wrote in homage to Edison in 1930.

For the utilities serving smaller communities, electric motor load growth was a fact of life in the period between 1900 and 1920. The Edison Electric Co. of Lancaster reported that its industrial customers in 1908 had 2,965 horsepower of electric motors connected to the utility's system. By 1914, the demand from electric motors alone had grown to 12,154 horsepower, a four-fold increase in six years. That demand doubled again between 1914 and 1918, when the company reported that its industrial customers had an electric motor load of 25,211 hooked up to the system.

Lancaster Steel Products, which produced cold-drawn steel in its Lancaster mills, used 2,000 horsepower

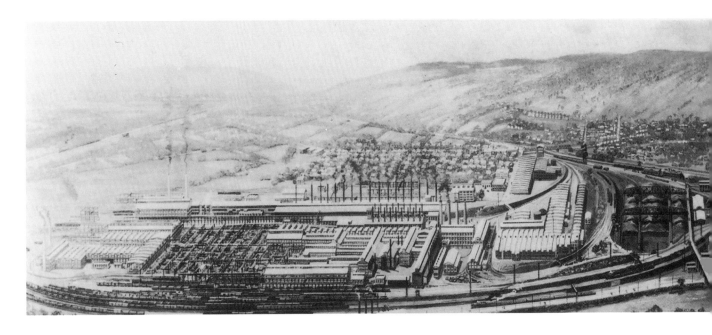

alone from electric motors at the time of World War I, and the John Farnum Cotton Mill's electric motors produced 1,500 horsepower. More than two dozen candy factories in and around Lancaster used more than 3,600 horsepower from electric motors to produce chocolate and caramels for America's sweet tooth. A wide variety of manufacturers, from cut-glass factories to creameries, hosiery mills to ice cream plants, printing houses to pumping plants, and tanneries to tobacco processors bought electric power from Edison Electric Co. to run their electric motors.

Edison Electric Co.'s transmission lines snaked out across the rolling southeastern Pennsylvania countryside, allowing manufacturers to locate their factories and mills in communities like Mechanicsburg, Millersville, Elizabethtown, Lititz and Manheim. The Lancaster company was able to meet increasing demand for industrial electric power after 1910, primarily because it was able to purchase power wholesale from the Holtwood hydroelectric generating station. The power then travelled 15 miles from the damsite to Lancaster by high-voltage transmission lines.

The growth in electric motor load from 1914 to 1918 at Edison Electric Co. of Lancaster illustrated a second reality faced by utility companies in Pennsyl-

vania in the second decade of the 20th century. Pennsylvania's industrialized economy would bear a disproportionate share of America's shift to a wartime

The silk and textile mills of the Lehigh Valley produced uniforms and apparel for American fighting men stateside and overseas.

economy following the congressional declaration of war on Imperial Germany in April 1917. The mills of Bethlehem Steel Co. would become America's armaments foundry during the war; already by 1915-1916, the grassy areas along the Lehigh River adjacent to Bethlehem's mills were packed with upright steel shells destined for shipment to the British Army on the Western Front.

Bethlehem Steel Co. was America's armaments foundry during World War I. *(photos courtesy of the Hugh Moore Historical Park and Museums, Inc.)*

The British government entered a $60 million order for munitions with Bethlehem on July 24, 1915. Most of the munitions were made at the company's Bethlehem and Sparrows Point mills, which required electric power from Pennsylvania producers. Bethlehem Steel Co. generated much of its internal electric power requirements, but as the war years dragged on, Bethlehem Steel Co. augmented its internal generation with power purchased from Lehigh Navigation Electric Co. through the steel mill's Quarry substation. The Pennsylvania Water & Power Co. also provided industrial electric power to Bethlehem Steel Co. The hydroelectric company sent power from its Holtwood station on the Susquehanna River to Consolidated of Baltimore, which in turn sold electricity to Bethlehem for use at the steel company's massive mill at Sparrows Point on the Baltimore Harbor.

The power demands of the wartime

In 1912, Harwood Electric Co. merged with Beaver Meadow Electric Co. and 10 other non-operating companies with a capital stock of $1,113,000 and outstanding bonds totalling $1 million.

Between 1900 and 1920, manufacturers like this silk mill demanded more power to run their electric motors. Load growth was over eight-fold during that time period. *(photo courtesy of Hugh Moore Historical Park and Museums, Inc.)*

economy were not limited to steel mills. The anthracite mines of northeastern Pennsylvania went into overtime production to provide hard coal for mills, factories, army bases and navy yards. The silk and textile mills of the Lehigh Valley produced uniforms and apparel for American fighting men stateside and overseas. Hundreds of factories across Pennsylvania converted to wartime production, making everything from automobile and truck parts to foodstuffs. All this increased production for America's defense needs created an unprecedented demand for Pennsylvania's electric utilities.

Another factor that had a major impact on the subsequent course of events in eastern Pennsylvania's electric utility industry was the geography of the state itself. Eastern Pennsylvania is bisected by mountains and valleys that generally run southwest to northeast. Much of the transportation network in the 19th century had been based along the region's rivers and canals, and what roads did exist at the turn of the century followed the valleys.

Consequently, the electric system in much of eastern Pennsylvania was valley-based. Transmission lines ran up and down the valleys from one coal-mining community to another, but transmission lines run across the mountain from one valley to another were limited before 1915, as were road and rail construction across the mountains. Transmission line technology had advanced rapidly during the early decades of the 20th century, but construction of the lines was still highly labor-intensive, requiring men and mules and wagons to place the wooden or steel

transmission towers.

Much of the development of the companies that preceded Pennsylvania Power & Light Co. was linear, with half-a-dozen companies in the same valley linked together by low-voltage transmission lines. But the small companies of the first two decades of the 20th century were generally unable to run lines across the mountains that hemmed in their service territories.

John Wise

Co., and for utilizing the waste fines from the anthracite mining process as boiler fuel. For both companies, wholesale electric power sales to neighboring utilities was simply an afterthought.

'Controlled by Purely Electric Interests'

With the exception of Lehigh Navigation Electric Co., Harwood Electric Co. and Pennsylvania Water & Power Co., the predecessor companies in what would become the PP&L service territory were isolated electric systems unable to interconnect with their utility neighbors.

Complicating the matter of geography was the question of utility politics. Pennsylvania public utility law forbade a company to operate in more than one township. The larger companies got around the law, which was designed to limit cutthroat utility competition, by setting up paper, nonoperating companies to obtain franchise or charter rights in a community. By 1915, technology and economics dictated that the economies of scale made available by large electric power systems were the most cost-effective and efficient method of delivering electric power to customers.

Finally, the development of an interconnected utility system in eastern Pennsylvania was hampered by the fact that two of the biggest utilities in the region were subsidiaries of coal-mining companies. Both Harwood Electric Co. and Lehigh Navigation Electric Co. had been set up for the specific purpose of electrifying the mines of the parent Pardee interests and Lehigh Coal and Navigation

As World War I approached, Calvin Pardee and his family, and John Wise and the board of managers of the Lehigh Navigation Electric Co. recognized the essential limitations of electric power develop-ment in eastern Pennsylvania.

In 1912, Harwood Electric Co. merged with Beaver Meadow Electric Co. and 10 other non-operating companies with a capital stock of $1,113,000 and outstanding bonds totalling $1 million. Early in 1913, the company acquired the Hazleton Electric Co., which had been formed a few months earlier by the consolidation and merger of the old Edison Electric Illuminating Co. of Hazleton; Freeland Electric Light, Heat and Power Co.; West End Electric Light and Power Co.; Hazleton Electric Light and Power Co. and nine nonoperating companies organized specifically to secure charter rights.

In 1913, the Pardees instructed Wise, their general manager, to negotiate a sale of Harwood Electric Co. to Lehigh Navigation Electric Co. Wise was named as general manager for both companies and

Downtown Hazleton.
circa 1920s

supervised the 1914 construction of the 66,000-volt transmission line across Broad Mountain that tied together the Hauto and Harwood plants. The purchase agreement called for Lehigh Navigation Electric Co. to buy 18,418 shares of Harwood Electric Co. from the Pardees for $45 a share, a total price of nearly $829,000. The Pardees received First Mortgage 30-Year Gold Sinking Fund bonds in lieu of cash, and Lehigh Navigation Electric Co. agreed to pay interest on the bonds beginning at two percent from July 1, 1913. The interest would increase by one-half percent per year until the bonds reached five percent. Lehigh Coal and Navigation Co. endorsed the bonds and guaranteed prompt payment of interest to the Pardees.

Wise, the new manager of both properties, had an entrepreneurial streak. In 1913, the year he negotiated the sale of Harwood Electric Co. to Lehigh Navigation Electric Co., eastern Pennsylvania experienced its most severe winter in decades. "In 1913, we experienced an open winter without much snow," Wise recalled in the early 1940s, "but the cold weather drove the frost into the ground to

a depth of five to seven feet. Thousands of water pipes were frozen, and electricity came to the aid in thawing them. Electric wires were connected to the water pipes and then the juice (was) turned on. Depending upon conditions, it took from one to 20 minutes to thaw the average-sized pipes and restore the water service."

Interestingly, the Pardees did not get out of the electric utility business once they had sold Harwood Electric Co. Early in 1913, just before the disposal of Harwood Electric Co., the Pardees organized the Schuylkill Gas and Electric Co. Located in Mahanoy Township of Schuylkill County, the new company consolidated and merged 12 small utilities operating in the southern anthracite field. The Pardees and A.W. Drake, their long-time associate in utility ventures, hoped to dispose of surplus electric power from the Harwood plant as well as to create a better integrated system to serve the needs of the southern anthracite field. In later years, the Pardees sued Lehigh Navigation Electric Co., feeling that they hadn't gotten full value for their sale of Harwood Electric Co.

The board of managers of Lehigh Navigation Electric Co. began to realize after 1915 that the utility tail was wagging the coal company's dog. The 1917 annual report of the Lehigh Coal and Navigation Co. noted that "your Board of Managers deemed it desirable that the further development of the project should be controlled by purely electrical interests, particularly as the rapid growth of the business required continuous heavy capital expenditures."

The expenditures had been significant almost from the time Lehigh Navigation Electric Co. had purchased Harwood Electric Co. In October 1914, the company had authorized more than $300,000 in capital improvements, including the construction of 22,000-volt steel tower transmission lines into the Lehigh Valley. Enlargement of the Siegfried substation and installation of a frequency changer for the Hauto plant totalled $125,000 alone. Meeting in Philadelphia on Oct. 16, 1914, the executive committee of the Lehigh Coal and Navigation Co. agreed to lend the electric subsidiary $390,000 for construction work, and approved the expenditure of $537,000 more as needed.

The executive committee of the coal and navigation company approved another $372,500 in loans to Lehigh Navigation Electric Co. in April 1915, bringing the total in loans from 1913-1915 to $1.3 million. In July 1915, Lehigh Navigation Electric Co. purchased an additional 9,100 shares of the common stock of Harwood Electric Co. from Alfred Pardee, bringing Lehigh Navigation Co.'s ownership to more than 28,000 of Harwood Electric Co.'s 30,000 shares.

The loans reached $1.5 million in late 1915, which depleted Lehigh Coal and Navigation Co.'s working capital to such an extent that the parent company had to incur a floating debt of $400,000. Lehigh Navigation Electric Co. asked the parent company for a reduction in the interest rate on the first mortgage notes to 3.75 percent and offered to give Lehigh Coal and Navigation Co. one-year notes in $100,000 denominations, placed through Brown Brothers and Chase National Bank of New York City.

When the one-year notes came due in October 1916, Lehigh Navigation Electric Co. had to request an extension of the $1.5 million already financed, plus another $750,000 in loans from the parent company, this time at an annual interest rate of five percent. By July 1917, the financial burden of Lehigh Navigation Electric Co. to the parent company had become so heavy that S.D. Warriner and the Lehigh Coal and Navigation Co. board of directors instructed William Jay Turner, the general counsel of the company, to sell the electric subsidiary.

The Electric Bond and Share Co.

The purchaser of Lehigh Navigation Electric Co. was one of the most aggressive electric utility holding companies in America in 1917. Electric Bond and Share Co. was headquartered in New York City, and it traced its origins back to the start of the General Electric Co. in 1892. In the early days, General Electric Co. was primarily an electrical equipment manufacturer, selling its products to the small town utilities that were springing up all across America in the last decade of the 19th century.

The electric utility business was extremely capital intensive in its early years, as the Lehigh Coal and Navigation Co. found out between 1907 and 1917.

(courtesy of the Hagley Museum and Library)

Generating plants had to be built, transmission lines had to be extended to nearby towns, and distribution systems had to be set up. Residential and commercial customers even had to be wired for electric lighting.

One year after General Electric Co. was formed, America experienced the Panic of 1893, perhaps the most severe financial downturn in American history, with the exception of the Great Depression of the 1930s. Business stayed in the doldrums until after the presidential elections of 1896, and utilities across the nation found themselves in financial trouble. Many of

Service in 1905 was frequently available only from dusk to dawn; storms often knocked power out for hours, if not days; and kilowatt-hour prices of 15-20 cents were not uncommon.

the early city utilities went under in the mid-1890s and were sold off by receivers to stronger neighboring utilities. General Electric Co. found itself holding first mortgages and equities for the equipment it had sold to failing utilities.

In 1905, General Electric President Charles Coffin assigned GE executive Sidney Z. Mitchell the task of organizing the utility stocks owned by General Electric Co. into a separate company. Mitchell had spent much of the previous 20 years in the Pacific Northwest running the Northwest Electrical Supply and Construction Co., which General Electric Co. had acquired in the 1892 merger with the Edison General Electric Co. Mitchell had traveled across the Northwest, from California to Washington and across into Idaho and Nevada, building generating plants and transmission networks, and reorganizing utilities that had fallen into the hands of receivers. Being something of a free agent, Mitchell also enjoyed a long association with Stone & Webster, the Boston firm instrumental in setting up the electric railway system in the Lehigh Valley.

Coffin, who had been Elihu Thomson's original backer in the General Electric Co.

merger, recognized talent when he saw it. He called Mitchell to New York in 1905 to share ideas about how to set up a separate company to reorganize the electric bonds and shares owned by General Electric Co. "It is interesting that, in this instance, it was not the man who sought the job," wrote Mitchell's son in 1960. "The man was found first, and helped to work out the organization to do the job. Mitchell then was not yet 43."

What Coffin had in mind was a company that could hold the stocks and bonds of the smaller utilities acquired by General Electric Co. since 1892. "Many of these securities were those of small companies and were quite unmarketable," Sidney A. Mitchell recalled his father telling him. "It had been the practice of General Electric to sell the securities of the larger companies which had a better financial standing to the United Electric Securities Co. of Boston or the Electrical Securities Co. of New York. These two companies, whose common stock was all owned by General Electric, would sell their own debentures and preferred stock to the public in Boston and New York, and with the proceeds of such sales purchase from the General Electric the securities of the better utility companies. United Electric Securities Co. and Electrical Securities Co. were purely investment companies and participated in management matters only when forced to by the failure of some electric operating company to meet its obligations. They provided an adequate method of indirectly selling the better securities which General Electric took in payment for its equipment. But General Electric still had the 'cats and dogs' that were disturbing Mr. Coffin and his fellow directors. At this point, they thought of Mitchell in the West. He had been dealing with 'cats and dogs.' Perhaps he could help."

Coffin and Mitchell reasoned that the Electric Bond and Share Co. could bridge the gap then existing in the electric utility industry between the electrified urban areas of the nation and the small towns still primarily dependent upon isolated lighting plants for their electric power needs. "In 1905 electric service of any kind was almost unheard of in rural areas in most of the smaller communities," Bond & Share reported in 1935. "Even in the larger communities service was subject to frequent interruptions and voltage irregularities, with poor and inadequate wiring."

Service in 1905 was frequently available only from dusk to dawn; storms often knocked power out for hours, if not days; and kilowatt-hour prices of 15-20 cents were not uncommon. "The development of the operating companies nearly everywhere was blocked and even their existence was often threatened by unworkable financial structures and mortgages with high interest rates and burdensome sinking fund requirements," Electric Bond and Share Co. wrote. "Very few companies were profitable and most of them were continually in financial difficulties. The securities of companies operating in smaller communities constituted such poor risks, not only from the standpoint of earnings, but also from the standpoint of property values, that they were unattractive to the investing public."

Between 1905 and 1920, S.Z. Mitchell

Sidney Zollicoffer Mitchell (above) organized PP&L in 1920. In 1905, Charles Coffin (below), then president of General Electric, asked Mr. Mitchell to take over the Electric Bond and Share Co. *(photos courtesy of Harris County Heritage Society)*

and the Electric Bond and Share Co. parlayed those "unattractive" shares in small-town utilities into a utility holding company that spanned the width and breadth of the United States. Bond & Share companies, organized under four sub-holding companies—American Power & Light Co., Electric Power & Light Co., National Power & Light Co. and American & Foreign Power Co. Inc.—controlled more than two dozen operating utilities in the United States and electric and gas subsidiaries in 13 foreign countries.

The predecessors of such utilities as Pennsylvania Power & Light Co., Washington Water Power Co., Utah Power & Light Co., Idaho Power, Houston Lighting & Power Co., New Orleans Public Service, Omaha Public Power District, Mississippi Power & Light Co. and Florida Power & Light Co. were all Bond & Share operating companies at some time between 1905 and 1938. From its offices on Rector Street in New York City, Electric Bond and Share Co. operated interconnected grids that tied power networks together in seven separate regions of the country, ranging from the Pacific Northwest to South Florida.

Electric Bond and Share Co. wasn't the

"In 1905 electric service of any kind was almost unheard of in rural areas in most of the smaller communities." —Electric Bond and Share Co.

only organization to centralize utility operations into a holding company structure. In Chicago, Samuel Insull, Thomas Edison's former associate, started the Middle West Utilities Co. in 1912. Middle West Utilities Co.'s first acquisition was Central Illinois Public Service

pany had become one of the most common forms of utility ownership in the United States.

The Lehigh Power Securities Corp.

The acquisition of Lehigh Navigation Electric Co. by Mitchell's Electric Bond and Share Co. in September 1917 was a complex transaction in which Bond & Share retired Lehigh Navigation Electric Co.'s debt, issued stock in a new company (the Lehigh Power Securities Corp.), and effectively took control of electric power development in the anthracite region. Mitchell appeared before the Lehigh Navigation Electric Co. board of directors on Sept. 12, 1917, to explain the transaction. Sidney Z. Mitchell was elected to the board of directors of Lehigh Navigation Electric Co., which operated as a subsidiary of Lehigh Power Securities Corp., and S.D. Warriner retained his membership on the boards of Lehigh Navigation Electric Co. and Harwood Electric Co.

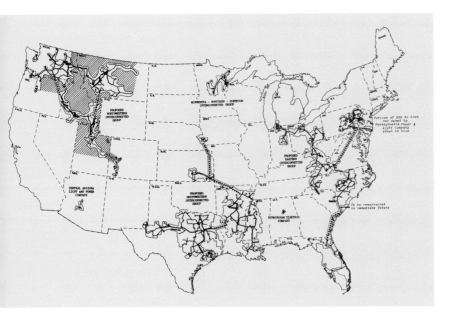

Electric Bond and Share Co. transmission lines created interconnected power networks along the East Coast, South Central region and in the Mountain West. *(photo courtesy of Electric Bond and Share Co.)*

Co. The Insull company spread across Illinois, Indiana and Iowa, buying up electric and gas utilities and electric street railway systems. Five years after its inception, Middle West Utilities Co. was serving 131,000 electric and 43,000 gas customers in 400 communities in 13 states.

In the east, the House of Morgan created the Niagara-Hudson Power Corp., which provided electric power service to hundreds of communities in New York, New Jersey and Connecticut. Financier Howard C. Hopson's Associated Gas & Electric Co. operated utilities across the Midwest and the East, including the Rochester Gas & Electric Corp. Expanding through the acquisition of electric street railway systems in such metropolitan areas as Washington, D.C., Milwaukee, Cleveland, St. Louis and San Francisco, the North American companies eventually wound up serving electric customers in 1,500 communities in 10 states. By the time America entered World War I, the electric utility holding com-

There was little doubt, however, that Mitchell was calling the shots after September 1917. Mitchell and Warriner both attended the board meetings of Lehigh Navigation Electric Co. through 1917 and 1918, but it was clear that Electric Bond and Share Co. was now the dominant partner. In June 1919, Mitchell, Warriner and Bond & Share officials met in Allentown to discuss future expansion plans for Lehigh Navigation Electric Co. Mitchell laid out an ambitious expansion plan that called for the merger of Lehigh Navigation Electric Co. and Lehigh Valley Power & Light Co., which operated the electric street railway and interurban systems in the Lehigh Valley.

Mitchell proposed exchanging $1.5 million in preferred stock in the new company for the $641,700 in outstanding stock of the Lehigh Valley Light & Power Co. The $3 million in outstanding stock of the Lehigh Navigation Electric Co. was exchanged for $2,178,000 of the new company's stock. "The complexity of the transactions," wrote utility historian Thomas Parke Hughes, "suggests why many utility heads at the time were known more for their financial ingenuity than for their ability to solve technological and managerial problems."

Under the terms of the merger plan, the Hauto plant was valued at $1,770,000, and the Siegfried-to-Allentown tie line was valued at $175,000. Mitchell noted that expansion of the Hauto plant and associated transmission lines would more than double the value of the new company.

The Bond & Share executive also outlined plans to create an entirely new company. "Agreement is now being prepared and it is expected to be submitted to the (Pennsylvania) Commission this week covering the merger of Industrial Power Co. (consisting of seven township companies with charters from Hauto to Allentown) with the Stroudsburg Co. under the new name of Lehigh Industrial Power Co.," Mitchell told Warriner and the Lehigh Coal and Navigation Co. board. "It will probably take about three weeks to get this through if no objections are encountered. We propose to promptly follow this merger by the further merger of the Lehigh Valley Light & Power Co. with all the North Central group of properties except Hagerstown (Maryland), and concurrently therewith—or shortly thereafter as may at the time be deemed most expedient after full conference with you and Mr. Turner—to likewise merge this company with the Harwood properties. It has been proposed to call this final company Pennsylvania Power & Light Co."

Mitchell proposed to finance the new venture by having PP&L and Lehigh Industrial Power Co.—essentially the old Lehigh Navigation Electric Co. group of companies—issue joint five-year, six percent ("or if the lawyers approve seven percent") bonds. Mitchell noted that the bonds would be issued under carefully drawn safeguards so as to "facilitate sale of these bonds to the public on the most advantageous terms. If this is not done and everything is deferred until the final merger has been put through, the delay is bound to cause serious operating embarrassment and will be very expensive."

Once the sale of bonds had been placed, Mitchell intended to deed all the property held by Lehigh Industrial Power Co. to Pennsylvania Power & Light Co. "We have already very successfully completed two pieces of finances in this way, one in Montana and one in Carolina, and as a matter of information I am sending you herewith, under separate cover, the papers relating to the Carolina financing which may be of interest to you or Mr. Turner."

Lehigh Coal and Navigation Co. went along with the Bond & Share plan because the capital investment required to realize the full efficiencies of the Hauto and Harwood plants in the post-World War I era was beyond the scope of what was essentially a regional anthracite mining and railroad company. Warriner and Lehigh Coal and Navigation Co. were amply compensated for giving up control of the Pennsylvania electric utility properties. As late as 1939, the company held 700,000 shares of National Power & Light Co. stock, the subholding company that Mitchell had set up to control Pennsylvania Power & Light Co.

For S.Z. Mitchell, the acquisition of the Lehigh Coal and Navigation Co. utility properties and the merger with Lehigh Valley Light and Power Co.—the new company added the article "The" to distinguish it from the old company— was the key to creating an interconnected grid in central and eastern Pennsylvania, one of the most heavily industrialized regions in the United States, under the control of the Electric Bond and Share Co. Through the early months of 1920, Mitchell continued to consolidate contiguous utility properties into the growing Pennsylvania Power & Light Co. grid. Directors of the Northern Central Gas Co., Columbia and Montour Electric Co., Northumberland County Gas & Electric Co., the Harwood Electric Co., the Schuylkill Gas & Electric Co. and

Through the early months of 1920, Mitchell continued to consolidate contiguous utility properties into the growing Pennsylvania Power & Light Co. grid.

Pennsylvania Lighting Co. all agreed during the spring of 1920 to join The Lehigh Valley Light & Power Co. and fold their utilities into the Pennsylvania Power & Light Co.

The Lehigh Valley Power & Light Co., Harwood Electric Co. and Schuylkill Gas and Electric Co. were all part of the Pardee and Lehigh Coal and Navigation Co. properties, with the exception of the Lehigh Valley Transit Co., which served Allentown and street railway customers in the Lehigh Valley. The other properties merged into PP&L were considerably smaller. Columbia and Montour Electric Co. provided electric and gas service in Danville and Bloomsburg, along with electric service in Berwick. Northumberland County Gas & Electric Co. provided electric and gas service in Sunbury, along with electric service in Milton. Northern Central Gas Co. provided gas service in Milton and Williamsport. Electric Bond and Share Co. acquired the securities of the three companies from Wallbridge and Co., an investment banking firm with offices in New York and Philadelphia.

Pennsylvania Lighting Co., the last of the seven operating companies merged into PP&L in 1920, provided electric and gas service to customers in Shamokin, and electric service to customers in Mount Carmel. Electric Bond and Share Co. acquired the securities of Pennsylvania Lighting Co. from Chandler and Co., a Philadelphia investment banking firm.

Both Wallbridge and Co. and Chandler and Co. sold their interest in the four operating utilities to the Electric Bond and Share Co. for the same reason given by Lehigh Coal and Navigation Co.: the capital investment required to keep up with the growth of electric power demand in Pennsylvania was beyond the ability of the investment bankers to

The growth of industrial demand during World War I was also fueling a population boom in eastern Pennsylvania; the population of Lehigh and Northampton counties alone increased 20 and 25 percent respectively between 1910 and 1920.

finance it. The growth of industrial demand during World War I was also fueling a population boom in eastern Pennsylvania; the population of Lehigh and Northampton counties alone increased 20 and 25 percent respectively between 1910 and 1920.

"The result of this increased industrial activity was to create heavy demands on the electric plants for power in all classes of service—residential, commercial and industrial," PP&L reported at the time of the 1920 merger. "As shown by the proceedings before the Pennsylvania Commission, which resulted in the granting by that Commission of the approval of the consolidation and merger, each of the constituent companies had mortgages covering their respective properties, and it was found to be impossible to finance from this source the additions necessary to supply the demand in the territory. The necessities of the situation required a new corporation which would present a simplified structure and a unified security to attract the necessary new capital. The greater diversity and larger operations would thus make possible the offering of a funded obligation which would appeal to a broader market."

That "simplified structure and a unified security" was embodied in Pennsylvania Power & Light Co. On April 12, 1920, the agreement of consolidation and merger was signed by all parties concerned. The Pennsylvania Commission signalled its approval on June 1, and Letters Patent were issued by the Governor three days later. On June 12, Mitchell convened the first board of directors meeting of the Pennsylvania Power & Light Co. in Allentown.

In a little over three years, Electric Bond and Share Co. had consolidated nearly 70 electric and gas utilities serving 115,000 customers in 370 communities of eastern and central Pennsylvania. The formation of PP&L in 1920 was the springboard for rapid growth in the decade ahead.

S.Z. Mitchell and the Electrical Industry

Sidney Zollicoffer Mitchell is known as the man who created the modern public utility holding company. *(illustrated by Brent Schaefer © 1995)*

Sidney Zollicoffer Mitchell was one of the giants of the electric utility industry during the early part of the 20th century. The man who organized Pennsylvania Power & Light Co. in 1920, Mitchell had created the modern public utility holding company with the formation of the Electric Bond and Share Co. in 1905. His creative financial genius was responsible for the establishment of dozens of operating U.S. electric utilities from one end of the country to the other.

M.L. Ramsay, a newspaperman and early propagandist for the Rural Electrification Administration, thought Mitchell a shadowy character. "Mitchell was ever the power industry's man of mystery," Ramsay wrote in *Pyramids of Power*, his 1937 best-seller on the history of the electric utility industry. "Outside of Wall Street and his own industry he was virtually unknown. Loathing publicity, he was uncommonly successful in avoiding it."

The "man of mystery" was a native of Alabama, born in the early days of the Civil War. Mitchell's family were planters, and Confederate generals Albert Sidney Johnston and Felix Kirk Zollicoffer were family friends, hence the young Mitchell's first and middle names. Years later, Mitchell developed an instant friendship with Gen. Harry Trexler, his fellow director at PP&L, when Trexler inquired if the Electric Bond and Share Co. chairman was named after Johnston and Zollicoffer.

The young man from the red clay hills of east central Alabama went off to the U.S. Naval Academy in 1879, graduating Annapolis with the Class of 1883. At the age of 21, Mitchell was assigned for sea duty aboard the *U.S.S. Trenton*. His assignment was to install the first electric lighting system aboard a U.S. Navy ship, and although the cotton insulation covering the electric wires had a disconcerting tendency to short-circuit and catch fire when wet, Mitchell was able to get the Brush arc light generator aboard ship working well. During a stopover at Gibraltar, the crew delighted in blinding British vessels arriving in the harbor with the ship's arc searchlight.

Mitchell resigned his commission in the Navy in 1885 and joined the Edison Electric Illuminating Co. in New York. Working in Edison's machine shops and on his wiring squads was equivalent to a graduate degree in electrical engineering; and when Henry Villard, one of Edison's chief financial backers, decided to give up the franchise for Edison power plants in the Pacific Northwest, Edison tapped Mitchell to go to Seattle and take over the job of selling Edison systems in Washington, Oregon, Idaho, Alaska and British Columbia.

Washington was still a territory in late 1885 when Mitchell and his Annapolis classmate Frederick H. Sparling set up shop at 629 Front Street in Seattle. For most of the next 20 years, Mitchell "dug postholes, organized companies, bought equipment and sold stock." Mitchell installed incandescent and arc lighting systems and electric street railways across the Northwest for Edison, and after 1892 for General Electric Co. Along the way, Mitchell became great friends with Charles Stone of the Boston firm of Stone & Webster, whom he had met while helping organize a street railway system in Tacoma, Wash.

Mitchell's success had come to the attention of Charles Coffin, the shoe manufacturer from Lynn, Mass., who had bankrolled Elihu Thomson and helped to set up General Electric Co. in 1892. Coffin called Mitchell to New York in 1905 and asked him to take over the Electric Bond and Share Co., a holding company that General Electric Co. had set up to organize and hold stock in operating utilities nationwide that GE had acquired as mortgage security for installing its equipment.

Investment bankers of the time called the small-town securities in the Bond & Share portfolio "cats and dogs," and the shares that Mitchell inherited included stock in such companies as the Anniston Electric & Gas Co., Albany and Hudson Railway and Power Co., Chicago Edison Co., Cleveland Electric Illuminating Co., Fall River Electric Light Co., Laramie Electric Gas, Light &

Fuel Co. in Wyoming, Omaha Electric Light & Power Co., Puget Sound Electric Railway, Tonawanda Power Co., Cape Fear Electric & Power Co. in North Carolina, Union Electric Co. of Dubuque, and the Twin City General Electric Co. of Ironwood, Mich. The Bond and Share portfolio also included stock from foreign firms, such as electric street railway systems in Great Britain and the Thomson-Houston Co. of France.

Mitchell mixed the "cats and dogs" together into a utility holding company that was in many ways the model for corporate development in the first third of the 20th century. He reasoned that small, scattered electric utilities would benefit from a centralized management, including engineering, purchasing and accounting. Electric Bond and Share Co. typically provided those services for operating utilities, charging an annual fee of between 1.6 and 2 percent of gross revenues.

'More Interconnection'

During World War I, Bernard Baruch and the members of the U.S. War Production Board came to Mitchell for advice about how to make the nation's utility industry more efficient and how the government could encourage construction of more power plants. "You don't need more generators," Mitchell replied. "What you need is more interconnection. All stations keep an idle generator as a spare for insurance against breakdowns. Tie these stations together, and the idle capacity in the better station will be put to work. Furthermore, when Station A is operating at maximum capacity, Station B, 50 miles away, may be operating at half capacity. And when Station B is working at full load, Station A may have plenty of spare power. By utilizing your spare units and diversifying the load it should be possible to increase the capacity of the connected system as much as 50 percent."

Pennsylvania Power & Light Co.'s rapid expansion during the 1920s is evidence of Mitchell's theory of interconnection. Mitchell's

management philosophy also stressed the fact that sales in operating utilities should increase by six to eight percent annually, and that small generating stations are in and of themselves inefficient. He preached to all who would listen that small contiguous operating companies in each state should be merged into one large company. His financial rule of thumb operated from the assumption that each dollar of increased sales necessitated the investment of $5 in new plant; for the holding company to earn a nine percent return on its investment, the common stock of the operating company had to be attractive to small investors.

S.Z. Mitchell used all these management philosophies to build Electric Bond and Share Co. into one of America's premier utility holding companies. He retired as CEO of Electric Bond and Share Co. in 1933 amid the clamor of the New Deal for punitive regulatory measures against the holding companies. Samuel Insull's Middle West Utilities Co. had collapsed into receivership in the spring of 1932, and Congress would pass the Public Utility Holding Company Act two years following Mitchell's retirement.

By the time S.Z. Mitchell died in February 1944, the operating companies of Electric Bond and Share Co. were beginning to be spun out into independent publicly traded companies. Mitchell's foresight in creating large, efficient statewide utilities as part of the Bond & Share empire made the federally mandated process smoother than it otherwise might have been. "Through Mr. Mitchell's organizing genius in creating and integrating the Electric Bond and Share system of operating companies, he brought to millions of people who had never enjoyed them before the benefits of electric and gas service," the board of Electric Bond and Share Co. eulogized its fallen chairman on Feb. 25, 1944. "Largely to his boundless energy and creative talents may be attributed the preeminence which the United States now holds in the utility field, a preeminence which has served our country well in peace and magnificently in war."

11

Consolidation

Edward K. Hall,
PP&L's first
president.

When Electric Bond and Share Co. took over the management of the operating units of the Pennsylvania Power & Light Co. in June 1920, the first task facing Sidney Zollicoffer Mitchell, P.B. Sawyer, Gen. Harry Trexler, Edward K. Hall and other members of the management team was consolidation of the far-flung generation, transmission and distribution systems of the newly formed company into a regional, integrated electric utility.

PP&L's system extended from the anthracite region in the northeastern part of the state through the industrial belt of the Lehigh Valley and back up the

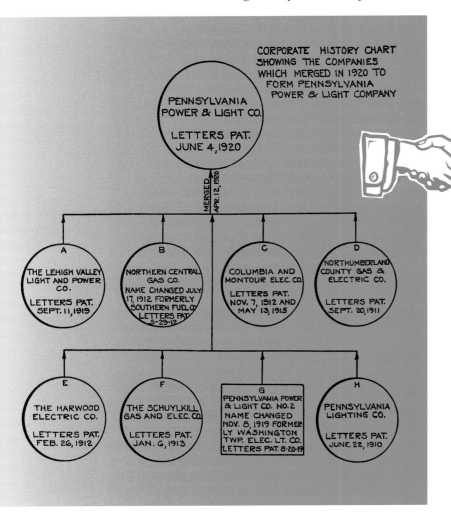

CORPORATE HISTORY CHART SHOWING THE COMPANIES WHICH MERGED IN 1920 TO FORM PENNSYLVANIA POWER & LIGHT COMPANY

PENNSYLVANIA POWER & LIGHT CO.

LETTERS PAT. JUNE 4, 1920

MERGED APR. 12, 1920

A
THE LEHIGH VALLEY LIGHT AND POWER CO.
LETTERS PAT. SEPT. 11, 1919

B
NORTHERN CENTRAL GAS CO. NAME CHANGED JULY 17, 1912 FORMERLY SOUTHERN FUEL CO. LETTERS PAT. 5-29-12

C
COLUMBIA AND MONTOUR ELEC. CO. LETTERS PAT. NOV. 7, 1912 AND MAY 13, 1915

D
NORTHUMBERLAND COUNTY GAS & ELECTRIC CO. LETTERS PAT. SEPT. 20, 1911

E
THE HARWOOD ELECTRIC CO. LETTERS PAT. FEB. 26, 1912

F
THE SCHUYLKILL GAS AND ELEC. CO. LETTERS PAT. JAN. 6, 1913

G
PENNSYLVANIA POWER & LIGHT CO. NO. 2 NAME CHANGED NOV. 8, 1919 FORMERLY WASHINGTON TWP. ELEC. LT. CO. LETTERS PAT. 8-20-19

H
PENNSYLVANIA LIGHTING CO. LETTERS PAT. JUNE 22, 1910

PP&L acquired the franchises and property of dozens of small utilities between 1920 and 1923. This chart shows the initial merger of companies that formed PP&L.

Susquehanna River to Sunbury and Northumberland County. The utility operated generating plants, electric street railways, and gas plants, and sold gas and electricity to residential, commercial and industrial customers throughout the central and eastern portions of Pennsylvania. One of the first things that Mitchell accomplished following the 1920 merger was the organization of PP&L as a subsidiary of National Power & Light Co., one of the major holding companies of Electric Bond and Share Co.

After 1921, National Power & Light Co. provided PP&L with engineering, construction, management and financial services; much of the construction that PP&L contracted for during the 1920s was

handled by the Phoenix Utilities Co., the construction arm of Bond & Share and National Power & Light Co.

National Power & Light Co. was one of four subholding companies of Electric Bond and Share Co., and for all intents and purposes, controlled only the Lehigh Power Securities Corp. and the seven operating companies merged to form Pennsylvania Power & Light Co. Besides National Power & Light Co., Electric Bond and Share Co. also controlled the American Power & Light Co., Electric Power & Light Corp. and American & Foreign Power Co. Inc. Electric Power & Light Corp. controlled the United Gas Corp. and six other operating gas utility subsidiaries. American Power & Light Co. controlled 17 different operating companies across the country, including Houston Lighting & Power Co., Minnesota Power & Light Co., Utah Power & Light Co., Florida Power & Light Co., New Orleans Public Service, and the Washington Water Power Co. American & Foreign Power Co. Inc. controlled electric and gas utility subsidiaries operating in 13 foreign companies.

Mitchell's top lieutenant at National Power & Light Co., Paul Backus Sawyer, was essentially in charge of the PP&L consolidation. Sawyer delegated authority for the overall running of PP&L to the company's first president, Edward K. Hall. An AT&T executive from nearby New York City, Hall took the train to Allentown once a week to sign papers and oversee operations. Day-to-day running of the newly consolidated utility was entrusted to the capable hands of John S. Wise, the Lehigh Navigation Electric Co. engineer who had supervised construction and operation of the Harwood and Hauto plants.

Sawyer, a native of Lafayette, Ind., and a 1900 graduate of Purdue University, had ample utility experience by the time of PP&L's formation in 1920. Sawyer started with the Des Moines, Iowa, Edison Light Co. as a timekeeper shortly after the turn of the century, worked his way up and joined Union Electric Co. of Dubuque as general manager in 1911. The next year, Sawyer was named vice president and general manager of the Utah Power & Light Co. in Salt Lake City. Utah Power & Light Co. was a subsidiary of the Electric Bond and Share Co. In the years before World War I, Sawyer supervised construction of hydroelectric dams along the mountain streams of the Wasatch Range and the interconnection of Utah Power & Light Co.'s system with that of Idaho Power, another Electric Bond and Share Co. subsidiary, to the north.

Sawyer came to New York in 1914 to work for another utility holding company. In 1917, Mitchell hired him to oversee the Lehigh Power Securities Corp. interests for National Power & Light Co. Sawyer spent the three years prior to 1920 supervising the merger and acquisition of the PP&L predecessor companies. He was closely associated with the management of PP&L until his election as president of National Power & Light Co. in 1941, after which he essentially oversaw the preparation of PP&L for its emergence as an independent New York Stock Exchange company following World War II. Sawyer died in April 1946 in St. Luke's Hospital in New York City.

Mitchell's philosophy in setting up holding companies basically stated that the operating utilities should spread the risk. Thus, a downturn in the economy in one region would be offset by an economic resurgence in another region. On a national scale, that meant that a failure of the orange crop in Florida could be recouped by electric power sales to the iron ore industry in Minnesota.

Mitchell's secondary purpose was to provide a central service organization to the operating utilities, thus standardizing the supply of service and running the operating utilities in the most cost-efficient manner possible. The executive officers for each operating utility kept watch over their charges from the Electric Bond and Share Co. offices at 71 Broadway in New York. At the executive offices, several departments provided

direct services to PP&L and the other operating utilities.

The corporate department was in charge of legal matters, along with issues involving finances and mortgages. The engineering department rendered general engineering services, consultation and advice, while the rate department offered general analyses of rate policies and development of rate schedules. The duties of the secretarial department were generally analogous to those of a modern investor relations department, while the commercial department acted as a clearinghouse for general sales and merchandise information for the operating utilities.

Electric Bond and Share Co.'s accounting department dealt with accounting classifications, systems, procedures and forms, and the tax department advised operating utilities with respect to federal and state taxation policies. The treasury department was responsible for the temporary investment of the operating utilities' surplus funds, and the statistical department assisted the operating companies in the preparation of annual and interim reports. The insurance department's duties included negotiations of policy contracts and the analysis of insurance laws and regula-

Paul Backus Sawyer was essentially in charge of the PP&L consolidation.

tions. The purchasing department was responsible for negotiating and executing purchase agreements in quantity for the operating utilities.

Unlike Pennsylvania Power & Light Co. in later years, the holding company period of the company's history, especially during the 1920s, was characterized by a small administrative staff in the corporate and operating headquarters at Allentown and Hazleton. For all intents and purposes, the company staff worked

127

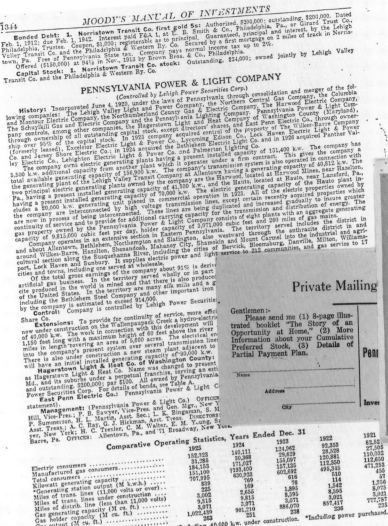

mated at 650,000," the manual informed potential utility investors. "Electric power and light usage is supplied to more than 62,700 consumers in 100 communities, of which 15 are served at wholesale, and gas service to more than 15,900 customers living in 12 cities and towns." PP&L served a concentrated territory that included the "Allentown-Bethlehem-Northampton-Slatington industrial section, one of the most industrially important, prosperous and densely popu-lated districts of the state. It extends west-ward through the heart of the anthracite coal district in and around Hazleton, Shenandoah, Shamokin and Mount Carmel, into the industrial and agricul-tural section along the Susquehanna River around Milton, Danville, Bloomsburg, Berwick, Sunbury and Williamsport."

Poor's and Moody's noted that "in this territory, there are many diversified lines of industrial activity, including iron and steel works, anthracite coal mines, steel car and automobile works, silk mills, cement plants and other important manufactories. Among the many large plants supplied with electric power by the company are those of the Bethlehem Steel Co., American Car and Foundry Co., International Motor Co., the Lehigh Coal and Navigation Co., Lehigh Valley Coal Co. and 23 other coal mining companies and nine large cement manufacturing companies."

The concept of diversified risk as outlined by Mitchell and Electric Bond and Share Co. was already in some evidence in the PP&L territory in 1921. Anthracite coal production from Pennsyl-

It was wise to invest in the young PP&L with its service territory including "one of the most industrially important, prosperous and densely populated districts of the state," according to the 1921 Poor's and Moody's consolidated manual.

out of the Electric Bond and Share Co. offices at 71 Broadway in New York City.

'An Extensive Territory in Eastern Pennsylvania'

The public utility section of Poor's and Moody's consolidated manual for 1921, PP&L's first full year of operation, validated Mitchell's goal of establishing an integrated regional utility in Pennsyl-vania. "The company owns and operates electric power and light and gas proper-ties in an extensive territory in Eastern Pennsylvania with a population esti-

vania mines had reached its peak during 1917, the year that America went to war. By 1922, anthracite production from the Pennsylvania fields had fallen to 55 million tons, little more than half the production at the industry's 1917 peak. The industry's decline in the 1920s was due to a number of factors, including industry-wide labor problems in the immediate postwar period, the substitution of other fuels for anthracite and the increasing costs of mining deeper, less accessible seams of anthracite. Because Mitchell had included properties outside the anthracite area in the 1920 combination, PP&L was far better able to grow and meet expanding electrical demands in the 1920s.

Internally, Electric Bond and Share Co. used the early 1920s to integrate its generation, transmission and distribution systems. New generating units were immediately ordered for Hauto and Harwood plants, the base load generation for the PP&L system. Both plants were expanded during 1921; addition of a 12,500-kilowatt unit at Harwood brought that plant's capacity to 41,500 kilowatts, and installation of a 20,000-kilowatt turbo-generator at Hauto in 1921 upgraded the plant's capacity to 50,000 kilowatts. A similar unit was installed in 1923, bringing Hauto's capacity to 70,000 kilowatts.

The Allentown plant formerly operated by the Lehigh Valley Transit Co. was upgraded with installation of a 12,500-kilowatt generator in 1917, shortly after its acquisition by Electric Bond and Share Co. A second, similar unit was installed in 1920 following the merger, increasing the plant's capacity to nearly 39,000 kilowatts.

Of more importance to the integration of the new system was the construction of high-voltage transmission lines. At its inception in 1920, PP&L consisted of 37 isolated electric systems or isolated supply groups. Only 10 of the 37 isolated systems—principally the systems of the Lehigh Navigation Electric Co.—had been tied together prior to the 1920 merger. Expansion of the Hauto, Har-

wood and Allentown steam stations, coupled with construction of backbone 66,000-volt transmission lines, allowed PP&L to close small, inefficient, isolated power plants.

Ties to the Pennsylvania Lighting Co., which served customers in the anthracite region, were strengthened in 1921 when an existing 66,000-volt line running out of the Hauto station was tapped and extended. Soon after, PP&L shut down the 1,800-kilowatt Mount Carmel station and the 3,400-kilowatt Shamokin station. During 1922, a double-circuit, 66,000-volt steel-tower transmission line was built between the Harwood plant and Wilkes-Barre, where crews installed a stepdown substation. The 11,000-kilowatt River station in Wilkes-Barre was converted to use as a peaking unit, and was shut down soon after PP&L's acquisition of the Wilkes-Barre properties in 1923.

Dozens of small, inefficient power plants were retired by PP&L during the period 1920-1925. The construction of beefed-up transmission facilities made the retirements possible. "The integration of the various acquired properties into one unified system rendering standard service involved more than simply connecting the properties together by electric lines," company engineers noted in 1935. "It was generally necessary to change over the old company's facilities to make them conform to Pennsylvania

---

"in this territory, there are many diversified lines of industrial activity, including iron and steel works, anthracite coal mines, steel car and automobile works, silk mills, cement plants and other important manufactories."—Poor's & Moody's

---

Power & Light Co. standards of service, and in many cases the acquired facilities had to be substantially rebuilt in order to make them conform to the construction standards of the Pennsylvania Power & Light Co.'s system."

The conversion work involved a number of tasks, including changing over from direct current to alternating current operation; changing from 25-cycle operation to 60-cycle operation; changing two-phase operation to three-phase operation; upgrading nonstandard voltage systems to standard voltage; changing DC Magnetite arc light systems to series incandescent operations; replacing nonstandard AC series incandescent systems with standard 6.6-ampere series operation; and changing obsolete multiple systems of street lighting to standard 6.6 ampere series systems.

PP&L also continued to acquire other utility systems during the period. As early as 1921, the Lehigh Power Securities Corp. had acquired control of the Eastern Pennsylvania Railways Co., serving street railway customers in Pottsville and surrounding Schuylkill County. Eastern Pennsylvania was a 1906 creation of the engineering firm of John G. White & Co., and between 1909 and 1922, the company acquired the franchises of some 40 light, heat, power and street railway companies in the anthracite regions of Schuylkill and Columbia counties. East Penn Electric had been tied to the PP&L system by low-voltage transmission lines even prior to 1920, but the ties were strengthened by the construction of 66,000-volt lines in 1923 and 1925.

It was 1925 before PP&L acquired full operating control of the Eastern Pennsylvania properties and their more than 200,000 customers, but the acquisition brought the company a major new source of generation. In 1923, the White Co. interests built the Pine Grove steam

Despite the industry's decline by the 1920s, anthracite was vital to PP&L's growth for the manufacturing of gas and steam as well as generating electric power. This brochure from the 1920s highlights the importance, history and usage of anthracite to PP&L's service area.

electric station in a beautiful valley 18 miles from Pottsville. The Pine Grove plant utilized pulverized anthracite from the culm banks scattered about the vicinity, and it was the first generating station in the country to utilize pulverized anthracite as fuel. PP&L upgraded the facility in 1926 by installing a 30,000-kilowatt turbo-generator with 400-pound boilers.

PP&L acquired the franchises and property of dozens of small utilities during the 1920-1923 period, including those located in Stroudsburg, Mauch Chunk, Mahoning Township of Carbon County, Kulpmont, Shamokin, Mount Carmel, Barry, East Cameron, Conyngham Borough, Snydertown, Upper Augusta, the Borough of Freeburg and Gregg. Most of the acquired companies operated dusk-to-dawn residential and streetlighting service; most were also located adjacent to recently built PP&L high-voltage transmission lines.

Financing Expansion

The growth of PP&L during the early consolidation period took major capital investment. In order to finance the construction of the generating plants and transmission system, PP&L executed and delivered its First and Refunding Mortgage in February 1921. Bond issues under the mortgage followed in rapid succession: $8 million at seven percent interest in February 1921, $7 million at five percent interest on Oct. 1, 1922, and $4 million at six percent interest on Sept. 1, 1923. The 1921 issue was used to liquidate floating debt and finance property additions, while PP&L earmarked the 1922 issue for additions to the Hauto and Harwood stations. The 1923 issue was used to acquire properties in Wilkes-Barre and Williamsport.

PP&L experienced rapid growth in demand and kilowatt-hour sales between 1920 and 1923. At the time of the merger, the company had 62,759 electric and 15,653 manufactured gas customers.

The Harwood Steam Electric Station was the largest plant on the system until Hauto SES was built.

HARWOOD ELECTRIC CO

Hauto Steam Electric Station's source of plant cooling water was Lake Hauto. Though the plant is now gone, Lake Hauto remains a central eastern Pennsylvania landmark.

Above: *The Hauto turbine room. circa 1920s*

Right: *Hauto Steam Electric Station was not a "mine-mouth" plant like Harwood. Coal was delivered by train and, as this photo shows, conveyed into the upper level of the plant, at which point gravity took over.*

Three years later, both classes of customers had doubled to 124,962 electric customers and 34,207 manufactured gas customers. Total kilowatt-hour sales during the period went from 390.6 million in 1921 to 527.8 million in 1923. Significantly, nearly 400 million kilowatt-hours of electricity in 1923 were designated for industrial customers. The company's electric power revenues jumped from $9 million in 1921 to $13.2 million two years later.

Standardizing rates was an issue of immediate concern in 1920. With more than 60 operating companies coming together to form PP&L, the profusion of rates was confusing, to say the least. At the beginning of its integrated operations, PP&L had inherited some 571 different rates from its predecessor companies; they appeared in 102 separate tariffs on file with the Pennsylvania Public Service Commission. "The form of charges in these rates varied widely and included flat rates, step rates, block rates with minimums, demand or service charges which were fixed or varied with connected load or demands," the rate department reported in 1935. "In many cases, particular industries such as coal, cement, pumping and manufacturing

were given special class rates because of size, time of use, load factor or nature of use."

Complicating the matter of rate standardization even further was the fact that many of the rates in existence in 1920 had been established prior to the creation of the Pennsylvania Public Service Commission in 1914. For rate standardization purposes, that meant rates were "dictated by municipal ordinances, by the demands of local authorities, and by the companies' own rate policies. Knowledge in the art of rate making in the early days of the industry was meager, and the management of each company had its own rate making theories. As a result, it was found that the rate of one acquired company was unusually high for lighting purposes and correspondingly low for industrial purposes, while the rates of another acquired company would be just the opposite."

'Ice by Wire'

In addition, there was an almost complete lack of promotional rates. Electric Bond and Share Co. rectified

The Pine Grove Steam Electric Station was built in 1923 and acquired by PP&L in 1925. It was the first generating station in the country to utilize pulverized anthracite as fuel. *(illustration by Brent Schaefer © 1995)*

that situation early on. PP&L was already heavily involved in merchandise sales and residential load growth promotion during the 1920-1923 period. In June 1921, the company advertised an electric washer and wringer for $100. They could be purchased from the company for $2.50 down, with up to one year to pay the balance. Other PP&L promotions of the period advertised electric irons for $1 down and electric vacuum cleaners for $5 down.

PP&L operated merchandise sales floors in all its district offices, which were

refrigerators; company advertisements called it "ice by wire."

Residential wiring was a particular target of the early promotional efforts. "Any building, no matter how long built, may be wired now, without damaging the floors and without removing the plaster," a September 1921 newspaper advertisement promised. "Wires are fished through the partitions, thus concealing them and giving you the lighting outlets at any points you desire, as well as base plugs wherever you desire." For its residential wiring campaign, the company developed sales allies with area contractors; in June 1922, it announced a program to wire homes in Wilkes-Barre in conjunction with the 17 contractor members of the Wilkes-Barre Electric Association.

Pennsylvania Power & Light Co. achieved a real measure of success in its consolidation efforts during the 1920-1923 period. The company managed to integrate dozens of predecessor operating companies into a unified electric utility system serving a large portion of central and eastern Pennsylvania. It expanded generation and extended transmission, standardized rates, created a promotional presence in its franchise territory and established organization and procedures through its parent, the Electric Bond and Share Co.

Within the comparatively short period of three years, Pennsylvania Power & Light Co. had laid the groundwork for the explosive growth the company would experience for the remainder of the decade.

This photo shows the Stroudsburg office merchandise display from July 1924. The framed posters in the picture proudly proclaim that the company never missed paying a dividend to its stockholders.

open six days a week and Saturday evenings. The company's line of merchandise included the Hotpoint Electric Range, which had been invented by North Dakotan George A. Hughes and displayed for the first time in 1910 at the National Electric Light Association annual convention in St. Louis, Mo. Servel was a popular line of electric

The Life and Times of E.K. Hall

Edward Kimball Hall
*(photo courtesy of
Dartmouth College Library)*

Pennsylvania Power & Light Co.'s first president was a renaissance man of early 20th century business history, a correspondent of U.S. presidents, one of the founders of the modern game of football, a vice president of the giant American Telephone & Telegraph Co. and a teacher and lecturer at one of the nation's most prestigious business schools.

Sidney Zollicoffer Mitchell, the chairman of Electric Bond and Share Co. in New York City, tapped Edward Kimball Hall to be the first president of PP&L in June 1920 because of Hall's expertise in the field of business. Years later, John S. Wise Jr.—operations manager under Hall from 1920 to 1928, and Hall's successor as president of PP&L—remembered that Bond & Share had picked Hall for the PP&L job because he was a "top man in the fields of organization and financing."

One month shy of his 50th birthday, Hall was vice president for personnel and public relations at AT&T in June 1920 when he accepted the position of PP&L's first presidency. In an intriguing twist, Hall retained his vice presidency with AT&T and took the train weekly from New York to Allentown to oversee operations at the new Pennsylvania electric utility. Most of Hall's utility career had been spent in the telephone business, but from 1917 to 1919, he had served under Mitchell as a vice president of Bond & Share in New York City.

A Prairie Native and Corporate Lawyer

Hall was born July 9, 1870, in the farming community of Granville, Ill., in the north central part of the state just east of the Illinois River. The son of Charles Prentiss Hall and Lucia Cotton Kimball Hall, E.K. Hall traced his lineage on his mother's side of the family to the Pilgrim founders of the Massachusetts Bay Colony. His father had been a captain in the Fourteenth New Hampshire Volunteer Infantry Regiment during the Civil War, ending the hostilities as commander of Fort Pulaski at the mouth of the Savannah River in the spring of 1865.

Following the war, the senior Hall taught school in Illinois before returning to his native New Hampshire in 1878. Young Hall attended grade and high school in Hinsdale, N.H., before enrolling at St. Johnsbury Academy in Vermont. In the fall of 1888, Edward Kimble Hall entered Oberlin College in Ohio; the following year, he transferred to Dartmouth College at Hanover, N.H.

At Dartmouth, Hall excelled at football, which became a lifelong passion for him. Hall played end at Dartmouth and was captain of the powerful 1891 football squad. While captain, he also served as the on-field coach and lettered in track and baseball, besides football. In need of money to go on to law school, Hall took a job following graduation as football coach and acting physical education director at the University of Illinois in Champaign-Urbana.

Hall soon discovered that football in the west was somewhat different from football in the east. During 1892, the 12-1 Illinois football squad played six games across the Midwest in a barnstorming tour that lasted an incredibly short eight days. "More than once," the *Dartmouth Alumni Magazine* reported in 1950, "the coach had to enter the game as a much needed substitute. Only one game of this strenuous season was lost."

During the two years he spent at Champaign-Urbana, Hall was the sparkplug for instituting intercollegiate track meets in the Midwest, similar to the events that were then taking place among college teams on the East Coast. He organized the first intercollegiate championship at Chicago in 1894. When the Illinois team he coached took first place, the team honored their coach by voting to run under the green color of Hall's Dartmouth alma mater.

In 1895, Hall had saved enough money from his coaching job to enter Harvard Law School. While at Harvard, he was on the editorial board of the *Harvard Law Review*, and he received his law degree in the spring of 1896. In his only other contact with Pennsylvania prior to accepting the presidency of PP&L, Hall practiced law in Scranton for a year-and-a-half following law school before returning to Boston to form a legal partnership with Samuel F. Powers.

The Boston firm of Powers & Hall became one of the most respected legal establishments in New England

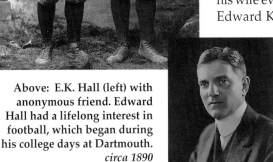

Above: E.K. Hall (left) with anonymous friend. Edward Hall had a lifelong interest in football, which began during his college days at Dartmouth.
circa 1890

Right: Edward Hall received his law degree from Harvard Law School in 1895.
(photos courtesy of Dartmouth College Library)

during the first decade of the 20th century. Hall spent 15 years practicing law in Boston, and it was during this period that he raised a family. He married Sally Maynard Drew of Lancaster, N.H., on July 1, 1902; Hall's father-in-law, Irving W. Drew, would become a United States Senator from New Hampshire in 1918. Hall and his wife eventually had three children, Dorothy, Edward K. and Richard Hall. Dorothy, now Mrs. Lawrence Leavitt, is in her 90s and lives in Norwich, Vt., immediately across the state line from Dartmouth.

The Boston years were busy ones for Ed and Sally Hall. The young lawyer served as outside legal counsel for the New England Telephone & Telegraph Co., and in 1907 he was elected to the board of aldermen in his home of Newton, Mass., just outside Boston. An ardent fly-fisherman, Hall found time to exercise his angling interests each summer during a family vacation in the northwoods of Maine. But it was his passion for football that brought Edward Kimball Hall's organizational abilities to the attention of the nation at large.

College Football Czar

Upon hearing that Ed Hall had died at Dartmouth in 1932, Herbert O. "Fritz" Crisler, then football coach at Princeton University, noted that "football men in the Middle West, like those in the East, have always looked upon Mr. Hall as one of the wisest and most devoted servants of the cause of amateur sport. He was a stabilizing force in football."

Tributes flooded into Hanover, N.H., from the world of college football. "Two figures stand out pre-eminent in the development of American football, Walter Camp and Ed Hall," wrote Walter R. Okeson from the athletic department at Lehigh University. "Together they worked to develop the open game, and on Walter Camp's death,

Ed Hall carried on. His last great contribution was to revise the rules so as to give protection to the players...."

Herbert Stegeman, athletic director at the University of Georgia, told *The Atlanta Journal* that he thought Ed Hall "was the most important figure in football with the possible exception of Mr. (Amos Alonzo) Stagg." The accolades for Hall's organizational ability were in response to the quarter-century that PP&L's first president spent in refining the rules of college football. By the turn of the century, college football had become America's most popular sport, with as many as 40,000 fans cheering on their favorites.

In the East, Yale, Harvard and Princeton dominated the college football scene. When Walter Camp's Yale squad defeated Princeton 23-4 in 1905, the game in New Haven was the crown of the New York social season. In the Midwest, "the Giants of the Midway" of the University of Chicago, coached by Amos Alonzo Stagg, created a football dynasty in the Windy City.

But the primitive football played in the early years of the century exacted a fearsome toll on the participants. Played like rugby with minimal padding, football developed a reputation for brutality, killing and maiming numerous collegians each season. The situation reached a head midway through the 1905 season when Columbia University announced it was abolishing the sport in the wake of several much-publicized gridiron casualties.

The carnage on the gridiron came to the attention of the sport's number one fan, President Theodore Roosevelt. Roosevelt used the "bully pulpit" of the presidency to suggest reforms in the intercollegiate rules. The U.S. President met with college presidents in early December, who in turn sent representatives to New York to discuss the formation of a rules committee for intercollegiate college football.

The National Collegiate Athletic Association (NCAA) had been formed by 28 colleges and universities earlier in 1905, and it was the NCAA that oversaw the establishment of the new rules committee. Walter Camp of Yale headed the seven-man committee, which also included Stagg of the University of Chicago and Parke Davis of the University of Wisconsin. Hall was selected as a member of the committee, representing the business community and alumni.

Hall became the committee's secretary in 1907 and its chairman four years later. He championed the introduction of the forward pass, which came to prominence in 1913 when Gus Dorais and Knute Rockne teamed up to make the University of Notre Dame a football powerhouse in the Midwest. Hall also was a strong voice for the abolition of the flying wedge and mass momentum plays that had sent so many collegians to the hospital.

Parke Davis, the University of Wisconsin coach and one of Hall's colleagues on the rules committee, wrote years later that it was his happy privilege "to serve 10 years of this period as a member of the committee and thereby to acquire directly a profound appreciation of the abilities and activities of Ed Hall as one of the makers of collegiate football."

Thursday, November 8, 1951

HANOVER, N. H.   Page 3

Edward Hall, '92, Named to Gridiron Hall of Fame; Devoted Life to Football

Announcement has been made by the Honors Court of the Football Hall of Fame at Rutgers that Edward K. Hall '92, Dartmouth player and noted coach, is among those selected to the roll of gridiron greats.

End and captain of the powerful 1891 squad, Hall compiled a memorable record in Hanover. Beyond football, he was captain and manager of the track team, a member of the baseball varsity and a Phi Bete.

Often hailed as "The Father of Modern Football," Hall was a well-known official and served as a member of the National Football Rules Committee for 25 years, until his death in 1932. During this period he was chairman for 21 years, secretary for four.

Following his graduation from Dartmouth, Hall coached football and acted as physical director at the University of Illinois for two years. From there he entered business and law, rising to the position of vice-president of American Telephone and Telegraph.

Long active in Dartmouth affairs, Hall was a member of the Board of Trustees for two terms and was one of the founders and long-time members of the DCAC.

He also served as chairman of the fund-raising committees for the Alumni Gym and Yale Bowl.

Both of Mr. Hall's sons attended Dartmouth, and Dick's House is named in honor of his son Richard who died in his sophomore year. Upon retirement from business, Hall made his home in Hanover and lived in close touch with the College until his death.

137

Utility Executive

For more than a quarter-century, E.K. Hall made his reputation as the nation's czar of college football. But during much of that period, Hall was also establishing his credentials as one of America's savviest utility executives. Hall was the prototype of the modern utility executive, combining the law, public relations and human resources into the professional practice of utility public affairs.

When he joined New England Telephone and Telegraph Co. in Boston in 1912 as vice president in charge of public relations, his duties included appearing before the utility commissions, lobbying state legislatures, filing rates, advertising, and relations with subsidiary companies.

Hall summed up his business philosophy with four words: contact, conference, confidence and cooperation. "The management has to get acquainted with its people," he wrote years later. "That is Contact. You talk things over. That is Conference. You talk together long enough, and inevitably, if both sides are honest, and they usually are, that conference will breed Confidence. Just as soon as you get con-

Hall corresponded frequently with Presidents Taft and Coolidge.

fidence, then it is easy to get Cooperation."

Hall's work with New England T&T brought him to the attention of Charles B. Coffin and Sidney Zollicoffer Mitchell, the executive management team at Electric Bond and Share Co. in New York City. In February 1917, Hall announced he was leaving the Bell System to become the vice president of personnel and a director of Bond & Share.

Hall arrived in New York at about the same time that Mitchell was setting up the Lehigh Power Securities Corp. to run the Hauto steam electric station and other Pennsylvania properties that Bond & Share was in the process of acquiring.

Hall's active tenure with Bond and Share lasted slightly more than two years, although he remained a director of the electric utility holding company until his retirement in 1930. Early in World War I, Mitchell lent Hall out to the Committee on National Public Utility Commissions, and later in the war, Hall served as business director of the Committee on Education and Special Training.

Following the war in 1919, H.B. Thayer, the chairman and president of AT&T in New York City, enticed Hall back to the telephone business, "to study the problems of public relations and personnel, in which work he has been eminently successful in suggesting and working out plans for the application of team play throughout the personnel of the entire Bell System."

Hall's emphasis on teamwork was an outgrowth of his lifelong fascination with collegiate athletics. In many ways, he was years ahead of his time, a utility executive who sounded thoroughly modern in his assessment of corporate success. Parke Davis, his longtime rules committee colleague, noted that in his business career at AT&T and PP&L, Hall "labored unceasingly to develop ways and means to bring out the best in each individual employee and to weld the performances of each into that effective teamplay upon which successful group accomplishment depends. Each employee, he urged, should be made to feel he was as necessary a part of the organization as the president."

PP&L's first president corresponded frequently with other CEOs, including at least two presidents of the United States. William Howard Taft, president from 1908 to 1912, and later a Supreme Court Justice, was a frequent visitor to the Halls' home in Montclair, N.J., during the World War I years. In early 1928, the Halls dined at the White House with President and Mrs. Calvin Coolidge; the couple had known each other in Boston when Hall was vice president at New England T&T.

E.K. Hall married Sally Maynard Drew on July 1, 1902. Here, several years later, they pause for a photo before an unfinished new house. *(courtesy of Dartmouth College Library)*

Hall's competence was so widely recognized in the utility industry that Mitchell was able to prevail upon Thayer to let the AT&T vice president serve as the part-time president of PP&L from 1920 to 1928. Those early years were critically important for the Pennsylvania utility. Under Hall's tutelage, PP&L consolidated a group of electric and gas companies serving central eastern Pennsylvania and acquired an additional 39 companies serving Wilkes-Barre, Williamsport, and Schuylkill, Carbon and Luzerne counties between 1923 and 1928. The company built the Wallenpaupack hydroelectric project in 1925 and helped electrify Pennsylvania's anthracite coal mining industry.

It was during Hall's presidency that PP&L negotiated with Scranton Electric Co. for the construction of the joint-venture Stanton Steam Electric Station, and it was Hall who got the ball rolling for the construction of the Tower Building in Allentown in 1928. Hall's background as a lawyer and lobbyist served the company well during the mid-1920s when Pennsylvania Gov. Gifford Pinchot's "Giant Power" program suggested the municipalization of the state's electric utility industry.

On the occasion of Hall's retirement from the Bell System in 1930, D.H. Morris, one of his colleagues on the AT&T executive management team, noted that "there is an old adage which says, 'If you have a hard job to do, pick a good man to do it.'" Ed Hall had a hard job to do at PP&L; S.Z. Mitchell picked a good man to do it.

Final Years

Ed Hall left corporate life in the spring of 1930. He was 60 years old, and he had passed on the presidency of PP&L two years before to John Wise. "All of us have to quit sometime," he told the *New York Telegram* of his decision to retire from AT&T, adding that "there are severances I shall make that I regret."

Even though retired, Hall intended to stay active. He and his wife sold their home in Montclair, N.J., and built a home on the campus of Dartmouth, his alma mater. "It's peaceful up there in the White Mountains," he told journalists. "There the soil smells sweet; there are trees and lakes and streams—and the old college." He had agreed that spring to serve as a lecturer in the Tuck School of graduate management at Dartmouth, but the return was also sentimental. In 1924, Hall's son Richard had died suddenly of infantile paralysis while an undergraduate at Dartmouth; the Halls had recently donated the funds for a new student infirmary, Dick's House, in memory of their son.

Hall's time back at Dartmouth was all too short. Shortly after returning to his alma mater, he began suffering from heart trouble. Early in the morning of Nov. 10, 1932, he suffered a massive

EDWARD KIMBALL HALL PASSES AWAY AT HOME

Pres. Hopkins Comments On College's Great Loss

Before leaving Hanover yesterday morning, President Hopkins made the following comment on the death of Mr. Hall:

"In the personal shock of news of Ed Hall's death I cannot go into details of my sense of loss. For over three decades I have treasured our mutual friendship. In sports, in business, in college affairs, formally and informally, and always socially and personally, we have played and worked together. I have never known him to do a questionable thing or to countenance a mean one. No words can express my sense of loss."

Heart Attack Brings to End Life of Former Officer Of Great Company

DEVOTED TO COLLEGE

Dartmouth Mourns Decease Of Well-Known Alumnus And Liberal Donor

Edward Kimball Hall, formerly vice-president of the American Telephone and Telegraph Company and since 1930 resident lecturer in the Amos Tuck School of Business Administration of Dartmouth College, died at his home here early yesterday morning. Mr. Hall had been suffering from heart trouble for several weeks and death came suddenly as a result of an acute heart attack.

Mr. Hall was born in Granville, Ill., on July 9, 1870. He entered Dartmouth in the fall of 1889 from Oberlin College and graduated in 1892. He studied law

Edward Hall died at his Dartmouth home in 1932 at the age of 62.

heart attack and died at his home in Hanover, N.H.

Tributes flowed in from across the nation, and his obituary was carried in *The New York Times*, *The Boston Herald* and numerous other national newspapers. "Words do not describe men like E.K. Hall," R.M. Hofer wrote in the nationally syndicated *Industrial News Review*. "They were born with a spirit of kindliness in their makeup, and they are the driving force and inspiration for the thousands of lesser personalities with whom they come in contact. They carry our social and business life forward on a constantly higher plane." It was a fitting epitaph for PP&L's first president.

Interlude: The 1920s

This home-built paddlewheel steamboat pushed barges of "river coal" to Holtwood, for sale to Pennsylvania Water & Power Co. *circa 1925*

In many ways, utility work hasn't changed all that much in the past 75 years. Steam still turns turbine blades to create electricity, and steel towers carry copper conductors across the land to deliver that electricity to end-use consumers. Meters record the electric power usage in homes and factories, and the electric bill arrives every month like clockwork. Rates are set by the power company and approved by the Public Service Commission, and an office staff is responsible for accounting, auditing, investment, financial relations,

PP&L employees in the 1920s were involved with a much more labor-intensive society.

public affairs and advertising. Line crews maintain the company's transmission and distribution system, and power plant and substation employees maintain the utility's generation system.

What has changed dramatically in three-quarters of a century is the nature of the work. PP&L employees in the 1920s were involved with a much more labor-intensive society. Line crews—many of them from outside contractors and known as "boomer linemen"—used pike poles and hemp to wrestle wooden transmission poles and crossarms into place. Trucks were almost nonexistent. Crews drove wagons with a team of horses, and meter readers made their rounds on foot or on bicycle. Since hard

in Boston Ledgers, huge, unwieldy account books that had to be muscled from shelf to desk. The entries were made with fountain pen and ink in a precise handwriting that sometimes amazes historians.

Power plant work was hard, dirty and dangerous. It wasn't until immediately before World War I that power plant engineers discovered an efficient, cost-effective method of pulverizing coal, so coal cars had to be unloaded by hand. Likewise, boilers were stoked by hand. Ash had to be removed from the clean-out pits with shovels.

'Slice into a Wire and Listen for the Buzz'

In a 1970 interview, Bill Thomas recalled that "an 18-man crew in my early days did the work of a five-man crew today. That's how mechanized tools and new technology have made our jobs easier. I saw some fellows who would take a skinning knife, slice into a wire and listen for the buzz to determine if there was juice in the lines. Those were the days when there were 2,300-volt lines all over the place."

Thomas started work for Harrisburg Light & Power Co. on July 6, 1920, just one month following the official merger of PP&L in Allentown. Thomas would work for Harrisburg Light & Power Co. eight years before the firm was acquired by PP&L in 1928. When he joined the Harrisburg utility as a line crew helper, Thomas was 15 years old and just out of the eighth grade. There was no training program as such. "When a new fellow would come on our crew,"

The few company line trucks available in the 1920s were made by PP&L. Back then, utility companies couldn't buy ready-made specialized truck bodies; the company had to design and build its own. Notice the wooden water keg attached to the front of the cab.

hats weren't introduced until the post-World War II era, linemen soaked felt hats in water to make them stiff and able to at least absorb a blow.

People lived close to their place of work. Private automobiles for most employees were still decades in the future, and employees who had to travel to work most often took one or more of the streetcar lines that criss-crossed central and eastern Pennsylvania. Office workers made their entries

Safety equipment was in its infancy. "The only tools the company gave us were a pair of rubber gloves." —Bill Thomas

Thomas told Jim Marsh of the *PP&L Reporter*, "there was no extensive job training. The rest of the men would take him and put him to the test right away. If there were eight men setting and rigging new poles, the new man would watch the first seven; then it was his turn, and he just had to go up and do it. If he didn't pull his share, he didn't last long on that crew."

Safety equipment was in its infancy. "The only tools the company gave us were a pair of rubber gloves," Thomas said, "and we tested them ourselves. We blew in the gloves, rolled them, squeezed them and spun 'em around. If the air didn't leak out, we figured they were okay." Thomas, who retired in 1970 and died seven years later, was the third of four generations to work for PP&L and its predecessors. John Thomas, his father, worked for the company from 1913 to 1939 and retired as a general foreman at Harrisburg. His grandfather, also named John Thomas, was a PP&L labor foreman from 1920 to 1934.

Jack W. Thomas, Bill's son, started working for PP&L in 1949. He told an interviewer in 1993 that his great-grandfather actually worked for his grandfather in Harrisburg in the 1920s. "He was general foreman in Harrisburg at the time," Thomas recalled, "and my great-grandfather had the labor crew. I often remember a story they

Jack W. Thomas started working for PP&L in 1949. His father, grandfather and great-grandfather previously worked for the company. *circa 1994*

Just 32 days before the October crash on Wall Street in 1929, these workers at Holtwood were concentrating on how to unload a large transformer for Unit 8 in the hydro station.

Norman M. "Mo" Snyder started as a clerk at PP&L in 1922 at the age of 16.
circa 1994

told. On rainy days, when they were in the barn, they'd get together and play cards, and they were playing poker. They weren't supposed to gamble.

"So they were playing poker. And my grandfather walked in on them, and of course, my great-grandfather saw him coming. He says, 'Well, I'll name trump: diamonds. Diamonds are trump. I have 30 meld.' And my grandfather said, 'Pop, I know you don't know anything about pinochle.' Yeah, my granddad often told me about that."

Snyder recalled that the application simply asked for basic information: name, church attended and the like.

This homemade Ford-powered locomotive moved homemade coal cars around the Millersburg Steam Electric Station in the 1920s. The driver is Fred E. Schorr Jr. with his son, Blaine. Fred Sr. and Blaine's son, Larry, also worked for the company. The family's influence spanned from the company's beginning to 1991 when Larry Schorr retired from the Brunner Island Steam Electric Station.

'For Medical Purposes'

Applying for a job with the power company was somewhat less complex than it is today. Norman M. "Mo" Snyder started work as a clerk with PP&L just after his 16th birthday. During the winter of 1922, Snyder had attended business school at Eighth and Hamilton in Allentown. His instructor told him to go down to PP&L since the company was looking for a bookkeeper. "I said, 'OK, I'll go down,'" Snyder told an interviewer. "I went to Room 208. That was on the east side of the corner building at Eighth and

Hamilton Street, the southwest corner. And I went there to 208, and there's a fellow in there by the name of Russ Reinert. He's an oldie. He said, 'You'll have to fill out this application.' And he gave me a sheet of paper the size of an ordinary letterhead."

The application simply asked for basic information: name, church attended and the like. There were no tests administered; Snyder was asked to give the name of his minister as a reference. Snyder recalled that there was a question about alcohol use, since Prohibition was then in force in America. "If you used alcohol, you'd say, 'Yeah, for medical purposes,'" Snyder said. When asked his salary requirement, he told Reinert that he'd work for whatever he was worth. Reinert put down $50 a month.

Since he wasn't yet 16, Snyder was told to check back with PP&L on his birthday. "I didn't go back on my birthday," Snyder recalled. "So my dad gets a telephone call from the Pennsylvania Power & Light Co. one day, and they say, 'Hey, where's that Norman? Where's that son of yours?'" Snyder started work with PP&L on May 24, 1922. "The first job I did was in this Room 208," Snyder recalled. "The auditors from the Electric Bond and Share would come in there, and they'd put me to work as the ledger boy. I had to carry the ledgers out. Some of them were this big and weighed maybe 10, 20 pounds."

Snyder was thankful that he had an office job with PP&L. One of his uncles had worked for the Lehigh Valley Light & Power Co. when Snyder was a child. One of his earliest memories was touring the company's plant on Front Street in Allentown at the age of 10. "They showed me the power plant," he said. "And they showed me the turbine and the generator and the big fly wheel, and the belts were this wide that ran from the turbine to the generator. I saw these guys coming into the plant. They were black from the coal pile. They would haul the coal in with a wheelbarrow, dump it in front of the boilers, and the guys would stoke this furnace, you know, by hand."

'A Family Attitude'

J. Ford Fritzinger started as a time-keeper at Hauto plant in 1922, the same year that Norman Snyder began work at the Allentown office of PP&L. Born in Mauch Chunk, he had worked in a bank for $80 a month when Sam Robbins, the chief clerk in Hauto's generation department, called him and offered a job. His starting salary was $125 a month, "the biggest raise I ever got in my life," Fritzinger recalled. "I did the steno-graphic work," Fritzinger said. "God knows, I never was a stenographer though. But I did the stenographic work for the chief clerk and the general super-intendent and stuff."

When Fritzinger went to Hauto, the plant was still operating on 25-cycle. Hauto provided electric power for the mines of the Lehigh Coal and Navigation Co., along with power for the electric street railway lines that ran up and down the valleys of the anthracite region. Fritzinger remembered that there was a cemetery on the hill above Lansford. "Now then," he said, "it was quite a steep hill between Lansford and Summit Hill, where the trolley car went up. So when a trolley car (went up the hill)—and at that time, they had a funeral car—everybody got in. So that got pretty loaded to go up this hill. So when that time came, you had a drag on the power. The load increased, you know, and you had to be careful (or) you'd blow a fuse. Well, the way the fellows did it at that time, somebody from Lansford said, 'Funeral going up the mountain.' They went around, and they had a two-by-four or something bigger than that, and they put it in the switch so the switch couldn't open up while the funeral went up the mountain. That was the fuse. Ha!"

Fritzinger particularly remembered the sense of family that the workers at Hauto

J. Ford Fritzinger started as a timekeeper at the Hauto plant in 1922 for $125 a month. *circa 1994*

In the 1920s and 1930s, before mechanized post-hole augers were available, digging foundation holes for transmission lines was far more labor intensive.

Frederick W. Kuehn received a call from Fritzinger in 1929 to come and work at PP&L. Kuehn gave notice at New York Power & Light Corp. and started at Hauto in January of that year. *circa 1994*

felt in the 1920s. Fritzinger made the acquaintance of several of the men on the boiler repair gang, two of whom had been on the Hauto plant's original construction crew. Many a time, the two men told Fritzinger, they'd be called out in the middle of the night. "We'd have to put our shoulders under the one corner of the plant while the other fellows put the bricks in, see," the men told the new timekeeper. "You know, one of the things that people say since I've been out down there is that we don't have that old family attitude that we used to have. I'm not sure about that. I think

Kuehn recalled, "We'd go out there and rip our clothes off and jump in naked. There was nobody around there, you know. All men, you know."

a predecessor of Niagara Mohawk Power in 1929—when he got a call from Fritzinger to inquire about his availability for work. Kuehn, who had been born in Lehighton and had graduated from high school in Palmerton, knew who Fritzinger was. "He was a chief clerk," Kuehn recalled. "He hired me. That's the way things were in those days. He called me, and I said, 'OK, I'll be down,' because I was getting sick of New York Power & Light Corp. They had me out there knocking rust off cars at Amsterdam Generating Station, and Amsterdam was a hard-coal-burning plant."

When Kuehn started at Hauto in January 1929, one of his first jobs was to go out and read the dam level at the pumphouse of the lake that supplied the plant with cooling water. The outflow water from the plant was downright warm, even in winter, and sometimes the temptation was just too much. "I used to go in the water, noontime," Kuehn recalled. "We'd go out there and rip our clothes off and jump in naked. There was nobody around there, you know. All men, you know."

The mostly men—and some women—who worked for PP&L in the 1920s may not have had the equipment and technological know-how enjoyed by today's work force. But they knew how to get the job done, and how to have fun in the process.

This billboard appeared throughout PP&L's service area in 1965. It emphasizes the company's growth as well as sense of community and family, which started in the 1920s and continues today.

there's a family attitude down there today."

Getting a job at PP&L in the 1920s was often a case of who you knew. Frederick W. Kuehn was working for the New York Power & Light Corp.—

13

The Roaring Twenties

PP&L's first "General Office," the Buckley Building at Eighth and Hamilton streets, Allentown, in early 1920s.

Five years after its founding, Pennsylvania Power & Light Co. was growing and expanding across central and eastern Pennsylvania. In 1923, it had acquired the properties of the Wilkes-Barre companies, which it had operated under lease since the 1920 merger. Other 1923 acquisitions included the Excelsior Electric Light & Power Co., the Lycoming Edison Co., the Lock Haven Electric & Power Co. and the Jersey Shore Electric Co. In 1924, PP&L acquired the Bethlehem Electric Co., and by 1925, it was negotiating for purchase of the Panther Valley Electric Co., the Lehighton Electric Light & Power Co. and the Palmerton Lighting Co.

Herbert Hoover, then U.S. Secretary of Commerce, warned in a 1928 speech, "neither our national nor our state governments are...equipped for the task of government operation of utilities." By November of that year, Hoover was making headlines as a presidential candidate.

PP&L reported 152,000 electric consumers and 31,000 manufactured gas consumers in 1925, up more than 20 percent on the electric side since 1923 and nearly 10 percent on the gas side for the same period. Generation station output was 708 million kilowatt-hours, a jump of more than 102 million kilowatt-hours in two years; by 1925, PP&L had 1,064 miles of transmission lines of more than 11,000 volts in operation or under construction—a more than 30 percent increase from the less than 800 miles of high-voltage transmission in operation or under construction in 1923. Distribution showed similar growth, with 3,002 miles of distribution line in operation, 1,100 miles more than the 1,895 miles in operation at the end of 1923.

This 1922 photo shows the state-of-the-art meters and switches in Harwood Steam Electric Station's control room. Harwood Electric Co. was one of the eight companies that was consolidated to form PP&L in 1920.

'As Dark as Egypt's Night'

Centralization and efficiencies made possible by the 1920 merger led to profitable utility operations. Gross earnings in 1925 totalled $18.2 million, up more than $4 million since 1923. Net income of $8.2 million for the year was up by more than a third from the $6.07 million reported in 1923.

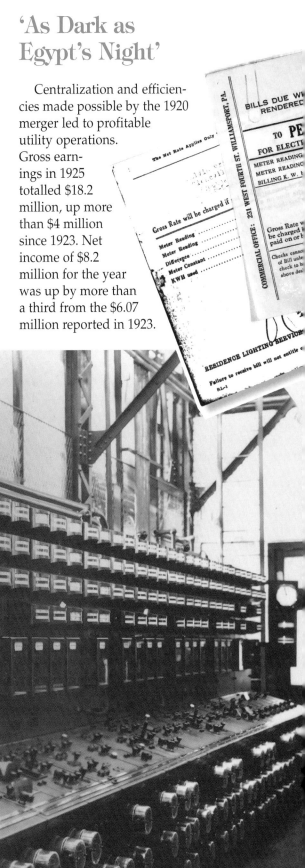

PP&L paid $2.3 million in preferred dividends in 1925, more than double the $1.126 million paid in 1923.

PP&L's profitability was proving attractive to investors. The company established a customer ownership campaign shortly after the merger in 1920 and encouraged its customers to buy preferred stock in the utility. Samuel Insull, who had been Thomas Edison's secretary at the time of the first three-wire installation in Sunbury and later went on to head Commonwealth Edison in Chicago and Middle West Utilities Co., had established the practice of selling utility stock to employees and customers in the 1910s. By the 1920s, utilities all over the country, including PP&L, had adopted the practice.

"Never was the condition of public utilities better than it is today," the business section of the *Allentown Call* noted in 1924, "and nowhere in the United States is there a territory so compact, so diversified in industry and so thoroughly knitted together for a super-power system with all its ramifications than the Lehigh Valley. Investors have been sensing this sort of thing, and there has been a good deal of local pride in the investment in securities that stood for improvements making for the growth and development of the communities in which people live."

The business editors were impressed, in particular, by the strides that had been made in electrification of the Lehigh Valley. "Thus, there are communities of the Lehigh Valley," the editors wrote, "which 20 years ago were as dark as Egypt's night after sunset but today scintillate by night with homes brightly illuminated, in which many dwellers are investors in this light and power company. They have seen what the company means and does. They have been putting their money to work while it has been improving their lot as well. Mail-men would be surprised to know the value of the dividend checks that they carry into many small towns every three months. And the size of the checks is increasing, for security holders are adding to their investments as rapidly as they can."

The editors painted a rosy picture of the future. "The prospect for the future is even greater than the splendid state," the article continued. "Every city and town in the valley is growing in size and importance. Intensification and concentration of business are easily to be noticed. This growth produces increased earnings per unit of operation for the public utility operation, and consequently the growth and tendency of the times favor an enhancement of the securities of the public service corporation. In a general way, this is true of the public utility securities. It is particularly true of the local company because of excellent management, unexcelled territory and other favorable factors."

PP&L served 31,000 manufactured gas consumers in 1925.

Utility stocks in the 1920s were the equivalent of high technology stocks in the 1980s and 1990s.

Boom Times

The *Call*'s business editor wasn't alone in his glowing assessment of Pennsylvania Power & Light Co. The 1920s were the golden age of investor-owned utility expansion in the United States. Fueled by technological advancement and the innate economic strength of the public utility holding companies, the industry went on a decade-long binge of mergers and acquisitions unparalleled either before or since. Wall Street reacted favorably. Utility stocks in the 1920s were the equivalent of high technology stocks in the 1980s and 1990s.

In its Jan. 2, 1926, issue, *Electrical World Magazine* called the events of 1925 in the electric utility industry a "record trend to centralized management." A total of 560 companies were involved in mergers during 1925, 153 of which were acquiring utilities. The 407 utilities acquired during the year had an aggregate capitalization of nearly $2 billion, equal to about one-quarter of the total capitalization of the electric light and power industry. "The companies acquired were not confined to any one section of the nation," the magazine reported, "and in many instances, the acquired companies operated in several states and even in widely separated sections of the country."

Activity in Pennsylvania was actually somewhat slow during the year. Pennsylvania Power & Light Co. acquired the East Penn Electric Co. during 1925. Across the state, General Gas & Electric Co. acquired the assets of the Towanda Gas & Electric Co., the Northern Pennsylvania Power Co. and the Saylorsburg Light & Power Co. in Monroe County. In the Pittsburgh metropolitan area, the Standard Power & Light Corp. acquired the Pittsburgh Utilities Co., the United Railway Investment Co. and the Philadelphia Co., another utility investment subsidiary.

If merger and acquisition activity in Pennsylvania was slow during the year, it was almost unrestrained in neighboring New York. That wasn't surprising, given the fact that a large number of the electric utility holding companies in the United States in the middle to late 1920s were headquartered in New York City. Besides Electric Bond and Share Co., such utility giants as American Electric Power Co., American Gas & Electric Co., Associated Gas & Electric Co., Henry L. Doherty & Co., Engineers Public Service, Federal Light & Traction Co., National Public Service Co. and the J.G. White Management Corp. all called New York City home. In addition, the Mohawk-Hudson Power Corp., one of the region's major holding companies, had headquarters in Albany.

Mohawk-Hudson Power Corp. was particularly active in acquisitions during 1925. The company bought small utilities in and around the communities of Cohoes and Gloversville, the Utica Gas & Electric Co. and the Adirondack Power & Light Co. in Schenectady. New York State Electric & Gas Co. bought 15 small distribution utilities in central New York, and the Buffalo, Niagara & Eastern Co. consolidated its control of utilities in and around Buffalo on the Niagara Frontier. The North American Co., a holding company that controlled utilities from Union Electric Co. in St. Louis to The Milwaukee Electric Railway & Light Co. and Potomac Electric Power Co. in Washington, D.C., moved into the New York market with its acquisition of Western New York Electric Co. in Jamestown.

'Which Kings Could Not Command'

The reason for the wave of mergers and acquisitions during the mid-1920s was complex. General business conditions in Pennsylvania and the United States were favorable for utility growth, low interest rates, and utility credit conditions which encouraged mergers

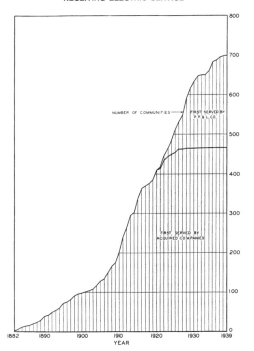

PENNSYLVANIA POWER & LIGHT COMPANY
NUMBER OF COMMUNITIES OF OVER 100 POPULATION
RECEIVING ELECTRIC SERVICE

This graph is evidence of the explosive growth in the utility industry during the first part of the 20th century.

and acquisitions. "Many small private plants and many small municipal plants have been purchased and merged into a coordinated system," *Electrical World* observed early in 1927. "Other properties of the same character have been absorbed by expanded transmission systems. These small properties have been taken over purely on an economic and service basis. The large modern system, with efficient power production sources, with the advantages offered by diversity, skilled management, interconnection and ample financial resources has been able to offer customers on small properties cheaper and better service."

In a 1925 address in Louisville, Ky., to the public relations committee of the National Electric Light Association—then the industry's trade association—Samuel Insull pointed out the strides that had been made in the slightly more than four decades since Thomas Edison had inaugurated central station electric service at Pearl Street in New York and Sunbury station in Pennsylvania. "Here is an industry that has risen in 40-odd years from the status of a laboratory experiment to the gigantic proportions represented by a cash investment of $6.6 billion, gross revenue last year of $1.35 billion, municipal, county, state and federal taxes paid to the amount of $1.35 million, and regular daily service to more than 16 million customers," Insull told his audience, "an industry that has made the magic of electric service a commonplace of everyday life; an industry that supplies conveniences and comforts to the day-laborer which kings could not command only half a century ago; an industry that has made electricity, the wonder-worker, more useful, more economical to use, and more easily accessible to more users, here in the United States, than it is anywhere else on earth."

By 1925, *Electrical World* estimated that all cities, towns and villages in the United States having a population of 5,000 or more people had access to electric central generation service. The more than 16,500 communities of more than 5,000 people served by central station generation represented 90 percent of the urban area of the country and contained a population

"Here is an industry that has risen in 40-odd years from the status of a laboratory experiment to the gigantic proportions represented by a cash investment of $6.6 billion, gross revenue last year of $1.35 billion, municipal, county, state and federal taxes paid to the amount of $1.35 million, and regular daily service to more than 16 million customers." —Samuel Insull circa 1925

of 66 million people at mid-decade. The fact that the majority of people living in communities served by central station generation still did not get electric service, and the fact that seven million Americans living in the more than 36,500 communities of less than 5,000 population were most often without electric service of any kind would become a thorny issue that Pennsylvania Power & Light Co. and the rest of the industry would have to confront during the latter 1920s and the early 1930s.

After riding a crest of popularity in the years before World War I, the municipal electric utility industry in America tailed off dramatically during the 1920s. In 1902, municipally owned plants supplied nearly eight percent of all the electric

Bethlehem Electric Co. was one of the companies PP&L acquired in 1923. As was the case with many early utility companies, acquisition and industry growth led to power plant closings. Bethlehem customers were served by PP&L and the vacant building became the home of Chick's Auto Service. *(illustration by Brent Schaefer © 1995)*

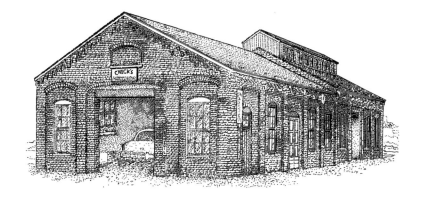

current supplied to consumers in the U.S.; 20 years later, the ratio was down to less than five percent and diminishing. Pennsylvania in particular and America in general were electrified by investor-owned holding companies during the decade.

Again, the reasons are complex, but the fact that Republican administrations in Washington, D.C., held power from 1920 to 1932 made it difficult for municipal utilities to increase their share of generation except in such bastions of prairie populism as Nebraska, Iowa and Minnesota. "Neither our national nor our state governments are planned or equipped for the task of government operation of utilities," U.S. Secretary of Commerce Herbert Hoover warned in a 1928 speech, arguing that municipal generation of electric power was a "19th century dream."

Electric power generation, transmission and distribution enjoyed perhaps the greatest expansion during the 1920s. The consolidation of holding company control of the industry made possible a spurt of growth unparalleled in the industry's history. With major expansions in 1925 and 1928, and the continued extension of its high-voltage transmission system across central and eastern Pennsylvania, PP&L participated in that enviable record of growth.

Lines Across the Land

On a Saturday night in the last week of September 1923, the citizens of Bloomsburg gathered on the main street of the Columbia County community to celebrate the city's new streetlights. It was county fair week in the Susquehanna River town, and the streets were packed with late afternoon and early evening fairgoers. At precisely 7 p.m., W.R. Rhoads, the manager of the Pennsylvania Power & Light Co., and Willie Law, the local president of the Bloomsburg Rotary Club, turned the switch that placed the new streetlighting service into operation. As the lights illuminated downtown Bloomsburg, the first notes of a concert given by the Elks Band floated across Market Square.

The *Bloomsburg Morning Press* reported that "so light it was that small print could be read anywhere on the street, the long stretch of street ablaze with light, with the lights up the Normal Hill a fitting climax, (was) a thing of real beauty." The

Bloomsburg before and after new streetlights were installed. Bloomsburg was served by Columbia and Montour Electric Co. prior to PP&L.

thousands of spectators in town for the fair witnessed, according to the president of the town council, the "rebirth" of downtown Bloomsburg. "Bloomsburg did far more than install a new lighting system," the *Morning Press* editorialized. "It proved that it could clean its business section of offending awnings, signs, poles, wires and other obstructions and that there could be real cooperation in a worthwhile achievement."

That worthwhile achievement, however, could not have been accomplished without the active assistance of Pennsylvania Power & Light Co. For it was PP&L's aggressive program of high-voltage transmission line extension and equally aggressive merger and acquisition activity during the decade that made effective streetlighting in places like Bloomsburg a reality. In the mid-1920s, dozens of communities like Bloomsburg were still served by isolated central station plants, tied together by frequently unreliable low-voltage transmission systems. Between the spring of 1928 and the end of 1930, Pennsylvania Power & Light Co. acquired many of these smaller systems and integrated them into the expanding high-voltage transmission grid serving central and eastern Pennsylvania.

Most of the companies purchased in the 1928 and 1930 mergers were small and undercapitalized. Typical of the properties was the Jamestown Electric Co. Organized to provide electric service to a portion of Mahanoy Township in Carbon County in 1900, Jamestown Electric Co. in 1928 served a population of some 2,400 people and competed directly with Mauch Chunk Heat, Power and Electric Lighting Co. for customers. In 1926, Lehigh Power Securities Corp. acquired the stock of Jamestown Electric Co.; two years later, the property was merged into PP&L.

Also acquired in 1926 by Lehigh Power Securities Corp. was the stock of the Big Spring Light & Power Co. Serving the Borough of Newville in Cumberland County, Big Spring Light & Power Co. operated a small hydroelectric facility on Conodoguinet Creek after 1913. The small

hydro station near Newville was equipped with three 45-inch Samson upright water wheels operating under an eight-foot head, one 75-kw Ft. Wayne generator, and one 135-kva Allis-Chalmers turbo-generator, both of which were three-phase, 60-cycle alternating current units. The company was acquired by McGovern & Co., a New York investment banking firm, which then sold the company to Lehigh Power Securities Corp.; PP&L soon retired the hydro station and integrated Big Spring Light & Power Co. into the electric grid.

Another small utility acquired in 1928 was the Middlesex Electric Light, Heat & Power Co. Serving customers in Middlesex and Balfour villages and surrounding portions of Middlesex Township of Cumberland County, the company was organized in 1922 and built a distribution system to serve approximately 35 customers. Middlesex Light, Heat &

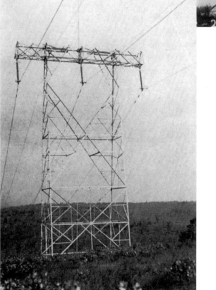

The network of high-voltage transmission lines stretching across the land made it possible to operate the most economical generating stations at the highest load factor, which made it possible to bring effective streetlighting to places like Bloomsburg in the mid-1920s.

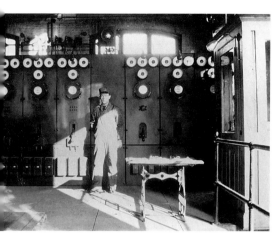

This unknown Harrisburg Light & Power Co. employee is standing in front of the 6,900-volt switch and meter board that monitored the plant. Notice the desk made out of a board on sewing machine legs.
circa 1913

Power Co. purchased its power requirements from the United Electric Co., which owned a 13,000-volt line passing near the village. Lehigh Power Securities Corp. acquired the stock of the company and merged it into PP&L two years later.

In April 1928, PP&L acquired stock in a number of properties, most of which were not integrated into the company's system until the 1930s. One property that was integrated almost immediately following the 1928 acquisition was the Harrisburg Light & Power Co. The electric utility serving the state capital and environs was one of the larger properties acquired during the merger activity in the late 1920s.

Organized in 1913, Harrisburg Light & Power Co. was an outgrowth of numerous utilities serving Harrisburg and surrounding Dauphin County areas, including the Excelsior Electric Co. of Harrisburg, the Harrisburg Light, Heat & Power Co., the Paxtang Electric Co. and the Steelton Light, Heat & Power Co. Predecessors of Harrisburg Light &

Power Co. had been providing arc and incandescent electric lighting service to Harrisburg since the 1883-1884 period.

Unlike most utility properties acquired during the 1920s, Harrisburg Light & Power Co. served an urban industrialized area of more than 125,000 people. The utility operated its own generation, and distributed electric power in Dauphin County that was delivered to outlying areas by a high-voltage transmission system. At mid-decade, Harrisburg Light & Power Co. reported nearly 25,000 electric meters connected, an increase of more than 40 percent since the end of the first World War.

The utility burned 158,669 tons of coal a year at its Cedar Street and Ninth Street steam electric generating stations, both of which had been upgraded during the mid-1920s. Harrisburg Light & Power Co. had an aggressive program of under-grounding distribution service in metropolitan Harrisburg, and the utility also provided steam to more than 1,000 customers in the downtown area.

In the mid-1920s, Harrisburg Light & Power Co. extended a 13,200-volt transmission line from Cedar Street through Steelton and Highspire to the northern

Changing Arm. This Crew took down static wire on S-M Lines Nov. 1920

ABRASION MOULDING

4000 V. DISTRIBUTING LINES
METHOD OF PROTECTING WIRES
THROUGH TREES

Growth of Business Harrisburg Light and Power Company

Kilowatt Hour Sales

	Power	Light	Total
1913	2,677,696	6,517,276	11,995,090
1914	3,909,915	7,191,025	13,735,122
1915	6,957,197	7,611,637	17,238,930
1916	11,773,661	8,492,224	23,850,150
1917	13,786,608	9,765,260	27,717,115
1918	20,097,308	9,524,797	34,354,320
1919	18,565,084	9,580,359	32,519,455
1920	20,751,471	11,926,130	38,253,704
1921	19,916,335	11,972,267	38,731,309
1922	(6 month estimated) over		45,000,000

Increase in Number of Consumers for Electric Service

1913	7461	1918	13908
1914	8290	1919	15084
1915	9444	1920	16975
1916	12321	1921	18411
1917	13402	1922—July 1st	19032

There was connected to the **Harrisburg Light and Power Company's** Electric Distribution System on Dec. 31st. 1921—739,716—16 C.P. Equivalents.

As an illustration and proof of the value of Electric Service in the home there was connected on Dec. 31st. 1921—140292—16 C.P. Equivalents, in domestic electric appliances as, Washing Machines, Vaccuum Cleaners, Irons, Toasters, and Heating Cooking Utensils.

Steam Heat Service

Steam Heat service was supplied during 1921-1922, to approximately 800 Consumers amounting to 368,743,000 lbs. The street distribution required to supply this service is approximately 33,000 feet of mains varying in size from 20 inches to 4 inches.

limits of Middletown Borough, and then easterly to the vicinity of Hummelstown. Transmission lines of 6,900-volt capacity were extended from the Harrisburg system to Pleasant View, Speeceville and the industrial load required by the Air Reduction Co. In addition to its internally generated power, Harrisburg Light & Power Co. purchased large blocks of power from the hydroelectric stations located along the nearby Susquehanna River, including York Haven and Holtwood.

'Tend Toward Greater Efficiency and Reduction in Operation'

The newly organized Harrisburg Light & Power Co. window display in 1913.

H. Root Palmer, vice president and general manager, outlined the reasons that Harrisburg Light & Power Co. agreed to be acquired by Pennsylvania Power & Light Co. "We cannot overlook our recommendations of last year that additional capacity should be given consideration to be installed and available for the 1925 season," Palmer told shareholders in the company's 1924 annual report. "Had there been available only the hydro capacity and the unreliable supply of Ninth Street capacity as obtained during the season of 1923 and 1924, we would have been able to supply our demands from our Cedar Street plant only when the entire generating capacity was in operating condition. We would again recommend early and favorable consideration to this increased capacity, which would be not only an insurance of continued service but tend toward greater efficiency and reduction in operation."

Pennsylvania ended the decade with another wave of merger activity. On Dec. 31, 1930, the Allentown utility acquired another two dozen companies, mostly small electric and gas utilities. The newly acquired utilities served customers across the length and breadth of the service area, including Lancaster, the Conestoga Valley, Donegal, New Kingston, Penns Creek, Lititz, New Parryville and Wrightsville.

Pennsylvania Power & Light Co. was able to grow and expand during the 1920s for a number of reasons. It served a growing industrialized area of central and eastern Pennsylvania, it had the strong financial backing of the Electric Bond and Share Co., and with the addition of the big Wallenpaupack Creek hydroelectric project, it had generating capacity to spare.

The 1928 and 1930 Expansions

Pennsylvania Power & Light Co. achieved a major expansion of its system in the late 1920s when it acquired dozens of small companies in two separate acquisitions in 1928 and 1930. Companies acquired in 1928 included:

Ariel Light, Heat & Power Co.
Benton Hydro-Electric Co.
Big Spring Light & Power Co.
Denison Electric Co.
East Penn Electric Co.
Franklin Township-Carbon Electric Co.
Honesdale Consolidated Light, Heat & Power Co.
Hummelstown Water & Power Co.
Jamestown Electric Co.
Juniata Public Service Co.
Middleburg Light, Heat & Power Co.
Middlesex Electric Light, Heat & Power Co.
Millville Electric Light Co.
Montgomery and Muncy Electric Light, Heat & Power Co.
Montoursville Electric Light Co.
Mount Pocono Light and Improvement Co.
Orangeville-Columbia Power & Light Co.
Panther Valley Electric Co.
Parryville Electric Co.
Paupack Electric Co.
Prompton Electric Co.
Prospect Rock Electric Light, Heat & Power Co.
Ringtown Light, Heat & Power Co.
Schuylkill Electric Co.
Stockertown Light, Heat & Power Co.
Tatamy Light, Heat & Power Co.
The Beach Lake Electric Light Co.
The Citizens Electric Light & Power Co. of Hughesville, Pa.
The Clymer Power Co.
The Coopersburg Electric Light, Heat & Power Co.
The Macungie Electric Light, Heat & Power Co.
The United Electric Co.
Varden and Lake Ariel Light, Heat & Power Co.
Weissport Electric Co.
White Haven Light, Heat & Power Co.

Lock Haven Steam Electric Station was one of hundreds of small power plants acquired by PP&L through mergers. Lock Haven was merged with PP&L on Sept. 24, 1923.

In 1928, PP&L acquired stock in a number of other Pennsylvania companies, although the properties of many of these utilities weren't actually acquired and integrated until later. The companies whose stock was acquired in 1928 and the year the properties were actually acquired include:

Central River Coal and Supply Co.
   (Liquidated Dec. 31, 1934)
East Penn Traction Co.
Harrisburg Light & Power Co.
   (property acquired in August 1928)
Hummelstown Water Supply Co.
Juniata Land Co. (Liquidated Dec. 31, 1934)
Juniata River Water Power Co.
   (Liquidated Dec. 31, 1935)
Lehighton Electric Light & Power Co. (Feb. 14, 1938)
Mauch Chunk Gas Co. (April 30, 1929)
New Parryville Consolidated Gas Co.
   (Dec. 31, 1930)
Pine Grove Electric Light, Heat & Power Co.
   (Nov. 30, 1935)
The Carlisle Gas & Water Co. (Nov. 30, 1935)
Watts Water and Power Co.
   (Liquidated Dec. 31, 1935)

Under the terms of a contract dated Nov. 1, 1930, PP&L acquired another 27 companies, including:

Conestoga Valley Electric Co.
Donegal Gas Co.
Edison Electric Co.
Farmers Electric Co.
Farmers Electric Co. of Conestoga Township
Farmers Electric Co. of Manor Township
Farmers Electric Co. of Martic Township
Farmers Electric Co. of Pequea Township
Farmers Electric Co. of West Hempfield Township
Gas Company of Northumberland
Halfpenny and Grove, Inc.
Hartleton Power & Light Co.
Hubley Electric Co.
Intercourse Electric Co.

Laurel Park Power & Light Co.
Lititz Gas Co.
Naomi Pines Electric Co.
New Kingston Electric Light, Heat & Power Co.
Penns Creek Hydro Electric Co.
Pequea Electric Co.
Pioneer Electric Light Co.
Sherman Valley Electric Light, Heat & Power Co.
The Citizens Electric Co.
The Lancaster Electric Light, Heat and Power Co.
The Lancaster Gas Light and Fuel Co.
The Mount Nebo Electric Light Co.
Wrightsville Light and Power Co.

Pennsylvania Power & Light Co. closed out the decade with two more acquisitions. On Dec. 31, 1930, the company acquired the stock of the Columbia Gas Co. and the Conestoga Terminal Co. The actual property of Columbia Gas Co. wasn't acquired until Nov. 30, 1935, and Conestoga Terminal Co. wasn't integrated into the PP&L system until Aug. 1, 1934. The two years between 1928 and 1930 produced significant expansion for Pennsylvania Power & Light Co. There wouldn't be comparable expansion for the company again until the mid-1950s.

14

White Coal in the Poconos

At the time of construction in 1906, Holtwood Dam on the Susquehanna River was to be the largest dam ever built in the U.S., exceeded only by the Aswan Dam in Egypt.

Hydroelectric development on the nation's rivers and streams reached its peak during the 1920-1940 period. That development was most common along waterways that had been dammed with rock crib structures during the 19th century. Those improvements were commonly used for the passage of logs and other river traffic; shoreside contraptions of pulleys and ropes ran sawmills and gristmills.

McCall's Ferry Power Co. started
construction on what would be Holtwood
Dam in 1906. It was completed in 1910
after the company reorganized as the
Pennsylvania Water & Power Co.

The construction of the massive Niagara hydroelectric project on the St. Lawrence River at the end of the 19th century proved the feasibility of using cheap, clean and efficient hydroelectricity to power North America's cities. Dozens of hydroelectric projects were constructed from 1900 to 1920, each in its own way advancing the technological frontiers, and each claiming at least some superlative: longest dam, highest dam, biggest turbine.

The Holtwood Dam on the Susquehanna River at McCall's Ferry was one of those "superlative" hydroelectric projects—the world's longest. Others that captured the nation's attention included the Thomson hydroelectric project and Keokuk on the Mississippi River. Built in a secluded valley of the St. Louis River in the Minnesota uplands above Lake Superior between 1900 and 1907, Thomson provided power to the Duluth Edison Electric Co., the utility that served the rapidly growing port city of Duluth, Minn., and that would become a subsidiary of the Electric Bond and Share Co. in the years just prior to the first World War.

Holtwood was soon supplanted as the longest dam in the world by the mile-long Keokuk Dam on the Mississippi River, which was built between 1911 and 1913 by Stone & Webster, the Boston engineering consulting firm that had been involved in early Lehigh Valley traction companies. Built on the Des Moines Rapids on the Mississippi for the Mississippi River Power Co., the Keokuk hydroelectric project provided electricity for consumers in St. Louis downstream.

By 1920, hydroelectric engineering firms like Stone & Webster, H.M. Byllesby, Mead and Seastone, J.G. White Management Corp. and C.T. Main had begun to perfect the development and installation of hydroelectric dams and powerhouses. Holding companies like the Electric Bond and Share Co. operated hydroelectric construction subsidiaries, and a number of large electric utilities, including Pacific Gas & Electric, Duke Power, New England Electric and Alabama Power established their own in-house hydro-electric engineering and construction departments.

"A larger number of hydroelectric plants came on line or were significantly upgraded between 1920 and 1930 than during any decade before or since," hydroelectric historian Duncan Hay noted in *Hydroelectric Development in the United States, 1880-1940*, the definitive history of the industry published by the

Dozens of hydroelectric projects were constructed from 1900 to 1920…each claiming at least some superlative: longest dam, highest dam, biggest turbine.

Edison Electric Institute in 1991. "The nuances of converting waterpower into electricity and transmitting the resulting energy had been worked out over the preceding 25 years. Indeed, a de facto standardization had evolved in hydroelectric plant design to the point that most plants built during the 1920s looked very much like their neighbors."

Hay, the curator of the New York State Museum, pointed out that "standardization in hydroelectric plant design was the product of several factors, including cumulative experience, national and regional technical periodicals, the growing influence of consulting

capacity in the Pacific Northwest, spurred by the massive
hydroelectric projects on
western rivers during the Great
Depression, had shot up to
nearly 14 million kilowatts.
The Mid-Atlantic states were
still in second place, but just
barely ahead of the intermountain states and the
Tennessee River Valley in the
east South Central region.

The reason for the
decreasing share of hydroelectric power capacity in the Mid-
Atlantic states was twofold. For one
thing, Pennsylvania coal, both anthracite
and bituminous, was in abundant supply.
For another, most of the more suitable
hydroelectric sites in the region had
already been developed by the 1920s.

One of those sites was along Wallenpaupack Creek in Pennsylvania's Pocono
Mountains. Meandering out of the wild
mountains in Pennsylvania's northeast
corner, Wallenpaupack Creek had been
the site of a massive lake in prehistoric
times. But the dike that had plugged one
end of the valley had broken in more
recent geologic times, allowing the stream
to run unfettered through its upland
basin.

The Lenni-Lenape, or Delaware
Indians, who populated the rugged
Poconos before the European colonization
of Pennsylvania called the Wallenpaupack "the swift and slow water."
The name captured the stream's capri-
cious character, one writer for *Commonwealth Magazine* noted in 1951, "miles of
quiet pools extending to the turbulent
falls and rapids in the last mile of its
former descent from Wilsonville to where
it joins with the Lackawaxen River at
Kimbles."

Engineers from the Electric Bond and
Share Co. were quick to recognize the
potential waterpower capacity of the
Wallenpaupack basin. By 1923, they had
worked out engineering plans for a
concrete and earth dam 1,250 feet across
Wallenpaupack Creek. Some 70 feet high,
the dam near Wilsonville would back up

**Damming up the
meandering mountain
creek in the mid-1920s
created Lake
Wallenpaupack, a
source of power and
play.** *circa 1971*

engineering and management firms,
holding companies and corporate consolidations. The results of these influences
are visible in power stations built during
the 1920s but their roots go back to the
beginnings of commercial electric power."

'Swift and Slow Water'

With the exception of New York, most
of the better hydroelectric sites in the
Mid-Atlantic states had been developed
by 1920. Hydroelectric power accounted
for about four billion kilowatt-hours of
generation in the Mid-Atlantic region in
1920, roughly one-third of the 12 billion
kilowatt-hours of
electricity generated
in the region. The
four billion kilowatt-
hours of hydro-
electric power
generation in the
region compared
favorably with the
rest of the country in
1920; only the
waterpower-rich Pacific Northwest had
greater hydroelectric capacity at the time,
and it generated minuscule amounts of
power from coal.

By 1940, hydroelectric power generation in the Mid-Atlantic states had
nearly doubled to just under eight billion
kilowatt-hours. Coal-fired generation in
the region, however, had skyrocketed to
28 billion kilowatt-hours. Hydroelectric

> *Hydroelectric power
> accounted for…roughly
> one-third of the 12 billion
> kilowatt-hours of electricity
> generated in the region.*

Wallenpaupack Creek into a 5,760-acre reservoir one mile wide, 13 miles long and 60 feet deep. "The hand of man is to create for Pennsylvania its largest lake," the *Allentown Morning Call* reported in its Sunday morning editions of Oct. 14, 1923. "Scarce 70 miles away from Allentown, a gigantic development is about to be begun that will result in the creation of a lake 12 miles long, 51 miles in circumference, more than two miles wide and containing 216,000 acre-feet of water."

In a full-page article on the front of the newspaper's feature section, the reporter for the *Morning Call* waxed eloquent about the potential of the new water-power development. "But it is the people who are going to perform this work of change upon the topography of

installed in the Wallenpaupack power-house were designed to supplement PP&L's coal-fired generation at Hauto and Harwood. Wallenpaupack was designed as a peaking plant, since continuous operation of the hydro station would draw down the reservoir behind the dam in two months or less.

A reporter visiting the site in the fall of 1923 noted that "at present the only evidence of the giant plan to be found outside of those keen minds that have conceived it…(is) stakes here and there about the topography of Wayne County

Wayne County, Pennsylvania, and the purposes for which it is to be done, that Allentonians are particularly interested," the *Morning Call* reported. "The former are the Pennsylvania Power & Light Co., the extensive electric system which serves the greater portion of Eastern Pennsylvania, and whose main offices are located in Allentown. The latter is even more directly concerned with the happiness and prosperity of the Lehigh Valley since this immense new lake that is to be born is to send the energies which its water possesses by reason of a 373-foot fall into the Lehigh Valley in the form of electric current and thus aid in the efficient operation of the industrial interests here located."

The two 22,000-volt turbo-generators

with bits of colored bunting depending from them, and signifying things to the hundreds and more surveyors and engineers who are scattered over the 240 square miles of the drainage area, the vanguard of workers soon to come."

Crews started moving into the Wallenpaupack basin in the spring of 1924. Before the work was completed and the reservoir was filled two years later, some 2,700 workers would be employed clearing the land, building the dam and the powerhouse, installing the three-and-a-half mile flow line and creating an

Wallenpaupack hydro-electric station was put into service as a peaking plant in 1926.

Insert: Dam at Lake Wallenpaupack.

Harwood Steam Electric Station in 1921. The Wallenpaupack powerhouse was designed to supplement coal-fired generation at Hauto and Harwood.

industrial oasis in the middle of the Pocono wilderness.

The actual engineering and construction of the project was handled by Phoenix Utility Co., an Electric Bond and Share Co. subsidiary formed in 1919. Phoenix Utility Co., named for the mythical bird that rises from the ashes, was an experienced engineering and construction contractor by the mid-1920s. The Bond & Share subsidiary engineered and built eight separate hydroelectric projects across the United States during the 1920s. Besides Wallenpaupack, Phoenix Utility Co. engineers built the Fond du Lac hydroelectric project on the St. Louis River and the Blanchard hydroelectric project on the Upper Mississippi River for Minnesota Power & Light Co. in 1924 and 1925. Built in the shape of an arch 80 feet high and 500 feet long, the Fond du Lac Dam plugged a steep valley of the St. Louis River and is still considered to be one of the finest examples of its kind on the North American continent.

Other Phoenix Utility Co. projects included Powerdale on Oregon's Hood River in 1923; Soda on Idaho's Bear River in 1924; Cutler on the Bear River in Utah in 1927; Lake Chelan on Washington's Chelan River in 1928; Tillery on North Carolina's Yadkin River in 1928; Morony on the headwaters of Montana's Missouri River; and Walters on the Pigeon River in North Carolina, both completed in 1930.

Until 1928, Pennsylvania Power & Light Co. essentially had no construction department. Besides the construction crew at Wallenpaupack, Phoenix Utility Co. handled all construction work at Hauto and Harwood, and supervised transmission line crews across the system. "In my time at Hauto," recalled Ford Fritzinger, "which was 1922 to 1931, Phoenix was putting in the Unit Four and Five generators. I remember that they were a part of the Electric Bond and Share Co., which is known as EBASCO today. I lived in Mauch Chunk (the present-day Jim Thorpe), and a Mr. Waterman, who was in charge of the Phoenix operation at Hauto, used to be my passenger to and from work."

The formation of a PP&L distribution construction crew in 1928 was the beginning of the end for Phoenix Utility Co. Electric Bond and Share Co. was increasingly sensitive to criticisms of holding company control following the 1928 Federal Trade Commission hearings. By the early 1930s, Bond & Share operating utilities were establishing internal construction departments and pulling functions formerly performed by Phoenix Utility Co. in-house.

At the end of 1932, Phoenix Utility Co. turned over its accounts in Pennsylvania

It took two years and 2,700 workers to build the dam at Wallenpaupack, from 1924 to 1926.

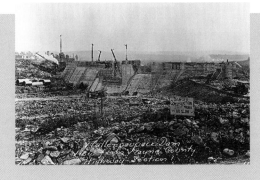

to PP&L; early the following year, Phoenix cancelled its contract with PP&L and turned back equipment it had leased from the Allentown company. The nearly 250 Phoenix Utility Co. employees assigned to work with PP&L were absorbed into the Pennsylvania Power & Light Co. Construction Department.

The Green Goose

Two of the Phoenix Utility Co. engineers working on the Wallenpaupack project from 1924 to 1926 were A.E. Silver and A.C. Clogher. Silver was an electrical engineer on the project, and Clogher was the hydraulic engineer for Wallenpaupack. In the summer of 1926, they wrote up their observations for *Electrical World Magazine*.

In three parts, the two engineers explained the development and construction of the hydroelectric project in the Pocono Mountains. They described to their readers how the power station itself was built, the layout of the substations at Wallenpaupack and Siegfried, and the construction of the 220,000-volt transmission system that tied the hydroelectric project into the PP&L grid.

"The station has been laid out so as to require a minimum of operating attendance," the Bond & Share engineers wrote, "and an attempt was made to group all auxiliary equipment and all control and indicating apparatus on one floor in plain view of the operator and within easy access. This was completely accomplished with the exception of the exciters, which are direct-connected and are mounted on top of the generators, and the exciter rheostats, which are operated from the control room. This results in the second floor being the operating floor, with the third floor purely a maintenance and repair floor, where all types of equipment from waterwheels to transformers can be easily handled and dismantled."

Located on the Lackawaxen River adjacent to the Erie Railroad, the substructure for the powerhouse was built on ledge rock, except for one corner of the building, which was supported on steel and concrete piles. Still in service today, the powerhouse itself is 130 feet long and 75 feet wide. The structural steel frame

> *The actual engineering and construction of the project was handled by Phoenix Utility Co., an Electric Bond and Share Co. subsidiary formed in 1919.*

weighs 220 tons, and the powerhouse contains 6,100 yards of concrete. The walls are faced with 330,000 bricks.

Inside the powerhouse, two I.P. Morris vertical reaction turbines develop 28,500-horsepower apiece. The turbines utilize 330 feet of head and run at 300 r.p.m. The turbines are connected to the

Westinghouse vertical generators by a shaft 39 feet long. The two generators are rated at 20,000 kilowatts apiece, generating 11,000 volts of three-phase, 60-cycle alternating current. The generator shaft is cushioned by 40-inch Kingsbury thrust bearings. A complete shop and garage are located about 200 feet west of the powerhouse, and a village for the operators of the station, consisting of six tile and stucco houses, was located about one-quarter mile west of the station along the road to Hawley.

Perhaps the most striking landmark at the hydroelectric station is the 2.4 million gallon Johnson differential-type surge tank, dominating the hill above the powerhouse. Rising 135 feet above the surrounding countryside, the surge tank in later years was affectionately known to Wallenpaupack operators as "the Green Goose," so named for its coat of green paint. The surge tank was the terminus

for a wood-stave flow line extending from the reservoir intake more than 3-1/2 miles away. With a 14-foot diameter, the flow line—made out of Douglas fir staves from the Pacific Northwest—rested on nearly 2,300 steel and concrete saddles. The water delivered to the surge tank from the flow line passed into two plate steel penstocks, each 414 feet long and eight feet, nine inches in diameter. The penstocks deliver water to the turbines some 300 feet down the hill from the surge tank.

The construction of the dam, tailrace, flow lines, surge tank, penstocks and powerhouse between 1924 and 1926 was a gargantuan task. "Material for the earth embankment for Wallenpaupack Dam and for Tafton Dike was secured from borrow pits near the structures," Silver and Clogher wrote in *Electrical World Magazine*. "Gravel from a hill near the dam provided excellent aggregate for all of the concrete for the job, after being washed, screened and reassembled.

"A standard-gage (sic) construction railroad was built from the Honesdale branch of the Erie Railroad at the generating station to the dam. This railroad paralleled the flow line and wall used for placing all the materials in the pipe and its foundation. There were no unusual problems in the construction of the development, but it was necessary to construct the tailrace bridge without interfering with traffic on the Erie Railroad, this traffic being extremely heavy, as it is a direct route from the anthracite coal regions to New York."

Major construction equipment used during the two-year project included four 40-ton locomotives operating on four miles of railroad spur and hauling two flat cars and eight dump cars. There was also a gasoline section motor car in use on the railroad tracks. The crew used two 5-ton Caterpillar tractors, three 1.5-yard steam shovels, five 3/4-yard steam shovels, a 13-ton road roller, four road graders and two 30-ton locomotive cranes. Crews moved construction equipment onto the site in the spring of 1924 and began actual construction work on May 1, 1924. Just over 25 months later, on June 3, 1926, the two units at Wallenpaupack hydroelectric station went on line.

Upgrading the Siegfried Substation

The construction of the Wallenpaupack hydroelectric project was only one component of the mid-1920s expansion of the PP&L system. To use the electric power generated at Wallenpaupack, PP&L had to upgrade both its transmission system and series of substations serving the eastern Pennsylvania grid. "The transmission of the output from the 40,000-kwh Wallenpaupack generating

station over the 65 miles to Siegfried does not, in itself, warrant a 220-kv installation," Silver and Clogher wrote in their after-action report. "Several years ago, when the present system was being organized through the consolidation of several smaller systems, a development looking to the future growth was worked out. This plan was based upon the building up of a 66-kv, 60-cycle network for transmission and main distribution duty, with a later step of 220-kv as a standard trunk voltage."

The Phoenix Utility Co. engineers decided that it wouldn't be economical to transmit electric power from Wallenpaupack over 66-kv circuits. They also expected to bring additional energy into the

By the 1940s, like a giant garden soaker hose, the original 14-foot diameter wooden flow line began to leak generous amounts of water. For that reason, it was replaced by a steel pipe in the 1950s.

Dark as a coal bin at midnight is a fair description of working conditions inside the Wallenpaupack flow line. Here workers repair the head gate, which separates the lake from the rest of the line. circa 1957

Prior to construction of the Wallenpaupack to Siegfried line, high voltage transmission lines were not designed well enough to withstand the sheets of ice that were typical of the region's storm season. These towers along the Harwood-Hauto line couldn't hold up to the storm of Dec. 6-7, 1914.

PP&L system from possible steam and hydroelectric stations to be built along the Susquehanna River. Another possibility that the engineers weighed was the installation of additional generating capacity at Wallenpaupack.

The key to upgrading the utility's system was the expansion of PP&L's Siegfried substation, 10 miles north of Allentown and 65 miles south of Wallenpaupack. Siegfried operated at 66,000 volts, and upgrading the substation to 220,000 volts involved major expansion work, including the installation of the world's largest-capacity single-phase transformers. Unlike today's air- and oil-cooled transformers, the water-cooled transformers installed at Siegfried in 1926 consisted of huge units resembling giant water tanks, approximately 10 feet in diameter and 15 feet high. The substation even had a spray pond to handle its water cooling needs.

"At Siegfried, water is pumped from deep wells into supply mains, which connect in multiple into a storage tank, a spray pond reservoir and the transformer distribution manifolds," Silver and Clogher explained. "The feed into the spray pond reservoir is controlled by a float valve. The normal supply into the transformer manifolds is from an addi-

tional main direct from the spray pond reservoir. The water level in the storage tank is approximately 120 feet, and in the spray pond reservoir approximately 100 feet above the base of the transformers."

But it was the 220,000-volt line between Wallenpaupack and Siegfried that tested the ingenuity of the Electric Bond and Share Co. engineers who designed it. "In undertaking the design of this line, it was recognized that excessively heavy sleets prevail through the territory to be traversed," Silver and Clogher explained. "A careful study showed that the severity and frequency of the sleet loads were greatest above an elevation of about 1,000 feet, and especially so over the highest ridges."

The Electric Bond and Share Co. engineers came up with what later observers called "an elegant solution" to the sleet problem. They used clamps to hold the conductors firmly to the steel transmission towers under normal circumstances. But under the line loading and line breakage conditions experienced in sleet storms, the clamps in the suspension anchor would slip and give the line slack, thereby keeping the tower from being toppled. "It was recognized that repair of a tower failure is far more serious than repair of a conductor failure and that a high-strength conductor of the order required, if firmly attached to supporting towers of sufficient strength to withstand the unbalanced pull of one or more broken conductors, would cause these towers to be excessively heavy and expensive," Silver and Clogher noted. "The conductor attachment therefore incorporates a clamp designed with a grip adequate for any differential in tension in the conductor while intact, but which will slip and relieve the tower at an unbalance of tension well under that which would occur with the conductor broken."

For corner and dead-end structures, the engineers substituted strong, simple, straight steel girders that stand vertically and are held in position by strong guy wires, much the same way that telecommunications towers are held safely in position today. "The mast of the guyed structure for angles and dead ends is a fabricated steel column terminating in a ball-and-socket support at the base to avoid all bending stresses," Silver and Clogher reported. "It was designed in standard sections of such lengths as to enable assembling in any desired overall height in increments of approximately five feet."

Construction of the Wallenpaupack to Siegfried line was a trendsetter in another important area of high-voltage transmission line operation. Between 1926 and 1930, Pennsylvania Power & Light Co., Electric Bond and Share Co. and General Electric cooperated in a landmark study on lightning using the Wallenpaupack-Siegfried 220,000-volt line as one of the major facilities for the investigation.

Before 1926, transmission line engineers operated from the assumption that "lightning involved a bound charge on the earth due to cloud field, the sudden release of this charge and generation of steep wave-front and high-voltage surges," PP&L engineers Edgar Bell and F.W. Packer reported in a 1942 paper before the American Institute of Electrical Engineers (AIEE). "Because of this general conception, overhead ground wires were not considered worth their cost, and tower-footing grounding was seldom talked of."

In its first 18 months of operation, the Wallenpaupack-Siegfried line was not equipped with overhead ground wires. The line "operated very poorly," Bell and Packer reported, with 27 lightning trip-

outs. "In addition, lightning caused a Wallenpaupack transformer to fail within 3-1/2 months, and a second transformer failed three weeks later. The line was then operated at 66-kv, and all transformers at Wallenpaupack and Siegfried were rebuilt at the factory."

During 1927, a total of 24 line miles of the Wallenpaupack-Siegfried line were equipped with conventional overhead ground wires spaced 10 feet, six inches above the conductors. That didn't stop the trip-outs entirely, but it was a big help. By the 1930 storm season, the engineers were supplementing the overhead ground wire with buried tower footing grounding cable. Insulator flashovers, a common problem during the 1910s and 1920s, declined dramatically, dropping from 74 a year to 20 a year on the Wallenpaupack-Siegfried line.

Lightning investigations continued on the Wallenpaupack-Siegfried line through

---

Between 1926 and 1930, Pennsylvania Power & Light Co., Electric Bond and Share Co. and General Electric cooperated in a landmark study on lightning using the Wallenpaupack-Siegfried 220,000-volt line as one of the major facilities for the investigation.

---

the 1930s. The 65-mile line across the rugged terrain of the Pocono Mountains advanced the theory and science of high-voltage transmission networks in the United States, and proved to be the backbone of the growing Pennsylvania Power & Light Co. system.

Moving the Purdytown Cemetery

The inundation of a hydroelectric reservoir typically entails at least some relocation of residents. Farms, barns, roads and other infrastructure in the path of the rising water must be moved to higher ground. When Lake Wallenpaupack filled in during the summer of 1924, Pennsylvania Power & Light Co. was faced with the ticklish task of moving an entire cemetery to higher ground.

At first, PP&L staff thought there were approximately 20 bodies buried in the Purdytown cemetery on what was then known as the Maud Andrews property in Paupack Township of Wayne County. But by the time the cemetery was moved to a new site along the Wilsonville-Lakeville Road in Paupack Township, contractors had identified 54 bodies in the 100-year-old burial ground.

In a June 10, 1924, Wayne County court order, Pennsylvania Power & Light Co. was given authorization to move the Purdy Cemetery about one-half mile, out of the path of the waters backed up by the dam being built near Wilsonville. The family cemetery had been abandoned for at least 50 years, and PP&L had advertised in the local *Hawley Times* its intentions of moving the cemetery that summer. Since "no relatives or friends of the dead having asked for permission to remove the remains at their own expenses," the court ordered that PP&L could remove the bodies at its own expense. PP&L contracted with Hawley undertaker George Teeter to move the bodies from the Purdy Cemetery to the new burial ground. Teeter was to be paid a flat rate of $450 for moving what was originally estimated to be 20 bodies. Work on relocating the Purdy Cemetery began the third week of August.

At first, rumors in the surrounding communities suggested that workmen had found no bodies. "It has been reported that workmen have been unable to find any trace of coffins or bodies in a large number of graves," a news item in the *Sunbury Daily Item* of Aug. 20, 1924, reported. "Is the removal of markers and tombstones equivalent to removal of bodies from their graves?"

In reality, the opposite was the case. Teeter and his crew found human remains in nearly every grave. Tracing burial records in the county courthouse, Teeter found that the earliest burials in the Purdy Cemetery dated to 1810. Elder William Purdy, the pastor of the Baptist Church of Palmyra and his wife Rachel, the people for whom the cemetery was named, were buried within four years of each other between 1824 and 1828. All told, there were considerably more than 20 burials in the cemetery. "After the old site was thoroughly cleared of trees and underbrush in preparing to open the graves, it was found that there were more graves there than the original count seemed to show when Mr. Teeter and I made this count together," PP&L's W.C. Anderson wrote John Wise in Allentown on August 7. "There are 27 or 28 well-marked graves having one or two stone markers each, instead of 20 as we previously thought were there, and there are plain indications of still more graves which are not so distinctly marked with the names of individuals buried in them."

All told, there were 56 graves in the Purdy Cemetery. In a commentary on the child mortality rate in the 19th century, at least 30 of the bodies in the cemetery were infants or children. PP&L agreed to pay Teeter $20 per body for moving and reinterring the bodies in the cemetery, and the job was essentially completed by the end of August 1924. It was one of the more unique relocation efforts of the hydroelectric era in Pennsylvania.

(illustration by Brent Schaefer © 1995)

15

Electrifying the Sinews of Production

The combination of refined electric motors, expansion and development of high-voltage transmission networks, and the emergence of large central stations, like Hauto, made it possible for manufacturers to electrify factory floors in the early 1900s.

The 1920s consolidation of the electrical systems serving central and eastern Pennsylvania made possible the rapid electrification of industry in the Pennsylvania Power & Light Co. service territory. By the mid- to late-1890s, electric power began to serve a host of demands for motive power in emerging U.S. industries. Processes like electrochemicals, electroplating and arc welding—all of which would assume increasing importance in the automobile and truck manufacturing industries—were particularly suited to the adaptation of electric power. Electric utilities were particularly interested in adding industrial load to their system, since factories typically improved the daytime load of central station electric power plants, which in the early days ran to meet the peak demand of the evening lighting load.

The emergence of large central station generating units like Hauto and Harwood during World War I, and more importantly, the technological development of high-voltage transmission networks, made industrial loads increasingly attractive to utilities like PP&L. Finally, the refinement of the electric motor opened up a world of opportunity for the electrification of the factory floor. "The ability to match each machine with an appropriate motor opened endless possibilities for factories to mechanize

---

Assembly of a Model T Ford in the spring of 1913—before Ford installed his first assembly line—took more than 12 hours of labor. One year later, ...assembly took one hour and 33 minutes.

Factory electrification revolutionized production of the automobile, which led to mass production assembly lines.

and reorganize work according to the popular principles of scientific management," electric utility historian Harold L. Platt wrote in 1991.

Electric motors were primarily responsible for increased productivity in American manufacturing after about 1910. Their precision made design improvements in machinery a reachable goal for industrial engineers. The electric motor, noted *American Machinist* in 1916, "permitted far more precise testing and experimentation than had been possible before." The electric motor also led to design modifications in factory machinery that provided increased flexibility over the steam-driven belt apparatus that had powered most factory floors in the late 19th century. It was little wonder that American manufacturers placed orders for a quarter million electric motors in the year 1909 alone.

Since each machine could have its own motor drive, factories no longer had to be

built three and four stories high to accommodate steam boilers and moving lines of vertical belts. Flexibility in factory design also was enhanced by the addition of electric cranes, ventilating systems, elevators and lighting systems.

The introduction of the electric motor in the first three decades of the 20th century was epitomized by Henry Ford's installation of the nation's first moving assembly line at his Rouge plant outside Detroit in 1913. David Nye, an electric utility historian who has written extensively on the electrification of the nation's manufacturing sector, pointed out that Ford combined five practices in the installation of his first moving assembly line. "The combination of these five practices," Nye wrote, "—subdivision of labor, interchangeable parts, single-function machines, sequential ordering of machines and the moving belt or line—defines the assembly line.

"Factory electrification was the necessary precondition before these elements could be improved individually and then welded together into a new form of production." Indeed, the new form of production brought about a quantum leap in productivity on the factory floor. Assembly of a Model T Ford in the spring of 1913—before Ford installed his first assembly line—took more than 12 hours of labor. One year later, after Ford had shocked the American business community by offering workers at the Rouge plant a $5 daily wage, assembly of a Model T took one hour and 33 minutes.

For Pennsylvania Power & Light Co., the electrification of the industrial base of central and eastern Pennsylvania during the 1920s was a symbiotic relationship that characterized the company's destiny for much of the next half-century. As the electric company made more electric power available, the factories in the utility's service territory rapidly absorbed the surplus electric power. As industry continued its rapid pace of electrification, PP&L continued the capital investments that made more and more electric power available for industry.

An Industrial Colossus

The Pennsylvania Power & Light Co. service territory in the 1920s was admirably suited for industrial expansion. Colonial ironmongers had located their foundries and beehive coke ovens in the valleys of central and eastern Pennsylvania because of the abundance of natural resources and the transportation networks that linked the region to the population centers of Philadelphia and New York. Anthracite coal mining had been a mainstay of the region's economy since Josiah White had founded the Lehigh Coal and Navigation Co. in the early decades of the 19th century, and Charles Schwab had made Bethlehem and the adjacent Lehigh River Valley a center of integrated steelmaking in the first decade of the 20th century.

North and east of Allentown, the Portland Cement industry had made eastern Pennsylvania synonymous with cement production in the United States. Allentown boasted a thriving truck-manufacturing industry, and towns up and down the Lehigh River had thriving silk mills at the turn of the century. Communities like Wilkes-Barre, Harrisburg and Hershey pointed with pride to a diverse economic base, including everything from the machine-tool industry to chocolate to glassmaking and leather tanning. All would be transformed in the 1920s and the 1930s by the addition of bountiful supplies of low-cost, efficient industrial electric power. "Pennsylvania uses as much power in industry as any two states in the United States," Walter F. Rittman and Sumner B. Ely reported to Gov. Gifford Pinchot's Giant Power survey in 1923. "In the year 1922, this energy amounted to approximately 13 billion kilowatt-hours…. This means that the manpower of the commonwealth was augmented by water and fuel power equivalent to 2,000,000 horses working continuously day and night throughout the year. Five counties alone use more power than the entire state of Ohio."

Rittman and Ely reported that by 1922, more than 25 percent of the power consumed by energy in Pennsylvania was provided by electric utilities from central-station generating units. "The recent developments in industry have been for the industries to purchase more and more of their power in the form of electric energy from large central-power generating plants," they noted. "Except under special conditions, the small, isolated power plant appears to be doomed. The trend has been to substitute electrical power for mechanical power."

The value of Pennsylvania's manufactured products in 1922 was second in the U.S. only to New York. The 4.63 million horsepower installed in Pennsylvania industry in 1922 was 15.25 percent of the nation's total. Yet Pennsylvania's population was only 8.15 percent of the U.S. population. Of the nearly 13 billion kilowatt-hours of energy consumed in 1922, slightly more than three billion

> *By 1922, more than 25 percent of the power consumed by energy in Pennsylvania was provided by electric utilities from central-station generating units.*

Bethlehem Steel Co., along with the rest of the iron and steel industry, burned millions of tons of Pennsylvania coal to make electric power for its mills and shops. *(photo courtesy of Hugh Moore Museum and Library)*

kilowatt-hours were generated and sold by the state's electric utilities.

In 1928, the Allentown Chamber of Commerce conducted a survey of business and industry in the Lehigh Valley. The Chamber reported that Pennsylvania Power & Light Co. had an installed capacity of 280,000 kilowatts from five large steam plants and one large waterpower facility. The company had access to another 750,000 kilowatts from interconnections it had established with neighboring utilities, including the Philadelphia Electric Co. "Allentown is now ready to serve the largest industries with an adequate supply of power," the chamber survey concluded. "The growth of Allentown can well be illustrated by the fact that the number of customers supplied by the company increased 230 percent in the 10 years from 1916 to 1926, and the consumption of electricity in the same period increased 326 percent."

Industries in the Mid-Atlantic region in 1919 were already deriving 35 percent of their energy needs from purchased electric power driving electric motors. The survey noted that in PP&L's service territory in 1919, electric motors had already made substantial inroads on the factory floor. In Lehigh County, the federal survey counted 1,540 electric motors operated by purchased electric power, more than nine times the 161 steam engines reported in the survey.

There were more than 1,000 electric motors reported in Dauphin County, compared with 157 steam engines, and the 560 electric motors in Northumberland County outnumbered the 95 steam engines by a margin of five to one. In Schuylkill County, electrification of the anthracite mining industry was reflected in the fact that electric motors driven by

purchased power outnumbered steam engines five to one.

Electrifying the Portland Cement Industry

The electrification of the cement industry in the Lehigh Valley during the 1910s and 1920s was a Pennsylvania Power & Light Co. success story. "The Lehigh District in Pennsylvania not only witnessed the founding of the industry but soon became the largest Portland cement-producing center in the country," a 1929 industry brochure reported. "By 1890, the mills in the Lehigh Valley produced 60 percent of the total output of the United States. By 1900, this figure had increased to 72.6 percent."

The cost of transporting bulk cement to population centers outside the Mid-Atlantic region soon led to the construction of Portland Cement plants around the country, and a corresponding drop in the percentage of Portland Cement produced in the Lehigh Valley. The valley's proportion of national production dropped to 34 percent in 1910 and to just over 25 percent in 1920. Still, the 23 mills located in the Lehigh Valley accounted for 40 million barrels of annual production in 1920, making the Lehigh Valley the largest cement-producing region in the United States.

The Lehigh Portland Cement Co. was the valley's largest producer. Founded in 1897 by Gen. Harry C. Trexler, John Ormrod and Col. E.M. Young, the company built its first mill in North Whitehall Township the following year. Trexler, who had already established himself as an investor and executive with the electric street railway companies serving the Lehigh Valley, became the first president of Lehigh Portland Cement Co. During the first 10 years of his presidency, the company built a total of seven plants, five in the Lehigh District and two in Indiana. During the 1910-1920 period, another

Col. Edward M. Young

Gen. Harry C. Trexler, along with John Ormrod and Col. E.M. Young, founded the Lehigh Portland Cement Co. in 1897. In this photo, Trexler (right) talks with Allentown Mayor Malcolm Gross at the groundbreaking for the Americus Hotel in July 1926. (photo courtesy of the Morning Call)

eight plants were built or acquired from other companies, stretching across the country from Pennsylvania to Washington state.

High on Trexler's list of priorities for the industry was electrification of production. By 1919, cement production in the Mid-Atlantic region, which for all intents and purposes was confined to the Lehigh Valley, utilized more than 3,000 electric motors, generating nearly 130,000 horsepower of energy. Nearly 2,000 motors—about two-thirds of the total—were run on power purchased from an electric utility supplier, the vast majority coming from Pennsylvania Power & Light Co. Northampton County, where the bulk of the cement manufacturers were located, had the fourth largest amount of installed industrial horsepower in the state, as reported in the 1923 Giant Power survey.

Portland Cement manufacture was perhaps as energy-intensive as any industry in the United States at that time. Limestone was first quarried and then fed through electric-driven crushers capable of reducing rock the size of a piano.

Secondary crushers reduced the rock to a uniform size capable of passing through the grinding mill. "The next major step involves heating the raw materials to temperatures between 2,400 and 2,800 degrees Fahrenheit," a 1937 newspaper article explained, "at which they melt—reaching the point of 'incipient fusion' in scientific terms. This process takes place in huge cylindrical steel kilns from 8 to 14 feet in diameter and from 125 to 325 feet long. These kilns lined with fire brick are mounted with the long axis nearly horizontal, inclining slightly with the discharge of the lower end and revolving slowly. The finely ground materials are fed into the higher end. At the lower end of the kiln, there is a roaring blast of flame produced by blowing powder coal, oil or natural gas into the kiln."

The waste-heat from the kilns accounted for the large number of electric motors run by current generated in the plant. In 1919, cement producers consumed some two million tons of Pennsylvania coal, and captured the waste heat from the firing process in the kilns to run generators to power more than 1,000

Portland Cement manufacture was perhaps as energy-intensive as any industry in the United States at that time.

The 23 Portland Cement Co. mills in Lehigh Valley made it the largest cement-producing region in the U.S. in 1920. *(photo courtesy of the Lehigh County Historical Society)*

electric motors. Gen. Trexler's Lehigh Portland Cement Co. was on the cutting edge of a technology that later generations of engineers would identify as "cogeneration."

Way Down in the Mine

The state's two biggest industries, iron and steel and coal mining, were well on the way to being electrified in the 1920s, with one major difference. The iron and steel industry, in keeping with its traditional development as an integrated industry, generated much of the power it used internally in the 1920s. The state's number one county for industrial energy consumption was Allegheny County in and around Pittsburgh, the home of U.S. Steel and other giant steel manufacturers. Like the cement industry, the iron and steel industry burned millions of tons of Pennsylvania coal in its steel-making process and used both waste heat and straight coal-fired generation to make electric power for its mills and shops. U.S. Steel and Bethlehem Steel Co., which was located in the Pennsylvania Power & Light Co. service territory, would not supplement their own internally generated electric power requirements with purchased power until the onset of World War II in the 1940s.

The anthracite coal industry on the other hand had a long tradition of buying power from Pennsylvania Power & Light Co. and other electric utilities. Both the Harwood and Hauto plants had originally been owned by coal companies, and anthracite producers had begun electrifying their mines and collieries as early as the turn of the century. "Mine owners had many uses for electricity," David Nye noted in *Electrifying America*. "Electric lights gave safe illumination that did not exhaust scarce oxygen supplies. Electric alarm systems signaled danger or disaster. Electric drills were more portable than

In 1919, cement producers consumed some two million tons of Pennsylvania coal, and captured the waste heat from the firing process in the kilns to run generators to power more than 1,000 electric motors.

other drills."

Electricity eliminated the need for the huge pipes used to transport steam and compressed air in the mines, and portable electric pumps kept Pennsylvania's deep-shaft anthracite mines free of water. Electric hoists were easily installed and could haul more coal to the surface than steam hoists of similar size. By 1904, General Electric had developed a strong business in mining machinery sales, with most of its sales coming from the anthracite and bituminous coal mines of Pennsylvania and West Virginia. "The greatest single change electricity made in the mines was the elimination of mules, which were replaced by more powerful electric locomotives," Nye explained. Electromotive power brought about as much of a transformation underground as it did above ground with the electric street railway systems of central and eastern Pennsylvania.

PP&L targeted the region's anthracite mines as potential customers all through the 1920s. A typical effort came to fruition in the fall of 1930 when the company entered into a long-term contract to supply the Philadelphia and Reading Coal and Iron Co. with its electrical requirements, amounting to 30,000 kilowatts, and with a prospect of reaching 60,000 kilowatts. As part of the negotiations for the new contract, PP&L agreed to buy the equipment and facilities that the anthracite company had used for generating its internal electric power requirement.

By 1930, the anthracite coal industry in Pennsylvania was well into what would be a decades-long decline. Pennsylvania Power & Light Co. had helped electrify the sinews of the state's industrial production during the 1920s, and industrial electrification would pick up during the 1930s, even though the Great Depression would throw an economic damper over the rapid pace of industrialization. By the 1930s, the waterpower resources of the Susquehanna River would be developed further, leading to the increased electrification of the industrial and rural segments of southeastern Pennsylvania's economy.

The General

Long before Americans got in the habit of calling David Sarnoff, the ruthless executive of RCA/Victor, "the General," the only "General" most Pennsylvanians knew was Harry Clay Trexler. Traction magnate, cement company executive, soldier, philanthropist and benefactor to Allentown and the Lehigh Valley, Trexler was one of the founders of Pennsylvania Power & Light Co. His wide variety of business interests, his lifelong concern with conservation and his sense of civic responsibility marked Trexler as a unique representative of the Progressive era in Pennsylvania society. When he died in an automobile accident in November 1933, the *Allentown Morning Call* eulogized what it called the city's "first citizen. He had a new conception of the responsibilities of wealth, but better than that, he loved to do good for his fellow men."

Harry Clay Trexler was born in Easton on April 17, 1854. It was seven years before the outbreak of the Civil War, and the Lehigh Valley was enjoying one of its periodic boom times. Allentown and surrounding areas were the hub of a thriving iron smelting industry, and the region's immense anthracite coal deposits were rapidly being opened up by canals and railroads. Trexler's father moved to Allentown soon after Harry's birth and started a very successful lumber business.

Trexler entered the family lum-

General Trexler rides proudly on his white horse, Jack o' Diamonds, in the October 1918 Liberty Bond Parade. *(photo courtesy of the Morning Call)*

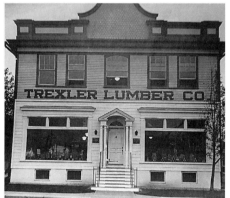

The Trexler Lumber Co. was started by Harry Trexler's father. The Allentown lumber company became one of the city's best-known businesses. *(photo courtesy of the Morning Call) circa 1928*

ber business at a difficult time in Allentown's history. The region's iron industry evaporated during the 1870s when the introduction of the Bessemer process—and its need for bituminous metallurgical coking coals—resulted in a relocation of the bulk of the iron and steel industry to the Monongahela River Valley on the other side of the state. At the same time, the Pennsylvania-German culture in which Trexler had grown up gradually gave way—first to the more dominant English influence of the region, and second, to the waves of immigration that began to leave their mark in the 1880s.

Trexler built the Trexler Lumber Co. of Allentown into one of the city's best-known businesses. The firm had timber operations in the Williamsport region, sawmills and timber lands in Mississippi, North Carolina and Virginia, and distribution yards in Portsmouth, Va., and Newark, N.J. But by the 1890s, Trexler was convinced that the building industry—his primary market—would increasingly rely on structural steel instead of longleaf yellow pine for its raw material. Structural steel, which was being made in Bethlehem, required Portland Cement for a base.

In 1897, Trexler, John D. Ormrod and Col. E.M. Young formed the Lehigh Portland Cement Co. and built a mill in North Whitehall Township. Over the next third of a century, Allentown and the surrounding Lehigh Valley would become the cradle of the American Portland Cement industry, thanks in part to Trexler's leadership.

Trexler also got involved early on in building the utility infrastructure of the Lehigh Valley. Trexler's utility interests included the electric, water and telephone services in Allentown. He also consolidated a number of the financially unsuccessful electric street railway ventures of the area into the Lehigh Valley Transit Co., serving as the firm's president prior to the merger with Pennsylvania Power & Light Co. in 1920. Trexler's reputation for financial acumen led Sidney Zollicoffer Mitchell to ask the Allentown resident to serve on PP&L's first board of directors. Later, Trexler served on the board of directors of National Power & Light Co., one of the subholding companies owned by Mitchell's Electric Bond and Share Co.

For much of his adult life, Trexler served with the Pennsylvania National Guard. In 1916, when President Woodrow Wilson mobilized the National Guard for border duty during the Mexican insurrection, then Colonel Trexler served as quartermaster for the Pennsylvania units, at one time writing a personal check to cover the payroll for troops departing for border duty at El Paso, Texas. During World War I, Trexler, by then a General, again mobilized Pennsylvania troops for service in Europe; he retired as a Brigadier General with full military honors at the age of 65 in April 1918. At the age when most men slow down and sit back, Trexler continued his activities full-bore past the age of 65. From his offices in the Young Building at Hall and Hamilton streets in Allentown, Trexler supervised his growing empire of businesses. The Lehigh Portland Cement Co. remained the nerve center of Trexler's business inter-

General and Mrs. Trexler in 1933. *(photo courtesy of the* Morning Call*)*

ests, but there were countless other investments to watch over. From the turn of the century on, Trexler had been buying land outside Allentown, and by 1918, his Trexler farms and orchards were famous all over the Mid-Atlantic states. People drove from miles around to see Trexler's herd of bison at the farms.

Trexler's ownership interest in the Lehigh Valley Traction Co. translated into a significant investment position in National Power & Light Co., the Bond & Share subholding company that controlled PP&L. In 1917, Trexler exchanged his 6,290 shares of common stock and 2,100 shares of preferred stock in the transit company for 49,000 shares of common stock in Lehigh Power Securities Corp., the original vehicle Bond & Share used in the formation of PP&L. In the early 1920s, Trexler's shares in Lehigh Power Securities Corp. were transferred for 49,000 shares in National Power & Light Co.

From 1924 to 1931, Trexler invested heavily in electric utility stocks, often pledging collateral in the cement company to Philadelphia banks for cash loans. "If you want to experience a short winter," the General told his longtime aide, Nolan Benner, "just put your note in the bank in December to come due the first of April."

All through the 1920s, Trexler served on PP&L's board of directors, and after 1925, he also served on the board of directors of National Power & Light Co. in New York. Trexler and Paul B. Sawyer, the National Power & Light Co. executive responsible for PP&L, developed a lasting friendship. Sawyer valued Trexler's common sense advice about utility matters. According to Benner, Trexler was primarily responsible for the selection of John Wise as the second president of PP&L. At the company's board meeting in New York City in the fall of 1928, the matter of a replacement for E.K. Hall, PP&L's first president, came before the directors. Trexler suggested Wise. Mitchell agreed that Wise had all the qualifications, but he opposed the former Harwood Electric Co. engineer for a simple reason: Wise was too short.

At five feet, five inches, Wise just didn't have the imposing stature for the job a six-footer would have, Mitchell explained. Directors were asked to bring additional suggestions to the next board meeting. Trexler, who still thought his suggestion had been the right choice, told Wise of Mitchell's objections when he returned to Allentown.

Wise reminded General Trexler, a military man, that the biblical David who slew Goliath, Napoleon Bonaparte and Gen. U.S. Grant were all approximately five feet, five inches tall. Trexler asked Wise to dictate a memo to that effect, and he made sure to read the memo to the directors at the next board meeting. The vote to name Wise, the company's operating manager, as president was unanimous.

Trexlertown farms and orchards were famous all over the Mid-Atlantic states. Here, Trexler admires his orchard. (*photo courtesy of the* **Morning Call**) *circa 1920s*

A Legacy for the Ages

On Nov. 16, 1933, Trexler came to his office at the Young Building at the usual time and announced to Benner that he had to attend a National Power & Light Co. board meeting that day in New York. Benner told him that Route 22 East had some icy patches, but the General replied that he thought the sunshine later in the day would melt the ice. He called for his Cadillac coupe, and his chauffeur picked him up about 10 a.m.

On the return trip to Allentown, the Cadillac slid on a patch of ice and collided with an oil truck in Wilson Borough just outside Easton. The 79-year-old Trexler was taken to the Easton Hospital and lingered through the night before dying just before 4 a.m. on Nov. 17, 1933. Trexler's chauffeur, who survived the accident, later told Benner that George Frazier, a Philadelphia banker who served on the board of directors of National Power & Light Co. with Trexler, cornered the General on the street outside the company's corporate headquarters at Two Rector Street and suggested that the

Harry Clay Trexler was born in Easton on April 17, 1854, and died at age 79 on Nov. 17, 1933.

two men get dinner in New York and take the late train down to Frazier's home. "Your chauffeur can call for you in the morning," Frazier told Trexler that November evening. "George, I'd like to accept your invitation," Trexler told his fellow director, "but I promised my wife that I would return in time to have dinner with her." Ironically, Frazier survived Trexler by only a week; he was killed when his automobile collided with a streetcar in the Elkins Park section of Philadelphia.

It seemed that half of Allentown turned out for the General's funeral, and for good reason. After bequeathing $150,000 to each of his two brothers, various smaller bequests to his loyal staff and providing for his widow (who would live until 1935), Trexler left the bulk of his estate to a charitable trust. Benefiting were Lehigh County hospitals, churches, institutions for the handicapped, the Young Womens' Christian Association, Boy Scouts "and any other worthy organizations which have for their object, and which truly serve, the benefit of mankind."

Trexler also directed that following his wife's death, Springwood, his Allentown estate, be given to the city of Allentown for use as a public park. Trexler's wild game park in Upper Whitehall Township was similarly given to Lehigh County for use as a park. Trexler's estate left $250,000 for the perpetual maintenance of Springwood and $150,000 for the perpetual maintenance of the game park property.

A measure of the high regard in which Trexler held his colleagues at PP&L and National Power & Light Co. was the fact that all three people who witnessed Trexler's last will and testament were affiliated with the Allentown utility. Paul B. Sawyer, the general manager of National Power & Light Co., C.M. Walter, PP&L's treasurer, and Samuel Weil, Sawyer's personal secretary, all witnessed the will on April 15, 1929.

Harry C. Trexler was exactly the type of person needed by early 20th-century America. A business executive, entrepreneur and philanthropist, he endeavored to leave the world a little bit better than he had found it. "Of such characters who served well their fellow men," the Morning Call concluded in its editorial eulogy, "the ancients made gods and demi-gods. Allentown, in his lifetime, esteemed General Trexler as its first citizen. In death, it treasures him as its most precious memory."

16

River of Power

The turbulent Susquehanna River is an ideal power source. This photo was taken just below Holtwood Dam during the flood of 1936.

Since 1910, the Susquehanna River has fueled the Holtwood plant and the growing community of the same name.

Unlike many river systems, the Susquehanna River was far from tapped out as a power source in the latter 1920s. Philadelphia Electric Co. proved that point eloquently in 1928 when it built a massive hydroelectric facility on the river at Conowingo, just south of the Maryland border. As far back as the first decade of the century, John Abbett Walls had contemplated building a hydroelectric dam at the site just above the Chesapeake Bay, but Walls' Pennsylvania Water & Power Co. had eventually decided to build a hydroelectric facility at McCall's Ferry, farther north on the river.

Philadelphia Electric Co. had embarked on a crash program of building coal-fired generation in the decade following World War I. The use of electricity in the home by residents of Philadelphia, America's third largest city in the 1920s, had skyrocketed after 1910. Philadelphia Electric Co.'s customer base had nearly tripled in the 1920s, from

Residents of Holtwood collecting old clothes for Belgian Relief in the fall of 1918. The coal-fired electric boom of the 1920s was just stoking up.

103,000 customers in 1918 to 306,000 customers five years later.

Like residents in Allentown, Scranton and Lancaster, customers were no longer content with single electric lights on drop cords. Increased appliance usage had caused demand to rise dramatically on the Philadelphia Electric Co. system, and the company responded by significantly adding to its power generation.

In 1918, the company built two units of its four-unit Chester station south of the city; an additional two units were added in 1924. A total of 180,000 kilowatts was added in six units at the Delaware station between 1920 and 1924; and Units 10 and 11 at the Richmond station came on line in 1925 and 1926. The two Richmond units added 120,000 kilowatts to Philadelphia Electric Co.'s generation mix.

Philadelphia Electric Co. also was beginning to supply power to neighboring utilities. In 1923, the Philadelphia utility installed a high-voltage tie between the Delaware station and the Camden substation of Public Service Electric and Gas across the Delaware River. PSE&G was in dire need of additional generation, and the 26,000-volt underwater cable helped, since Philadelphia Electric Co. was able to carry some of the rapidly growing industrial load in Camden.

Philadelphia Electric Co. and the utilities in the Mid-Atlantic region were struggling to keep up with demand in the 1920s. For the Philadelphia utility, the obvious solution was to add generation on the Susquehanna River. As early as 1916, Philadelphia Electric Co. and Pennsylvania Water & Power Co. had begun to study expansion of the river's hydroelectric resources, spurred in part by the Pennsylvania Railroad's wartime decision to electrify its main line between New York and Washington.

Through the mid-1920s, crews working for Philadelphia Electric Co. built the massive Conowingo hydroelectric dam. By 1928, what was then the second largest hydroelectric plant in the United States—after Niagara Falls—was on line.

Conowingo's seven generating units had a total capacity of 252,000 kilowatts. The construction involved the demolition of the steel railroad bridge across the Susquehanna, an event that was extensively covered in the nation's press. Construction of the hydroelectric dam also entailed building two 220,000-volt transmission lines to Plymouth Meeting

As early as 1916, Philadelphia Electric Co. and Pennsylvania Water & Power Co. had begun to study expansion of the river's hydroelectric resources.

substation, three 66,000-volt lines from Plymouth Meeting into the city of Philadelphia, and a 33,000-volt line to serve local customers in Hartford and Cecil counties, Maryland.

A run-of-river plant, which meant that it had no appreciable reservoir storage of its own, Conowingo produced a substantial percentage of Philadelphia Electric Co.'s system requirements through the 1930s and 1940s; as late as 1980, Conowingo provided close to 5 percent of the utility's generation mix. During periods of high flow, the plant was run as a baseload station. During the low flow periods of late summer and fall, Conowingo served as a peaking plant.

With the completion of the Conowingo plant in 1928, the generation picture in the Mid-Atlantic region brightened considerably. But the Susquehanna was still capable of generating even more hydroelectric power. First, however, the river would be put to use generating electric power from one of the more unique fossil fuel deposits in the United States, anthracite coal fines that clogged the Susquehanna River bottom from above Harrisburg all the way to Lake Aldred, the impoundment behind Holtwood Dam.

The Manor Coal Washing Plant

Pennsylvania Water & Power Co. had long studied a site at Safe Harbor, eight miles above its dam at Holtwood. By 1930, the Baltimore-based firm had 20 years of experience running Holtwood. That experience included building one of the most unique fossil fuel generating stations in the nation's electric utility history.

Ever since J.S. Battin had invented the first mechanical coal breaker at Minersville in Schuylkill County in 1845, millions of tons of culm—anthracite coal fines and wastes—had washed down the Susquehanna River all the way to the Chesapeake Bay. Early in the 20th century, the river frequently ran black all the way from Wilkes-Barre to McCall's Ferry. Coal is slightly heavier than water, and coal the size of sand created bars all the way to Harrisburg. Below the state capital, the anthracite wastes were finer than silt.

As early as the 1890s, entrepreneurs began dredging the river from Harrisburg south to recover the coal wastes. Dredged and dried, the culm that washed downriver was a perfectly acceptable boiler fuel. Residents of Harrisburg used the fuel to heat their homes, and industries in the Susquehanna Valley increasingly turned to culm to fire their boilers.

As early as 1909, dredgers reported recovering 107,800 tons of coal from the waters of the Susquehanna. By 1940, the recovery had reached nearly a million tons a year. Residents of Harrisburg joked that the fleet of dredging boats docked in the river near the state capital was the Susquehanna Navy.

Still, the millions of tons that continued to wash down the river from the anthracite regions farther north began to cause problems for Pennsylvania Water & Power Co.'s Holtwood Dam. The buildup of culm in Lake Aldred behind the dam began to concern Pennsylvania Water & Power Co.'s engineers. They feared that siltation would interrupt the river's flow past the dam. In 1925, Pennsylvania Water & Power Co. built an innovative coal-fired generating station at Holtwood to correct the problem of coal siltation.

Pennsylvania Water & Power Co. formed the Holtwood Coal Co. and the Anthracite Production Corp. to dredge coal out of the river, build a coal washing plant at the

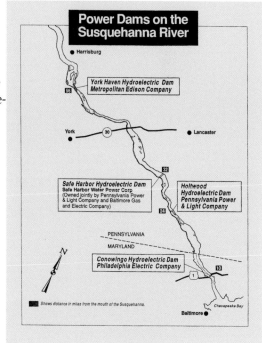

Cross Section through the Holtwood Power House

Power Dams on the Susquehanna River

Harrisburg

York Haven Hydroelectric Dam
Metropolitan Edison Company

York · 30 · Lancaster

Safe Harbor Hydroelectric Dam
Safe Harbor Water Power Corp.
(Owned jointly by Pennsylvania Power & Light Company and Baltimore Gas and Electric Company)

Holtwood Hydroelectric Dam
Pennsylvania Power & Light Company

PENNSYLVANIA
MARYLAND

Conowingo Hydroelectric Dam
Philadelphia Electric Company

Chesapeake Bay

Baltimore

Shows distance in miles from the mouth of the Susquehanna.

Cross Section through the Safe Harbor Power House

Holtwood hydroelectric site and burn the recovered coal in an adjacent steam electric generating facility.

Prior to the construction of the first units at the steam plant at Holtwood, most steam generation units in the United States burned coal on a grate.

The Manor coal washing plant, as it was known at the time, was unique. Holtwood became the only power plant in the world to combine both a hydro-electric station and fossil-fueled station on the same site. Sternwheel dredges contracted by Pennsylvania Water & Power Co. plied back and forth across the waters of Lake Aldred, dredging coal and providing raw material for the Manor coal washing plant.

(Below) The Holtwood Steam Electric Station in 1924.

(Inset) Holtwood in 1910, one of the most unique fossil fuel generating stations in electric utility history.

Perhaps the biggest problem facing the Penn Water engineers in 1924 and 1925 was how to burn the coal recovered from the river. Prior to the construction of the first units at the steam plant at Holtwood, most steam generation units in the United States burned coal on a grate. The fine sizes of river coal recovered by the Lake Aldred dredges dictated an alternate method of combustion.

From the time that John Abbett Walls and Frederick Allner decided to build a steam station at Holtwood, they suspected that the solution lay in blowing pulverized anthracite into the boiler. Skeptics scoffed and said that the winds blowing down the Susquehanna River Valley would blow down the chimneys, forcing smoke and flame out the bottom of the boilers.

Walls and Allner assigned John R. Baker to study blower-type furnaces. Baker discovered that there was only a handful of blower-type furnaces in the United States, including a small, pilot-type plant at Lykens, Pa., and a larger unit at Warren, Ohio. Baker selected the best properties of the two plants and

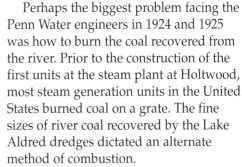

incorporated them into the design for the boilers at the Holtwood station. Walls and Allner backed their engineer's plans and went ahead in 1924 with the construction of boilers fired by pulverized anthracite.

The coal washing plant necessitated some different procedures for the Pennsylvania Water & Power Co. crews. Early on, crews began purchasing paperboard barrels full of white, natural, undyed rubber balls about the size of tennis balls. The balls were captured between two screens on the top floor of the plant, and their purpose was to prevent caking of mud in the first step of the separation process.

The dredging crews were also witness to some interesting phenomena on the Susquehanna River. Jim Geiling, a longtime dredging crew member, recalled that it was an annual treat to see chunks of river ice bob to the surface during the dredging season. Broken ice floes in some years created ice ridges many feet higher than normal river level during the winter's freeze-thaw cycle. The weight of the ice on top of the resulting ice ridges, usually behind the dam or at the narrowest part of the river, caused large ice cakes to be driven down into the mud beneath the river bottom.

In the spring and early summer, when the dredge began its annual work in earnest, the churning action on the river bottom would dislodge some of the ice chunks deposited months earlier, much to the delight of the crews on the dredge and tug.

Tom Yezerski, another longtime dredging crew member, reported that the constantly shifting mud and coal deposits frequently buried plant matter beneath the river bottom, where decay produced pockets of methane and other noxious gases. When the dredge disturbed any of these gas pockets, eruptions of stench would bubble up from the river bottom, sometimes spectacularly and sometimes in the form of a bubble trail, but always annoyingly odiferous. Yezerski and his co-workers called it "river flatulence."

The Manor coal washing plant was successful almost from the start. Much of the coal recovered from the river during the 1920s and early 1930s was passed across shaking tables, which used water sluiced over riffles to separate coal and sand. But even though the recovery was considered highly successful for that time and place, Pennsylvania Water & Power Co. engineers were convinced that the recovery process could be improved.

G.W. Spaulding of the company's coal recovery team suspected that even finer river coal could be recovered by the Manor coal washing plant. In 1939, Spaulding and his team began studying the use of vibrating screens and flotation cells for the recovery of very fine coal. Pennsylvania Water & Power Co. worked with the Battelle Institute of Columbus, Ohio, and the U.S. Bureau of Mines research laboratory at College Park, Md., to study the problem of fine coal recovery.

Eventually, the Pennsylvania Water & Power Co. experiments used a combination of fuel and pine oils in the flotation process. The utilization of even finer river coal allowed the company to expand its steam generation capacity at Holtwood through the 1940s and 1950s. The Manor coal plant, and the use of anthracite silt, survived into the 1970s when the supply dwindled to the point it was no longer economical to "mine" the river.

(Above) River dredging to recover and sell the coal that had washed down the Susquehanna began in the late 1800s. (Inset) Just before the more modern Manor plant was built, quality control operators at Holtwood visually monitored the washing process to make sure the coal was clean and good enough for the boilers. *circa 1948*

Jim Geiling. *circa 1993*

Tom Yezerski. *circa 1994*

Safe Harbor

As the nation slid into the Great Depression, President Herbert Hoover, a former engineer himself, summoned the nation's utility executives to Washington, D.C., in the winter of 1930. The New York Stock Exchange had collapsed just weeks earlier, and President Hoover wanted utility executives to accelerate capital investment programs in order to jump-start the ailing U.S. economy.

One of those projects was the construction of the Safe Harbor hydroelectric facility on the Susquehanna above Holtwood and Lake Aldred. Safe Harbor, at the conjunction of the Susquehanna River and Conestoga Creek, had a long and proud history prior to the 1930 decision to build a hydroelectric dam at the site. As far back as 1695, William Penn had selected 16,000 acres in the vicinity for the construction of a city to rival Philadelphia, but the rock and island-studded channel of the river precluded shipping from Chesapeake Bay.

Rivermen often steered for the "safe harbor" of deep water just off the mouth of Conestoga Creek, and the name stuck. Over the years, the community of Millersport grew up at the safe harbor site, with a number of taverns reported at the waterfront community as early as 1811. By the middle of the 19th century,

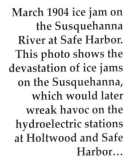

William Penn.
circa 1690s

Millersport was known on the maps as Safe Harbor.

Through the Civil War, the Safe Harbor Iron Works provided employment for residents of the community. Built in the late 1840s following the discovery of iron ore in the area, the Safe Harbor Iron Works produced iron rails for the railways then being built across Pennsylvania and the Mid-Atlantic region.

The floods that periodically ravaged the Susquehanna Valley dictated the course of events at Safe Harbor. Devastating floods in 1865 closed the Iron Works and destroyed the dam crossing the Susquehanna. Destruction was so complete that the owners did not reopen the Iron Works until the 1879 completion of a mile-long railroad spur to connect with the Columbia and Port Deposit Railroad.

The Panic of 1893 caused further disruption at the Iron Works, although by 1895, the region had recovered enough that a new match factory had opened in an abandoned iron rolling mill. But once again, weather proved to be the deciding factor in determining the future of Safe Harbor and the Conestoga Valley.

In the spring of 1904, a massive ice jam worked its way down the Susquehanna. The ice ridges pushed higher and higher as ice and water continued to inch downriver. Conestoga Creek proved to be a perfect vent for the miles-long ice jam. Ice rose ever higher in Conestoga Creek,

By the middle of the 19th century, Millersport was known on the maps as Safe Harbor.

March 1904 ice jam on the Susquehanna River at Safe Harbor. This photo shows the devastation of ice jams on the Susquehanna, which would later wreak havoc on the hydroelectric stations at Holtwood and Safe Harbor...

and the floes took out the Columbia and Port Deposit Railroad bridge across the creek. The match factory was washed away, and dozens of houses were crushed by the ice. For all intents and purposes, the community of Safe Harbor ceased to exist.

Selection of Safe Harbor as the site for a massive new hydroelectric facility in early 1930 was the culmination of nearly 15 years of study by Pennsylvania Water & Power Co. But instead of undertaking the project on its own, Penn Water went to its Baltimore neighbor and best customer, Consolidated Gas & Electric. Consolidated, the predecessor of Baltimore Gas & Electric, had been buying wholesale electric power from Holtwood since shortly after the hydroelectric facility began in 1910. In 1927, Penn Water and Consolidated had signed a 43-year contract, which included provisions for coordinating generation and transmission procedures of the two companies.

In January 1930, Consolidated and Penn Water formed the Safe Harbor Water Power Corp. as the outgrowth of two predecessor companies that had been formed as part of the October 1927 agreement between the two companies. Under the terms of the 1930 contract, Consolidated was to receive two-thirds of the power generated by the new hydroelectric facility; Pennsylvania Water & Power Co. was to receive one-third of the generating capacity.

The $30 million Safe Harbor project was designed and constructed under the supervision of engineers from both Penn Water and Consolidated. Work on the dam and powerhouse began in the spring of 1930, and up to 4,000 men—many of them unemployed—were put to work building the Safe Harbor project.

The Largest Propeller-Type Water Wheels in the World

The engineers building Safe Harbor selected Kaplan Turbines for the project. Then the largest propeller-type water wheels ever built in the United States, the Kaplan turbines were extensively tested in Penn Water's hydraulic test laboratories at Holtwood. One item of special interest to the Penn Water engineers was the problem of cavitation; the immense pressure against the turbine blades and the attendant swirling water was capable of causing extensive pitting.

"Research is no stranger to executives and engineers of the Pennsylvania Water and Power Co.," a reporter from *Power Magazine* wrote in July 1934. "They have

Charles Proteus Steinmetz is said to have visited the Holtwood hydroelectric station. Holtwood was, after all, one of the great engineering marvels of Steinmetz's day.

...havoc at Safe Harbor hydroelectric station in January 1978.

1934 to serve the Pennsylvania Railroad, and the final unit—also 25 cycles—went on line in 1940, again to serve the railroad's needs.

Safe Harbor Water Power Corp. linked the new hydroelectric facility to Baltimore by a pair of 230,000-volt high transmission lines. Early in 1931, construction crews completed the first line to the Baltimore utility's Westport substation. Two years later, a second line was completed from the hydro plant to Consolidated's Riverside generating station. Shortly before the project started, in the summer of 1932, Consolidated began planning the extension of the Safe Harbor transmission link from Riverside to Potomac Electric Power Co.'s substation in Takoma Park, Md.

The contractor for the transmission line from Riverside to Takoma Park tapped into a unique labor pool for the line's construction. In the summer of 1932, some 11,000 veterans of World War I had descended upon Washington, D.C., demanding that the federal government pay them a bonus for their service during the Great War. Many of them hungry and unemployed, the "Bonus Marchers" set up camp on the marshy flats of the Anacostia River in the nation's capital. Late in July 1932, the Roosevelt Administration ordered the U.S. Army to disband the Bonus Marchers. Shortly before the troops began burning the makeshift tent camp, representatives of the contractor visited the camp on the Mall and hired Bonus Marchers to help build the tie line from Riverside to Takoma Park.

The completion of the first units at Safe Harbor in 1931 brought to an end the hydroelectric development of the Susquehanna River in Pennsylvania and Maryland. But the transmission ties that radiated out from Safe Harbor ushered in a new era of electrical interconnection in the Mid-Atlantic states.

(Top) The discharge flume of the hydraulic testing lab Pennsylvania Water & Power Co. built in anticipation of the Safe Harbor plant. After Safe Harbor designs were developed at the lab, manufacturers began to visit Holtwood to contract for tests and experiments. The lab was dismantled shortly after World War II.

(Right) Back in 1937, patroling transmission line rights-of-way was likely one of the more enviable jobs. This particular line is the Conestoga-Perryville line, which still carries electricity from Safe Harbor hydroelectric station to power Conrail electric locomotives.

had long and successful experience in design and operation of the Holtwood plant, where many modern ideas regarding hydro-operating practice and economics have been developed. This work has proved that an engineering research department, properly organized and directed, is one of a company's most valuable assets, which it is desirable to maintain on a permanent basis."

The cavitation experiments at the Holtwood hydraulic laboratory allowed the Safe Harbor crews to upgrade the Kaplan turbines in the initial units from 38,500-horsepower to 42,500-horsepower. Penn Water even went to the trouble of inviting German engineers, who had had more experience with the Kaplan propeller-type turbines, to the hydraulic laboratory to help with the cavitation studies.

The first two units of Safe Harbor were completed and transmitting power to Baltimore by the first week of December 1931. By 1933, an additional three units were on line at Safe Harbor. The first five units were all 60-cycle units to serve Consolidated of Baltimore. A sixth unit of 25 cycles was completed in

Impressive not only in size and modernization, the Safe Harbor hydro-electric station was known for its spotless appearance.

109 Dredge

"You can't call the Susquehanna a lazy river," wrote Mary H. Cadwalader in *The Baltimore Sunday Sun Magazine* of Sept. 19, 1948.

Not only did the river produce hydroelectric power at Holtwood, Safe Harbor, York Haven and Conowingo, it also yielded nearly 200,000 tons a year of anthracite coal fines for steam generation at Holtwood. From the time that the Manor coal washing plant went on line in 1925, a river fleet of tugs and dredges scoured the river bottom from March to December each year for river coal suitable for burning in the Holtwood plant's steam electric boilers.

Even though actual dredging ceased during the winter months each year, the 80 members of the River Coal Production Group of Pennsylvania Water & Power Co. labored to keep the river coal fleet of dredges, barges, tugs, steamboats and towboats in tip-top condition for the dredging season ahead. When the ice finally went out on the Susquehanna in March each year, the crews worked around the clock, seven days a week, lifting coal-laden silt from the bottoms of Lake Aldred and Lake Clarke.

For nearly 30 years, the flagship of the river fleet was *109 Dredge*, a 24-foot-wide hull with a cutter, dredge bucket and suction hose affixed to its superstructure. *109 Dredge* went into service in 1925 at the time that the Manor coal washing plant came on line, and was enlarged and extensively remodeled in 1951 in anticipation of the construction of a new coal washing plant above Safe Harbor.

109 Dredge was towed to its assigned spot on Lake Aldred each spring by one of the sternwheel steamboats in the river fleet. Throughout the spring, summer and fall each year, the sternwheel steamboats shuttled back and forth between the dredge and the Manor coal washing plant with barges full of silt and river coal.

To recover 200,000 tons of river coal a year from the Susquehanna, the crews of the River Coal Production Group had to dredge up more than 400,000 tons of river bottom. "Our production represents the output of a medium-sized, modern anthracite coal mine," Billy Crook of Penn Water's River Coal Production Group told the readers of *Hydro Hi-Lines* in a March 1953 article.

During the annual dredging season, only floods and dense fogs interrupted the river fleet's task. A flow of 150,000 cubic feet per second, not an uncommon occurrence during the spring melt, was enough to send the river fleet to shelter. "Susquehanna River fogs are notorious," Crook recalled in 1953. "Sometimes they're so heavy, a man can't see six feet in front of him. When this occurs, we head for the nearest shore and tie up, waiting for it to lift."

The end of an era for the river fleet came in 1953 when *117 Dredge* was placed into service. In 1952, Pennsylvania Water & Power Co. had begun a $10 million expansion program, the crown jewel of which was the construction of a second coal washing plant on the ridge above Safe Harbor. Designed to handle 4,500 tons of silt a day pumped through a 180-foot tunnel and up a 65-foot shaft to the new coal washing plant located on the bluff 275 feet above the unloader, the 1953 expansion project vastly increased the amount of river coal available for the Holtwood Steam Electric Station's boilers.

117 Dredge was capable of more than doubling the output of 200,000 tons a year recovered by *109 Dredge* and the steam dredges. Gone were the wooden barges, replaced by 800-ton steel barges. The steam-driven sternwheeler navy that had plied the waters of Lake Aldred and Lake Clarke for nearly 30 years was a historical footnote following the 1953 expansion.

17

PNJ

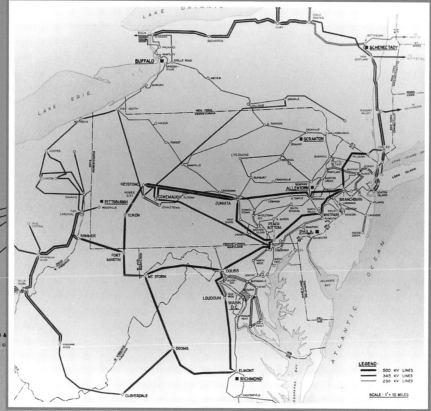

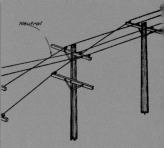

PJM Interconnection map. The Pennsylvania-New Jersey (PNJ) Interconnection was expanded into Maryland creating the PJM Interconnection.

The theory and practice of electric utility interconnection on the North American continent got its start in the Mid-Atlantic region shared by Pennsylvania Power & Light Co., Philadelphia Electric Co. and Public Service Electric & Gas Co.

The high-voltage capacity, intercompany power grid is an American innovation that can trace its roots to the formation of the Pennsylvania-New Jersey Interconnection in 1928, the world's first fully integrated power pool. The three utilities linked their system together with a backbone 230,000-volt transmission ring that was a state-of-the-art transmission network in the late 1920s. Indeed, much of the American power grid wouldn't be able to duplicate the technological sophistication of the Pennsylvania-New Jersey network until the post-World War II era, some two decades later.

The PNJ interconnection in the 1920s often evolved by trial and error. The three original partners in the interconnection served rapidly growing industrial, commercial and residential loads in adjacent parts of Pennsylvania and New Jersey, and the state of generation in the mid-1920s was such that large baseload generating units were coming into common usage.

PP&L's experience with the construction of Wallenpaupack hydro in 1925 was typical, as was Philadelphia Electric Co.'s construction of the first units at Conowingo on the Susquehanna in 1928. Baseload hydroelectric units completed across the United States in the 1920s were often built by construction crews employed by utility holding company subsidiaries like the Phoenix Utilities Co.

Baseload fossil fuel plants were also increasingly common as the decade progressed. PP&L had experience through its predecessors in building baseload plants like Hauto and Harwood. Transmission technology was advancing

The three original partners in the interconnection served rapidly growing industrial, commercial and residential loads.

rapidly, and all three utilities were aggressively pursuing the acquisition of small-town utilities in the two states through extension of the "high line." The Allentown utility also entered into a joint venture partnership with Scranton Electric Co., a subsidiary of the giant American Gas & Electric holding company, to build the Stanton steam electric generating station south of Scranton in 1925.

On the Susquehanna River, Pennsylvania Water & Power Co. embarked in the mid-1920s on the construction of its innovative Manor coal washing plant and adjacent Holtwood Steam Electric Station. For all intents and purposes, the Mid-Atlantic region's electric power grid was beginning to take shape by the late 1920s.

The region served by the three utilities was adaptable to the concept of regional interconnection. Public Service Electric & Gas Co.'s generation in the southern half of its service territory was inadequate in the mid-1920s, and the New Jersey utility had already contracted with Philadelphia Electric Co. in 1923 for a 26,000-volt underwater cable to serve customers in Camden, across the Delaware River from Philadelphia.

The peak loads for both Philadelphia Electric Co. and Public Service Electric & Gas Co. occurred at the same time of day and year, primarily because both utilities were serving large urban loads. PP&L, which served a mixture of industrial and small-town

The Stanton Steam Electric Station was built in 1925 as a joint venture between PP&L and the Scranton Electric Co. The Stanton plant was home to the shortest railroad in the world— just three miles long. *(illustration by Brent Schaefer © 1995)*

industrial loads, experienced peaks at different times of day and year from its neighboring, big-city utilities.

Philadelphia Electric Co.'s plans to develop the waterpower resource of the Susquehanna at Conowingo in the mid years of the decade dictated that the three utilities come to some kind of interconnection arrangement. Conowingo was a run-of-river plant, and the hydroelectric resources in the three states needed coordination with steam generating plants to balance load and demand. The stream flow on the Susquehanna was notoriously fickle, and Philadelphia Electric Co. couldn't afford to depend upon Conowingo from a pure reliability standpoint.

American Superpower Corp.

In October 1923, Sidney Z. Mitchell of the Electric Bond and Share Co. joined with executives of utility holding companies from across the country and investment bankers to form the American Superpower Corp. American Superpower was a response to the post-World War I problems that had plagued the utility industry, primarily the technological difficulties inherent in interconnecting large-scale, fragmented power systems and the lack of investment capital to finance the creation of regional power grids.

"New problems of regulation are constantly arising out of the growing system of interconnection and the

consequent future fluidity of electric power," American Superpower Corp.'s annual report noted in 1925. "There are new problems of corporate relationship which accompany such physical interconnection, and there is a multitude of expanding questions of market and supply—these are among the broad problems in the solving of which the American Superpower Corp. is interested. In addition, there are many specific problems of engineering, administration, public relations, finance and law in which through the abilities and cooperation of its directors, the successful practices of any

Philadelphia Electric Co. (PE), *circa 1907.* PE, PP&L and Public Service Electric and Gas Co. of New Jersey created the Pennsylvania-New Jersey Interconnection in 1928. *(courtesy of Philadelphia Electric Co.)*

American Superpower was a response to the post-World War I problems that had plagued the utility industry.

Built in 1904, the York Haven hydro-electric station is the oldest operating electric generating station in Pennsylvania.

This 1903 photo of Philadelphia Electric Co.'s Schuylkill station shows coal being unloaded from barges that were brought upriver by tug boats. *(courtesy of Philadelphia Electric Co.)*

Philadelphia Electric Co.'s Chester station in the 1950s. *(courtesy of Philadelphia Electric Co.)*

of the companies represented on its directorate may be passed on to other companies."

In the end, American Super-power Corp. became little more than an investment arm of the holding companies involved. But the company's formation indicated a desire on the part of these utilities to cooperate on matters relating to potential interconnection.

The technological problems of interconnection were particularly complex. At the turn of the century, central stations were initially interconnected with alternating current transmission, usually at 6,600-volt and 13,200-volt levels. Metropolitan Edison Co.'s York Haven hydroelectric plant on the Susquehanna went into service in the summer of 1904; it transmitted electricity at 4,800 volts to the community of York Haven, and later at 23,000 volts to the city of York, Pa.

Pennsylvania Water & Power Co.'s Holtwood station was interconnected with Baltimore's Consolidated Gas & Electric Co. after 1910 via a double-circuit, 70,000-volt transmission line, although the original transmission link was 25-cycle rather than 60-cycle. A 60-cycle, 66,000-volt line from Holtwood to Consolidated's Highlandtown substation was placed in service in 1913.

That same year, Public Service Electric & Gas Co. had interconnected much of its northern New Jersey service territory with a 13,000-volt transmission grid. In 1917, Philadelphia Electric Co. interconnected its Chester and Schuylkill coal-fired generating stations with a twin-circuit, high-capacity 66,000-volt transmission line.

PP&L's interconnections with neighboring utilities began in 1923. That year, crews connected the company's 66,000-volt system at South Lebanon with Metropolitan Edison Co.'s 110,000-volt system at South Reading. In 1925, PP&L interconnected its Wilkes-Barre substation with the Plymouth generating station operated by UGI's electric division. The next year, ties were completed between UGI's Hunlock generating station and PP&L's Berwick substation. PP&L created additional ties with UGI in 1928 when it interconnected the Stanton generating station with UGI's Swoyersville substation.

Still, in 1923 the Mid-Atlantic region was essentially unconnected electrically. PP&L had no interconnections with PSE&G and none with Philadelphia Electric Co. The Allentown utility was interconnected with Pennsylvania Water & Power Co., Scranton Electric Co., UGI and Metropolitan Edison Co., and Pennsylvania Water & Power Co. also had interconnections with Philadelphia Electric Co. and the Consolidated system in Baltimore. PSE&G had yet to interconnect its northern and southern systems.

Much work remained to be done before the utilities in the region could begin large-scale interconnection, however. Development of effective systems controls were an integral part of the evolution of interconnected transmission. As early as 1923, Philadelphia Electric Co. began to assign regulation to its Schuylkill, Chester and Delaware steam electric stations. The following year, the Philadelphia utility provided its system operators at four steam electric generating plants with a graphic display to measure output and system frequency; the company used a master clock manufactured by the Warren Telechron Co. of Ashland, Mass., to synchronize its system.

PP&L installed frequency control equipment at Wallenpaupack hydroelectric station in 1928 to control two 20-megawatt units at the hydroelectric station in the Pocono Mountains. Frequency control and system synchronization were necessary first steps toward integrating the large-scale transmission systems in the Mid-Atlantic region.

Forming PNJ

With technological solutions to the problems of large-scale interconnection either in place or on the horizon, PP&L, Philadelphia Electric Co. and PSE&G began moving toward a formal power pooling arrangement. In 1923, the

(Left) PP&L's Berwick Steam Electric Station was connected with UGI's Hunlock generating station in 1926.

(Below) The Delaware Steam Electric Station. *circa 1924*

three utilities hired Maj. Malcolm MacLaren of Princeton University's electrical engineering department to study load diversity in Pennsylvania and New Jersey. The diversity factor was important, and simply represented the ratio of the potential maximum load to the actual peak load. MacLaren reported back that the three utilities were compatible in load diversity and should consider forging tighter interconnections. In response, PP&L, PSE&G and Philadelphia Electric Co. appointed a committee to act upon MacLaren's report.

MacLaren reported in February 1924 that the three utilities could avoid 130 megawatts of installed capacity in 1925 if the three systems were pooled.

Joseph B. McCall was president of Philadelphia Electric Co. in the 1920s when PNJ was formed. *(courtesy of Philadelphia Electric Co.)*

W.C.L. Eglin

Dr. N.E. Funk

Essentially, MacLaren reported in February 1924 that the three utilities could avoid 130 megawatts of installed capacity in 1925 if the three systems were pooled. MacLaren based his estimates on a 1924 peak load of 1,010 megawatts. With construction of 200 miles of high-voltage transmission, the utilities could save $2.8 million the first year because of the load diversity. Another $700,000 a year in production costs could be saved, he reported.

In August 1925, the three utilities issued a report that recommended setting up a formal power pool. Committee members closely followed events in Connecticut that summer when three small predecessors of Northeast Utilities formed the Connecticut Valley Power Exchange to pool power resources for customers in Turner's Falls and Springfield, Mass., and Hartford, Conn. Members of the committee that studied Dr. MacLaren's report included Norbert G. Reinecker of PP&L, S.Z. Mitchell and C.E. Groesbeck of Electric Bond and Share Co., Joseph B. McCall and W.C.L. Eglin of Philadelphia Electric Co., and Farley Osgood and N.A. Carle of Public Service Electric & Gas Co. Osgood of PSE&G chaired the committee, and his name adorned the committee's report.

The Osgood Report extended MacLaren's study through 1935. It reported that gross savings of power pooling over a six-year period would come to $45 million. Costs were estimated at $26.2 million, for a net savings of $18.7 million for the period, or more than $3 million a year. Osgood's committee recommended that the three utilities follow through and set up a formal pool.

On Sept. 16, 1927, the three utilities signed a memorandum of agreement establishing the Pennsylvania-New Jersey Interconnection. While there were no models existing for setting up a formal, regional power pool, there were comparatively few political or philosophical differences separating the three partners. PP&L was a subsidiary of the Electric Bond and Share Co. holding company, while PSE&G was controlled by J.P. Morgan's United group of utility companies. At the time of the agreement, Philadelphia Electric Co. was in the process of being acquired by United Gas Improvement Co.

The purpose of the arrangement, according to Dr. N.E. Funk, Philadelphia Electric Co.'s vice president of engineering and the Philadelphia utility's first representative to the pool's management committee, was to take advantage of "predictable diversity" between PP&L's morning peak in October and PSE&G's and PECO's evening peak in December. PP&L's annual peak, Funk noted, was attributable to the run-up in anthracite mining in anticipation of the winter heating season, while the other two utilities reached their annual peak in the Christmas shopping season.

The three chief executives of the partners signed the pooling agreement, and while simple in scope, it served as the model for utility pooling arrangements for more than a generation. In essence, the agreement called for the establishment of committees responsible for planning and coordinating the delivery of the lowest cost electric power available to the three members of the pool. Each utility appointed members to the pool committees, and the operating committee, which had overall responsibility for the pool, required unanimous agreement for any policy decisions taken that affected the pool.

Meetings of the operating committee were rotated among the headquarters of the three companies, and were held alternately in Allentown, Philadelphia and Newark. The agreement did not require the pool committee to undertake the responsibility of building and owning generating stations and

On Sept. 16, 1927, the three utilities signed a memorandum of agreement establishing the Pennsylvania-New Jersey Interconnection.

transmission lines. That was left to the individual member utilities.

Building the Ring

The keystone of the PNJ agreement involved the construction of a ring of 220,000-volt transmission lines some 210 miles in length across the two states. The ring was modeled on the 220,000-volt transmission line built by Phoenix Utilities Co. crews from Wallenpaupack to Siegfried substation in 1925-1926, the first such 220,000-volt line in Pennsylvania. Each of the partners agreed to build two transmission lines to the other two partners; construction costs were split three ways among the partners. Because geographical ownership of the transmission ring was not divided equally, Philadelphia Electric Co. agreed

to pay PP&L $10,000 annually and PSE&G $140,000 annually.

Siegfried was one of three anchors for the PNJ transmission ring. Roseland substation, approximately 50 miles west of Newark, was PSE&G's terminal on the system, while Plymouth Meeting substation, approximately 25 miles northwest of Philadelphia, was PECO's terminal on the PNJ system.

The PNJ operating committee recommended the construction of single-circuit steel tower lines with 14-16 insulator strings. Phoenix Utilities Co. crews completed the first link in the ring, the Wallenpaupack to Siegfried segment, in 1926, even before the signing of the formal agreement. Phoenix Utilities Co.

> *Each of the partners agreed to build two transmission lines to the other two partners; construction costs were split three ways among the partners.*

The PJM control room in Valley Forge. *circa 1963*

crews built a line shortly after from Towamencin Township to Siegfried and also built a line from Lambertville to PSE&G's New Jersey territory; PSE&G crews, meanwhile, had built a line west from Roseland substation to a point near Lambertville. PECO crews linked Plymouth Meeting substation with Siegfried in 1928, the same year that Conowingo came on line.

The 86-mile link between Roseland substation and Plymouth Meeting substation was placed in service in 1931, and the next year, the transmission ring was closed with completion of the line from Roseland to PP&L's Bushkill substation near Wallenpaupack.

During the latter part of the 1920s and the early 1930s, the three member participants of PNJ all established transmission ties with neighboring utilities. PP&L established ties with Metropolitan Edison Co.; Philadelphia Electric Co. was linked with Atlantic Electric and Delmarva Power; and PSE&G established ties with New Jersey Power & Light. South of the PNJ system, Safe Harbor Water Power Corp. established ties with Consolidated Gas & Electric Co. outside Baltimore.

The formation of PNJ and the completion of the 220,000-volt transmission ring in Pennsylvania and New Jersey was a landmark accomplishment in American electric utility history.

Initial plans of the PNJ operating committee had called for the creation of an administration and load dispatching staff at Siegfried substation, but the onset of the Great Depression shelved those plans. Philadelphia Electric Co. was responsible to the pool for frequency and time error control, and generation for all systems was dispatched manually. The system was divided operationally north and south, and communications took place over leased, dedicated telephone circuits.

Late in 1927, George Keenan, chief system operator for PP&L, was appointed PNJ's first superintendent. Keenan served as chairman of the operating committee, and he divided his time between PP&L's system operations facility in Hazleton and the PNJ office at Philadelphia Electric Co.'s headquarters in Philadelphia. In 1932, Keenan was recalled by PP&L and replaced as superintendent of PNJ by H. Webster Phillips of Philadelphia Electric Co.

Through the initial meetings of the operating committee from 1928 to 1930, the PNJ member companies struggled with establishing load and operations schedules. At the seventh meeting of the operating committee in May 1930, the committee established a 12 percent installed reserve requirement for its members. Prior to the interconnection, each of the partners had maintained an 18 percent installed reserve, so the 12 percent reserve represented the major savings that had been predicted by Maj. MacLaren back in 1924.

The formation of PNJ and the completion of the 220,000-volt transmission ring in Pennsylvania and New Jersey was a landmark accomplishment in American electric utility history. For the first time on the North American continent, integration of large-scale electric utility systems under separate ownership proved feasible in both theory and practice.

"The integrated and centrally controlled PNJ power pool differed from the mergers and utility holding company structures that were then proliferating," Thomas Parke Hughes observed in *Networks of Power*. "In concept, it can be compared to the confederation of 19th century railroad systems that were formed to facilitate cross-country traffic cooperation. The utility managers and engineers who operated the power pool began to see the PNJ as electrically one company, but financially and organizationally a committee of peers negotiating planning and operations. The PNJ brought the economic benefits of a large system and at the same time preserved the utilities' corporate identities."

The Shortest Railroad in the World

When PP&L and Scranton Electric Co. entered into a joint venture agreement to build the Stanton steam electric station on the west bank of the upper Susquehanna River Valley three miles north of West Pittston from 1925 to 1927, PP&L wound up owning the shortest railroad in the world.

The Stanton plant, which first went on line in March 1927, consisted of two 50,000-kilowatt units separated by an imaginary center line. One of the units was owned and operated by PP&L; the other was owned and operated by Scranton Electric Co., a subsidiary of the American Gas & Electric holding company.

The two original units at Stanton—a third unit was added in 1953—were fired by eight stoker-fired boilers burning No. 3 and No. 4 buckwheat anthracite coal. The two units provided steam at 640 p.s.i. and 735 degrees Fahrenheit, although reheated steam could be pushed to 750 degrees Fahrenheit. Combined, the two units consumed close to 1,350 tons of local anthracite coal a day.

The coal arrived at the Stanton plant via the West Pittston-Exeter Railroad, a three-mile-long shortline railroad that was at one time the shortest chartered railroad in the United States. Owned and operated as a subsidiary by PP&L, the West Pittston-Exeter was founded in the early 1920s by the Exeter Power Co. to haul coal to Stanton plant. But when PP&L emerged as a joint venture partner in Stanton station in 1925, ownership of the railroad passed to the Allentown utility and Scranton Electric Co. After PP&L acquired Scranton Electric Co. in 1955, it took over 100 percent ownership of the West Pittston-Exeter.

A load of empty cars are hauled back to the Lehigh Valley Railroad, three miles from the Stanton plant. At right is the Susquehanna River.

The WP-E connected with the Lehigh Valley Railroad at Forest Castle and the Erie Lackawanna Railroad at West Pittston. The nearest connection point was 2.92 miles from the Stanton plant railyard, and the WP-E operated much the same as its far larger neighbors, filing tariffs with the Interstate Commerce Commission and submitting to the regulation of the Pennsylvania Public Utility Commission.

The basic cargo of the WP-E over the years that Stanton plant operated was anthracite coal, although the railroad developed a thriving trade in coal ash during the 1930s and 1940s. Originally, Stanton plant gave carloads of coal ash to the Pennsylvania Highway Department for use on icy highways. In the 1930s, anthracite ash was discovered to be an excellent material for the construction of concrete block; at one time, during the Great Depression, Stanton plant was selling anthracite ash (which was hauled to the mainline by the WP-E) for more than the $2 a ton it was paying for its supply of buckwheat anthracite.

Ironically, the WP-E almost never got off the ground. Old No. 1, a coal-fired steam engine, pulled into the Stanton railyard on its inaugural run on the next-to-last day of December 1925. The locomotive and its load of 10 cars—which were to begin stockpiling coal in anticipation of the early 1927 start-up at the plant—were some four days late to Stanton.

On Dec. 26, 1925, the locomotive had been crossing the Susquehanna River on a makeshift barge. The barge had given way, and the locomotive took a detour into the Susquehanna River. It required heavy equipment from the Lehigh Valley Railroad

(Courtesy of Charles V. Touhill, Pittston, PA)

and took three days to extricate No. 1 from the bottom of the river and send it on its way to Stanton.

Robert Berninger, who transferred to Stanton as a test engineer for American Gas & Electric Co. in 1927 and retired in 1962 as plant superintendent, recalled in 1976 that unloading the coal cars of the WP-E was one of the hardest jobs at the plant. Often, the coal was frozen solid when it arrived at Stanton. "The men had to pour hot water on the cars to thaw the coal so it could be handled," Berninger told the *PP&L Reporter*.

Until the purchase of Locomotive No. 6 in 1950, the WP-E was a steam railroad all the way. Nos. 1 and 2 were comparatively small 20-ton switch engines. No. 3 was a 40-ton behemoth, but No. 4 was the locomotive that generations of Stanton workers remember as the workhorse of the line.

Built in Dunkirk, N.Y., in 1906 by the American Locomotive Works, No. 4 was a 72-ton, six-wheel-switcher, a 0-6-0 in railroad parlance. Built for the Baltimore and Ohio Railroad, No. 4 was sold to the Ohio Power Co. in 1924 and pressed into service at Ohio Power Co.'s Philo plant as a switch engine. In 1929,

Ohio Power Co. sold the engine to the WP-E, where it served until being replaced by the railroad's first diesel electric locomotive in 1950. Five years later, the WP-E sold No. 4 to a junk dealer for scrap.

Old No. 4 lived on, however. Berninger removed the locomotive's bell before it went to the scrapyard, and in 1962, he gave the 15-inch diameter, cast iron bell to John Davidson, PP&L's longtime Scranton and Harrisburg manager. Following Berninger's death, Davidson donated the bell to the Pennsylvania Anthracite Heritage Museum in Berninger's name.

Stanton plant survived No. 4 locomotive by some 17 years. Scheduled to be removed from service in October 1972, the plant was inundated by the floodwaters of the Susquehanna during Hurricane Agnes in June of that year. Water flooded the subterranean levels of the plant and surged some 15 feet above ground level, effectively destroying the plant's effectiveness. In 1974 and 1975, Stanton plant was razed by crews of the Interstate Wrecking Service. Along with the plant went the trackage of the West Pittston-Exeter, once the shortest railroad in the world.

John S. Davidson (left) chats with author Bill Beck during the 1993 shareholders' meeting in Harrisburg. He died in June 1994, not quite a year before his invaluable historical recollections would be published in this book.

18

The Tower Building

The PP&L Tower. *circa 1928.*

Behind the Silk and Linden street sign, peaking over the rounded top of the former Hess's Department Store parking lot ramp, stands Allentown's famous skyscraper, the PP&L Tower. *circa 1994*

In the late winter of 1994, Allentown residents were shocked when one of the city's newest office buildings cracked in the center and literally self-destructed.

Sometime in the early morning hours of February 23, the ground beneath Corporate Plaza at Seventh and Hamilton shifted, and the city's newest big downtown building settled into a sinkhole.

"The building's rounded corner bulged like a tight shirt on a fat man," *Morning Call* columnist Frank Whelan wrote of what he had seen walking to work along Hamilton Mall that morning. "Pieces of glass hung out of the window frames. As I got closer, it was clear that a large crack had opened in the center of Seventh Street. It had half swallowed a streetlight. The flower bowl was almost at street level."

The culprit, Whelan wrote, "was a sinkhole, one

of the facts of life of the Lehigh Valley. Limestone caverns honeycomb the city and the entire region. Around the turn of the century, a man claimed to have actually walked from one end of Allentown to the other in them."

The loss of Corporate Plaza—the building had to be demolished soon after—immediately caused questions to be raised about the structural integrity of PP&L's General Office building at the corner of Ninth and Hamilton. Known to generations of PP&L employees as "the Tower Building," the 23-story skyscraper, when it was completed in 1928, was the tallest building between New York City and Pittsburgh. For many, the Tower Building has been a Lehigh Valley landmark.

Whelan put many of the fears to rest

when he reported that the 66-year-old building rests on solid bedrock. Back in 1927, engineers had sunk caissons seven feet in diameter well into the bedrock before construction of the tower had begun. Steel I-beams were inserted into the caissons, which were then filled with concrete. The Tower Building, Whelan reported, is as solid as the bedrock upon which it rested.

Allentown's First Skyscraper

Allentown almost wasn't selected for the general headquarters of Pennsylvania Power & Light Co. Following consolidation in 1923, the company was headquartered in Allentown's Buckley Building, at 802 Hamilton Street. But the newly consolidated utility quickly outgrew its quarters in the Buckley Building, and by 1925, company executives were considering what to do next.

Geographically, the directors were leaning toward locating the general office in Hazleton. The anthracite area was booming in the mid-1920s, and Hazleton was pretty close to the center of the service territory. PP&L director Alvin Markle, an anthracite company executive and native of Hazleton, tried to convince his fellow directors to locate the company's headquarters in his hometown.

Allentown had its champions on the board. Gen. Harry Trexler was particularly anxious that the PP&L headquarters be located in the Lehigh Valley. Trexler's numerous business interests were in Allentown, and he argued to fellow board members that since Electric Bond and Share Co. had become interested in the company in 1917, the effective operating headquarters of the company had been on Hamilton Street in Allentown.

The Bond & Share contingent on the board weighed in on the side of Trexler. Sidney Z. Mitchell, Paul B. Sawyer and E.K. Hall were no doubt swayed by the argument that Allentown was served by

In 1994, Allentown's Corporate Plaza was devastated by a collapsed sinkhole. This caused great concern for many, including PP&L's general office building employees. (*courtesy of the* Morning Call)

Frank Whelan, historian and Allentown *Morning Call* columnist, reported that the Tower Building rested on solid bedrock.

direct rail connections from New York City; Electric Bond and Share Co. executives could get on the train at Grand Central Station in New York and be in Allentown less than two hours later.

Once the decision was made to locate in Allentown, the directors quickly came to the secondary decision of selecting a site at Ninth and Hamilton streets. Originally, the directors wanted to purchase property on the southwestern corner of the intersection. The property was owned by Nathan Martin and his sister. Martin had the reputation of being a recluse, and Trexler sent Nimson Eckert, a close personal friend of the Martins, to inquire about buying the property at a reasonable price. "The Martins say they don't want to sell because they would not know what to do with the money," Eckert reported back to the board.

The property across the street, on the northwestern corner of the intersection, was available, and PP&L took an option in 1925. At the suggestion of Mitchell, the firm retained the New York architectural firm of Helmle, Corbett and Harrison to design what would become known as the Tower Building. Six well-known architectural firms, including two from Allentown, were invited to submit bids for the design of the Tower Building.

Helmle, Corbett and Harrison had already designed numerous buildings, including the Bush Terminal and the Chamber of Commerce Building in New York, the Bush Building in London and the George Washington Masonic National Memorial in Alexandria, Va.

Harvey Corbett and Wallace K. Harrison came to Allentown to design the new building. Born in 1895 in Worcester, Mass., Harrison was a high school dropout who studied at the Ecole des Beaux Arts in Paris

following World War I. In 1921, he returned to New York to join Helmle and Corbett. Although he gave much of the credit for the design of the PP&L Tower to Corbett, the Tower Building was Harrison's first major skyscraper project in a long and illustrious career.

"That building, the first skyscraper I ever worked on, has always seemed to me the perfect illustration of why the skyscraper was the logical answer to the changing business scene in this country," Harrison told an interviewer in the 1950s.

> *"The Martins say they don't want to sell because they would not know what to do with the money."—Nimson Eckert*

The skyscraper that Harrison and Corbett designed was 322 feet high, more than three times as tall as the Soldiers and Sailors Monument in Allentown. With its long perpendicular lines, fluted coping at the corners and progressive setbacks, the design was one of two examples of art deco architecture in Allentown. More importantly, the 23-story skyscraper was the prototype for art deco architecture in New York City. Harrison would go on to incorporate much of the design of the PP&L Tower into his design of Rockefeller Center. Later, Harrison would

Allentown's Buckley Building (right corner) at 802 Hamilton Street was PP&L's first home office from 1923 to 1928. *(photo courtesy of the Lehigh County Historical Society)*

8th and Hamilton Streets, Allentown, Pa.

serve as the lead architect for the United Nations Building and Lincoln Center.

Snakes Underground

Hegeman-Harris Co. of New York was named as general contractor for the project, and foundation work got underway in October 1926. Hegeman-Harris Co. also served as the general contractor for the 34-story Tribune Tower in Chicago, and the firm was well aware of the subterranean streams that flowed beneath Allentown and the Lehigh Valley.

Subcontractors included the Gunvald Aus Co., handling steel design and inspection of fabrication and erection; Clyde R. Place, mechanical and electrical engineer; Daniel E. Moran of Moran, Maurice and Proctor on foundation work; H.N. Crowder Jr., electrical wiring; D'Arcy Ryan of General Electric, handling exterior floodlighting; and W&J Sloane, interior decoration.

Engineers for Hegeman-Harris Co. determined that support piers needed to be sunk 125 feet to find suitable anchorage in the bedrock below Ninth and Hamilton. As sidewalk superintendents congregated along the Ninth Street side of Hess's department store to watch activity in the growing hole, crews operating a steam shovel loaded a procession of dump trucks with dirt and rock from the excavation site. Theatergoers at the Pergola Cinema across the street noticed that the excavation went on late into the evening during the fall of 1926.

In the spring of 1927, the excavation

Construction on the Tower started with negotiations in 1925, excavation in 1926, construction in 1927 and finally occupation in 1928. These photos show the construction progress from December 1926 to July 1927.

crews were down 62 feet. Excavation halted momentarily one spring morning when crews reporting to work found a four-foot snake "alive and kicking in the watery bottom of the caisson. The zoologist at Muhlenberg College, Dr. Henry Bailey, could not explain the presence of the snake so far underground except that it had followed a subterranean stream," reported the *Allentown Call-Chronicle*.

The 48 concrete piers averaged 78 feet in depth before hitting bedrock. Foundation experts who examined the bedrock in the fall of 1926 expressed the opinion that the foundation was capable of supporting as much as a 40-story building.

By the fall of 1927, the superstructure of the 23-story building was towering over the Allentown skyline. A reporter for the *Philadelphia Inquirer* marveled at the audacity of PP&L in building such a big city structure in a small town like Allentown. "Emulating the example of this and other large construction centres," the reporter noted, "the smaller cities of this country are going in for skyscraper building. This is particularly in evidence in Allentown, where one of the tallest, as well as most modern office structures in Pennsylvania, is nearing completion."

Steel erection had started on Jan. 28, 1927, and the first concrete floor arches were poured five weeks later. Brickmasons started laying the first brick walls on April 8, 1927, and completed the job at the end of the summer.

The Tower Building operated a frontage on Hamilton Street of 100 feet and a depth of 130 feet on Ninth Street. The top of the flagpole above the building was 382 feet above sea level. The building contained 184,522 square feet of usable space in 21 office floors, a sales and display floor with a mezzanine, an elevator, a penthouse

The elegant interior of the Tower included six elevators which could safely transport passengers from the first floor to the 22nd floor in just 30 seconds.
circa 1928

Electrically operated through motor-generator sets, the six elevators could operate at a speed of 650 feet per minute.

and a basement with a mezzanine. Construction for the Tower Building was $3.2 million, with another $676,000 going for purchase of the site. Today's conservative estimates for replacement cost range well above $70 million.

Terrazzo, Marble and Limestone

The exterior of the bottom two stories was New Hampshire granite and Indiana limestone, with bronze work at the doors and windows. Above the second floor, the exterior was brick with hollow tile furring, faced with light tan pressed brick. An exterior floodlighting system installed by General Electric made the Tower Building visible at night from almost any point in the Lehigh Valley.

Inside the building, the interior was richly appointed. The reinforced concrete floors in the display room, the main corridors above the first floor and the stairwells were surfaced with terrazzo. Walls in the washrooms were Tennessee Marble to a height of seven feet, and the main corridors were surfaced with Bottachino Marble. The offices were floored with what the designers called "battleship linoleum."

The building contained six elevators, three on either side of the main corridor. Five of the elevators carried passengers; the sixth was designated as a freight elevator. Electrically operated through motor-generator sets, the six elevators could operate at a speed of 650 feet per minute, whisking passengers from the

first floor to the 22nd floor in 30 seconds or less. Doors and safety gates were operated by compressed air.

Two steel stairways with terrazzo treads and landings extended the full height of the building through fireproof towers. Piping was also carried through the full height of the building with service shafts providing access at each floor. A ventilating system was also contained in the building's service shafts, as were the electrical and telephone wiring.

The building was equipped with two large steel tanks for firefighting, one on the penthouse level and the other on the 13th floor. A fire alarm system was tied to the signal system of the Allentown Fire Department. Like PP&L's Hauto and Harwood stations, the Tower Building derived its heat from anthracite coal. The vapor-vacuum type heating system was supplied from three 150-hp horizontal return tubular boilers fired with No. 2 buckwheat anthracite coal.

The building boasted the first Private Automatic or "dial system" exchange in Allentown, installed on the sixth floor by the Lehigh Telephone Co. "The building exchange is a duplicate, on a small scale, of the Central City Exchange and provides a complete intercommunicating system for the building, is convenient in operation, and results in a maximum of efficiency," the company reported in 1928. "Facilities for direct communication with any subscriber supplied by the local City Exchange are provided over 24 trunk lines between the building and the telephone company's central office."

The office layouts on the various floors were similar, with a private corner office for the department head, a waiting and meeting room, and a room for stenographers. The rest of the floorspace was left undivided, with hollow, movable partitions for the most flexible layout.

"The penthouse consists of two floor levels," the company reported, "the lower of which contains the refrigerating plant, the elevator signal system and one large office. The upper level houses the elevator machinery, elevator control equipment and water tanks. The basement houses a substation for supplying electric light and power to the building and to customers in the immediate vicinity. Here are also located the heating plant, pump room, switchboards, a repair shop and an incinerator. Storage vaults and stock rooms are provided in both the basement and basement mezzanine."

Like Going Into the Taj Mahal

Pennsylvania Power & Light Co. opened its new Tower Building to the public on July 16, 1928. "The public yesterday had its first opportunity to see the new Pennsylvania Power & Light Co. building, the imposing structure which somehow better than anything else in the city gives expression to the progressive spirit of Allentown," the reporter from the *Morning Call* described the new downtown landmark for the newspaper's readers.

"While at night it almost seems a phantom palace with the illuminated crown, during the day and particularly yesterday since its doors were first opened to the public, it appears as though it had been uprooted from some huge metropolis and set down in the heart of Allentown—or again, as many people who came to see the office yesterday declared, 'you just can't imagine you're in Allentown—you think you're in New York, or some such place.'"

During the open house celebration, the sales floor was decorated with floral tributes from the Lehigh Valley Electric Association, the Walters-Genter Co., the Edison Electric Appliance Co., Westinghouse and the Lehigh Valley Electrical Contractor's Association. The Hess's Department Store gave the utility a silver and black screen, depicting the new building, which had resided in the department store's display window

The exterior of the Tower is as impressive as the interior with details like this sculpture by Alexander Archipenko on the building's east side.

Saxon Scheirer

through much of the spring.

For PP&L employees, the new building was an eloquent statement that the Allentown utility had arrived to take its rightful place in the business community of the Lehigh Valley.

"It was like going into the Taj Mahal," retiree Saxon Scheirer told the *PP&L Reporter* in 1978, adding that his sales department had been among the first to move into the new building in January 1928. "The sales office where I worked was above a ladies apparel store between Seventh and Eighth on Hamilton. There was another location between Eighth and Ninth streets above a soda and confectionery store where the purchasing and general stores personnel were. The District Office and many of the general office people were located in a building on the northwest corner of Eighth and Hamilton streets. And there were several other locations in downtown Allentown, too. We were all over the place. Of course, the company at the time also had 52 district offices in 11 divisions."

For Scheirer and the other employees, "it was a tremendous feeling when we

"…many people who came to see the office… declared, 'you just can't imagine you're in Allentown —you think you're in New York, or some such place.'"
—Morning Call. circa 1928

than a couple of stories. On the 13th floor where we were, you could see for miles. It really made us all recognize the size of Allentown and its growth. It gave everyone a new vista."

Particularly impressive for the employees was the space and the amenities. "The spaciousness of the floors really was a big plus factor and a tremendous source of pleasure to us," Scheirer recalled. "In the old building where we were, we had room for one extra chair. If more than one appliance representative came to visit us, someone had to stand. In the new building we actually had a receptionist, and we had a waiting room filled with benches and chairs.

"Our air conditioning in those days was fans. Westinghouse had just come out with a new type of metal fan that was installed in the Tower Building. The fans in the other old buildings had big brass blades. They were so noisy you had to shut them off to carry on a phone conversation.

"The elevators were a sensation to be in. The elevators at the time were the fastest-moving elevators in the United States. When you went whizzing up or down in one of them, it was quite a thrill. In fact, the entire building was quite remarkable."

The old gentleman who bought PP&L common stock on the strength of his belief that the Tower Building represented the arrival of the electric utility industry was right. By 1928, electricity was "here to stay" for residents of central eastern Pennsylvania.

Trolleys ran along Hamilton Street in May 1928 despite torn-up roadways.

State-of-the-art for its day—(counterclockwise from top) the Tower office areas, switchboard, motor-driven water pumps and massive steam heat boilers. *circa 1927*

began working in the Tower Building. It was the biggest skyscraper in the entire Lehigh Valley. I really believe the building helped to sell the company, which was less than 10 years old at the time, to the public. When you told people you worked for PP&L, they now knew who you were talking about. I remember one fellow who bought some PP&L stock because he said that seeing the Tower Building convinced him that electricity was here to stay."

Scheirer particularly remembered the view. "One of the things that impressed us was the view you had from the building," he recalled. "None of us had ever seen the town from anything higher

One for the Encyclopedia

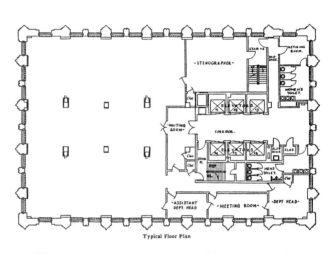

Typical Floor Plan

Because of its unique construction and design, the Tower Building was featured in the 1930 edition of *The Encyclopedia Britannica*. Chief among the attributes cited by *Britannica* was the fact that the building's concrete floors were joined with the steel frame to form a single unit instead of being supported by thick, costly exterior walls.

But the Tower Building accumulated a whole host of superlatives. In 1928, Pennsylvania Power & Light Co. published a brochure on its new building and listed some of the quantities involved in the construction:

Excavation for basement	12,700 cubic yards
Excavation for caissons, rock	1,100 cubic yards
Excavation for caissons, earth	300 cubic yards
Number of caissons	48
Structural steel	3,300 tons
Rivets	250,000
Face brick	1,024,000
Common brick	1,823,000
Piping	42 miles
Cement	104,200 bags
Sand	18,900 tons
Stone	5,400 tons
Form lumber	576,600 board feet
Granite	10 carloads
Marble	20 carloads
Reinforcing steel	2,400 tons
Hollow tile	270,000
Windows	897

Glass	20,000 square feet
Hollow metal doors	500
Plastering	55,000 square feet
Conduit for lighting and power	30 miles
Wire for lighting and power	182 miles
Telephone cable	84 miles
Bronze work	40 tons
Terrazzo floor	18,000 square feet
Tile floor	9,300 square feet
Asbestos pipe covering	23 miles
Heating system radiation	45,000 square feet
Linoleum	10,000 square yards
Electric lighting fixtures	1,635
Telephones	225
Venetian blinds	348
Window shades	561
Paint	1,650 gallons

Add to the above list the equipment used, including three low-pressure boilers, 15 house pumps, a filtration system, five water storage tanks with a total capacity of 25,000 gallons, six elevators, three ventilating fans, a water softening plant and eight transformers, and it's easy to see why the editors of *The Encyclopedia Britannica* included the Tower Building in the 1930 edition.

Shades Properly Drawn

For generations of PP&L employees, one of the first things taught when they come to work in the Tower Building is how to draw the shades properly at night.

The practice goes back to the very earliest days of the Tower Building. On May 1, 1928, well before the official public open house, H.R. Bell, superintendent of buildings, sent a memo to Harry Ferguson, secretary to Norman G. Reinicker, general superintendent of PP&L.

"It has been brought to my attention that all of the shades on your floor are not being pulled down to the proper level," Bell wrote. "For instance, last night the only rooms where the shades were pulled down properly were Mr. Reinicker's private offices and the meeting rooms. In your room, the shades were up and the windows open about a foot from the top. In the large room, all the shades were left up."

Bell suggested that Ferguson appoint a person from the department to see that shades were at the proper level in the evening and Saturday at noon "so that the building will set forth a neat appearance from the outside."

Bell was fighting a losing battle with the shades, and in the summer of 1928, the Building Department took over the shade detail. But cutbacks during the Great Depression caused PP&L to delegate window shades once again to personnel in the various offices of the building.

"The Building Department has in the past delegated a man to go through the entire building after office hours to see that windows are closed, shades properly drawn and lights turned out," a general office memo of May 1, 1931, pointed out. "Effective today, this practice will be discontinued, and it is, therefore, up to the individual employees to take care of the windows at his or her desk. The last employee out of the office should check up on all windows and lights."

Bell and the Building Department were also concerned with the appearance of the sales floor and sales mezzanine. Outside salesmen or demonstrators were prohibited from being on the sales floor after business hours, and there were a host of regulations to be adhered to concerning curtains and lights in the Sales Department.

Sales personnel were instructed to turn on window and sales floor lights "full at dark. Watch Hess Brothers—always be sure to turn lights on before they do." Curtains were to be closed between midnight and 1 a.m. and opened between 5 a.m. and 6 a.m. Lights were to be left burning all night over the investment counter, the contract and information counter, the cashier cages and in the vestibules. Lights were also to be left on for at least one-half the mezzanine floor.

Elevator etiquette was another area of concern to the Building Department. Elevator operators were instructed to wear their uniforms at all times, even on weekends. They were allowed to wear their uniforms out of the building at lunch but were asked to keep the uniforms in their lockers when leaving for the day.

PP&L personnel who pressed both the "up" and the "down" buttons on the elevators were a point of personal aggravation to the Building Department. The elevators were such an attraction that personnel frequently rode them to the top floor and then back down at the end of the day.

Smoking and chewing gum were particular banes of the harried Building Department personnel. At a meeting of department heads in the new building on April 11, 1928, Bell reported that "men and women drop chewing gum into drinking fountains, causing them to clog, (and) men frequently drop cigars and cigarettes on floors of elevators and on stairways."

In a follow-up report to the April 11 meeting, W.L. Davis, the company auditor, noted that "there is no smoking in the General Accounting Department  during working hours, and this will account for the fact that cigars and cigarette butts are sometimes found in the halls. A cuspidor in the hall might remedy the situation. While on this subject, you might be interested in knowing that we have had one waste basket catch fire already; hence, the 'No Smoking' rule in the Accounting Department will be enforced."

19

The Sales Department

Walking into the lobby and sales floor of the PP&L Tower Building was like walking into a grand hotel. Notice the four vacuum cleaners ready for demonstration on an oriental rug.

When PP&L opened its brand new Tower Building for public inspection in the summer of 1928, "Meet me on the Mezzanine" was the theme that the Allentown utility adopted for its retail customers.

The five-day open house at the 23-story Tower Building included entertainment and refreshments on the balcony floor,

This view greeted visitors to PP&L's brand-new Allentown General Office when it opened in 1928. Notice the elegant display of electrical appliances.

demonstration structure of the Hoover vacuum cleaner.

"There are numerous other unusual displays showing the very newest types and models in electric appliances and furnishings, including the up-to-date colored General Electric refrigerators and other creations in the world of electricity as applied to the modern home."

Beautiful, Yet Simple and Dignified

The brochure handed out to visitors at the open house instructed retail customers to enter the building on the Hamilton Street side, since that entrance led "into the spacious and well-appointed sales and appliance display room. The sales and appliance display room is spacious, and its decorations, fittings and appointments are beautiful, yet simple and dignified.

"The terrazzo floor is of a color combination which blends well with the natural walnut panelling on the walls and columns. This panelling extends to a height of about 11 feet on the walls and on the columns to the high ceilings. The ceiling is finished in recessed panels and together with the walls above the wood panelling is decorated in simple style and color to blend with the walnut trim and wainscoting. Ornamental chandeliers supply subdued but well-distributed light over the entire room.

"Appliances are displayed in floor cases, on tables and on other furniture designed especially for the purpose. Cashier's cages, Customers' Service Bureau and Investment Department offices are located at the rear of the room. Rooms for the display of appliances in operation in a model electric kitchen, as well as the Appliance Sales and Service Department are included.

"A mezzanine floor extending over the rear portion of the display room provides a large waiting and retiring room for the convenience and comfort of the patrons and the public, a special display section

which was destined to serve as a retail show floor for nearly half-a-century. Edith Hutchison, the Chicago-based home economist and dietitian for the Edison Electric Appliance Co., gave lectures every hour on the hour during the five-day celebration, demonstrating Hotpoint appliances and the recently introduced Servel electrically refrigerated water cooler.

Waffles and coffee were served daily on the mezzanine to those in attendance, and the retail floor was open until 9 p.m. on Thursday, Friday and Saturday of the open house week.

"Among the unusual features of the display room," noted the reporter from the *Allentown Call*, "are a huge model of the Hotpoint automatic iron weighing 150 pounds (the ordinary size weighs six); a cutaway demonstrator model of the Prima electric washer with the never-crush wringer rolls, and a remarkable

and several offices. Decorations and furnishings on this floor are in keeping with those on the main display floor."

The attention to detail in the display room and Sales Department floor was typical of the importance that electric utilities attributed to merchandise sales in the 1920s. The electrification of American society after 1900 was made possible to a great extent by the introduction of electrical home appliances. As early as the 1890s, electric fans, toasters and resistance heaters were in common use in American homes.

In 1910, George Hughes, a North Dakotan who had grown up with a family-owned utility business, demonstrated an electric stove at the National Electric Light Association annual convention in St. Louis. Four years later, Hughes joined the Hotpoint Co. of Chicago, which made an iron with a small extra heating coil in its nose, which kept the point of the iron hot for ironing around buttons. In 1918, Hotpoint merged with General Electric's Edison Electric Appliance Co.; over the next quarter-century, the Hotpoint stove was introduced into well over a million American homes.

Early marketing efforts for electric appliances were primitive, to say the least. Hotpoint's Hughes often related the story of the door-to-door appliance salesman early in the century who would ring the bell, lay an iron on the doorstep and "run like hell."

One problem early in the century that precluded the marketing of electric service was the large number of unwired homes in urban areas like Allentown, Scranton, Philadelphia and New York. The National Electric Light Association, the forerunner of the Edison

Electric Institute, sponsored several "Wire Your Home" campaigns for member companies in the first decade of the 20th century. To forestall the problem of unwired homes, electric utilities sold the Clement Electric Service Table, a single unit that contained a service connection with meter and push-button main-switch for furnishing limited service for flat irons, fans, hot plates and lights.

As late as 1921, PP&L announced a house-wiring promotion for existing buildings and resi-dences. "No damage to floors, and without removing plaster," advertisements in the service area newspapers promised. "Wires are 'fished' through the partitions. We have arranged with the city's experienced

> *One problem early in the century that precluded the marketing of electric service was the large number of unwired homes in urban areas like Allentown, Scranton, Philadelphia and New York.*

Advertisements from 1921 promoting house wiring and labor-saving appliances.

Grace A. Raker, former PP&L home economist. Opportunity for women at PP&L expanded in the 1920s in the Home Economics and Home Service departments.

wiring contractors to do the wiring at low prices. We pay them when work is completed—you pay us in monthly installments covering a period of one year."

Building Load

Pennsylvania Power & Light Co. and its predecessors established a strong sales and marketing effort for electric appliances early in the 20th century. The sales and marketing effort, which blossomed in the 1920s, provided an opportunity for the advancement of female employees.

As early as 1913, the Scranton Electric Co., which would become a part of PP&L in 1954, operated an appliance counter on the first floor of its general office in the Board of Trade Building. The counter was staffed by female sales per-sonnel, many of whom would go on to staff the utility's Home Economics and Home Service departments in the 1920s and 1930s.

Mae Phillips, a salesperson at Scranton Electric Co.'s appliance counter in 1913, explained to readers of American Gas & Electric Co.'s *AGE Bulletin* that many of the customers at the appliance counter were housewives who felt more comfortable dealing with female sales personnel. Phillips also noted that Scranton Electric Co. was engaged in sophisticated marketing efforts to sell appliances in 1913, including cooperative advertising campaigns.

"I consider the splendid cooperative advertising campaign being conducted by the appliance manufacturing companies one of the real big forces that are bringing this department more and more to the

The sales and marketing effort, which blossomed in the 1920s, provided an opportunity for the advancement of female employees.

front in the central station industry," Phillips said.

For much of the fall and early winter of 1913, Scranton Electric Co. conducted a vacuum sweeper campaign. The company ran coupons in the local newspapers, which were good for an $11 discount on the $39 price of the electric sweeper. Customers put $9 down and agreed to pay $3 a month on their electric bill; as an enticement for the Christmas season, Scranton Electric Co. threw in two small appliances of the customer's choice.

"The Appliance Department is more and more becoming one of the big factors in securing and holding residential business," Phillips pointed out in 1913, "and that means additional company revenue."

By the 1920 formation of PP&L, utilities across the country had established formal sales departments charged with selling appliances and lighting to residential customers. PP&L formed its Merchandise Sales Department in the summer of 1920, shortly after the company itself was formed.

Merchandise Sales moved into something of a vacuum in the PP&L service territory. Through the first two decades of the century, electrical contractors often sold appliances as a sideline. The contractors frequently lacked the financial backing or the promotional expertise to sell what was essentially a consumer durable, and PP&L moved decisively to establish a formal marketing presence in the area.

"Even in the later 1920s and 1930s," the company explained in 1970, "when many dealers were promoting and selling various electric appliances, they had neither the time nor manpower, nor could they afford the cost of pioneering customer acceptance of such appliances as refrigerators, ranges and water heaters. Thus, it became PP&L's job to pioneer the use of electric appliances and equipment as they became available."

PUT IT ON YOUR LIGHT BILL

Electric consumption jumped dramatically in the period between 1916 and 1926. Nationally, the number of homes wired increased nearly threefold from 1917 to 1926, from 5.8 million to 15.3 million. In 1915, the average American home wired for electric service consumed 260 kilowatt hours per year. That figure spurted to 293 kilowatt hours in the year following the end of the Great War.

In the early 1920s, the Merchandise Sales Department advertised, sold and financed wiring, electric light bulbs, portable lamps, electric washing machines, irons, vacuum cleaners, heating pads, curling irons, room heaters and sewing machines. Electric washing machines of the time, which included a motor-driven wringer and a brass and wooden tub, were advertised at $2.50 down with up to a year to pay the balance. Electric irons sold for $1 down, and vacuum cleaners could be purchased for as little as $5 down.

Because of its background as an Electric Bond and Share company, many of the appliances sold and promoted by PP&L were made by General Electric. GE pioneered many of the larger appliances such as refrigerators, electric ranges and washing machines, and by the mid-1920s, the General Electric "Monitor Top" refrigerator was a common sight in PP&L's Merchandise Sales Department showrooms. Prior to 1922, Hotpoint electric stoves, like Henry Ford's Model T, came in

any color the customer wanted, as long as it was black; that year, Hotpoint brought out a white porcelain enamel stove that soon became all the rage in central eastern Pennsylvania.

PP&L's showrooms, which were located in the Tower Building and at each of the utility's district offices, were open six days a week, including Saturday evenings. On Christmas Eve, the field sales staff worked until late in the evening delivering electric appliances to customers.

The Merchandise Sales Department was responsible for advertising appliances, an activity which picked up steam dramatically in the 1920s. A 1922 Hometown Advertising Conference sponsored by the department elicited positive responses from customers in the service territory. "It's about time the public got to know what PP&L is doing," one newspaper advertising executive noted. "It's the best thing I ever saw," another respondent replied. "I like the way employees are featured in the ads."

> *"...it became PP&L's job to pioneer the use of electric appliances and equipment as they became available."*

Display area of electrical appliances in the Allentown Electric Light & Power Co. office. *circa 1910*

(Inset) Table display of Mazda light bulbs.

The Merchandise Sales Department also used the emerging medium of radio to reach its customers, and it sponsored increasingly sophisticated demonstrations of appliances in its showrooms. In May 1922, the department ran advertisements in the *Bethlehem Times*

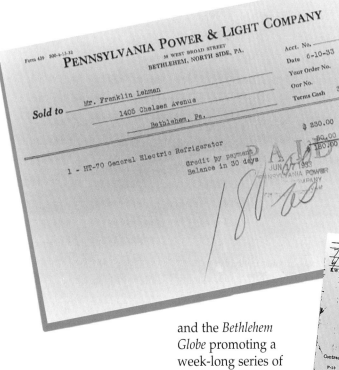

and the *Bethlehem Globe* promoting a week-long series of electric cooking demonstrations conducted "by an expert demonstrator from the Hughes Hotpoint Factory." The demonstrations ran from 2-5 p.m. Monday through Friday and from 2-8 p.m. on Saturday.

The success of the cooking demonstrations led to the 1929 expansion of the Merchandise Sales Department to include a Home Service Department. "Its purpose was to demonstrate the care and use of the various electric appliances both in the home and by public group demonstration," a 1970 history of the department noted. By the mid-1930s, the 56 women in the Home Service Department made up one of the largest such

departments among investor-owned electric utilities in the United States.

Expansion in the 1930s

The opening of the Tower Building in the summer of 1928 coincided with PP&L's first electric refrigerator sales campaign. Electric refrigeration for the home had become a reality two years before when General Electric first introduced its Monitor Top model. PP&L added a line of electric ranges in 1932.

The expansion of the Merchandise Sales Department during the 1930s was an anomaly of electric utility expansion during the decade. The collapse of the stock market in October 1929 ushered in the Great Depression, and although economic conditions deteriorated dramatically in Pennsylvania and the rest of the nation, kilowatt-

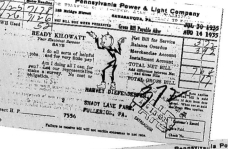

hour sales kept rising for most utilities, including PP&L.

Millions of Americans were unemployed, and the unemployment rate in the Lehigh Valley throughout much of the early 1930s topped 25 percent. But 75 percent of the working population was employed, and the depressed economic conditions kept inflation in check for more than a decade. The result was strong consumer demand for electric appliances.

From 1920 to the onset of World War II, PP&L engaged in a great, nationwide social experiment that led to the electrification of the American home.

Early in the 1930s, the Merchandise Sales Department expanded, hiring specialists in electric ranges, water heaters, gas ranges and commercial equipment. PP&L also instituted a Dealer Cooperative Program during the decade, helping electric appliance and equipment dealers to sell more product. By 1938, the Dealer Cooperative Program accounted for more than $10 million in sales a year, 88 percent of which was attributed to dealer sales. In 1938 alone, the program resulted in the sale of 18,100 refrigerators and 4,000 electric stoves to PP&L customers.

Better lighting was one area of retail and commercial sales and marketing that the electric utility industry had not previously concentrated upon. In the early 1930s, lighting fixtures in many PP&L homes were little better than they had been 20 years before. The ceiling fixtures often consisted of a lamp cord extension to which was attached a socket containing a 25- or 50-watt light bulb with a shade.

To remedy the sometimes dismal lighting situation in American homes, the National Electric Light Association inaugurated the "Better Light-Better Sight" program in 1933. PP&L adopted the program the next year, sending forth "a sizable force of personnel" to make personal calls on customers and conduct demonstrations to promote and sell the value of better lighting; a popular sales technique of the program was to inform parents of the value of better lighting for their children's homework.

From 1920 to the onset of World War II, PP&L engaged in a great, nationwide social experiment that led to the electrification of the American home. In the space of little more than two decades, the operation of the typical home went from a highly labor-intensive activity to one that was dependent more upon machinery than elbow grease. Increasingly, the labor-saving aspects of home electrification freed housewives for employment outside the home, a trend that would become much more sharply pronounced during the World War II years.

"Good results were attained through sales efforts to increase the use of services by existing customers and to extend them to new customers," PP&L concluded about its Merchandise Sales Department activities in 1938, the last year of the Great Depression.

Perfect Coffee by a Perfect Method

WITH Electricity in Your Home endless Comforts and Conveniences are afforded by the use of

Electrical Appliances

These ads are from one of PP&L's predecessors, the Edison Electric Co.

Industrial Sales and Area Development

There is a perhaps apocryphal story from the early days of PP&L's history that the chief clerk of the Industrial Sales Department climbed the stairs to the roof of the Tower Building each morning and checked the horizon in the surrounding Lehigh Valley. If he spotted smoke rising from factory chimneys in the valley, he noted the approximate location and turned the information over to the department's sales personnel to find out the exact location and to contact the owner about the benefits of industrial electric power.

The formation of PP&L's Industrial Sales Department in 1928 coincided with the opening of the Tower Building in Allentown, so the story could well be true. PP&L formed the department from members of the Commercial Department, and the early mission of industrial sales personnel was to identify service area businesses that still generated internal electric power and try to convince them to buy industrial power from the Allentown-based utility. Smoke rising from a factory chimney was a tip-off that coal-fired boilers were at work in the facility's basement.

Personnel from the Industrial Sales Department were also busy during the 1930s converting industrial facilities in the service territory from 25- to 60-cycle electric power. Industrial Sales personnel from Allentown canvassed the territory, helping factory owners convert to 60-cycle power. Increasingly, trained personnel were assigned to the field divisions to assume similar responsibilities in the areas outside Allentown.

As industrial sales became a more important part of the company's revenue stream in the 1930s, the department was expanded. Specialists were added to the sales force, and as the decade wore on, the department developed expertise in a number of fields, including the application of electricity to such industries as textiles, water pumping, iron and steel, cement, sand, gravel and slate quarries. The department also became much more involved in the fields of commercial lighting and refrigeration.

The Benefits of Area Development

In 1929, the year after the formation of the Industrial Sales Department, PP&L assigned an executive from the department to work full-time with area and industrial development.

The concept of utility area development work can be traced to Sidney Z. Mitchell, Electric Bond and Share Co.'s founding chairman. Mitchell had long been convinced that utilities could not move their generation and transmission facilities to another state or region if the local economy turned sour. Accordingly, he argued that utilities should make every effort to strengthen the economy of their service territories by attracting new industry and retaining the industrial base they already had.

The formal establishment of an area development function in 1929 made PP&L one of the first utilities in the nation to create such a department. In the mid-1930s, PP&L assigned a full-time industrial development representative to the New York area and a second representative to the Philadelphia area. The representatives called on industrial and commercial executives in the two metropolitan areas, trying to convince them of the benefits of locating manufacturing facilities in central eastern Pennsylvania. In 1937 alone, 55 new industrial plants were located in Pennsylvania Power & Light Co.'s service territory, partly as a result of the company's industrial development efforts.

That same year of 1937, PP&L combined its industrial sales, area development and merchandise sales functions into a General Sales Department.

In 1937 alone, 55 new industrial plants were located in Pennsylvania Power & Light Co.'s service territory.

20

Giant Power

Franklin D. Roosevelt's New Deal Administration led to a national restructuring of the utility industry in the 1930s. (*photo courtesy of AP/ Wide World Photos*)

While Pennsylvania Power & Light Co. was consolidating its operations in the early 1920s, the American electric utility industry was undergoing a political upheaval unprecedented in its history.

Technological advances in steam electric power generation and transmission and the economic organization of the industry into a holding company structure were obscured by political battles on both the national and state levels. The political wars that characterized the decade led to a national restructuring of the utility industry in the 1930s when the New Deal administration of Franklin D. Roosevelt passed landmark legislation outlawing the holding companies.

Many of the early battles were fought in Pennsylvania. The Progressive administration of Gov. Gifford Pinchot conducted a decade-long campaign to restructure the industry within the state. Pinchot's Giant Power proposal was modeled on the public power initiatives of Sir Adam Beck, which had resulted in the formation of Ontario Hydro in nearby Canada during the early years of the 20th century.

In essence, Pinchot's Giant Power proposal called for the construction of state-owned, mine-mouth generating plants in the coalfields of the western part of the state. Pinchot proposed transmitting the power back east to the state's population centers by a state-owned transmission grid.

Ironically, Giant Power never took hold in the 1920s, partly because the utilities in the eastern part of the state already had a large capital investment in generation and transmission facilities, and partly because the technology wasn't quite advanced enough to support what a later generation of engineers called "coal by wire." But Giant Power, at least in its proposal to ship coal-fired electric power eastward via high-voltage transmission lines, exists today in parts of Pennsylvania Power & Light Co.'s service territory. The Keystone and Conemaugh projects of the 1970s essentially followed the model that Gifford Pinchot had suggested half a century before.

Gifford Pinchot— forester, Pennsylvania governor and outspoken critic of the electric power business. (*photo courtesy of the* Morning Call)

The Political Background

Gifford Pinchot was elected governor of Pennsylvania in 1922, following the death the year before of the state's conservative Republican boss, Boies Penrose. Penrose had dominated state politics for more than a decade, and although a Republican himself, Pinchot had solid credentials as a Progressive dating back to his work in Theodore Roosevelt's administration. Pinchot, who had been trained as a forester, made his reputation as a reformer, tirelessly campaigning for the restructuring of the U.S. Department of the Interior. At Pinchot's urging, Roosevelt transferred oversight of national forests from Interior to the Department of Agriculture.

As a forester, Pinchot was also interested in the development of hydroelectric sites on federal land. As early as 1903, Pinchot convinced Roosevelt to veto a bill granting permission for an investor-owned electric power company to build a dam and hydroelectric station on the Tennessee River at Muscle Shoals, Ala.

Pinchot's campaign to reserve federally owned waterpower sites for public development led to the passage of the Federal Water Power Act of 1920. The site at Muscle Shoals that Pinchot was instrumental in getting Roosevelt to reject for water power development in 1903 would later become the linchpin for the creation of the Tennessee Valley Authority.

Pinchot's election as governor of Pennsylvania in the fall of 1922 brought about an upheaval in state politics. Pinchot's two terms as governor (1923-1927 and 1931-1935) resulted in a great deal of administrative reorganization. During his first term alone, he brought about the creation of the Pennsylvania Department of Forests and Waters and instituted conservation measures in the state. Pinchot liquidated the state debt, created a state budget system and established a state employees' retirement system. On the social side, he reformed mental health practices, tightened state election laws and spearheaded a largely unsuccessful campaign to enforce prohibition laws.

But it was Pinchot's interest in electric power development that most characterized his first term in office. According to M. Nelson McGeary, Pinchot's biographer, his "two main objectives as Governor of Pennsylvania…were the regulation of electric power and the enforcement of prohibition."

Pinchot, who once called power company executives examples of "greedy, unreasoning selfishness," feared the creation of an uncontrolled national monopoly in the electric power business. He criticized power companies in the state for high rates and for their lack of rural line extensions. Prior to his inauguration in the spring of 1923, the incoming Pennsylvania governor met with Morris L. Cooke, a Philadelphia engineer who had established a reputation as a champion of publicly owned power developments in the United States. Pinchot and Cooke went to the Pennsylvania legislature during the 1923 session with an ambitious plan to study the best ways to secure a cheap and abundant supply of electric power in the state.

The legislature appropriated $35,000 for a landmark study of the state's electric power industry. Cooke was in charge of the study, and when the 480-page Giant Power report was publicly released in the spring of 1925, it set off a political battle in Pennsylvania that foreshadowed the national utility battles of the 1930s.

Basically, Cooke and his engineers had been charged with the mission of conducting "an outline survey of the water and fuel resources available for Pennsylvania, and of the most practicable means for their full utilization for power development, and other related uses; also to recommend, in outline, such policy with respect to the generation and distribution of electric energy as will, in the opinion of the board, best secure for the industries, railroads, farms and homes of this commonwealth, an abundant and cheap supply of electric current for industrial, transportation, agricultural and domestic use."

> *His "two main objectives as Governor of Pennsylvania... were the regulation of electric power and the enforcement of prohibition."*
> —*M. Nelson McGeary, Pinchot's biographer*

What Cooke and the Giant Power Survey Board discovered was that some 90 percent of the electricity generated in the state was derived from coal. A total of 19 holding companies operated in the state, providing electric service to 5.4 million residents living in 58 counties. The Philadelphia Electric Co. (renamed PECO Energy Co. in 1994) provided service to a population of nearly 1.95 million people living in the City of Brotherly Love and its suburbs. Pennsylvania Power & Light Co., a subsidiary of the Electric Bond and Share Co., provided local service to a population of almost 835,000 people in the central and eastern portions of the state. Together, the two holding companies provided electric service to more than 50 percent of the state population.

Cooke and the Board proposed a reorganization of the entire system of generating and transmitting electric power within the state. The Survey Board correctly noted the "Great Growth in the Use of Electricity." Cooke himself pointed out that in 1900, 10 percent of the total industrial power of the state was electrically driven. At the time of his report, the figure had increased to 65 percent, and the Philadelphia engineer estimated that the figure would be 90 percent by 1940.

The Giant Power Survey Board pointed out that it was technologically feasible to transmit power long distances over high-voltage transmission lines and asked if that were the case, then why should the electrical power industry haul coal by rail from the western coalfields to the generating stations back east? Cooke and his

> *When the 480-page Giant Power report was publicly released in the spring of 1925, it set off a political battle in Pennsylvania that foreshadowed the national utility battles of the 1930s.*

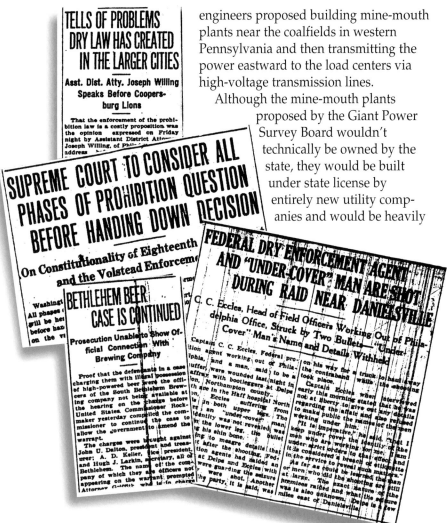

engineers proposed building mine-mouth plants near the coalfields in western Pennsylvania and then transmitting the power eastward to the load centers via high-voltage transmission lines.

Although the mine-mouth plants proposed by the Giant Power Survey Board wouldn't technically be owned by the state, they would be built under state license by entirely new utility companies and would be heavily

Prohibition in the mid-1920s drew more public attention than the Giant Power plan. *(courtesy of the Morning Call)*

regulated. Under the Giant Power plan, the investor-owned power companies would be reduced to the status of local distribution companies; decisions on plant construction and operation would be made by a state board, as would generation and transmission planning decisions.

Giant Power was also synonymous with social engineering. Cooke, who went on to design and head the Rural Electrification Administration for President Franklin D. Roosevelt in the mid-1930s, used the Giant Power survey to

advance the idea of rural electrification. Pinchot was also interested in the concept of reversing the industrialization of the cities. Giant Power, he predicted, would spread the electric power load into less urban parts of the state and halt industrial concentration, mass factory labor and the spread of slums in urban areas.

The Superpower Response

Giant Power never took hold in Pennsylvania for a number of reasons. For one, Pinchot's popularity had carried him to the Governor's mansion in Harrisburg in the fall of 1922 but had worn thin by 1926; he was handily defeated in the fall elections by an electorate that was more interested in enforcement of prohibition and the reorganization of state government than ambitious new ventures in electric power generation. Giant Power needed a friend in the statehouse to have any chance of public acceptance after 1926.

Then too, there were technological and economic reasons for Giant Power's failure. Although Cooke, Otto Rau and the other engineers of the Giant Power Survey Board had proposed a network of high-voltage transmission lines heading back east from the bituminous coalfields in the western part of the state, high-voltage transmission was still in its infancy in 1924.

It was only in 1927 that PP&L, Philadelphia Electric Co. and Public Service Electric & Gas Co. signed an agreement establishing the Pennsylvania-New Jersey Interconnection. The backbone of the PNJ was a 220,000-volt ring system that interconnected the three utilities outside Philadelphia, and that landmark utility interconnection wasn't fully accomplished until 1930. In later years, when American utilities did begin to construct mine-mouth generation plants and ship the power to load centers, the high-voltage lines were typically operated at 400,000 and 500,000 volts, a transmission level far beyond the capabilities of utility engineers of the mid-1920s.

Philadelphia Electric Co. rejected the report on the grounds that the transmission assumptions were not technologically feasible. G.M. Gadsby of the Pennsylvania Electric Association echoed the complaints of Philadelphia Electric Co. "Economic law must control" the development of utility systems, he wrote in the *National Electric Light Association Bulletin,* noting that many of the technological advancements proposed by the Giant Power Survey Board were still experimental.

Giant Power's assumptions on coal were also suspect. PP&L and Philadelphia Electric Co. between them used about one million tons of Pennsylvania bituminous coal a year in 1924, and the vast bulk of that was used by PECO for its Chester and Delaware River gener-

ating stations. Nearly 100 percent of Philadelphia Electric Co.'s bituminous coal came from the Clearfield district in central Pennsylvania and not from the western coalfields.

By the mid-1920s, Philadelphia Electric Co. was well along with its plan to diversify its generation mix, principally through the construction of the massive Conowingo Dam and hydroelectric station on the Susquehanna River below Holtwood. PECO, for its part, wanted to diversify its generation mix because of the unreliability of its coal supply, not the cost of transporting it. In 1917-1918, the utility experienced coal shortages when the federal government nationalized the railroads serving Philadelphia. The following year, the utility again experienced a disruption in

PP&L's Hauto facility was affected by the turmoil of the early 1920s.

Philadelphia Electric Co.'s Conowingo Dam was an example of the company's and the industry's move towards diversification. (*courtesy of Philadelphia Electric Co.***)**

John L. Lewis, of the United Mine Workers, led thousands of miners out on strike. This was just one of the coal-related problems the Pennsylvania utilities had to deal with in the early 1920s, which created the move towards diversification. (*photos courtesy of AP/Wide World Photos*)

its coal supply when John L. Lewis of the United Mine Workers led thousands of miners out on strike against the bituminous operators. A coal 1922 strike and the continuing shortage of coal cars arising from the wartime demand on the railroads contributed to a dramatic increase in the cost of Pennsylvania

bituminous coal; in 1922, the Philadelphia utility actually resorted to purchasing coal in England and shipping it to the United States.

The high price of bituminous coal in Pennsylvania in the early 1920s was a function of extraordinary events arising from wartime emergencies and labor unrest and not from high rail rates, as the Giant Power Survey Board reported. Anthracite use also weighed against adoption of the Giant Power plan. PP&L's Harwood and Hauto generating stations were in the anthracite fields. Scranton Electric Co. was another heavy user of anthracite coal, and Pennsylvania Water & Power Co. was then in the process of completing its coal-washing plant at Holtwood to process anthracite culm and fines washed down the Susquehanna River. None of the utilities that burned anthracite in their boilers paid inordinately high transportation rates for their fuel.

By 1924, utilities in the northeastern corridor already had their own counterpart to Giant Power. In 1921, William S. Murray, a young engineer, had been commissioned by the Department of the Interior, Pinchot's old nemesis, to write a report on the electric power situation in the Northeast. Murray's report, entitled "A Superpower System for the Region Between Boston and Washington," coined the word "Superpower" for the concept of building large coal-fired, steam-electric generating stations in the region and interconnecting them with high-voltage generation lines. By 1924, midwestern utility magnate Samuel Insull appropriated the word for his Super-Power Co. of Illinois, an ambitious joint venture that called for building a huge coal-fired generating unit in the small community of Powerton, Ill.

Unlike Giant Power, Superpower proposed an expansion of the electric power grid along the lines of the status quo. Utilities would build and own the generating stations, and undertake joint ventures to build the transmission lines necessary to deliver the power. U.S. Secretary of Commerce Herbert Hoover followed up Murray's report with the formation of a Northeastern Super Power Committee made up of utility executives, federal government officials and state representatives. Pinchot and Cooke grudgingly took part in the initiative.

telegraph would die from want of current. Where would the people go? Certainly not to the theaters. They would be dark and lifeless. They could go only to their homes and there experience the

> *"What would happen if...millions of electrons should go on strike and electrical energy cease to flow.... First, the lights would go out.... Where would the people go?... They could go only to their homes and there experience the reminiscences of one hundred years ago by the light of a tallow candle."*—Survey Graphic

Electric Power May Pile Cities Higher Than Ever

Although eventually unsuccessful in its home state, Giant Power sparked debate around the country. The report was released in 1925 amid tremendous media interest. Widely circulated, the 480-page report occasioned great comment in the press. The initial run of 20,000 copies was soon distributed, and national magazines like the *Annals of the American Academy of Political and Social Science* and *Survey Graphic* devoted entire editions to the issues raised by the report.

Predictably, much of the response focused on the social aspects of utility restructuring. "The relation electric utilities throughout the country bear to the communities they serve is brought home if we ask the question: What would happen if the millions of electrons should go on strike and electrical energy cease to flow," the editors of *Survey Graphic* asked in their March 1, 1924, issue. "First, the lights would go out, but that is not all. Electric traction would stop. Sixty percent of the factory workers would be thrown out of work. The elevators in the office buildings would cease running. The newspapers would cease circulation. After a few hours, the telephone and the

reminiscences of one hundred years ago by the light of a tallow candle."

The editors of *Survey Graphic*, in commenting on Giant Power, came down on the side of the social engineering end of the electric utility equation. "Electric power may pile cities higher than ever unless we make use of the opportunity it holds out," they wrote. But at the same time, they put their finger on a phenomenon that was beginning to worry the American body politic.

"The chairman of the board of directors of a great American corporation recently remarked to some friends that one of the most difficult problems in our democracy arose out of the widening gap between the technical expert and the average voting citizen," the editors noted. "This observation is especially pertinent in the field of electricity. It is illustrated by our popular habit of referring to such pioneers as Edison as 'electrical wizards.' Electricity is such a subtle commodity, at once so beneficent and so terrifyingly destructive, that we regard it and its high priests with a kind of awe."

That gap identified by the editors of *Survey Graphic* in the wake of Gifford Pinchot's Giant Power survey would only widen as the nation slipped into the Great Depression.

President Herbert Hoover with the First Lady in 1932. As U.S. Secretary of Commerce in the 1920s, Hoover worked on the formation of a Northeastern Super Power Committee made up of utility executives, federal government officials and state representatives. (*photo courtesy of AP/Wide World Photos*)

The Saga of Morris Llewellen Cooke

The architect of Gifford Pinchot's Giant Power survey was a Philadelphia engineer whose ideas on the public ownership of electric power continue today in the form of nearly 1,000 rural electric cooperatives that derive their existence and authority from the federal Rural Electrification Administration.

Morris Llewellen Cooke was an engineer by training and a Philadelphian by upbringing. A disciple of Frederick W. Taylor, the late 19th century management guru, Cooke believed that Taylor's principles of scientific management could be applied to the electric utility industry. Cooke found comfort in the belief that engineers could release human beings from the demands of manual labor and provide the fruits of scientific accomplishment to society at large. "I am a public engineer and not a private engineer," he once said. "I believe all engineers in time will come to this platform."

Cooke first came to the attention of the nation's electric utility industry in 1911 at age 39 when he was appointed director of public works in the office of Philadelphia Mayor Rudolph Blankenburg. The engineer wasted little time in making his mark. He hauled his predecessor into court on corruption charges and then took on United Gas Improvement Co., the city's gas utility, over the matter of gas rates.

Cooke was convinced that the city's two main utilities, UGI and Philadelphia Electric Co., "mulcted and fleeced the public," and in 1913, he set out to lower Philadelphia Electric Co.'s rates. When the city council refused to appropriate money for Cooke's campaign against the electric utility, he filed suit against Philadelphia Electric Co. as a private citizen, charging the company with high rates and inefficient operation.

When Gifford Pinchot approached Cooke about serving as the executive director of the Giant Power Survey Board, the Philadelphia-based engineer was enjoying a successful career as a management consultant to the public power business. Cooke's innovative suggestions in the Giant Power report, and his forceful personality, built his reputation as one of America's foremost thinkers on the role of electric power in society.

Cooke had grown increasingly opposed to the investor-owned utilities, allying himself with Sen. George W. Norris of Nebraska, the great proponent of public power in the 1920s. Cooke reserved particular venom for the holding companies, once referring to Samuel Insull and Electric Bond and Share Co.'s Sidney Z. Mitchell as the "alpha and omega" of the electric power industry.

In 1931, New York Gov. Franklin D. Roosevelt named Cooke a trustee of the New York Power Authority. Cooke followed Roosevelt to Washington, D.C., a year later, and quickly became involved with the New Deal brain trust that surrounded the former New York governor. Increasingly, Roosevelt relied upon Cooke for advice in restructuring the electric utility industry, a campaign promise he had made during the 1932 election.

In 1934, Cooke, then serving as an advisor to a federal commission studying flooding in the Mississippi Valley, composed a "12-minute memo" for Roosevelt and Secretary of the Interior Harold L. Ickes. The short, lucid memo outlined the

Frederick W. Taylor's principles of scientific management inspired Morris Cooke, the architect of Gifford Pinchot's Giant Power survey. (*photo courtesy of the Hugh Moore Historical Park and Museum*)

reasons why government involvement in rural electrification was important to the New Deal. In the second week of May 1935, Roosevelt signed an executive order establishing the Rural Electrification Administration and named "this big boy from Philadelphia" as its first administrator.

The suggestions that Morris L. Cooke had made concerning rural electrification in the Giant Power report of 1925 had finally borne fruit on a national level.

The Great Depression

For Pennsylvania Power & Light Co. and the nation's electric utility industry, the world changed dramatically on Oct. 29, 1929. "Black Tuesday," as it has become known to posterity, ushered in the Great Depression. The collapse of Wall Street that long-ago day was one of the seminal events of the 20th century.

The market had been weak most of September and October 1929. Stocks had dipped and regained value, and market observers were predicting by the middle of October that Wall Street would recover from the fluctuations that had been so evident earlier in the month.

The collapse of Wall Street on Oct. 29, 1929, led to the Great Depression of the 1930s. Throughout the decade, Allentown's *Morning Call* reported the effects on the Lehigh Valley and the citizens of Pennsylvania. (*courtesy of the Morning Call*)

AMELIA EARHART

New York Gives Noisy Welcome To Ocean Flier

In an era of unemployment and food shortages, an inspirational story about aviator Amelia Earhart Putnam was uplifting. "The first woman to fly the Atlantic, the first to fly it alone and the first pilot, man or woman, to cross it twice in an airplane," reported the *Morning Call* on June 21, 1932. (*courtesy of the Morning Call*)

Utilities were...able to avoid plant closings and mass layoffs, although wage cutbacks were a common occurrence during the dark days of the mid-1930s.

On Thursday, October 24, 12.9 million shares traded hands as the market headed downward with a vengeance. The problem was margin trading. Millions of Americans maintained margin accounts, and as long as the market kept rising, everybody made money. But when the market started dropping at the end of the month, small investors were forced to make good on their margin calls.

The market stabilized on Friday, October 25, and Saturday, October 26, (which was a half-day on Wall Street), but the real skid began on Monday, October 28. Losses totaled $14 billion on that one day alone, on just under 10 million shares traded. Tuesday dawned amidst near panic conditions on Wall Street. Before the day was over, 16.4 million shares had been traded at huge losses. Millions of small investors, many of whom had held previously rock-solid utility stocks, were wiped out.

For that one day, the losses totaled $15 billion. For the month of October 1929, losses on Wall Street were a mind-boggling $50 billion. In just under two months past Labor Day, the leading industrial stocks traded on the nation's securities markets had lost 40 percent of their value.

Ironically, the onset of the Great Depression was initially hardly felt by electric utilities like Pennsylvania Power & Light Co. The reason was simple. Electric power was a growth industry, and although 25 percent of the working population was unemployed in the depths of the Great Depression, three-quarters of the population still had jobs. Those who had jobs were helped by the fact that the economy experienced a prolonged period of wage-price stagnation. Demand for electric appliances like washing machines, refrigerators and stoves stayed relatively high during the 1930s. Load continued to grow, even during the darkest days of the Great Depression, and utilities were for the most part able to avoid plant closings and mass layoffs, although wage cutbacks were a common occurrence during the dark days of the mid-1930s.

Still, Pennsylvania Power & Light Co. definitely felt the effects of the Great Depression on its operations. For one thing, the tremendous growth in kilowatt-hour sales and revenues tailed off dramatically after 1930. For another, the company's reliance on industrial power sales—as high as 70 percent of generation mix in the mid-1920s—was affected by plant shutdowns in the Lehigh Valley and the anthracite fields.

As early as 1930, PP&L's revenue growth slowed considerably. Through the late 1920s, gross earnings had risen significantly. In 1927, the company reported gross earnings of $21.47 million. With the addition of 105,000 new customers in 1928, gross earnings leaped to $26.61 million, nearly a 25 percent increase. In 1929, the gross earnings figure was $30.2 million, close to a 20 percent increase from the 1928 figures.

The double-digit increases in gross earnings characteristic of the late 1920s came to a skidding halt in the early 1930s. Gross earnings of $31 million in 1930 were up just three percent from the year before. The increase was slightly better—about 4.5 percent—on gross earnings of $32.4 million in 1931.

The December, 1930, addition of substantial properties in Lancaster County increased PP&L's customer base and revenues. A note in the 1931 annual report pointed out that revenues for the year would have been just over $35 million had the new customers been included for the entire calendar year. The reality was that 1930 was the last year in a number of years that revenue increased.

By 1931, revenues of $34.99 million were actually below what they had been the year before, when the new customer base from Lancaster was included. Revenues dropped again in 1932, to $33.62 million, and the slide continued in 1933 when revenues totaled $32.75 million. It was only in 1934 and 1935 when revenues topped $34 million each year that revenues regained the level they had reached in 1930.

The devastating economic conditions in Pennsylvania and the nation were compounded for PP&L by political factors. In 1933, the Pennsylvania Public Utilities Commission ordered the Allentown utility to reduce its general residential rates. "Revenues declined due to rate reductions and to general business conditions in the territory served," Paul B. Sawyer, chairman of the board, reported to shareholders in the spring of 1934, "while on the other hand, the company was subjected to new forms of taxation and to further restrictive regulation of the working hours of employees. To offset, as far as possible, the adverse effects of these added burdens, the company found it necessary extensively to readjust its operating practices and procedures. Notwithstanding these burdens and the difficulty of obtaining a sufficient amount of additional business to offset the business lost, the company has been able to maintain its usual high standard of service to the public."

PP&L's experiences during the Great Depression were hardly unique. Utilities across the country struggled with the debilitating economic conditions. In the eight years between 1929 and 1937, the national income dropped from $79 billion in 1929—an all-time high—to $68 billion in 1937, a 14 percent decrease. Industrial production dropped even more during the period, 15 percent in eight years.

But PP&L and the utility industry began a recovery after 1934 that would continue for the next four decades. During the 1929-1937 period, the electric utility industry nationwide added 2.85 million customers, increased average residential energy consumption by 67 percent and cut the average residential kilowatt-hour rate by more than 30 percent.

By the late 1930s, the industry was well on the way to recovery.

Photos of Allentown slum buildings provided visual documentation for the U.S. Housing Authority, which intended to replace the buildings with 36 one- and two-story row houses. (*photos courtesy of the* **Morning Call**)

In 1937, average residential consumption of electricity increased 10 percent, from 727 kwh to 797 kwh. Rates were cut an average of six percent for the year and the industry reported adding 800,000 residential customers during the year.

"The job of disseminating the blessings of electricity among the people is still far from complete," C.W. Kellogg, president of the Edison Electric Institute, reported to members in April 1938. "We are indeed happy as an industry in being able to feel that the results of our sales efforts mean so much in added comfort, safety and convenience and decreased drudgery to our millions of customers."

The Decline in Industrial Production

The WPA put men to work on projects like the construction of Allentown's Cedar Beach. *circa 1937 (photo courtesy of the Lehigh County Historical Society)*

Even though PP&L and the industry managed to recover from the Great Depression by the late 1930s, there were difficult years in the Lehigh Valley during the early part of the decade. The city of Bethlehem passed out seeds to more than 400 families to stave off famine. More

than 2,000 men and women were employed on public works projects in Bethlehem in 1934, and 500 families were evicted that year for nonpayment of rent. Bethlehem raised $17,000 from charity in 1933 to employ residents on the city woodpile. In Easton, the local trust company took possession of more than 2,300 homes from residents who were unable to continue paying their mortgages.

In a sense, residents of the Lehigh Valley were luckier than most citizens. The area had a strong, diversified industrial base. Mack Trucks Co., Bethlehem Steel Co. and the silk mills survived the Great Depression better than many industries. Allentown was the hub of a regional marketplace serving the entire valley. The commercial district along Hamilton Street boasted a variety of shopping facilities, including the Hess Brothers Department Store, S.S. Kresge, McCrory's and Woolworth's.

Bethlehem Steel Co. was a case in point. After suffering through the worst two years in its history in 1932 and 1933, when steelmaking capacity was reduced to 17 percent, the company cut costs by

reducing and restructuring long-term debt. Through an innovative shared part-time work program, more than 20,000 workers were kept on the payroll through the darkest days of the Depression.

By the mid-1930s, the company had adopted a strategic plan for future expansion. Between 1935 and 1938, the Bethlehem steelmaker spent nearly $93 million on modernization and capital expansion, including construction of a 25-ton electric furnace for making alloy steel at the Bethlehem works, the addition of an electric heat-treating department, the installation of a forging machine in an expanded drop-forge building and an enlargement of the corporate office building. The company's increasing reliance on industrial electric power outstripped its internal electric generation, and Bethlehem Steel Co. began to forge stronger ties with Pennsylvania Power & Light Co. during the decade. By 1937, Bethlehem Steel Co.'s work force of 107,000 was at an all-time high.

If economic conditions in the Lehigh Valley were better than in the nation at large, conditions in the anthracite region reached a crisis point during the early 1930s. Demand for anthracite had been dropping steadily all through the 1920s, as consumers switched to fuel oil and natural and manufactured gas for heating purposes. More efficient heating equipment created a market for soft coal and coke in the big cities of the Northeast and New England; by the mid-1920s, soft coal was selling for as much as $7 a ton less than anthracite.

Conditions during the 1930s were particularly depressing in the Wyoming Valley. Collieries and breakers from Wilkes-Barre to Nanticoke shut down or drastically curtailed operations as demand slackened. Workers in the

Lines were a common site in the depression era. This crowd waits for Benesch's furniture and goods store to open for its "Back to Prosperity Dollar Sale"…better here than the soup kitchen lines. (*photo courtesy of the* Morning Call)

Allentown looking west down Hamilton Street in 1938 or 1939. Notice the PP&L Tower Building in the background. (*photo courtesy of the Lehigh County Historical Society*)

anthracite fields made 72 cents an hour for a 10-hour day, but most anthracite workers were only employed two days a week, and the take-home pay of $15 a week wasn't enough to maintain a standard of living. Things were in an upheaval in the Wyoming Valley in 1934-1935 when the United Anthracite Miners, a splinter group from the United Mine Workers, went to war with the parent union.

More than 2,000 men and women were employed on public works projects in Bethlehem in 1934, and 500 families were evicted that year for nonpayment of rent.

The decline of the anthracite region in the 1930s had been swift and sure. In 1917, the year America entered World War I, anthracite production had topped 90 million tons, an all-time record. For

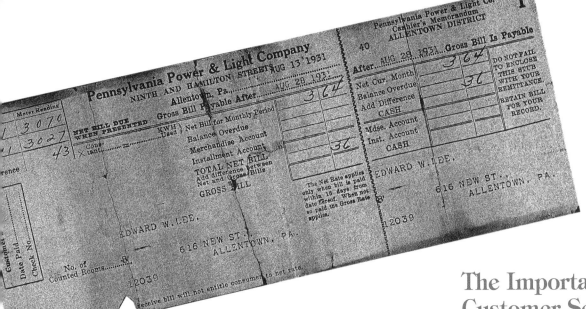

much of the 1920s, with the exception of the strike year of 1922, production fluctuated between 65 million and 75 million tons, but dropped precipitously in the early 1930s. By 1932-1933, annual production averaged 43 million tons, 30 million tons less than at the beginning of the 1920s.

Although production rebounded late in the decade to the 47 million ton level, anthracite would never again reach the production levels of the World War I era. The sharp decline during the decade had implications for Pennsylvania Power & Light Co. The closing of dozens of collieries and breakers, and the subsequent dispersal of populations from anthracite communities represented a loss of load for the utility in the Wyoming Valley. But the loss of load was offset to a certain extent by the increasing electrification of the remaining mines. By 1935, PP&L itself was the largest single user of anthracite in the world, consuming more than one million tons of anthracite a year in the boilers of its steam electric generating stations.

By 1935, PP&L itself was the largest single user of anthracite in the world, consuming more than one million tons of anthracite a year in the boilers of its steam electric generating stations.

The Importance of Customer Service

Pennsylvania Power & Light Co. in 1935—as the Great Depression wound down—was a well-run, thriving organization. The company supplied electric, gas and steam heat service in 28 counties of Pennsylvania, an area larger than the states of New Jersey and Rhode Island combined. The total population of 1.67 million in the service territory lived in a total of 658 communities, and 87 percent of the customers served lived in communities of 2,500 or less.

Total electric sales to customers topped 1.3 billion kilowatt-hours, a 269 percent increase in 20 years. Rate reductions since 1930 totaled more than $23.6 million. PP&L preferred stock was owned by more than 48,000 people, most of them residential customers of the company.

One bright spot in the company's business outlook was the increase in PP&L's gas business. By 1935, the utility was providing manufactured gas to 29 communities, four more than it had served with gas in 1917. During the 1920s, the company had embarked on an ambitious program to interconnect communities with gas transmission lines. As a result, the company operated 15 gasworks in 1935, two less than in 1917. But the more efficient gasworks operated in 1935 were capable of producing 138 percent more gas than the larger number of gasworks 18 years earlier.

PP&L also entered the natural gas business during the 1930s. The discovery of a natural gas field at Tioga in 1930 led

PP&L to build a 55-mile gas transmission line from the gas fields to Williamsport, where it connected with existing transmission mains. By 1932, customers in Williamsport, Milton and Sunbury were being served with natural gas. Gas appliances in the three communities were converted to the use of natural gas at the company's expense, and monthly gas bills were reduced approximately 20 percent. After 1932, PP&L acquired leases in the Tioga field and began drilling natural gas wells of its own, an activity that continued until the early 1940s.

PP&L continued to render steam heating service in the cities of Wilkes-Barre and Harrisburg as a by-product of electric generation in the two communities. Between 1920 and 1935, the company sharply increased the number of steam heating customers in the two communities and boosted the amount of steam sold by more than 100 percent.

Promotion and customer service continued to be bulwarks of the company's business. "The increased use of service which brings about such low rates," the company pointed out in 1935, "has been hastened by a promotional program which has directed the customer's attention to the advantages to be obtained from the use of electricity."

Throughout the 1930s, the company targeted commercial and small industrial customers for increased use of electric power. PP&L called the program "purchased service" and pushed it hard during the decade. As late as 1930, large numbers of small businesses and factories still used coal-fired boilers for their electric power needs.

"Purchased service is clean," noted Douglas C. Hornig, a PP&L sales representative based in Allentown. "Cleanliness is smart merchandising; a spick and span shop attracts customers and makes them feel at home. Employees appreciate a clean place of business. It creates a cheerful atmosphere in which to work."

PP&L touted purchased service's appeal to comfort, convenience, safety and economy. "Purchased service is odorless," Hornig continued. "There is no danger of offending customers with an unpleasant atmosphere. Employer and employee like to work in comfortable, healthful surroundings."

For much of America, the Great Depression was a seminal event in the nation's history. For the first time since the Panic of 1893, Americans questioned the essential underpinnings of the national economy. That utilities like Pennsylvania Power & Light Co. came through the crucible of the changing economic conditions of the decade in such good shape was an affirmation of electric power's growing role in a modern society. But the economic conditions were only one factor in the paradox of electric utility growth during the Great Depression. The political and social components of electric utility growth during the decade created a set of circumstances that would present the industry with its greatest challenge in the mid-1930s.

Douglas C. Hornig, PP&L sales representative in Allentown during the 1930s.

By 1935, the utility was providing manufactured gas to 29 communities, four more than it had served with gas in 1917.

THE COST OF MY SERVICES HAS BEEN GREATLY REDUCED SINCE OCTOBER 1ST 1935!

TO LOWER PRICE LEVELS

CLOTHING

HOUSE RENT

EGGS

BEEF

PORK

GROCERIES

TO HIGHER PRICE LEVELS

NOW...MUCH MORE ELECTRIC SERVICE FOR YOUR DOLLARS

The 1936 Floods

As if economic conditions during the 1930s weren't enough to turn utility executives' hair gray, the weather conditions over much of America during the decade only served to compound the misery of the Great Depression.

Farmers in Pennsylvania and up and down the East Coast struggled with drought in 1930. By 1932, the drought had moved west into the Great Plains, and much of the midsection of the country was plagued by dust storms in 1933 and 1934. Millions of tons of topsoil blew away from Texas north to the Dakotas. In central South Dakota in 1933, streetlights came on at noon as the sun was obscured by blowing dust.

For much of the nation east of the Rocky Mountains, the year 1936 was particularly memorable from a meteorological standpoint. The year opened with bitterly cold, record low temperatures from Montana to Pennsylvania. Ironically, many of the places that reported record low temperatures in January 1936 reported record high temperatures in June and July of the same year; temperatures topped 100 degrees that summer as far north as Duluth, Minn.

Ice buildup on York County shore.

For Pennsylvanians, however, 1936 was the year of the floods. Snowpack in the headwaters of the Susquehanna River had built up to unprecedented levels during the cold winter of 1935-1936 as major snowfalls blanketed Pennsylvania and New York in January and February. A sustained thaw in February and early March sent a wall of ice and water down the swollen river.

"Heavy accumulation of snow lay on the ground at the end of the freeze," Pennsylvania Water & Power Co. reported in 1936. "Thawing weather melted much of this snow, filling the streams and saturating the ground. Finally, heavy rains washed off the remaining snow and ice and caused the already swollen streams to rise faster and higher than forecasters at first thought possible."

Ice dams formed in the river and its tributaries during the first week of March, and more than an inch-and-a-half of rain fell on the ice-clogged rivers from March 10-13. By March 13, the river had flooded parts of Harrisburg's uptown and west suburbs. Then the heavens really opened up. For the period March 15-20, rainfall on the Susquehanna Basin averaged four inches, with nearly six inches reported from stations

Battling the Depression in Pennsylvania included drought in 1930 and the floods of 1936. These photos show the ice buildup at Safe Harbor in March of 1936, the destruction of the deflection wall at Holtwood, inspection of the broken wall in mid-April, and finally rebuilding the wall that July.

on the Juniata River.

The north branch of the Susquehanna was the first to feel the full brunt of the flood. On March 16, the river at Wilkes-Barre stood at 17 feet at noon. Within 36 hours, the river had risen to 25.77 feet, and by midnight of March 18, the north branch had risen to 32.75 feet. For the next 15 hours, the crest inundated Wilkes-Barre and flooded the Wyoming Valley all the way to Nanticoke. Early in the morning of March 20, the river reached its highest level at 33.1 feet and then slowly began to recede.

Hundreds of Repair Crews

As the flood slowly approached its crest in the Wyoming Valley, Pennsylvania Power & Light Co. marshalled forces to keep utility service going in the valley. "In anticipation of the flood crisis," a grateful observer from Wilkes-Barre wrote later in 1936, "Pennsylvania Power & Light Co. started the machinery for the mobilization of several hundred pumping outfits from scattered points in its territory and concentrated them at strategic locations; gathered hundreds of gas, electric and steam heat repair crews; established commissaries at which an army of workers were fed and housed; placed orders for supplies of repair material of a wide variety, such as transformers, gas and electric meters, miles of wire, tons of cable, hundreds of pairs of rubber boots, medicines, foods and countless other necessary items and arranged for their transportation by special train and convoys of motor trucks from New York, Philadelphia and many other points and at the same time handled hundreds of other details."

PP&L's preparations spared customers in the Wyoming Valley prolonged outages, although crews would be busy repairing distribution facilities and gas mains in Wilkes-Barre until summer. But Wilkes-Barre and the Wyoming Valley weren't the only communities affected by the 1936 floods. Sunbury, at the confluence of the north and west branches of the Susquehanna, was under six to 12 feet of water. Homes a mile north of the river were under water in Williamsport, and much of the downtown caught fire during the height of the flood.

Nor was the Susquehanna the only river in the Mid-Atlantic region to suffer the ravages of flood. Downtown Johnstown was under water after a gauging station on the Kiskiminetas River recorded a river level of 47.2 feet, the highest water ever recorded on the river. River levels at Pittsburgh, at the confluence of the Allegheny and Monongahela rivers, also hit an all-time high: 46 feet. Water in the Golden Triangle area of downtown Pittsburgh was 20 feet deep in places. At Easton and Phillipsburg on the Delaware River, waters were 10 feet above flood stage and the highest they had been in the two communities since the flood of 1903.

A gas depot southwest of Wilkes-Barre.

A Bald Eagle Creek home ripped from its foundations.

The Day They Saved the Power Plant

The floods worked their way down the Susquehanna, cresting at nearly 30 feet at Harrisburg on March 19. Gas mains and power lines were left in what one observer called "pitiable condition," and cleanup began in earnest on March 21. Cleanup was complicated by the fact that the flood waters had washed away the west shore end of the Walnut Street Bridge.

Farther downstream, the flood and ice jam flowed toward the recently completed Safe Harbor Dam and the Holtwood Dam. As early as the first week of March, the ice entered Lake Clarke above Safe Harbor and had begun to pile up against the dams.

By March 19, the peak of the flow had reached Safe Harbor and Holtwood. In September the year before, the flow past the two dams had averaged 2,100 cubic feet per second (cfs), a somewhat typical late summer flow. On March 10, the flow past Holtwood had surpassed 100,000 cfs; three days later, the flow had increased more than fivefold, to 520,000 cfs. On March 19 and 20, the average flow was 780,000 cfs. The peak flow was estimated at an unprecedented 850,000 cfs. Water gushed over the Holtwood Dam in a wall more than 19 feet high.

Water lapped against the hydroelectric station and the coal washing plant as early as March 13,

but crews were able to sandbag the facilities and keep everything operating. But news of the crest moving downriver from Harrisburg spurred Pennsylvania Water & Power Co. to redouble efforts to contain the damage.

"The work of preparation for the flood was started early on the 18th by regular Holtwood forces, which were later augmented by men from Safe Harbor, transmission line employees, and laborers who were hired during that day," Pennsylvania Water & Power Co. reported in a commemorative booklet later in 1936. "To quickly secure the extra help that was needed in this work, use was made of the Lancaster Broadcasting Station. The employment of temporary labor, including many former employees and special employees of the transmission line department, on the 19th and 20th, totaled 360 men."

As it was, the efforts of hundreds of extra workers were of more value during the cleanup. Early in the morning of March 19, the deflection wall at Holtwood failed, sending water cascading into the tailrace. The surge of water knocked out several transformers, and water flooded into the high-tension bus rooms, causing the live buses to flash over and short out. Although confusion reigned in the Holtwood plant, station service was restored within 30 minutes, and Safe Harbor picked up 60-cycle service dropped by Holtwood. Miraculously, Pennsylvania Water & Power Co. maintained service to its customers.

Crews labored for weeks to shovel silt out of the Holtwood plant and to dry out transformers and other equipment, and it was summer low-flow conditions before crews could rebuild the deflection wall at Holtwood. The dam at McCall's Ferry had been on line for more than a quarter-of-a-century, and even old-timers had never seen anything remotely like the floods of March 1936. But through it all, Pennsylvania Water & Power Co. handled everything the river could throw at it.

22

Lines to the Farm

By 1935, PP&L district representatives served 8,200 farm customers, which was 75 percent of all PP&L rural customers.

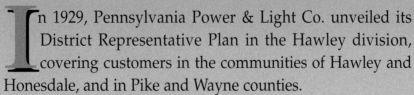

In 1929, Pennsylvania Power & Light Co. unveiled its District Representative Plan in the Hawley division, covering customers in the communities of Hawley and Honesdale, and in Pike and Wayne counties.

The idea of the plan, according to Norman G. Reinicker, general manager of the Allentown-based utility, was to better serve the company's small town and farm customers. Under the District Representative Plan, one PP&L employee was assigned the duties of meter reader, service man, bill distributor, collector, appliance demonstrator and salesman for 700 to 900 customers. "He must handle complaints and explain rates," Reinicker explained, "and be a general, all-around utility man."

In rural areas, the district representative was supplied with a panel truck painted in the usual red and black PP&L color scheme and inscribed with the district representative's name below the company logo. Inside the truck were compartments to carry small appliances, lamp bulbs and repair parts. Lug nuts on the floor of the truck locked a range and refrigerator in place, ready for the district representative to display and exhibit to rural customers.

In a spring 1934 letter to customers in the Fogelsville district, Allentown Division Manager Charles E. Oakes explained that the district representative would be "glad to show you how to read your meter and how to replace fuses properly. If you wish, he will also inspect your elec-

trical appliances, explain the best way to use them and if necessary, make minor adjustments and repairs on them which are so frequently neglected in busy households. This cooperation is given gladly, so that you may get the most economical and beneficial service from the electricity used. This representative will also read your meters monthly and give you dependable information on new appliances in which you may be interested."

The District Representative Plan was extended to the Mt. Pocono district in 1930 and expanded dramatically thereafter. By 1935, 141 district representatives were looking after the needs of 120,000 PP&L customers, 40 percent of the company's residential customer base. Among the customers served by

The District Representative Plan was a commitment by PP&L to provide better, personal customer service. As these 1936 newspaper clips show, PP&L was not only interested in expanding transmission lines but also its customer service program—both city and rural. (*courtesy of* the Morning Call)

district representatives were 8,200 farm customers, 75 percent of the nearly 11,000 rural customers served by PP&L.

The District Representative Plan was a hallmark of Pennsylvania Power & Light Co.'s commitment to customer service. "There is no more crying need today than that for mutual understanding between the customer and the company," Reinicker told delegates to the annual convention of the Pennsylvania Electric Association in September 1935. "It seems to me that the only way to obtain the customer's complete understanding and confidence is through personal contact."

But the plan was also a recognition of one of the essential paradoxes of Pennsylvania Power & Light Co. service during the 1930s. Although some 70 percent of the company's kilowatt-hour sales were to industrial customers in the Lehigh Valley and the anthracite coal regions, nearly half of the company's 300,000 residential customers lived on farms or in small towns. During the 1930s alone, PP&L energized more than 7,500 miles of rural lines across central and eastern Pennsylvania.

Shortly after its formation, PP&L was already serving farm customers. Predecessors had been serving farm customers since before the turn of the century; one farm in what is now the northwest section of Allentown started receiving electric power in the 1890s from a PP&L predecessor. By 1926, the company was serving 26,000 rural and farm customers (the company at the time made no distinction between farms and residential customers living on the outskirts of small towns). In 1923, the company assigned Charles E. Oakes, a young engineer from Oregon recently hired from the Federal Power Commission, to specialize in engineering farm electrification applications. For much of the 1920s, Oakes served as the secretary of the Joint Committee on Rural Electrification, a group of representatives from Pennsylvania utilities and farm organizations.

Oakes found that rural lines in the 1920s were typically built by extending the existing distribution systems, using

the same kind of construction. He initiated a long-range planning program which dictated that rural lines would be located so they could reach the maximum number of potential customers. PP&L's Engineering Department developed a type of distribution construction that lent itself readily both to low initial cost and low conversion cost as it became necessary to increase the capacity of existing facilities to take on scattered large size loads.

Pennsylvania Power & Light Co. crews embarked upon a program of building three-phase, 11,000-volt, 4-wire rural lines designed for 450-foot spans using high-strength conductors. Transformers and service installations were supplied from a single-phase, 6,900-volt, 2-wire rural line. The secondary service wires, with 115-230 volts, were attached immediately below the primary neutral.

At the beginning of 1926, PP&L service territory had less than 1,000 miles of rural lines. In the latter 1920s and 1930s, PP&L built some 7,600 miles of rural lines in its service territory, half of all the distribution line construction the utility under-

In 1935, Allentown Division Manager Charles E. Oakes and 141 district representatives were responsible for 120,000 PP&L customers. Mr. Oakes went on to become the company's third president.

"It seems to me that the only way to obtain the customer's complete understanding and confidence is through personal contact."
—Norman Reinicker

took during the era and approximately 30 percent of the total rural lines existing in the state by 1939.

By the time the state farm census was conducted in 1935, PP&L was serving 25,500 farm customers. Those farm customers made up approximately 57 percent of the total number of farms in the company's service territory. The company reported to the Pennsylvania Public Utilities Commission that an additional 4,120 farms were located along existing lines but had not yet been connected to those lines. "It is apparent that electric service is available to approximately 66 percent of the total number of farms in the area," the company reported in 1939.

Expansion Into Lancaster

In 1930, Pennsylvania Power & Light Co. completed the last major acquisition of the early stages of its history. The December 1930 merger of 21 operating companies in the Lancaster area added customers in practically all of Lancaster County, and a substantial portion of the suburban area outside the city of Reading in Berks County. Companies serving adjoining parts of Lebanon and Chester counties were also added to the PP&L fold. The population of the territory served was approximately 200,000, with 60,000 people then living in the City of Lancaster.

In 1923 many of the farms that were electrified derived their electric power from internal generation, like steam engines and windmills.

Edison Electric Illuminating Co. of Lancaster, which provided service in Lancaster and surrounding boroughs and townships, was the major acquisition in the 1930 merger. Stocks in the properties had been acquired by Lehigh Power Securities

Corp. throughout the 1910s and 1920s, and the 1930 merger into Pennsylvania Power & Light Co. was done partly to incorporate "paper" or "township" companies to protect charter rights in territory already occupied or to provide electric power in the territory not already served by PP&L or any other utility.

Under Pennsylvania law, a corporation organized to supply electric light, heat and power was originally chartered with respect to only a single subdivision, such as a city, borough or township. As a result of the Pennsylvania law, many utility corporations were organized by operating companies merely to obtain charter rights in a particular territory. These companies, which often owned no generating or transmission facilities, were commonly referred to as "paper" or "township" companies. Under the law, a utility corporation like Pennsylvania Power & Light Co. could succeed by merger or consolidation to obtain the rights granted by charter to an unlimited number of such separate corporations. Between 1920 and 1939, PP&L merged and consolidated more than 800 separate predecessors, many of them "paper" or "township" companies.

The 1930 merger added a substantial number of rural and farm customers in Lancaster, Chester and Berks counties. Some of the primarily rural electric companies added in 1930 were the Conestoga Valley Electric Co., the Farmers Electric

Co., the Intercourse Electric Co. and the Pioneer Electric Light Co.

The corporate history of the Conestoga Valley Electric Co. is typical of the rural and farm electric companies incorporated into the PP&L system. Serving customers in East and West Earl, Brecknock, East Cocalico and Ephrata townships of Lancaster County, Conestoga Valley Electric Co. was incorporated in the summer of 1916. Like many of the other small town utilities in central and eastern Pennsylvania, Conestoga Valley Electric Co. incorporated four "paper" companies: the Bowmansville Electric Co., Earl Electric Co., the Murrell Electric Co. and the West Earl Electric Co.

PP&L's efforts to upgrade service to rural and farm customers is graphically illustrated by the progress of rural line construction in Colerain Township of Lancaster County. In 1930, when PP&L acquired the Lancaster County properties, there were no electric power lines serving farmers in the township. By 1935, PP&L had built and energized approximately 10 miles of farm line in the township, and five years later, almost 20 miles of energized farm lines served the township.

Even with the Great Depression affecting business and commerce in Pennsylvania, PP&L's rural and farm line program accelerated during the 1930s. While the addition of farm customers slowed during the 1932-1934 period from an average of 1,100 additions a year during the late 1920s, additions picked up significantly after 1935. In 1936 and 1937, the company added more than 11,000 farm customers and some 20,000 rural customers. During those two years alone, PP&L crews built and energized nearly 2,300 miles of farm and rural lines.

The 1930s rural lines construction program was unique for investor-owned utilities. Nationwide, the total of farms served by investor-owned power companies was half that of PP&L—about 27 percent. Only Wisconsin Power & Light Co. in Madison, Wis., had a record of rural electrification that approached that of PP&L. In 1930, the Wisconsin utility had 7,721 rural customers, nine times the

rate of six years before.

The rural lines program instituted by Charles E. Oakes in 1923 also brought about technological developments. At the beginning of the rural electrification program, PP&L was serving an average of 17.3 rural customers per mile of line.

By 1939, the company's rural lines were serving an average of 11.2 customers per mile, an indication both of the more sparsely settled territories in which rural line extensions were being made and of the technological advancements of distribution line design and construction.

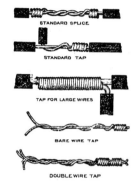

The Politics of Rural Electrification

Electrifying the nation's farms was a priority of the nation's Progressive political movement during the 1920s and 1930s and culminated in the creation of the Rural Electrification Administration (REA) by President Franklin D. Roosevelt.

As early as 1921, the National Electric Light Association (NELA), the trade group representing the nation's investor-

Rights-of-way like this one are the electric highways to rural and farm communities.

CHRONICLE and NEWS
New Year Prosperity Edition
JANUARY 1st, 1929

WITH GIANT STRIDES THE GREAT SPIRIT
OF PROGRESS RIDES TOWARD A
* GREATER LEHIGH VALLEY *

1929   1929   1929

1929 started out with great promise for the Lehigh Valley as portrayed in the New Year Prosperity Edition from the local newspaper. (*courtesy of the* Morning Call)

owned electric utility industry, began to address the problem of rural electrification. "The farmer can, does and will use more current per customer than the customer in the city," Grover Neff, an executive with Wisconsin Power & Light Co., told delegates to the 1921 NELA annual convention. "The rural business is very important to the utility. The farmers are rapidly learning the value to them of electric service and are demanding it. I think, therefore, that the utilities and electrical associations, and especially this association, should take steps to develop a practical plan for financing farm lines and

to ascertain the fundamental factors upon which to base a proper rate."

NELA responded by forming a Rural Lines Committee and appointing Neff as its first chairman. Working with the American Farm Bureau, the NELA Committee formed the Committee on the Relation of Electricity to Agriculture (CREA). PP&L's representative to CREA was Charles E. Oakes, who struck up a lifelong friendship with Neff.

In the 1920s, CREA sponsored national and foreign farm power surveys, surveys of central station and isolated power plant service to farmers and experimental work on the uses of electricity in the field of agriculture. CREA members in the Upper Midwest sponsored well-publicized farm electrification experiments in the early 1920s at Red Wing, Minn., and Renner, S.D.

Still, farm electrification was a long way from being achieved in the 1920s. Nationally, only 348,000 of an estimated 6.5 million farms had any electric service at all in 1923, and many of the farms that were electrified derived their electric power from internal generation, like steam engines and windmills. In 1924, the relative lack of rural electrification nationwide became a political issue in Pennsylvania.

The Giant Power survey commissioned by Pennsylvania and approved by the Pennsylvania General Assembly indicted the state's power companies for "an almost negligible start on the electrification of rural Pennsylvania." Morris Cooke, executive director of the Giant Power Survey Board, reported that Pennsylvania farms were ill-served by the state's power companies. Of 202,250 farms in the state in 1923, Cooke reported, only 12,452 had access to public utility service. There were 11,132 farms in the state with their own farm lighting plants, and an additional 7,085 farms operated small coal-gas plants for lighting. More than 170,000 farms—85 percent of the state's total—had no modern means of illumination or motive power at the time.

"There appear to be two chief reasons for this failure of the electrical industry to cope with this part of its problem," Cooke wrote. "First, absorption in meeting the very great and urgent demands for power in the large industrial centers; and second, rate schedules in which farmers were classed with urban domestic customers." Those farmers lucky enough to be located in proximity to a utility distribution line often paid as much as 15 cents per kilowatt-hour for their electric power. As a result, farms that were wired to a central generating station were characterized by low average consumption—typically 50 kilowatt-hours per month or less.

Cooke and the engineers he gathered together as part of the Giant Power survey team estimated that the cost of designing and building 20,000 miles of pole line would be something less than $30 million and would make service available to the occupants of 75,000 farms in the state. During the 10 years following

the release of the Giant Power survey report, PP&L alone designed and built more than 10,000 miles of rural and farm lines in its service territory.

Cooke ignited a national debate about rural electrification with the findings of the Giant Power Survey Board. Writing in the March 1, 1924, issue of *Survey Graphic,* he noted that power companies were not necessarily opposed to serving rural loads. "Within the electrical industry there is a growing interest in this rural load," he admitted. "While in size it does not compare with the industrial, it is broadly speaking an 'off peak' load and is not as subject to seasonal fluctuations or to the variations due to the business cycle as is the industrial load. But the industrial load because of its relatively large volume is, and probably always will be, the great consideration in laying out transmission lines and therefore the Giant Power survey is making an effort to determine probable industrial demand 10, 20 and 30 years hence."

Rural electrification once again became

Rural electrification once again became an issue in Pennsylvania politics in the heated 1930 gubernatorial race.

©HVAS

an issue in Pennsylvania politics in the heated 1930 gubernatorial race. Gifford Pinchot, whose term as governor from 1922 to 1926 had resulted in the creation of the Giant Power Survey Board, ran on a platform that called for the abolition of the Pennsylvania Public Utilities Commission. The PPUC, Pinchot charged, was a captive of the public utilities themselves, and as such, approved rates that were injurious to the economic health of the state's ratepayers, particularly in rural communities.

By the time of the 1930 elections, Cooke had moved on to New York State, where he advised Gov. Franklin D. Roosevelt on utility matters. When Roosevelt moved to Washington, D.C., in 1933, he brought Cooke with him. Two years later, Roosevelt asked Cooke to serve as the first administrator of the Rural Electrification Administration.

Given his experiences in Pennsylvania, Cooke was loath to call upon the investor-owned utilities to help the federal government electrify rural America. Instead, Cooke opted for a model that utilized locally owned farmer cooperatives to accomplish the electrification goals of REA. Ironically, many of the technologies that REA used to bring electric power to the farm were borrowed from the pioneering efforts made by Charles E. Oakes and the rural lines department of Pennsylvania Power & Light Co. during the 1920s and 1930s.

Ironically, many of the technologies that REA used to bring electric power to the farm were borrowed from the pioneering efforts made by Charles E. Oakes and the rural lines department of Pennsylvania Power & Light Co. during the 1920s and 1930s.

The Irrepressible
Reddy Kilowatt

For generations of PP&L customers, the most recognizable symbol of the Allentown-based utility was a stick figure with lightning bolts for limbs, wall sockets for ears and a light bulb for a nose.

Reddy Kilowatt served as a symbol for Pennsylvania Power & Light Co. for nearly half-a-century, from 1934 until 1981. During that period, millions of Pennsylvanians identified Reddy with their power company.

They weren't alone. Reddy served as an ambassador for hundreds of electric utilities in the United States and abroad. In many ways, Reddy Kilowatt signified electric power for much of America.

Reddy's creator was Ashton Collins, a New Orleans native who was working as assistant commercial manager for Alabama Power Co. in 1926. Collins was

Ashton Collins, creator of Reddy Kilowatt. (*photo courtesy of The Reddy Corporation International*)

searching for a way to humanize the idea of electricity as a servant for the utility's customers when he happened to look out the window and see a flash of lightning against the Alabama mountains.

Collins thought he saw arms and legs in the lightning flash, and he sketched out a stick figure with a light bulb nose and curled-up toes. Collins used Reddy's prototype in Alabama Power Co.'s advertising, and realized he had a concept that might be of interest to electric utilities across the country. He left Alabama Power Co. to set up his own firm and began licensing Reddy Kilowatt to other utilities.

Eight years later, Collins hit pay dirt. Philadelphia Electric Co. signed on as Collins' first client in 1934, and Pennsylvania Power & Light Co. followed suit a short

By the mid-1950s, Reddy Kilowatt was used by more than 200 U.S. utilities and by 40 companies in some 16 foreign countries.

time later that year. In the next four years, utilities across the country, including Ohio Edison, Gulf Power, Alabama Power Co. and Minnesota Power & Light Co. all adopted Reddy Kilowatt as an advertising "spokesperson."

By the mid-1950s, Reddy Kilowatt was used by more than 200 U.S. utilities and by 40 companies in some 16 foreign countries.

Reddy's very saturation of the U.S. market caused a number of utilities to reexamine their use of the ubiquitous spokesperson. In the 1930s and 1940s, many Pennsylvanians thought Reddy belonged only to their electric company. But as each new customer adopted the lightning bolt figure, Reddy's effectiveness for brand identification grew weaker. By the 1960s, Reddy's use in PP&L was confined to the business cards of employees who still had a soft spot in their hearts for Ash Collins' cartoon creation.

When PP&L switched to a hometown advertising image in the 1970s, Reddy's universal presence was no longer required. On Dec. 31, 1981, PP&L let its 47-year contract with Reddy Kilowatt lapse. And a little piece of utility history lapsed with that contract expiration.

Reddy Kilowatt served as a symbol for Pennsylvania Power & Light Co. for nearly half-a-century, from 1934 until 1981.

The Death Sentence

This collage of newspaper clips represents the political atmosphere in Pennsylvania during the tumultuous 1930 gubernatorial race. (*courtesy of the* Morning Call)

Politics dominated the activities of the American electric utility industry during the 1930s. Pennsylvania Power & Light Co. found itself embroiled in political battles on the state and local levels during the decade. Electric Bond and Share Co., the holding company that owned and operated PP&L and numerous other utilities around the country, was at the center of a decade-long fight to politically restructure the way utilities generated, transmitted and distributed electric power.

Electric utilities were a major issue in the 1932 presidential elections, and President Franklin D. Roosevelt was swept into office on a promise to break up the holding companies. During the New Deal, the federal government interjected itself into the affairs of the industry. The Roosevelt Administration proved itself a major champion of public power, creating the Tennessee Valley Authority (TVA) and the Rural Electrification Administration (REA) and signing into law the landmark Public Utilities Holding Company Act of 1935.

The reasons for the shift in favor of public power during the decade are many and complex. The inability of many investor-owned utilities to follow the lead

---

The Roosevelt Administration proved itself a major champion of public power, creating the Tennessee Valley Administration (TVA) and the Rural Electrification Administration (REA) and signing into law the landmark Public Utilities Holding Company Act of 1935.

---

of PP&L and extend their lines into rural areas was a sore point when millions of Americans still lived on the farm. The very size of the holding companies— a handful of holding companies controlled well over half the generating capacity in the nation—did not sit well with many Americans, who opposed big business on principle. Finally, Americans were reacting—as they did again in 1992—against the 12-year Republican occupancy of the White House from 1921 to 1933 and the resulting *laissez faire* attitude toward business.

The bankruptcy of the Middle West Utilities Co. empire in April 1932 gave the populist politicians a figure to ridicule. Samuel Insull, the British-born immigrant who had worked for Thomas Edison at the time of the three-wire demonstration at Sunbury in 1882, had moved on to Chicago in the 1890s. There, he had made Commonwealth Edison a model of the modern big-city utility. During the 1920s, Insull had bought central stations, traction companies and manufactured gas plants across the nation's midsection, consolidating them into the Middle West Utilities Co., one of the most successful of the decade's holding companies. By 1930,

Middle West Utilities Co. and its subsidiaries were providing four billion kilowatt-hours of electric power to more than 6.3 million customers, stretching from Oklahoma to New Jersey and from Florida to Maine.

Insull was under fire in the U.S. Senate in the late 1920s for his generous support of political candidates, and when the stock market collapsed in 1929, the Chicago utility magnate found himself financially stretched. Insull had carried on a quarter-century feud with J.P. Morgan and the New York banking interests, and when bond payments came due in the fall of 1931, Middle West Utilities Co. defaulted.

The resulting bankruptcy impoverished many of the small stockholders who had purchased shares in Middle West Utilities Co. and its operating utilities. Insull had pioneered the practice of selling common shares to the public in 1919, and utility stocks during the 1920s, and shares in the holding companies were considered so safe that they were commonly recommended for the portfolios of "widows and orphans."

The wreck of Middle West Utilities Co. happened in the midst of the 1932 presidential campaign. Most utility executives supported Herbert Hoover, the Republican candidate and a noted engineer himself. But Hoover's administration had been ineffective in dealing with the Great Depression, and Franklin Roosevelt, who had fought Morgan and the utility holding company interests during his four years as governor of New York from 1928 to 1932, turned the Insull bankruptcy to his campaign's advantage.

Roosevelt called the wave of mergers and consolidations in the utility industry during the 1920s "a new kind of economic feudalism," and he predicted the holding companies would "have to be combated just as was the power of the old barons and the earlier kings." At a campaign stop in Minnesota, Roosevelt left little doubt about whom he blamed for the Depression. "It is an unfortunate fact," he said, "that largely through the building up of a series of great mergers and a series of great holding companies, the capital structure, especially in the case of the electric utilities, has been allowed to expand to an extent far beyond the actual and wise cash investment."

Insull was the perfect foil for Roosevelt's charges of greed and corruption in the utility industry. "The Ishmaels and the Insulls, whose hand is against every man," Roosevelt described the Chicagoan in a September 1932 speech at Portland, Oreg., in which he advocated the public ownership of waterpower sites in the American West.

The 1930 race for governor pitted Gifford Pinchot against the utility industry. Utilities lost. (*courtesy of the Morning Call*)

Pennsylvania Politics

Closer to home, PP&L and the state's utilities fought several battles during the 1930s. The tumultuous 1930 gubernatorial election pitted Gifford Pinchot and the state's progressives against the state's utilities. Pinchot, who had been out of office since 1927, campaigned on an anti-utility program. The Republican Party had become fragmented during the 1920s, and as many as three factions tried to take control of the state party. Joseph R. Grundy, president of the Pennsylvania Manufacturer's Association and a power in the state party, threw in his lot with Pinchot. In the Republican primary, the Pinchot and Grundy forces defeated the other major wing of the party, headed by William S. Vare, leader of the Philadelphia Republican organization and a spokesman for the state's utilities.

Victory in the 1930 Pennsylvania primary was sweet revenge for Pinchot. The forester had been defeated by Vare in a three-way contest for the Republican senatorial nomination in 1926. Vare had gone on to win the November general

election, but had never officially held the seat in the U.S. Senate. Pinchot had charged that the utilities had spent millions of dollars on Vare's campaign. The charges were picked up by Sen. James Reed of Missouri, who had his eye on the 1928 Democratic Presidential nomination.

The Reed Committee, which also included Sen. Robert M. LaFollette Jr. of

---

Pinchot's uncompromising stand in favor of Prohibition was popular in rural Pennsylvania, and his opposition to the utilities struck a chord in working-class neighborhoods of Philadelphia, Pittsburgh and Allentown.

Wisconsin—a longtime Pinchot ally—held hearings in 1926 and 1927 and eventually refused to seat both Vare and Frank L. Smith of Illinois, who had been helped to victory in November 1926 by the large campaign contributions of Samuel Insull.

Pinchot's victory in the 1930 Republican gubernatorial primary was helped by the entry of a liberal faction in the race. Throughout the fall, Pinchot hammered on the utility issue, pledging to replace the Pennsylvania Public Service Commission with a new Pennsylvania Public Utilities Commission. Pinchot's campaign specifically targeted utilities, promising that in his administration, utility return on equity would be tightly controlled at eight percent. Ironically, Vare and the state's utility and banking interests wound up supporting the Democratic Party nominee for governor in the fall elections.

In the end, Pinchot won the election by a slim plurality of 58,000 votes. Pinchot's uncompromising stand in favor of Prohibition was popular in rural Pennsylvania, and his opposition to the utilities struck a chord in working-class neighborhoods of Philadelphia, Pittsburgh and Allentown.

But Pinchot's victory wasn't the disaster that the utilities had predicted. Ever the pragmatic politician, Pinchot had thrown in his lot with Grundy and the state's manufacturing segment; Democratic politicians claimed that GOP stood for "Grundy Owns Pinchot." In the end, Pinchot did replace the Public Service Commission with a new Public Utilities Commission, but threats to traditional utility operations in Pennsylvania during the 1930s were far more likely to come from Washington, D.C., than Harrisburg.

For PP&L, the most spirited opposition faced during the decade came from the city of Bethlehem. For much of the 1930s, Robert Pfeifle, the outspoken mayor of Bethlehem, pushed for the creation of a municipally owned utility in the steel city. As early as 1927, PP&L had announced an increase in the city's annual water pumping station and

streetlighting rates from $23,000 to $44,000. After the city council rejected the increase, PP&L compromised with a rate of $33,000 for the pumping station and streetlights.

When bids were opened in January 1933, Pfeifle and the Bethlehem City Council informed PP&L that the city was considering buying diesel engines to provide municipally owned power for the streetlights. "Not that I am advocating public ownership of all utilities," Pfeifle said in his 1933 message to the community, "yet it is my belief that if the city owned and served our citizens with those necessities of life, the profits now going to a few people throughout the country, would, to a large extent, offset our total taxation. I have arrived at the above conclusion as a result of investigation and study of what has actually occurred in many communities throughout our country."

Pfeifle and PP&L skirmished over the municipal power issue for four years, from 1933 to 1937. Suits and countersuits flew back and forth, and the matter eventually went all the way to the Pennsylvania Supreme Court. In April 1935, the federal Public Works Administration appropriated $135,000 in loans and grants for the proposed city power plant. PP&L filed a bill for injunction in the Court of Northampton County, charging that the city had exceeded its bonding limits in accepting the PWA money.

Pfeifle, while publicly praising the municipal power plant as the "beginning of a New Deal electrically for the consumers of Bethlehem and a fine yardstick to measure the local power company's excessive rates," was more pragmatic in private. To a friend, he admitted that he didn't care if the municipal power plant never ran. "I want it there as a threat if the power company continues to raise its rates," he said.

In November 1935, a Northampton County Judge ruled in favor of PP&L, and a 1936 Pennsylvania Supreme Court decision reaffirmed the lower court's ruling that the Bethlehem City Council had exceeded its borrowing capacity. In October 1937, the city and PP&L entered into a new contract for streetlighting and water pumping, a contract which was $4,700 a year less than the contract PP&L and the city had negotiated back in 1933.

The Wheeler-Rayburn Act

If Pennsylvania Power & Light Co. had been preoccupied during the 1930s by political battles on the state and local levels, its parent was coping with a far more serious threat on the national level. With the 1935 passage of legislation sponsored in the Senate by Burton K. Wheeler of Montana and in the House of Representatives by Sam Rayburn of Texas, Electric Bond and Share Co. and the rest of the holding companies were forced to divest themselves of their operating utilities.

At the end of the 1920s, Electric Bond and Share Co. was at the height of its power and influence. From its offices at Two Rector Street in New York, Bond &

Share controlled Lehigh Power Securities Corp., the immediate parent of Pennsylvania Power & Light Co., and six other large holding companies: American Gas & Electric Co., American Power & Light Co., Utah Securities Corp., National Securities Corp., National Power & Light Corp. and Electric Power & Light Corp.

Electric Bond and Share Co. utilities provided electric power to consumers from the Pacific Northwest to Pennsylvania, and from Minnesota to Florida. In the 19 years between 1905 and 1924, Bond & Share acquired hundreds of companies in Pennsylvania and around the country.

> *In April 1935, the federal Public Works Administration appropriated $135,000 in loans and grants for the proposed [Bethlehem] city power plant.*

Thanks to Mayor Pfeifle, in 1937 PP&L lowered its streetlighting and water pumping contract by $4,700 a year from its 1933 contract. These photos show Bethlehem in the early 1930s when Pfeifle was battling the utility. *(photo courtesy of the Morning Call)*

Bethlehem mayor Robert Pfeifle pushed for the creation of a municipality-owned utility. He settled for a lower rate contract with PP&L. The next battle for the company would be the Wheeler-Rayburn Act. (*courtesy of the* Morning Call)

By 1935, Roosevelt felt comfortable enough with the way the economic recovery was proceeding to begin his long awaited campaign against the holding companies.

Most were located in small towns and consolidated into regional utilities, but Bond & Share subsidiaries served customers in such then large cities as Harrisburg, Lancaster, Duluth, Omaha, Fort Worth, Dallas, Houston, New Orleans, Memphis and Knoxville.

During the nearly 20 years that General Electric controlled Electric Bond and Share Co., the utility holding company reported earnings of $39 million, with nearly one-third of that coming in 1925 alone. The earnings for the holding company were over and above those of the subholding companies like Lehigh Power Securities Corp. and the individual operating companies.

The election of Franklin D. Roosevelt in November 1932 spelled the beginning of the end for the holding companies. In 1927, the Federal Trade Commission had begun hearings into the operation of the electric utility holding companies. Over the next eight years, FTC examiners looked into the books of 18 holding companies (including Electric Bond and Share Co.), 45 subholding companies (including Lehigh Power Securities Corp.) and 91 operating companies (including PP&L). Findings were reported in 40,000 pages of testimony and exhibits in 84 volumes.

Slowly at first, and at an increasing pace as the Great Depression worsened, the nation's press headlined the findings of the FTC examiners. By the time Insull's Middle West Utilities Cos. went into receivership in April 1932, public enthusiasm for doing away with the holding companies was at a fever pitch. Roosevelt, however, had other worries with which to contend. For the first two years of his administration, the priority was digging the nation out from under the debris of the Great Depression.

By 1935, Roosevelt felt comfortable enough with the way the economic recovery was proceeding to begin his long awaited campaign against the holding companies. Supreme Court Justices Louis Brandeis and Felix Frankfurter both urged Roosevelt to attack the holding company problem, and early in 1935, Roosevelt assigned Thomas Corcoran and Benjamin V. Cohen—both former law clerks for Frankfurter—to draft holding company legislation.

Roosevelt, who called holding companies "a 96-inch tail wagging a four-inch dog," endorsed the legislation in his annual message to Congress. The next month, he publicly urged its passage in one of his Fireside Chats. The so-called Wheeler-Rayburn bill, however, languished in committee through much of the spring of 1935.

The holding companies marshalled their forces for an attack on the legislation. "The legal department of Electric Bond and Share Co., in conjunction with attorneys for various subsidiaries, were inundated with work in preparing witnesses and oral and written presentations in opposition to the passage of this law and by way of suggesting vital amendments," recalled William W. Staplin, then an attorney in Bond & Share's legal department. "Of particular concern were the so-called 'death sentence' provisions which would have required the breaking up and dissolution of holding companies unable to qualify as approved integrated systems operating within a single area, the necessity of restructuring the capital accounts of all the subsidiaries and compliance with all the other extreme requirements and restrictions of the act. The mere size and number of subsidiary holding and operating companies would indicate the problems created for the Electric Bond and Share Co. system in this regard. All members of the department were involved to a greater or lesser extent in facing these problems."

The House and Senate wrangled over the "death sentence" for much of the spring and early summer. In August, Sen. Alben Barkley of Kentucky was chosen to introduce compromise language in the stalled bill. Barkley's compromise directed the Securities and Exchange Commission to permit a holding company to control more than one integrated holding system if the additional systems were unable to stand alone as independent utility operations. It also directed the SEC to set up simplified integrated utility systems. It did not drop the controversial "death sentence."

Still, the compromise language was enough to break the logjam in Congress, which wanted to adjourn in order to escape the hot August weather in Washington, D.C. On August 22, the bill sailed through Congress, with the House voting for passage 219-142. Four days later, Roosevelt signed the Public Utilities Holding Company Act of 1935 into law.

A State of Utter Confusion

The utility holding companies were in a state of shock. "Following passage of the Public Utility Act of 1935, the electric and gas utility industry was in a state of utter confusion," Staplin recalled. "The provisions of this law were so far-reaching and drastic as to leave company executives uncertain as to its impact and as to what course to follow. The demands upon the legal department of Electric Bond and Share Co. were such as to require almost around-the-clock efforts.

"A meeting of the top executives and lawyers of Electric Bond and Share Co. and its subsidiaries was held at the office of Electric Bond and Share Co. at which Frank A. Reid and Samuel W. Murphy presided, and at which Mr. John W. Davis (the firm's outside counsel) expressed the opinion that at least two-thirds of the provisions of the Act, including the death sentence, were unconstitutional."

Davis was proved wrong three years later. In a case that was argued before the Supreme Court of the United States by Reid & Priest, the outside firm that Reed, Murphy and Staplin formed to handle Bond & Share matters in the wake of the holding company act, the high court affirmed the constitutionality of the 1935 legislation. The holding companies would be forced to divest themselves of their operating subsidiaries.

But interestingly enough, the divestiture would take nearly a decade and a half to be accomplished. World events had intruded upon the parochial politics of utility regulation. War clouds were gathering across both Europe and Asia in 1938, and Roosevelt knew that he would have to depend upon the utilities for defense electric power production during any expected hostilities.

Franklin D. Roosevelt, "Mr. Fix the Economy" during the early 1930s, had become "Dr. Win the War" by the late 1930s.

> *"Of particular concern were the so-called 'death sentence' provisions which would have required the breaking up and dissolution of holding companies unable to qualify as approved integrated systems operating within a single area, the necessity of restructuring the capital accounts of all the subsidiaries and compliance with all the other extreme requirements and restrictions of the act." —William W. Staplin*

An Engineer's Engineer

He was an engineer's engineer.

John Shreve Wise Jr., Pennsylvania Power & Light Co.'s second president, pioneered many of the engineering innovations that made the Allentown utility one of the most progressive engineering companies of its kind in the country. Wise oversaw construction of the Harwood and Hauto steam electric plants in the early decades of the century. His championing of the Coxe traveling grate made it possible to burn anthracite coal as fine as granulated sugar, and he pioneered the concept of increasing current through transmission lines to reduce icing. In the 1930s, Wise demonstrated the feasibility of using two wires instead of four in rural distribution line, cutting the per-mile cost from $2,200 to $1,000.

Wise was named to succeed Edward Kimball Hall as PP&L's president in 1928. He guided the company through the Great Depression and World War II before retiring and relinquishing the presidency to Charles E. Oakes in 1945.

Born July 17, 1877—two years before Thomas Edison demonstrated the feasibility of incandescent electric lighting—Wise was the son of a prominent Philadelphia family. "When he was born in Philadelphia in 1877," the *Allentown Morning Call* editorialized at Wise's death in 1974, "not a room in that city or anywhere else in the world was lighted by electricity. The incandescent bulb that made this kind of interior lighting possible wasn't invented until a few years later."

John Wise graduated from Eastburn Academy in Philadelphia in 1894, spending his summers sailing his 15-foot Cricket class boat at the family's home at Longport on New Jersey's Great Egg Harbor Bay. He and boyhood friend Smedley Darlington Butler, a

John Shreve Wise, PP&L's second president.

Marine Corps general during World War I, established a record for 15-foot sailboats that has stood for more than a century.

At the age of 17, Wise entered the University of Pennsylvania, graduating in 1898 with a B.S. degree in electrical engineering. During his junior and senior years, he was coxswain of Penn's eight-oar varsity crew. Following graduation, the diminutive Wise volunteered for service in the Spanish-American War; he was rejected because he was only five feet, six inches tall.

Wise went to work for the Philadelphia Electric Co. in the summer of 1898, firing boilers, climbing poles and pulling cable. In early 1899, he was accepted at the General Electric Training School at Schenectady, N.Y. Known as "the test," the two-year training program gave young engineers the practical experience they would need to work for an operating electric utility.

Wise recalled working 12-hour shifts, seven days a week, with only an occasional Saturday off during the two years he was enrolled in "the test" at Schenectady. He completed his two years at General Electric with six months practical experience in the firm's plant at Lynn, Mass.

After leaving GE, Wise worked for the Electric Company of America at its utility in Atlantic City, N.J., and at the Auburn Light, Heat and Power Co. in Auburn, N.Y. In 1906, Alfred Pardee, a friend of Wise's father, invited the young engineer to Philadelphia to discuss building a plant at the Lattimer and Harwood mines in the anthracite region of Pennsylvania that would burn waste coal for fuel.

The plant that Wise designed and built at Harwood and manned with a crew that he trained was the first public utility power generating facility in the U.S. to burn coal at the mine mouth and transmit the power generated by high-voltage transmission lines. The plant was built adjacent to the Harwood Coal Mines, and a five-mile double-pole line was completed to nearby Hazleton. Wise's adaptation of a traveling grate invented by plant employee Eckley Coxe was instrumental in getting the new plant up and running.

"These culm banks were the size of mountains," Wise recalled years later in a newspaper interview. "A lot of good coal went to waste. Eckley B. Coxe invented a traveling grate, and it burned coal all right. But he died before he finished the design."

Wise tinkered with the balky grate, and his improvement led to the success of the Harwood plant. In essence, Wise redesigned the grate to allow a fivefold increase in the amount of air passing over it. "I was in the boiler room one day," Wise told a newspaper reporter in 1969, "and saw that the tops of the grate had burned off. I decided that was wrong; that the grates were getting too hot. If it wasn't for that grate design, there might not have been a PP&L."

130 Million Tons of Coal

Years later, Wise, who was then 90 years old, took a birthday telephone call from Jack Busby, one of his successors as chief executive officer of PP&L. "He told me that since 1907, they'd used 130 million tons of coal to generate electricity," Wise said. "He said he thought I'd be interested. I was, and I was pleased."

Wise helped consolidate the Harwood Electric Co. between 1909 and 1912, and the next year,

represented the Pardee interests in negotiating a merger between Harwood Electric Co. and the Lehigh Navigation Electric Co. Lehigh Navigation Electric Co. was building the Hauto plant at the time, and Wise was named general manager of both companies. He completed construction of the Hauto plant, trained the staff and built a 15-mile high-voltage transmission line across Broad Mountain to tie Harwood and Hauto together in a regional grid.

Following Electric Bond and Share Co.'s formation of Lehigh Power Securities Corp., the holding company for its Lehigh Valley interests, Wise was sent to Allentown in 1917. Three years later, he was named operating manager for the newly consolidated Pennsylvania Power & Light Co. One of Wise's monuments is the Allentown General Office Tower, which he conceived, planned and completed during the 1920s.

When E.K. Hall, PP&L's first president, announced

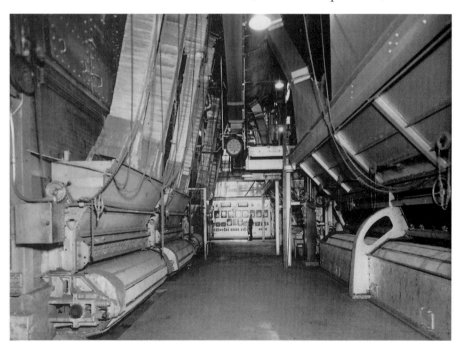

John Wise finished and refined Eckley Coxe's traveling grate design to reduce coal waste. The traveling grates burned lump coal, while today's boilers burn finely pulverized coal. This photo from the Cedar SES boiler room shows the odd-looking coal-feed chutes which are part of the Coxe traveling grate system.

his intention to retire from public life and move to Dartmouth University in 1928, Wise was named the company's second president and appointed to the PP&L board of directors. The choice was excellent. Wise had supervised the engineering work that saw PP&L expand greatly through consolidation and merger during the 1920s. There was no one in the company who knew the system better.

John Wise's presidency lasted 17 years. He helped consolidate the gains that the company had made during the 1920s, and guided PP&L across the shoals of the Great Depression. Wise also deserves credit for integrating the PP&L system into the Pennsylvania-Jersey-Maryland (PJM) Interchange during the 1920s and 1930s, the nation's first power pool. Wise's chairmanship of the Pennsylvania Joint Committee on Rural Electrification from 1927 to 1936 put PP&L in the forefront of utility efforts to electrify rural America.

(illustration by Brent Schaefer © 1995)

One of Wise's monuments is the Allentown General Office Tower, which he planned, conceived and completed during the 1920s.

The HPF&WFA

Eligible for retirement in 1942, John Wise remained in the presidency for the duration of World War II, retiring in May 1945. In the 29 years remaining to him, he established a reputation as one of the finest dry-fly anglers on the East Coast; during the spring and summer months, he could frequently be found fishing on the Upper and Lower Tunkhannock, the Tobyhanna, Wagner's Run, Beaver Creek and other trout streams of the Pocono Lake Preserve.

Wise's Tall Timbers Camp atop the Poconos was the site of the annual convention of the Hazleton Pickerel, Fly and Worm Fishing Association of

Allentown, Pa. In 1959, fellow members of the HPF&WFA immortalized their octogenarian founder with a descriptive limerick:

> *Old Man Wise near eighty-two*
> *With Power and Light in his past*
> *Now looks forward each day*
> *To the trout he will play*
> *That rise to the flies he will cast.*

Wise stayed active well into his 90s. His wife Adele died in January 1970, shortly after their 67th wedding anniversary, and the former PP&L chairman lived at home in Allentown's Livingston Apartments until the day he died. "I didn't stop driving until I was 90," Wise told a reporter in 1969. "Used to drive out to California to see my daughter. But I quit. Felt a man 90 years old should stop driving."

In 1968, Wise attended the 70th anniversary reunion of the class of 1898 at the University of Pennsylvania. "In the parade around Franklin Field I carried the flag, the class flag," Wise recalled. "Some students helped carry the other two fellows. Today, there are only seven left out of the class, and only two of them are on their feet."

John S. Wise died in Allentown on Aug. 13, 1974, at the age of 97. In an editorial marking his death, the *Allentown Morning Call* listed the many accomplishments and achievements "of this very notable, very energetic, very colorful man who for so many years did so much to promote the development of this community and the elements that brought prosperity to its people.

"All of them are the marks of a great American. John Wise was one of them."

24

World War II

THE MORNING CALL FIRST

ALLENTOWN, PA., MONDAY MORNING, DECEMBER 8, 1941

Japan Attacks Hawaii, Guam, Philippines, Causing Heavy Damage and 350 Deaths; Roosevelt May Ask Declaration of War

Enemy Planes Bomb Islands In Philippines

Japanese Forces Invade Malaya Near Singapore

Panama Canal Zone Is Placed On War Footing

Arbitration Board Awards 'Union Shop' to Workers In Nation's Captive Mines

F. D. R. to Address a Special Session of Congress Today; U. S. Warship Reported Afire

Company and industry battles of the 1930s took second seat when Japan declared war on the United States. (*courtesy of the Morning Call*)

O n Nov. 25, 1939, a small item appeared in the back pages of the *Allentown Morning Call*. It noted that "John Wise, this city, president of the Pennsylvania Power & Light Co. was invited yesterday to meet with the National Power Policy Committee in Washington, D.C., next month to discuss methods 'of meeting the country's future power demands.'"

Wise's invitation to the nation's capitol came at the personal behest of Harold L. Ickes, the portly Chicago lawyer who headed the U.S. Department of Interior. No friend of the investor-owned utility industry, Ickes' sudden invitation to Wise and the chief executive officers of about 50 other private utilities around the country was an example of the changed relationship between the New Deal and the electric utility industry.

Chicago lawyer Harold Ickes' sudden invitation to the CEOs of about 50 private utilities around the country in 1939 was the industry's official call to prepare for war. *(courtesy of the Morning Call)*

Ickes had told Wise that the meeting would take up much of the month of December. A different set of utility executives was arriving in Washington to meet with the National Power Policy Committee on each of three days—December 5, 12 and 19; Wise was asked to arrive on the 19th. The discussions, he was told, involved "a meeting of minds with the utility officials on the extent to which they could meet demands in the event of a continued industrial upturn and at the same time assure adequate facilities for national defense."

The timing of the committee meetings was no coincidence. When Wise found out about the meetings, it was less than two months since German Panzer divisions had sliced into Poland. Within days of the invasion of Sept. 1, 1939, both Britain and France had declared war on Germany. America was still officially neutral and would remain that way for more than two years. But the Roosevelt Administration clearly foresaw that the United States would eventually be drawn into the conflict. Making certain that there would be enough electric power to keep America's war industries running smoothly was a Roosevelt Administration priority after 1938. If America were to serve as the "Arsenal of Democracy" during the global war with Germany and Japan, then abundant supplies of electric power were absolutely essential to keep the arsenal running.

World War II was perhaps the watershed event of the 20th century for American society. The nation was transformed in ways that weren't always fully apparent at the time. Women entered the work force in droves, and the war accelerated the movement of both white and black Americans from the farm to the city. Government's involvement in the economy reached unprecedented levels, and the baby boom that began in the closing days of the war created a pent-up demand for goods and services that continued unabated until the early 1970s.

The war had a major impact on PP&L and the nation's utilities. Hundreds of employees left for the armed services, and women often took their places in the office and power plants. Merchandise sales were restricted because of shortages of steel, rubber and copper wire, and PP&L held its system together with baling wire and band-aids while meeting the incessant demand for industrial electric power from the anthracite mines and defense plants in the Lehigh Valley. The conversion of the region's industrial base to defense production laid a solid framework for the postwar boom in the economy of central and eastern Pennsylvania.

Women entered the work force in droves as their husbands, fathers and sons went off to war. From left: Women working as machinists at L.F. Grammes. (photo courtesy of the Lehigh County Historical Society) *Women preparing wheels for painting at Mack plant.* (photo courtesy of Mack Truck Co.) *PP&L office worker.* circa 1940s

On the Eve of WWII

Pennsylvania Power & Light Co. on the eve of World War II was an important cog in the industrial economy of central and eastern Pennsylvania. The utility had come through the difficult years of the Great Depression relatively unscathed. Although the well-publicized problems affecting Electric Bond and Share Co. and the other major U.S. electric utility holding companies commanded the lion's share of newspaper headlines during the mid- to latter-1930s, PP&L's operations were basically unaffected by the political woes of the parent company.

Early in 1941, John Wise announced a $5 million construction program to strengthen the utility's generating capacity. The bulk of the dollars earmarked for the expansion were designated for a 35,000-kilowatt peaking unit at Hauto plant. The company placed an order with Westinghouse Electric and Manufacturing Co. for the high-pressure topping turbine, which was expected to be operational by the fall of 1942. Also announced as part of the expansion program was the addition of a 15,000-kilowatt unit at the company's Cedar steam plant in Harrisburg.

Wise told *Electrical World* that the power plant expansion programs were a part of the company's policy of keeping well ahead of the requirements of its customers and always being prepared to meet anticipated power requirements. He told the magazine that both Hauto and Cedar plants were strategically located, and that the additional power produced would be available to customers throughout the service territory.

Wise also noted that PP&L was the world's largest user of anthracite, consuming 1.5 million tons of fuel per year. The expansion at Hauto, he added, would boost the plant's consumption of anthracite to more than 500,000 tons a year, making Hauto the largest and most modern anthracite burning plant in the world.

Allentown and the Lehigh Valley continued to be the industrial engine that drove demand for electric power. The region was noted for the manufacture of Portland Cement, trucks and buses, silk and rayon cloth, industrial machinery, furniture, metal tools and steel. By 1940, the Lehigh Valley was third in the state behind Philadelphia and Pittsburgh in industrial production, wages paid and value of products manufactured.

Nearly 25,000 industrial workers were employed by 260 separate manufacturing units in the city of Allentown. Capital

> *By 1940, the Lehigh Valley was third in the state behind Philadelphia and Pittsburgh in industrial production, wages paid and value of products manufactured.*

invested in local industry topped $60 million and the value of products manufactured was $65 million. The industrial payroll in Allentown in 1939 was $20 million. In addition, Allentown and the Lehigh Valley were becoming a center of distribution for companies nationwide due to the region's proximity to both Philadelphia and New York City.

Allentown was efficiently served by four railroads, making it possible to reach any point in the country over more than 200 fast-freight routes. The four lines maintained more than 4,000 miles of trackage in the city and operated railyards with a capacity of more than 10,000 cars. The community enjoyed rapid interurban service to Philadelphia and the anthracite regions, and the new Allentown-Bethlehem Airport offered scheduled air service to Cleveland, Chicago, Detroit and numerous other U.S. cities.

For the most part, PP&L's political problems were over. The company had spent much of the 1930s doing battle with Pennsylvania Gov. Gifford Pinchot and Bethlehem Mayor Robert Pfeifle, but those problems had essentially been resolved by 1940. In the Harrisburg area, PP&L line crews engaged in several fights with their counterparts from the Rural Electric Cooperatives of Dauphin and Cumberland counties.

"The battle of the pole holes" took place in later January 1941 and pitted PP&L crews against 50 or so Cumberland County farmers. In the winter of 1940, PP&L started stringing power lines into the Big Spring area of the county in order to serve local farmers. A group of farmers in the area, however, had already taken steps to organize a rural electric cooperative and objected to the line, which was to extend from Oakville to Newville.

When PP&L crews finished their day's work in the area, digging holes and setting distribution poles. The disaffected farmers came out at night and filled the holes. The drama would be played out again the next day, and again the next night. Several times in mid-January 1941, the dueling shovelers stayed at it until 1:30 in the morning. Finally, in late January, PP&L called off its crews and indicated the company's willingness to relocate the line and let the farmers purchase their power from the rural electric cooperative.

Day of Infamy

Battles over REA territory became totally irrelevant on Dec. 7, 1941. That Sunday afternoon in the Lehigh Valley, Pennsylvanians joined their compatriots across the country in disbelief as they listened to the first radio accounts of the Japanese attack on the U.S. Naval Base at Pearl Harbor, Hawaii. The "Day of Infamy" that President Roosevelt described so eloquently the next day in his war message to Congress had finally arrived. After watching much of Europe and Asia consumed by the fires of conflict during the previous two years, America was finally at war itself.

The war planning that had been going on since at least 1938 meant that PP&L and the nation's utilities were able to make a fairly smooth transition to defense electric power production. Pennsylvania, with its tradition of industrial production, was transformed into one of the major arsenals of the American war effort.

In Berwick, in Columbia County, the

American Car and Foundry Co. converted its railroad freight car assembly lines to the manufacture of tanks and armored vehicles. By war's end, 15,224 tanks would roll off the Berwick assembly lines. The Keystone Ordnance Works rose from farm fields in Greenwood Township of Crawford County, and a giant TNT manufacturing plant was built near Alvira, on the border of Lycoming and Union counties.

Electric power was the key to a smooth conversion to defense production. "Electricity is the mainspring that turns the wheels of our factories, mills and mines," *Business Week* editorialized in 1943. "It is the tireless arm that grinds our grain, weaves our cloth, pumps our water, builds our planes, our guns, our ships, our cars, our trucks and tanks…."

The Spiders Look Like Tanks

For Pennsylvania Power & Light Co., the most obvious impact the war had was in the number of employees called to military duty. By 1943, 933 men and women of the PP&L family had answered the call to the colors. Three employees had been killed in the line of duty. By the next year, 1,088 employees had been called to military duty; "seven have made the supreme sacrifice," the annual report noted, "that free men may stay free." Before the war was finally over in the summer of 1945, well over 20 percent of the company's pre-war work force had seen military duty.

Employees scattered to the far reaches of the globe in support of the war effort. Pvt. George

Lehigh County recruits receive typhoid inoculations. (*photo courtesy of the* Morning Call)

The first troops to leave Allentown and serve in combat with the highest distinction were the members of the 213th Coast Artillery National Guard. circa 1940 (*photo courtesy of the* Morning Call)

Ludwig wrote friends in the Harrisburg division in 1943 that he was stationed in the Hawaiian Islands. "The mosquitoes are getting larger and flying at a longer range," Ludwig wrote. "The ants eat all the candy, and the spiders look like tanks."

In 1943, the vast majority of PP&L employees in service were still in training or stationed in the continental United States. Harrisburg division employee Capt. James M. Brown was stationed at Bolling Field in Washington, D.C. Pvt. Oliver Hartman of the Walnut Steam Electric Station was undergoing training at

Fort Belvoir, Va., while George Belford of the Transmission Department was in training at Fort Sampson, N.Y.

Two years later, PP&L employees were all over the world and frequently in the thick of the fighting. In the spring of 1945, Pvt. Ray B. Howard reported to friends at the Walnut Street station that he was spending time in Paris before moving up to the front. George Ludwig wrote Harrisburg colleagues that he was in the Philippines, and Dudley Grove of the Second Street office let friends know that he was stationed in Australia. Emory N. "Nels" Miller reported that he had enjoyed his "cruise" over to Great Britain. Miller would see combat as his unit chased the retreating Nazis into Bavaria.

Many of the PP&L employees called to the colors enjoyed a busman's holiday while in the service. Lt. Col. Donald

Before the war was finally over in the summer of 1945, well over 20 percent of the company's pre-war work force had seen military duty.

The U.S.S. Allentown as it was christened in Milwaukee, Wis.'s, Froemming Shipyard on July 3, 1943, by Miss Joyce E. Beary of Allentown. (*photos courtesy of the Lehigh County Historical Society*)

Himes of Harrisburg compared his utility service in Germany to that which he was more familiar with at PP&L. "My copy of the company bulletin arrived yesterday," he wrote back to Harrisburg in the spring of 1945. "I didn't have a chance to read it until late last night. I finished it from one end to the other, the last six pages by flashlight.

"We had just moved our bivouac into a location where the public utilities were kaput…and my own generator went out while I was reading. I have two Kraut 15 kw diesel generators (captured). They are mounted on trailers and have been very useful. I use one for lighting my command post and the houses, cellars or barns the men occupy, and the other for power for my shop equipment, i.e., welding, radio-telegraph and telephone repair, motor maintenance, etc. They are 120-240-380 volt types.

"The one used for lighting we have revised to 110-220, since practically all Germany is 220, and we can get (by hook, or crook, or plain confiscation) radios, bulbs, etc., of that voltage. One interesting note: many of these towns have D.C. current and practically all of their appliances are built with a switchover for either type. All electric stores I've seen have been four-wire, three-phase. They also put a mercury-type amp meter in each house when using D.C."

The Home Front

The employees left behind on the home front had to cope with wartime shortages of personnel and material. Female employees were hired in record numbers and took positions formerly reserved for males. Female employees worked in stores and as meter readers, jobs they had never held in the pre-war company.

Procedures changed dramatically almost as soon as the U.S. entered the war. On Dec. 10, 1941, PP&L President John S. Wise sent a memo to all division and department heads, asking them to

"tighten up 100 percent on guards (and) refuse strangers admission to property." U.S. Army, Navy and Federal Power Commission representatives were to be let on to PP&L property but "these representatives must be identified and escorted through the property."

By June 1942, wardens had been assigned to each floor of the Tower

Building in Allentown. A number of employees had completed the American Red Cross standard and advanced First Aid courses, and a dispensary was located on the building's 12th floor. Wardens were responsible for coordination of the building's work force during air raid alerts.

Besides the increased security activities, home front employees threw themselves into the war effort, organizing writing campaigns for fellow employees in service, serving on draft boards and planting Victory Gardens.

"Company employees continued to

Home front efforts included bandage making by nurses and volunteers in the PP&L Tower lobby and aircraft spotter duty at Breinigsville Aircraft Spotter Post 29-B. (*photos courtesy of the Lehigh County Historical Society*)

take leading parts in all home-front war work," the company's 1944 annual report noted. "Where, at the outbreak of the war, the emphasis was on such things as Civilian Defense and the Aircraft Warning Service, the present-day employee home-front cooperation is reflected in War Bond purchases, Blood Bank donations, and contributions to the Red Cross, Community Chest and similar deserving organizations. The support of company employees in time, effort and money to these causes has been very generous."

Employees also had to cope with shortages, both on and off the job. In the spring of 1943, the War Production Board tightened up supplies of scrap copper, a critical material for the electric utility industry. Appliance sales dropped precipitously as the war effort consumed iron and steel supplies previously designated for the consumer durables market. The company fleet dealt with gasoline and tire shortages, and employees coped with sugar, meat and coffee rationing.

World War II was a critical juncture in the history of the electric utility industry. After the political battles of the 1930s, the war effort had the effect of unifying the industry. In addition, the industrial-

ization of the war effort provided a much-needed boost to utility revenues, especially at PP&L, which served one of the most heavily industrialized regions in the U.S.

By early 1945, PP&L was looking forward to the return of peacetime conditions. "Although most of the company's large industrial customers have no serious physical reconversion problems, industrial loads may temporarily decline as peace approaches. The company's new business programs will include measures calculated to offset any decline in industrial business through cooperation with industrial customers in their efforts to secure new business, through the development of new commercial interests within the territory and through promotion of new and additional uses of utility services among present customers."

The company needn't have worried about prospects for the future. Pent-up demand for new appliances and industrial utility service caused by the Great Depression and the war propelled Pennsylvania Power & Light Co. on the greatest expansion in its history in the quarter-century following 1946.

The Rise of the Industrial Sector

For Pennsylvania Power & Light Co., World War II was a five-year struggle to provide electric power to the defense industry in central and eastern Pennsylvania.

Much of the Lehigh Valley and the anthracite region of Pennsylvania enjoyed an unprecedented industrial boom during the war years. "Industrial business, generally, in 1943 exceeded all previous records," PP&L reported

Almost 4,700 military E.H. cargo trucks were made in Allentown from 1940 to the end of 1944 at the Mack International Motor Truck Co. (*photo courtesy of Mack Truck Co.*)

in early 1944. "There were extremes of both high and low production among various classes of industry. Steel production, for example, was very high whereas cement production was low, due largely to restrictions on new construction. There was a slight decrease in the number of electric customers served due mainly to closing of commercial establishments because of wartime restrictions. The increase in sales of electricity and gas to industrial customers at the lower steps of the industrial rates is indicated by the fact that the percentage increase in sales exceeds the percentage increase in revenues from these sales."

Gross operating revenues of nearly $51 million in 1944 were 50 percent more than in 1934, just 10 years before. The reason for the jump in gross revenues was simple. Central and eastern Pennsylvania was a key component in America's arsenal of democracy.

Literally hundreds of war plants began to spring up in PP&L territory shortly after the Japanese bombs stopped falling on Pearl Harbor. Mack International Motor Truck Co. in Allentown, a company industrial customer since before 1920, secured contracts to make trucks, tank transmissions, tractor-trailers, diesel trucks and wrecker chassis. The Trojan Power Co. in Allentown

geared up to produce explosives, nitro starch, ammunition components and chemical explosives.

Bethlehem Steel Co. on its own accounted for hundreds of defense contracts during the war. The complex of big steel mills straddling the Lehigh River in Bethlehem produced everything from shell forgings to bar steel to ammunition components to railway rails and splice bars for the Allied defense effort. Bethlehem Steel Co.'s war contracts totalled more than $21.4 million in 1941 alone.

One major unheralded war industry of the Lehigh Valley was silk and textiles. Old-line Allentown companies like Modern Clothing Co., Phoenix Silk Corp. and Queen City Textile Corp. helped outfit the millions of American men and women in uniform. The mills in Allentown cranked out hundreds of products, including wool and khaki trousers, underwear, mosquito netting, flannel shirts and serge coats.

The company's Williamsport and Susquehanna divisions were particularly critical to the war effort. The Lycoming division of the Aviation Manufacturing Corp. in Williamsport produced airplane wheels, engines, parts and propellers. In Berwick, in PP&L's Susquehanna division, the giant American Car and Foundry Co. had dozens of contracts for war work. The company's plants made pontoon equipment, drive sprockets, tanks and components, railroad cars, engine supports, turret castings and links for tracked vehicles.

Even before the war started, PP&L's defense industrial business had skyrocketed. In June 1941, six months before the attack on Pearl Harbor, industrial customers in the company's 10 divisions had secured $135 million in defense contracts.

The rapid increase in defense industrial production at the beginning of the war put strong pressures on PP&L's generating capacity. The company announced in 1940 that it intended to install 31,250 kilowatts of generating capacity at Hauto Steam Electric Station. But defense needs across the country intervened, and by the spring of 1941, PP&L was beginning to get worried about meeting its 1942 deadline for installing the two new generators at Hauto.

In a May 21, 1941, letter to Edward R. Stettinius, director of priorities in the federal Office of Production Management (OPM), PP&L President John S. Wise Jr., argued for the swift expedition of the company's request for the additional generation.

Queen City Textile Corp. of Allentown, along with the region's other silk and textile mills, went into high gear during the war to produce trousers, underwear, mosquito netting, flannel shirts and serge coats. *circa 1940 (photo courtesy of the* **Morning Call***)*

"Comprehensive load-capacity studies and analyses indicate that, due to the rapidly increasing and expanding National Defense activity, this additional capacity will be required by the Fall of 1942," Wise wrote. "Manufacturers with whom orders have been placed have advised that the scheduled in-service date of Aug. 1, 1942, will be jeopardized if materials are not received in time to fit into their production schedules."

As it was, OPM was unable to release materials in time for Westinghouse to meet the August 1942 deadline for installation of the Hauto generators. Stettinius,

who would later serve FDR and Harry Truman as Secretary of State, was able to do the next best thing. Aware of the critical importance of central and eastern Pennsylvania to the war economy, Stettinius expedited PP&L's request. In the process, OPM allowed PP&L to increase the size of the generators slated for Hauto.

In 1943, two new generators totaling 41,250 kilowatts of capacity were placed in service at Hauto. Pennsylvania Power & Light Co. was able to provide electric power to defense industries in its service territory, in the process doing its part to help win the war.

25

Interlude:
PP&L People in 1945

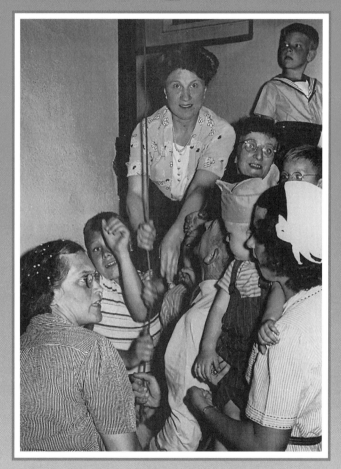

After President Truman's official announcement of the victory over Japan at 7 p.m. on Aug. 14, 1945, bells were rung by jubilant Allentonians. (*courtesy of the* **Morning Call**)

The end of World War II in 1945 marked the 25th anniversary of Pennsylvania Power & Light Co. PP&L had undergone momentous change during its first quarter-century, and the people who kept the lights burning in central and eastern Pennsylvania were witness to political, economic, social and technological trends that were not even thought of when the modern utility was incorporated in 1920.

Cpl. Martin P. Henninger

Pvt. 1st Class Aldon R. Dorney

Seaman 1st Class Carl Derr

The company in 1945 was faced with the daunting task of absorbing more than 1,000 employees expected to return from military service.

The 25th anniversary year was typical in the two significant changes it brought to the Allentown utility. PP&L absorbed hundreds of men and women returning from the service into its work force, and the utility entered upon the postwar era with a new management team in place at the Allentown General Office Tower.

As early as the spring of 1944, the company had begun laying plans for the reintegration of returning veterans into the company work force. The company's philosophy was simple and to the point. "The company needs its employees who are in military service and wants them back," PP&L noted in the summer of 1945. "The company plans to reinstate and reemploy those who are honorably discharged and capable of working."

Employees had begun trickling back from service in 1944. By the end of that year, 63 former company employees had returned from military service. In accordance with company policy, the 1944 annual report to shareholders noted, they "were reinstated and placed in jobs as good as or better than the ones which they left."

The company that veterans returned to in 1945 had changed during the war. Benefits had improved dramatically since 1940. By the end of 1944, 5,077 employees—96 percent of the company's work force—had enrolled in the PP&L Employee Group Insurance Plan. The company's group insurance contract covered death and disability, and by the end of 1944, there was $22,157,000 worth of insurance in the plan.

An Employee Retirement Plan was also in existence by 1944. There were 3,678 employees participating in the retirement plan, out of a total of 4,176 employees eligible to participate. At the end of 1944, 330 former employees had been retired under the plan.

Every department of the company contributed employees to the war effort, including 117 from the General Office departments,

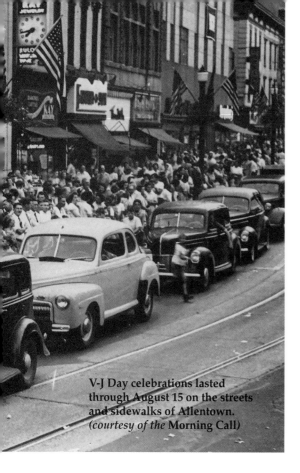

V-J Day celebrations lasted through August 15 on the streets and sidewalks of Allentown. (*courtesy of the* Morning Call)

Still, the company in 1945 was faced with the daunting task of absorbing more than 1,000 employees expected to return from military service. All told, 1,144 employees had answered the call to the colors. Every department of the company contributed employees to the war effort, including 117 from the General Office departments, 313 from the operating departments, 249 from the divisional departments and 465 from the Construction Department.

"There is no means of forecasting the total number of employees who will return or the number who will return during any given time interval," the company noted in the summer of 1945. "A relatively small but constant number may return from month to month or the fortunes of war may release large numbers at irregular intervals. The problem of reinstating those who return may be

serious in some departments, while presenting no difficulty in others. Management must be prepared to consider their application for reemployment, regardless of when they return.

"The problem requires serious attention and the job of fitting each returning veteran into our organization can be turned to the company's advantage by utilizing the skill and training which many of these veterans have acquired. A well balanced plan for the employment of veterans will react favorably on public relations."

As it was, the absorption of returning veterans into the company work force was accomplished in a swift and smooth manner. The fortunes of war dictated that returning veterans were absorbed over a relatively long period of time. Most employees who returned and claimed their old jobs came back between the end of the war in Europe in May 1945 and the beginning of 1946.

In 1945, 410 war veterans were reemployed, 330 at compensation levels higher than what they had been paid when they left for the service. A total of 228 returning war veterans were placed in or subsequently promoted to higher positions than they held before entering the service. By the end of 1946, approximately 900 employees had returned to PP&L from the military.

Additional numbers of returning veterans opted to continue their education, taking advantage of the G.I. Bill of Education that had been passed by Congress in 1944. Employees who returned and

Lt. Thomas F. Hall

Pvt. Keith E. Keenly

Chief Pharmacist Artie R. Leh

313 from the operating departments, 249 from the divisional departments and 465 from the Construction Department.

T/5 Robert C. Keiper

Cpl. Kermit Steckel

Pvt. Roland L. Hertzog

went to college were absorbed back into the work force in 1947, 1948 and 1949. A small number of former employees elected to continue their careers in the military, or sought work elsewhere in the country.

Finally, the rapid conversion to a peacetime economy worked in the company's favor. Pent-up consumer demand for housing, automobiles and consumer durables meant that the war industries of the Lehigh Valley and the anthracite region were quickly converted to peacetime use. Pennsylvania

Power & Light Co. spent much of the latter half of the 1940s gearing up for one of the most significant expansions in the company's history.

On Dec. 31, 1945, PP&L had 5,734 employees on active duty, a gain of nearly 10 percent over the preceding year, with much of the increase coming in the last three months of the year as veterans returned to work. Nearly eight of 10 company employees had more than five years of service, and more than one in four (28 percent) had been with the company for 20 years or more.

Proudly we pay tribute to the men and women of this Company who have answered the call to colors.

Seven have made the supreme sacrifice . . . that free men may stay free.

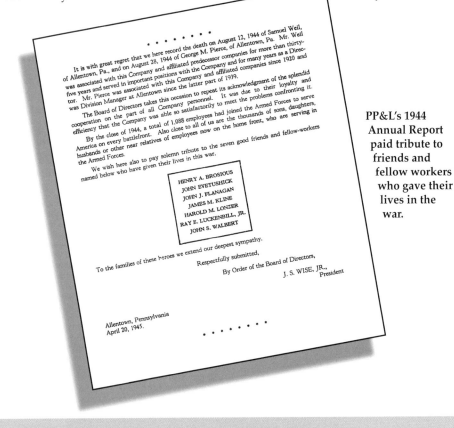

It is with great regret that we here record the death on August 12, 1944 of Samuel Weil, of Allentown, Pa., and on August 28, 1944 of George M. Pierce, of Allentown, Pa. Mr. Weil was associated with this Company and affiliated predecessor companies for more than thirty-five years and served in important positions with the Company and for many years as a Director. Mr. Pierce was associated with this Company and affiliated companies since 1920 and was Division Manager at Allentown since the latter part of 1939.

The Board of Directors takes this occasion to repeat its acknowledgment of the splendid cooperation on the part of all Company personnel. It was due to their loyalty and efficiency that the Company was able so satisfactorily to meet the problems confronting it.

By the close of 1944, a total of 1,088 employees had joined the Armed Forces to serve America on every battlefront. Also close to all of us are the thousands of sons, daughters, husbands or other near relatives of employees now on the home front, who are serving in the Armed Forces.

We wish here also to pay solemn tribute to the seven good friends and fellow-workers named below who have given their lives in this war.

HENRY A. BROSIOUS
JOHN EVETUSHICK
JOHN J. FLANAGAN
JAMES M. KLINE
HAROLD M. LONZER
RAY E. LUCKENBILL, JR.
JOHN S. WALBERT

To the families of these heroes we extend our deepest sympathy.

Respectfully submitted,

By Order of the Board of Directors,

J. S. WISE, JR.,
President

Allentown, Pennsylvania
April 20, 1945.

PP&L's 1944 Annual Report paid tribute to friends and fellow workers who gave their lives in the war.

Veterans returned to a company that had undergone significant changes in the executive ranks during 1945.

During 1945, $13.2 million was paid to employees in wages and salaries.

Changes at the Top

Veterans coming back from military service returned to a company that had undergone significant changes in the executive ranks during 1945. After 38 years of service with PP&L and its predecessors, John S. Wise Jr. stepped down as the company's president. Wise had been eligible for retirement in mid-war, but he had promised Paul B. Sawyer of the National Power & Light Co., the utility's immediate holding company, that he would stay on until the end of the war.

Wise's successor as the third president of PP&L was Charles E. Oakes, president of the Birmingham Electric Co. in Alabama from 1939 until 1945. Birmingham Electric Co., which would shortly become a part of Alabama Power Co., was a sister utility to PP&L in the Electric Bond and Share Co. family, and Oakes had spent 16 years with PP&L between 1923 and 1939.

The board of directors was increased in 1945 from five to nine members. Joining the board were D.H. Brillhart, president of the Union Bank and Trust Co. of Bethlehem; Sawyer of National Power & Light Co.; George Ross Hull of the law firm of Hull, Leiby and Metzger in Harrisburg; and Ira A. Hawkins, Jr., of the New York law firm of Simpson, Thacher and Bartlett.

A.D. Root, a 30-year veteran with Electric Bond and Share Co., joined PP&L as vice president and treasurer, while L.K. Bingaman was elected secretary of the company. Bingaman, who had started in the power business with the Edison Electric Illuminating Co. of Sunbury in

Charles E. Oakes succeeded John Wise to become PP&L's third president in 1946.

1907, had been assistant secretary and assistant treasurer of the company since its incorporation. Harry Ferguson, who had served as assistant to the vice president and general manager, was appointed operating manager.

Ferguson, a 1916 mechanical engineering graduate of the University of West Virginia, had joined PP&L as a power plant engineer in 1920, the year the company was incorporated. For a number of years, Ferguson had served as the assistant to Norman G. Reinicker, the company's longtime vice president and general manager.

Reinicker's illness and death in January 1946, coming on the heels of Wise's retirement, severed the link between the PP&L of 1945 and the PP&L of 1920. A 1911 mechanical engineering graduate of Cornell University, the Baltimore-born Reinicker had served as a power plant engineer with the Detroit Edison Co. following graduation. From 1915 to 1918, he had been chief assistant for power plants at New York Edison Co. During World War I, he was superintendent of power for the Old Hickory Powder Co. in Nashville, Tenn., a subsidiary of the DuPont Co. In 1919, Sidney Z. Mitchell had brought Reinicker to Allentown to serve as superintendent of operations for the Lehigh Navigation Electric Co., one of the major predecessors of PP&L.

From 1920 until he fell ill in the fall of 1945, Reinicker was John Wise's right-hand man. He was the company's first

After 38 years of service with PP&L and its predecessors, John S. Wise Jr. stepped down as the company's president.

Over the years, Wise entrusted Reinicker with the day-to-day operation of the company. Reinicker represented PP&L in the planning sessions for the implementation of the 230,000-volt transmission ring that led to the formation of the PNJ Interconnection.

superintendent of operations, and in 1925 was made PP&L's general superintendent. When Wise was elected the company's second president in 1928, Reinicker was named general manager; seven years later, he added a vice presidency to his title. Over the years, Wise entrusted Reinicker with the day-to-day operation of the company. Reinicker represented PP&L in the planning sessions for the implementation of the 230,000-volt transmission ring that led to the formation of the PNJ Interconnection, and he supervised construction of the Wallenpaupack hydroelectric station. Wise and Reinicker had been instrumental in seeing to it that PP&L became the world's largest single consumer of anthracite coal during the 1920s.

Norman G. Reinicker, PP&L's vice president and general manager until his death in 1946.

Reinicker's death in January was followed three months later by the death of Paul Backus Sawyer. The company's first vice president and general manager in 1920, Sawyer had gone on to work for the National Power & Light Co., the Electric Bond and Share Co. subholding company that had responsibility for PP&L. The longtime chairman of the board of directors of PP&L, Sawyer had been elected to the newly independent PP&L less than a year before he died. The deaths of Reinicker and Sawyer were ironic, coming in the year in which PP&L finally broke its connections to the holding company era. When returning veterans came back to PP&L in 1946, it was to a company that was no longer the subsidiary of a holding company.

The Peace Dividend

World War II brought immense changes in the way that utility line workers went about their business. Pennsylvania Power & Light Co. generation plant workers and transmission and distribution line crews benefited from new tools and techniques that had been developed for American fighting men during the war.

Take the matter of protective headgear. The steel battle helmet worn into combat by American troops in the European and Pacific Theatres of Operations was adapted for use by utility workers in the years after the war. From the turn of the century to the early 1950s, PP&L line crews made their own hard hats, soaking felt fedoras in brine and water until they were stiff as boards.

The development of injection-molding techniques during the war provided the key to making a lightweight, strong hard hat for line crews and power plant workers. Modeled on the steel battle helmet, with the addition of a molded lip to protect the forehead, hard hats began showing up in PP&L power plant locker rooms in the early 1950s.

Those first hard hats were made of injection-molded fiberglass. Shoestring-like cords sewn through the shell held a leather suspension inside the helmet. By the early 1960s, molded plastic hard hats began to be introduced at PP&L.

Another wartime innovation that began to show up in PP&L's arsenal of tools was the tracked vehicle. The American Army had ridden to the front in half-tracks during the war. The half-tracks were essentially 10-ton trucks with a series of bogie wheels and tracks where the rear wheels should have been. For PP&L, which had to maintain transmission line corridors in some of the most rugged country east of the Rocky Mountains, the

Cpl. Wilbur F. Roth in 1943 wearing a steel battle helmet. After the war, combat helmets like Corporal Roth's were modified for utility workers to use.

idea was a natural.

In 1947, PP&L line crews modified an old Ford truck with tracks in place of the rear wheels. For much of the late 1940s, the crews used the truck, which they dubbed a "weasel," to reach transmission lines in rugged terrain in the Pocono Mountains. In the 1960s, crews used an updated snowtrack vehicle to maintain power lines in snowy conditions.

One procedure that utilities like PP&L copied from the Army, the Navy and the Marines was the U.S. military's emphasis on training. Millions of GIs and sailors had received their introduction to military life in basic and advanced training, and utilities like PP&L were quick to see the benefit of establishing training programs for new employees.

In 1947, Pennsylvania Power & Light Co. established its On-The-Job Training Course for Linemen. The training program was a concentrated course on electrical construction and maintenance work combining study in the theory of electricity with actual field application of the classroom work. The program was coordinated through the Veterans Administration, since most of the enrollees were former GIs who had previously been employed with the company. In its first year of operation, the program trained 85 employees at schools in Hazleton, Williamsport, Harrisburg, Lancaster and Allentown. Upon completion of the program, graduates became linemen third class and were assigned to a PP&L line crew.

Some utilities created Cadet Engineer programs in the late 1940s and early 1950s that were modeled on the military's WWII Officer Candidate Schools.

Utilities like Wisconsin Power & Light Co. and Northwestern Public Service, both former subsidiaries of the Insull Middlewest Utilities holding company structure, were particular champions of the Cadet Engineer concept.

One wartime technological innovation of immediate benefit to utilities was the development of mobile radio telecommunications equipment. The armored divisions of Gen. George S. Patton Jr. had maintained unit cohesiveness during the invasion of France and Germany with mobile radio telecommunications.

Immediately after the war, PP&L began outfitting its fleet of line trucks with mobile radio sets that had been developed during the war. By late 1947, the utility had 19 mobile radio units in its fleet of line trucks. The first real test of the system came on New Year's Day 1947 when a massive sleet storm crippled central and eastern Pennsylvania.

One company line foreman spent three days in the field helping crews restore service to the more than 80,000 suburban and rural customers left without power in the storm. "I don't know when we'd ever have finished all we had to do without this amazing short cut," the line foreman described the use of the mobile radio equipment in restoration of service. "Instead of wasting needed hours in hunting trouble, we could put all of our time directly to the important job of getting service back to our customers."

A lineman who started work with the company in 1920 wouldn't necessarily notice great changes in operations in the years just after the war. Linemen were still outfitted with leather boots, toolbelts and spikes, and the A-frame boom trucks of the late 1940s were only a marginal improvement over the primitive line trucks of the early 1920s. But change was having an impact on the way line workers did their jobs, and those changes would become far more pronounced during the 1950s and 1960s.

From the turn of the century to the early 1950s, PP&L line crews made their own hard hats, soaking felt fedoras in brine and water until they were stiff as boards.

26

The Big Board

In 1940, PP&L was preparing for divestiture, and by 1946, stockholders gladly received dividends.

War's end brought about a major change in the way PP&L did business. The Public Utilities Holding Company Act, which had been passed by Congress 10 years before, required utility holding companies, with certain exceptions, to divest themselves of operating utilities. The U.S. Supreme Court had ruled favorably on the constitutionality of the legislation in 1938, but the intervention of World War II—and the nation's need for a strong electric utility industry to provide defense electric power—had slowed the process of divestiture.

But with the end of the war, the breakup of the holding companies picked up speed. Between 1945 and 1950, the vast majority of utility operating subsidiaries of holding companies in the U.S. were spun out as independent, investor-owned stock companies.

In actuality, Pennsylvania Power & Light Co. had been preparing for divestiture from National Power & Light Co., the subholding company of the Electric Bond and Share Co., since shortly after the 1938 Supreme Court decision had been announced. As early as December 1940, PP&L submitted a reclassification of its plant, property and equipment to the Federal Power Commission and the Pennsylvania Public Utility Commission.

The reclassification document involved massive amounts of work by the company's auditors and accountants, and resulted in the compilation of about a dozen volumes of data for the two commissions. Reclassification was critical to the process of establishing a stock price for the proposed independent, investor-owned utility; only by determining what

PP&L had paid for the plant, property and equipment of its more than 800 predecessor utilities could the utility establish a realistic opening price for the company's common stock.

The company continued with its reclassification activity throughout the war. In 1941, the U.S. Securities and Exchange Commission (SEC) raised questions about the restatement of the company's plant and investment, surplus, capital and other accounts. In November 1941, the SEC put limits on the dividends that PP&L could pay to its shareholders, which at the time consisted primarily of National Power & Light Co. and Electric Bond and Share Co. The company was enjoined from paying dividends equivalent to more than 25 percent of the net earnings available for common stock after June 1, 1941.

At the same time, PP&L agreed to write down $575,000 of its $9.15 million investment in the Wallenpaupack hydro-electric project, at the request of the

> *Between 1945 and 1950, the vast majority of utility operating subsidiaries of holding companies in the U.S. were spun out as independent, investor-owned stock companies.*

In the early 1940s, as PP&L prepared for divestiture, plants like Wallenpaupack were evaluated to determine a realistic stock price.

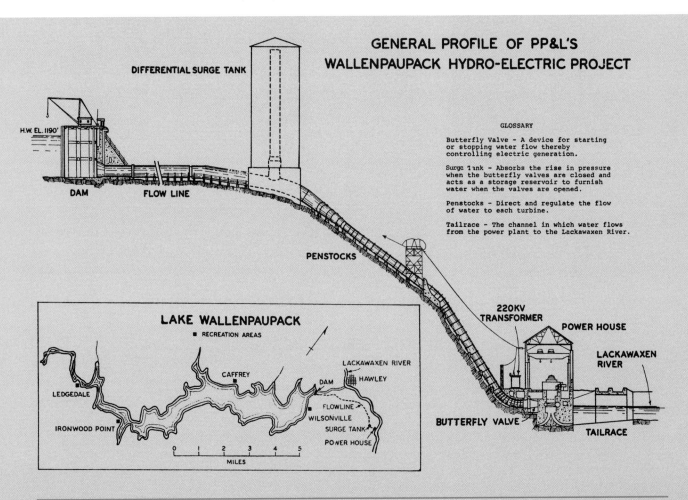

GENERAL PROFILE OF PP&L'S
WALLENPAUPACK HYDRO-ELECTRIC PROJECT

DIFFERENTIAL SURGE TANK

H.W. EL. 1190'

DAM   FLOW LINE

PENSTOCKS

GLOSSARY

Butterfly Valve - A device for starting or stopping water flow thereby controlling electric generation.

Surge Tank - Absorbs the rise in pressure when the butterfly valves are closed and acts as a storage reservoir to furnish water when the valves are opened.

Penstocks - Direct and regulate the flow of water to each turbine.

Tailrace - The channel in which water flows from the power plant to the Lackawaxen River.

220KV TRANSFORMER

POWER HOUSE

LACKAWAXEN RIVER

BUTTERFLY VALVE

TAILRACE

LAKE WALLENPAUPACK
■ RECREATION AREAS

LEDGEDALE

CAFFREY

IRONWOOD POINT

LACKAWAXEN RIVER

DAM   HAWLEY

FLOWLINE

WILSONVILLE

SURGE TANK

POWER HOUSE

0   1   2   3   4   5
MILES

Federal Power Commission. The FPC ordered that $540,000 of the amount be charged against earned surplus. The FPC later reduced the disallowed costs in the Pocono Mountains hydroelectric project to $500,000, slightly more than five percent of the total cost of the project. Some utilities at the time were forced to write down as much as 25 percent of the cost of hydroelectric projects.

In June 1943, the FPC notified the company that further proceedings would be necessary to straighten out the Wallenpaupack accounts. But winning the war came first. "Due to the war emergency, however, further action will be postponed for the time being," FPC auditors notified PP&L on June 19.

In preparation for the impending divestiture from National Power & Light Co., PP&L began consolidating subsidiary operations of its own. At the annual shareholders' meeting in May 1944 in Allentown, the company reacquired 15,469 shares of $7 preferred stock in the Lehigh Valley Transit Co. These shares were valued at $97.50 apiece. As part of the transaction, PP&L acquired the Allentown Steam Electric Generating Station from the transit company for $1.9 million.

By 1944, both the end of the war and the end of PP&L's 25-year existence as a holding company subsidiary were in sight. National Power & Light Co. had been ordered by the SEC to liquidate its holdings in 1942 and was in the process of achieving that goal by year-end 1944. PP&L had reached an accommodation with the Pennsylvania Public Utility Commission on its proposed reclassification of accounts, agreeing to amortize $1.75 million a year for 15 years in an Electric Plant Acquisition Adjustment account.

The final piece to the divestiture puzzle involved retiring debt and cleaning up the PP&L balance sheet. Between 1939 and 1944, the company reduced long-term debt $5.43 million, consisting of $4.25 million in 2-5/8 percent 10-year notes and $1.18 million in first mortgage bonds, 3-1/2 percent series due in 1969.

New Ownership

On Dec. 31, 1945, National Power & Light Co. took the first step in a two-year program of divestiture of ownership in Pennsylvania Power & Light Co. The holding company surrendered for cancellation almost 1.2 million shares of common stock in PP&L and transferred to the company all the outstanding capital stock of the Edison Illuminating Co. of Easton, which PP&L subsequently sold for $425,000 to General Public Utilities.

PP&L issued and sold more than 1.8 million shares of its common stock at $10 per share, raising $18,187,190 of new capital, which was used to retire old preferred stocks. More than $60 million in preferred stock was exchanged for $44 million in new 4-1/2 percent preferred stock; the balance was paid in cash with the proceeds from the common stock sale at the redemption price of $110 per share and accrued dividends.

At year end, PP&L stock was owned by approximately 8,500 shareholders, many of them living in the company's service territory. National Power & Light Co. still owned about 29 percent of the company, and Electric Bond and Share Co. owned 34 percent of the company's common stock. But that would change during the next two years.

The 1945 change in ownership was most immediately apparent in the public face PP&L presented to the investment community. For 25 years, PP&L had produced a 10-page annual report to shareholders that included only a bare-bones financial picture of the company's annual progress. Printed on

The difference between PP&L's bare-bones, no-frills 1944 annual report and the expanded, illustrated 1945 annual report is more than graphic. The change is one of audience—from holding company officials to investment community.

For 25 years, PP&L had produced a 10-page annual report to shareholders that included only a bare-bones financial picture of the company's annual progress.

inexpensive white paper, the annual report was designed to be circulated only to holding company officials in New York.

The 1945 annual report said volumes about the company's new ownership structure. The 36-page report was printed on heavy stock and included an architect's rendering of the company's proposed new Sunbury Steam Electric Station on the cover. Inside, the two-color report included a montage of photographs of the company's service territory, charts and graphs, and a full-color map of PP&L's service territory.

By the next year, company President Chas. E. Oakes was able to announce to PP&L shareholders that "a significant change has taken place in the ownership of our common stock. National Power & Light Co. and Electric Bond and Share Co. have practically completed disposition of their holdings of common stock of this company. As a result, our stock is currently owned by approximately 70,000 stockholders with no stockholder holding as much as seven percent (of the stock)."

Electric Bond and Share Co. had disposed of its holdings in PP&L during a two-week period in early 1947. Bond & Share had priced the 1,010,000 shares of PP&L common stock at 17-1/2, well below the $21 a share the stock was trading for at the beginning of the year. Still, the run-up in PP&L stock price made the Bond & Share offer highly attractive to the investment community; PP&L's common stock price had essentially doubled in little more than a year's time, and the more than one million shares offered by Bond & Share were snapped up in less than two weeks.

Electric Bond and Share Co. had also disposed of 808,000 shares of American Gas & Electric Co., the parent company of Scranton Electric Co. Again, Bond & Share had sold the AG&E shares at a discount of nearly 20 percent. The holding company had discounted the shares of both issues for a good reason. It needed to raise $73 million in cash prior to early March to retire its $5 and $6 preferred stock. At the time of the early 1947 AG&E

Anna G. Ludwig, homemaker

Oscar L. Drumm, farmer

By 1946, there were nearly 70,000 PP&L stockholders, of which two-thirds lived in Pennsylvania.

Catherin Payne, nurse

Oliver D. Williams, businessman

Charles K. Farwell, PP&L meter reader

and PP&L issues, Electric Bond and Share Co. announced to the market that its - National Power & Light Co. subsidiary was preparing to dispose of its interest in Birmingham Electric Co. and Carolina Power & Light Co.

A final secondary offering of 153,753 shares of PP&L was made by Electric Bond and Share Co. on March 13, 1947. Before the New York Stock Exchange closed that afternoon, a group of brokers headed by Lehman Brothers purchased the entire block at a much less discounted price of $20 a share. The brokerage syndicate included First Boston Corp., Kidder Peabody and Co., and Merrill Lynch, Pierce, Fenner and Beane.

The strong market in PP&L stock in 1946 and 1947 wasn't at all uncommon for utilities in the postwar period. Nearly 15 years of depression and war had created pent-up demands in the capital markets. Holding companies disposed of more than $250 million in utility stocks between the summer of 1945 and 1946 alone.

Selling the Company

Not since the 1920s had Pennsylvania Power & Light Co. actively sold stock to the investing public. The Depression, the Holding Company Act and the War had brought a halt to public sales of stock. Following divestiture, PP&L once again became active in selling its stock to the public. Key to the strategy was a public relations campaign that stressed the Allentown utility's image as a hometown business.

"A far reaching change has taken place in our ownership," Chas. E. Oakes told company workers in the *1946 Report to Employees*. "Where last year there was but one common stockholder, there are now more than 40,000 and a total of about 70,000 common and preferred stockholders. Important to us, 24,000 of these stockholders are among our customers here in central eastern Pennsylvania. Over 1,500 are our fellow employees.

"Yes, ours is a hometown business,

These promotional kits from 1944 were packed with posters, a booklet, news releases, newspaper advertisements, stickers, business cards and more. Not since the 1920s had PP&L been so keyed up about marketing.

manned and managed by local people with a real community of interest between us and the folks we serve. As a result, all of our business policies… employee relations, public relations, rate, commercial, financial…are made here, and by local people."

By 1947, Oakes was able to report that "an important trend developing in our security ownership is that more and more Pennsylvanians are becoming stockholder-partners in our business. More than 80 percent of our preferred and nearly 43 percent of our common stocks are now held by Pennsylvanians."

Oakes stressed to employees in 1947 and 1948 the importance of PP&L as an investment. Pointing out that the total plant account in 1947 had reached $234.5 million, Oakes noted that "somebody, and in our case a great many somebodies, put up the money which we used to buy these things…and they must be paid a wage for the use of their money.

"From this invested money came this company and its plants, lines and

FIRST-HAND INFORMATION BROUGHT DIRECT TO HOME-TOWN STOCKHOLDERS

Following 1948 annual meeting in April, President Chas. E. Oakes held a series of regional meetings throughout the Company's service area. Aided by Company officials, the year's operations and future plans were presented to many stockholders not able to attend annual meeting.

This page out of the 1948 annual report shows PP&L President Charles Oakes and an assembly of local shareholders. That year, Oakes and his management team held seven regional meetings to unveil plans for the Sunbury Steam Electric Station.

other tools. From putting these tools to work came our jobs. From jobs well done came growing business and earnings… and most important to all of us, good wages and greater opportunities. Meanwhile, from earnings came dividends and some money which was left in the business to pay a portion of the cost of construction of new facilities. From our continued ability to furnish efficient public service to our customers…and to pay good wages to employees…and to meet current business expenses and financial obligations…and to provide a reasonable wage for the use of investors' savings… we have built our reputation as a sound and stable business."

PP&L's "reputation as a sound and stable business" was on display during 1948. In a series of annual meetings for local shareholders, Oakes and the company's management team took to the road to inform local shareholders of the company's progress and to unveil plans for the company's proposed Sunbury Steam Electric Station. The seven regional meetings in the spring of 1948 were designed to acquaint shareholders with the company's business and to introduce the company to potential local investors.

At a meeting in the Lycoming Hotel in Williamsport, Oakes told 250 local investors that the company's revenue in 1947 was more than $58.75 million, up 9.7 percent from the previous year. At Sunbury, Oakes told a packed gathering at the Masonic Temple banquet hall that the

company's expansion program was designed to meet the electrical power needs of a region "destined to become one of the most highly industrialized areas of the United States." In Wilkes-Barre, 250 anthracite region shareholders crowded into the Admiral Stark Room of the Hotel Sterling to hear PP&L's president note that more than 60,000 shareholders owned the nearly three million shares of company stock outstanding.

Oakes' tour of the region in May 1948 was symbolic of the customer service and

---

Adding urgency to the necessity of selling stock to the investing public was the fact that the electric power load was growing rapidly in central and eastern Pennsylvania in the latter 1940s.

---

marketing tradition that PP&L and its predecessors had exhibited for much of the 20th century. As an investor-owned utility, PP&L had to adapt to new realities in the postwar world. Adding urgency to the necessity of selling stock to the investing public was the fact that the electric power load was growing rapidly in central and eastern Pennsylvania in the latter 1940s. For much of the next 15 years, the lion's share of equity sales would be invested back into an ambitious and aggressive construction program to keep up with the booming power demand.

A Westerner Who Came East to Head PP&L

Charles "Charlie" E. Oakes

Charles E. Oakes, Pennsylvania Power & Light Co.'s third president, was a westerner. Born before the turn of the century, he was raised in the mountains of northeastern Oregon. Among Oakes' earliest memories of growing up in Enterprise, Ore., was seeing Chief Joseph as an old man, the paramount chief of the Nez Perce tribe who had led the U.S. Army on a merry chase across the intermountain west in the 1880s. Oakes grew up in Enterprise, a small farming community, and was salutatorian of his three-member graduating class at the Enterprise High School.

Oakes went off to what was then the Oregon State Agricultural College—later Oregon State University in Corvallis—in 1911, graduating in 1915. Two years later he received his master's degree in mechanical engineering with a minor in electrical engineering from Cornell University, Ithaca, N.Y. He was to live and work in the East and Mid-South for the remainder of his long life.

Oakes had two offers of employment when he left Cornell with his master's degree. He had taken electrical engineering at Oregon State and Cornell, and Westinghouse, the giant electrical manufacturer, offered him a job in its Pittsburgh facilities. He chose another offer from the Bureau of Standards in Washington, D.C., because it paid $5 more per month. Since the U.S. had just entered World War I, the Bureau of Standards was instrumental in testing munitions and armaments for the rapidly deploying American army.

Following the war, Oakes transferred to the newly created Federal Power Commission in Washington, D.C. Oakes wooed and wed Anna Margaret A. Buckley of Meriden, Conn.; soon after their March 1923 wedding, the newlyweds pulled up stakes and moved to Allen-town, where Oakes had been hired as a Pennsylvania Power & Light Co. rate engineer. "He developed during his Washington years a healthy disrespect for the way government conducts business," remembers his daughter, LoisAnn Oakes, who still lives in Allentown.

Oakes, who always signed his name "Chas. E. Oakes," worked for PP&L for 16 years in the 1920s and 1930s, starting out in the Rate Department on Eighth Street. He was among the first employees to occupy an office in the new General Office Tower at Ninth and Hamilton, and worked his way up to district manager and later general manager in Allentown.

LoisAnn Oakes recalled that her father sold electricity by visiting Grange meetings in Lehigh County and the coal regions when PP&L focused its sales efforts on rural electric power development during the 1930s. "It was typical of him to wear a three-piece suit, white shirt and tie every day," she said.

By 1938, Oakes felt that he was stagnating in his job at PP&L, that his career path was blocked at the Allentown utility. He discussed this with his wife, Anna, and decided to borrow on his life insurance and go out to the West Coast to find work. He was particularly interested in Pacific Gas & Electric Co. in California.

Oakes told P.B. Sawyer, his mentor, of his plans, and Sawyer, PP&L's liaison with the Electric Bond and Share holding company, advised Oakes to wait a few months before doing anything so drastic. The industry was in a state of flux in 1938. The U.S. Supreme Court had just ruled favorably on the constitutionality of the Public Utilities Holding Company Act of 1935, setting into motion the inevitable breakup of holding companies like Electric Bond and Share Co.

Oakes Goes to Birmingham

Early in 1939, Electric Bond and Share Co. tapped Oakes to head Birmingham Electric Co., its electric utility subsidiary in northern Alabama. Birmingham Electric Co. would later become a part of Alabama Power Co. He was expected to spend two years in Alabama, and was charged with keeping Birmingham Electric Co. from becoming part of the Tennessee Valley Authority, the big municipal power and economic development organization created by President Franklin D. Roosevelt in 1936.

Due to the onset of World War II, Oakes spent six years in Birmingham, helping to supply Birmingham's steel industry with electric power and helping to integrate the city's utility into the Alabama Power Co. system. In 1945, Oakes was asked to return to Allentown as president of PP&L following the retirement of John Wise. Oakes was truly PP&L's first postwar president; the announcement of his appointment on May 9, 1945, was buried in the back pages of area newspapers that reported the end of the war in Europe the day before.

Like many of the nation's electric utilities, PP&L had struggled to meet demand during the war. The utility was limping along, wringing kilowatts from the steam generation facilities and the Wallenpaupack hydroelectric plant it had built during the period of expansion during the 1920s. But the onset of the Great Depression in the 1930s stifled demand for nearly a decade, and the difficulty of acquiring construction materials during the war kept PP&L from building new generation facilities.

Oakes had a deep-seated belief in the value of electric power and a keen understanding of financial matters. In an address to the 18th annual convention of the Edison Electric Institute in June 1950, Oakes accurately

Chas. E. Oakes graduated from the Oregon State Agricultural College in June 1915.

When John Wise retired in 1945, Chas. E. Oakes became PP&L's president.

predicted the impact that the equity markets would have on utility expansion during the 1950s. "Of particular interest is the trend which developed in the last half of 1949 toward a greater use of equity securities in financing planned construction of the electric companies," Oakes told delegates to the Atlantic City convention. "Of the total of $543 million in funds obtained, $293 million came from the issuance of preferred and common stocks, which, including the earnings retained and invested during the same period, results in more than 60 percent of the total financing done by equities."

Oakes' longtime interest in public relations—especially in the area of economics education—was a model for other utilities struggling to deal with the new realities of operating in the public arena as stand-alone entities, rather than as subsidiaries of holding companies. "Though we have been successful in solving the problem of production," he told colleagues in 1953, "we have not done as well with this one of beliefs. It is of primary importance in this area of ideas that the public be made more conscious of the nature of economic forces and the individual's importance in their creation."

Oakes presided over an ambitious building program in the postwar years that was perhaps unparalleled in PP&L's history. During his presidency, PP&L built the Sunbury Steam Electric Station on the Susquehanna River, started work on Martins Creek Steam Electric Station and took its first tentative steps in the field of atomic power. In 1955, Oakes informed what was then the Atomic Energy Commission that PP&L intended eventually to build a nuclear station financed entirely with private funds.

During Oakes' tenure at PP&L, the customer base increased from 439,000 to more than 700,000. The utility's plant grew from $20 million in 1946 to more than $50 million 11 years later. Generating capacity increased during the Oakes years from 448,000 kilowatts to 1.3 million kilowatts.

Oakes was a strong proponent of the investor-owned utility industry at a time when public power—in the form of federal hydroelectric projects in the west and rural electrification—was taking an increasing share of the electric power business. In 1951, Oakes appeared before the Senate Finance Committee in Washington on behalf of the Edison Electric Institute to argue that the corporation income tax be applied to public power entities.

It was on Oakes' watch that PP&L expanded in other directions besides the construction of generation facilities. In 1954, the company merged with the Pennsylvania Water & Power Co., bringing the giant Holtwood hydroelectric facility onto the PP&L grid. The next year, the Allentown company announced its merger with the Scranton Electric Co., which served much of the anthracite industry of northeastern Pennsylvania.

The 1950s and 1960s were years of immense change for Pennsylvania Power & Light Co.

(Top) **Working in PP&L's Rate Department, Chas. E. Oakes found time to be father and friend to his oldest daughter, JeanClaire.** *circa 1929*

LoisAnn, the youngest Oakes daughter, is an accomplished singer. Here, she cuts the ribbon to open Bethlehem's Pennsylvania Playhouse on Oct. 23, 1965.

Under Oakes' leadership, the company established a reputation for successful utility economic development unequalled in the industry. It was also during the 1950s that PP&L's focus on marketing residential and commercial electric resistance heating established the company as a leader in that field.

Oakes was unstinting in his service to his community. During his years as PP&L CEO, he served as state campaign chair of the American Cancer Society, as a member of the executive board of the Lehigh Council of the Boy Scouts of America, as president of the Allentown Hospital Association and as a member of the Governor's Council of Business and Industry, among other positions. He served his industry as president of the Edison Electric Institute in 1947. As chair of a State Department Agency for International Development study commission, he made recommendations for the development of the electric power industry in Iran.

Oakes was awarded honorary doctoral degrees by Muhlenberg College in 1950 and by the University of Scranton in 1962. The next year, he received a special citation at Lehigh University's Centennial Convocation.

Oakes relinquished the presidency of PP&L in 1963 but continued as the utility's chairman until his retirement in 1967. Charles E. Oakes died in Allentown on June 5, 1977, at the age of 84. He served as president and/or chairman of the board for 22 years, nearly one-third of the company's modern history.

The Postwar Expansion

When completed, the Sunbury Steam Electric Station on the shores of the Susquehanna River was the most modern, state-of-the-art generating station in Pennsylvania and the world's largest anthracite-burning plant.

In less than a lifetime, the Edison Electric Illuminating Co. of Sunbury grew from an inventor's dream in 1883 to PP&L's Sunbury plant in 1949.

In his forecast for the *Allentown Evening Chronicle* at year-end 1948, PP&L President Chas. E. Oakes noted that 116 new industries had moved into the company's service area during the year, making a total of 374 since V-J Day in August 1945.

"This means," Oakes pointed out, "more people, more new homes and commercial establishments and an improved market for local farm products." The new industries in the PP&L service territory and the expansion of industries already on the company's lines translated into 13,000 new electric customers during the year.

COMMERCIAL SALES DEPT.

FARM SALES DEPT.

INDUSTRIAL SALES DEPT.

RESIDENTIAL SALES DEPT.

The postwar era meant thousands of new electric customers. Marketing efforts enlisted the help of Reddy Kilowatt.

Oakes told the *Chronicle* that the demand for electricity since the early 1930s had annually exceeded that of the previous year, with only a slight drop in the record demand at the end of the war. "But by December 1946, an all-time high had been reached," Oakes added. "This was exceeded again and again in 1947. The year 1948 was no exception. On November 22, the maximum one-hour use exceeded last year by more than seven percent. This was 74 percent ahead of 1939, the last normal prewar year."

The trend had become apparent as early as 1946, the first full year following the end of the war. Anthracite production had maintained its wartime pace during the year, and the cement industry in the Lehigh Valley continued its march toward capacity production, fueled by the prospect of increased highway and bridge construction in the postwar era. The textile industry had increased its use of electric power during the year by 20 percent, the greatest industrial increase on the PP&L system. Only steel failed to operate at capacity in 1946, and that was primarily due to supply problems; the industry was plagued during the first year after the war by an inability to secure enough metallurgical coking coal, steel scrap and pig iron. The steel industry in the Lehigh Valley, however, predicted production at 90 percent of capacity in 1947 and 1948, once raw material supplies were straightened out.

After dipping slightly in late 1946, PP&L customers' hourly use reached an all-time high on Dec. 17, 1946. The 550,000 kilowatt-hours recorded the week before Christmas in 1946 didn't stand up long as an hourly record. The record for the highest peak load in the company's history was set again in 1947. The 1948 peak load of 654,089 kilowatt-hours reached in December 1948 was 7.3 percent greater than the 1947 record and more than 100,000 kilowatt-hours higher than the December 1946 peak. In each month of 1948, the maximum hourly customer use exceeded that of the corresponding month of the previous year.

By 1948, the peak load on the system was up more than two-and-a-half times in 15 years. "In spite of these extraordinary demands for electricity," the 1948 annual report noted, "we successfully maintained an adequate supply of power. Customers' demands were met by close attention of our personnel to plant operation and careful scheduling of maintenance. Never before has the coordinated use of interconnections with neighboring utilities been as important an aid in meeting customers' service requirements."

Sunbury

By 1948, it had been more than half a decade since PP&L had added generating capacity at Hauto and Harwood. To the load planners, that must have seemed like an eternity. The big baseload units in the anthracite region were getting older. In 1948, John S. Wise had been retired for three years; the plant he had built in Carbon County in 1907 had already logged more than 40 years of service.

Fortunately for the operating departments, PP&L was getting ready at year-end 1948 to place its first new baseload unit in production since the 1920s. As early as the end of the war in 1945, PP&L announced construction of a large power plant on a site on the Susquehanna River near Sunbury. The selection of Sunbury for the Sunbury Steam Electric Station resonated with PP&L tradition. It was at Sunbury that Thomas Edison had proved the feasibility of a three-wire incandescent system more than 60 years before.

The Sunbury Steam Electric Station was planned as a state-of-the-art facility that would have made Thomas Edison proud. "This plant will incorporate the most modern features to provide high efficiencies and low operating costs," the company announced to shareholders in the spring of 1946. "It will use pulverized coal as fuel. The plant will be strategically located with respect to the electric system development, interconnections with the systems of adjoining companies and to both the anthracite and the bituminous coal fields."

The site for the Sunbury Steam Electric Station had been acquired in 1924, more than 20 years before the plant was actually announced. The 259-acre site on the west bank of the Susquehanna, 3-1/2 miles below the confluence of its west and north branches at the city of Sunbury, was well suited to serve the PP&L system.

Sunbury was in the center of the western half of the company's service territory, equidistant between Williamsport and Harrisburg. The site at Shamokin Dam was easily served by mines in the nearby anthracite fields; Sunbury's boilers could be served by truckload deliveries from anthracite mines in the Shamokin and Mt. Carmel areas. The site was also situated on the Reading Railroad's lines, which allowed it to receive coal from the bituminous fields in western Pennsylvania. Finally, the Susquehanna River provided all the cooling water the new plant would need. In full operation, Sunbury station used 135 million gallons of water a day, a consumption equal to the daily requirement of metropolitan Washington, D.C.

The impetus for the new coal-fired power plant went back two decades. As

"In spite of...extraordinary demands for electricity," the 1948 annual report noted, "we successfully maintained an adequate supply of power...never before has the coordinated use of interconnections with neighboring utilities been as important an aid in meeting customers' service requirements."

The site for the Sunbury station was acquired in 1924. *(illustration by Brent Schaefer © 1995)*

early as the mid-1920s, P.B. Sawyer, the president of National Power & Light Co.; John S. Wise; and Norman G. Reinicker had put together the first studies that called for a new baseload power plant on the Susquehanna. The Great Depression and the breakup of the holding companies shelved the early plans, but PP&L acquired additional land at the site through 1936. The increase in wartime demand gave new urgency to the generation planning process.

In the early 1940s, Wise appointed a team to update the original studies and design a new coal-fired plant for the Sunbury site. George M. Keenan, vice president of Engineering and Construction, headed a team that included M.D. Engle from Mechanical Engineering; S.C. Townsend from Electrical Engineering; A.E.M. Shafer; and E.E. Chubbuck and C.E. Lewis from the Construction Department. The design and construction team worked throughout the war with Ebasco Services Inc., the outgrowth of the old

This generator for Unit One arrived at Sunbury in April 1948.

Phoenix Utilities Co., and in 1945, the surviving entity of what had been the Electric Bond and Share Co.

Generators from General Electric

In 1945, PP&L ordered two 75,000-kilowatt generators from General Electric Co. Rated at 13.8 kilovolts, the 3,600-rpm, hydrogen-cooled generators were hooked to 250-kilowatt, 250-volt flywheel type exciters driven by 350-horsepower induction motors. The following year, PP&L ordered two 75,000-kilowatt, 3,600-rpm, tandem compound, double flow, condensing type turbines from General Electric Co. At the same time, the company ordered two condensers from Westinghouse plus all the corollary equipment that goes into making up a modern steam electric generating station: cooling water systems, feed water systems, coal handling systems, dust and ash handling systems, pumps, compressors, valves and the like.

The costs for the new plant were a then eye-popping $1.8 million for the two generators and $4.7 million for the steam generating equipment from Westinghouse and Foster-Wheeler Corp. The steel used in construction was sufficient to produce 6,500 automobiles, and more than three million bricks—enough to complete 200 large homes—were used in construction. Steel towers, 136 feet high and crossing the Susquehanna on a 1,500-foot span, would carry Sunbury power into the PP&L transmission grid.

Groundbreaking took place in 1946. The new plant was a massive undertaking. Besides the fully enclosed turbine and generator building, construction crews had to build two

66,000-volt switchyards, a scale and gatehouse, an office and service building, a water treatment plant, a control house and an intake house. Providing for the coal that the plant would burn was a construction project in itself. Crews had to lay railroad tracks, clear coal storage and ash disposal areas and build a car dumper, yard service building, thaw shed, crusher house and stacker runway.

Enclosing much of the property was a 30-foot dike, insurance against the legendary floods along the Susquehanna. "Much of the area was originally brush-covered river bank, inundated whenever the Susquehanna reached flood levels," the company noted in a press release. "Giant earthmoving equipment literally turned the terrain upside down. A dike more than 1-1/2 miles long and 30 feet above low water level protects the area from the Susquehanna River at highest-on-record flood levels."

During peak construction in 1948 and 1949, more than 1,500 workers were employed on the project. Approximately 80 percent of the construction work force was from the local area; unlike the hydro-electric construction projects of the first three decades of the century, housing did not have to be supplied for the construction crews or the operating staff.

As the largest anthracite-burning utility in the world, PP&L intended to burn anthracite in the boilers at Sunbury. Most of that anthracite would be trucked into the plant, although the utility did build rail-handling equipment to burn a mix of bituminous coal when the moisture content of the anthracite was too high. All told, nine miles of railroad track were required to serve the plant. The Reading Railroad extended its tracks from Shamokin Dam, opposite Sunbury, to the northern boundary of the plant, while the Pennsylvania Railroad built a line from Selinsgrove to the southern boundary of the plant.

The coal-handling system at Sunbury, however, was different than that at Hauto or Harwood, where a bin and feeder system was in use. Sunbury would be the first of PP&L's plants to utilize a direct-firing system in the boilers. Each of the eight coal pulverizers at the plant used 40 tons of steel balls to grind 13-1/2 tons of coal an hour as fine as talcum powder.

The direct-fired system eliminated storage bunkers in use at the other plants. "Sunbury paved the way for use of a

Crews began construction on the Sunbury station in 1946.

The steel used in construction was sufficient to produce 6,500 automobiles, and more than three million bricks—enough to complete 200 large homes—were used in construction.

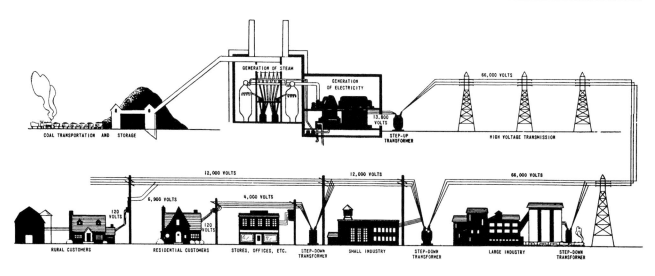

single process in power plants, where drying, pulverizing and feeding of coal to the boilers are combined into a single process that is cleaner and uses less machinery than before," PP&L noted in 1989 for the 40th anniversary of the Sunbury station.

Two miles of rubber conveyor belts shuttled the coal from the plant's 114-acre coal yard to the ball mills. At capacity, 800 tons of coal an hour could be moved to the plant on the conveyors. At full opera-

tion, the boilers consumed 4,500 tons of coal per day. Sunbury was the first direct-fired steam electric generating station in the U.S. and served as the model for the next generation of coal-fired plants in the utility industry.

'The Greater Progress of the Commonwealth of Pennsylvania'

Pennsylvania Power & Light Co. dedicated the first unit at Sunbury on June 21, 1950. Beneath a striped tent, more than 350 guests—including business and civic leaders and representatives of the utility industry—turned out for a

(Right) On Aug. 17, 1949, longtime employee Clinton W. Bell eased open the throttle of Sunbury's Unit One for the first time.

(Below) Inside Sunbury.

guided tour of the plant, followed by a luncheon hosted by PP&L.

Keynote speaker for the day was Harold Stassen, president of the University of Pennsylvania and a former Republican presidential candidate. Stassen, a former governor of Minnesota and a longtime friend of PP&L president Chas. E. Oakes, chose to address the economic freedoms that Sunbury represented and that Americans had recently fought World War II to maintain.

"I should like first of all to make this point this afternoon," Stassen noted, "that if America is to retain its economic freedom, those who have positions of economic leadership must push forward with courage and vision and efficiency to meet the needs of the people. And because they have done just that, I particularly commend Mr. Oakes and his associates of the Pennsylvania Power & Light Co. for recognizing that responsibility by their action in building this very modern plant to supply efficiently and economically, the future needs of the people of Pennsylvania."

Stassen lauded the completion of the Sunbury plant "for the greater progress of the Commonwealth of Pennsylvania," and he credited Oakes and the staff of PP&L for making him feel right at home. "I appreciate very much Mr. Oakes' gracious introduction," he said, "and, just to indicate the thoroughness with which he and his associates prepared for this occasion, I might say that I had hardly stepped into the plant this morning for our introductory walk through it and observation of it and lectures upon it when one of his engineer employees stepped up and said to me, 'I'm from Minnesota.' They really wanted me to feel at home, but I can hasten to assure him that I have become so acclimated to this great keystone state of Pennsylvania that I can really feel at home with a Pennsylvania audience, even though no Minnesotans are present."

As part of his remarks, Oakes dedicated a small wooden building immediately adjacent to the turbine and generator building to signify the contribution

(Top) Sunbury Steam Electric Station looking southeast from the coal yard. *circa 1953*

The coal-yard staff at Sunbury gathered in front of the plant's newest diesel yard locomotive for a picture to commemorate the plant's 40th anniversary in 1989.

made by Thomas Edison to the utility industry at nearby Sunbury two-thirds of a century before. "Within but a short distance of here, there was constructed in 1883 a small electric plant with the first 'three-wire' system of supply. On July 4, 1883, Thomas Alva Edison closed the switch, illuminating by electricity the interior of what is now the Edison Hotel in the nearby city of Sunbury, the first commercial building in the world to be lighted in this manner."

Oakes promised that PP&L would continue meeting the strong demand for electric power in central and eastern Pennsylvania. "It has been repeatedly said that the country faces a power shortage," Oakes said. "In the entire history of Pennsylvania Power & Light Co., despite the changing economic conditions through years of peace or war, electricity was never too little nor too late for our customers. There never has been, nor is there now a power shortage. And this growing Sunbury

Four days after the [Sunbury] gala dedication, elements of the Inmun Gun—the North Korean People's Army—streamed across the 38th Parallel into South Korea.

intention that there will not be a power shortage here. Already we are well along the way on an important addition to this plant."

PP&L's dedication of the Sunbury plant was more timely than both Oakes or Stassen knew. Four days after the gala dedication, elements of the Inmun Gun— the North Korean People's Army— streamed across the 38th Parallel into South Korea. Before the summer was out, the United States would be leading a coalition of United Nation's troops to stop communist aggression in Asia. The three-year war on the Korean Peninsula would put new demands on the industrial base of central and eastern Pennsylvania.

PP&L turned steam into the first of the two big 75,000-kilowatt turbines at Sunbury in August 1949. In November, steam was turned into the second unit. Both units went commercial late in the year, and in the nick of time. By the dedication of the new plant the next summer, electric power demand in PP&L's service territory had accelerated past the record levels it had reached in the late 1940s. In July 1950, kilowatt-hour sales jumped 13.4 percent over what they had been in July 1949. The increase was 18.2 percent in August, and nearly 25 percent in September, reflecting defense industry needs in central and eastern Pennsylvania arising from the Korean War.

The Storm of the Century

The 1948 storm showed PP&L that it had the tools to cope with the worst that Mother Nature could throw at it.

New Year's morning dawned cold, rainy and wet across much of central and eastern Pennsylvania in 1948. New Year's revelers were still in bed when the rain began to change to sleet and then to freezing rain in the Lehigh Valley.

There is no weather phenomenon short of a hurricane or flood that is more destructive of the electric utility infrastructure than ice and freezing rain. Ice coats tree limbs and power lines. When the load gets too great, tree limbs buckle and fall across distribution lines. Iced-up transmission and distribution lines can snap like worn rubber bands.

By early afternoon, most of the Lehigh and Panther valleys were encased in a sheath of ice. Lines were down across much of the eastern half of PP&L's service territory. The hardest hit areas were in the Allentown, Bethlehem, Pottsville, Hazleton and Schuylkill divisions. By early afternoon, most of Allentown, Bethlehem and Hazleton were without power entirely; communities in the Panther Valley were cut off by the storm, and hospital emergency rooms performed surgery by flashlight.

Weather conditions were optimal for the storm, which had developed the last week of December in the Midwest and had followed an irregular course across northern Illinois, Indiana and Ohio into Pennsylvania. The surface temperature in the Lehigh and Panther valleys was just below freezing and the air aloft was just above freezing, which kept the precipitation from turning into either rain or snow.

Convoys of Trucks

Dispatchers at PP&L's operating headquarters in Allentown had been watching the storm since early New Year's morning. Throughout the day, convoys of line trucks began wending their way across the hills and valleys of central Pennsylvania, headed for the stricken Lehigh and Panther valleys. Before service was fully restored later that week, more than 800 company personnel from Harrisburg, Williamsport, Susquehanna, Lancaster, Wilkes-Barre, Schuylkill and Pottsville divisions would join their compatriots in the Allentown, Bethlehem and Hazleton divisions.

In the system control room atop the General Office Tower in Allentown, dispatchers located line trouble by means of private telephone and FM radio. Crews worked 'round-the-clock in the trouble room of the Allentown Service Depot to marshall forces for the fight to restore service. Trouble room crews received damage reports from the line crews in the field and from customers in the storm area. After cataloging the reports for the most efficient handling, the trouble room crews dispatched line crews to the damaged areas.

Employees from the General Office Tower and the Allentown and Bethlehem divisions who normally wouldn't be called in on outage duty, braved the slick—in some cases impassable—streets to come in and help. There was plenty of work to do. Commercial people arranged for sleeping quarters and food supplies for the

out-of-town line crews. Marketing personnel manned the telephone bank in the General
Office Tower, taking complaint
calls and informing customers of
restoration progress.

Safety and meter department employees
guided out-of-town crews to trouble spots. Engineering
department staffers provided on-the-spot design assistance in the field. Residential, inventory and appraisal
department employees roamed the icy streets of Allentown and Bethlehem, doing the door-to-door legwork
of checking service facilities. Operating headquarters
staff personnel worked 'round-the-clock to find manpower for the hardest-hit areas and to coordinate the
flow of supplies and material with the stores department.

To fight the ice conditions in 1948, PP&L crews had
one tool that was unavailable before the war—a fleet of
mobile radio-telephone trucks. A number of technologies
that were developed for U.S. combat troops in World
War II were adapted by the nation's utilities in the postwar era. Hard hats—an outgrowth of the G.I. helmet—
came into wide use among line crews following the war.
Radio trucks, a staple of U.S. armored divisions in
Europe, soon became standard operating equipment for
electric utilities.

PP&L began installing FM mobile radio-telephone
equipment in its line trucks right after the war. The 1948
ice storm proved once and for all the success of the concept. Telephone lines were down throughout the region
from early New Year's morning; some smaller communities in the Panther Valley didn't have their telephone
service restored for several weeks.

PP&L pressed 19 mobile radio-telephone trucks into
service during the storm. With an estimated
90,000 customers out-of-service at the height of
the storm—most of them in rural and suburban
areas outside Allentown, Bethlehem and
Hazleton—the radio-telephone trucks proved
invaluable.

"Not only did these radio-telephone trucks
save endless hours in searching out available

means of communication, but eliminated the waste of attempts by line
crews in locating trouble under the
ever-changing storm conditions," PP&L
reported later that spring. "Constant contact with the trouble room also efficiently
coordinated the routing of proper supplies
and personnel to each of the individual jobs."

One veteran lineman was amazed at how much more
efficient the crews were with the radio-telephone trucks.
"I don't know how we'd have finished all we had to do
without this amazing shortcut," the lineman observed
after the storm. "Instead of wasting needed hours in
hunting trouble, we could put all of our time directly to
the big important job of getting service back to our
customers."

The New Year's Day ice and sleet storm in the Lehigh
and Panther valleys was one of the worst winter storms
PP&L had experienced since its 1920 incorporation.
Before service was restored, the cost of the New Year's
Day storm had soared to more than $300,000, an
immense sum when wages and operating expenses for
the year totaled less than $43 million.

Still, the 1948 storm showed PP&L that it had the tools
to cope with the worst that Mother Nature could throw
at it. "More than 800 company employees from all
departments and from all parts of the system worked
practically around-the-clock in the five-day battle with
the storm," company president Chas. E. Oakes wrote in
the *1948 Report to Employees.* "All of us were represented.
Every department in the company had a share and made
a real contribution toward getting service restored with
the greatest possible speed.

"Once again, our people won for themselves a fine
reputation for alert all-out devotion to duty. To
their credit, there was not a serious accident
among our crews during the entire period.
Nowhere in the nation has there been a finer
record of top-flight performance. The efforts
made in restoring service added immeasurably
to the ever-growing public appreciation of our
company."

28

Merger with Scranton Electric Co.

Pennsylvania Power & Light Co. entered the 1950s with new and growing confidence. Although it had been on its own for less than five years, the Allentown-based utility was participating in the remarkable postwar resurgence of central and eastern Pennsylvania.

The 150,000-kilowatt Sunbury plant was equivalent to nearly one-third of the generating capacity of the entire PP&L system. But it was apparent even before the first two units at Sunbury went on-line in 1949 that more generating capacity must be added. Construction had begun in the fall of 1949 on a 100,000-kilowatt addition to Sunbury, and before 1950 was over, PP&L announced the addition of a fourth unit at Sunbury—a 150,000-kilowatt behemoth that brought the total generating capacity of the Shamokin Dam facility to 425,000 kilowatts.

PP&L purchased the Scranton Electric Co. in 1953 after 28 years as a joint venture partner in the Stanton Steam Electric Station.

The construction of six new transmission lines, totaling 133 miles, brought the total of transmission lines built and energized since 1945 to 224 miles—the largest transmission construction project since PP&L had completed its portion of the PNJ 220,000-volt transmission ring in the late 1920s.

The increase in kilowatt-hour sales at the dawn of the 1950s was spread over all classes of the company's customers. By late 1950, PP&L was supplying electric power to 4,200 industrial customers, who provided about 35 percent of the company's electric revenues. Industrial sales totaled $24.4 million in 1950, of which about 25 percent was derived from sales to anthracite mining customers. Close to another 25 percent came from iron, steel and metal products customers, while cement and quarry customers accounted for

$2.6 million a year in sales. Textile and apparel customers accounted for $3.45 million a year in sales.

The company's sales to the anthracite industry illustrated two contrasting phenomena. PP&L's kilowatt-hour sales to the industry had shot up from the 105 million kwh level at the beginning of the war to nearly 160 million kwh in 1948 as the industry electrified its operations. But production in Pennsylvania dropped off precipitously at the end of the war; production went from 63.7 million tons in 1944 to 42.7 million tons in 1949. The health of the anthracite industry would become a major concern of PP&L before the end of the 1950s.

The postwar boom in kilowatt-hour sales wasn't just due to industrial expansion. After 15 years of depression and war, home appliance sales literally skyrocketed in the five years following the end of the war. In 1946, before wartime restrictions had been fully lifted, 19,676 refrigerators had been sold in the company's service territory. Five years later, 62,355 refrigerators had been sold to PP&L customers. The story was much the same for ranges, water heaters, home freezers and electric washing machines and promised future growth for PP&L's residential electric revenues.

An appliance that didn't even exist at the end of the war proved to be one of the hottest sellers in central and eastern Pennsylvania in the five years following

---

The onset of the Korean War in 1950 resulted in increased sales, both to industrial customers and to the U.S. military establishment.

The March 1953 company publication, *Hydro Hi-Lines*, **saluted employees who had entered the Armed Services.**

| Willard J. Neff | Fred T. Buswood | Fred E. Stevenson | Diller M. Gaul | Roy A. Stauffer |

1946. Gen. David Sarnoff had introduced television at the New York World's Fair of 1939, but the new appliance hadn't gone into commercial production until 1946. That first year, only 236 sets were sold in the PP&L service territory. By 1950, 35,415 sets had been sold to PP&L customers.

PP&L was also reaping benefits from the television boom on the industrial side of the ledger. RCA's major tube factory was located in Lancaster. During the war, the Lancaster facility was built with U.S. Navy financing and produced 2,000 different types of radio tubes, totaling more than 20 million tubes by 1945. During the postwar era, the big plant was converted to the manufacture of television tubes. By the mid-1950s, the RCA plant in the Pennsylvania Dutch country was the largest television picture-tube manufacturer in the world.

The onset of the Korean War in 1950 resulted in increased sales, both to industrial customers and to the U.S. military establishment. The U.S. Army cranked up the Susquehanna Sub-Depot of the Letterkenny Ordnance Department to make war weapons for Army ground forces once again. Known during World War II as the Pennsylvania Ordnance Works, the Susquehanna Sub-Depot of the Letterkenny Ordnance Depot was on wartime footing through 1953. PP&L also sold electric power to the U.S. Army Reserve Training Center in Loyalsock Township of Lycoming County, the U.S.

JANUARY 2, 1949

Chinese Premier Urges Redoubled Peace Efforts

Nanking, (AP)—Premier Sun Fo in a radio address yesterday urged the Chinese people to "give their organized support to the peace effort, so the Communists will realize what the people desire and will cease military action in the interests of their countrymen."

At the same time, Sun told soldiers at the front, they must not be distracted by the government's announcement that it desires peace, but must "redouble their efforts in order to win peace."

Aims at Support

Sun's statement, transmitted over the central broadcasting facilities, was seen in this Red-threatened Chinese capital as an effort to gain public support for the government's current "peace offensive."

"I shall devote my highest effort to bringing about peace for the welfare of the people," Sun declared, "but peace cannot eas-

Courtesy of the **Morning Call**

Army Reserve Training Center in Pottsville, and the Marietta Transportation Corps Depot. In 1955, shortly after the end of the war in Korea, Marietta was purchasing $40,000 worth of electricity from PP&L per year.

The Greatest Business on Earth

After being out of merchandising for nearly 20 years, PP&L returned to the business with a vengeance in the early 1950s. The completion of the first two units at Sunbury, and the announcement that even bigger units were on the drawing board, led to a resurgence of marketing activity. In 1950, the company unveiled its three-phase sales program. As the company said in its 1950 marketing brochure, "1950 will serve as the first of the series of years of creative selling to develop a greater pile of needs, solved by further application of electricity in eliminating obsolete production, business and living standards."

In 1951, the company followed up its 1950 sales promotion efforts with "Operation Grip." That stood for the Grass Roots Impact Plan, and its purpose was to sell residential home appliances. PP&L sales personnel were assigned quotas, including 20,000 electric ranges, 9,000 home freezers, 1,800 electric dishwashers and

Eugene W. Gainer   Charles Bachman Jr.

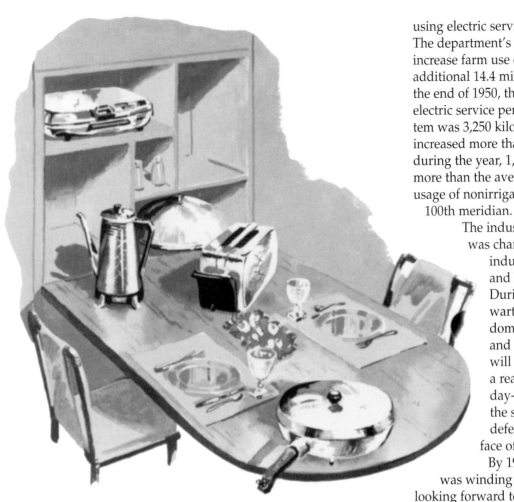

I'll Cut Laundry Time Down to Minutes a Week!

1,500 electric dryers. Quotas were actually below those of 1950, primarily because the Korean War had resulted in government regulations on credit purchases.

New to the quota list were electric dishwashers. Two new lines of electric dishwashers had been introduced late in 1950. "The national advertising and promotion to be placed on these new lines by their respective manufacturers and distributors and a substantial increase in the number of dishwasher sales outlets will be effective in increasing sales of this appliance," the marketing department informed sales personnel.

Farm sales were another emphasis of the 1951 program. "Although approximately 35,800 farms are served by our company," the marketing department noted, "it does not mean they are using electric service to its fullest extent." The department's 1951 objective was to increase farm use of electric service an additional 14.4 million kilowatt-hours. At the end of 1950, the average annual use of electric service per farm on the PP&L system was 3,250 kilowatt-hours. That increased more than 400 kilowatt-hours during the year, 1,000 kilowatt-hours more than the average kilowatt-hour usage of nonirrigated farms east of the 100th meridian.

The industrial sales department was charged with helping industry "to produce guns and butter at their best. During the period when wartime conditions predominate, manufacturing and processing industries will be hard put to maintain a reasonable hold on their day-to-day business and at the same time help with the defense effort—all in the face of a controlled economy."

By 1953, the war in Korea was winding down, and PP&L was looking forward to increased consumer spending. The 1953 sales program was headlined "the greatest business on earth," and carried a circus theme. Sales promotional tools for the year included an increased emphasis on appliance demonstrations, the "light-conditioned home" program, lectures and movie showings on electrical living applications, the Edison Electric Institute (EEI) sales training course, more than 550 classroom demonstrations of electrical appliances for home economics departments in schools, special electric appliance purchase opportunities for PP&L employees and PP&L's all-electric kitchen and laundry planning service.

At the same time, PP&L began to investigate selling the General Office Tower and building a new headquarters in suburban Allentown. In late 1952, the advertising and publicity department quietly circulated a study which suggested disposing of the General Office Tower and moving outside the city. The problem was traffic.

"The present location is the center of one of the worst traffic problems in the central city area," the report concluded, "a situation amplified by inclement weather when the building is unapproachable by as much as 20 minutes at a time. Parking facilities for employees (and) customers are inefficient. Visitors from other parts of the territory waste time gaining entry to the building."

The study had other complaints with the landmark at Ninth and Hamilton streets. "Certainly conditions have changed tremendously since our present General Office building was constructed in the late twenties," the study continued. "In a matter of five years or even less, the company found that the lighting intensities of this almost new building were of an earlier day. Ten years after the building was constructed, we found it antiquated from an air conditioning viewpoint…. The skyscraper building has become outdated and inefficient for our type of operation."

The study noted that numerous companies, including General Foods, General Electric Co., Union Carbide, Time Inc. and American Telephone & Telegraph Co. had moved out of crowded Manhattan into suburban Long Island, New Jersey or Connecticut. Metropolitan Edison Co. had recently moved into a suburban location outside Reading, and Central Hudson Gas & Electric Corp. was in the process of doing the same thing in Poughkeepsie.

A central assumption of the study was that the General Office Tower could find a buyer in the Allentown market. The authors noted that real estate and construction consultants had advised that "our present office building could be sold for sufficient moneys to pay for the lands and construction of a suburban office building."

The study suggested two locations for a brand-new suburban headquarters complex: northwest of the city of Allentown and adjacent to the new high-speed bypass of Route 22 leading from Easton to Harrisburg. In either case, the new building would "be a maximum of three

stories high, fully equipped with modern lighting and air conditioning, and include in its facilities in addition to those incorporated in the present office building a 1,400-seat and a 200-seat auditorium, employee cafeterias, a 1,000-car parking lot, outside recreation facilities, and available adjacent space for various servicing facilities," including banks, barber shops, hairdressers, gas stations and the like.

In the end, the 1952 suggestion to move to suburban Allentown was deferred until a more serious proposal was undertaken in the 1960s. Part of the

Despite Gen. David Sarnoff's introduction of the television at the 1939 New York World's Fair, it took nearly 10 years before the new appliance made its way into the homes of PP&L customers.

After being out of merchandising for nearly 20 years, PP&L returned to the business with a vengeance in the early 1950s.

reason for the inaction was purely pragmatic. By the time the report was widely circulated to PP&L's executive management team following the first of the year in 1953, the Allentown-based utility was looking seriously at its first major acquisition since 1930.

North to Scranton

PP&L's May 1953 offer to purchase the Scranton Electric Co. was a delayed result of the Public Utilities Holding Company Act. American Gas & Electric Co., one of the major holding companies and the parent of Scranton Electric Co., reorganized in the 1930s as the American Electric Power Co. AEP was one of a handful of

exempt holding companies under the terms of the 1935 Public Utilities Holding Company Act. What that meant was that the bulk of AEP's system, which served customers in West Virginia, Ohio, Michigan and Kentucky, was interconnected. But to comply with the Act, AEP had to divest itself of operating companies that were not connected to the AEP backbone system. Since Scranton Electric Co. was well east and north of the main AEP system, it had to be sold to bring AEP into compliance with the 1935 Act.

PP&L's offer of May 22, 1953, to acquire Scranton Electric Co. in an exchange of stock made eminent sense. The Allentown electric utility's transmission lines were already interconnected in a number of places, and the two utilities served the same kind of customer mix. Since 1925, the two utilities had been joint venture partners in the Stanton Steam Electric Station.

Scranton Electric Co. served the city of Scranton and the surrounding anthracite region of northeastern Pennsylvania. The company had transmission ties with PP&L in the Pittston and Peckville areas, and its customer mix in the postwar era looked much like that of PP&L. In 1952, residential service accounted for 37 percent of the company's sales, while industrial service accounted for 39 percent of sales and commercial service accounted for 16 percent of sales.

Like PP&L, the company's business had been increasing steadily since the war. Revenues had totaled nearly $11 million in 1952, almost double the $6.3 million reported in 1943. Scranton Electric Co. had acquired the neighboring Abington Electric Co. in 1950, and its record of reducing rates to customers made it doubly attractive to Pennsylvania Power & Light Co. Between 1943 and 1952, the company's average kilowatt-hour rates declined almost one-half cent, from 3.9 cents to 3.5 cents. Net income for 1952 was $1.7 million, equivalent to a 15 percent rate of return.

"A summary of our operations and business performance indicated that the past year was one of accomplishment, progress and encouraging gains in sales volume and customers," Clarence Nagle, president, wrote shareholders on Feb. 5, 1953, "one during which the company met fully its many and exacting public responsibilities."

The Pennsylvania Power & Light Co. offer involved the exchange of one share of the PP&L common stock for two shares of the common stock of Scranton Electric Co. Preferred shareholders of Scranton Electric Co.'s 4.4 percent series were offered a one-for-one exchange for each share of PP&L's 4.4 percent series preferred. Shareholders owning Scranton Electric Co.'s 3.35 percent preferred were offered three-quarters of a share of PP&L's 4.5 percent preferred for each

share, or could exchange one share of the 3.35 percent series preferred for two shares of PP&L common stock.

By July 15, 1953, 91 percent of the common stock of Scranton Electric Co., along with 91 percent of the preferred stock of the Scranton utility, had been deposited for exchange under the terms of the May 22 offer. Exchange agents for the offer included the Scranton Lackawanna Trust Co. and Third National Bank and Trust Co., Scranton; Chemical Bank & Trust Co. and Irving Trust Co., New York; and Girard Trust Corn Exchange Bank and The Pennsylvania Company for Banking and Trust, Philadelphia.

"As previously announced," PP&L President Chas. E. Oakes wrote Scranton Electric Co. shareholders, "it is planned that toward the end of this year action will be taken to merge the Scranton Electric Co. into Pennsylvania Power & Light Co., subject, of course, to necessary corporate and regulatory approvals."

As usual, corporate and regulatory approvals took longer than first estimated, and it was 1956 before Scranton Electric Co. was fully integrated into the PP&L system. By that time, PP&L had already made another ambitious acquisition, beefing up its postwar generating capacity with the purchase of the Pennsylvania Water & Power Co. and its hydroelectric facilities on the Susquehanna River.

Reddy Kilowatt wasn't the only one selling PP&L's services. In 1951 the push in marketing included assigned quotas for PP&L sales personnel of 20,000 electric ranges, 9,000 freezers, 1,800 dishwashers and 1,500 dryers.

The Thermos Bottle Locomotives

One piece of power plant equipment that was instantly recognizable to several generations of steam station operators and staff was the "thermos bottle on wheels." From the early 1940s through the 1970s, the fireless steam locomotives used to shuttle coal cars around the power plants were a fixture at most of PP&L's steam stations, but most prominent at Hauto and Sunbury Steam Electric stations.

Called "thermos bottle locomotives" by power plant staff, the switch engines did resemble giant thermos bottles. The thermos bottle locomotives ran on stored heat. When being readied for service, approximately three-quarters of the boiler was filled with hot water. Steam was then admitted under pressure—which could go as high as 350 pounds per square inch (psi)—and some of the captured heat was transferred to the water, raising the water temperature above 212 degrees Fahrenheit. Since the steam pressure in the boiler was much greater than the atmospheric pressure, the superheated water didn't boil.

When the throttle was opened to move the engine, some of the steam left the boiler, passed through the cylinders and was vented out the stack. The steam remaining in the boiler expanded, thereby decreasing the pressure. As the pressure decreased, the superheated water began to boil, and some of it turned to steam, which then replenished the supply. The process continued over and over until the water temperature and steam pressure became too low. Once the boiler pressure dropped to around 50 psi, the engine had to be recharged. Generally, each charge of steam was good for about four hours worth of operation, depending upon the demands on the engine.

First manufactured at the turn of the century, the fireless steam locomotives were made by several companies. The Heisler Locomotive Works of Erie, Pa., made Locomotives No. 4093 and 4094, in use at Hauto plant from the early 1940s to the closing of the plant in 1969. No. 4094, which was also known to Hauto crews as "Engine D," was a 95-ton, 0-8-0 fireless steam locomotive with four drive wheels on each side. At the time of its retirement in 1969, Engine D was the largest of 45 fireless cookers in operation in the United States. Engine F was a smaller six-wheel counterpart to Engine D.

The fireless cookers in operation at Sunbury Steam Electric Station were manufactured by the Porter Locomotive Works of Pittsburgh. At one time in the late 1960s, PP&L had six fireless cookers in operation, more than any other company in the country. Sunbury operated three of the Porter locomotives, while the coal plant at Holtwood operated one of the Porters, and Hauto operated the two Heislers.

The fireless locomotives were used to shuttle hopper cars of anthracite coal within the plant yards. As PP&L's coal-fired stations got bigger and more efficient in the 1960s, the thermos bottle locomotives were gradually replaced by diesel-electric locomotives for switching work at the plants.

Following the shutdown at Hauto in 1969, PP&L donated Engine D to the Pennsylvania Historical and Museum Commission for use at the Railroad Museum of Pennsylvania in Strasburg. In 1973, PP&L donated Hauto's Engine F to the Carbon County Tourist Promotion Agency.

29

PW&P
Comes Aboard

John T. Kauffman, second from left, poses here with Purdue University classmates. As a recent graduate, Kauffman began his career at Pennsylvania Water & Power Co. in 1950.

John T. Kauffman. *circa 1990*

John T. Kauffman went to work for the Pennsylvania Water & Power Co. in the summer of 1950. PP&L's recently retired CEO was then a mechanical engineering graduate of Purdue University. A U.S. Navy veteran of the Okinawa campaign, Kauffman had spent a couple of years in the Merchant Marine following the war and then had completed his engineering degree at Purdue. A New Jersey native, he wanted to move back east after school. Pennsylvania was particularly attractive, because his parents were from the Pottstown and Reading area.

These early Holtwood Village homes were part of the "town" Pennsylvania Water & Power Co. built for the people running Holtwood hydroelectric station. Built in 1924 along the hillside, these homes were known as the "old village" after a "new village" of brick homes was built at the top of the hill in 1950.

After writing to dozens of utilities in the Mid-Atlantic states, Kauffman received an offer from the Pennsylvania Water & Power Co. He and his Indiana-born wife packed up the car with all their worldly belongings and headed cross-country to southeastern Pennsylvania. "Took all our belongings," he said, "and put them in our little old car."

After finding rental lodgings in Lancaster, Kauffman started work with PW&P as a junior test engineer in July 1950. Pennsylvania Water & Power Co. was then in its 40th year of operation, and Kauffman found the work both interesting and exciting. "I was intrigued," he said, "because Penn Water at that time was dredging coal out of the river and burning it in its old boilers. And the hydro, you know, was real intriguing. It kind of looked like a real neat combination of coal recovery and hydro and steam generation."

Penn Water still ran both Holtwood and Safe Harbor, and the company's offices were in Lancaster in the Fulton National Bank Building, immediately across the street from the Greist Building, PP&L's headquarters in Lancaster following the 1955 merger with PW&P. Penn Water's engineering and administrative offices were located in Baltimore's Lexington Building, the headquarters of Baltimore Gas & Electric Co.

Kauffman recalled his first day of work

"Most of the people in the plant lived in the village. Or they lived in the Safe Harbor village. Or they had been back and forth between the two, because it was a single entity. In fact, one time in my career, before I went into the steam plant, we were getting paid by both Safe Harbor and Holtwood. You'd get two pay envelopes. It would be half in here and half in there."—John T. Kauffman

Holtwood.
(illustration by Brent Schaefer © 1995)

43 years previously as though it had been the day before. "We all hopped in the car and went up to Safe Harbor," he said. "And they had a 21-foot Steel-Craft bay cruiser with a fathometer in it, a recording fathometer. It was a beautiful summer morning, and I can remember sitting in the back of this boat, charging up the Susquehanna River thinking, 'You know this working's pretty good.'"

Penn Water at the time was planning the construction of what would be Unit 17 at Holtwood. Critical to that process was determining whether or not enough coal was being washed down the river to feed the mammoth anthracite-fired boilers that were planned for Unit 17. "What we did was we went up the river, and the river was laid out in a grid system. Then we used to run the grids with a fathometer to determine how much coal came in. We did a lot of work with that. We took samples out of the bottom, analyzed the samples and we used to run tests to determine suspended samples in the silt in the flow."

Kauffman worked analyzing river samples for about six months. "Of course, about that time they were going to build Holtwood 17," he recalled. "So I got transferred to the steam plant department, and there I was sort of a results engineer. Because of the impending construction, I really did a lot of work with the development of training modules. I ended up training all the operators for the plant and so forth."

Shortly after starting work at Penn Water, Kauffman and his wife moved from Lancaster to Quarryville. But most of the people he worked with every day lived in the village. "The village was bustling," he said. "Most of the people in the plant lived in the village. Or they lived in the Safe Harbor village. Or they had been back and forth between the two, because it was a single entity. In fact, one time in my career, before I went into the steam plant, we were getting paid by both Safe Harbor and Holtwood. You'd get two pay envelopes. It would be half in here and half in there."

Penn Water in the early 1950s operated pretty much as it had for the preceding 40 years. The utility was primarily a wholesale generator of electric power, selling to other utility and industrial customers. Penn Water was a one-third partner in Safe Harbor; Baltimore Gas & Electric Co. controlled the other two-thirds ownership. Major customers included Baltimore Gas & Electric Co., PP&L, Philadelphia Electric Co. and the Pennsylvania Railroad. Baltimore Gas & Electric Co. resold some of its power from Safe Harbor on a long-term contract to Potomac Electric Power Co. in Washington, D.C.

By the early 1950s, John Abbett Walls and the talented group of engineers—including Frederick A. Allner, Axel Bang and Hugo Lowy—he had brought with him in 1910 to build and run the Holtwood plant had all retired or were nearing retirement age. Walls was still working out of the Baltimore office, and although pulling back from day-to-day control of Penn Water, he still exerted an enormous amount of influence on the company. It was through Walls' efforts in January 1951 that the company began publishing *Hydro Hi-Lines,* a monthly newspaper for employees. In an editorial in the first issue, Walls called up memories of the day in October 1910 when the first power was generated at Holtwood, admitting that "not always do affairs within the two companies flow with the speed of electricity; it has taken us that long to get around to this event, the first issue of the company's magazine."

Perhaps the most flamboyant character of the company's latest years was D.I. Smith, superintendent

In 1951, John Abbett Walls *(above)* of Pennsylvania Water & Power Co. was instrumental in the development of the monthly employee newspaper, *Hydro Hi-Lines.*

Robert R. Fortune *(circa 1976)* and Austin Gavin represented PP&L on the joint venture board established to oversee the Susquehanna River hydroelectric plant during negotiations between PP&L, PW&P and Baltimore Gas & Electric Co.

W. Roger Small Jr. beloved superintendent of the Holtwood plant.

of the steam plant in 1950. "David Isaac Smith," recalled John Kauffman. "Everybody called him D.I. He was a ripper of a manager, you know. We're going to do it, we're going to do it now, and don't give a hoot about anything. Go get it done. But he was a great guy, and he ended up being a lot of the spark plug in building Holtwood 17."

'My wife thought it was the end of the world'

Smith was superintendent of the steam plant in 1955 when one of the most significant events in Penn Water history occurred. Pennsylvania Power & Light Co. announced it was purchasing Pennsylvania Water & Power Co. and merging it into the parent organization.

It was the second major acquisition by the Allentown utility in little more than a year.

The news hit employees at Holtwood and Safe Harbor like a ton of bricks. "My wife thought it was the end of the world," Kauffman recalled, "because we had just bought a house and we just bought all new carpets for the house. The next day, they said the company was sold, and she read it in the *Lancaster New Era*. She says, 'Oh, my gosh, after we spent all that money, now where are we going?'" Kauffman's memory of the event is that "it was not common knowledge. That was done pretty close to the vest."

The negotiations for PP&L's acquisition of Penn Water carried on for more than a year. They were conducted at the highest levels of PP&L, PW&P and Baltimore Gas & Electric Co. Chas. E. Oakes handled most of the negotiations for PP&L, and he usually dealt with John Abbett Walls of Penn Water and Charles P. Crane, the president of Baltimore Gas & Electric Co.

Oakes and his directors had agonized over the decision to acquire Penn Water. The reason was simple. Pennsylvania Water & Power Co. and Baltimore Gas & Electric Co. fought like cats and dogs. A long-running rate dispute had consumed the two companies during the late 1940s and early 1950s.

"It was terrible," said Austin Gavin, then an attorney in PP&L's legal department. "There was litigation, and they fought about everything. And they got a great deal of publicity. It was written up as one of the examples of corporate feuds. I think it was known throughout the electric utility industry. It was widespread."

Gavin was too junior an employee in the legal department at the time to be privy to the negotiations. But even a junior attorney in the legal department was savvy enough to figure out that there was more than a little concern on the part of the directors and management that a PP&L tender offer for Penn Water might well embroil the company in the fight with Baltimore Gas & Electric Co.

"And finally, PP&L decided, after a considerable split of opinion as to whether or not we were going to walk into and take over that fight," Gavin said. "It turned out that we got along fine with Baltimore, and there was no problem at all."

Roger Small, a Baltimore native who took a temporary job at Safe Harbor following his 1934 graduation from Johns Hopkins with a bachelor's degree in electrical engineering—and retired 45 years later—remembered that at least three companies were evaluating Penn Water in the fall of 1954: PP&L, Philadelphia Electric Co. and Metropolitan Edison Co. Small added that it was no secret to

At least three companies were evaluating Penn Water in the fall of 1954: PP&L, Philadelphia Electric Co. and Metropolitan Edison Co.

mid-level management at the time that Penn Water itself wanted to sell.

"They initiated the move," Small said of Penn Water, "because they figured that with the steam plant in there was no further hope of much expansion at that time. They felt that if they didn't do something then when they were in a good position, they'd miss their opportunity. In the case of a forced sale, they wouldn't bring as much. So they took the initiative on the thing. I knew some of the people. I didn't know the PP&L people who came around, but I knew some of the Metropolitan Edison people who came around making a survey of the place."

PP&L's bid for Penn Water had to be acceptable to Consolidated of Baltimore, which would soon change its name to Baltimore Gas & Electric Co. To help administer the ownership structure of Safe Harbor, PP&L and Baltimore Gas & Electric Co. agreed to set up a joint venture board to oversee the Susquehanna River hydroelectric plant. "They would have two (people) on the board, and we would have two on the board," Gavin explained. "Bob Fortune and I for a long

time were representatives of PP&L on the board, which did nothing at all, really. Routine matters. We had no problem whatsoever with Baltimore. But there had been a lot of concern throughout the company as to whether or not we were being foolish to step into the middle of that fight and whether it could be ended. But

---

The complex agreement that Oakes negotiated with Pennsylvania Water & Power Co. was submitted to shareholders of both companies at special meetings on Dec. 15, 1954.

---

fortunately, they did it."

The complex agreement that Oakes negotiated with Pennsylvania Water & Power Co. was submitted to shareholders of both companies at special meetings on Dec. 15, 1954. Both parties hoped to be able to consummate the agreement by mid-year in 1955.

"Among other things," Oakes reported in the 1954 annual report to shareholders, "the agreement of merger stipulates that

This photo taken at the Nov. 30, 1954, retirement luncheon for Al Borgealt pictures from left, PW&P President G.W. Spaulding, Frank Goldenberg, Al Borgealt, John Abbett Walls and Nathan B. Higgin, president of Safe Harbor.

RETIREMENTS

Pennsylvania Power & Light Co. will provide $7.6 million cash to redeem all Penn Water's outstanding preferred stock. It will issue one-fourth share of its 4.40 percent Series Preferred Stock and one-half share of common stock for each share of Penn Water's common stock. The company will receive all property and assets of Penn Water and will assume all debts and liabilities of Penn Water.

"Also, the company will increase the number of its directors, from 10 to 11, with the additional directorship to be filled by Mr. Joseph S. Young, presently a director of Penn Water and president and a director of Lehigh Portland Cement Co." One former Penn Water director had left for bigger and better things shortly before the merger. Prescott S. Bush, a Connecticut investor who had been elected to the board of Penn Water in 1941 and had served as chairman of the board during the postwar years, was elected to the United States Senate in the November 1952 elections. Bush resigned from the board on Dec. 4, 1952; 36 years later, his son, George Herbert Walker Bush, would be elected President of the United States.

Following the shareowners' meetings in December 1954, two events of some significance occurred that had a material impact on the merger. The Federal Power Commission approved Penn Water's new contracts on a unit rate basis for service to its electric utility customers, including PP&L. "This action simplifies Penn Water's rate schedules and in this respect is a helpful step toward accomplishment of the merger," Oakes reported.

"Also, the company and Consolidated (of Baltimore) have agreed, subject to the merger becoming effective, upon an overall settlement of all the various disputes and litigation between Penn Water and Consolidated. This agreement will make

With the help of a crane, these men rotate into proper position the 127-ton stator for the No. 17 generator unit at Holtwood.
circa 1954

it possible to dispose of all such controversies promptly after the merger. One of the items agreed upon is the sale to Consolidated of Penn Water's Maryland subsidiary, thus assuring that the company's operations will continue to be located entirely within the state of Pennsylvania."

One piece of important accounting was accomplished early in 1955. Penn Water sold the 87,720 shares of Consolidated of Baltimore that it owned, and used the net proceeds of approximately $2.8 million to reduce outstanding bank loans. In the process, it removed one of the few serious impediments remaining to the merger, given the fact that Baltimore Gas & Electric Co. did not want to see its stock transferred from Penn Water to PP&L.

Twenty years after Holtwood's anthracite-burning Unit 17 went into operation, flue-gas scrubbers were installed. *circa 1974*

Unit 17

While merger preparations were proceeding in the fall of 1954 and winter of 1955, Penn Water was getting ready to unveil the world's largest anthracite-fired boiler. No. 17 generating unit turned over for the first time on April 30, 1954. It was synchronized the next day, underwent various shakedown operations during the month of May and went into commercial operation at midnight, June 6, 1954, at 66,000 kilowatts.

By July, contractors from Western Knapp Co. and Ebasco Services Inc., many of whom had lived at Holtwood with their Penn Water crews for two years

and more, had scattered to the four winds. "All that is left of Ebasco now is an office group which is paying the remaining bills, disposing of excess material and finishing up the inventory of everything which went into the new

No. 17 generating unit turned over for the first time on April 30, 1954. It was synchronized the next day, underwent various shakedown operations during the month of May and went into commercial operation at midnight, June 6, 1954, at 66,000 kilowatts.

plant," *Hydro Hi-Lines* noted in July 1954.

With Unit 17 in service, Penn Water had substantially completed its $25 million postwar expansion program. "The task of designing and constructing our new steam generating unit and the new coal recovery and washing facilities at Safe Harbor was one of major magni-

---

The Holtwood hydro facility had a generating capability of 100,000 kilowatts, and PP&L's one-third share of Safe Harbor brought on line almost another 80,000 kilowatts.

---

tude," Operating Superintendent G.W. Spaulding told employees. "Because of our use of 'river coal,' the facilities from dredge to boiler were different from those generally in use. This made that work both more interesting and more difficult. Our past experience in the recovery, preparation and use of river coal was of great assistance."

A reporter for the *Baltimore Evening Sun* toured the facilities on May 26 in the company of R.L. Bortner, Penn Water's vice president of property and public relations. The reporter pronounced himself satisfied that

"Mr. Bortner is confident that there is no job too big for his 768-member family to take on. The 50 carloads of coal that daily appear from beneath the river's surface are substantial indications that he may be right."

The Penn Water merger proceeded to closing on the same schedule that Oakes had predicted in the 1954 annual report to shareholders. The merger was completed effective June 1, 1955; ironically, the Penn Water merger was completed nearly eight months before the Scranton Electric Co. merger, even though PP&L had been working on that merger for more than two years.

Addition of Penn Water to the PP&L system provided a major boost to the company's mid-1950s generation expansion plan. The Holtwood hydro facility had a generating capability of 100,000 kilowatts, and PP&L's one-third share of Safe Harbor brought on line almost another 80,000 kilowatts. The Holtwood steam units, bolstered by the addition of Unit 17, had a rated capability of 106,000 kilowatts. Overnight, PP&L had added the equivalent of a Sunbury Steam Electric Station to its system.

With territorial expansion satisfied, the next world for PP&L to conquer was atomic.

The Holtwood Lab

In its 45-year history as an independent company, Pennsylvania Water & Power Co. pioneered a number of innovative techniques and procedures that were adapted by hydroelectric projects all over the world.

Chief among the innovations was Penn Water's establishment of a research laboratory at the same time that Safe Harbor went on line in 1934. The impetus for the creation of the laboratory was the installation of the Kaplan turbines at Safe Harbor. Originally rated at 38,500-horsepower capacity, the two turbines had the largest capacity in the world at the time.

John Abbett Walls pushed for the establishment of a laboratory, partly because company engineers were convinced that the capacity of the two turbines could be pushed even higher, and partly because the sheer size of the turbines would result in excessive cavitation, in which large turbine blades were eaten away by pitting from water action.

During much of 1934 and 1935, two eminent German scientists, Dr. D. Thoma and Dr. Wilhelm Spannhake, were sent to the Holtwood laboratory by the German manufacturer to oversee the testing of the Kaplan turbines. At the time, none of the four U.S. turbine manufacturers had a laboratory for testing various aspects of turbines, the principal concern being cavitation in the larger turbine blades.

Word of the Holtwood laboratory soon got around the industry. When federal government engineers began planning to install even larger Kaplan turbines in its Bonneville power project on the Columbia River, "not

Kaplan runner at Safe Harbor. *circa 1931*

The first Kaplan turbine runner arrived at Safe Harbor in the fall of 1931 via a specially designed railroad car.

The impetus for the creation of the laboratory was the installation of the Kaplan turbines at Safe Harbor.

only were the results of our test and studies requested by outside engineers, but the use of the Holtwood hydraulic laboratory, built at Mr. Walls' instructions, was made available to all comers." During World War II, the U.S. Navy used data developed by the Holtwood laboratory's experiments on Kaplan turbine blades to conduct cavitation studies on Navy submarine propellors.

"Research is no stranger to executives and engineers of the Pennsylvania Water & Power Co.," *Power Magazine* editorialized in its July 1934 issue. "It is only natural then that the company built a research laboratory when it decided to go ahead with Safe Harbor, which, because of the equipment to be installed involved many problems on which complete information was not available. This laboratory has paid its way several times in providing fundamental data necessary for proper design and operating procedure."

A generation earlier, Penn Water had pioneered the use of cameras to take aerial photographs of transmission line rights-of-way. "During the First World War," Arch Crane, the editor of *Hydro Hi-Lines,* wrote in a 1955 article, "the Army had found that there were no suitable cameras for taking photographs from airplanes, and as a result, an

This aerial view of Holtwood was taken in 1955. The plant's laboratory was one of the first research and development facilities. During World War II, data developed at the lab was used to conduct cavitation studies on Navy submarine propellors.

inventive genius named Sherman Fairchild formed the Fairchild Aerial Camera Co. to produce aerial cameras and to make aerial photographs.

"Mr. Allner met Sherman Fairchild, and together they decided that aerial maps would be very helpful in laying out rights-of-way and building transmission lines. Accordingly, when the company was ready to proceed with the construction of the lines from Holtwood to York and Holtwood to Coatesville in 1923, the routes were mapped from the air by Fairchild's company. Today, the use of such maps is standard practice in the industry."

Penn Water's record of innovation between 1910 and 1955 was unparalleled in the industry. PP&L, which had already demonstrated its commitment to research and development with its anthracite-fired power plant program, was able to build on that record in the years ahead.

The Nuclear Imperative

PP&L's 1955
annual report
cover illustration.

The cover of PP&L's 1955 annual report to shareholders served notice to the financial community that the Allentown utility had made some major strategic decisions during the year concerning the future of generation planning.

The cover depicted a turbine-generator, a substation, power plant control room graphs and transmission lines. Tying the elements together on the cover was a multicolored atomic particle. PP&L had entered the nuclear age.

"In July 1955, the company announced its intention to build an atomic-electric power plant," Chas. E. Oakes noted, "providing that such a plant be found to be competitive with a fuel-burning generating plant. Satisfactory progress is being made on essential research and development work, which is being conducted jointly with Westinghouse Electric Corp."

The company's decision to investigate atomic power was a direct result of the increase of business in 1954 and 1955. The annual report noted that all-time records were established during 1955 in several important phases of company operations. System output for the year totaled 6.25 billion kilowatt-hours, and as it had every year since the end of World War II, PP&L established a new peak load—1.275 million kilowatts on Dec. 20, 1955.

Operating revenues for the year totaled $120.365 million, a gain of more than $11.1 million over 1954 revenues. Penn Water had been absorbed into the system in June; had Penn Water been a part of the company's system for the entire year, the revenues would have been nearly $123 million. Cash on hand at the end of the year was more than $20 million, and the amount committed to the company's 1955 construction program exceeded $31.4 million. The company certainly felt itself in a position to finance an atomic energy project in 1955.

Atomic Power

PP&L's interest in building what was then called an atomic power plant was part of an industry-wide fascination with tapping the possibilities of the atom in the postwar period. The atomic age had been ushered in just 10 years before, when *Enola Gay*, a B-29 Superfortress, had dropped the first atomic bomb over Hiroshima, Japan, in August 1945. The fearsome potential of the atom as a weapon of war had been symbolized in the mushroom cloud that all but obliterated Hiroshima—and, three days later, Nagasaki.

In the postwar years, Americans learned that the atomic bomb had been conceived, fabricated and tested in a top-secret federal government effort called The Manhattan Project that culminated in the events of August 1945. Thousands of Americans and European refugees had toiled at top-secret government installations near Oak Ridge, Tenn.; Hanford, Wash.; and Los Alamos, N.M., to design and build the atomic bomb.

Too Cheap To Meter

Americans also learned in the postwar years that uranium, the radioactive fuel that provided the explosive power for the atomic bomb, was capable of heating water into steam for electric power production. As the Atomic Energy Commission (AEC) gradually revealed the secrets of the atom in the early years of the Eisenhower Administration, a new emphasis took hold, one which stressed the use of atoms for peace.

In 1951, the first known useful electricity produced from atomic energy was generated at the AEC's National Reactor Testing Station in Arco, Idaho. Slightly more than 100 kilowatts was produced in the test project, enough to operate the pumps and other reactor equipment and to provide lights for the building housing the reactor. Technicians under

Dr. Walter H. Zinn drew enough heat from liquid metal in the breeder reactor to produce steam for a small turbine. Zinn emphasized that the test was simply that, and that no comparisons could be made between producing electricity from the breeder reactor and more conventional sources.

President Eisenhower committed his administration to the peaceful development of the atom. In 1953, Eisenhower told the United Nations that the U.S. intended to build a nuclear reactor to demonstrate the feasibility of atomic energy.

By 1955, AEC's Power Demonstration Reactor Program was drawing interest from electric utilities nationwide. The aim of the program was to bring private resources into the development of engineering information on the performance of nuclear power reactors and to advance the time when nuclear power would become economically feasible. Under the program, AEC made a commitment "to subsidize industry by waiving the AEC charges for the loan of source and special nuclear materials."

Already in 1955, electric utilities across the country had moved swiftly to capitalize on the AEC's offer to open its research and development efforts to private industry. AEC had announced early that year that it intended to spend $500 million over three years on the development of atomic power reactors as heat sources for electrical generation. Of that sum, $225

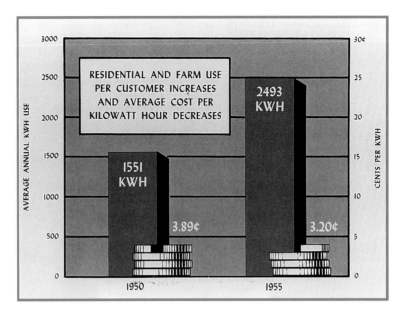

million would be spent on government research and development of power reactors, and $75 million would be allocated as subsidies to private industry. A total of $200 million was earmarked for military-type reactors for submarine and ship propulsion.

Early in 1955, six atomic energy projects were in various stages of planning or completion. Duquesne Light Co. of Pittsburgh, Westinghouse and Stone & Webster were building a pressurized water reactor at Shippingport, Pa., in the western part of the state. Ground was broken for the

> *The company's decision to investigate atomic power was a direct result of the increase of business in 1954 and 1955.*

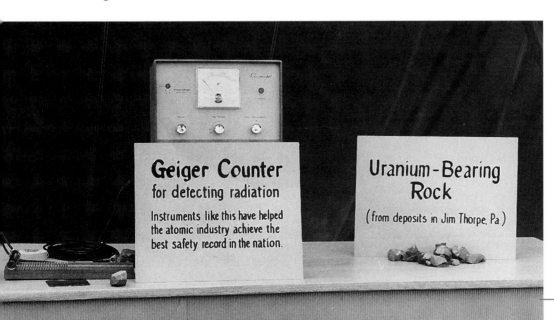

Geiger Counter
for detecting radiation

Instruments like this have helped the atomic industry achieve the best safety record in the nation.

Uranium-Bearing Rock

(from deposits in Jim Thorpe, Pa.)

Stressing the safety of nuclear power, this Geiger Counter and uranium sample were displayed at the dedication of Brunner Island Steam Electric Station in 1961. Six years before, Chas. E. Oakes announced the company's nuclear interest. It wouldn't be until 1971 when PP&L announced it was building the Susquehanna nuclear station.

315

Harley Collins.
circa 1980s. **Collins was one of the few engineers selected to join the Pennsylvania Advanced Reactor (PAR) Team in the 1950s.**

Shippingport project in September 1954, and when the project was completed in 1957, it would be the first commercial reactor in the United States.

The Argonne National Laboratory, Allis-Chalmers and Sargent & Lundy were getting ready to break ground on an experimental boiling water reactor at Argonne's laboratories northwest of Chicago, and Argonne was also a partner in an experimental fast breeder reactor project slated for Arco, Idaho. North American Aviation Inc. was experimenting with a sodium graphite reactor near Santa Susana, Calif., and Oak Ridge National Laboratory was experimenting with homogeneous reactors at its Tennessee facilities.

Utilities across the country were forming study teams to investigate the feasibility of nuclear energy. By the spring of 1955, a total of 20 utility and industry study teams had been set up in the U.S. They ranged from the Atomic Power Development Associates Team—which included future nuclear utilities like Cleveland Electric Illuminating Co., Consolidated Edison, Consumers Power, General Public Utilities, Toledo Edison, Boston Edison, Long Island Lighting and Hartford Electric Light Co., not to mention such industrial giants as Ford Motor Co., Bendix Aviation, Babcock & Wilcox and Allis-Chalmers—to the study team set up by the Consumers Public Power District of Columbus, Neb. Other study teams were headed by Pacific Gas & Electric, General Electric, Monsanto, the Tennessee Valley Authority, Westinghouse, Bethlehem Steel Co. and Kaiser Engineers.

Some groups had already gone beyond the study team phase. The Yankee Atomic Electric Co., a consortium of Boston Edison, Hartford Electric Light Co. and nine other New England utilities, was

By the spring of 1955, a total of 20 utility and industry study teams had been set up in the U.S.

awaiting Massachusetts Department of Public Utilities' approval of a stock issue to begin construction of a small nuclear facility to be located in New England. Yankee Nuclear would go on line in 1960 at Rowe, Mass.

That spring of 1955, Consolidated Edison in New York had announced plans to go it alone on the construction of a nuclear generating station at a site near Peekskill, N.Y., on the Hudson River. Walker Cisler, the charismatic chief executive officer of Detroit Edison, was rumored to be lining up financing for a nuclear project in southern Michigan.

The American Nuclear Society was getting ready to hold its first annual meeting in June at Penn State, and conferences were being announced almost weekly. The Atomic Industrial Forum (AIF) held its "Atomic Energy—The New Industrial Frontier" conference at the Mark Hopkins Hotel in San Francisco on April 4-5, and the Association of Electrical and Chemical Engineers took a look at nuclear engineering during their conference at UCLA in late April. AIF sponsored another forum—this time on a realistic appraisal of atomic energy—at the Waldorf Astoria in late May, and the industry's first-ever trade fair was held at the Sheraton-Park Hotel in Washington in late September.

The promise of atomic energy was too rich for utilities to ignore. The only real stumbling block in the 1950s was the insurance industry's hesitation to insure multimillion dollar nuclear projects at a time when the technology was as yet unproven commercially. In 1957, Lewis L. Strauss, chairman of the AEC during the Eisenhower Administration, convinced Congress to pass the Price-Anderson Act, which essentially limited utility liability in case of an accident at a nuclear plant. By the early 1960s, Glenn T. Seaborg, President John F. Kennedy's appointee to head the AEC, was describing the future of atomic electric power as "too cheap to meter."

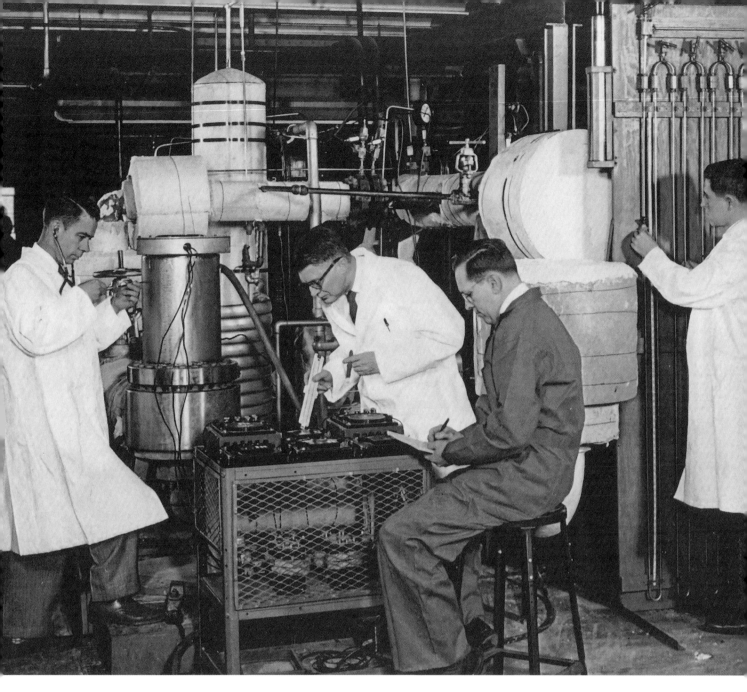

The Pennsylvania Advanced Reactor

Pennsylvania Power & Light Co.'s approach to nuclear power was typical. The company took pride in its technology culture and engineering expertise. When it came time to consider joining an atomic energy study team, PP&L elected to throw in its lot with Westinghouse rather than join the industry consortiums that were forming almost monthly in 1954 and 1955.

On Aug. 30, 1954, President Eisenhower's signing of the Atomic Energy Act authorized utilities to possess nuclear material for commercial purposes. Just over two months later, in November, PP&L joined with Westinghouse to conduct a research and development program to determine the feasibility of utilizing the new energy source on PP&L's power supply system.

The first step undertaken by the partners was to survey the various types of reactors that might be adapted to power generation. At first, PP&L thought its Westinghouse affiliation might qualify it to build the first pressurized water reactor, but Westinghouse had already made a commitment to bid on the reactor, which

Between 1955 and 1958, the PAR team of engineers spent about $15 million on nuclear research and development.

Norman W. Curtis.
circa 1980s. Curtis, a
second generation
PP&L worker, was
selected to join the
PAR project in 1955.

would be built between 1954 and 1957 at Shippingport, Pa., with Duquesne Light Co. and Stone & Webster as partners. Westinghouse then suggested that PP&L join it in potential commercial development of a homogeneous reactor being developed at Oak Ridge.

Jack Busby recalled squiring a group of PJM executives to meet with Hyman Rickover, the founding father of the nuclear Navy, at midnight in Morristown, N.J., to discuss the homogeneous reactor. The irascible Rickover "makes Ross Perot look like a quiet, unemotional team player," Busby said. "His majesty was treating us like a bunch of schoolboys. It was an impressive performance."

In August 1955, the two companies signed a pact to develop the Pennsylvania Advanced Reactor (PAR). Soon after, Union Carbide Nuclear Co. joined the group as a potential fuel reprocessor. Engineers throughout PP&L were selected to join the project.

One of those picked was Norman W. Curtis. Now retired and living in Lower Macungie Township outside Allentown, Curtis was a second generation worker at PP&L. Born in Allentown, he had moved with his parents to Freeport, Maine, as a young man when his father left PP&L because of Depression cutbacks. In 1959, Curtis, then a University of Maine graduate, joined PP&L.

"Oh, the first three years, to a large degree I was living out of the trunk of my car, and worked the Susquehanna River from Lancaster up to Williamsport, over to Honesdale and down through the coal regions," Curtis recalled. For the next two years, Curtis helped build the Hosensack substation. In 1954, he heard about PP&L's joint venture study team with Westinghouse.

"It was still a closed society," Curtis described the nuclear fraternity in 1954. "Nobody knew what was involved, except that the military gates were opening a little bit, and the utilities were invited to go through military-type security clearance for a few people and get some seed money going in terms of technology exchange."

Tempted by what he had heard, Curtis, a physics major in college, applied for the project. In 1955, he was assigned to PAR. "I joined a number of people in Allentown, up in the tower, 23rd floor, where we had our secret sanctum going up there," Curtis said. Besides Curtis, members of the team included Bill Frederick, John West, Bill Gibbard, Jay Meikrantz, Harry Search and Chuck Repp, among others.

"We kind of cut our teeth on what we could learn about the commercial atomic power bit," Curtis said. What the group learned was that it wanted to bid on the Shippingport project. "We lost that bid," Curtis explained, "came in second, I guess, then succeeded in winning the worst bid of all, which was for the homogeneous reactor, which of course turned out to be a total fiasco by the time we got done with it."

Much of the work for the PAR was carried out at Westinghouse's Commercial Atomic Power Activities Laboratory in Pittsburgh. Curtis and the other members of the PAR team scattered to Oak Ridge and the Sandia laboratories in New Mexico to work with AEC scientists on the technology. PAR, Curtis said, "was a technology that was just too far out for the time. Too many materials problems. Impossible challenges with regard to maintenance and plant design. We just didn't know any better."

The homogeneous reactor created problems from the start. "The field we were dealing with was acid," Curtis said. "Hydrochloric acid with uranium sprinkles. And you had to contain that in

What the group learned was that it wanted to bid on the Shippingport project. "We lost that bid, "came in second, I guess, then succeeded in winning the worst bid of all, which was for the homogeneous reactor, which of course turned out to be a total fiasco by the time we got done with it."—Norman W. Curtis

the piping system and maintain it, with all the problems of radiation and pressure and so forth."

By 1957, PP&L and Westinghouse had spent $5.5 million on the PAR. That year, they asked the AEC to provide $7 million for future research and development during 1958 and 1959. Congress was slow to appropriate the money, and although Baltimore Gas & Electric Co. had indicated a willingness to join the project in 1958, the total outlay for the two initial partners was well over $9 million.

"In late 1958, it became apparent that in several important problem areas we were not obtaining information at a rate sufficient to obtain the objectives of the 1958-1959 program," Dr. W.E. Johnson, the project manager for Westinghouse's atomic power department, told a congressional subcommittee. "In addition, it appeared that there was essentially nothing that could be done to correct this."

The problems, Johnson explained, concerned "gaseous recombination," the effects of irradiation on slurry properties,

reactor vessel hydraulics, corrosion-erosion, stress corrosion, reactor startup and plant layout and design. Cooling the reactor vessel was a particular problem. "Only through tests on a prototype reactor can the true magnitude of the problem be determined," wrote Johnson and S.C. Townsend, his PP&L counterpart in the PAR project. "For this reason, project engineers and scientists again questioned the feasibility of proceeding directly with full-scale plant construction."

On Dec. 16, 1958, PP&L and Westinghouse announced the suspension of the PAR project "because construction of a large scale aqueous homogeneous plant was technically infeasible at that time." The PAR project had come under the jurisdiction of Jack K. Busby, who had succeeded Oakes as president, and once the meter had climbed over $9 million, Busby went to Pittsburgh in late 1958 to assess the status of the project.

"Busby saw the money going down the tube with this thing," recalled Harley Collins, then a member of the PAR team,

Chas. E. Oakes (left) and Jack Busby, who succeeded Oakes as president in 1958. They appeared together again in the 1960s to underscore PP&L's commitment to building newer and better facilities to serve the growing economy of the service area. Behind the men is a panel showing the first unit at Brunner Island and a figure of $60 million, the amount earmarked for 1964-1968 construction projects.

319

It became Busby's painful duty to serve as the hatchet man for PAR.

PP&L's 1954 service area.

"and so he came out to Pittsburgh and he got the whole group together for dinner. And he asked us what we thought about it. Well, by the time he left that evening, I think he had made the decision. That was it. And the project shut down, which was a good decision."

It had been a painful decision for Busby, who had shepherded the project for Oakes ever since PP&L had decided to commit to PAR back in 1955. PP&L had selected the cream of its engineering work force to join the PAR study team, more than 30 employees all told. "The concept was that nuclear power was going to be a very important part of our future," Busby said in a 1992 interview.

But it was obvious after three year's work that the problems associated with the homogeneous slurry reactor—although an excellent concept—were going to preclude commercial development for decades, if not longer. It became Busby's painful duty to serve as the hatchet man for PAR.

But Busby's actions didn't terminate PP&L's interest in nuclear power. "We were in the right stable," he said, "but we had the wrong horse. And we were building young people with nuclear savvy." Accordingly, Busby established an atomic power group in the Engineering Department.

Early in 1959, Norman Curtis was called back to Allentown along with John West and Bill Gibbard "to become a three-man think tank, and our assignment was to track the state of the art. It was recognized that the concept we had nibbled at was too far out in the future. But other projects were coming along. More and more utilities were making commitments. And our job was to track the technology and the politics and the economics and act as a source of information for company management, if and when it might be time later to make another move."

The service provided by the atomic power group became invaluable a decade-and-a-half later when PP&L decided to proceed with the Susquehanna nuclear project.

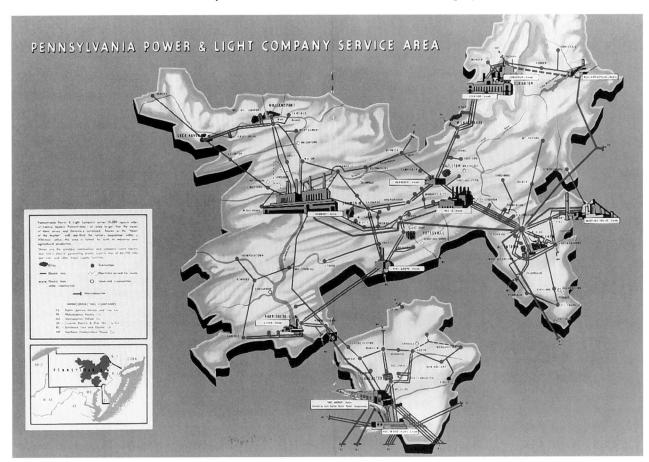

PENNSYLVANIA POWER & LIGHT COMPANY SERVICE AREA

Shippingport

Before it embarked upon the PAR project with Westinghouse, PP&L had investigated the possibility of joining other utilities in the Pennsylvania-New Jersey (PNJ) power pool to submit a proposal to the Atomic Energy Commission (AEC) to build a pressurized water reactor in Pennsylvania.

PP&L's Jack Busby, then the company's vice president for Legal affairs, joined other PNJ executives in a 1954 midnight meeting with Adm. Hyman Rickover to discuss the PNJ bid. Rickover, who was then overseeing the development of reactors aboard vessels for the U.S. Navy, threw cold water on the proposal. "Rickover made it very clear that he was concerned about the PNJ consortium's ability to make decisions," Busby said. "We didn't even have a project manager appointed."

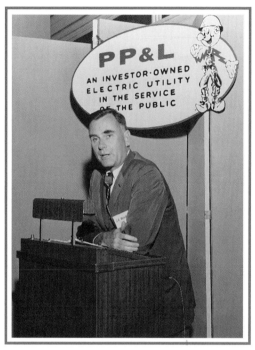

Young Jack K. Busby. *circa 1961.* As PP&L's vice president of Legal Affairs in 1954, Busby negotiated with the U.S. Navy's Adm. Hyman Rickover about the Pennsylvania-New Jersey power pool's interest in submitting a proposal to the Atomic Energy Commission to build a pressurized water reactor.

The AEC, Busby said, "had a widespread demonstration reactor program. It was an ambitious, aggressive, expensive, well-intentioned program. It provided financial incentives, but expected utilities to put in money."

PP&L was shocked when Duquesne Light Co. went it alone and submitted a proposal to AEC for a pressurized water reactor. The company was even more shocked when the AEC accepted the proposal.

An important factor in the selection of the Pittsburgh utility as the lead agent for what would become the Shippingport nuclear plant was the fact that Westinghouse had huge facilities in Pittsburgh. Nevertheless, Busby said, "it came as a terrible shock to us. My pride was hurt."

The genesis for the Shippingport reactor, which was located on the Ohio River 35 miles northwest of Pitts-

burgh, was the nuclear propulsion program being developed by Rickover for the U.S. Navy. Lewis L. Strauss, AEC commissioner in 1954, wanted a Westinghouse reactor that was being developed for a prototype aircraft carrier to be adapted for civilian use. He prevailed upon Westinghouse to find a utility partner to prove the feasibility of the civilian application. Westinghouse joined with hometown Duquesne Light Co. to submit the Shippingport application.

The AEC fronted 85 percent of the cost of building Shippingport. In September 1954, President Dwight D. Eisenhower waved a "magic wand" from a Denver television studio to inaugurate groundbreaking at the Shippingport site, halfway across the country.

A little over three years later, on Dec. 2, 1957, the 60,000-kilowatt Shippingport atomic power plant "went critical," becoming the first commercial nuclear power plant in the United States. The largest of six civilian nuclear plants authorized by the AEC, Shippingport was described by a *Saturday Evening Post* editor as "a $110 million showpiece of the atomic age." Shippingport's output was enough to provide electric power for a city of 120,000 people.

Following Shippingport, atomic power plants experienced a near exponential increase in size. In 1959, two years after Shippingport went critical, Commonwealth Edison started up Unit 1 of Dresden atomic power station. The 207,000-kilowatt unit in central Illinois was more than three times the size of Shippingport and was the first nuclear power reactor totally financed by a private utility. In 1964, just seven years after Shippingport went on line, economy of scale had made its presence felt in nuclear engineering. That year, Jersey Central Power & Light ordered its Oyster Creek unit, a 650,000-kilowatt behemoth that dwarfed Shippingport. The rush to nuclear energy was on.

Shippingport remained opera-tional for a quarter-century. Shut down in 1982, the reactor was dismantled, shipped by barge down the Mississippi River, through the Panama Canal and eventually up the Pacific Coast to the federal nuclear reservation at Hanford, Wash., where it was entombed in 1989.

The genesis for the Shipping-port reactor, which was located on the Ohio River 35 miles northwest of Pittsburgh, was the nuclear propulsion program being developed by Rickover for the U.S. Navy.

31

Martins Creek

Martins Creek
Power Plant
Dedication
October 12, 1954

Addresses by:

The Honorable
Edward Martin
United States Senator,
Commonwealth of Pennsylvania

Chas. E. Oakes
President,
Pennsylvania Power
& Light Company

PENNSYLVANIA POWER & LIGHT COMPANY

In the early summer of 1957, Chas. E. Oakes addressed the Downtown Athletic Club in New York City. It was a traditional financial briefing for the members, many of whom were employed by Wall Street's investment community. Oakes had addressed the group in 1951 and again in 1954. The 1957 address would be his last; later that year, Oakes was succeeded as PP&L president by Jack K. Busby.

The news that Oakes relayed to the members of the Downtown Athletic Club was that of unbridled growth. In the three

To meet growing demands in the postwar era, Martins Creek Steam Electric Station was built under the leadership of Chas. E. Oakes.

years since Oakes had last spoken to the club, PP&L had absorbed Scranton Electric Co. and Pennsylvania Water & Power Co. The new additions, coupled with the internal growth in customers, revenues and demand that PP&L was experiencing in its service territory—22 percent of the state's land area, 20 percent of Pennsylvania's population, 25 percent of the state's farms and 15 percent of Pennsylvania's industrial base—was putting unprecedented strains on the company's operations.

> *"This is evidenced by the fact that since 1946, use of service has increased 241 percent, with a resulting gain in revenue of 141 percent, while number of customers increased 29 percent."*
> —*Chas. E. Oakes*

"A part of the increase in residential and farm revenues is due to an increase in the number of customers served and to the substantial increase in use by existing customers," Oakes told members of the club. "This is evidenced by the fact that since 1946, use of service has increased 241 percent, with a resulting gain in revenue of 141 percent, while number of customers increased 29 percent."

What Oakes was in essence explaining was the simple fact that residential and

farm kilowatt-hour usage was increasing at a rate more than eight times faster than the number of customers. Even though PP&L had gotten out of the business of directly merchandising appliances during the Great Depression, the number of appliances in use on the system continued to increase dramatically.

PP&L was by no means alone in its attempts to cope with postwar growth. The decade following World War II was a golden age for America's electric utility industry. Skyrocketing demand was fueled by a labor shortage, low interest rates and a dramatic rise in the gross national product. For the first and only time in the nation's history, a family of four could live comfortably on the salary of a single wage earner.

The second message that Oakes left with the group was that residential and farm electric power rates were actually going down. While kilowatt-hour usage was up 241 percent, the company's revenues had only increased 141 percent. Economies of scale in electric power plant construction and operation had made it possible for PP&L to generate significantly more electric power to meet demand, while reducing the kilowatt-hour rate for that electricity.

The story was similar for PP&L's commercial and industrial customers. The number of commercial customers had increased by 26 percent since 1946, but kilowatt-hour usage had climbed 126 percent. Oakes attributed the rise in commercial business to the "population move into the suburban areas and the consequent growth of roadside businesses. With the movement to the suburbs has come new opportunities for improving the standards of doing business. The results of our promotional activities in this direction have been particularly noticeable in the newer buildings and neighborhood shopping centers which are characterized by higher quality, greater quantity and more effective use of lighting, while air conditioning, in old buildings as well as new, has become a necessity in up-to-date business establishments."

The Role of the Pennsylvania Turnpike

The growth of the suburbs was related to state and federal roadbuilding programs that were unequalled since the Good Roads movement of the 1920s. As early as 1940, Pennsylvania had begun construction of the Pennsylvania Turnpike, a controlled access, four-lane highway stretching 360 miles across the southern third of the state. The Pennsylvania Turnpike crossed about 85 miles of the southern section of PP&L's service territory and connected the state with the Ohio Turnpike on the west and the New Jersey Turnpike on the east. By the time the Northeast Extension opened in 1957—running 110 miles north to south from Scranton to Philadelphia and literally traversing the eastern third of PP&L's service territory—there were more than 20 million automobiles registered in Pennsylvania.

The success of the Pennsylvania Turnpike in dispersing the state's population into suburban areas was not lost on the federal government. In 1956, the year prior to Oakes' appearance at the Downtown Athletic Club, President Dwight D. Eisenhower signed legislation creating a $33 billion, 41,000-mile national system of interstate and defense highways.

The existence of the Pennsylvania Turnpike system—and the promise of even better roads nationwide—also provided a boost to Pennsylvania's industrial economy. "In the 1946 to 1957 period, industrial revenues almost doubled," Oakes noted. "This largely is attributed to—first, the increase in number and capacity of the manufacturing establishments served; and, second, the rising use of electricity per man-hour by industry in recognition that electric power is one of the best means of increasing employee productivity."

Oakes stressed that "PP&L is not a one-industry company. Industrial revenues are well distributed and thoroughly diversified. The result is a high degree of revenue stability. The recent decline in

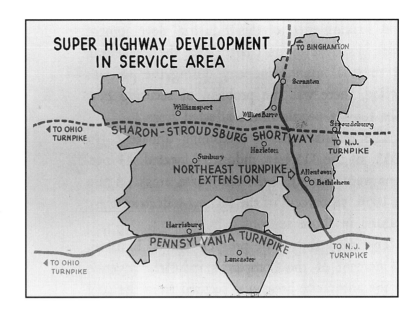

anthracite mining appears to have spent itself."

Indeed, anthracite mining in 1957 appeared to be the only PP&L industrial segment that wasn't participating in the continuing postwar boom. Down 16 percent in electric revenues in 1957 from its 1946 high of $8.4 million, the region's anthracite mines were, in effect, a casualty of cheap petroleum and cheap electricity.

But the rest of PP&L's industrial customers were experiencing tremendous gains in productivity. Using 1946 as a baseline, Oakes pointed out that electric revenues were up 336 percent for chemicals, 144 percent for cement and quarries, 201 percent for lumber and products, 223 percent for metals and

> The existence of the Pennsylvania Turnpike system—and the promise of even better roads nationwide—also provided a boost to Pennsylvania's industrial economy.

As part of the 1954 diamond jubilee, electric utilities sponsored public awareness programs like "You Are There," which ran on CBS-TV and was hosted by Walter Cronkite.

183 percent for paper and printing.

"The record shows good gains from the various industrial groups," Oakes said. "Our sales people work closely with the industries throughout the area, helping them adapt electric power so they can hold and better their competitive positions."

The same held true for PP&L. The company spent much of the 1950s involved in an ambitious construction program that wouldn't, for all intents and purposes, be completed until the mid-1970s. Between 1957 and 1961 alone, PP&L budgeted $193 million for construction, of which about 45 percent—or $85 million—was committed to new generation. By the time Oakes spoke at the Downtown Athletic Club, PP&L was putting the finishing touches on the Martins Creek Steam Electric Station and beginning to plan seriously for Brunner Island, the next in the series of coal-fired units that went on line between 1946 and 1970.

Construction of Martins Creek Steam Electric Station in February and March 1953.

Martins Creek

Even before the completion of the Sunbury Steam Electric Station, PP&L was already planning future generation to meet demand on the system. Sunbury proved to be an admirable baseload generation plant, but its location in the north central portion of the company's service territory dictated that other steam electric generation units be located in the eastern portion of PP&L's service territory.

As early as 1951, PP&L's System Power and Engineering Department had settled on a 483-acre site just off Rte. 611. Ten miles above Easton and three miles east of Martins Creek on the banks of the Delaware River, this would be the site of its next steam electric generating station.

"PP&L's power load studies indicated future need for substantial additional generating capacity in the eastern part of its service area even before the third unit of PP&L's Sunbury plant was in regular service and while the fourth unit was still in the blueprint stage," the company noted in 1954. "With tremendous quantities of water needed for cooling the spent steam and changing it back to water, a location along the Delaware River was a foregone conclusion in meeting the huge requirements of this giant future steam electric station."

Martins Creek was planned as a baseload generating unit larger than anything already installed at Sunbury. The plant in Mount Bethel Township would have the distinction of hosting the largest single turbine-generator on the PP&L system when the plant first went on line in 1954. And Unit One—rated at 132,500 kilowatts—would be joined by Unit Two, a unit of similar size, two years after first going on line.

Martins Creek was a departure for PP&L in three important respects. The company pioneered community development efforts by keeping area residents fully informed of its plans to build the new multimillion dollar plant. It built the first "outdoor type" unit constructed as far north as the Mid-Atlantic and New

The plant in Mount Bethel Township would have the distinction of hosting the largest single turbine-generator on the PP&L system when the plant first went on line in 1954.

England states. After nearly 50 years of building anthracite-fired coal plants, Martins Creek depended on Pennsylvania bituminous coal for its boiler fuel.

"Recognizing that the building of a multimillion dollar power plant brings a great influx of construction workers into an area, as well as increased traffic from

(Above) **Cross-section of Martins Creek 1.2 million lb./hr. steam generator for Unit No. 1.** *circa 1954*

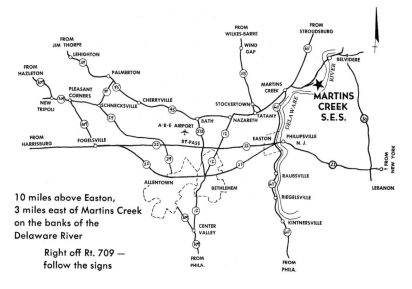

10 miles above Easton, 3 miles east of Martins Creek on the banks of the Delaware River

Right off Rt. 709 — follow the signs

incoming material and supplies, the Pennsylvania Power & Light Co. conducted a 'Howdy Neighbor' get-together recently in the Centerfield School Auditorium, Martins Creek, Pa., in order to acquaint residents of that community and Lower Mt. Bethel Township with plans and problems attending construction of the Martins Creek Power Plant on the Delaware River," the Edison Electric Institute reported in June 1952.

PP&L's openness in dealing with the local community paid dividends. More than 500 people assembled in the Centerfield High School auditorium, which was decorated with displays illustrating the Allentown utility's growth during the postwar period. They heard Chas. E. Oakes report that Martins Creek was part of a $288 million construction budget for the period from 1945 to 1955.

Oakes noted that more than $10 million in orders had already been placed

for the new Martins Creek unit, which would cost more than $30 million when the first unit went on line a little more than two years in the future.

Other speakers for the evening included James C. Knowles, vice president of the Lehigh division; George M. Keenan, vice president and recently elected company director; Bert C. Seitzinger, project manager in charge of the Sunbury plant construction; Harry T. Jansen, assistant project manager; Richard Forbes, superintendent of the Martins Creek plant; and Steven Nemeth, chairman of the board of supervisors of Lower Mt. Bethel Township. That afternoon, Knowles had impressed a future generation of PP&L customers when he briefed an assembly of Centerfield High School students on the new plant, and the job opportunities it afforded residents of the community.

At the Howdy Neighbor meeting, Oakes, Knowles, Keenan and the others described the uniqueness of the first Martins Creek unit. "This station is one of the first 'outdoor' type steam electric stations built in the northeast and the first on the

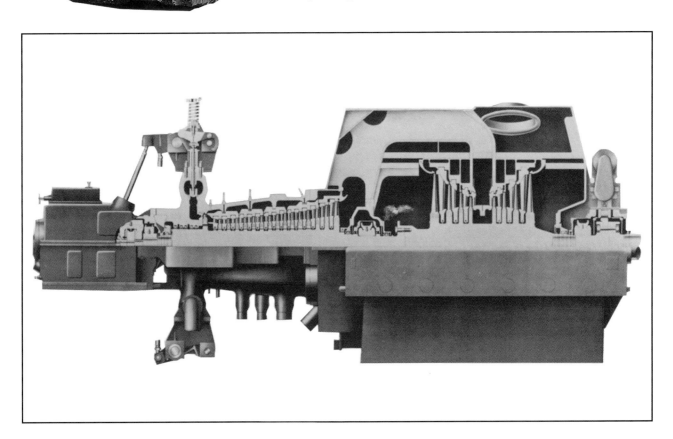

PP&L system," Knowles and Keenan told the crowd. "The major equipment, including the turbine-generator, steam generating unit, forced and induced draft fans, precipitators, stand pipes, car unloading facilities, thaw pit, coal bunkers, air ducts and breechings are installed out-of-doors."

Outdoor generating stations had been installed elsewhere in the United States ever since the end of World War II. But the outdoor units were usually more suitable to southern climates, and they traditionally were fired by oil or natural gas. Houston Lighting & Power Co., a sister utility to PP&L in the Electric Bond and Share Co. family during the 1920s and 1930s, refined the concept of the outdoor units in its postwar building boom, especially following the 1947 construction of its Greens Bayou gas-fired plant.

The great advantage of outdoor units was the speed with which they were built. Mrs. B.P. Sergeant, a Martins Creek resident and a PP&L shareholder since 1923, took the controls of a steam shovel in July 1952 and broke ground for the new plant. Just 25 months later—on Aug. 13, 1954—Unit One was synchronized and on line with the PP&L system.

Martins Creek was the first power plant on the PP&L system specifically designed to burn bituminous coal. The company took pains to stress that "PP&L remains the largest single user of anthracite in the world…using, as one company, more than the combined consumption of a single industry such as railroads, steel, textiles and the like. The present anthracite consumption is at the rate of some 2 million tons a year."

The switch to bituminous was necessary, given the continuing decline of the state's anthracite industry. Diversity of fuel supply protected PP&L from the drop-off in anthracite production, but it was a costly switch. Transportation costs were up sharply, since bituminous had to be rail-hauled from the fields in western Pennsylvania. Average fuel costs rose from 13 cents per million Btu in 1946—when the company was running literally all of its boilers on anthracite—to 23 cents

per million Btu a decade later. PP&L estimated that the average fuel cost would be nearly 35 cents per million Btu by 1964.

Still, the economics of the declining anthracite industry dictated the diversification of fuel mix. By 1956, PP&L was burning just over one million tons of bituminous a year, equal to 28 percent of the company's coal consumption. In his 1957 address to the Downtown Athletic Club, Oakes estimated that PP&L's bituminous consumption would double to more than two million tons in 1965, equal to 50 percent of the utility's coal consumption.

This brand-new 65-ton vulcan diesel-electric yard locomotive went to work shuttling coal cars at Martins Creek in August 1953.

Mrs. B.P. Sergeant, a Martins Creek resident and a PP&L shareholder since 1923, took the controls of a steam shovel in July 1952 and broke ground for the new plant. Just 25 months later—on Aug. 13, 1954—Unit One was synchronized and on line with the PP&L system.

Martins Creek was a study in superlatives. Unit One generated enough electricity to run electric refrigerators in 2.5 million homes. Its water consumption of 60,000 gallons a minute was twice the total water requirements of Allentown, Bethlehem and Easton. The 30,000 yards of concrete used in the construction of

Unit One was enough to build a 17-mile-long highway 18 feet wide from Martins Creek to Stroudsburg. More than 300,000 cubic feet of air a minute, heated to 600 degrees Fahrenheit, was required to keep the fires in the boiler going.

Martins Creek was dedicated following official inspection tours on Saturday,

Visitors tour the new Central Control Room at Martins Creek in August 1954.

Oct. 16, 1954. The Korean War had been over for more than a year, but in far-off Vietnam—a place most Americans would have been hard put to identify on a map—Ho Chi Minh assumed power in Hanoi after an eight-year struggle with the French. In Washington, D.C., Sen. Joseph R. McCarthy, a Wisconsin Republican, was rooting out supposed communists from the government.

Pennsylvania U.S. Sen. Edward Martin told 600 visitors at the Martins Creek dedication that PP&L's newest power plant was a symbol of the struggle to create and maintain a free enterprise system in the United States. "We are meeting here today to dedicate a great power plant which, in itself, depicts the continuing growth and development of America," Martin said. "It stands as a symbol of enterprise, ingenuity, industry, invention and America's faith in the future."

Martin's speech also referenced the fact that the plant was being dedicated

one week shy of the time 75 years earlier when Thomas A. Edison had proved the feasibility of the incandescent electric light. Senator Martin paid tribute to 75 years of progress in his address.

"The inventions of Edison and others, under America's free enterprise system, have given our country unparalleled benefits," Martin said. "Their work in the last 75 years has made working and living conditions more efficient, more convenient, and more comfortable. Every home, every industry and every walk of life has been improved. Our inventors have had so much to do with our country's productivity and in giving us the highest living standard ever known in the world.

"Today, electric power is the lifeblood of our nation. Yet, it is such a small item in the average household budgeting. It is also such a small part of the operating cost of a business. Today, we can hardly realize that three generations ago the world was without electricity. Homes and offices were illuminated by gas or kerosene lamps. Machinery was run by steam or water power. Cooking was done on wood or coal stoves. Food was kept in ice boxes or spring houses.

"Foresight and planning have characterized the electric industry throughout its history. Here at Martins Creek today we see evidence that these qualities are still in full flower."

The senator didn't mention it, but foresight and planning were even more evident at PP&L as Martins Creek began to pick up system baseload. A second Martins Creek unit was already under construction, and the company was ready to break ground on an even larger baseload unit in the southern portion of the service territory, at Brunner Island on the Susquehanna River. PP&L engineers were even then refining the science of high-voltage transmission, turning the PJM power pool into one of the most efficient bulk power delivery systems on the continent.

The Construction Department

The changeover from Phoenix Utilities Co. to the PP&L Construction Department is shrouded in mystery. From 1920 until the Great Depression, PP&L power plant and transmission line construction was handled by Phoenix Utilities Co., a subsidiary of the parent Electric Bond and Share Co. Bond & Share provided construction services to all of its operating subsidiaries through Phoenix Utilities Co., building coal-fired power plants, hydroelectric facilities and high-voltage transmission lines across America.

Phoenix Utilities Co. built the entire Wallenpaupack hydroelectric project, the Siegfried substation and additions to Hauto and Pine Grove plants in the 1920s and early 1930s. In 1933, Bond & Share turned over construction responsibility from Phoenix Utilities Co. to PP&L; on Jan. 30, 1933, John S. Wise formally accepted responsibility for PP&L construction in a memo to P.B. Sawyer of National Power & Light Co., the Bond & Share subholding company that was the parent for PP&L.

Passage of the Public Utilities Holding Company Act of 1935 forced Electric Bond and Share Co. to divest itself of its operating subsidiaries. Although PP&L didn't become a New York Stock Exchange company until after World War II, it already had more than a decade of construction experience under its belt.

In 1985, the late Arthur W. Moore, whose last job before retirement from PP&L was overseeing the construction of the North Building in Allentown, was asked about the changeover from Phoenix Utilities Co. to the PP&L Construction Department. "We didn't know what was going on," Moore reported. "All we knew was that we went to bed one night as Phoenix Utility employees,

The Construction Department grew from 250 Phoenix Utilities Co. employees hired by PP&L in the 1940s to more than 2,000 employees in PP&L's own Construction Department in the 1960s. These linemen are going through a training exercise at PP&L's Walbert Training Center in the 1980s.

and the next morning, we woke up and we were PP&L employees."

Few of the employees were inclined to question the change, because it happened during the Great Depression, when most people were just happy to have a job. "The important thing to us was that the paychecks kept coming," Moore said.

J. Ford Fritzinger, a 1966 retiree, said in 1992 that he was equally in the dark about the changeover. "I don't really know how it happened," he said, "and as chief clerk at the Hauto plant, I had many contacts with the Phoenix people. In my time at Hauto—1922 to 1931—Phoenix was putting in the Units 4 and 5 generators. I lived in Mauch Chunk, and a Mr. Waterman, who was in charge of the Phoenix operation at Hauto, used to be my passenger to and from work. In spite of all of that close contact, I still couldn't explain how the change came about."

Following the changeover, PP&L retained its field headquarters for the Construction Department in Hazleton. Everett P. Welch, a 1965 Construction Department retiree, recalled in 1985 that "in those days, the equipment mostly consisted of concrete mixers, air compressors and jackhammers."

Welch also recalled that flexibility was a hallmark of

From 1945 until the completion of the Susquehanna nuclear station, PP&L's Construction Department managed the most aggressive building program in the company's history.

the Construction Department. "A painter didn't have to paint all the time," he said. "He could rig a transformer one day and paint another. You found something else for them to do when their 'usual' job was slack. With all that cross-training, and everybody knowing what it felt like to do the other guy's job, we had a special feeling of fellowship."

From its inception in 1933 until the end of World War II, PP&L's Construction Department did far more maintenance than actual construction. But the postwar building boom proved the wisdom of creating the Construction Department. From 1945 until the completion of the Susquehanna nuclear station, PP&L's Construction Department managed the most aggressive building program in the company's history.

The original Construction Department consisted of about 250 Phoenix Utilities Co. employees who were hired by PP&L. Beginning in the late 1940s, the Construction Department began overseeing the contractors who were building the company's new postwar generating stations, including the Sunbury, Martins Creek, Brunner Island, Montour and Susquehanna Steam Electric stations.

In the 1960s, PP&L's Construction Department totaled more than 2,000 employees. The department began taking on maintenance jobs in power

Don't look down! Construction Department employees work on 500,000-volt transmission line. *(Inset)* Everett P. Welch retired from the Construction Department in 1965.

plants that had traditionally been performed by independent contractors. "Power plant people saw the benefit immediately," the *PP&L Reporter* noted in a 1985 story. "Here was a work force with a wealth of varied experience and talent, with the kind of dedication that only PP&L people could muster on a job."

32

Brunner Island

BRUNNER ISLAND S.E.S.
Plant Location and
Access Routes

Brunner Island,
PP&L's second
semi-outdoor,
bituminous coal-
burning plant,
went into
operation
in 1961.

O ne of the factors that influenced PP&L's response to the rapid increase in demand during the postwar period was the company's reliance upon one of the most sophisticated interconnected transmission networks on the North American continent.

PP&L's
BRUNNER ISLAND
PLANT
TURN RIGHT
½ MILE

The intermediate-pressure turbine rotor for Brunner Island Steam Electric Station's Unit 1 was unloaded at the construction site in 1960.

The Pennsylvania-New Jersey Interconnection agreement, which had been signed by PP&L, Philadelphia Electric Co. and Public Service Electric & Gas Co. on Sept. 26, 1927, in anticipation of completion of the 220-kv ring around Philadelphia was upgraded during the 1950s into one of the nation's premier power pools.

As early as 1949, the operating group of PNJ had recognized that certain sec-

tions of the agreement required revisions. For one thing, the four General Public Utilities (GPU) operating companies in the Mid-Atlantic region were effective associates in the pool through interconnection agreements with PSE&G. For another, Baltimore Gas & Electric Co. and Potomac Electric Power Co. were pressing for membership in the pool.

The three partners in the PNJ system

had all undergone major postwar building programs. PP&L had added the Sunbury and Martins Creek Steam Electric Generating stations and was in the process of building Brunner Island on the Susquehanna. PSE&G was in the process of completing a similarly aggressive building project; Philadelphia Electric Co. capped off the first phase of its postwar building program with completion of Units One and Two of the 600-megawatt Eddystone Steam Electric Station in 1960. Eddystone's steam conditions of 5,000 psi and 1,200 degrees Fahrenheit with two reheats to 1,050 degrees Fahrenheit were the highest pressures ever attempted in a utility boiler installation.

The members of the pool had also dramatically upgraded their transmission networks in the late 1940s and 1950s. In 1953, GPU began the integration of its operating systems with the construction of 230,000-volt transmission from Humelstown to Middletown Junction to

South Reading to Hosensack, which created a tap on the line from Plymouth Meeting to Siegfried. In September 1954, Pennsylvania Water & Power Co. completed a 230,000-volt line from its Manor substation to MetEd's Middletown Junction substation.

All the activity on the PNJ system led to the first major change in the pool in nearly three decades. On Sept. 26, 1956, 29 years to the day after the formation of the pool, the operating group signed a five-party agreement that created the Pennsylvania-Jersey-Maryland (PJM) power pool. The PJM pool added Baltimore Gas & Electric Co. and the GPU system to the original three members of the pool and created a backbone 230,000-volt transmission network that criss-crossed the Mid-Atlantic states and provided members with the assurance that they could tap the immense bulk power supplies in the region.

On Sept. 26, 1956, 29 years to the day after the formation of the pool, the operating group signed a five-party agreement that created the Pennsylvania-New Jersey-Maryland (PJM) power pool.

Brunner Island.
(illustration by Brent Schaefer © 1995)

Randolph C. Ryder Jr. a 13-year-old PP&L shareowner, turned the first spadeful of dirt for the new Brunner Island plant in January 1958.

The Decision to Build Brunner Island

Even with the existence of the PJM transmission network, PP&L continued to struggle in its attempt to keep up with spiraling electric power demand in central and eastern Pennsylvania. With the completion of Sunbury and Martins Creek in the early to mid-1950s, the company had diversified its generating capacity geographically, providing ample power for the northern, western and eastern segments of its service territory.

Through the 1940s, the southern segment of the PP&L service territory was the most rural section on the system. The vast majority of the company's farm customers were located in the York, Lancaster and Harrisburg regions. But the postwar years brought a huge expansion to Harrisburg, the home of Pennsylvania's state government. Huge manufacturing facilities, like RCA's television tube factory outside Lancaster, brought thousands of new residents to the area.

PP&L was in negotiations to acquire Pennsylvania Water & Power Co. as early as 1954, but even with the acquisition of Holtwood and partial ownership of the Safe Harbor hydroelectric facilities, PP&L was predicting the need for additional generating capacity in the south in the late 1950s and early 1960s. For one thing, much of the Holtwood and Safe

In July 1954, about the same time that PP&L dedicated the first unit of its Martins Creek plant, crews started topographic surveys for a new power plant on the Susquehanna River, about 15 miles downstream from Harrisburg.

Harbor capacity was already under contract to wholesale customers. For another, planners expected to see continued sharp growth in the Lancaster-Harrisburg corridor.

In July 1954, about the same time that PP&L dedicated the first unit of its Martins Creek plant, crews started topographic surveys for a new power plant on the Susquehanna River, about 15 miles downstream from Harrisburg. The 766-acre site for PP&L's next power plant was located in East Manchester Township of York County, on the west bank of the river. Less than a mile upriver was Metropolitan Edison Co.'s York Haven hydroelectric station, the site of the first hydroelectric facility built on the river in 1895.

The initial two units at the Brunner Island station were the biggest yet planned for the PP&L system. Unit One was a 344,000-kilowatt turbine generator, planned for commercial operation in June 1961. Unit Two was even larger—397,000 kilowatts—and was planned for commercial operation in October 1965. Unit One alone was twice the generating capacity of the first two units at Martins Creek. Original cost for the first two Brunner Island units was also the largest PP&L had ever incurred: $47.7 million for Unit One and $34.7 million for Unit Two.

Groundbreaking for the first two units of the new power plant took place in January 1958. Randolph C. Ryder Jr. a 13-year-old PP&L shareowner, turned the first spadeful of dirt. Ryder's participation was symbolic of the company's commitment to meeting future generating needs in central and eastern Pennsylvania.

"He represents our customers of tomorrow and from all indications, his formal act here today, as big as this Brunner Island plant will be, symbolizes only the beginning of a great new electrical age," PP&L Chairman Chas. E. Oakes said at the groundbreaking ceremony. "For at this moment, we already look ahead to the need for power plant capacity that by 1970 will be double what we now have."

Like Martins Creek, Brunner Island

was designed as a semi-outdoor plant, primarily because of the necessity of getting the unit into commercial operation as soon as possible. Also like Martins Creek, Brunner Island was designed to burn Pennsylvania bituminous coal. Unlike Martins Creek, the new plant was designed to use the only cross-compound turbine-generator on the PP&L system. The cross-compound design incorporated two turbine-generators operating as one and fed from a common steam source. PP&L's Engineering Department noted that the new design "is more efficient and economical than the conventional design in units of this large size."

Construction on the first unit at Brunner Island proceeded on schedule through 1958 and 1959. However, in 1960, the story was different. In July, boiler makers at the Brunner Island construction site walked off the job in a dispute with boiler manufacturers. Ninety-eight days later, in early November, the boiler makers settled on a new contract and returned to work. PP&L announced that the early 1961 completion date for Brunner Island was being moved back to March or April.

The importance of getting Brunner Island into commercial operation was underscored by problems with company generating facilities late in 1960. In September, the 160,000-kilowatt Unit Two at Martins Creek was pulled out of service for repair of damage to the steam boiler. Crews worked around the clock to return the unit to service on December 18.

In November, Unit Two at Sunbury suffered a short circuit in the generator station. The 87,500-kilowatt unit experienced severe damage and had to be rewound on location. The unit

was out of service for more than 60 days at the end of the year, although there was one bright spot to the outage. The four-year inspection and overhaul of the turbine was moved up from April 1961 to coincide with the outage.

Annual Meeting in the Round

As it was, Unit One was all but completed by the April target date, although commercial operation didn't take place until June 1961. Along with a formal dedication—like the one at Martins Creek several years before—PP&L decided to unveil the new plant at the company's 1961 annual shareholders' meeting. Invitations went out in the late winter of 1961; shareholders in the Philadelphia area

The week before the 1961 annual shareholders meeting unveiling Brunner Island, the Soviets were making headlines for orbiting the earth. (*courtesy of the Morning Call*)

PP&L President Chas. E. Oakes (left) welcomes Pennsylvania Gov. David L. Lawrence to the official dedication ceremonies at Brunner Island Steam Electric Station in July 1961.

Pennsylvania Governor Lawrence addressed the crowd inside the 25,000-square-foot striped green and white tent. (*photo courtesy of the Lancaster Intelligencer Journal*)

could ride a special chartered train to Brunner Island.

Monday, April 17, 1961, dawned bright and sunny. The spring of 1961 had been wet and miserable in southeastern Pennsylvania, and company officials were concerned that inspection tours of the new Brunner Island station would be curtailed by the weather. But 24 hours before the shareowners were scheduled to arrive at the plant, the clouds lifted, the sun came out and the temperature began to rise into the 60s. Electric heaters installed in the 25,000-square-foot striped green and white meeting tent were run full blast the night before to dry out the moisture from more than two weeks of rain at the site.

More than 2,500 shareowners showed up for the annual meeting at Brunner Island, shattering the record of 1,500 people set at the annual meeting two years before. More than a few of the shareowners arrived on the train from Philadelphia with transistor radios glued to their ears. Late the week before, Yuri

The official dedication for Brunner Island Unit One took place on July 12, 1961. More than 1,100 guests turned out on a beautiful summer day.

Gagarin had circled the earth in the Soviet spacecraft *Vostok I*, becoming the first man ever to orbit the globe. Earlier that day, several thousand Cuban exiles had landed on a beach at Cuba's Bay of Pigs. Hourly radio news bulletins followed the first foreign policy crisis of John F. Kennedy's presidency.

At the conclusion of the meeting, which was held in the round, shareowners took a guided tour of the 300,000-kilowatt turbine-generator. Exhibits and explanatory signs were located along the route; some 25 specially designed displays and exhibits explained PP&L's business, from atomic power to electric home heating. More than 100 company employees participated in the meeting arrangements. Duties ran the gamut, the *PP&L Reporter* explained, "from parking cars to pouring coffee, from staffing the press room to explaining plant facilities and from stringing wires to greeting guests."

Once the shareowners departed, PP&L Construction Department and contractor crews began to prepare the big turbine-generator unit to go on line. But the foul weather that had plagued the construction crews since the previous fall dealt a final surprise to Brunner Island early in the second week of May.

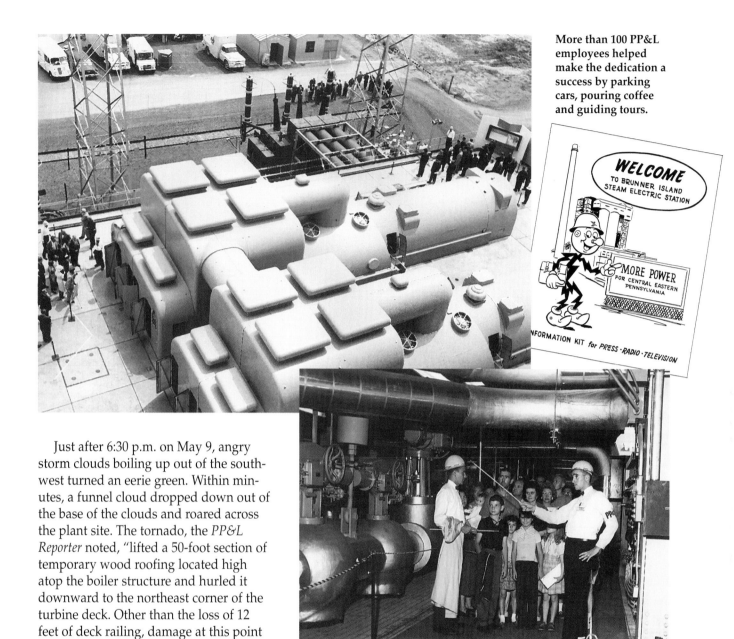

WELCOME TO BRUNNER ISLAND STEAM ELECTRIC STATION

MORE POWER FOR CENTRAL EASTERN PENNSYLVANIA

INFORMATION KIT for PRESS · RADIO · TELEVISION

Just after 6:30 p.m. on May 9, angry storm clouds boiling up out of the southwest turned an eerie green. Within minutes, a funnel cloud dropped down out of the base of the clouds and roared across the plant site. The tornado, the *PP&L Reporter* noted, "lifted a 50-foot section of temporary wood roofing located high atop the boiler structure and hurled it downward to the northeast corner of the turbine deck. Other than the loss of 12 feet of deck railing, damage at this point was light.

"However, a piece of roofing slammed into the 'C phase' portion of the service transformer at ground level, knocking out service to equipment and crews at work in the plant." Fortunately, damage was light. By the next evening, replacement parts had been installed and the service transformer was back in operation. During the outage, crews energized the plant's main transformer so that work could continue. All told, only about 12 hours were lost in the final preparation for start-up. On May 13, 1961, the first steam was admitted to the turbine-generator. Brunner Island was finally on line.

The Very Cornerstone...

With the addition of Unit One at Brunner Island, the first phase of PP&L's postwar construction program was essentially complete. In less than 15 years, PP&L had added more than one million kilowatts of coal-fired generating capacity with its Sunbury, Martins Creek and Brunner Island stations. The Penn Water acquisition added 285,000 kilowatts of coal-fired and hydroelectric generating capacity, while the addition of the Suburban Steam Electric Station and half of Stanton—both of which were part of the Scranton Electric Co. acquisition—gave PP&L the electric power supply it needed to meet the ever-increasing demand for electricity in central and eastern Pennsylvania.

The official dedication for Brunner Island Unit One took place on July 12, 1961. More than 1,100 guests turned out on a beautiful summer day. They heard Pennsylvania Gov. David L. Lawrence laud electric power development in the state as the "very cornerstone of our present and future progress."

Had Lawrence, the former mayor of Pittsburgh, known about the next generation of coal-fired steam electric stations—plants that would be built in western Pennsylvania's bituminous coal fields and that would transmit their power eastward by high-voltage transmission lines—he might have referred to electric power development as the "keystone" of our present and future progress.

The control room at Brunner Island in 1961.

The 1958 Storm

The winter of 1958 was a season to remember. In late February, PP&L's service territory was buried under as much as 29 inches of snow. Drifts of up to 25 feet in the Poconos closed roads and made travel all but impossible across the northern half of the state. But the snow that fell in the February storm was dry and granular. Only 300 PP&L customers lost power during the storm.

That wasn't the case just one month later. A fast-moving storm swirling northeastward out of Virginia blanketed Pennsylvania, New Jersey, Long Island and Massachusetts with as much as 38 inches of wet, heavy snow. More than 1.6 million electrical customers in the Mid-Atlantic states found themselves without power for up to a week.

The first flakes of snow began falling across the Lehigh, Lancaster, Harrisburg and Central divisions late in the afternoon of Wednesday, March 19. The temperature hovered at the freezing mark, and a layer of ice and heavy snow began to accumulate on company transmission and distribution lines. By early Thursday morning, snow and ice up to 14 inches thick covered conductors across the service territory.

"Damage to company lines in Lancaster County was at an all-time high," PP&L reported in the wake of the storm. "Several steel towers on the 66,000- and 110,000-volt circuits out of Holtwood and 220,000-volt circuits on the river crossing at Safe Harbor collapsed in

PP&L's Holtwood plant suffered unbelievable damage to what were considered sturdy steel towers.

ungraceful heaps. Lines in several tight little sections of Lancaster County were in shambles.

"For a mile, two miles, and sometimes three miles in a row, every pole was in some way damaged... snapped through, split, canted, or cross-arms splintered, or dangling or down completely. Span after span of wire lay on the ground. Clinging, leaden weight had humbled sections of sturdy line that only a few years back had weathered a hurricane practically undamaged."

The first trouble calls came into PP&L early Thursday morning. Before the storm was over, more than 205,000 PP&L customers were without power at one time or another. As it had done in the New Year's Day storm 11 years before, PP&L marshalled its forces to get power back to customers. Line and construction crews from trouble-free areas, as well as outside contractor crews, were rushed in to help support the forces already at work.

"First steps were those which

These helicopters helped find trouble spots and airlift line crews and equipment to restore service in remote areas of PP&L's service territory.

would restore either super-critical locations such as hospitals or the greatest number of customers in the shortest time," the company reported. "This was followed by picking up the outlying, the unreported and the tight little pockets of extra-special trouble."

One technological innovation that helped line crews restore service was the use of helicopters. PP&L contracted for a two-seat helicopter from Miller Aviation in Pittsburgh to fly over the affected areas and help locate trouble spots. A U.S. Army helicopter, called into service under the state's special emergency decree, flew in from Fort Eustis. The big helicopter proved its worth when it airlifted a PP&L crew and a half-ton of equipment into an isolated valley in the Lehigh division, where the crew restored service to a 66,000-volt transmission line.

By midnight Thursday, PP&L's quick response had reduced customer outages to half what they had been

A total of 2,500 company employees had served on storm duty.

early in the afternoon. The vast majority of the 105,000 customers still out of power had it restored by Monday. It took close to a week to restore the final 2,200 customers and 170 miles of line, all in Lancaster County.

A total of 2,500 company employees had served on storm duty. A task force of more than 150 employees remained on duty for a week in the Route 322 area below Ephrata and in the Holtwood section of Lancaster County. "Looking up against the graying mid-week evening sky, it seemed every pole came equipped with a busy lineman," PP&L wrote in a special storm edition of the *PP&L Reporter*.

"The company's storm fighters did a magnificent job. The hours were endless. The work grueling. The task herculean. But the morale was superb and the accomplishments amazing in their rapidity."

A Winter Peaker in a Summer Pool

By 1964,
12 buildings
qualified for
PP&L's All-
Electric Building
Award.

This crowd
warms up under
an outside
electric space
heater in the
mid-1960s.

Pennsylvania Power & Light Co. entered the 1960s with adequate generating capacity and plans to add more in the years ahead. The company enjoyed strong residential, commercial and industrial growth, thanks to continued strength in the postwar Pennsylvania economy.

But beyond economic growth, PP&L controlled its own destiny in the field of load growth. Beginning in 1960, the company began an aggressive marketing campaign designed to

PROOF—
ELECTRIC
HEATING
COSTS
ARE LOW

MR. and MRS. DONALD M. STONER, N.7th Street, Millintown.

only $142.02

Now everyone can enjoy flameless quality-heating.

**The Joy of Total Electric Living
Starts with Electric Home Heating**

The full enjoyment of any home comes only when you cease to be a slave to it. In the total electric home, electric servants not only take over back-breaking, tedious chores but eliminate such tasks to begin with.

Take electric home heating for example. Since electric heat is flameless, it's as clean as electric light. There's nothing to burn to create soot and grime, and so walls and furnishings stay brighter longer.

Electric home heating offers COMFORT-PLUS even on the coldest, windiest days. You get gentle warmth

all over . . . and with resistance types of heat you can enjoy room-by-room control.

Best of all, PP&L's special low rate makes electric heating a bigger bargain than ever . . . now it's as low as 1.35¢ per kilowatt-hour!

More than 4,000 PP&L customers . . . in new homes, older homes, mobile homes and apartments . . . are already enjoying FLAMELESS electric home heating. Why not you, too? See your Recommended Reddy Kilowatt Electric Home Heating Dealer or call PP&L today!

add tens of thousands of electric resistance heating customers during the decade. Unlike most electric utilities during the period, PP&L pegged its growth to electric heating. Utilities all across the U.S. in the 1960s geared their residential and commercial growth to air-conditioning; consequently, most of the utilities in the country gravitated toward a summer peak during the 1960s. PP&L established itself as a winter peaker after 1965, a phenomenon that has continued for 30 years.

Following a special study in the late 1950s, PP&L decided in late 1959 to aggressively promote electric heating for homes. "This decision is now being announced to residential field sales personnel and to potential company allies," PP&L announced on Dec. 7, 1959, "including builders, architects, equipment manufacturers and distributors, electrical contractors and electric home heating dealers."

In 1961, when PP&L began its concerted effort to sell electric heat to its customers, there were slightly more than 1,000 electric home heating customers on the company's system. By 1964, that number had increased six-fold and it doubled to nearly 14,000 electric home heating customers by early 1967. More importantly, new construction in the PP&L service territory was increasingly built with electric heating. In 1962, only nine percent of new dwelling units were heated electrically. Five years later, the number of new dwelling units with electric heat had more than quadrupled, to 38.2 percent.

PP&L sold its electric heat program under the slogan "flameless electric heating." The utility promised "draft-free comfort, clean as electric light, minimum attention needed and maximum flexibility." Part of that flexibility involved the multitude of installations available to customers. In the 1960s, the company sold electric home heating through ceiling cables, wall panels and baseboard units.

"Electric home heating is so wonderful because it gives you the comfort you want without many of the problems of other heating systems," a 1961 brochure explained. "And being *flameless,* electric heat is unmatched for cleanliness, safety and modernity. It is steady, even heat. It can be controlled separately in each room to meet family living habits…78 degrees in the baby's room, 65 degrees in your bedroom, 72 degrees in the living room, for instance. There are no furnace, ducts, pipes, radiators or chimneys, thus saving valuable space for better living."

PP&L residential customers raved about the comfort of electric heat. "It was the most comfortable winter we've ever had—absolutely," wrote Mr. C.L. Mentzer of Valley View, Pa., in 1961. "Electric home heating lets us use all of our basement and keeps our home cleaner," wrote Joseph M. Ludlum of Paxtang, while Mrs. Richard R. Branda of Bethlehem was impressed with the fact that her family could "keep temperatures at a lower level and still be comfortable."

Electric heating was also particularly adaptable to commercial applications. In 1964, Allentown opened its new city hall and municipal building. The heart of the electric heating system for the 107,000-square-foot structure was two 175-ton electric heat pumps that provided the heating and cooling necessary to operate the building. "The main building's five floors, as well as the adjoining three-story police headquarters, benefit from the well-designed electric heating and lighting systems," PP&L explained in a 1964 brochure, "which, taken together, provide a high comfort level, utilizing all heat available."

As the 1960s progressed, PP&L marketing efforts paid off with sharply increased commercial electric heating installations. Offices, schools, churches, restaurants, stores and motels across the service territory shifted to electric heat from PP&L. In the late 1960s, dozens of commercial establishments, including the Pennridge Medical Arts Building in Sellersville, the Wallenpaupack Joint High School in Hawley, Wheeler's Diner in Allentown, Woolworth's in Shenandoah, the Landis Valley Motor Inn in Lancaster and Tabernacle Baptist Church in Williamsport all chose to build with electric heat.

Commercial installations had even more electric heat options than residential customers. Besides ceiling cable, wall units and baseboard heaters, commercial customers were able to avail themselves of in-duct heaters, radiant units, electric furnaces, unit ventilators, heat pumps and hot water units. PP&L's marketing department sold the reliability of "year-round climate control."

During 1963, the Edison Electric Institute established the All-Electric Building Award. The award was designed to appropriately recognize industrial and commercial buildings used for manufacturing, processing, retail operations, warehousing and institutional buildings, schools and churches in which electricity

was the only service used for heating, cooling, lighting and other basic functions. PP&L was quick to adopt the program for its service area, and within a year, 12 buildings in the area had qualified for the new award.

In 1962, only nine percent of new dwelling units were heated electrically. Five years later, the number of new dwelling units with electric heat had more than quadrupled, to 38.2 percent.

The 1967 Sales Marketing Meeting at the George Washington Motor Lodge in Allentown. Vice President Emmet R. Molloy (r) announced Robert J. Galgon's sales reward for a job well done.

The promotion of flameless electric heat was a success for PP&L. Schools, offices and others were switching to electric heat and being awarded for their efforts with the All-Electric Building Award as shown above being presented to Lancaster's Duke Convalescent Residence. *circa 1960s*

Rates and Finances

One of the keys to PP&L's success in selling electric home and commercial heating during the 1960s was economy of scale. As the company brought new, efficient coal-fired power plants on line, it was able to reduce rates to its customers. As more customers took advantage of those low rates and shifted to electric heat, demand went up and Wall Street put a premium on the company's stock, allowing PP&L to qualify for lower interest rates the next time it had to go to the markets to borrow money to build new power plants.

In late June 1961, PP&L went to the Pennsylvania Public Utility Commission with a new tariff designed to create a better all-round climate for promoting the advantages and benefits of electric power. "A principal feature of the tariff," the company said in its filing application, "is that it will make available, for the first time, a separate and more attractive rate for residential customers who use electric energy as the exclusive source of home heating in addition to cooking and water heating." The new tariff offered electric home heating at a rate of 1.65 cents per kwh, compared with a rate of 1.8 cents to two cents per kwh under the company's then-current residential rate schedule.

PP&L's residential electric heating rate stayed at 1.65 cents per kilowatt-hour for less than nine months. In February, the company filed new tariffs with the Commission, effectively lowering the heating rate to 1.5 cents per kilowatt-hour. "The company's new rate for the total electric home is next to the lowest in the entire state," the company told employees in February 1962. "Pennsylvania Electric Co.'s rate, which is the lowest, is only about seven dollars a year less for a typical installation."

Rates kept going down through the mid-1960s, helped immeasurably by the commercial operation of larger, more efficient generating units at Martins Creek and Brunner Island. In May 1963, the company went back to the PUC, this time with a $3 million residential rate decrease. "There are some vitally important reasons for the recent series of rate cuts," the *PP&L Reporter* explained. "For one, the company fully believes that the flameless electric way is the best way for our customers. At the same time, it is quite evident that the type of energy the customer uses for heating his home determines what he chooses for his other energy needs." Spaceheating under the new tariff dropped to 1.35 cents per kwh.

In the four years between 1961 and 1965, PP&L reduced rates seven separate times. The total rate reductions saved customers $13.3 million, about equally split between industrial, residential and commercial customers. By 1965, the residential spaceheating rate had been reduced to a penny per kwh, a little more than half the residential rate schedule in 1959, just six years before.

"It is worth mentioning that during the period when these rate reductions were being made, the company has continued to earn a fair rate of return on invested capital," Jack Busby told the 18th annual convention of the Financial Analyst's Federation in Philadelphia in May 1965. "Further rate reductions should not change this pattern.

"It is also worth mentioning that while some part of these depreciation and rate changes may be attributed to tax savings, they have been mainly attributable to productivity gains of the business—derived from better growth and more efficient use of capital and more efficient operating practices."

Busby promised the financial analysts "further rate reductions in 1966 and following years within a tentative goal which calls for $20-$22 million of aggregate rate reductions in the 1961-1970 period." Busby identified two principal reasons for the major emphasis on rate reductions. "We deemed it unhealthy and undesirable for the company to have rates which were above national average levels," he explained. "Lower rates were absolutely essential if we were to have better growth in the sale of electricity in the important competitive markets. Our guiding theme has been to do a better job of penetrating the market available to us because we knew we could not rely on riding the wave of the population explosion."

Busby's emphasis on marketing struck a chord with the investment community. By the mid- to late-1960s, Wall Street was discovering PP&L. An early 1966 research report by Carl M. Loeb, Rhoades & Co., a New York brokerage house, noted that PP&L's common stock was selling at $35 a share, nearly 17 times the estimated 1966 earnings and paying a four percent yield on the dividend of $1.44.

Loeb, Rhoades & Co. went on to say that it considered "the shares attractive in the utility group." The company also gave favorable ratings to the industrial potential in PP&L's service territory, citing RCA's decision to build a 300,000-square-foot plant to manufacture color television tubes near Scranton. PP&L's service territory had recorded employment gains of more than eight percent, the report noted, and the region's unemployment rate of five percent was below the U.S. average of 5.2 percent.

In the summer of 1968, G.H. Walker & Co., another New York investment banking firm, was even higher on the stock. The price by that time had fallen to $29 a share in the wake of inflationary pressures and the nation's economic difficulties in trying to carry on the Vietnam War without shifting to a wartime economy.

"In recent years," the G.H. Walker & Co. report pointed out, "this company has achieved a remarkable transformation in that its rate of load growth is now one of the fastest in the Northeast after having been one of the slowest during the fifties. This change, partly brought about by the improved economic environment of the service area, was mainly due to an accelerated rate of growth in usage per customer stemming from a series of voluntary, promotional rate reductions made in the early sixties."

In the four years between 1961 and 1965, PP&L reduced rates seven separate times.

One of the things that had scared investors away from PP&L common stock in the late 1950s and early 1960s was the utility's dependence upon industrial sales to the state's rapidly declining anthracite mining industry. By 1968, that was no longer the case, as pointed out by *Financial World Magazine* in its August 28 issue.

"Cities like Scranton conjure up vistas of anthracite mining, and thus it's important to bear in mind that PP&L has successfully weathered the impact of the decline in the hard coal industry," the editors noted in their recommendation of the utility's stock. "As a matter of fact, only 2 percent of the utility's total industrial kilowatt-hour sales was attributable to

Keystone Steam Electric Station—located in western Pennsylvania—was designed as a mine-mouth plant to send electric power back to eastern Pennsylvania and New Jersey as Gifford Pinchot had envisioned 40 years before with the Giant Power program. *circa 1968*

anthracite mining last year, as against 33 percent in 1950.

"Declining sales to the hard coal miners have been more than offset by sales to new industries which have located in system territory. In this connection, it should be noted that the service area is favored by a much greater than average number of interstate and limited access highways, which permits overnight shipping to most metropolitan centers in the Northeast."

The Keystone Cemented in Place

In its August 1968 report, G.H. Walker & Co. noted that "between now and 1970, the company will spend $335 million on construction, with probably an additional $200 million in 1971 and 1972." Much of that construction expenditure was for big new additions to Martins Creek and Brunner Island, but the company was also

involved in a joint venture construction project in western Pennsylvania.

The Keystone Project was an initial 900,000-kilowatt capacity coal-fired power plant located along the Chestnut Ridge, 10 miles west of Indiana in western Pennsylvania's Armstrong County. Jointly owned by Atlantic City Electric, Delmarva Power & Light, Jersey Central Power & Light, Baltimore Gas & Electric Co., PSE&G, Philadelphia Electric Co. and PP&L, the $190 million project was slated for start-up in 1967, with a second similar unit scheduled to come on line one year later.

Like the Giant Power program envisioned by Gifford Pinchot 40 years before, Keystone was designed as a mine-mouth plant. Electric power would be transmitted back to eastern Pennsylvania and New Jersey by more than 600 miles of high-voltage transmission lines. Parallel 500,000-volt circuits ran 225 miles east from Keystone to PP&L's service territory near Philadelphia, where the power was fed into the interconnections of the New Jersey and Maryland utilities in the consortium.

"A key factor in making the big plant and long lines practicable was development of an integrated program under which PJM companies are contracting to take specified amounts of the plant's output," the *Edison Electric Institute Bulletin* reported at the project's announcement in late 1962. "Keystone is expected to consume over 160 million tons of Pennsylvania bituminous coal over its life, and use as much as 4.7 million tons annually through at least the first 10 years of operation."

Keystone was part of a much larger mine-mouth program, which would tap the immense bituminous coal reserves of western Pennsylvania in the late 1960s and early 1970s. At the same time that PP&L and its PJM partners announced construction of the Keystone station, Allegheny Power System announced its intention to build a 500,000-kilowatt steam electric station on the Monongahela River near Morgantown, W.Va. A second, even larger unit was scheduled for con-

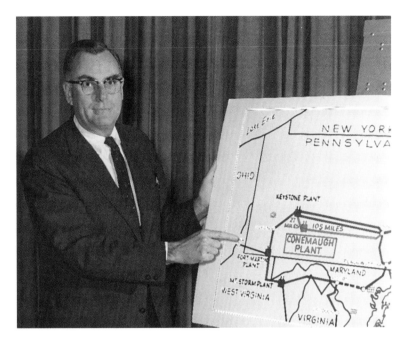

PP&L President Jack Busby points out the strong power grid that would be created when both the Keystone and Conemaugh plants went on line and interconnected with other major utility plants. *circa 1968*

struction in Huff County, about 11 miles west of Johnstown.

That second unit, which would become known as Conemaugh Station, broke ground in 1966. The partners in what would eventually become two 900,000-kilowatt units included all the original partners in Keystone, with the addition of UGI Corp. and Potomac Electric Power Co., both new members of PJM in the late 1950s and early 1960s.

Keystone and Conemaugh marked a watershed in the electric power development of Pennsylvania and the Mid-Atlantic region. Power plant economics changed dramatically in the years after 1965. Inflation, sharply higher interest rates and America's over-dependence upon foreign oil all conspired to drive construction costs up and consumption down during the 1970s. Not only that, PP&L and America's electric utilities had to contend with a massive failure of the nation's electric power transmission grid.

> *Jointly owned by Atlantic City Electric, Delmarva Power & Light, Jersey Central Power & Light, Baltimore Gas & Electric Co., PSE&G, Philadelphia Electric Co. and PP&L, the $190 million project was slated for start-up in 1967, with a second similar unit scheduled to come on line one year later.*

Coal-o-Watts

PP&L called its shift to Pennsylvania bituminous coal as a generating fuel "coal-o-watts." The shift, which took place during the 1960s, lessened PP&L's dependence upon the declining production from the state's anthracite fields. But the shift to bituminous coal had one big drawback: the bituminous fields were a long way from the PP&L power plants.

At Sunbury—the baseload plant which went on line in the late 1940s and early 1950s—anthracite coal could be delivered from the nearby fields by truck. Fuel costs were kept low by this efficient delivery system. But Martins Creek and Brunner Island—the baseload plants which went into commercial operation during the 1960s—were much too far from the bituminous fields in the western part of the state to deliver coal by truck.

Rail hauls of up to 250 miles one way were necessary to feed the big boilers of Martins Creek and Brunner Island, and later, Montour plant. The solution was a unit train system.

Unit coal trains had been pioneered by the Southern Co. in the late 1950s, and they offered the option of delivering coal in a dedicated trainload from the mine to the power plant. Since there were no intermediate stops or handling of the coal cars, the railroads quickly developed cut-

rate unit train tariffs for their utility customers.

In 1963, PP&L signed an agreement with the Pennsylvania Railroad for unit train coal delivery from western Pennsylvania to Martins Creek and Brunner Island. "The integral train offers several opportunities to reduce shipping costs," explained Philip W. Siekman, general services vice president, "the greatest being in speeding up the 'turn-around,' where empty cars are returned to their original shipping point in four or five days as compared with the former 14-30 days."

Siekman estimated that the unit train concept would save the utility as much as 30 percent of its annual $20 million fuel shipment costs. The 100-car unit trains were unique in their Pennsylvania roots. The cars were built for PP&L by the Bethlehem Steel Co. and were pulled by locomotives running over Pennsylvania Railroad tracks. Each train hauled in excess of 7,000 tons per trip, and each of the two 100-car trains was scheduled to haul one million tons of coal per year.

PP&L inaugurated the service on June 18, 1964, when the first train pulled into the Brunner Island plant with a load of coal from the Tunnelton Mine in Indiana County. H. Beecher Charmbury, the state's secretary of mining, cited the unit train as "a significant first by three outstanding

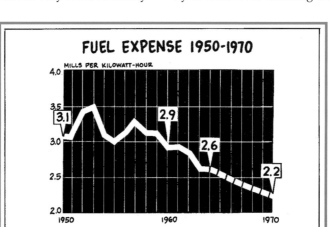

These graphs from Jack Busby's 1965 presentation to the Financial Analysts Federation show the direction PP&L saw itself going over the next five years from where it came the previous 20 years.

Pennsylvania companies—PP&L, the Pennsylvania Railroad Co. and Bethlehem Steel Co. Such cooperation and innovation exemplify the progressive industrial spirit which typifies the new Pennsylvania."

W. Parker Stuart, Pennsylvania Railroad Co.'s coal traffic manager, called PP&L's system "the first true unit train because it is the first where the cars are owned by the customer and are kept together as a unit to be shuttled back and forth by the railroad."

Savings to PP&L were immediate and significant. The 74 cars built by Bethlehem Steel Co. had cost $1 million, but PP&L's costs of operating the unit train were as much as $1.80 a ton less than conventional transportation. In little more than six months, PP&L had recouped the cost of its investment in the coal cars.

In the fall of 1965, PP&L took delivery of an additional 136 coal cars from Bethlehem Steel Co. The new cars allowed the company to increase its per-trip load from 7,000 tons to 10,000 tons. The new cars also allowed

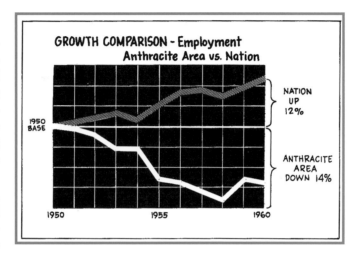

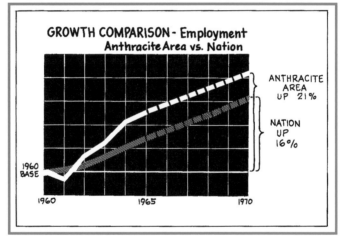

PP&L to add a second unit train to its fleet. To prepare Brunner Island plant for handling the unit trains, the company installed a new $700,000 rotary car dumper at the big baseload plant on the Susquehanna River.

The unit train concept helped PP&L get a handle on coal transportation costs that were getting out of control in the early 1960s. "We can also say that we are successfully dealing with the difficult problem of converting from our former fuel supply of nearby anthracite to comparatively remote bituminous fuel," Jack Busby told the 18th annual convention of the Financial Analysts Federation in Philadelphia in May 1965. "Our procurement arrangements, coupled with delivery by unit trains, are enabling us to make this wholesale transition while holding the cost of delivered fuel pretty close to 22 cents per million Btu. When the heat rate gains are taken into account, substantial savings in fuel expense are being realized."

The Computer Era Begins

PP&L's new computer center in 1962.

The 1964 inauguration of unit coal train service to Brunner Island and Martins Creek was only one of a number of cost containment measures that came to fruition in the 1960s. The other was the increasing computerization of PP&L operations.

PP&L had switched to a revolutionary punchcard billing system in 1944, while war still raged in Europe and the Pacific. That first system was the forerunner of the computer. It was big, bulky and slow, but it began slowly to eliminate the need for hand-sorting of the hundreds of thousands of monthly bills that were mailed to customers.

The computer had gotten its start in World War II as a machine capable of breaking enemy codes. The punchcard processor took over other repetitive types of operations during the 1950s, including customer accounting, payroll and property records. PP&L engineers were familiar with the concept of computers, but the first true computers didn't arrive on the scene until late in the 1950s. Until that time, transmission and power plant planning engineers took the train up to Schenectady, N.Y., where they used General Electric's Network Analyzer, working out transmission line and synchronization problems in week-long sessions.

"In the late 1950s, we obtained computers that were useful not only for PP&L's business applications, but could perform vital company engineering calculations as well," Floyd F. Beisel of the Computer Department wrote in 1968. "So, following the business world's established pattern, we began developing nonbusiness applications for the system being developed. The computer capability and lack of randomly accessible storage precluded the current interdepartmental task force approach that results in the ultimate integrated systems."

Those first real computers in the 1960s were limited in their amount of memory and took up most of the seventh floor of the company's General Office Tower in Allentown. When the company's computer center opened late in 1960, its first order of business was transferring the company's 733,000 customer billing accounts from the old postcard-punchcard system to computerized envelope billing.

The new computer center was the pride and joy of the newly established Computer Department. The main components of the ultra-modern center in 1962 consisted of an IBM 1418 Optical Scanner, four IBM 1401 satellite computers and an IBM 7070 mainframe computer.

The roomful of equipment in the computer center was state-of-the-art technology for 1961. The IBM 1418 Optical Scanner was the first one installed anywhere by IBM, and it could read up to 400 documents a minute. The IBM 7070 and the four satellite computers could perform 30 simultaneous equations involving up to 54,000 multiplications and additions every 19 seconds. The printer could turn out what was then the astonishing figure of 600 lines of type in one minute.

It was little wonder that PP&L's 1962 emblem promised "efficient public service."

34

Blackout

20 Million in U.S., Canada Without Electricity As Massive Power Failure Hits Northeast

Mild Attack Possible
Eisenhower Resting, Chest Pains Probed

Grid System Disrupted Near Niagara
Communications, Traffic Snarled

N.Y. at a Grotesque Halt

850,000 Trapped in Subways

Prison Riot   Utility Experts 'Pretty Well Agreed'

U.S. Paratroopers Pull Out of Zone D

The blackout was a crisis like no other for the utility industry. The Allentown *Morning Call's* Nov. 10, 1965, headline said it all in a nutshell. *courtesy of the* **Morning Call**

In the early evening of Tuesday, Nov. 9, 1965, Ray Erickson was returning to New York from a utility meeting in Cleveland. As the Convair 880 banked over Long Island for its final descent into La Guardia, the land below suddenly went dark. The glow from the lights of Manhattan, visible 30 miles out to sea, was gone. Everything below was an eerie black, punctuated only by the occasional beam of a car's headlights.

Erickson, then a manager in the Corporate Communications Department at Central Hudson Gas & Electric, remembered looking out the window of the plane and thinking that World War III must have started.

It hadn't. But New York City and much of the northeastern U.S. was experiencing a massive power failure unprecedented in the nation's history. Erickson's plane was diverted south to Baltimore. He was just one of the 30 million people whose lives were disrupted by the worst power failure in the nation's history.

Newsweek called it "the most colossal power failure in history." At just after 5:16 p.m. that afternoon, a backup protective relay on a 230,000-volt transmission line connecting Ontario Hydro's Adam Beck plant on the Niagara River with metropolitan Toronto opened up. The line disconnected from the Ontario Hydro system, and like the water at nearby Niagara Falls, the electricity flowed outward and sought its own level. In the way was a big generating station owned and operated by the Power Authority of the State of New York on the U.S. side of the international boundary. Within seconds, electric

Engineers at Consolidated Edison, the big electric utility serving New York City, had momentary hopes of averting the crisis, at least for the metropolitan New York area. They had minutes to make the choice between disconnecting Consolidated Edison from the transmission grid and trying to meet the sudden cascading demand coming down from Canada. They elected to try the latter. It didn't work.

Between 5:24 and 5:28 p.m., the New York metropolitan area went dark. In 12 minute's time, most of the states of New York, Connecticut, Rhode Island, Massachusetts, Vermont and New Hampshire, along with much of the province of Ontario, were without power.

In New York City alone, more than 800,000 commuters were stranded on 630 subway trains at the peak of the evening rush hour. Metropolitan Transit crews led groups of passengers out of the underground subway tunnels, lighting the way with flashlights. Above ground, rush-hour traffic from New York north to Boston was snarled, as traffic lights winked out.

Paul Schock had just returned to his room on the 14th floor of the Americana Hotel when the blackout hit. Schock, a PP&L advertising representative, was in Manhattan to attend an American Management Association seminar. After walking down 14 dark flights of stairs to the lobby, he and other guests managed to get sandwiches prepared by candlelight in the hotel's kitchen. Schock confessed himself "just as surprised as anyone else that something like this could happen."

> *In 12 minute's time, most of the states of New York, Connecticut, Rhode Island, Massachusetts, Vermont and New Hampshire, along with much of the province of Ontario, were without power.*

power from the 3,200-megawatt Adam Beck and PASNY generating stations was out of phase with the rest of the interconnected network in Canada and the U.S.

Transmission engineers called the resulting phenomenon "cascading," as the thousands of megawatts of runaway electric power overwhelmed transmission lines from Canada's Georgian Bay to the Atlantic Ocean. At 5:17 p.m., Buffalo and Rochester were out. One minute later, the lights in Boston went down.

The Aftermath

The vast majority of the 30 million victims of the Northeast Blackout had power restored by midnight, and only a handful of residents of the area were without power the morning of Wednesday, November 10. The Federal Power Commission had ruled out sabotage within hours of the disruption. But that didn't mean society wasn't looking for someone to blame.

PP&L was barely affected by the blackout. Less than 5,000 of PJM's six million customers lost power during the blackout; all were located on the Pennsylvania-New York border. "Service was restored to most of them within minutes," PJM reported to FPC Chairman Joseph Swidler the week following the blackout. "The longest interruption of any PJM customer was one hour and 14 minutes. No major problems were encountered in the restoration of service to these customers."

Still, for PP&L and the rest of the electric utility industry, the Northeast Blackout had been an uncomfortable and highly visible reminder that no technology was absolutely foolproof. Since the creation of the modern utility industry in the 1920s, electric power engineers and executives had prided themselves on system reliability. Back in the 1920s, the holding companies had stressed reliability when they attempted to sell small-town utilities on the benefits of hooking up to the highline.

Like most utilities, PP&L had developed emergency procedures to restore power in the wake of nat–ural disasters. The 1936 floods on the Susquehanna River, the 1947 ice storm and the 1958 blizzard had all tested PP&L's ability to restore service in trying circumstances; and PP&L had come through the crises with flying colors.

But this was different. This was a massive power failure in clear weather that disrupted the lives of millions of people. The venerable *New York Times* spoke for millions of Americans when it editorialized on the scope of the problem the second morning following the blackout. "After Tuesday's failure, the utilities are on trial," *The Times* pointed out. "They must give a complete account of what went wrong. And they must see to it that the public will never again be faced with the helplessness that comes from a total failure of power."

America's electric utility industry geared up to identify the problem and fix

it. Jack Busby, PP&L's president, was named by FPC Chairman Joseph C. Swidler to the Commission's Advisory Committee on Bulk Power Supply, and started a series of meetings that would consume much of his time through the rest of 1965 and most of 1966. Busby and PP&L also worked closely with the

SPECIAL BULLETIN

WASHINGTON, D.C., JUNE 8 -- I AM IN WASHINGTON ATTENDING THE HEARINGS BY THE FEDERAL POWER COMMISSION ON THE MONDAY, JUNE 5, BLACKOUT. I MAY BE REQUIRED TO STAY THROUGH TOMORROW. NONETHELESS, I DID WANT EVERYBODY BACK HOME IN THE COMPANY TO KNOW HOW MUCH MANAGEMENT APPRECIATES THE JOB BEING DONE BY EVERYONE IN PP&L. ALL OF US ARE THRILLED ALSO WITH THE CONTINUING EFFORTS IN THE SUSQUEHANNA DIVISION WHERE DAMAGE TO UNITS AT THE SUNBURY PLANT IS CONTINUING TO KEEP THAT AREA IN VERY CRITICAL SHORT SUPPLY. ALL TOLD, A MAGNIFICENT JOB HAS BEEN ACCOMPLISHED. MUCH WORK STILL REMAINS TO BE DONE IN ANALYZING WHAT HAPPENED AND WHY -- AND MOST IMPORTANT, HOW TO PREVENT IT FROM EVER HAPPENING AGAIN. THIS LAST POINT IS OUR REAL RESPONSIBILITY -- AND WE IN PP&L ARE GOING TO MEET THAT RESPONSIBILITY.

SINCERELY,

JACK K. BUSBY

State Council of Civil Defense in Harrisburg to integrate service restoration planning with the state and other Pennsylvania electric utilities.

In December 1965, the FPC submitted its initial report on the outage to President Lyndon Johnson. The 101-page report blamed an incorrect setting of a relay at the Adam Beck plant near Niagara Falls for the blackout. W. Ross Strike, chairman of the Ontario Hydro-electric Commission, accepted the blame for the outage in a statement issued in Toronto.

"There can be no absolute assurances that outages of the November 9 magnitude will not recur," the report concluded. "On the other hand, there is no reason why operating equipment and techniques cannot be improved to the point where

Just when they thought everything was under control, another blackout. This time it affected about two-thirds of PP&L's customers. Jack Busby, PP&L's president, lauded employees for their efforts in restoring service and went on to assign three specialists to work on an exhaustive study of the problem.

After the 1965 blackout, Jack Busby was named to the Federal Power Commission's Advisory Committee on Bulk Power Supply. By December of that year, the commission submitted its 101-page report on the outage to President Lyndon Johnson.

For the second time in 19 months, the densely populated East Coast of the United States had suffered a catastrophic power failure.

the likelihood of recurrence would be so remote that it would not constitute a major worry to either the industry or the public. We believe the many steps already taken by the utilities on their own initiative together with implementation of our recommendation for immediate and long-term measures can achieve that goal."

An interim FPC report in November 1966, a year after the blackout, recognized Busby's group for the work they had done in investigating computerization of system security. "We anticipate many further opportunities for using computers in power system control," the Commission noted in its November 1966 interim report, "including the prompt indication of specific actions to be taken to avoid exceeding stable and safe operating limits of generating and transmission facilities."

One utility recommendation that did come out of the November 9 blackout was the 1968 creation of the North American Electric Reliability Council (NERC). In the 1970s, NERC assumed responsibility for development and maintenance of national standards for interconnected transmission systems, a function that in the past had been performed by regional groups like the North American Power Systems Interconnection Committee. As the oldest power pool on the North American continent, PJM was a

charter member of and prime mover behind NERC.

For its part, PP&L sharpened its response to storm-related outages. On Friday, March 18, 1966, the temperature was a sunny 68 degrees in Allentown. On the 14th floor of the General Office Tower, in the company's emergency control room, operators coped with a three-day snow, ice and windstorm. It was all a drill with simulated conditions, and it was conducted jointly with operators from Philadelphia Electric Co., West Penn Power and New York State Electric & Gas Co.

"Being prepared is a watchword at PP&L, and because of the nature of our business, the company must be prepared to cope with any and all emergencies—snowstorms, real or imaginary, may arise at any time," the *PP&L Reporter* noted in its coverage of the drill. Less than 15 months later, on another sunny spring day, the drill became real for PP&L and PJM.

Another Jolt for the Utilities

Shortly after 10 a.m. on Monday, June 5, 1967, it happened again. This time, runaway power cascaded across the Mid-Atlantic region, interrupting a large portion of PJM. Some 13 million customers in Pennsylvania, New Jersey and Maryland were without power for varying periods during that day; about two-thirds of PP&L's customers were affected by the outage.

Only the fact that Israeli armored forces were locked in combat with the Egyptian Army in the Sinai Desert kept the PJM outage from becoming national front-page news. As it was, President Lyndon Johnson must have felt himself star-crossed. For the second time in 19 months, the densely populated East Coast of the United States had suffered a catastrophic power failure.

Johnson, who as a young congressman had taken pride in bringing a rural electric cooperative to his district in Texas, sent a strong message to the electric utility industry. "A nation which is dependent on an uninterrupted flow of electric power cannot tolerate area-wide blackouts," Johnson said in his June 6 statement to the nation. Not even the deepening crisis in the Middle East could mask the president's concerns about the reliability of the nation's bulk power supply.

This time it was Pennsylvania Power & Light Co. at the eye of the storm. During the 1965 blackout, PP&L had enjoyed the luxury of being a concerned bystander. In the June 1967 blackout, the Allentown utility suffered a severe outage which affected more than 565,000 customers.

The troubles were traced to the opening of Philadelphia Electric Co.'s 230,000-volt transmission line between Nottingham and Plymouth Meeting. The line was transmitting power from Conowingo, Peach Bottom and the yet-to-be-completed Muddy Run pumped storage facility on the Susquehanna. The 230,000-volt line overloaded, overheated, sagged into a distribution line and arced over. Automatic protection devices up and down the line tripped, and within minutes, the Philadelphia Electric Co. system began to shut down. The collapse of the Philadelphia Electric Co. system sent power cascading into the PJM interconnections; PP&L lost most of its system in a matter of minutes following 10:20 a.m. "On Monday things got pretty hot for poor old Reddy Kilowatt," an editorial cartoon in Sunday's *Allentown Call-Chronicle* deadpanned.

PP&L was already facing a tight load picture for the summer of 1967. Even though the Allentown utility was a winter peaking system, the rest of the members of the PJM pool were summer peakers. The tight capacity system in the pool stemmed from slowed construction on two major power plants in the pool. Vietnam's toll on the American economy was reflected in a shortage of men and material for utilities undertaking construction projects.

Power plants that had taken three to

four years to put on line in the early 1960s now took more than five years. The two largest units behind schedule in June 1967 were Keystone Unit One and PSE&G's big nuclear power plant at Oyster Creek, N.J. Both had originally been scheduled for commercial operation in late 1966 or early 1967.

The June 5 outage hit PP&L like a ton of bricks. At 10:22 a.m., all the units at Brunner Island, Stanton, Hauto and Wallenpaupack tripped. A minute later, units at Martins Creek and Suburban station tripped, and three units at Sunbury went down at 10:28 a.m.

Outages were widespread across the PP&L system. The city of Allentown was without power altogether, and most of the northern half of the service territory was also down. Ironically, Lancaster and Harrisburg were never interrupted; and there were two separate interruptions. The first lasted until shortly after noon,

As these reports reflect, despite the disruption the outages caused, PP&L forged ahead with construction and transmission improvements.

PP&L President Jack Busby 10 years after that fateful day in 1965.

All told, PP&L racked up $824,000 in expenses from the one-day system outage.

when PP&L managed to restore about 60 percent of its load.

The system crashed a second time at 12:15 p.m. Norman W. Curtis, Hazleton-based superintendent of system operations for PP&L, briefed Federal Power Commission officials in Washington throughout that afternoon about the utility's efforts to restore power.

At 1:10 p.m., PP&L's system generating capacity was back up to 950 megawatts, about half the estimated load for early afternoon on a day in June. Brunner Island Unit One was carrying around 200 megawatts of load, and crews were frantically trying to restart Brunner Island Unit Two. Crews were beginning a second restoration at both Martins Creek and Sunbury.

By 2:00 p.m., PP&L had restored all of its 220,000-volt backbone system and had restored interconnections to GPU, Philadelphia Electric Co. and PSE&G. Most of the local city load was coming back rapidly; Allentown, Scranton and Wilkes-Barre were all 90 percent restored, Curtis told the FPC. By 3:30 p.m., Curtis could report that "we have restored approximately 95 percent of our customers." At 6:20 p.m., the crisis was over. Curtis reported that, with the exception of two large industrial customers on standby and one 12,000-volt distribution circuit, the entire PP&L system was once again up and running.

Damage to the PP&L system was significant. Units One and Two at Sunbury sustained bearing failures during the outage and were down for repairs most of the summer. The cost of repairs, after insurance payments, and the cost of replacing power from the two units for six weeks was $500,000. All told, PP&L

racked up $824,000 in expenses from the one-day system outage.

Company President Jack Busby lauded employees for their efforts in restoring service. "Certainly if there is any reason to reflect with optimism on the day and those which followed, it was the response of employees to the situation," Busby said the week following the outage. "I have seen outstanding examples of employee service—and they are gratifying. However, from what has been accomplished in customer restoration work, it is obvious that many, many unheralded efforts were made and will probably continue."

Investigations into the outage continued through 1967 into 1968. PP&L assigned three specialists to work with a PJM engineering team on an exhaustive computer study at General Electric Co.'s Schenectady works. Engineers were unable to come to any conclusive determinations regarding the computer simulation, but efforts to strengthen transmission ties in the PJM region intensified. The 500,000-volt line from Philadelphia Electric Co.'s new Peach Bottom nuclear station to Whitpain was put in service weeks after the outage. A 500,000-volt line from Juniata to Branchburg was well under construction by the end of the summer, and ground was broken for a 500,000-volt line from Branchburg to Whitpain early in the fall of 1967. That summer, PP&L completed 220,000-volt lines from Sunbury northeast to Jenkins substation and southwest to Juniata.

Finally, PP&L commissioned a public opinion poll to get consumer reaction about the blackout. On the whole, customers were understanding. "The overall conclusion that one can make from the Bucci opinion poll is that the public has been most tolerant in this case and that there are no serious consequences as far as individual customers are concerned," the *PP&L Reporter* noted in its wrap-up of the outage. "It needs no polling, however, to know that the blackout did develop major problems for some businesses.

"The very simple moral is: This kind of interruption better not happen again."

Jack Busby: A Legend In His Own Time

If any of PP&L's current or retired employees is worthy of being called a living legend, it would have to be Jack Busby.

President of Pennsylvania Power & Light Co. from 1957 until his retirement in 1979, Jack Kemp Busby put an indelible stamp on PP&L. During the more than two decades Busby took the helm of PP&L, the company completed its postwar building program and entered the nuclear age. Busby was the model for the chief executive officer who knew how to delegate and who understood how important it was to put the utility's best public face forward.

As comfortable with power plant workers as he was with senators and CEOs, Busby's skill in dealing with people both inside and outside the company is still the subject of awed respect among those who worked with and for him from 1957 to 1979. His support of Operation Understanding in the 1970s went a long way toward humanizing PP&L for both internal and external audiences.

Busby was movie-star handsome, with bushy eyebrows that were the subject of a cartoonist's dreams; his craggy facial features were as instantly recognizable to a generation of Pennsylvanians as were the facial features of mine worker's leader John L. Lewis to an earlier generation of Keystone State residents. Mention the word "Jack" to PP&L employees of the 1960s and 1970s, and they know instantly whom you are identifying.

An earnest young Jack K. Busby addresses a small group of bankers and brokers at Honesdale in October 1961.

Jack Kemp Busby was born in Chicago, Ill., on June 16, 1917, the son of Leonard A. and Esther Boardman Busby. Busby's father was a Chicago traction executive who died in 1930 when his son was just a teenager. The Chicago bank that was a trustee for the senior Busby's estate lost huge amounts of money during the Great Depression, and Busby, his sister and his mother had to cope with sharply reduced financial circumstances until the bank made good on the estate in the mid-1930s.

Busby attended the Chicago Latin School and Hotchkiss, a Connecticut preparatory school. He received his bachelor of arts degree, magna cum laude, from Princeton in 1938 and earned his bachelor of law degree from Yale in 1941. That same year, Busby was admitted to the New York Bar and became associated with Simpson, Thacher and Bartlett in New York City. Throughout the 1930s and 1940s, Simpson, Thacher and Bartlett had done work for numerous electric utilities, including Pennsylvania Power & Light Co. and its holding company, Electric Bond and Share Co. The New York firm specialized in legal affairs for the electric utility industry.

As it did for most people of Jack Busby's generation, World War II intervened in his career. Shortly after going to work for Simpson, Thacher and Bartlett, Busby left for the U.S. Navy. "I went on to active duty in the Navy as a distinguished apprentice seaman-in-training," Busby recalled, "and then went to one of the 90-day wonder schools and in due course got on destroyers. I spent from mid-1942 to early 1946 in the destroyer Navy."

Busby returned to Simpson, Thacher and Bartlett following the war and worked with the New York law firm until 1951. In October 1947, Busby married Elise Hohle of New York City, a fellow attorney at Simpson, Thacher and Bartlett. The New York firm served as outside counsel for PP&L in the postwar years, and when PP&L's top corporate counsel suffered a heart attack in 1951, Busby was asked if he would take the job.

"Their top lawyer had a heart attack, and they were looking for someone," Busby recalled in a recent interview. "The firm that I was working for then was outside general counsel for the company, so that was a factor in my being identified as a possible source of filling that vacancy in their in-house legal staff. That transpired in 1951."

At rest in his office. *circa late 1970s*

Jack Busby in the mid-1970s preparing to go down into the Greenwich Mine near Ebensburg, Pa., one of PP&L's former bituminous coal properties.

Busby served as general counsel of the company until 1954, when he was named vice president and general counsel. In 1956, he became executive vice president and a director of the company, and the following year, Jack Busby was named president of the company to succeed Chas. E. Oakes. In 1964, he added the title of chief executive officer to his position description. In early 1977, Busby relinquished the presidency to Robert K. Campbell and was named chairman of the board, a position he held until his retirement two years later.

In the 1960s, Busby presided over a vigorous program of area and economic development in central and eastern Pennsylvania. PP&L's programs were helped by the fact that the utility reduced its rates by more than $15 million during the 1960s. Management became immeasurably more difficult during the 1970s. PP&L was whipsawed by the energy crisis, double-digit inflation and skyrocketing rates as it attempted to keep up with the surging demand for electric power in its service territory.

Still, Busby managed to guide PP&L skillfully across the rocks and shoals of 1970s utility economics. Busby spearheaded completion of the Keystone Project, a consortium of utilities that built baseload mine-mouth steam generation plants in the coal fields of western Pennsylvania and shipped the power east to the load centers via high-voltage transmission lines. It was also on Busby's watch that the ambitious postwar expansion of PP&L's generation base was completed.

Perhaps the most important contribution that Jack Busby made to Pennsylvania Power & Light Co. was his championing of the Susquehanna nuclear project. As far back as the 1950s, PP&L had established an atomic energy group in its Engineering Department. It was during Busby's presidency that PP&L signed a contract with General Electric Co. for reactors, and committed to building the Susquehanna station on the Susquehanna River near Berwick. PP&L's Construction Department built the plant, a mammoth undertaking.

Busby's position on nuclear power was eloquently stated in his most recent interview. "The position we always took was that it is a resource that should not be thrown away when you come to developing power supply for this country. It has its limitations. It has its questions, but we need it. In the long run, we're going to need it."

Busby's first wife was killed in a tragic automobile accident outside Allentown in April 1966. Busby married the former Mary Rose McWilliams of Boston, Mass., in 1969. The couple are now retired and live in Pinehurst, N.C.

35

A Good Place to Do Business

PP&L foresters worked with 139 community groups in 33 areas to plant more than a quarter-million seedlings in 1964 and 1965.

Operation Trees was PP&L's solution to restore the anthracite region's landscape, which had been marred by years of mining.

For PP&L, the driving force behind industrial and economic development efforts during the 1960s was the anthracite region. Between 1961 and 1965 alone, PP&L's aggressive marketing efforts resulted in the addition of more than 500 businesses in the service territory.

The decline of Pennsylvania's anthracite production had become worrisome to PP&L executives as early as the mid-1950s. In 1946, 73 percent of the company's industrial power revenue in the anthracite region had come from the coal-mining industry, while only 27 percent was derived from all other industrial customers. The industry had recovered from the abrupt collapse in mining during the Great Depression, thanks primarily to increasing demand during World War II. Mines and collieries in the region produced 50 million tons for the last time in 1948. Production then went into a precipitous decline, halving each decade through the 1950s, 1960s and 1970s. From 1962 to 1984, annual production year-to-year increased only twice; declines in production were registered in each of the other 20 years.

The reasons for the decline were varied. In a sense, the region never recovered from the Great Depression. The opening up of massive bituminous fields in western Pennsylvania following the war fueled the postwar expansion in utility

These boys are ready to plant seedlings as part of PP&L's Operation Trees.
circa 1964

steam generation, and cheap oil from the Middle East took away much of anthracite's home heating business in the Mid-Atlantic region. Higher labor costs in the anthracite regions, coupled with uncompetitive coal company pricing policies, led to further evaporation of the market.

"Employment in mining dropped catastrophically with the decrease in production," Bucknell University geographer Ben Marsh wrote in 1987. In 1920, 175,000 miners toiled underground and in the breakers of the anthracite region. More than 95 percent of the mining jobs were lost in the region between 1925 and 1985. Population of the mining towns dropped 20 percent between the peak in the 1920s and 1950, while another 20 percent of the population was lured away to factory jobs in the Mid-Atlantic region during the 1950s. Population decline averaged 10 percent each decade during the 1960s and 1970s.

By the 1960s, the towns of the anthracite region were in serious decline. The winding mountain roads of eastern Pennsylvania passed through places like Shamokin and Tamaqua, Mt. Carmel and

The company's goal for 1965 was 300,000 seedlings, with plans to plant a total of one million trees by the end of the decade.

From 1962 to 1984, annual [coal] production year-to-year increased only twice; declines in production were registered in each of the other 20 years.

Unit coal trains transported coal from mines to power plants as part of a cooperative effort between the Pennsylvania Railroad and PP&L. *circa 1964*

Ashland, and Shenandoah, Frackville and Mahanoy City, but the postwar boom had passed them by. Every year in June, the Trailways and Greyhound bus terminals were crowded as the year's crop of high school graduates set out to find a better life in Philadelphia, Allentown or New York City. Dominated by culm banks spread out across the ridges, the anthracite towns shrunk back to a main street populated by churches and taverns; often, the most prosperous business in town was the local funeral parlor.

Only the intervention of the region's charismatic congressman saved the industry from going out of business altogether. Daniel J. "Dan" Flood, whose

anthracite went to West Germany each year during the 1960s, and as late as the 1980s, the military was still burning half-a-million tons of anthracite a year at its West German bases.

PP&L's efforts to diversify the economy of the anthracite region began in earnest in 1946. Over the next 17 years, a total of 750 industries were encouraged to locate in the region. Although most were small businesses, they created job opportunities for more than 56,000 residents. The resulting $214 million annual payroll went a long way to remedy the problems of the declining anthracite mining industry.

PP&L's efforts to diversify the economy of the anthracite region began in earnest in 1946. Over the next 17 years, a total of 750 industries were encouraged to locate in the region.

The Hazleton service center located in the heart of PP&L's anthracite region in 1950. Its oldest buildings housed a World War I munitions plant. PP&L turned the source of armaments into an electric service maintenance facility for the surrounding region. Between 1940 and 1949, John S. Davidson served as manager of the Hazleton division.

11th Congressional District cut through the heart of the anthracite region, managed in 1962 to create an artificial demand for anthracite by writing an amendment that required the U.S. Department of Defense to burn hard coal at military installations in West Germany. Flood, a longtime member of the defense subcommittee of the House Appropriations Committee, made no apologies for the piece of outrageous pork he had engineered into the Defense Department's permanent budget; one million tons of

'Indissolubly linked with the area it serves'

For PP&L, the decline of the anthracite industry in the postwar period was a challenge that had to be undertaken if the company's area development program was to succeed. Industrial development—the attraction of new businesses and the creation and retention of jobs for area residents—had been a staple of the

L.W. Heath, executive vice president of PP&L, recruited John S. Davidson in 1937.

For most of five decades, Davidson served as the unofficial cheerleader for the anthracite region. His efforts with PP&L's area development departments and with local industrial development programs paid off in thousands of jobs for residents of the state's northeastern corner.

company's area development efforts since the mid-1920s.

Oakes said it best in 1957 when he noted that "the cumulative effects of our long-range area development efforts are founded on the premise that the business of the company is indissolubly linked with the area it serves." The creation of new jobs and payroll would lead to the overall economic strengthening of PP&L communities, and in the process expand and develop present industries, stimulate the location and development of new industries, develop agricultural-industrial facilities, promote the area's summer-winter resort resources and develop and conserve the region's natural resources.

A good example of how those goals could be integrated into a successful area development program was PP&L's 1963 inauguration of Operation Trees. PP&L called Operation Trees "a practical self-help program for beautifying the anthracite area," and the idea behind it was simple.

"Years of mining operations have left their mark on the area," the company pointed out. "The appearance of what otherwise was, and in some places still is, attractive landscape is marred by spoil banks, culm banks and the scars of strip mining. Though the scars are evidence of the region's extensive and continuing contribution to progress, they are, at the same time, becoming an increasingly greater deterrent to accelerating the area's economy."

The solution, PP&L observed, was to plant trees in the anthracite region. "The anthracite area has had many tools to work with," the company explained,

"plant sites, shell buildings, low-cost financing, a supply of capable and willing workers, friendly people, convenience to the nation's largest markets, transportation, schools, housing, and a willingness to cooperate among communities."

But by the early 1960s, the environmental ethic was making its presence felt in the field of industrial development. All other things being equal, industries frequently factored quality of life into their plant location decisions. Working in conjunction with the Northeastern Forest Experiment Station of the U.S. Department of Agriculture, PP&L undertook an extensive research project in the northeastern section of its service territory. Company foresters examined soil conditions, tree types and moisture needs in the anthracite region, all as a part of the company's program to improve the physical environment of the anthracite region.

In 1964, PP&L made more than a quarter-million seedlings available in the area. Trees were planted in 33 areas by 139 community groups under the supervision of PP&L foresters. The company's goal for 1965 was 300,000 seedlings, with plans to plant a total of one million trees by the end of the decade.

The Irrepressible John Davidson

The anthracite region is an insular place where everyone knows everyone else's business. It's also a place where the measure of a man is taken firsthand, be it in his work, his contributions or his play. Finally, it's a place with an innate mistrust of corporations, a mistrust born of bitter labor-management struggles and the socialist leanings of the first generation of immigrant miners. It is also a mistrust that is taken in at the breast and passed along from generation to generation.

Given that background, it would seem impossible for the residents of the anthracite region to take in an executive from

the big-city electric utility in far-off Allentown. But several generations of anthracite region residents knew John S. Davidson as "Mr. PP&L."

The son and grandson of electric power pioneers, Davidson served as manager of the Hazleton division from 1940 to 1949, vice president of the Scranton division from 1957 to 1967 and vice president of the Northeast division from 1967 until his retirement. For most of five decades, Davidson served as the unofficial cheerleader for the anthracite region. His efforts with PP&L's area development departments and with local industrial development programs paid off in thousands of jobs for residents of the state's northeastern corner.

Davidson remained interested in anthracite region development until his death in 1994. Born in Vermont in 1907, Davidson moved with his parents to Portland, Ore., as an infant. Davidson's father worked for the Electric Bond and Share

Co.—his grandfather had started a power plant in Port Huron, Mich., about the time that Thomas Edison was perfecting his incandescent lighting system—and the family moved to Omaha in 1917, where his father ran Electric Bond and Share Co.'s Nebraska Power Co.

Davidson grew up in Omaha and started working summers through high school as a laborer on steam turbine overhaul jobs at Nebraska Power Co. In 1931, he graduated from Colby College in Maine with a B.S. degree and returned to Omaha, where he was hired to do sales and cashier work in Nebraska Power Co.'s South Omaha electric shop. From 1932 until he left Nebraska Power Co. in 1937, Davidson worked a variety of jobs, including stints in the company's power plants, merchandising and new business departments.

In February 1937, L.W. Heath, executive vice president of Pennsylvania Power & Light Co. and a longtime friend of

John S. Davidson (center), vice president, and Herbert D. Nash (right), manager of business development of the Scranton division, accept the 1963 President's Award from PP&L President Jack K. Busby.

The Hazleton power control center in 1953.

Davidson's father, approached the younger Davidson about job opportunities at PP&L. The Allentown utility was just then setting up a department to sell air-conditioning, and Davidson had already had experience selling air-conditioning with Nebraska Power Co. The offer was for $225 a month for three months, with a raise to $250 a month thereafter.

Heath, who ran the commercial department at the time, wanted his sales personnel to have practical experience. For the first several months Davidson was at PP&L, he worked in the company's manufactured gas plant at Carlisle, staying in the Molly Pitcher Hotel at night and cleaning out flue gas traps and digging ditches for gas mains during the day.

After a long summer working in the gas plant, Davidson came back to the Allentown Commercial Department. His job title was assistant to the vice president-commercial, and he did a variety of tasks for Heath. In 1940, Heath asked him to go to Hazleton as division manager. Davidson and his wife

Davidson marshalled the resources of Pennsylvania Power & Light Co. toward a single-minded dedication to diversifying the economy of the anthracite region.

had just had a baby, and the couple had bought a small house in Allentown. For several months, Davidson commuted back and forth.

It was during his tenure in Hazleton that Davidson began to make his mark in area and industrial development activities. Davidson shepherded the division, which contained PP&L's Operations Center, through the difficult days of World War II. When the war ended, he was one of the first to foresee the decline of the anthracite industry. In 1947, Davidson convinced the city and its Chamber of Commerce to form the Hazleton Industrial Development Corp.

Davidson was elected to head the corporation, and he soon spearheaded a drive to raise $500,000 in cash as an incentive for business attraction in the community. "I heard that the Electric Auto-Lite Co. was thinking about building a plant, and they were located in Toledo, Ohio," Davidson recalled. "So I went out to Toledo and interviewed and told them that we would be interested. But before that we decided that if we were going to do anything industrial, we would have to raise some money."

Hazleton raised $658,000, and in 1948, the Electric Auto-Lite Co. announced it was going to build a major new factory in the community. "It is a monument to the efforts of Mr. Davidson and a small number of associates who landed this industry, which is expected to give employment to a large number of people," the local newspapers editorialized when Davidson was promoted to vice president of the Harrisburg division in the fall of 1949.

Chairman for LIFE

Eight years later, Davidson was back in the anthracite region, this time as vice president of the Scranton region. By 1957, the region was, in the words of the poet Edna St. Vincent Millay, "dying inward from the edges." Abandoned collieries and coal breakers littered the landscape, and thousands of residents left for jobs in the big cities of the East Coast and Mid-Atlantic regions. Unemployment in Lackawanna County was 16.4 percent.

Davidson marshalled the resources of Pennsylvania Power & Light Co. toward a single-minded dedication to diversifying the economy of the anthracite region. Scranton was a clannish community, and there were still hard feelings in town about PP&L's acquisition of Scranton Electric Co. Davidson went to see Ben Filmore, president of the Hudson Coal Co., and one of the community's pillars, and told him that PP&L's word was its bond. "And he looked at me," Davidson said, "and he said, 'Mr. Davidson, I've been in this coal business for 40 years, and I've learned not to trust a blasted soul. Good day!'"

Davidson and Filmore got to be good friends. When Chas. E. Oakes sent Davidson into Scranton, he had a list of eight things he wanted his new vice president to accomplish. Close to the top of the list was establishing better relations with the *Scranton Times*. The *Times* was owned by the Lynett family of Scranton, and Ed Lynett had thrown out of his office just about everybody from the General Office Tower that Oakes had sent to see him.

Davidson, an Episcopalian, soon noticed that Lynett took a particular interest in Scranton University. Formerly known as the College of St. Thomas, the university was run by Jesuit priests and was strapped for cash in the late 1950s. "I said to Mr. Oakes, well one of the first things we got to do is show some financial interest in the University of Scranton, because Mr. Lynett is very, very interested in it," Davidson recalled. Soon after, Oakes called Davidson to tell him that he was bringing up a check for $20,000 for Father John J. Long, the president of the university. Davidson got to be friends with Ed Lynett, and when the publisher died in the 1960s, the Scranton division vice president sponsored Lynett's son for membership on the board of the North-

eastern Bank of Scranton.

With a network of contacts established, Davidson went to work to revitalize Scranton's industrial development efforts. Davidson reflected the PP&L philosophy that the community had to have ownership in an economic development project for it to be truly effective.

Two years after arriving in Scranton, Davidson was named general chairman of the 1959 Lackawanna Industrial Fund Enterprises (LIFE) campaign to raise $1.5 million to bolster the area's industrial development program. Like the Hazleton Industrial Development Corp. 12 years before, LIFE under Davidson's leadership was phenomenally successful. The $1.5 million was raised in eight weeks; major contributions came in from the community's banks, PP&L and its Scranton division employees, the Scranton family and the *Scranton Times*.

> *John S. Davidson typified the can-do spirit of PP&L's aggressive industrial and area development efforts in the 1960s.*

The *Evening News* in far-off Harrisburg lauded "Lackawanna's do-it-yourself spirit," and John Davidson took the message of Scranton's can-do spirit to companies around the country in the years to come. The $1.5 million raised by LIFE and John Davidson provided the seed money for the Keystone Industrial Park, a full-service facility that attracted manufacturers and distributors to the anthracite region in the 1960s. By the end of the decade, more than 5,000 Scranton residents were working in the Keystone Park, and the unemployment rate was less than half what it had been in 1958.

John S. Davidson typified the can-do spirit of PP&L's aggressive industrial and area development efforts in the 1960s. Davidson and his cohorts helped transform central and eastern Pennsylvania in the postwar years and made the words "PP&L" and "industrial development" synonymous for a generation of Pennsylvanians.

The Trane Trip

In 1988, Joseph X. Flannery, columnist for the *Scranton Times*, reminisced about John S. Davidson's 30-year association with Lackawanna Industrial Fund Enterprises (LIFE) organization. Then 81 and long retired from PP&L, Davidson had just stepped down as vice chairman of LIFE.

"It is somewhat of a miracle that the Scranton area even exists," Flannery wrote, "let alone boasts an unemployment rate lower than many other parts of the state. Who caused this miracle? Well, there are a lot of heroes—too many to name. But let me advance one, John Davidson, who, on Friday, will sever his last link with the on-going program of wooing industries here."

Flannery went on to detail how Davidson had taken the reins of LIFE in 1959 and helped raise $1.5 million for economic development in little more than two months. He recounted how Davidson had become president of the Scranton Chamber of Commerce in 1962; and he told the story of how Davidson had enticed Trane—the big Wisconsin-based heating and air-conditioning firm—into locating a plant in Scranton's Keystone Industrial Park.

Davidson, Flannery wrote, "was trying to convince the Trane Co. to surrender its plant on Davis Street to move to the Keystone Industrial Park in Dunmore. He had intervened at a local bank to set up the financing for the McKinney Manufacturing Co. of Pittsburgh to move to the Davis Street plant. But first he had to convince Trane officials at LaCrosse, Wis., to move to a new plant in the industrial park."

> Davidson "was trying to convince the Trane Co. to surrender its plant on Davis Street to move to the Keystone Industrial Park in Dunmore.... But first he had to convince Trane officials at LaCrosse, Wis., to move to a new plant in the industrial park."
> —Joseph X. Flannery

Davidson's trip to Trane in Wisconsin was the stuff of which industrial development legends are made. The PP&L vice president asked Joe Sproul, a local contractor, to accompany him to answer technical questions that might arise. It was late November, and the two men flew to Chicago, where they were to change planes for LaCrosse. A major storm was sweeping across the country, and the flight into the Windy City was bumpy and turbulent. When they arrived in Chicago, they learned that all commercial flights to the north and west had been cancelled.

"I had a meeting in LaCrosse the next morning with the chairman of the board, and I chartered a twin engine Beechcraft airplane," Davidson recalled. "The guy was very reluctant about even flying. It was snowing to beat the band, the weather was terrible with rain and sleet, but anyway we got on the plane, and they had a kerosene heater on the plane."

Things quickly went from bad to worse. "It was cold as the dickens, and the thing was going this way and that," Davidson continued. "Joe was lying on the floor and the kerosene heater tipped over. I had this wet raincoat on, and I jumped up and put it right over the heater and put the fire out."

The plane made it to LaCrosse, and Davidson and Sproul checked in to the Holiday Inn. The next morning, John Davidson got the Trane chairman's agreement to put a major new plant expansion into the Keystone Industrial Park.

36
Interlude:
PP&L People in 1970

Radios, hydraulics, plastics and helicopters dramatically changed utility operations in the 1960s and 1970s.

Pennsylvania Power & Light Co. celebrated its 50th anniversary as a modern corporation in 1970, and it's likely that Edward Kimball Hall and John S. Wise, the company's first two presidents in the 1920s, would still have recognized the operation that Jack Busby was running half-a-century later. However, it's doubtful that Hall, who died in 1932, and Wise, who was then living in retirement in Allentown, could believe the tremendous strides made in utility techniques, procedures and equipment in the relatively short space of 50 years.

The day hydraulically driven augers were invented was a great day for linemen and construction workers. This digger demonstrates its efficiency in Stroudsburg in the summer of 1957.

Helicopters enabled crews to set transmission towers in remote and rugged terrain, as well as patrol transmission line rights-of-way and personnel transportation.

Hydraulics and plastic transformed the business of construction and maintenance of distribution lines and low-voltage transmission lines

For line crews, the quarter-century between 1945 and 1970 had been years of almost unremitting progress. Hydraulics and plastic transformed the business of construction and maintenance of distribution lines and low-voltage transmission lines. Increasingly after the 1960s, high-voltage transmission line crews used helicopters to set transmission towers in the rugged terrain of central and eastern Pennsylvania.

PP&L and other utility line crews dug holes for poles in the late 1940s and early 1950s with a hole-digging truck, essentially a vehicle that had been rigged up with a hydraulically driven auger on the back end. Once the hole had been dug, a line truck with an A-frame on the back was maneuvered into place. Crews armed with pike poles then manhandled the poles into the ground.

The auger and the A-frame were distinct improvements over the previous method, in which crews with long-handled shovels dug the hole and then maneuvered the pole into place with pike poles. Still, setting poles in the 1950s was dirty, exhausting, labor-intensive work.

That all started to change in the early 1960s when PP&L began to equip its line fleet with hydraulic line trucks. The new trucks had room for four line crew members in the cab and carried a hydraulic attachment on the bed that used a hydraulic boom to drill the hole, pick up a pole and hold it steady while dirt was being tamped around it. With other attachments, the hydraulic boom was easily convertible to raise transformers, pull line and jack out poles.

By the end of the decade, PP&L had replaced its fleet of line trucks with hydraulic-boom model trucks. Lightweight plastics also began to make their presence felt in line work during the decade. Plastic replaced the wood in "hot sticks," the lineman's tool used to handle electric conductors and switches. Hot sticks had to be kept dry, and plastic hot sticks could be transported on a rack outside the truck and wiped dry with a cloth before use. Cotton handlines were also replaced with plastic rope, primarily because the synthetic rope had the same or higher tensile strength as cotton rope but did not absorb water.

Late in the 1960s, hydraulics technology and plastics were combined when molded fiberglass-reinforced buckets were fitted on the end of a truck's hydraulic boom. Ladders quickly became a thing of the past, as linemen in the fiberglass buckets were able to work more safely and closer to hot wires.

Plastic also began to appear in hard hats during the 1960s. The new lightweight plastics had the dielectric strength, could withstand maximum impact and were several pounds lighter than the molded fiberglass hard hats that were still common in the late 1950s and early 1960s. By 1969, PP&L made hard hats available as protective equipment for all employees.

For transmission line crews, the advent of helicopter haulage during the 1960s

The transformation of PP&L's utility trucks from the 1920s to the 1940s to the 1990s.

was a godsend. As early as the winter storm of 1958, PP&L had used leased helicopters to ferry line crews into isolated valleys for line maintenance and repair. But with the construction of the 500,000-volt transmission line from Keystone Unit One to the Harrisburg division in 1966, PP&L leased a big chopper to help transmission line crews pour concrete foundations for towers on the Susquehanna River crossing. When crews had to string transmission line over a strip mine pit near Stockton in the spring of 1966, helicopters were again called to the rescue.

Helicopters had been used for transmission line patrol ever since 1960, and the flying machines proved so valuable during the decade that PP&L decided to lease rather than rent. In July 1969, the company announced it was leasing a Bell JetRanger, primarily to shuttle personnel around the 20-county service area.

"If on a given day," the company explained, "four company personnel were sent in four separate vehicles and directions to Montour and Brunner Island generating plants and Harrisburg and Williamsport, they normally would be on the road about 16-1/2 hours for the round trip. Through proper scheduling, the travel time by helicopter could be cut to about six hours.

"Such efficient scheduling would lead to more productive use of about 11 hours, which would be cut from travel time. The

Using a hot stick, this lineman is able to safely reach out and close a switch on the line to restore power after a spring storm in 1975. At the end of the 1960s, wood hot sticks were replaced with plastic for a lighter weight, more practical tool.

Construction training—with a heavy emphasis on safety—at the Walbert Training Center in 1985.

With the development of larger power plants and higher voltage transmission lines in the postwar period, utilities had to be even more aware of the safety ramifications of operating procedures.

objective is to get to the job and get it done."

The Importance of Safety

PP&L stressed getting to the job and getting it done, but increasingly, the company stressed getting the job done safely. Working around electric power has always been inherently hazardous, and PP&L emphasized safety from the beginning of its corporate existence. In the 1930s, utilities like PP&L pioneered resuscitation and artificial respiration methods that entered general use in the society at large.

But with the development of larger power plants and higher voltage transmission lines in the postwar period, utilities had to be even more aware of the safety ramifications of operating procedures. For much of the 1960s, PP&L's TOPS program was a model for the utility industry. TOPS stood for "This Outfit Produces Safely," and it was part of a three-pronged project that included an accident investigation procedure and disciplinary policy. With 1,400 employees in the Construction Department alone in the late 1960s, employee safety was a mandatory company interest.

The TOPS program was responsible for a record of more than one million man-hours without a lost-time accident in the Construction Department in 1967. But PP&L learned the hard way that it couldn't rest on its laurels where safety was concerned. There were 111 total company accidents during January 1968, the worst monthly accident record in four years. In the spring of that year, PP&L instituted a formal program of tailboard conferences for line crews so that they could discuss the safety aspect of any job in detail before starting work.

Social trends also affected the way PP&L did its job as the 1960s gave way to the 1970s. The entry of women into the workforce was a trickle in the 1960s, but became a flood after 1970. Although women had been a part of PP&L's workforce since the 1920s, most had been clerical employees. Increasingly after the late 1960s, women professionals began joining the company in significant numbers.

In 1968, Carole Petrusic and Lynn Green, both of Bethlehem, became PP&L's first female cadet engineers. The two women, electrical engineering students at Drexel Institute in Philadelphia, spent two six-month training periods with PP&L working with lines and substation engineers. "Theory is fine," both women observed, "but you don't really understand it until you get out on the job. That's what makes going to Drexel and working at PP&L so great; your job training supplements the book knowledge."

PP&L was ahead of the power curve on another social trend in 1970: adherence to environmental principles. America celebrated the first Earth Day in April 1970 and PP&L had already begun to develop a formal environmental policy. By 1970, PP&L was already screening its transmission and substation facilities, landscaping parklands in its service territory, undergrounding distribution lines and erecting new "slimline" transmission towers.

"The company is recognized as one of the leaders in the industry in environmental activities," the *PP&L Reporter* noted in November 1970. "And as

Joseph Grusetskie, PP&L safety and health consultant, shows off one of the many TOPS decals demonstrating the company's commitment to safety awareness. *circa 1980s*

The TOPS program was responsible for a record of more than one million man-hours without a lost-time accident in the Construction Department in 1967.

Another sign of changing times… women's roles at the company began to change from primarily clerical to professional in the 1960s. Here, Sharon M. Grim adjusts her firefighter helmet before attacking a fire at the Luzerne County Fire School. She was an employee at the PP&L Susquehanna nuclear plant. *circa 1980s*

another positive indication of our deep concern for moving ahead with these programs, the company recently established an environmental development group working out of the General Office that will coordinate future programs and improvements in many areas related to our environment."

PP&L committed $40 million over a five-year period beginning in 1970 to help the company comply with accepted standards for clean air, clean water, a natural

---

In 1968, Carole Petrusic and Lynn Green, both of Bethlehem, became PP&L's first female cadet engineers.

---

landscape, recreational areas and healthful area development. "As a responsible member of the communities we serve," the 1970 annual report to shareholders noted, "we would be foolish to ignore the warning signs nature has provided for us."

PP&L entered its second half-century of operations in 1970 with clear goals in mind. "In PP&L we are an activist people with a strong tradition of positive approaches," Jack Busby wrote in the 1970 annual report. "We shall continue in this pattern in meeting our responsibilities: For improved earnings. For a more satisfactory power supply. For qualitative regional development. And for greater career and job satisfaction for employees."

37

From Coal to Nuclear

PP&L construction workers finish work on a 10-ton steel reinforcing bar cage for a 34-foot-deep foundation to hold a transmission line pole as part of the Montour-Susquehanna line relocation project to make room for the Susquehanna nuclear plant. *circa 1978*

The last big coal-fired steam electric plant PP&L built in the postwar period was Montour Steam Electric Station. Located on a 1,163-acre site in Derry Township of Montour County near Washingtonville, Unit One was announced at a June 5, 1967, meeting of the Rotary Club in Danville, the county seat, by company President Jack Busby. Unit One, Busby said, would be in the range of 765,000 kilowatts, equal to the largest unit that PP&L Construction Department crews were then installing as the third unit at Brunner Island.

Busby told the Rotarians that the company's decision to build Montour was influenced by "our belief that the northern tier of counties in our service area has a great growth potential because of their excellent combination of people, power, land and water and an important network of new highways—particularly Interstate 80, which provides a direct artery to the huge seaboard megalopolis and major eastern seaports. These advantages place the region at the confluence of trade and transportation and gives it the unique distinction of being able to serve markets north, east, south and west."

Busby's announcement of the new

capacity addition was serendipitous, to say the least. PP&L had been predicting electricity supply shortages for the summer ever since the spring, and earlier that Monday, PP&L and the PJM system had been rocked by a catastrophic power failure reminiscent of the great Northeast Blackout of November 1965.

For awhile early that afternoon, it looked like PP&L might have to postpone Busby's speech and the planned announcement of the Montour plant. But with the passage of the crisis in early afternoon, Busby decided to go to Danville for the Rotary Club speech. As it was, the Montour plant announcement

Montour Steam Electric Station. *(illustration by Brent Schaefer © 1995)*

was lost in the tidal wave of press coverage of the previous day's blackout.

Montour represented several significant firsts for Pennsylvania Power & Light Co. Unlike Brunner Island and Sunbury, the Montour plant was not located on a major river or stream. Instead, PP&L bought 2,800 acres adjacent to the plant and dammed up a stream to create a 162-acre lake for the plant to provide an emergency water supply. The main supply of cooling water was pumped through a 12-mile-long pipeline, from its Susquehanna River source. Water for the big coal-fired unit would be circulated through a massive cooling tower at the site. The chimney-like structure rose 370 feet in the air and totaled 390 feet in diameter at the base. Inside, some 260,000 gallons of water a minute from the plant's condensers cooled in the massive structure.

The lake and surrounding acreage became the core of the Montour Preserve, a natural area maintained by PP&L, that contains three boat-launching ramps, three picnic areas and two scenic overlooks. The 162-acre lake was stocked with game fish by the Pennsylvania Fish Commission.

Environmental considerations were a high priority for the $100 million project. Like the early units at Martins Creek and Brunner Island, Montour was designed to burn Pennsylvania bituminous coal from a new mine being opened by the Barnes & Tucker Co. in the Barnesboro area of western Pennsylvania. The Penn Central Railroad would haul some two million tons of coal a year to the Montour County plant.

To help minimize social and environmental impacts of the 765,000-kilowatt plant site, PP&L established the Montour Project Committee, a six-member group of local citizens whose job was to monitor construction of the plant. "The primary objective is to nurture an understanding between the company and the area residents of each other's goals, and cooperate in achieving these goals in order to develop the area's economy and resources," the *PP&L Reporter* explained

early in 1969.

Groundbreaking for Montour Unit One took place on a warm spring morning in May 1968. Less than four years later, in March 1972, Unit One went into commercial operation. Unit Two came on line 13 months later. Combined, the two units at Montour added more than 1.5 million kilowatts of capacity to the PP&L system. They would be the last coal-fired baseload generation units built by the Allentown utility in the postwar period.

Coal and the Environment

Jack Busby's June 5, 1967, announcement of the Montour plant was significant in another regard. As PP&L struggled with the aftermath of the PJM blackout and capacity problems in the PJM region, the company wasn't exactly sure that the second unit at the Montour site would be fueled by coal.

"The site has capacity for two units," Busby said in his speech to the Danville Rotary Club, "of which this will be the first unit. We are not prepared to say today whether the second unit will be a coal unit or a nuclear unit or exactly when that second unit will go in. But we do plan to build two units at our Susquehanna site, and we plan to build two units here."

Busby's mention of "that Susquehanna site" was a reference to PP&L's announcement the previous month that it intended to build a two-unit nuclear station at a site in Salem Township, Luzerne County, about seven miles upriver from the community of Berwick. "We are planning new

This bulldozer is dwarfed by the 370-foot chimney-like cooling tower at Montour Steam Electric Station.

Ground-breaking for Montour Unit One took place on a warm spring morning in May 1968. Less than four years later, in March 1972, Unit One went into commercial operation.

This young man catches a big one at the Montour Preserve. *circa 1970s.* The man-made lake was stocked with game fish by the Pennsylvania Fish Commission.

The Montour facility was the first PP&L generating station to use natural draft cooling towers.

conventional coal-burning units, pumped-storage hydro projects and further nuclear units," Busby told the Berwick Kiwanis Club in a May 2, 1967, address. "Also, we are already participating in the construction of two large mine-mouth, coal-fired plants in the western Pennsylvania soft-coal fields and installing combustion turbine additions to our system at strategic locations."

PP&L's decision to "go nuclear" was precipitated by a number of factors, both environmental and financial. Through the 1960s, coal-fired plants represented a lower capital cost than nuclear plants for construction, although nuclear fuel during the decade was less expensive than coal. In the mid-1960s, General Electric Co., Westinghouse, Babcock & Wilcox

and Allis-Chalmers—the major nuclear reactor equipment manufacturers—had experienced a flood of orders. What had been a buyer's market turned into a seller's market literally overnight.

The cost of money was going up, an important consideration for construction projects that were averaging $150 million apiece in mid-decade. Through the early part of the 1960s, PP&L could go to the capital markets and get short-term construction financing for 4-1/2 percent interest. By 1967, the interest rate on short-term construction financing had gone above six percent and was predicted to go higher.

Finally, there were real concerns in Allentown about the future of coal combustion and transportation. Pennsylvania was already seeing environmental activism in the late 1960s, and the grass roots concern about the environment would bear fruit during President Richard M. Nixon's administration. Between 1969 and 1974, Congress would pass, and Nixon would sign into law, landmark clean air and clean

> *The lake and surrounding acreage became the core of the Montour Preserve, a natural area maintained by PP&L that contains three boat-launching ramps, three picnic areas and two scenic overlooks.*

water legislation. In 1970, Nixon also created the U.S. Environmental Protection Agency (EPA). Early in the decade, EPA began to zero in on coal, identifying sulfur dioxide as a prime culprit in contributing to air pollution.

PP&L was already experiencing environmental problems with its Sunbury station, which little more than a decade before had been the company's most modern plant. "We know we have an air pollution problem there which we must cope with," Busby said in 1967. "They're anthracite-burning units and the matter of controlling stack emissions with anthracite seems to have at the moment stumped everybody." The stack emission problem was so vexing that PP&L prepared plans to place the first two units at Sunbury on curtailed operation in 1968.

Finally, coal transportation continued to bedevil PP&L. As more bituminous units had come on line in the 1960s, coal transportation costs continued to soar. By 1967, PP&L was burning more than five million tons of coal a year, and paying 24.4 cents per million Btu. That cost was projected to rise to more than 34 cents per million Btu by 1970, and much of the increase was directly attributable to the cost of hauling coal from western Pennsylvania's bituminous fields to the PP&L power plants, which were located as much as 250 miles east of the coal fields.

The Wreck of the Penn Central

What was even more worrisome to PP&L management was the precarious state of the Pennsylvania Railroad. By 1967, the Pennsy was barely treading water. That year, the railroad, buffeted by years of losses in passenger revenues and lack of maintenance, floated a survival plan that called for a merger with the

These students spend a day away from their classroom to learn field botany at PP&L's Montour Preserve. *circa 1970s*

Community programs like Maple Syrup day, and the Braille Trail were just a few examples of Montour Preserve's positive impact. circa 1970s

Bob Compton of PP&L's Corporate Communications Department retired in 1994 after 21 years writing about and for the Susquehanna facility.

The changing of the guard at Montour… in January 1977, outgoing Montour Superintendent Ken Krach (left) passes the torch of responsibility on to Dan Sachse.

New York Central, another basket case in the late 1960s.

The U.S. Supreme Court's ruling on Jan. 18, 1968, that the merger could go through under the name of the Penn Central Transportation Co. gave PP&L and other captive shippers some comfort, but some utilities began ordering fleets of locomotives so they could run their own unit trains. Through much of the next five years, PP&L executives sweated out what quickly became apparent as a disastrous merger. In 1970, the Penn Central filed for bankruptcy, the largest American company to go into receivership since the Great Depression.

Jack Busby perhaps said it best when he explained PP&L's decision to diversify its generation mix to a roomful of Danville Rotarians in the spring of 1967. "At the same time, we felt that it was not wise to put all your eggs in one basket," Busby said. "That is why we have also committed ourselves to a nuclear plant…."

Going Nuclear

It took three and one-half years of planning before PP&L could unveil plans for its nuclear-powered Susquehanna Steam Electric Station. On Sept. 24, 1970,

the company called a press conference at the Briar Heights Lodge near Berwick. Invited were media, community leaders, educators, business, government, and industry and labor officials representing the Berwick area and the northern tier of counties in the company's service territory.

By then, it was estimated to cost more than $500 million to build and install Susquehanna's twin 1.1 million-kilowatt boiling water reactors (BWR). Company President Jack Busby explained that the decision to go nuclear was governed by several factors. The tight power situation in the Mid-Atlantic region that had become evident in the mid-1960s had grown more acute by 1970; PP&L expected peak demand on its system to grow 150 percent by 1980. Then, too, lead times for nuclear plant construction had lengthened appreciably in the latter half of the 1960s, partly because of equipment shortages and increased scrutiny by the Atomic Energy Commission.

"The company must take positive action now to have the plants in service where they are needed," Busby told the media and other assembled guests. "Early phases of this building program— covering the addition of 3.4 million kilowatts by 1975—already are under way at a cost placed at one billion dollars."

Much of the three years that had elapsed since PP&L had announced it was going to build a nuclear station on the Susquehanna site had been taken up in investigating the type of reactor the company wanted to operate. "A nuclear reactor basically is an atomic furnace," the *PP&L Reporter* explained to employees in the October 1970 issue, and the type of furnace that PP&L would buy required thousands of employee-hours of research. Late in 1969, PP&L had solicited bids for the two reactors. Three nuclear equipment suppliers submitted bids for pressurized water reactors, and General Electric Co. submitted a bid for a BWR.

General Electric Co. had the exclusive U.S. license to make BWRs, and the big electrical equipment manufacturer had sold its first BWR unit in Illinois in 1959.

Since that time, G.E. had placed 15 other BWRs into commercial operation and had orders for 42 more units. "The plants have performed with a high degree of safety, reliability and service and have accumulated about 70 reactor years of operating experience since operations first began," the *Reporter* assured employees.

Since its initial foray into atomic power more than 15 years before, PP&L had kept alive at least the nucleus of an atomic department in Allentown. Although the company's participation in the Pennsylvania Advanced Reactor project in the 1950s had been aborted, PP&L had remained interested in nuclear power development.

In 1958, the company had joined with 50 other investor-owned utilities to support the development and prototype construction of a high-performance nuclear power plant under the name of the High Temperature Reactor Development Associates. Five years later, PP&L and 21 other investor-owned utilities formed the High Temperature Gas-Cooled Reactor Fuel and Fuel Cycle Development Program. The company began beefing up its Atomic Power Department after 1965, and by 1967, it was co-hosting in-depth, four-week nuclear power seminars at Muhlenberg College in Allentown.

What was different about nuclear plant construction and operation was the licensing and permitting process. Through the 1950s and 1960s, PP&L had built coal-fired power plants with a minimum of regulatory oversight. Coal-fired units were put on line in an average two to four years from groundbreaking to commercial operations.

Nuclear plants were a different animal altogether. The AEC's division of licensing and regulation required two separate licenses—one to build the plant and one to operate it. When PP&L announced its decision to build two 1,050,000-kilowatt reactors at Susquehanna, it began preparations for submitting a formal application to the AEC. It would be 13 long years before Unit One at Susquehanna "went critical" and began commercial operation.

The application process required a number of steps, and PP&L's plans were subject to public scrutiny every step of the way. PP&L's application, which quickly grew to a document several feet thick, was inspected by the AEC's Advisory Committee on Reactor Safeguards. The commission's Atomic Safety & Licensing Board held public hearings on the application in PP&L's service area before recommending approval. At that point, the five-member AEC ruled to accept the board's recommendation. Starting with reactors approved after 1970, operators had to file an Environmental Impact Statement with the U.S. EPA.

A Dark Cloud on the Horizon

Susquehanna was a truly massive undertaking. The company made its construction application to the AEC in April 1971. The construction permit was issued on Nov. 2, 1973, and an army of construction workers swarmed onto the site for the decade-long process of building Susquehanna.

By the time construction reached its peak in the late 1970s, more than 2,500 construction workers were employed at the Berwick site. Bechtel Power Corp. was the prime contractor for the largest construction job in the company's history, but

William A. Frederick, who retired in 1992, was manager of the proposed nuclear Susquehanna project when he conducted this news briefing in September 1970.

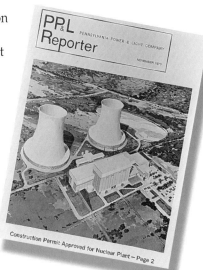

This November 1973 cover of the *PP&L Reporter* shows the architect's rendering of the Susquehanna Steam Electric Station.

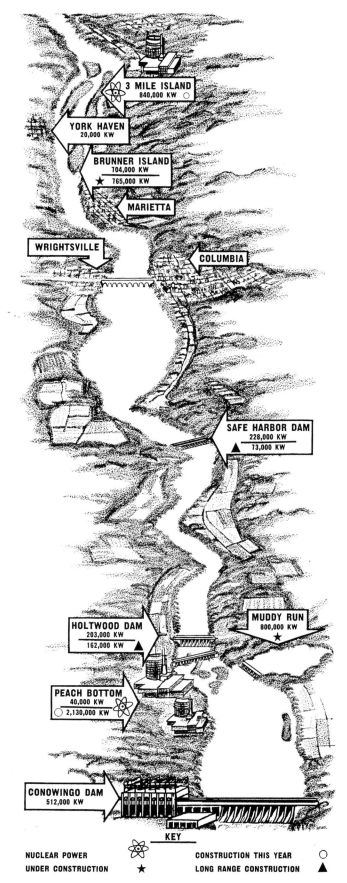

3 MILE ISLAND
840,000 KW ⦾

YORK HAVEN
20,000 KW

BRUNNER ISLAND
704,000 KW
★ 765,000 KW

MARIETTA

WRIGHTSVILLE

COLUMBIA

SAFE HARBOR DAM
228,000 KW
▲ 73,000 KW

MUDDY RUN
800,000 KW
★

HOLTWOOD DAM
203,000 KW
162,000 KW ▲

PEACH BOTTOM
40,000 KW ⚛
⦾ 2,130,000 KW

CONOWINGO DAM
512,000 KW

KEY

NUCLEAR POWER	⚛	CONSTRUCTION THIS YEAR ⦾
UNDER CONSTRUCTION	★	LONG RANGE CONSTRUCTION ▲

Pennsylvania nuclear power on the Susquehanna River in the 1960s.

in a sense, Susquehanna represented the finest hour for PP&L's Construction Department. Within weeks of the issuance of the construction permit, more than 100 Construction Department employees were assigned to the project to provide overall surveillance and supervision. Susquehanna was such a massive and lengthy undertaking that on-site Construction Department employees had their own newsletter—*From the Ground Up*—from 1973 to 1983.

One dark cloud was on the horizon when PP&L got construction under way. By late 1974, when construction crews had been on site for nearly a year, overall cost of the Susquehanna project was estimated at $1.385 billion. That was nearly three times the estimated cost when Jack Busby had announced the project back in 1970. Between 1974 and 1984, PP&L construction expenditures for generating capacity topped $4.3 billion. Much of that total was attributable to nuclear construction.

"The original estimate of the two Susquehanna units was not more than about 20 percent of the ultimate cost," recalled Bob Fortune, who retired as head of PP&L's Financial Department in 1984. "If management had known in advance what the ultimate costs would be, the units would never have been built."

Still, hindsight was a luxury that utility management didn't have the benefit of consulting in the 1970s. Susquehanna represented a huge sense of pride and accomplishment for PP&L. The experience of shepherding 2,100 megawatts of nuclear generation to commercial operation engendered a tremendous amount of esprit de corps among PP&L personnel.

"Susquehanna was essentially the end of the postwar building boom," explained Bob Compton of the company's Corporate Communications Department. Compton, who retired late in 1994, spent much of his 21-year career writing about and for Susquehanna Steam Electric Station. During that period of time, he saw Susquehanna grow to 25 percent of PP&L's 8,500 megawatts of generating capacity.

Nuclear Pennsylvania

P&L's 1970 decision to go nuclear and apply for a construction license for its Susquehanna Steam Electric Station was part of a trend that swept the American electric utility industry in the 1960s and 1970s. Nuclear power was widely seen as the solution to skyrocketing demand problems across the country and continuing utility concerns about supplies of coal and oil.

Early on, Pennsylvania utilities took a leading role in nuclear power development. Duquesne Light Co.'s

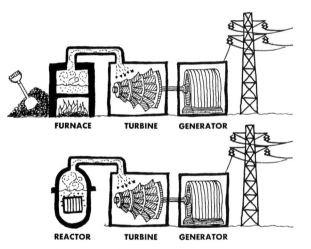

Steam-electric generation: fossil-fired and nuclear

Shippingport station was the first nuclear facility sited in the state back in the late 1950s. Philadelphia Electric Co. followed in 1960 with its application for the Peach Bottom nuclear station on the Susquehanna in York County, just north of PP&L's Holtwood and Safe Harbor hydroelectric facilities.

The original Peach Bottom reactor was built as part of the high-temperature gas-cooled prototype reactor consortium, a group of 52 investor-owned utilities that included PP&L. The 40,000-kilowatt prototype reactor went into service in 1967 and was retired in place eight years later after generating more than 1.3 billion

kilowatt-hours.

In 1968, Philadelphia Electric Co., Public Service Electric & Gas, Atlantic Electric and Delmarva Power announced an ambitious nuclear construction program, a series of four reactors for Pennsylvania and New Jersey. Two of the one million-kilowatt boiling water reactors were designated for the Peach Bottom site, and the remaining two reactors—both pressurized water types (PWRs)—were to be installed at Salem, N.J., in PSE&G's service territory. Philadelphia Electric Co. owned 42.5 percent of the four units.

At about the time that Philadelphia Electric Co. was bringing the prototype Peach Bottom unit on line—and PP&L was making its initial decision to go nuclear at Susquehanna—Metropolitan Edison Co. and its parent company, General Public Utilities (GPU), were getting ready to start commercial operations at Three Mile Island Unit One. Located on the Susquehanna River near MetEd's York Haven hydroelectric facility and PP&L's Brunner Island plant, TMI, as it would become known internationally a dozen years later, was just 10 miles from downtown Harrisburg.

Jointly owned by GPU's three subsidiaries—MetEd, Jersey Central Power & Light and Pennsylvania Electric

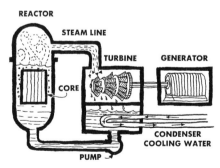

Boiling water reactor steam cycle

Co.—TMI Unit One was one of three Babcock & Wilcox PWRs that GPU envisioned building during the late 1960s and early 1970s. The other two reactors were to be built at Oyster Creek, N.J., on the Atlantic seashore in Jersey Central Power & Light's service area. But labor problems and other delays convinced GPU to locate the second of the two Oyster Creek units at Three Mile Island.

Another PJM member with nuclear aspirations was Baltimore Gas & Electric Co., PP&L's longtime partner in Safe Harbor. In 1967, BG&E committed to building twin reactors at Calvert Cliffs, described at the time as the largest single investment of private capital in the state's history.

With electric demand growing almost exponentially in the late 1960s, Philadelphia Electric Co. followed up its commitment to Peach Bottom and Salem in 1968 with the announcement that it planned to build two additional reactors—identical to the Peach Bottom BWRs—at Limerick, Pa. The two Limerick units were to be wholly owned by Philadelphia Electric Co. and were to go into service in 1975 and 1976.

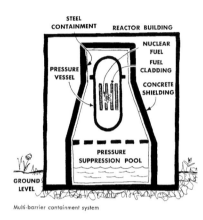
Multi-barrier containment system

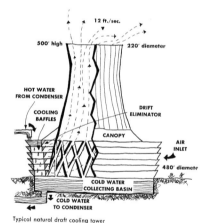
Typical natural draft cooling tower

erated by nuclear plants. In 1970, the year that PP&L announced its intentions to build Susquehanna, less than one million megawatt-hours of electric power were produced in the state's atomic reactors. Fourteen years later, the first full year of generation at Susquehanna Unit One, the state's electric customers were deriving 21 million megawatt-hours of energy from nuclear reactors.

Pennsylvania's experience with nuclear power in the 1960s and 1970s was reflected nationally. By 1974, 55 plants had operating licenses in the U.S., and another 63 plants had construction permits from the AEC. A total of 101 nuclear units were on order that year, and an additional 18 utilities had signed letters of intent for new nuclear plants.

Nuclear power accounted for eight percent of total U.S. electric capacity on Jan. 1, 1975, and the Atomic Industrial Forum, an industry trade association, estimated that nuclear power would account for

Nuclear-generated electric power provided an ever-increasing share of Pennsylvania's generation mix between 1970 and 1984. By the latter year, some 16 percent of the electric power generated in the state was gen-

12.8 percent of U.S. electric capacity in 1980 and 23.6 percent in 1985.

But that was before the world discovered a place named Three Mile Island.

A Billion-Dollar Year

News media from around the world flocked to the Three Mile Island site. (*courtesy of the Morning Call*)

Demonstrators protest outside the Danville Sheraton Inn on April 6, 1979, while PP&L executives meet with legislators and news media inside.

In the spring of 1979, Americans flocked to movie theaters to see Jane Fonda and Michael Douglas in a thriller about a meltdown in a nuclear reactor operated by a California utility. *The China Syndrome* was fiction—science fiction, really—but it tapped society's deep-seated fears about the often misunderstood power of the atom. The movie was also eerily prophetic.

In the early morning hours of March 28, 1979, a blast of super-heated steam erupted from a safety valve atop the reactor building of Three Mile Island Unit Two. The steam blast—not all that uncommon at the nuclear-powered steam electric station on the banks of the Susquehanna near Middletown, Pa.—was the start of a chain of events that would rivet world attention on the two-unit Pennsylvania nuclear plant in the weeks to come. It would also signal a sea of change in the fortunes of America's nuclear power industry.

For much of the morning of March 28, things went spectacularly wrong at the Pennsylvania reactor. What the Nuclear Regulatory Commission (the name of the Atomic Energy Commission had been changed in 1978 by President Jimmy Carter) clinically called "a feedwater valve transient" led to the complete disabling of the reactor and the subsequent buildup of a gas bubble inside the reactor containment building.

News media from around the world flocked to the site just downriver from Harrisburg. The plant's four big cooling towers became a symbol of society's fear of nuclear technology, even though the same kind of cooling tower had been built at PP&L's Montour coal-fired steam electric station just months before, and was therefore not something associated only with nuclear plants. Never before in the history of electricity had more news media attention been focused on the utility industry.

Unit Two had tripped shortly after 3 a.m. Nuclear Regulatory Commission (NRC) officials arrived at the site that afternoon and measured radiation of 12 millirems in the vicinity of the plant. The radiation leak continued the next day, and into Friday,

March 30. That Wednesday morning, PP&L had dispatched Bill Allen, Susquehanna's health physics supervisor, and Dennis Trout, health physics engineer, to TMI to assist MetEd with the crisis. On Thursday, eight additional PP&L health physics personnel arrived on site.

By then, the situation was serious—and deteriorating. PP&L sent nonessential employees home from Brunner Island, located just downstream from TMI, and suggested that employees who lived within 10 miles of the plant consider evacuating their families. Late that afternoon, PP&L activated its system emergency procedures.

The crisis peaked on Saturday, March 31, when Harold Denton, chief of reactor safety at the NRC, William States "Bill" Lee, the president and CEO of Duke Power in North Carolina—which was then the largest operator of Babcock & Wilcox pressurized water reactors—and a host of other government and utility officials entertained the possibility that the hydrogen bubble inside the Unit Two reactor containment building was capable of causing a core meltdown.

By Sunday, April 1, the hydrogen bubble had begun to shrink. The crisis was past. President and Mrs. Carter toured the stricken reactor, and the NRC began the lengthy review of reactor safety that characterized future development of the industry. On Monday, PP&L's new president, Bob Campbell, toured the company's Harrisburg service center to reassure employees that things were under control and that radiation

levels were within normal limits.

For Campbell and PP&L, the disaster at TMI couldn't have come at a worse time. The utility was deep into construction at Susquehanna, with more than 70 percent of the work at the big nuclear unit already complete. Metal siding was being installed on the top levels of the reactor building, and work was far enough along that construction crews had spent much of the bitter winter of 1978-1979 doing piping and electrical work indoors.

That Friday, April 6, Campbell had been scheduled to address Pennsylvania legislators at the Sheraton Inn in Danville. The meeting was an annual event, started five years before to brief legislators and media about the progress of Susquehanna construction. But in the wake of TMI, the April 6 meeting took on new significance for the Luzerne County community.

"By the time State Rep. Ted Stuban of Columbia County called the meeting to order, there were, including Stuban, nearly a dozen members of the House and one senator present. Three additional senators were represented by their staff members. There were also some two dozen representatives of both the print and broadcast media, as well as about 50 members of the public, some of them with anti-nuclear signs," the *PP&L Reporter* noted.

Campbell and John T. Kauffman, executive vice president of operations, told the sometimes hostile audience of legislators and media that PP&L would continue to stress openness and constant review of its operations as it moved toward completion and operating licensure at Susquehanna. "Campbell said the company is sparing no expense to see that Susquehanna operators will have the best possible training," the *Reporter* said. "Kauffman described the separate simulator building in which, aided by a computer, operators can study simulated accident conditions and learn appropriate corrective action. PP&L, he said, is one of only about three companies in the country to have such a facility."

PP&L's candor was able to defuse a tense situation, but it was painfully obvious following TMI that America's nuclear world had turned upside down.

The Real Risk

PP&L had been well aware of society's fear of nuclear power development when it decided to proceed with construction of Susquehanna Steam Electric Station. As early as 1972, Dick Lichtenwalner, Corporate Communications director, and Jack Busby had spent an afternoon discussing nuclear power risk strategies.

"One way of rationalizing this matter of risk from nuclear power development is to relate it, as Mr. Busby did on occasions, to the many risks the public is subjected to or voluntarily submits itself to in the course of everyday life," Lichtenwalner wrote Tom Ruddell in the Corporate Communications Department. Busby had suggested that the department investigate a number of different risks, including major industrial accidents like the 1947 Texas gas explosion, natural disasters like floods and hurricanes, aircraft and automobile travel and accidents around the home. Busby had suggested to Lichtenwalner that the risk statistics "could then be transported into meaningful exhibits."

But the real risk that PP&L would assume with its construction of Susquehanna was financial. The 1970s and early 1980s would witness a near unending PP&L pilgrimage to the nation's financial markets as it sold common and preferred stock, first mortgage bonds, debentures and notes, all in an attempt to finance the nearly $3 billion cost of building its first nuclear plant.

Debt and equity financing were already pronounced in the late 1960s as PP&L attempted to finance its ambitious postwar construction program. The company sold 621,266 shares of common stock in 1967, generating $18.6 million and another $16.7 million in 6-1/8 percent notes. The year that it decided to go nuclear, PP&L also sold $45 million in first mortgage bonds, carrying an interest rate of between 6-1/2 and 6-3/4 percent.

No financing was done in 1968, but the floodgates opened in 1969. For much of the next decade-and-a-half, PP&L was an almost constant visitor to the financial markets on Wall Street. From 1969 to 1977, the company raised more than $2.2 billion,

PP&L's new president, Bob Campbell. *circa 1980*

Campbell and John T. Kauffman, executive vice president of operations, told the sometimes hostile audience of legislators and media that PP&L would continue to stress openness and constant review of its operations as it moved toward completion and operating licensure at Susquehanna.

Richard H. Lichtenwalner, PP&L's Corporate Communications director in the 1970s

Thomas A. Ruddell III, PP&L Corporate Communications director in the early 1980s

"A write-off would have been a major disaster and could have bankrupted the company."
—Bob Fortune

primarily through the sale of common and preferred stock, first mortgage bonds and notes.

During that period, PP&L sold nearly 20 million shares of common stock in public offerings. Every year from 1969 to 1977, the company made a public offering of common stock, an average of 2.2 million shares a year.

Federal tax laws were changed during the decade to encourage employee stock ownership and dividend reinvestment plans. Between 1975 and 1977, PP&L made available an additional two million shares of common stock through its dividend reinvestment program. The company also provided 142,000 shares of common stock to the employee stock ownership plan, most of it allowed under federal tax regulations relating to utility construction programs.

What was all the more astounding to the old-timers at PP&L was that the 1969-1977 financings were dwarfed by the activity of the next seven years. Bob Fortune had come to PP&L from the audit department at Deloitte and Touche in the 1940s, and his task at PP&L in the late 1970s and early 1980s was to raise the money to finish completion of Susquehanna.

Things were under control through 1979, although construction cost estimates had increased by a factor of four since PP&L had filed its application for a construction license back in 1971. But the accident at Three Mile Island and the resulting government oversight of nuclear construction doubled and tripled construction time schedules.

Then, too, in the late 1970s, America was in the throes of one of the worst inflationary spirals in its history. Double-digit inflation was the rule rather than the exception, thanks to sharply increased energy costs and wage-price instability, and the cost of money was close to 10 percent by the end of the decade.

"Construction was committed and was in progress for several years prior to the Three Mile Island fiasco," Fortune recalled in 1992. "By that time, the commitment was so substantial that it never appeared practical to abandon the project. A write-off would have been a major disaster and could have bankrupted the company. So construction continued—expedited as much as possible—but that still required the raising of $4

to $5 billion of new capital in about seven years, from 1977 to 1984. This meant increasing the company's total capital structure by a factor of about eight to ten."

Fortune knew that he was faced with perhaps the biggest task in the company's history. "I recognized early that we had to maintain a respectable bond rating because at least half of the funds had to be raised by the sale of debt securities," Fortune explained. At the time, the company had a AA bond rating from both Moody's and Standard and Poor's.

A 20 Percent Prime Rate

"How could we keep the ratings with such a massive increase in debt?" Fortune asked himself. "The two most important factors to bond rating agencies were first, the percent of debt in the capital structure, which should be kept to 50-55 percent to maintain the investment grade rating. The second factor was the number of times interest was covered by income before interest charges. Three times was desirable, but the coverage could approach two times temporarily with prospects for recovery and still maintain an investment grade bond rating of ABB or higher."

One way to maintain an acceptable percentage of debt as well as a decent ratios was to sell substantial amounts of equity capital, a trend that PP&L had taken advantage of in the 1970s. The trend would accelerate dramatically in the late 1970s and early 1980s.

"We sold about 15 percent additional common stock every year," Fortune said, "which was the limit the market could absorb. This is because earnings for common stock had to increase at about the same percentage to support the additional shares. In spite of maintaining fairly good common stock earnings, the market price of the common stock became seriously depressed because of the flood of new shares, the numerous other electric utility stock offerings available for the same reason as PP&L's offerings and the high interest rates which occurred during the latter years of the 1970s and into the early 1980s."

Fortune called the run-up in interest rates at the end of the 1970s "a major handicap in financing during most of the period. They were the highest seen for at least the last 50 years. The prime rate at one time exceeded 20 percent."

One major problem of selling equity was the dilution that resulted. PP&L was selling common stock at discounts of up to 60 percent of book value. Dividend requirements for common approached 20 percent during the period—when the discount was taken into account. One solution to the problem was to sharply increase the amount of preferred stock sold.

"I don't see how the financing of the Susquehanna plant could have been accomplished without the large sales of preferred stock," Fortune said. "The situation called for the sale of substantial amounts of preferred stock—in violation of conventional wisdom and accepted financing policies. At one point PP&L had about 22 percent of preferred stock in its capital structure, when to exceed 10 to 12 percent was considered risky."

John Childs, a Wall Street expert in long-term financing, would single Fortune out at industry meetings. "He would always point me out and say, 'Don't do what Bob Fortune is doing. He's selling too much preferred stock. Never sell more than 12 percent.

It's too risky.'"

By the time Fortune retired on July 1, 1984, 31 months after his normal retirement date of September 1981, it was apparent that Susquehanna Steam Electric Station, and the massive financing needed to pay for it, was going to be successful. Unit One had come on line in 1983, and Unit Two would "go critical" just months following Fortune's retirement.

After raising billions of dollars—and flying in the face of conventional wisdom—PP&L had managed to weather the financing crisis in fine form. Although Standard and Poor's reduced the company's ratings to A, Moody's never lowered the rating below AA-.

Ironically, the difficulties encountered during the financing binge of the late 1970s and early 1980s laid the groundwork for a strong recovery of PP&L's capital structure in the mid- to late-1980s. "The sale of such an enormous amount of securities at high interest rates or preferred dividend premiums was quite a task," Fortune explained, "but it had major benefits in later years when a much lower interest rate environment prevailed. The savings resulting from refunding with lower-cost securities enabled strong earnings since the mid-1980s without the need for electric rate increases."

The accident at Three Mile Island and the resulting government oversight of nuclear construction doubled and tripled construction time schedules.

Susquehanna nuclear plant. *(illustration by Brent Schaefer © 1995)*

The Cost of Doing Business

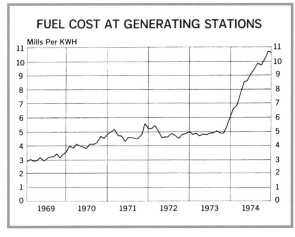

FUEL COST AT GENERATING STATIONS

Mills Per KWH

This graph tries to explain why
consumers pay more for less.

Inflation—the bugaboo of American business during the 1970s—wreaked particular havoc on the electric utility industry. For much of the decade, the industry was up to its eyeballs in inflationary alligators, primarily because of generation and transmission construction programs that had to be completed to meet the ever-growing demand for electric power.

PP&L had been involved in an almost unending construction program since it started building the first units at Sunbury Steam Electric Station in the immediate postwar years. But the period from 1945 to 1965 had been one of the most stable in American economic history. Interest rates moved in a narrow band from 4-1/2 percent to six percent during that period, and inflation rarely jumped more than a percent or two a year.

That all changed beginning in the late 1960s. The difficulty of trying to wage war in far-off Vietnam without making the sacrifices of converting to a wartime economy led to an inevitable wage-price spiral. In 1973, America's dependence upon foreign oil became frighteningly apparent when the Organization of Petroleum Exporting Countries (OPEC) embargoed Middle Eastern oil supplies; the cost of all domestic and foreign energy commodities skyrocketed in the years to come.

For PP&L, in the midst of a multibillion-dollar construction program, the resulting inflation would take a heavy toll. Already by 1970, inflation was making its presence felt in American society. Between 1964 and 1969, the cost-of-living index had risen by 21 percent, an average four percent annual increase. Food prices were up 20 percent for the period, and automobile repairs were up 23-1/2 percent. Services of all kinds were up

nearly 28 percent. Health care costs were already moving up sharply; the average cost of a semi-private hospital room had moved up 86 percent since Congress had passed President Lyndon Johnson's Medicare legislation back in 1964.

The cost of everything continued to go up during the decade. At the end of 1974, PP&L was paying an average of $25 a ton for coal on the open market, more than double the price it had paid in 1973. The nine million tons of soft coal that the company burned in 1974 cost $117 million more than it had the year before. A mile of double-circuit, 230,000-volt line using steel towers that cost $190,000 to build in 1972 cost $248,000 two years later.

Wages, the other major cost component of utility operations, were also undergoing significant upward pressure. PP&L settled the 1974 strike with the Employees Independent Association (EIA) and the International Brotherhood of Electrical Workers (IBEW) with a fairly typical wage agreement. Union employees settled for 8-1/2 percent the first year of the two-year contract and eight percent the second year. The year before, West Penn Power had settled with its employees for 8-1/2 percent; Duquesne Light Co.'s 6.88 percent wage settlement was the lowest for Pennsylvania utilities in the 1974-1975 period.

Wages and prices continued to rise during the decade. The cost of residential meters jumped 35 percent between 1973 and 1977, while incandescent streetlight assemblies jumped 43 percent and acetylene rose 51 percent in just four years. For PP&L, the cost of doing business had changed dramatically during the decade.

39

That Was No Lady

Tropical Storm Agnes devastated many communities throughout the PP&L service area. These photos show a line crew rowing down Harrisburg streets to reach flooded transmission poles and restore service.

In the popular mind, hurricanes and tropical storms are the occupational hazard of living in Florida or along the Gulf Coast of Mississippi, Louisiana and Texas. Utilities in those southern climes annually prepare their employees and customers to deal with the fierce storms that boil up out of the Caribbean or the Gulf of Mexico every autumn.

But the Mid-Atlantic and the East Coast regions of the United States are also prone to hurricanes and tropical storms. In the 20th century, dozens of killer storms have ravaged New England and the Atlantic Coast. On Sept. 21, 1938, the great Long

Island hurricane blasted across Long Island into Connecticut and didn't lose strength until it had devastated Massachusetts and Vermont.

More than 600 people were killed, and damage was estimated in excess of $350 million. Logging crews spent months cleaning up the massive forest blowdown in western Massachusetts and Vermont.

On the last day of August 1954, Hurricane Carol battered eastern New England. Sixty people lost their lives, and Providence, R.I., was under water for days; damage was estimated at $450 million. On Sept. 22, 1961, a dying Hurricane Esther was rekindled over the Gulf Stream and slammed into Cape Cod before petering out over Maine and Canada's Maritimes.

Pennsylvania Power & Light Co. had had firsthand experience with hurricanes and the damage they were capable of causing. Late in the afternoon of Friday, Oct. 15, 1954, Hurricane Hazel blasted into the southern half of PP&L's service territory with 84 mph winds and sheets of driving rain. The hurricane had come ashore early that morning at Myrtle Beach, S.C., and had devastated parts of North Carolina, Vir-

ginia and Maryland on her way north.

Before the fast-moving tropical disturbance had crossed the PP&L service area in a northerly direction into New York, more than 8,500 miles of line were down and 317,000 customers were without power. PP&L marshalled 149 of its own crews and 45 outside crews from power companies as far away as Massachusetts, Ohio, Michigan and Missouri. Hazel had done all its damage in the short span of about four hours. Unlike most tropical storms, Hazel's damage was from wind, not water; within 72 hours, literally all of the company's customers were restored to power.

Pennsylvanians, especially those who lived along the tempestuous Susquehanna River, were acutely aware of the flood danger posed by hurricane and tropical storm. Residents cast a wary eye to the south and east every hurricane season, especially in the months of August and September, the time of greatest likelihood for tropical disturbances. Typical was Tropical Storm Doria, which caused floods and high water all across southeastern Pennsylvania in the last week of August 1971.

But the National Weather Service cautioned that the hurricane season lasts from June until October. The next June, that warning was borne out in central and eastern Pennsylvania with tragic results.

The Most Damaging Storm Ever

Tropical Storm Agnes, the first of the 1972 season, was a full-fledged hurricane when her eye passed over the Panhandle of Florida just after noon on Monday, June 19, 1972. She weakened quickly as she passed inland and was quickly downgraded to Tropical Storm status. But a wide band of clouds and moisture curled far to the northeast ahead of the storm, and rain began that night in Tennessee, Kentucky and Indiana. The band of moisture took a sharp right over the Hoosier state and trended well east toward Ohio

Before Agnes had spent herself over the Susquehanna Valley late in the week, she dumped 18 inches of rain over parts of central and eastern Pennsylvania.

and Pennsylvania.

Before Agnes had spent herself over the Susquehanna Valley late in the week, she dumped 18 inches of rain over parts of central and eastern Pennsylvania. The Holtwood and Brunner Island plants were awash, and the state, along with Florida, Maryland, New York and Virginia, was declared a disaster area by President Richard M. Nixon.

Harrisburg, Wilkes-Barre, Sunbury, Scranton and dozens of other PP&L communities were devastated by the floods Agnes spawned. The $2.1 billion in damage caused by the storm, much of it in Pennsylvania, was the worst hurricane damage ever encountered up to that time. It was, as President Nixon called it, "the worst natural disaster in the whole of America's history."

Nixon flew over Harrisburg to survey the damage in the wake of the flood, no doubt reflecting on the capture just the week before of five burglars at an obscure Washington, D.C., address that became known to posterity as the Watergate Office Complex.

'A Large, Dirty Lake'

It started raining in Pennsylvania on Wednesday, June 21—the first day of summer. Four inches of rain fell that day, and it continued raining for the rest of the week. By Thursday, Harrisburg had recorded nearly a foot of rain, and Williamsport was inundated by 11 inches of precipitation. Weather forecasters issued flash flood warnings for the lower half of Pennsylvania.

On Friday, it was increasingly apparent that a disaster of historic proportions was shaping up for the Susquehanna and Wyoming valleys. At Wilkes-Barre, hundreds of volunteers, including quite a few PP&L employees, were sandbagging along the banks of the east branch of the Susquehanna. Their efforts were to little avail. Just after 10:30 that morning, the river surged over a 37-foot dike and inundated much of the Wyoming Valley beneath floodwaters

It was, as President Nixon called it, "the worst natural disaster in the whole of America's history."

Scenes like this from Bloomsburg fairground contributed to the $2.1 billion in damages caused by Agnes.

Despite their own personal losses, PP&L employees worked long hours restoring service and, in this case, rescuing a dog during the Agnes flood.

20¢ THE OBSERVER

Bob Hope tours flood-stricken Wyoming Valley area

To host giant television special to raise funds for flood victims

Hope for flood victims

(*courtesy of* Wyoming Valley Observer)

12 feet deep in places.

When the river finally crested at Wilkes-Barre at 7 p.m. Saturday—nearly 36 hours after breaching the dikes—it was 18 feet above flood stage and almost four feet higher than the official height of the levees. Writer Susan Stranahan described the Wyoming Valley as "a large, dirty lake"; 5,000 square miles were flooded, and the raging river washed out 200 bridges in Pennsylvania and New York.

Dozens of PP&L employees in the Wyoming Valley lost everything they owned. Bob Bellis' home on Oak Street about 300 yards from the Susquehanna dike was one of the first to go. Water reached nearly halfway up the walls on the second floor. "We'd been working 12-hour shifts every day to get service back to those who could take it," Bellis recalled shortly after the flood. "When things calmed down at work a little, about six days after the flood, the company gave me time off to clean up."

Marie Czoch, who had retired earlier in the year from the Sales Department in the Northeast division, evacuated her Wilkes-Barre home at the last minute. She and her husband made an ambulance out of the family station wagon and delivered two invalid neighbors to the Veterans Hospital in Wilkes-Barre. In the days after the flood, Wilkes-Barre lineman Jack Jescavage came across two elderly sisters exhausted by clean-up efforts at their home. The two women had lost all their appliances, and their two-wire residential electric service was ruined.

It would be weeks before electrical contractors could rewire their home, so Jescavage and Wilkes-Barre meter supervisor Matt Brady organized a rescue effort. The two men took up a collection, located a range and refrigerator for the two women, solicited donations and then supervised the installation of a 100-amp service for them. "I guess we sort of adopted the two little old ladies," Jescavage modestly told the *PP&L Reporter.*

'You've Got to Have an Emergency Plan'

Agnes wreaked havoc the length and breadth of the Susquehanna River. Much of Harrisburg was under water. Water lapped at the top of the first-floor windows of the Governor's Mansion, and the fires in the blast furnaces at Bethlehem Steel Co.'s big Steelton plant had been banked by the floodwaters. Even further downstream, water boiled over the Holtwood Dam, and Philadelphia Electric Co. engineers watched helplessly as water came within four feet of the top of the 92-foot-high Conowingo Dam, even as hydro employees opened the floodgates to let as much water as possible pass downstream.

The floods were particularly damaging to the PP&L system. Early in the storm, floodwaters knocked out Stanton Steam

At the height of the storm, about 130,000 PP&L customers were without service.

Electric Station in Scranton, the Holtwood Steam Electric Station and the Lock Haven combustion turbine. Bob Hoyt, area operating manager at Lock Haven, and five other employees holed up on the second floor of the Lock Haven Service Center and rode out the flood. They piled desks on top of tables, and records on top of the desks and saved most of the service center's documents, even though water in the street outside was 10 feet deep. The six men moved radio and telephone equipment to the second floor of the building and directed restoration work from the second-floor sanctuary.

Harrisburg and Wilkes-Barre were particularly affected by the storm damage. A number of substations in the two communities were put out of service, and water flooded the underground distribution networks serving the river cities. It was June 27 before PP&L crews were able to energize the Harrisburg underground system.

'The Pulse of the Island was Beating'

The bulk of the $11 million damage sustained by PP&L during the week-long disaster occurred at Brunner Island Steam Electric Station. Then the largest generating plant on the company's system, Brunner Island was completely inundated by the boiling waters of the Susquehanna River. By Friday afternoon, the big steam electric station was completely shut down, "its pump rooms under 17 feet of muddy water, its relays and switches soaked, its coal yard and feeder pits inundated, its motors slime-coated, all roads in and out of it closed by 10 to 12 feet of water and its communications with the mainland dependent on walkie-talkie pack radios," the *PP&L Reporter* described the mess below Harrisburg.

The last of 180 generation and 75 construction employees at the plant were evacuated at 2:15 that Friday afternoon, just 30 minutes before a wall of water crashed into the No. One pump room.

The Holtwood Steam Electric Station during and after floodwaters from Agnes flowed over the dam and into the plant.

A skeleton staff of 13 employees remained. Just after dawn on Saturday, a rented helicopter began ferrying mechanical and electrical crews into the flooded site. The men climbed down from the helicopter's ladder into the bucket of a front-end loader operated by Ben Smith, construction foreman, and were then ferried to the plant.

Working around the clock, the crews energized the transformer that supplied the 4-kv bus to the plant, which made available electricity for water treatment and supply, lighting and the big sump pumps in the basement of the plant. Literally hundreds of relays and switches had to be dried and tested before the pumps and other equipment could be restored to service.

By Sunday morning, helicopters were shuttling workers from the temporary staging area at the Northeastern Area High School in nearby Manchester. The choppers came and went in an unending stream, reminding some of the veterans in the crew of their days with the Air Cavalry in Vietnam. "I almost can't believe it," Edwin Mauk, wireman first class from the Lancaster Service Center, commented on the helicopter shuttle. "I never thought I'd ever see anything like this."

Once the pumps were operable that Sunday, crews faced the difficult problem of shoveling tons of mud out of the plant. Pumps had to be taken apart, washed, dried and put back together again. By Monday afternoon, 72 hours after the storm had first hit, "the pulse of the island was beating at an increasing rate. Motors were being taken apart and windings cleaned and checked, insulation was being tested, bearings were being inspected and talk was starting to be heard of when Brunner would be in full operation again," wrote Mike Piedmonte of the *PP&L Reporter* staff.

John T. Kauffman, PP&L's Generation Department head, was able to report on Tuesday, June 27, that "the bearings on all three of the main turbines have been inspected and found OK. We are now starting to check the turbine shafts for bowing." Kauffman noted that "our present estimate for return to service of all units at Brunner Island is 5 to 6 weeks; however, one unit may be back as early as July 10."

At the height of the storm, about 130,000 PP&L customers were without service, many because their meters had

been submerged by the floodwaters. One out of three of PP&L's 6,000 employees had been called into restoration service, and the control center in the General Office Tower in Allentown was the hub of emergency operations throughout the crisis. Control center teams worked round-the-clock, 12-hour shifts following the declaration of a system emergency at 1 p.m. on Thursday, June 22. The teams worked to coordinate line crews and plant personnel and directed equipment to the field from as far away as Colorado.

Hundreds of other PP&L employees did their part. Jim Marsh, now the director of Corporate Communications, was then a relatively new employee in the company's Communications Services Department. Keeping the lines of communications open among employees and customers was a vital task. That Saturday, Marsh flew over the Susquehanna River Basin, photographing storm damage and seeing the havoc up close with a reporter's eyes. Marsh then reported on the destruction from ground level on a damage inspection trip to Wilkes-Barre on Monday, as the floodwaters receded. Marsh worked 24 hours straight to help Editor Bernie Steber put together a special storm edition of the *PP&L Reporter*. "It was a humbling experience," Marsh recalled. "You'd be talking to people working up on a pole to restore electric service, when they didn't even know whether or not their own homes were still there. I was proud to work for an organization that had people with that kind of character."

In the end, Tropical Storm Agnes was the greatest natural disaster in the company's history. The fact that the death toll was so low—less than 100 people died in Pennsylvania, Maryland and New Jersey—was attributable to the gradual nature of the flooding. Just two weeks before Agnes vented her fury on the Susquehanna River Valley, nearly 300 South Dakotans died when a wall of water cascaded down from the Black Hills and swept into Rapid City and surrounding communities.

Everything In Their Power

Brunner Island Plant at Flood's Height

Once again, the professionalism of PP&L's people had come through in a crisis. "All of us share a feeling of great respect and appreciation for the PP&L men and women who worked so hard, showed so much guts, so much caring for others, so much imagination and daring, so much willingness to stay with it hour after hour, day after day, so much good humor and so much patience and readiness to serve in every way that would be helpful," Jack Busby wrote in the wake of the storm.

Busby's feelings were shared by many Pennsylvanians. "It gives me considerable pleasure to be able to commend your employees for the excellent job done during the current flood disaster in our Commonwealth," Gov. Milton J. Shapp wrote Busby the week after the flood. "I personally have seen the utility repairmen on the job day and night, and I know that they have done everything in their power to restore service to our citizens and our businesses."

That they had, but they'd been doing things that way for more than 50 years.

Noted as "a humbling experience," Jim Marsh (left) worked 24 hours straight to help Bernie Steber (right) put together a special storm edition of *PP&L Reporter*.

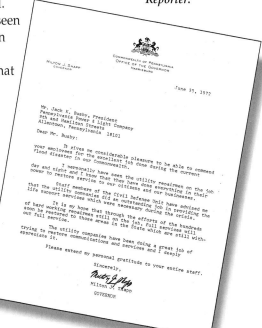

The Molly Maguires

During the 1960s and 1970s, PP&L was approached more than once by residential developers and customers to put a community's distribution system underground to make the community look as modern as possible. In the spring of 1968, company distribution crews placed a community's entire system underground, this time to deliberately make the town look as old-fashioned as possible.

The community was Eckley, a village of some 200 people just north of Hazleton, and the occasion was the filming of a Paramount Pictures movie, *The Molly Maguires.* Set in the anthracite region in 1876, the big-screen movie told the story of the Irish secret society that tried to overthrow Pennsylvania's 19th-century coal barons.

"In planning the color movie, Paramount insisted in achieving as much authenticity as possible and decided on the location at Eckley, a 'coal company-owned' village that most nearly resembled the environment of the 1870s," the *PP&L Reporter* noted. "Since there was no electric lighting then, Paramount contracted with PP&L to install underground electric service and remove all poles, overhead wiring and lighting."

John Luzenski and Donald Fritz of the company's distribution division were in charge of the job. The work began during unusually cold weather in February 1968 and involved removal of 2,000 feet of 2/0 copper, three-phase 12-kv primary and building 1,600 feet of 4/0 ACSR, three-phase 12-kv overhead line to bypass the village. An additional 2,500 feet of No. 4 copper, single-phase 12-kv line was replaced with underground lines and submersible transformers. A total of 90 buildings were provided with underground service; 84 of the buildings were on the town's main street.

PP&L crews camouflauged outside meters by building unpainted wooden boxes around them. Crews did encounter problems with ground frost and with a bed of rock beneath the town's asphalt roadway, which necessitated relocating a trench in one part of the town.

PP&L finished its work in April, and Hollywood took over the town for the spring and summer. Tourists flocked to the tiny community to watch cameraman James Wong Howe film a bevy of Hollywood stars, including Sean Connery, Richard Harris and Samantha Eggar. Paramount built the huge wooden breaker that dominated the outdoor set in the movie so that they could set it afire for one of the pivotal scenes.

John Luzenski worked in PP&L's distribution division when the call came in to install underground electric service and remove all poles, overhead wiring and lighting in the small community of Eckley. Paramount Pictures was coming to town to make a movie.

Only 86 inhabitants still resided in the town when Hollywood came calling in the spring of 1968. It's doubtful whether many of the patrons who saw the movie when it was released in 1969 knew of the key role that PP&L played in restoring the village to its 1870s authenticity.

40

Embargo!

In 1969, PP&L decided to expand Martins Creek Steam Electric Station with two oil-fired generators. As this photo shows, fuel oil was temporarily transported to Martins Creek by rail until a pipeline was built.

Americans learned to live with new realities in the 1970s. Perhaps the most difficult lesson for society to assimilate was the fragility of the nation's energy lifeline. During a six-year period from 1973 to 1979, America found itself questioning the essential soundness of its energy supplies. Almost overnight, the cost and availability of energy

Newspaper headlines on the oil crisis in the 1970s were not comforting to the utility industry. (*courtesy of the Morning Call*)

The 1979 fall of the Shah of Iran... and the subsequent capture of the Iranian government... under the Ayatollah Khomeini, led to a second oil embargo late in the decade.

supplies in North America were thrown into question. An economy that had run efficiently for more than a quarter-century on imported petroleum was thrown into chaos. The price of a barrel of oil doubled and tripled, and then doubled again. Long lines formed outside gas stations as Americans worried that their mobile way of life was about to change.

By 1969, oil had fallen to $1.40 a barrel, and much of the industrialized world was dependent upon supplies of cheap petroleum, most of it coming from the volatile Middle East. The outbreak of the Yom Kippur War in October 1973 threw world oil markets into chaos. The Organization of Petroleum Exporting Countries (OPEC) embargoed oil shipments to the United States and Western Europe, and prices surged as much as 130 percent during the last quarter of 1973.

Once set in motion, the upward spiral of oil prices continued for the remainder of the decade. The 1979 fall of the Shah of Iran, America's ally in the Middle East, and the subsequent capture of the Iranian government by Islamic fundamentalists under the Ayatollah Khomeini, led to a second oil embargo late in the decade. By that time, oil prices had topped $20 a barrel.

The rise in oil prices coincided with a decade-long run-up in inflation and interest rates. Oil wasn't the only energy commodity affected by the price increases. Natural gas producers, whipsawed by low prices through the 1960s and 1970s, had all but abandoned exploration for new sources. Bitterly cold winters in 1977, 1978 and 1979 caused the first spot shortages of natural gas since the 1930s and contributed to skyrocketing natural gas prices at the end of the decade.

Coal was not immune from upheavals in the energy markets; and that was an economic fact of life that planners at PP&L increasingly took into account. By the mid-1970s, the Allentown utility was burning

more than nine million tons of bituminous coal and one million tons of anthracite a year. The average cost of coal to the utility—at the mine—was $8 a ton in 1970. That price had increased to $12 a ton in the wake of the 1973 oil embargo, and it nearly doubled to $21 a ton by 1975.

'Mining it and Burning it'

The reason for the rapid jump in price was more complex than the increase in oil prices. "There are only two problems with coal," Jack Busby often told associates, "mining it and burning it."

Busby's facetious assessment of the difficulties of coal economics was more accurate than it first appeared. Much of the coal mined in Pennsylvania that was burned by utilities like PP&L was dug from underground mines by union miners. Throughout the 1960s and 1970s, costs for mine wages, equipment, capital costs and transportation all increased dramatically, the result of inflation and interest rate increases.

In 1972, the highest skill rate for a union job in one of Pennsylvania's mines worked out to $41.50 a day, not including fringe benefits, cost of living increases and overtime. Three years later, the figure was $57.20 a day, a 38 percent rise. Capital investment in mining equipment was increasing at an even steeper rate; the cost of a longwall continuous mining machine in 1975 was $250,000, 61 percent higher than the $155,000 the same piece of machinery had cost in 1972.

Capital costs—the dollars spent on capital items like machinery, office buildings, mine shafts and train-loading facilities—had tripled in a seven-year period. When the Rushton Mine, one of PP&L's bituminous suppliers, came on line in 1967, the investment per annual ton of production was $13. In 1974, two new mines came on line—the Greenwich Mine and the Oneida Mine. Their investment per annual ton of production was $34 and $45, respectively. Unit train costs were also escalating. The cost to transport a ton of coal in one of PP&L's fleet trains in 1972 was $2.87; three years later, that cost had jumped to $4.13.

Finally, environmental costs had begun to take an ever-increasing bite out of utility steam generation costs in the early 1970s. For the most part, environmental awareness is a modern phenomenon. The first Earth Day was celebrated in April 1970, and the environmental movement, which had begun to gather steam during the 1960s, sailed full speed ahead in the next decade.

Ironically, it was Richard M. Nixon who could most accurately be described as America's environmental president. During the late Mr. Nixon's slightly more than five years in office, America took giant steps toward a new environmental ethic. Congress passed, and Mr. Nixon signed into law, landmark clean air and clean water legislation between 1969 and 1974. It was during the Nixon Administration that the Environmental Protection Agency was established. Mr. Nixon's Christmas bombing of Hanoi, his 1970 incursion into Cambodia and the conspiracy surrounding the Watergate break-in obscure his record as the political

godfather of the American environmental movement.

Much of the impetus for the environmental movement nationally had come from the state level. Pennsylvania, with the establishment of its Department of Environmental Resources (DER), was a leader in the field. But for PP&L, complying with national and state environmental regulations was an increasingly expensive proposition, especially when it came to mining and burning coal. By 1975, the Allentown utility was spending $17 million to upgrade coal-cleaning equipment at its mines to comply with DER air quality requirements regarding sulfur content of coal burned.

No matter how expensive the cost of generating electricity at the beginning of the 1970s, electric power demand in the Mid-Atlantic region continued to grow, necessitating the addition of generating capacity. The problem of growth was particularly acute in the PJM region. In 1968, PJM member utilities were forced to reduce voltage on 14 separate occasions; that record was exceeded by 17 different voltage reductions in 1969. Late that year, PP&L

Throughout the 1960s and 1970s, costs for mine wages, equipment, capital costs and transportation all increased dramatically, the result of inflation and interest rate increases.

PP&L's oil tank-farm at Martins Creek provides fuel storage for the plant.

Martins Creek. *(illustration by Brent Schaefer © 1995)*

Austin Gavin,
PP&L executive vice
president. *circa 1970s*

decided to install new generating capacity on its system to forestall what was a worsening reserve situation on the PJM system.

Oil at Martins Creek

Environmental and cost reasons were behind PP&L's 1969 decision to expand its Martins Creek Steam Electric Station with two 800,000-kilowatt oil-fired generators. For the first time since the construction of Wallenpaupack hydro back in the 1920s, PP&L had elected to forego coal for a generating station. "At the time the decision was made in late 1969 to construct two oil-fired units at Martins Creek," the *PP&L Reporter* noted in 1973, "studies comparing the advantages and disadvantages of the two fuels indicated strongly that oil held the major advantages— among them, economics, environmental impact, diversification of fuel supply and increased reliability."

Already by 1969, utilities like PP&L were sharply aware of the environmental cost of burning coal. PP&L was faced with the decision to burn oil—which had relatively little sulfur content—or to install equipment that would remove sulfur

gases and particulates in order to burn coal. "The reliability of gas-removal and particulate-removing equipment wasn't proven then—and still isn't adequate," the *Reporter* pointed out late in 1973.

The addition of the oil-fired units at Martins Creek would boost the plant's total generating capacity to 1.9 million kilowatts and make the station the largest on the PP&L system. They would also solve a long-running problem with fly ash deposition from the plant's first two units.

In 1970, the company installed electrostatic precipitators on steel columns between the boilers and stack of the first two units. Essentially dust collectors, the precipitators were mounted 135 feet above the ground. With a dust-collecting surface of more than 165,000 square feet each, the precipitators were designed to eliminate the problem of fly ash emission at the big plant north of Easton.

The precipitators removed fly ash by passing flue gases between a series of electrically charged plates 30 feet high. As they moved through the electric field, the dust particles became charged themselves and adhered to the plates. At regular intervals, the plates were rapped automatically, which caused the dust to loosen and fall into hoppers below for removal.

"We are deeply concerned with the

The generator for Martins Creek's oil-fired Unit 3 began its voyage from Belfort, France, in the spring of 1974.

quality of the environment at our generating plants," PP&L Executive Vice President Austin Gavin reported in 1970, "and have gone ahead with this project even though we are preparing to convert the Martins Creek coal units to oil-fired operation within the next few years and will have no need for the precipitators there."

Interstate Energy

The expansion of Martins Creek was a departure for PP&L in several important respects. United Engineers & Constructors Inc. of Philadelphia was selected as construction contractor for the new two-unit plant addition at Martins Creek and the planned conversion of the existing units from coal to oil. Key to the environmental benefits of the new units was the planned construction of two 600-foot stacks to disperse combustion products and construction of massive cooling towers to lessen the amount of warmed water that would be released into the nearby Delaware River.

For the first time in its history, PP&L went offshore to order turbine-generators for the new oil-fired units. In May 1970, the company placed an order with M.A.N. of Nuremburg, West Germany, for the first two units, plus an option for a third unit. "We have been investigating the foreign equipment industry for about two years now," explained Willard U. Baum, PP&L vice president. "Our satisfactory findings abroad, plus the production schedules of domestic manufacturers prompted our order with M.A.N."

Baum added that U.S. firms were sharing in the bounty of the $350 million construction project. United Engineers & Constructors Inc. had already been named as construction contractor for the project, and PP&L planned to buy the boilers for the new addition from Combustion Engineering Inc. of Windsor, Conn. Gilbert Associates Inc. of Reading was selected as architect-engineers for the project.

"Maintaining the quality of the environment will be among our major concerns in the development of this project," Baum stated, adding that "we are already demonstrating this concern by spending nearly $20 million to install 99.5-percent efficient electrostatic precipitators on new coal-burning units and raising dust-collector efficiency at existing plants."

PP&L was also going offshore for fuel supply at its new Martins Creek units. In full operation, the two oil-fired units at Martins Creek would require about 10 million barrels of oil per year. Planners operated from the assumption that long-term contracts could most advantageously be made with foreign suppliers and that the oil would be delivered by tanker somewhere on the East Coast of the United States.

The big tank-farm terminal at Marcus Hook on the Lower Delaware River below Philadelphia soon presented itself as the most obvious place to take delivery of the foreign oil. But planners then had to determine how to get the fuel oil from Marcus Hook to Martins Creek.

Truck delivery would involve 160 trucks carrying 7,000 gallons per vehicle each day of the year to feed the boilers at Martins Creek. Rail delivery would involve two 50-car unit trains, with one trainload of more than one million gallons arriving at the plant each day. More than half the 107-mile trip each way would be on a single track line paralleling the Delaware River.

The third option—a pipeline from Marcus Hook to Martins Creek—was the most attractive option. "Pipeline transport offered substantial advantage," a 1970s background paper noted. "A buried pipeline is unseen and operation is noiseless. Oil is pumped as efficiently in good weather as in bad, in summer and winter.

Looking north, this photo of Martins Creek shows Unit 1 precipitator's inlet duct work. *circa July 27, 1970*

The addition of the oil-fired units at Martins Creek would boost the plant's total generating capacity to 1.9 million kilowatts and make the station the largest on the PP&L system.

Delivery by pipeline does not contribute to traffic jams or wear out public roads. It does not overload a railroad system. Importantly, pipelines have the best safety record of any carriers."

In December 1971, the Interstate Energy Co. applied to the Pennsylvania Public Utility Commission for a permit as a common carrier for the proposed pipeline from Marcus Hook to Martins Creek. The proposed 80-mile-long, 18-inch diameter pipeline, of which PP&L acquired ownership in March 1976, was designed to carry crude oil, No. 2 fuel oil and residual oil. Hearings, permitting and construction of the pipeline took nearly five years.

Unit No. 3 at Martins Creek went into commercial operation in May 1975, almost a year before the Interstate Energy Co. pipeline to the plant on the Delaware River was complete. Delays in the pipeline permitting and construction forced PP&L to start operations at Martins Creek with an interim delivery system. For nearly two years, the company leased three 50-car unit trains to deliver oil to the plant. PP&L had to pay $2.3 million to build a temporary rail-unloading facility at the plant; the monthly lease fee came out to $43,000.

The difficulty of securing permits for pipeline rights-of-way was minuscule in comparison to the white knuckles PP&L executives were subjected to in 1973 in the wake of the first Arab oil embargo. Already by September 1973—even before the outbreak of the Yom Kippur War in the Middle East— critics were calling into question PP&L's decision to go with oil-fired units at Martins Creek.

Austin Gavin, PP&L

executive vice president, answered critics in a September 1973 interview in the *PP&L Reporter.* It was neither practical nor feasible to convert the new units at Martins Creek to burn coal, Gavin pointed out. "This is because we are well down the road on the project," he said. "Construction of Unit 3, the first of the two units, which is scheduled to go into service early in 1975, is 55 percent complete. Construction of Unit 4, planned to go into service early in 1977, is about six percent complete."

To convert the units to coal-fired operation would have meant reducing the rated capacity of the units by half, Gavin reported. Even with escalating oil prices, annual operating costs of smaller coal-fired units would be as much as $7 million higher. Conversion would also mean that commercial operation of Unit 3 would be set back by as much as three years. That delay would mean additional rate increase requests in 1977 and 1978, averaging about 10 percent a year.

PP&L bit the bullet and continued with the construction at Martins Creek. As it was, oil prices did skyrocket in the wake of the Arab oil embargo. But the oil used at Martins Creek wasn't the light fuel oil that the media so frequently identified as the commodity under attack by the OPEC oil barons. Instead, PP&L was buying heavy bunker fuel oil in million-barrel contracts; PP&L was paying much less for its fuel than the prices so casually bandied about by the television network anchors.

Like anything else, what went up in price was bound to come down. After the supply scares of the 1970s, oil prices stabilized during the 1980s; by the end of the decade, prices had declined to $14 a barrel amid an actual oil glut.

Martins Creek had definitely achieved its goal of setting the company on a new environmental awareness path. The Delaware River Basin Commission, which compiled an environmental impact statement on the project, lauded PP&L's efforts. "The total adverse effect from the proposed action on the environment in the vicinity of the generating station both now and in the future is judged to be slight," the report concluded.

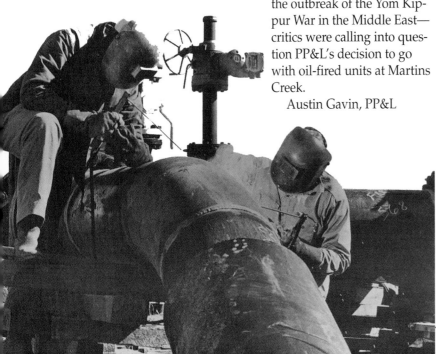

The End of an Era

Pennsylvania Power & Light Co.'s switch to bituminous coal in the 1960s and diversification to oil-fired generators at Martins Creek in the 1970s spelled the end of an era for two of the company's oldest anthracite-fired steam electric stations.

Hauto plant closed its doors in 1969 after 56 years of operation. Stanton plant followed suit in 1972 after 45 years of service. "It was an old and inefficient plant," John Chaplinsky, community service manager for PP&L's Northeast division, described Hauto for the media in early 1969. "Like an old car, it had become costly to operate. We needed the power it could generate, or we would have closed it sooner."

The plant that John S. Wise had helped design and build fell victim to economies of scale in the power generation business and to the new environmental realities of the 1960s and 1970s. With the new 765,000-kilowatt unit at Brunner Island expected to come on line during the summer of 1969, Hauto and Stanton had become expendable.

"Furthermore," Chaplinsky explained, "we have had problems limiting emissions of fly ash from Hauto's stacks. To reduce this emission to acceptable levels would have required an investment in collection equipment that was unwarranted by the age of the plant."

About 120 employees were affected by the shutdown at Hauto. Many of them were nearing retirement age, and most of the rest were placed in other positions around the system. In November 1968, more than 200 past and present employees of the plant gathered at the Summit Hill Rod and Gun Club to reminisce about a half-century of operations at the big anthracite-fueled plant in the Panther Valley.

Ninety-two-year-old John S. Wise was sanguine about the closing of the Hauto plant. In a 1968 interview with Len Kucinski of the *Sunday Call-Chronicle*, he noted that, "Hauto worked out fine and did its job. Too bad it's going. But you can't make money and give lower rates these days with inefficient equipment."

PP&L's Hauto plant closed in 1969 and was demolished after 56 years of operation.

Jack Busby explained that 14 acres of the 270-acre Hauto site would be retained for the Hauto substation. The remaining 256 acres "will be cleaned up," he said. "That is to say, the power plant will be demolished and the site cleared for other use, since we consider that the building has no value for industrial purposes. The coal stocks will also be cleaned up; the ash piles will be handled so that there is no dust nuisance, and our forestry group will take appropriate action to landscape the electric facilities and do reforestation on the hillside areas of the property that we own, where this is feasible."

Busby's announcement was considered good news in the Panther Valley. "Nobody is applauding the fact that 117 jobs will be lost or at least dislocated when the big power plant, now obsolete, shuts down," editorialized the *Tamaqua Evening Courier*. "But the decision not to let the plant stand around empty and deserted is well-taken. The company's latest plans to offset the economic loss represented by the closing of the Hauto plant amount to more good news in the story of the area's continuing resurgence."

Gentle Demolition Inc. moved on to the site early in 1969 and began dismantling the plant, piece by piece. Demolition took considerably longer than company planners first thought it would, primarily because of the skill with which John S. Wise had built the plant back in 1912-1913. Demolition crews discovered in tearing down Hauto that its walls were seven bricks thick and built around large steel beams.

Plans had been on the drawing board for years to dump the boilers at Stanton plant in October 1972. But nature intervened that summer. The flooding accompanying Tropical Storm Agnes inundated the plant. As soon as the flood-waters receded, demolition crews began to take the plant apart.

By 1976, the outer walls of the lower portion of Stanton were the only reminder that the site had once been a baseload power plant for PP&L and Scranton Electric Co. Only the skeletal steel shell of Hauto remained. It was truly the end of an era.

The Energy of Man

The onset of what is commonly referred to as the "Energy Crisis" was already apparent to power generation planners at PP&L and the utility industry in general as the 1960s drew to a close.

Double-digit electric power growth through the decade had stretched to the limit the industry's ability to deliver low-cost electric power. Inflation and interest rate increases were making energy supplies—both domestic and foreign—far more expensive than they had been in the past.

"The Energy of Man" was a three-car traveling train energy exhibit that toured PP&L's service area from 1971-1974.

To communicate the dramatic changes occurring in the nation's energy situation in the early 1970s, PP&L sponsored an innovative exhibit that traveled around the service territory. "The Energy of Man" was a three-car train that served as a traveling showcase for PP&L from 1971-1974. The 216-foot-long train was chock full of exhibits that traced U.S. energy innovation from Benjamin Franklin and Thomas Edison to nuclear power.

With its distinctive, 27-inch-high orange letters and its glossy white cars with an orange stripe, "The Energy of Man" was previewed to shareowners at the annual meeting on April 28 and unveiled to the public on May 3 in Berwick, near the site of PP&L's Susquehanna nuclear station.

"PP&L today is facing the greatest challenge in its history," Jack Busby said in dedicating the train. "We must support the quality of life by building vast new facilities essential to reliable electric service. At the same time, we must support the quality of life by minimizing the impact of our facilities on the environment. We can meet this challenge, but

only with understanding from the public we serve. It is to this understanding that we dedicate 'The Energy of Man.'"

The train began its initial tour of the system from May to November 1971. Provisions were made in the rear car for receptions, press conferences and a 44-seat meeting area for business and service groups and visiting school children. Sites selected for the 1971 tour included Berwick, Wilkes-Barre, Scranton, Hazleton, Bloomsburg, Strasburg, the Allentown Fair, Harrisburg, the Bloomsburg Fair, Williamsport, Sunbury, Pottsville and Bethlehem. While the train was parked at the siding in Bloomsburg in mid-June, it was open for special tours by employees attending the annual company picnic.

By the end of the 1972 season, "The Energy of Man" had brought PP&L's message to more than 200,000 people in the service area. The 1973 tour opened in Allentown in January and stayed the month of February at State College, where it was used as a classroom on wheels at Pennsylvania State University. The Penn State visit was jointly sponsored by PP&L, West Penn Power Co. and the Pennsylvania Electric Association.

When "The Energy of Man" was retired in the spring of 1974, it had traveled to 39 communities in PP&L's 10,000-square-mile service territory. More than 300,000 residents had toured the exhibit in those three years, validating Jack Busby's goal of fostering "understanding from the public we serve."

The 1980s: New Realities

Robert K. Campbell (left) succeeded Jack Busby as PP&L's chairman of the board, president and CEO in 1979.

Jack Busby stepped down as PP&L's chairman of the board on July 31, 1979. His 21 years as president and chief executive officer had placed an indelible stamp on the Allentown-based utility, and he had borne personal witness to momentous changes in the American electric utility industry.

Robert K. Campbell, Busby's successor, had been in place for two years, and was already proving to be a savvy utility executive. Campbell had skillfully orchestrated the PP&L response to the Three Mile Island crisis that spring of 1979, and would successfully guide PP&L's Susquehanna nuclear

station through the completion of construction and the start-up of commercial operations in the years ahead. With the completion of Susquehanna, PP&L closed the book on its ambitious—and expensive—postwar construction program.

Change in the utility industry had accelerated in the 1970s, and perhaps no change was more pronounced than the shift from energy consumption to energy conservation. Busby had understood the ramifications of that change early on. "I think if you sat down and did a little outside reading and did some outside talking with people, you couldn't help but be exposed to these ideas about energy waste, and they made a lot of sense," Busby said in an interview at the time of his retirement. "And of course, you had to start adjusting because you couldn't predict the time of the crunch."

Change in the utility industry had accelerated in the 1970s, and perhaps no change was more pronounced than the shift from energy consumption to energy conservation.

That summer of 1979, energy conservation was the watchword at PP&L. The Allentown utility, and the industry in general, was still feeling its way into the new energy realities brought about during the 1970s. The Arab oil embargo of 1973, double-digit inflation, energy prices that continued to ratchet upward and electric rates that followed suit had stood the conventional wisdom of economies of scale in the electric utility business on its head. Before the year was out, the nation would be rocked by a second oil embargo—this time emanating from far-off Iran.

Sharply increased electric rates during the decade had struck hardest at low-income customers and those on fixed incomes. By the summer of 1979, PP&L was stepping up efforts to help low- and fixed-income customers better insulate their homes and apartments. Following a pilot project conducted in the Lehigh division in 1978, the company bought six insulation-blowing machines and began to make them available to customers system-wide.

Seminars on "using energy wisely" were held around the system for industrial and commercial customers in the spring of 1979. At Harrisburg, more than 40 engineers and state energy coordinators attended a five-session Energy Management Action Course in May to learn how to conserve energy in state office buildings. Topics included controls; heating, ventilating and air conditioning (HVAC) systems; lighting systems; domestic hot water; heat recovery; and insulation.

PP&L's Generation Department wasn't above learning new tricks itself. At Brunner Island Steam Electric Station, an innovative aquaculture project used the warm water outflow of the big coal-fired plant to raise catfish. The project, which began on a 13-acre site south of the plant's switchyard in the summer of 1977, was producing pound-and-a-half catfish by the summer of 1979. "Benefits of farming the plant's warm water discharge are twofold," the *PP&L Reporter* explained in 1979. "First, fish convert feed to protein efficiently, providing an optimum supply of high quality food for people at the lowest possible cost of feed conversion, and second, it utilizes the 35 to 40 percent of heat energy that is normally lost from a power plant."

The need to conserve energy wasn't just an abstract policy-making exercise handed down from the top floors of the General Office Tower. Energy conservation affected everybody who worked for PP&L, not to mention everybody who purchased their electric power from the Allentown utility. In the summer of 1979,

In 1977, the Brunner Island Steam Electric Station began raising catfish using the plant's warm water outflow.

PP&L employees were acutely aware of the cost and scarcity of gasoline.

Mary Jo Semyon, a stenographer at Scranton, told the *Reporter* that she and her husband took the kids to monthly Phillies games by bus rather than car, and Ray Leaman, line foreman in construction, carpooled with five other employees from Lancaster to Cherryville every day. John Wieand, a clerk at the general office, revealed his solution to the gas crisis: riding his bike to work every day. "Maybe the gas situation is helpful in a way," Wieand mused, "because we need to learn to live a healthier life style."

The rate shock of the 1970s was addressed in a number of ways, not the least of which was a PP&L commitment to get a whole lot closer to its customers. In the summer of 1978, PP&L took the lead in forming a 16-member consumer advisory panel. Working in conjunction with Dr. Louis S. Meyer of the Pennsylvania Citizens Consumer Council, PP&L created the panel to address energy and other problems specifically relating to PP&L.

Members came from a wide variety of consumer action groups, including the Carbon County Action Committee for Human Services, Catholic Social Services, the Urban League, the Consumer Credit Counseling Service of Lehigh County and the American Association of University Women. Some of the representatives of the panel were frankly skeptical of PP&L's past consumer relations efforts.

But PP&L took the effort seriously, and the company was willing to take some criticism if that could improve its ability to reach out to consumers. Merlin Hertzog, vice president of Consumer and Community Services, and a PP&L representative to the panel, reflected the company's objectivity when he noted that "we plan to take a hard look at our performance as a company in response to consumers and also at the panels as representatives of our customers."

Busby reflected on the changes that had impacted PP&L during the 1970s, changes that were as significant as any the utility had faced during its history. "I

think there was a feeling during the '60s—not universally held by any means—that it was a fruit-picking period," Busby said before heading for a much-deserved North Carolina retirement. "There's lots of fruit out there. It's pretty easy to pick, so let's get some…. There was just an inadequate perception of things we should have been doing in the '60s to prepare for the '70s and '80s."

Busby described himself as a maverick—a description that would have been seconded by everybody at PP&L, not to mention the utility industry in general—and he said the company's greatest achievement during his tenure was maintaining its "strong, clear commitment of public service and community service. I think that was the way the company was when I came here, and I certainly hope it hasn't gone backwards in that respect."

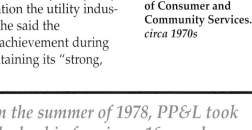

Merlin Hertzog, PP&L's vice president of Consumer and Community Services. *circa 1970s*

In the summer of 1978, PP&L took the lead in forming a 16-member consumer advisory panel to address energy and other problems specifically relating to PP&L.

Into the 1980s

The company that Bob Campbell inherited from Jack Busby in 1980 was still strong and vibrant, despite the challenges it had faced in the mid- to late-1970s. Operating revenues in 1980 were almost $887 million, and net income of $180 million provided a dividend of $2.12 per common share for each of PP&L's 45.6 million shareholders.

The 1980s were a decade of immense financial change. In 1981, the company topped the billion-dollar mark in operating revenues for the first time. Five years later, in 1986, revenues were double what they had been in 1981, reaching

Mary Jo Semyon, from the Scranton office, and other PP&L employees developed home front solutions to saving energy, like car pooling and public transportation. *circa 1970s*

Leon Nonemaker, PP&L's senior vice president of Division Operations. *circa 1970s*

The necessity to staff two new nuclear units, several new oil- and coal-fired units and a host of new positions created by computerization and energy conservation efforts resulted in a steady gain of employees.

Between 1980 and 1986, common stock increased by 29 million shares to 74.5 million shares.

nearly $2.2 billion. During the same period of time, net income climbed from $244 million in 1981 to $300 million in 1986. Dividends on common stock in 1986 were $2.58 a share.

But there was a lot more common stock on which to pay dividends. The financing program that had begun in earnest in the mid-1970s to pay off the massive costs of construction was predicated on the issuance of equity. Between 1980 and 1986, common stock increased by 29 million shares to a total of 74.5 million shares. Throughout much of the period, Allowance for borrowed Funds Used During Construction (AFUDC) averaged well over $100 million a year, reaching a peak of $172 million in 1982.

There were other realities to contend with besides those that were strictly financial. For one thing, the work force was growing. In 1980, there were just over 7,700 people on the PP&L payroll. The operations work force consisted of 4,875 people at year-end, and an additional 2,827 people were on the construction payroll. The construction work force topped out at 3,078 people in 1982, the

last full year of nuclear construction prior to the June 1983 commercial operation of Susquehanna Unit One.

The construction work force dropped by more than a third in the next few years, sliding in 1985 below 2,000 people for the first time since the mid-1970s. With no new baseload generation on the drawing boards after the early 1980s, the construction force stabilized at its 1985 levels for the remainder of the decade.

But the necessity to staff two new nuclear units, several new oil- and coal-fired units and a host of new positions created by computerization and energy conservation efforts resulted in a steady gain of employees throughout the period. While construction employment was falling by 1,100 people, operations employment jumped by 1,600 people between 1980 and 1985. Total employment, however, leveled off at just above 8,000 people for the remainder of the decade.

A change that was of even more import was the slowdown of kilowatt-hour sales in the early 1980s, the first drop since the days of the Great Depression. After missing the million-customer level by less than 500 customers in 1980, PP&L reported 1,006,570 customers in 1981. PP&L had placed its 500,000th customer on line in 1949, about the time that the first two units at Sunbury were coming into commercial operation. At the time, the average customer used 120 kilowatt-hours of electricity and paid 4.7 cents per kwh. A third of a century later, the average customer was using 800 kilowatt-hours of electricity and paying just less than five cents per kilowatt-hour.

But customers were actually using less electricity than they had in the recent past. From 1981 to 1982, total kilowatt-hour sales dropped from 22.9 billion kwh to 22.3 billion kwh.

Kilowatt-hour sales were actually up slightly in the commercial category, but they dropped off in both the residential and industrial categories. Industrial sales were off about eight percent for the year, partially because of fuel-switching caused by the energy crises of the late 1970s and

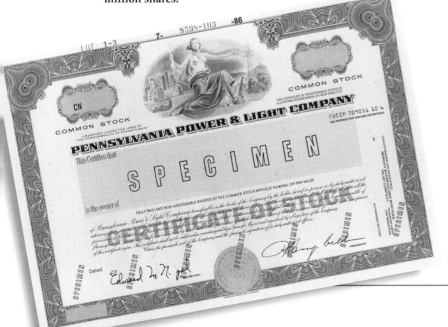

partially because of the delay in recovery from the recession at the end of the Carter presidency in 1979-1980.

It didn't help the company's kilowatt-hour sales that rates continued to climb in the early 1980s. The $101.3 million rate increase that the company was allowed to put into effect at the beginning of 1981 was the first general increase in four and one-half years.

"While we recognize that customers aren't pleased at the thought of paying higher electric bills, the increase is necessary for the company to remain financially healthy," explained Leon L. Nonemaker, senior vice president of Division Operations. "Even with the increase, PP&L customers pay among the lowest total electric bills of the seven major electric utilities in the state."

Better Ways

Given the drop in kilowatt-hour sales and the increase in electric rates at the beginning of the decade, PP&L continued to search for better ways to use electricity and supply it to customers. By 1981, the search had boiled down to three strategies:

- Conservation and energy/demand management programs.
- Improvements in existing plant capacity and efficiency.
- Experiments with industrial, commercial and residential alternative technologies.

In its 1981 mission statement, PP&L recognized what had—and what hadn't—changed about the generation, transmission and distribution of electric power. "While technology and the way we do our jobs have changed," Bob Campbell explained, "the company's mission—its reason for being in business—has remained virtually unchanged since it was founded in 1920. The bottom line is still to provide an essential service for nearly 2.5 million people in central eastern Pennsylvania."

The company's 1981 goals reflected the new realities of the electric power business and the changes "in technology and the way we do our jobs" that Campbell had described. Rate and financial goals were at the top of the list. Campbell called for maintaining financial strength in order to raise the capital necessary to finance the company's construction program at competitive rates.

Rate increases were to be held below the general level of inflation, and the company established a new "pioneer" rate geared to the purchase of electricity produced by alternative energy technologies. On the conservation front, the company set a target of an average 2.5 percent peak load growth, compounded annually for the period 1977 to 1995. The company also hoped to "explore, evaluate and encourage development of projects using alternate energy sources such as small hydro, solar, wind, refuse and cogeneration."

Development of a corporate coal supply strategy was a priority item, as was continuation of office automation, strengthening regional economic development efforts and examination of corporate contracting procedures and processes. On the personnel side, PP&L hoped to dramatically improve its slipping safety record and to identify employees with management potential.

But perhaps the top goal for 1981

While promoting electric water heaters in the 1970s, PP&L also encouraged conservation practices. This woman demonstrates insulation installation.

From 1981 to 1982, total kilowatt-hour sales dropped from 22.9 billion kwh to 22.3 billion kwh.

413

Commercial operation of PP&L's Susquehanna nuclear station was achieved on June 8, 1983.

involved Susquehanna Steam Electric Station. The target the company assigned to its 1981 goals was simply stated: "to bring the units into commercial operation in the second quarter of 1982 and the second quarter of 1983, respectively."

As it was, the timetable for completion of Susquehanna was off by just about a year. The Nuclear Regulatory Commission approved a 40-year operating license for Susquehanna in July 1982, and the first sustained chain reaction at Unit One was achieved at 11:17 a.m. on September 10. Two months and one week later, the first unit of the big nuclear plant generated its first electric power.

Following its November 16 synchronization with the rest of the PP&L generating system, Susquehanna reached 100 percent power for the first time on Feb. 4, 1983. The plant received a license for operation of its newly completed low-level waste holding facility on April 15, and commercial operation was achieved on June 8, 1983, at one minute after midnight.

"The timely completion and the safe and efficient operation of these new generating units continues to be the focus of the company's priorities," Campbell told shareholders early in 1984. "By the end of 1984, when both nuclear units are expected to be in commercial operation,

the company will have met its construction needs for major new generating capacity for at least the balance of this century.

"The company's strategy for the balance of the '80s is to market the effective use of this strong generating capability in a way that will help spark renewed economic prosperity in central eastern Pennsylvania."

Campbell's optimism was buoyed by internal analyses showing that the increased annual costs of operating Susquehanna would after five to 10 years be more than offset by the plant's lower fuel costs. Bill Hecht, then vice president for System Power, explained that nuclear fuel cost only half as much as coal, and far less than fuel oil. By taking advantage of nuclear baseload generation, PP&L would be able to sell electricity from its coal- and oil-fired units to neighboring utilities whose units operated less economically, thereby resulting in savings that would be passed on to PP&L customers.

"Because of its lower fuel costs, electricity from Susquehanna and from PP&L's least expensive coal-fired units will be used to meet most of our customers' energy needs," Hecht said of the company's strategy in 1983. "Other units with higher operating costs then will be available to provide electricity to other utilities."

The 1983-1984 completion of Susquehanna transformed PP&L and ushered in a new era of low-cost electricity for customers in central and eastern Pennsylvania. With more than two million kilowatts of nuclear generation on line and earning money, PP&L was finally free of the voracious capital needs that had confronted the company for more than a decade. In little more than three decades, the company had diversified its fuel supply to the point where it could generate electric power with hydroelectric turbines, coal, oil and nuclear fission. But meeting the needs of an equally diversified energy marketplace posed unique new challenges for PP&L in the years ahead.

The Campbell Years

Jack Busby spent 20 years as president of PP&L. When he relinquished the position in 1977, his successor was a surprise selection. Robert K. Campbell wasn't a PP&L employee, nor was he an electric utility executive.

Campbell came to the top job in Allentown from 20 years with Western Electric. A Chicago native, his background included engineering, administration and law. Campbell had come to Busby's attention when he was Allentown works manager for Western Electric. "He never had a large hat size," Busby recalled of his successor. "He had that midwestern Lincolnesque quality. He was a good listener and nonabrasive, and he had a way of absorbing information while retaining his own convictions."

Busby had told the board when he reached the age of 60 that he wanted his successor in place by the time he turned 62, and was adamantly opposed to appointing a caretaker chief executive. Busby also "got brave enough to tell the board that we would have to go outside for a successor. We had an obligation to make sure that we didn't have an ingrown culture."

Campbell fit Busby's description perfectly. He had received his B.S. in mechanical engineering from the Illinois Institute of Technology and his M.S. from the University of Illinois in Champaign-Urbana. Along the way, he picked up a master's in business administration from the University of Chicago and a law degree from Loyola University of Chicago.

Campbell joined Western Electric as a development engineer at the firm's Hawthorne works in Chicago in 1957. He was promoted through the ranks at Western Electric, serving in a number of managerial, administrative and public relations positions. In 1965, he joined Western Electric's new plant in Shreveport, La., as assistant manager of engineering; the next year, he was named manager of engineering at the Shreveport plant.

Robert K. Campbell, PP&L chairman from 1979 until his unexpected death in 1990.

Campbell came north to Allentown in 1967, then served as manager of Western Electric's Reading works. Busby explained that Campbell's technological and managerial background was attractive to the PP&L board of directors. "He had remarkably diversified experience with Western Electric," Busby explained. "We spent a lot of time talking about the value systems of the two organizations. I became very comfortable with his values."

Busby admitted that "it was a blow to a lot of people in the company when we recruited an outsider as president. But I felt strongly that we had to bring a fresh way of looking at ourselves. Still, bringing in a person in the starting role of president was a shock. But, Bob Campbell was an outstanding president."

An Outstanding President

Bob Campbell quickly proved equal to Jack Busby's confidence in him. At the comparatively young age of 47, Campbell was leaving two decades of experience in the telecommunications industry for the top job at an electric utility. Campbell's tenure at PP&L included some of the most tumultuous events in the company's history, including the successful conclusion to the company's struggle to get the Susquehanna nuclear station into commercial operation.

Campbell's introduction to the difficulties of electric utility management came early in 1979 when the Three Mile Island incident subjected Pennsylvania's nuclear utility industry to an international spotlight. Campbell skillfully created and managed five task forces to deal with the crisis.

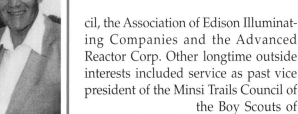

For much of the first half of the 1980s, the lion's share of Campbell's time was taken up with the fight to get Susquehanna licensed, operating and into the rate base. In 1983, Campbell presided over the unveiling of a major marketing and economic development effort, and the following year, the company announced a $2 million weatherization program for low-income customers, called WRAP, the Winter Relief Assistance Program.

Campbell's devotion to customer service was highlighted in 1986 when the utility he headed recorded the lowest complaint rate of any electric utility in the state. "At PP&L," Campbell noted, "concern for customers goes beyond being a reliable electricity supplier. It extends to being a neighbor who responds in time of need and financial hardship."

Campbell also wrestled with the financial aftershocks of the economic earthquake that shook the industry in the 1970s and early 1980s. "One of our primary objectives is to avoid base-rate increases for at least the remainder of the 1980s," Campbell vowed to shareholders at the company's 1987 annual meeting. A year later, he was able to report that "electricity sales, revenues, earnings and dividends were at their highest levels ever, and our electricity rates actually decreased. These indicators reinforce our belief that the strategies we put in place a few years ago are sound and serving us well."

Campbell found time for a host of civic and business duties outside his daily tasks at PP&L. He served as a member of the board of Harsco Corp., Consolidated Rail Corp. and AMP Inc., was a board member and past chair of the Pennsylvania Chamber of Business and Industry, and served on the board of the Pennsylvania Economic Development Partnership.

He was active in a number of electric utility associations, including the Electric Power Research Institute (EPRI), the Institute of Nuclear Power Operations (INPO), the U.S. Council for Energy Awareness, the American Nuclear Energy Coun-

cil, the Association of Edison Illuminating Companies and the Advanced Reactor Corp. Other longtime outside interests included service as past vice president of the Minsi Trails Council of the Boy Scouts of America, and membership in the Eastern Pennsylvania Chapter of the Nature Conservancy, the Pennsylvania Environmental Council and the Pennsylvania Society.

Robert Campbell with his family; above, with his wife Alvina and with his sons Joe, Tom and John.

In early June 1990, Bob Campbell was slated to become chairman of the Edison Electric Institute. But it was not to be. Few people outside the family knew that Campbell was diagnosed with liver cancer that spring of 1990. Employees were devastated in mid-June when Campbell, then 59, announced that he was stepping down for undisclosed health reasons; they were even more shocked when Campbell died on Saturday, June 16, 1990, at the Lehigh Valley Hospital Center.

More than 700 business, political and community leaders from the Lehigh Valley paid final respects to Campbell in services at First Presbyterian Church of Allentown on June 19. The Rev. Daniel Gambet, president of Allentown College, a PP&L board member and Campbell's best friend, told the congregation that the PP&L CEO had been well enough a few weeks before to shoot an 84 at the Saucon Valley Golf Club—and beat him by 18 strokes.

"He lived to see his three boys happily married and launched in successful careers," Gambet told the mourners. "He lived to hold three grandchildren in his arms and to help teach each of them to walk. He built his company, PP&L, into one of the finest electric utilities in the nation."

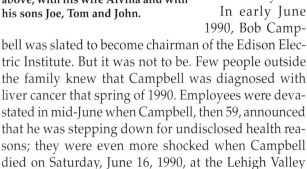

42

Poised for the 1990s

Lineman Thomas Rivera, pictured here on an aerial platform truck in Trexlertown, continued his work in PP&L's Construction Department as the company entered the most profoundly changing period in its history. *circa 1980s*

W ith the completion and commercial operation of Susquehanna Steam Electric Station's two units in 1983 and 1984, Pennsylvania Power & Light Co. marked a watershed event in its long history. For the first time since crews had begun building Sunbury Steam Electric Station in the years immediately following World War II, PP&L was no longer in a construction mode. It was a new age for the Allentown utility.

"The company enters this age with the strongest generating capacity it has ever known," PP&L noted in the summer of 1983, "especially low-cost energy from coal and nuclear units. Therefore, it is particularly important that PP&L's marketing position for the balance of the decade be clearly identified and communicated."

PP&L planned to couple its capacity surplus with "electric rates that are well below the regional and national average" to promote economic development in PP&L's service area and "to help reestablish a healthy economic climate in central eastern Pennsylvania."

The economic thrust was nothing new. PP&L had been emphasizing economic development ever since the 1920s. But by 1983, there was a new urgency to the company's efforts. With the addition of

With the addition of new generating capacity brought on line at Martins Creek and Susquehanna between 1975 and 1984, PP&L did have plenty of power to sell. The question was to whom it would sell that power.

nearly 4,800 megawatts of new generating capacity brought on line at Martins Creek and Susquehanna between 1975 and 1984, PP&L did have plenty of power to sell. The question was to whom it would sell that power.

The Decline and Fall of Big Steel

By the time Susquehanna Unit Two came on line in 1984, it was apparent that the American economy was in the throes of a change unprecedented since the Great Depression. "As PP&L entered the decade of the 1980s," the company laconically reported in 1983, "the country's economy continued to deteriorate. Plants were closing. Layoffs were occurring. Demand for steel and other basic products was down and electric sales to heavy industry declined."

The change away from a manufacturing-based economy had begun as early as the late 1960s. The Lehigh Valley's Portland cement industry was perhaps the first casualty of the changes sweeping the American economy, but iron and steel were by far the biggest victims. PP&L's planners and executives had to look no further than nearby Bethlehem to assess the changes that were going on in the American economy. For much of the 20th century, Bethlehem Steel Corp. had been the pillar of the Lehigh Valley's manufacturing economy. Aging industrial facilities that had been put into place at the beginning of the century, a flood of cheap foreign imports and contentious labor-management relations all combined to lay a triple whammy on the American iron and steel industry.

In the space of little more than a decade after 1975, America's domestic integrated steel industry began to unravel. Dozens of mills along I-80, from the Lehigh Valley west to Pittsburgh and the Monongahela Valley, then west again through Cleveland to Chicago and north to the iron ranges of Minnesota and

Michigan closed down. Furnaces were banked and abandoned. Hundreds of thousands of steelworkers were laid off from good family-wage jobs, most never to return to the mills.

Sales had begun to drop at Bethlehem in the mid-1970s. In 1977, the steel company that had anchored the Lehigh Valley economy for decades reported a net loss of almost $450 million, the largest single-year loss in U.S. corporate history until Chrysler Corp. eclipsed the record two years later.

Bethlehem recovered some of its lost momentum in the late 1970s, but the election of Ronald Reagan as President in 1980 was the harbinger of truly bad news for the iron and steel industry. As the Federal Reserve Board attempted to strangle Carter-era inflation, demand for steel products dropped precipitously. By the second quarter of 1982, Bethlehem and the other seven major domestic integrated mills reported a cumulative $700 million pretax loss. Industry capacity shrank as mills and blast furnaces closed. Output in 1982 was still only 42.5 percent of capacity. Bethlehem's big Sparrows Point plant finished the year at 40 percent of capacity.

Between 1977 and 1983, Bethlehem Steel's cumulative losses totaled $1.25 billion. Losses would actually accelerate in the period from 1983 to 1985, when the company lost another $1.5 billion. By mid-decade, more than half of the five-mile-long steelmaking complex along the Lehigh River had been abandoned. Bethlehem furnaces and mills at Lackawanna, New York and some at Sparrows Point, Md., were also shut down.

Bethlehem Steel was by no means alone in its agony. If anything, the suffering on the opposite end of the state was even greater than it was in the Lehigh Valley. The steel industry in the Monongahela Valley, the broad industrialized swath that reaches south from Pittsburgh to the West Virginia line, literally imploded between 1981 and 1987. U.S. Steel closed its Homestead, Duquesne and McKeesport works, changed its name to USX Corp. and bought an oil company.

Wheeling-Pittsburgh Steel shut its historic Monessen works in 1986, and J&L Steel tore down its Pittsburgh works. In 1981, 35,000 steelworkers made their living in the Monongahela Valley; six years later, fewer than 4,000 steelworkers were employed there.

It had frequently been said over the years that when Bethlehem Steel sneezes, the Lehigh Valley catches cold. In the early 1980s, Bethlehem Steel caught pneumonia, and the Lehigh Valley felt its effects. The big steel company's tax assessment was reduced by more than $14 million as part of local government's efforts to help Bethlehem recover from its fiscal woes, and property taxes all over the region had to increase sharply to make up the difference.

Thousands of steelworkers—some of them fourth and fifth generation employees—were laid off with dim prospects of ever being recalled to work. Steel-related employment in the Bethlehem area had peaked at 31,600 during World War II, but by the time the 1980s ended, there were fewer than 5,000 people at the Bethlehem works.

The loss of manufacturing employment rippled back into all segments of the local economy. Retail sales in Bethlehem and surrounding communities plummeted, and by 1986, the *Bethlehem Globe-Times* suspended its Sunday edition because of lack of advertising. Bethlehem Steel cut its annual contribution to the United Way by almost 60 percent, and the popular local director of the Bethlehem Area Chamber of Commerce had to leave his job because of budget cuts.

PP&L's President Bob Campbell noted that attraction and retention of job-producing industries was PP&L's "top priority." *circa 1980s*

In the space of little more than a decade after 1975, America's domestic integrated steel industry began to unravel.

Young Bill Hecht was PP&L's vice president of System Power when the new marketing focus was put in place in 1983. He was named vice president of Marketing and Customer Services in 1987.

"By 1983, it had become pretty clear to us that marketing made a lot of sense. It all seemed to tie together, and we wanted to make marketing a real sensible part of our business strategy."
—Bill Hecht

PP&L wasn't immune from the disaster that had befallen the region's steel and manufacturing base. By the end of 1982, sales of electricity showed a decline over 1981, the first time that had happened in more than half-a-century. Residential kilowatt-hour sales were off half a percent from 1981, commercial sales were up only one percent and industrial sales were down eight percent. Overall, kilowatt-hour sales were three percent lower than the year before.

Marketing Focus

It didn't take a genius to figure out that marketing and economic development had to become watchwords of the organization if PP&L were to avoid the hardships of some of its longtime industrial customers. Bob Campbell outlined PP&L's marketing strategy in a 1983 interview with the *PP&L Reporter*. "We will be increasing our efforts to attract and hold job-producing businesses in our service area, which had been suffering a disturbing loss of industries and employment in the recession of 1982-83," Campbell said. "There are over 124,400 people still without jobs in central eastern Pennsylvania."

Campbell noted that attraction and retention of job-producing industries was PP&L's "top priority. However, we'll be actively promoting efficient uses of electricity, especially where they can help industrial and commercial customers make choices on effective applications that give them an economic incentive or quality improvement. We'll also be promoting effective off-peak uses of electricity in residential applications. In that area, there often is a general lack of understanding of the efficiency and cost advantages of electricity."

To Bill Hecht, then the company's vice president of System Power, PP&L's new

marketing focus after 1983 was "very valuable. And it's just very good business for PP&L in the economic development front, recruiting new industry, making low-interest loans to non-profit economic development groups, really just laying out the risk capital to build a shell building, place advertisements in the plant-location trade press—all those kinds of activities that are more and more common now. PP&L has to be very, very aggressive in its economic development efforts."

It wasn't as if PP&L had abandoned marketing during its construction years, especially during the 1970s. But marketing had become eclipsed somewhat by the utility's conservation efforts during that decade. Congress had weighed in with the National Energy Policy Act (NEPA) of 1978, which codified many of the conservation initiatives that were then ongoing at PP&L and among America's electric utility industry in general. Five years later, however, it was becoming apparent that legislated conservation measures weren't the answer to America's energy problems.

"The marketplace forces didn't sustain the price of oil," Hecht explained. Far from zooming to $30 or $40 a barrel, the price of oil actually began declining in the early 1980s. The election of Ronald Reagan as President in 1980 led to a reassessment of Jimmy Carter's energy policy. In the early 1980s, Congress repealed many of the more draconian elements of NEPA, leaving utilities free once again to begin emphasizing marketing without worrying about meeting unrealistic federally mandated conservation targets.

"The marketplace disproved the concept that legislation would solve our energy problems," Hecht said. "By 1983, it had become pretty clear to us that marketing made a lot of sense. It all seemed to tie together, and we wanted to make marketing a real sensible part of our business strategy."

That didn't mean that PP&L would return to a 1960s or 1970s marketing effort. For one thing, electrotechnologies were changing dramatically in the early 1980s. Back in 1964 when Bill Hecht had joined PP&L as a junior engineer, the company was marketing electric resistance heating. "It put us in the enviable position of a winter-peaking utility in a summer-peaking pool," Hecht explained.

By 1983, the costs of providing electric heat were such that resistance heat was no longer the winner for PP&L it had been two decades earlier. But the considerable improvements in heat pump technology during that 20-year period presented a viable option to resistance electric heating. "We started to push heat pumps hard at that time," Hecht said, "along with off-peak thermal storage."

A CAN DO Spirit

Unlike steel and other manufacturing industries, the electric utility industry had a product that was in continuing strong demand in the early 1980s. In 1973, electricity supplied 25 percent of the energy used by industry. Just eight years later, that share had increased to 33 percent. The figures were closely paralleled in PP&L's case; between 1973 and 1981, industrial electric use grew 16 percent on the PP&L system.

For that figure to continue on its upward climb, PP&L had to replace the industrial jobs being lost in the heavy industrial sectors of the region's economy. For 1984, PP&L established a corporate goal of bringing at least 5,000 new jobs to the region.

PP&L's economic development efforts through the remainder of the decade involved neither brain surgery nor black magic. Successful economic development involved dogged determination, hard work, imagination and just a little bit of luck. In January 1983, PP&L kicked off its new economic development program by helping to coordinate a "Pennsylvania Night" promotion at a meeting of the Industrial Real Estate Brokers Association of Metropolitan New York at the New York Athletic Club. In attendance to tell

the brokers about Pennsylvania's advantages were Lt. Gov. William W. Scranton III and his father, the former governor and ambassador to the United Nations.

The company's Community Services Department was charged with spearheading PP&L's economic development efforts, including locating business prospects and securing project requirements, recommending locations that met those requirements, providing data required by businesses and industry to make location decisions and conducting inspection tours of possible plant locations and communities, in cooperation with local, regional and state groups.

Community Services expanded the company's national advertising campaign, placing advertisements in the *Wall Street Journal* and *INC Magazine*, establishing a toll-free 800-number response line and vastly increasing direct mail to target industries. "Central eastern Pennsylvania is an ideal location," explained Don Stocker, director of Community Services. "We're located in the heart of the eastern megalopolis, with more than 70 million people living within a 300-mile radius. We have an excellent transportation system, including a superior highway network and truck, rail and air service."

One of the community economic development groups that PP&L allied itself with for the effective delivery of economic development efforts on a regional basis was CAN DO, the Community Area-New Development Organization in Hazleton. Dr. Edgar L. Dessen, a Hazleton radiologist and PP&L director, had helped form CAN DO back in 1956 to diversify the Panther Valley from its longtime dependence upon the declining anthracite industry.

Over the years, CAN DO had financed five shell building projects in the Hazleton area, all with PP&L's help. "Not only did these buildings attract new industries," Dessen said, "but the 'merchandise on the shelf' attracted other

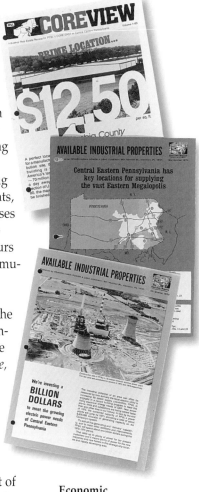

Economic development brochures along with other marketing materials were developed to attract business and industry to the PP&L service area.

The loss of manufacturing employment rippled back into all segments of the local economy.

Donald N. Stocker, PP&L's director of Community Services. *circa 1980s*

Edgar L. Dessen, M.D., Hazleton radiologist and PP&L director, helped form CAN DO.

Joseph C. Krum, director of Marketing and Economic Development. *circa 1980s*

industries who came to see the shell buildings and then were persuaded to erect other facilities more to their specifications."

Another local economic development initiative in which PP&L participated was SEDCO, the Schuylkill Economic Development Corp. in Pottsville. Like CAN DO, SEDCO's origins dated to the 1950s, but by the early 1980s, the organization was working hand-in-hand with PP&L to attract new business to the region, including Jetson Direct Mail Service, a new state prison and numerous hotel and motel facilities.

By 1987, PP&L was meeting and exceeding its goals of attracting 5,000 new jobs each year to the service area. Stable rates, abundant power and PP&L's personal touch created a host of success stories in the region. Increasingly, companies looked to central and eastern Pennsylvania for sites for distribution facilities, attracted by that 70 million-person market that was within half-a-day's drive of PP&L's service territory.

In 1984, the Economic Development, Community Services, Energy Conservation and Consumer Services departments were all merged together into a new Marketing and Economic Development Department.

Joseph C. Krum, director of Marketing and Economic Development, pointed out in 1987 that "in the years before 1984, our economic development efforts were bringing in about 2,500 jobs per year." Each new job,

Krum continued, produced about 25,000 kilowatt-hours of electric sales. "Our new objective was 5,000 net new jobs each year, which would add 125 million kilowatt-hours. We haven't been put to the real test yet. PP&L met its 5,000-job goal (in 1984, 1985 and 1986) in a generally expanding economy—a rising business cycle. Every business cycle turns downward eventually, and we're going to be hard put to maintain the 5,000 level when a downturn comes."

Krum's concerns were legitimate. Even though the recession of 1982-1983 was long over by 1987, Bethlehem Steel was still a long way from being out of the woods. PP&L's two largest industrial customers were the Bethlehem mills in the Lehigh Valley and at Steelton, near Harrisburg. Still, the big Lehigh Valley steelmaker was showing signs of life in 1987. It reported a second quarter net profit of $46.8 million, the highest since before the 1982 recession, and it reported significant new production efficiencies arising from the installation of continuous slab casters at its Sparrows Point and Burns Harbor, Ind., mills.

But the company's failure to modernize its Pennsylvania mills was troubling, as was Mack Truck's announcement late in 1986 that it planned to close its 5C heavy truck plant in Allentown, idling more than 1,800 workers—the vast majority of them PP&L customers.

Central eastern Pennsylvania went through an economic upheaval in the 1980s unprecedented since the Great Depression. PP&L refused to panic when the region's economy began a fundamental transformation. Instead, the utility rolled up its sleeves, went to work and created a marketing-based organization that was the envy of many of its peers in the electric utility business.

For 1984, PP&L established a corporate goal of bringing at least 5,000 new jobs to the region.

A Builder Takes the Helm

Shortly before he died of liver cancer in June 1990, Bob Campbell announced his retirement, effective July 1. As part of his announcement, he recommended to the board of directors that they name John T. Kauffman to succeed him. The board agreed with Campbell's final request and named Kauffman PP&L's chairman, president and CEO.

Kauffman accepted the responsibility, and in his first message asked employees help him "continue the policies and strategic direction that have been in place for a number of years and which have brought us a wide measure of success."

It was typical of the self-effacing Kauffman to ask employees to "continue your personal pursuit of excellence in all you do. There could be no more fitting tribute to Bob Campbell."

Kauffman, who had been named executive vice president and chief operating officer in October 1989, had spent his entire career with PP&L and its predecessor organizations. During the 1960s and 1970s, he had headed PP&L's Construction Department, with principal responsibility for the completion and start-up of the largest construction project in PP&L's history—the Susquehanna nuclear power plant.

Born in the Palisades area of northern New Jersey, Kauffman attended high school at Fort Lee, N.J., at the foot of the George Washington Bridge. When he left at the age of 16 in 1943, America was at war. Kauffman was accepted at Purdue University and after a year, he was accepted to the U.S. Merchant Marine Academy. He was sent for basic training to San Mateo, Calif., and was then assigned to a merchant vessel headed for the Pacific Theater. Kauffman spent much of 1944 in the western Pacific; his ship was attacked by a kamikaze during the invasion of Okinawa.

Following his wartime service, Kauffman was

John and Julia Kauffman in 1986. Mr. Kauffman succeeded Bob Campbell as chairman, president and CEO in 1990.

accepted at the U.S. Merchant Marine Academy in Kings Point, N.Y. He spent two years at Kings Point getting his engineer's rating and then went back to sea as a third assistant engineer on one of United Fruit's banana boats.

The boat hauled bananas "from Costa Rica," Kauffman recalled, "and then we'd run into Cuba and get sugar and run up to the east coast and back and forth." Kauffman worked the Mediterranean run for another company for awhile and then decided he'd better return to college to get his engineering degree. He enrolled back at Purdue, met and married Julia A. Crouch of Columbia City, Ind., and received his B.S. in mechanical engineering in 1950 from Purdue.

In the summer of 1950, Kauffman took a job with Pennsylvania Water & Power Co. at Holtwood, partly because his parents were originally from the Pottsville-Reading area. He loaded up his family in "our little old car and brought them east." Kauffman's first job was as a junior test engineer, a position he held for nine years. In 1959, he was promoted to superintendent of operations and shortly after transferred to Hazleton—PP&L acquired Penn Water in 1955—as plant betterment specialist. "We had a whole bunch of old plants then," Kauffman recalled in 1992, "and I used to go out and train the guys on how to shut them down in the evening and start them up in the morning as we brought the new unit on line."

Kauffman's sense of humor was legendary; the butt of many of the stories he told was John Kauffman—like the joke on himself about the time he was training personnel at Brunner Island. The safety valve on the deaerator had a tendency to blow and drench those standing below with water. One night, Kauffman walked out of the control room to the turbine deck and was soaked with water falling from above.

He walked back into the control room and told Arthur

John T. Kauffman in uniform as commodore of a yacht club on the Chesapeake Bay and as a young boy (right) showing first signs of engineering genius with an Erector Set.

Hummel, the shift supervisor, that "that safety is blowing on the deaerator again." Hummel got his hard hat and meandered out of the control room to take a look. He was back in less than a minute. "Ya dummy," he told Kauffman to the delight of the control room crew. "It's raining."

In 1964, Kauffman was promoted to construction superintendent—Electrical and Structural, a job he held for nearly seven years. "It was a great job," Kauffman said. "I was all over 10,000-square miles as we built new substations, installed new equipment and did maintenance at the power plants."

Kauffman became PP&L's power production chief about the time that Tropical Storm Agnes swept up the Susquehanna River Valley. "It was a mess," Kauffman described the storm clean-up. "All the electrical panels were filled with water and mud." Kauffman's next big job with PP&L came in 1973 when he was named to head System Power and Engineering. For the next decade, he was the man ultimately responsible for the construction and start-up of the Susquehanna Steam Electric Station, the biggest construction project in PP&L history, before or since.

"When we decided to build it," Kauffman said, "we didn't want to break new ground on the design. Philadelphia Electric Co. had already built Peach Bottom Two and Three. We wanted to use the same contractor to take advantage of their experience."

Then came Three Mile Island. Overnight, the rules of nuclear engineering, design, construction and operation changed dramatically. PP&L was at a point with Susquehanna where it could have abandoned the project and taken its losses. Many utilities at a similar point in nuclear construction did just that. But Kauffman pushed ahead with the project and saw it through to completion, even though he had been promoted to executive vice president in the mean-

time. He saw to it that the plant was completed right.

"It's a well-respected plant," Kauffman said in 1992. "We were just recently named one of the five best in the nation (by the NRC)." Kauffman made it a point to see to it that PP&L was as open as possible about its nuclear plant. "The community has been very receptive of Susquehanna. We worked to have those people understand what the plant was all about and that we cared about them. That's why it's open to tours. We have no secrets."

John T. Kauffman was a logical choice to succeed Bob Campbell in 1990. He served in the position of chairman, president and CEO for two years, stepping down at age 65 in 1992 to make way for his successor, William F. Hecht. "Although I will not be active in the day-to-day operation of the company," Kauffman said at the time of his retirement, "I am pleased that board members have asked me to stay on as a director. This will allow me to continue on as a PP&L representative in several community and education activities which are allied with PP&L's interests."

Those community and education activities included membership on the governing bodies of the Pennsylvania Chamber of Business and Industry, the Pennsylvania Business Roundtable, Pennsylvanians for Effective Government and the Eastern Pennsylvania Chapter of the Nature Conservancy. A longtime member of The Pennsylvania Society, Kauffman also served as past chairman of the Pennsylvania Electric Association.

On the civic front, Kauffman served on the boards of Pennsylvania 2000, Lehigh Valley 2000, the Lehigh Valley Partnership, the Lehigh Valley Business Conference on Health Care and the Advisory Committee of the Minsi Trails Council of the Boy Scouts of America. He served as co-chair of the Kutztown University Presidential Advisory Board and on the board of directors of the Hillside School for learning disabled children in his hometown of Emmaus.

The Challenge of Change

PP&L chairman, president and CEO Bill Hecht with a group of second graders at Montour Preserve in 1993.

PP&L produced its first comprehensive environmental report for shareowners, customers, employees and the public in 1993. It explained how the company provides reliable and economical electric service while protecting the environment.

Change is never easy to accommodate, but its very inevitability makes it perhaps America's most common workplace challenge. For much of its history, PP&L and its workers have had to deal with change. In the 1920s, change was embodied in the consolidation and centralization that resulted in hundreds of predecessor utilities being combined into PP&L. Change in the 1930s meant coping with the political realities of the breakup of the holding companies, and World War II brought about unprecedented change to PP&L in particular and the utility industry in general.

In the 1950s came the challenge of a construction program that transformed PP&L in little more than two decades. The energy crisis of the 1970s introduced conservation as an energy ethic, fostered by the environmental movement. The completion of Susquehanna and the essential closure of the construction era in the early 1980s changed the company's focus to a marketing emphasis that hadn't been seen around PP&L since the late 1920s.

While PP&L focused its attention on marketing in the late 1980s, the electric utility industry began to undergo another fundamental change—this time involving deregulation, competition and an actual restructuring of the way the industry delivered electric power to its customers.

The reasons for change were diverse, and not always readily apparent or understandable. Beginning with the Carter Administration in the late 1970s, government began a not-so-subtle shift away from regulation of business. Banks, airlines and trucking companies were the initial targets of deregulation, and the movement picked up steam with the election of Ronald Reagan as President in 1980. The 1978 passage of the National Energy Policy Act during the energy crisis of the 1970s laid the groundwork for the deregulation of the natural gas industry, which began to decouple gas supply and transmission from local distribution in the early 1980s.

The Natural Gas Policy Act of 1978 set into motion deregulation of the industry, and allowed drillers to recover the cost of exploration for new gas. By the mid-1980s, the industry had gone from a shortage to a surplus of gas, and prices retreated from their early 1980s highs. Instead of pulling back from deregulation, the Federal Energy Regulatory Commission redoubled its deregulatory efforts and prepared a set of rules that would effectively deregulate the industry by the early 1990s.

FERC Order 636 went into effect nationwide on Nov. 1, 1993. It basically said that pipeline companies—long the suppliers of gas to local distribution companies—could no longer sell gas direct to those local companies. Instead, local gas companies were free to make their own deals with suppliers or with neighboring gas utilities. More importantly, industrial gas customers could also buy gas direct from suppliers and use the gas system of the local distribution company to transport the gas.

Why Not Electricity?

The successful deregulation of the natural gas industry led observers of the electric utility industry to question why the same framework couldn't be applied to electric power. Industrial users had long argued that the natural monopoly of electric power transmission was outmoded in an increasingly competitive global economy. Utility executives argued equally passionately that if industrial customers were allowed to "cherry pick"—shop around among competing utilities for the cheapest rates—the stranded investment of electric power plants, substations and transmission lines would have to be paid for by those least able to pay, the utility's residential customers.

The situation was made all the more complex as the 1980s drew to a close by the rise of new players in the electric power business. The one section of the National Energy Policy Act of 1978 that had survived a decade later was the Public Utility Regulatory Policies Act. Known by the acronym PURPA, the act allowed creation of nonelectric utility companies to build and operate power plants. These Non-Utility Generators (NUGs) and Independent Power Producers (IPPs) were soon building electric power plants across the country.

By 1991, more than 4,500 non-utility generation projects had been proposed or completed in the United States. That same year, the U.S. Department of Energy estimated that electricity sales to utilities by independent companies would increase 7.4 percent a year during the 1990s, reaching 11 to 13 percent of U.S. electricity generation by the year 2010.

While the NUGs and IPPs built some cogeneration power plants specifically for industrial customers, they also built peaking and baseload generating units. Under PURPA, utilities had to purchase the electric power from these plants at avoided costs—the kilowatt-hour price calculated on the basis of how much the utility would pay for the power if it had built the plant for itself.

A Mature Industry

Then too, electric power was a mature industry by 1990. It had met the nation's demands for electric power in the period from 1950-1980, and there were those who questioned whether those demands would ever again reach the level of the 1960s. Indeed, electric power demand growth had dropped off from the seven percent annual rate that was so prevalent in the 1950s and 1960s to a rate approaching two percent a year in the 1980s.

Already by 1987, Wall Street was beginning to question the basic structural make-up of the industry. Edward J. Tirello Jr. the outspoken utility analyst of Shearson Lehman Brothers, floated the proposition in 1987 that the utility industry needed to rethink its regional orientation and consolidate into even larger super-regional utilities in order to achieve the economies of scale that had eluded the industry for more than a decade.

Tirello's prediction that the 225 U.S. investor-owned electric utilities would be merged into 50 surviving utilities within five years created a storm of controversy, and although Tirello's forecast proved to be at the least premature, it was clear that

some in the industry were taking the idea of consolidation to heart. In Iowa, Iowa Public Service merged with Iowa Power & Light Co. and later acquired the Iowa-Illinois Gas & Electric Co. The California Public Utilities Commission stepped in to prevent a merger between Southern California Edison and San Diego Gas & Electric Co.

In Indiana, the industry's attention focused in 1993 on the bare-knuckles brawl between Public Service Indiana and Indianapolis Power & Light. PSI and its charismatic chairman and CEO, James E. Rogers, announced a merger with - Cincinnati Gas & Electric Co. IPALCo., which felt itself threatened by the proposed merger, mounted a hostile takeover attempt of PSI. The normally genteel industry was transfixed by the specter of two electric utilities fighting it out in the public arena. The fight ended in the fall of 1993 when IPALCo. withdrew its hostile bid, but not before everybody in the

Training sessions like these are ongoing at PP&L. Training has always been important at PP&L to ensure that employees' skills are current and day-to-day operations are performed efficiently in an increasingly competitive environment.

By 1991, more than 4,500 non-utility generation projects had been proposed or completed in the United States.

As early as 1991-1992, PP&L's President Bill Hecht began planning and preparing the company for immense structural changes.

As the 1980s drew to a close, most electric utilities in the U.S. still depended upon their core business of generating, transmitting and distributing electric power for the lion's share of revenues.

electric utility industry realized that it wasn't the gentleman's club that it had long appeared to be.

Change manifested itself in a number of other ways as the 1980s gave way to the 1990s. Some utilities had been so severely impacted by the financial strains of nuclear building projects that they sought protection in bankruptcy court. Other utilities coldly assessed the limited potential for growth in their core business of electric power and elected to diversify into a host of related and nonrelated businesses.

The industry's diversification into everything from engineering subsidiaries to cable companies to coal mines to water companies required a different organizational structure so that rate payers would not be saddled with diversification costs. This trend to diversification led inevitably to the creation of dozens of holding companies to allow a corporate separation between regulated and nonregulated entities.

As the 1980s drew to a close, most electric utilities in the U.S. still depended upon their core business of generating, transmitting and distributing electric

power for the lion's share of revenues. Assessing the success of its natural gas deregulation experiment, Congress elected to further deregulate the nation's electric utility industry.

The passage of the National Energy Policy Act of 1992 opened the door to epochal changes in the electric utility industry. The act authorized transmission access for wholesale wheeling transactions, and overnight, the earth shifted beneath the feet of the industry. In 1994, the California Public Utilities Commission pushed the deregulation envelope even further, proposing a timetable for opening up electric utility competition in the Golden State. Under the proposed California regulations, industrial customers will be able to buy electric power from any supplier they choose within two years. By the year 2000, California residential customers will have the same right.

Cutting Back

The specter of competition produced two results, one unintended. For most of the postwar era, the nation's electric utilities had put a premium on reliability. Systems were designed with redundancy in mind, and since rates allowed utilities to recover reasonable costs, staffing levels were never called into question. But the completion of construction projects in the

A sampling of PP&L's people of the '90s—a time of many changes: Craig Merluzzi, Deborah Runkle, Edwin Solomon, Steven Williamson and Lynn Nehila.

1980s led to a decade-long period of rate stability. During much of the 1980s, utilities pared their work force by cutting back construction departments that were no longer needed.

But the potential for transmission access, deregulation and competition at the beginning of the 1990s led utilities to begin seriously cutting their work forces further. Competition meant that efficiency suddenly became a higher priority than reliability. With the wave of restructurings and consolidations that began to wash over the industry in the 1990s, utilities began to shed workers for the first time since the Great Depression.

Initially, attrition was the approved choice for reducing utility work forces. In the late 1980s and early 1990s, utilities all across the country instituted hiring freezes and offered early retirement programs to older employees. But by the mid-1990s, utilities were resorting to more radical measures. When Midwest Resources acquired Iowa-Illinois Gas & Electric Co. in 1994, the Des Moines-based company announced it was eliminating 650 jobs. Salaried employees of the two companies were required to reapply for their old positions.

The unintended consequence of competition in the electric utility industry emanated from Wall Street. Fear of competition moved Wall Street analysts to discount electric utility stocks. In 1994, FPL Group, the parent company of Florida Power & Light, further increased

Wall Street's concerns when it cut its dividend. Centerior Energy Corp. also halved its dividend, citing increasing competition and the unlikelihood of recovering increased costs with rate requests. In contrast to utilities that took the drastic step of cutting the dividend, many utilities had seen their dividend payout ratios approach the 90 percent level during the 1980s.

Reacting to the combination of rising interest rates and the anticipation of approaching competition, skittish investors began pulling away from utility stocks in the early- to mid-1990s. The Dow Jones Utility Average plummeted 15 percent in the five-month period from September 1993 to February 1994, a freefall which continued, albeit at a lesser rate, during the remainder of the year.

Pennsylvania Power & Light Co. was by no means immune to the changes that swept over the electric utility industry at the beginning of the 1990s. The changes that began in 1991 and are likely to continue into the 21st century are perhaps as significant as any the Allentown utility has faced in three-quarters of a century.

The changes that began in 1991 and are likely to continue into the 21st century are perhaps as significant as any the Allentown utility has faced in three-quarters of a century.

'Even More Wrenching Change'

"Undoubtedly," said Bill Hecht, "we're all undergoing change and will continue to undergo even more wrenching change.

Bill Hecht at the 73rd annual shareholders meeting in Harrisburg where he addressed "the rules of our changing business."

> *"These changes and increased competition in our business can be very beneficial to PP&L if we are ready to take advantage of those opportunities."*
> —William F. Hecht

And most people find change threatening. It's a human reaction. Some deal with it much more effectively than others, but we all find change to be threatening."

As early as 1991-1992, PP&L began planning for the immense structural changes that were already on the horizon. "We recognized that structural changes were likely to happen," Hecht explained. "We could not build a planning scenario in which that kind of structural change did not happen."

In 1992, PP&L pulled selected managers out of their jobs and gave them a strategic planning assignment. They were to assess the changes affecting the industry and report back on what PP&L needed to do to deal with those changes. "It was not an abstract, detached exercise," Hecht said. "They put together a strong case that confirmed generation no longer had to be a natural monopoly."

Many utilities concluded that distribution had to remain a natural monopoly, however, and even the National Energy Policy Act of 1992 recognized that fact. But if bulk power was traded as a commodity, then abundant supplies would bid the price down to variable costs. Conversely, in a short supply situation, customers would bid the price up. PP&L's strategic planning effort was leaning strongly to the former conclusion. "In most hours of the year," Hecht said, "there's an economic abundance of electric energy. That meant that the industry as a whole stood to have a shortfall of revenue. Our own experience with competition at the wholesale level indicated that the analytical models were borne out."

'The Rules of Our Business Are Changing'

Hecht outlined the changes to come when he told the 73rd annual meeting of shareholders in attendance at the Harrisburg Marriott on April 28, 1993, that "on the surface, these changes may seem like threats to our business, but we cannot afford to take a bunker mentality on this issue. The changes that are taking place provide us with many opportunities. These changes and increased competition in our business can be very beneficial to PP&L if we are ready to take advantage of those opportunities."

Hecht continued his remarks by noting that "the rules of our business are changing. The electric utility industry has entered a new age of opportunity. We can turn challenges into opportunities only by managing change.

"Understanding and managing change means that we must examine our strategic direction as a company on an ongoing basis; and we are doing just that. One thing is absolutely clear as we look to the future: the price of electricity will be at least partly deregulated. What does that mean for PP&L? It means that we will be in competition with others to sell our service. It means potential opportunities to sell our service in markets not now open to us. It means we will need to sharpen our pencils and our skills to take advantage of opportunities. It means that it will be increasingly important for us to be the lowest-cost regional supplier of electricity.

"In a more competitive marketplace, price will be an important factor in determining which utilities are winners and which are losers. We are in a good position to be one of the winners because we have already done a great deal to lower our costs, and still more is being done."

Managing change had become a way of life at Pennsylvania Power & Light Co. By the time the 1994 meeting of shareholders rolled around, PP&L had taken giant steps to restructure itself.

The Winter of 1994

A mid all the strategic planning for restructuring, reengineering, deregulation and competition, PP&L got a reminder in January 1994 that the utility business is still often a struggle with the forces of nature.

Some of the worst winter weather in the 20th century descended upon the nation's Mid-Atlantic and Middle Western regions during the third week of January. Coal piles at utility power plants from Indiana to New York froze into lumps of black ice the size of football fields, and rivers on the nation's East Coast froze for the first time in half-a-century, stranding oil and coal barges from New England south to Chesapeake Bay. Coal trucks couldn't get through to mine-mouth power plants because of ice and snow on the roads, and unit trains across the region ran behind schedule for weeks.

Utilities across the length and breadth of the PJM power pool instituted rotating blackouts to conserve precious electricity. The nation's Capitol was all but deserted on Wednesday, January 19, when the mayor of Washington, D.C., declared a power emergency, forcing businesses to close; federal government workers were sent home when federal buildings in the District closed down. For PJM power pool companies, it was the first time in 23 years that they had been forced to impose rolling blackouts—and the first time ever that blackouts had been required during the winter months. As far south as Virginia Power's service territory in the Tidewater State, blackouts of 15- to 30-minute durations were the rule rather than the exception.

It was cold. On January 19 and 20, temperatures plummeted in central and eastern Pennsylvania. Unofficial readings of -15 F at Allentown, -35 F at Berwick, -22 F at Harrisburg, -21 F at Wilkes-Barre and -20 F at Williamsport were more reminiscent of the High Arctic than Pennsylvania. It was even colder to the west. In Indiana early that week, the temperature reached an all-time record low of -36 F, and Lake Superior froze shore-to-shore for the first time in more than ten years.

Unprecedented Strains

The intense cold placed unprecedented strains on the region's electric power grid. PP&L set a new peak of 6.403 million kilowatt-hours between 6 and 7 p.m. on January 18, and PJM established a new winter peak of 41.35 million kilowatt-hours at about the same time—six percent higher than the old record, established just three days before. That night, PJM was forced to purchase more than three million kilowatt-hours from outside systems to meet the demand.

For PP&L and the PJM, the crisis peaked on Wednesday, January 19. At 3:15 in the morning, PJM declared a maximum generation emergency and began asking its customers to conserve energy by cutting interruptible customers, reducing voltage and preparing to institute rotating blackouts. PP&L requested reductions from its interruptible customers at 5:06 a.m., picking up about 170,000 kilowatts, and the total interconnection reduced demand another 800,000 kilowatts at 6:45 a.m., when it began cutting voltage by five percent. At 7 a.m., PJM called upon its members for further voluntary power use reductions, and five minutes later, the power pool began rotating power outages to balance demand with supply.

PP&L complied with the PJM request, blacking out 23,000 customers between 7:05 and 7:41 a.m. The company began broadcasting appeals to customers to conserve power until further notice. "The cold is taking its toll," John F. Sipics, the company's manager of System Operation, reported early that morning, "raising demand to record levels and hampering our ability to produce electricity. It is extremely important for customers to restrict their electricity use to essential services so we can continue to keep the homes and businesses of our region warm.

"Please turn off all unnecessary lights, appliances, televisions and electrical equipment. Put off using dishwashers, washing machines and dryers until we notify you that electricity supplies have returned closer to normal levels."

From Bad to Worse

Things went from bad to worse by mid-morning. After stopping the rotating blackouts at 7:41 a.m., power dispatchers breathed a sigh of relief, thinking that the crisis might be over. But a surge of demand just after 9 a.m. precipitated the biggest crisis of the day. Between 9:22 a.m. and 1:08 p.m., more than 250,000 PP&L customers were affected by rotating blackouts of anywhere from 10 minutes to half an hour. At noon, Pennsylvania Lt. Gov. Mark Singel announced a state disaster emergency and urged Pennsylvanians to practice voluntary electric conservation measures. Singel also asked businesses and other commercial operations to close until the crisis had passed.

As it was, the crisis passed during the day on Wednesday. PP&L's Wednesday peak came between 5 and 6 p.m., and it was less than 6,000 megawatts—about five percent less than the all-time record peak set the evening before.

PJM lifted voltage reductions Wednesday evening as customers in the Mid-Atlantic region

Frozen coal turned into black ice at Montour SES. *circa 1994*

heeded warnings and cut back electricity use dramatically. PP&L got a scare in the early hours of Thursday, January 20, when Unit Two at Susquehanna shut down because of high temperature readings in the generator cooling water system. By that time, however, the crisis had passed as temperatures began to warm up across the region. PJM lifted its call for voluntary power reductions on Friday morning, and when the Friday afternoon peak period passed, PP&L and the power pool were out of the woods at last.

Taken for Granted

Ironically, the media, government agencies and other pundits—many of whom had fought PP&L and its fellow utilities over transmission line routings that would have strengthened the pool in times of supply shortage—chastised the power companies for their response to the crisis. "We have all taken for granted that the lights will stay on," Pennsylvania Public Utility Commissioner Lisa Crutchfield said. "The situation in January 1994 should cause us all to realize that this is something that we cannot always take for granted."

Writer David W. Kirkpatrick made the intriguing observation from Harrisburg that "the electric utilities should be commended for their conduct in January, rather than criticized. The crisis was met, no one suffered any lengthy or damaging loss of power, and it is not likely that their critics could have done any better, even with hindsight."

For his part, Bill Hecht was proud of his colleagues at PP&L, many of whom braved icy roads, long hours and tough working conditions to limit the blackouts to a few hours on Wednesday. "It is my privilege to work with people who care about serving the customer as much as PP&L people do," Hecht said the week following the crisis. "You proved your dedication again last week—in a big way."

Restructuring for the Future

Service Improvement throuGH Teamwork (SIGHT) was developed as part of PP&L's 1994 restructuring initiative. Here, Crelia Anoia works with other members of the SIGHT team.

Employee Forum 92

Strategies for the Future
OCTOBER 22, 1992

PP&L President Bill Hecht understood that the key to restructuring included communicating change to employees and other interested stakeholders. With that in mind, Employee Forum was organized.

In 1994, PP&L accelerated the process of reinventing itself as a more customer-focused, more productive and more competitive company.

The Allentown utility took three significant steps during 1994 to prepare itself for the future. It restructured the top levels of its organization and set in motion a reengineering process for the rest of the company. It formed a new subsidiary to invest in energy projects outside its central eastern Pennsylvania service territory. In an effort to ensure that the company can continue

Robert D. Fagan heads PMDC.

to provide top-quality service to its customers, PP&L filed a rate increase request with the Pennsylvania Public Utility Commission—the first such request in a decade.

"For the long term, the most significant thing that we accomplished during 1994 was restructuring the top levels of the company," explained Bill Hecht, PP&L's chairman, president and CEO. "This is significant because top-level changes are the beginning of a process that will entirely revamp the way we provide service to customers."

Hecht realized in 1993 that the business he had made his life's work was no longer the industry he had come to know over 30 years of experience. "For years," he said, "the power business and the utility business were one and the same. But in the future, the utility business will definitely only be a part of the power business. Increasingly, the non-utility business will encompass generation."

Hecht made the decision that PP&L would be in the power business and would take advantage of the unregulated generation sector of the business. Accordingly, the company formed Power Markets Development Co., an unregulated subsidiary that will invest in electric facilities outside its service area. To get the new subsidiary started, PP&L invested $50 million from company profits. No rate payer dollars were spent to support the new subsidiary, which is headed by Schuylkill County native Robert D. Fagan, formerly an executive with Mission Energy Co.

Instead of setting up Power Markets Development Co. as a subsidiary of PP&L, the company announced in 1994 that it would form a holding company to serve as parent of the two subsidiaries. Power Markets Development Co. would be a sister company of the utility, an important distinction.

"We thought real hard about diversification," Hecht said. "For one thing, you want to be in a business you know something about. We're not interested in diversification for diversification's sake. And number two, you have to be realistic about the skills of your personnel in-house. You have to be willing to go outside and get really top-flight talent for areas you haven't been involved in before."

Increasing Rates, Cutting Costs

Hecht was quick to add that it isn't PP&L's intent to grow the diversification business to the point that the traditional utility business becomes less important. "We've still got more than $7 billion in operating assets."

The decision to increase rates was particularly difficult, Hecht said, but could no longer be avoided. In a sense, the increase in rates, the first in 10 years, was part of the company's commitment to its core business. PP&L experienced significant increases in costs to provide service to its 1.2 million customers. While internal cost-cutting measures helped to control costs in the early 1990s, they weren't able to offset cost increases completely.

On Dec. 30, 1994, PP&L asked the Pennsylvania Public Utility Commission to approve an increase of $261 million, or 11.7 percent of its base rates. PP&L's last base rate increase came in 1985. "Our record on rate stability is one few utilities can match," Hecht said early in 1995. "And we have reduced rates in the past to give customers the benefit of certain non-recurring cost savings. We will continue to cut costs, improve efficiency and make every effort to keep the rates as stable as possible."

Cutting costs had become a way of life at PP&L in the 1990s. One ongoing initiative is a reduction in the number of full-time employees. PP&L's work force decreased from 8,150 at the beginning of the decade to about 6,950 at the beginning of 1995. "We expect continued staffing level reductions as we streamline and reorganize our work force," Hecht explained. "We hope to continue the reduction through attrition, but we cannot rule out layoffs as a possibility in the future."

Late in 1994, an early retirement package was offered to employees 55 years of age or older. Of the nearly 850 people eligible for the package, 640 (75 percent) accepted early retirement.

The early retirement program illustrated the sometimes painful choices that utilities have been forced to make in the new competitive era. Late in January 1995, PP&L reported earnings of $1.41 per share of common stock for 1994, down about 32 percent from the $2.07 per common share reported by the company for the comparable period in 1993.

Substantially all of the reduction was traceable to one-time charges, including two major charges in the fourth quarter—a $43 million after-tax charge against net income for the voluntary early retirement program and a $40 million after-tax charge against net income related to a reevaluation of the book value of coal reserves held by a PP&L subsidiary. The two after-tax charges reduced 1994 earnings by a total of 54 cents per share of common stock.

"As we prepare for increased competition, we're making tough management decisions now that will help us in the long run," explained Ronald E. Hill, senior vice president—Financial. "These one-time charges are behind us now, allowing us to continue to move forward to be successful in the industry's new competitive atmosphere."

Hill noted that the utility had "very strong sales growth during 1994. We're especially encouraged by the increase in industrial sales, a strong sign of regional economic health." Overall sales to service area customers rose 4.1 percent, while industrial sales jumped 4.8 percent during 1994.

The early retirements were projected to save PP&L about $35 million per year in operating expenses, and as such, the program was forecast to "pay for itself" in about two years, Hill said. "The early retirement program is the most visible component to customers of our aggressive internal actions to prepare for change in our business, and to reduce our costs before having to ask customers to pay more for their electric service."

The Tip of the Iceberg

The most visible outcome of PP&L's restructuring program is the early retirement package, but Bill Hecht noted that there are "other things going on beneath the surface. And we've got to become dramatically more efficient in the utility business."

To that end, PP&L unveiled a new top-level structure for the Allentown utility in October 1994. "This new organization prepares PP&L for the more competitive future of the electric utility industry," Hecht said at the time. "The new structure is geared to providing high-quality, consistent and cost-competitive services to our customers."

A key component of the realignment was a functional approach to serving customers in PP&L's 29-county service area. The new organization replaced the company's five geographic operating divisions with three new departments— Electrical Systems, Customer Services and Marketing and Economic Development— all based on service provided to customers.

The geographical development of the PP&L system had followed the ridge and valley topography of central and eastern Pennsylvania, going back to the 19th century. When the PP&L system was put together in the 1920s, the technological improvements in long-distance, high-voltage transmission dictated that the company's operating structure follow geographic constraints.

"Systems that originally did not lend themselves to consolidation now do," Hecht explained, noting that the completion of the interstate highway system and the development of new communications

Ronald E. Hill, PP&L's senior vice president— Financial.

On Dec. 30, 1994, PP&L asked the Pennsylvania Public Utility Commission to approve an increase of $261 million, or 11.7 percent of its base rates. PP&L's last base rate increase came in 1985.

Bill Hecht as executive vice president in 1990.

technology have created opportunities for consolidation where none existed before.

"We had five operating divisions, each with marketing, operations, distribution, etc.," Hecht said. "We should have one distribution department, one marketing department. And when we have customer service concerns, the telephone may as well be picked up here in Allentown."

The functional rather than geographic organization of Division Operations will inevitably lead to more changes, Hecht said. PP&L serves several industry segments as part of its large industrial power customer base, including the iron, steel and pulp and paper industries. In the past, division marketing personnel dealt with those customers in their areas. "Why don't I have one marketing team learn the steel industry?" Hecht said. "And another one can learn the pulp and paper industry, and so on."

While the Division

The most visible outcome of PP&L's restructuring program is the early retirement package, but Bill Hecht noted that there are "other things going on beneath the surface."

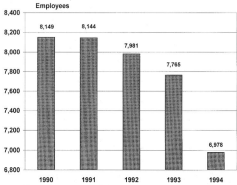

PP&L Employment Levels

Employees

Year	Employees
1990	8,149
1991	8,144
1992	7,981
1993	7,765
1994	6,978

Staff reductions like the early retirement program were projected to save PP&L about $35 million a year in operating expenses.

Operations changes were by far the most dramatic announced during the October 1994 restructuring, other changes were also announced at the same time.

A Mobile Work Force also was created, partly as a result of the new functional organization for Division Operations. In the past, construction workers had traveled from plant to plant, except that since nuclear work requires special training and skills, certain construction workers at Susquehanna generally stayed put. PP&L found itself often asking for volunteers on the fossil side of the business, and it discovered that the Distribution Department wasn't as mobile as it should be.

"It was another opportunity for us," Hecht said. "We decided we could take some of the construction people at Susquehanna and move them over to the Nuclear Department, all in an effort to eliminate duplication. Then we decided to create a mobile work force of the remainder of the construction workers."

Another initiative conceived as part of PP&L's restructuring was Service Improvement throuGH Teamwork (SIGHT). The company's SIGHT team presented its initial findings to top company and union officials in September 1994. A main feature of the recommendations noted that processes revolve around customers and focus on functions, not geography. SIGHT reported that PP&L can provide improved customer service with fewer people.

"There are some dramatic new initiatives in the information technology area that are now being developed by the SIGHT team," Hecht explained. "Their effort recognized early on how to design in parallel all the work processes that get services to our customers. In addition, we established the Nuclear Information Management System (NIMS) that is looking at record-keeping and how we develop formal work procedures on the nuclear side. Another initiative deals with the fossil plants along the same lines."

Another endeavor with a critical role to play during the 1994 restructuring was the Continuous Performance Improvement Process. Known inside the company by the acronym CPIP, the group put together teams of union and management employees and challenged them to identify opportunities to make the five fossil-fuel plants more competitive. Their suggestions and recommendations, most of which focus on reducing the cost of generation at each facility, will become blueprints for the future at each operation.

Anxiety and Consternation

Restructuring Pennsylvania Power & Light Co. from a geographically organized traditional electric utility in a natural monopoly environment to a functionally organized electric power supplier in a competitive environment won't happen overnight; and it won't happen without some element of upheaval. Moving the company from a staffing level of 8,150 at the beginning of the decade to 6,950 people four years later is in itself a real upheaval. But company management flatly predicts that staffing levels will be driven by reengineered work processes to somewhere between 6,000 and 6,500 people between 1995 and 1998. "All of this creates a fair amount of anxiety and consternation," Bill Hecht observed. "All of this means we have to plow new ground in human resources, essentially conducting a program in change management."

Key to that program is communicating change to employees and other interested stakeholders. PP&L has always been fairly adept at communicating change, dating back to the 1970s when Jack Busby took Operation Understanding on the road to explain to PP&L's constituencies what the company was doing in the face of energy shortfalls and rising rates. In the 1980s, Bob Campbell instituted the annual Manager's Conference, a yearly gathering of managers from around the system to hear top management give a state-of-the-company address.

"This past year, we expanded that as an Employee Forum," Hecht explained.

"We put together a vertical and horizontal cross-section of the organization—almost 1,000 people—and had a panel discussion of six employees selected at random."

The Employee Forum at the Kirby Center in Wilkes-Barre included nearly 40 questions from the six panelists and those in the audience. The majority of the questions, not all of them friendly, revolved around employee reduction and job security. "It was all designed as another piece of the communications effort that needs to go along with the restructuring if we're going to make it work," Hecht said in describing the forum.

A Fundamental Shift

Finally, the restructuring of Pennsylvania Power & Light Co. implies a fundamental shift in the company's financial strategies. In a regulatory environment, a

"There are some dramatic new initiatives in the information technology area that are now being developed by the SIGHT team," Hecht explained. "Their effort recognized early on how to design in parallel all the work processes that get services to our customers."

Andrew W. Gotwols, a station mechanic-electrical at Holtwood, and a member of the Market Price Clearing Team, which used CPIP principles to do its job. *circa 1990s*

PP&L's 1994 Employee Forum at the Kirby Center in Wilkes-Barre.

utility's finances are characterized by a high debt-to-equity ratio, high dividend payout ratio and long depreciation times.

"All of those things are called into question to the extent that we're unregulated," Hecht said, adding that PP&L has formulated financial strategies designed to grow earnings to decrease the dividend payout ratio and to increase equity. The 1994 charge against earnings for the early retirement program, the write-off of the coal properties and the rate increase filing were all designed to prepare the company financially for a nonregulated future. Other strategies call for decreasing depreciation times on some of the company's older fossil-fuel plants and recovering some regulated assets. "You can't charge tomorrow's customers in a non-regulated world," Hecht said.

Pennsylvania Power & Light Co.'s restructuring program was put into place on Nov. 1, 1994. "We worked restructuring down through the organization, hand-in-glove with the early retirement program," Hecht said. "We now anticipate continuous improvement as restructuring works its way downward. But there's a lot beneath the surface of this iceberg."

Change is hardly a stranger at PP&L. For 75 years in its present form—and decades before that for its predecessors—PP&L faced almost constant change. That change required both guts and grit. "I think there was a tremendous amount of courage that our predecessors showed," Hecht said. "They had real guts. The people who negotiated the early interconnection agreements had to have real guts. Tremendous guts. The people who did the financing for Susquehanna. Talk about real guts...."

Whether or not future generations look back upon 1994 and 1995 and decide that those who helped restructure PP&L showed real guts, it is certain they will agree that change came fast and furious for PP&Lers during those two years. "You know," Bill Hecht concluded, "we probably changed as much in 1994 as we did in any other single year of our previous history."

Bill Hecht:
Planning for the Future

Change and the future are synonymous, and William F. Hecht has been dealing with that reality for most of his 30-plus years at Pennsylvania Power & Light Co. PP&L's chairman, president and CEO since Jan. 1, 1993, Hecht is presiding over some of the most momentous changes in the company's 75-year-long history.

A native of Long Island, Hecht came to the Lehigh Valley for the first time to attend school at Lehigh University. "I finished my bachelor's degree in electrical engineering and came to work for PP&L and finished a master's degree in electrical engineering part-time."

Hecht's first job with PP&L in 1964 was as a graduate engineer trainee. After various engineering assignments in the company's System Planning and Lines and Substations departments, he was named manager of Distribution Planning in 1975. During those early years with the company, Hecht recalled being fascinated by the utility's generation of 25-cycle power.

"It was 25-cycle generation at Hauto and a 25-cycle circuit from Hauto all the way down into Bethlehem, to Bethlehem Steel," he said. "They took 25-cycle at three points—one with Hauto, another with a frequency changer at Freemansburg, which we owned at that time, and a third location was a frequency changer at a substation called Converter, which, for obvious reasons, they owned."

Growing Pains

Hecht also recalled that PP&L in 1964 was still experiencing some growing pains. As a graduate engineer trainee, he was exposed to multiple facets of the

William "Bill" F. Hecht, PP&L's chairman, president and CEO since Jan. 1, 1993.

company's business, working with a Williamsport line crew and a Scranton marketing operation, among others. When the 30-week training period was over, he was assigned to Holtwood as a plant engineer. "So after my last day of orientation," he recalled, "they gave me a $50 cash advance, which was supposed to last me a week, showed me how to fill out a petty cash voucher and gave me a road map and a list of places to go."

Another great difference between 1964 and the present is the change in the spatial relationship to the rest of Pennsylvania. "The transportation system in eastern Pennsylvania was not a shadow of what it is now," Hecht noted. "Interstate 80 was under construction. Pieces of it were beginning to open. When I worked in Williamsport, it was a three to three-and-a-half hour drive from Allentown. It was a long haul. And a tiring drive. So if you wanted to put in a day's work in Williamsport, you stayed overnight."

The Inevitability of Change

From 1976 to 1978, Hecht served as executive director of PP&L's Corporate Energy Planning Council and then spent five years as manager of System Planning. Because of the decade-long energy crisis and the huge nuclear construction program, Hecht got involved heavily in PP&L's conservation efforts. He can recall being awed by Jack Busby's management style.

In the latter 1970s, intervenors were constantly trying to get PP&L to abandon Susquehanna or convert it to a coal-fired unit. "They bought a share of stock and showed up at the shareowners meeting with a motion that we cancel Unit Two or convert it to coal," Hecht

said. "Nobody would second the motion. And Jack Busby seconded the motion so that the shareowners could vote on it—rather than to let it die without a second. And it blew my mind when he did that. He was the only guy who could have pulled that off. He was that kind of person."

Bill Hecht began his career at PP&L as a graduate engineer trainee in 1964. In 1975, he was named manager of Distribution Planning. In the '80s, he served as vice president of Marketing and Customer Services, vice president of Power Production and Engineering and senior vice president of System Power and Engineering.

From energy conservation in the 1970s and early 1980s, Hecht got his baptism by fire in Marketing and Customer Services in the 1980s. Named vice president of System Power in 1983, he also served as vice president of Marketing and Customer Services

Bill Hecht in Corporate Energy Planning Council where he served as executive director from 1976 to 1978.

ment effective Jan. 1, 1993, Hecht was tapped to succeed him as chairman, president and CEO following a lengthy process in which more than 20 candidates were assessed for their suitability for the job. Hecht, who works 9-1/2 hours a day, and sometimes through the weekend, was philosophical about the competition. "I think I can make a real contribution to PP&L," he told the *Philadelphia Inquirer* in the summer of 1992, "and I appreciate the opportunity to do that. At the same time, I would have continued to do a strong job, even if I weren't the successful candidate."

Hecht can get even more philosophical when talk turns to change and the impact change will have on the PP&L of the future. "Change is the standard," he said. "And we've been undergoing

"Our responsibility is to manage the business for the future as well as our predecessors managed it for us. And that means anticipating change and being involved in it."—William F. Hecht

and vice president of Power Production and Engineering before being named senior vice president of System Power and Engineering in 1989. At that time, he was appointed to the company's Corporate Management Committee (CMC). The following year, Hecht was named executive vice president—Operations and elected to PP&L's board of directors.

When John Kauffman announced his retire-

radical change throughout our whole history. The reason for our success today is the foresight of the people who came before us, who managed change. They weren't just keeping the store, if you will. It wasn't a momentum kind of management. Our responsibility is to manage the business for the future as well as our predecessors managed it for us. And that means anticipating change and being involved in it."

Thanks for the Memories

L iterally hundreds of PP&L employees, retirees and friends contributed memories and memorabilia to the successful completion of *PP&L: 75 Years of Powering the Future*. It might be an almost impossible task to recognize everybody in print, but here's at least an honest attempt.

75th Anniversary Committee

Chris Allen	John Biggar	Bob Compton	Dorothy Eyer	Roger Gilbert
Bob Gombos	Mike Kroboth	Jim Marsh	LoisAnn Oakes	Janice Osborne
Donald Simmons	Bernie Steber	John Trimble	Paul Wirth	

Bob Compton's Interviews

Austin Gavin
   As gracious as ever, Austin provided a wealth of information.

Merlin F. Hertzog
   Merl made the best cup of coffee I had during this project and surprised me with the breadth of jobs he held before becoming a senior vice president.

William F. Greenwald
   Bill is a Lehigh Valley financial executive who offered recollections of Chas. Oakes.

Ruth V. Ruppert
   Ruth is a PP&Ler who was interviewed to get a local employee's outlook on the Three Mile Island incident in 1979.

James K. Anderson
   Jim is an oil wildcatter from whom we sought information on Chas. Oakes.

Robert A. Patterson
   Bob knew Chas. Oakes from the standpoint of Pennsylvania State University, where Oakes was a board member.

Charles E. Hartman
   "Wash" was a safety man in Lancaster with many recollections of Construction Department activities in the area.

Frederick W. Kuehn
   Fred is a courtly gentleman who offered recollections of PP&L from an engineer's standpoint.

Brooke R. Hartman Sr.
   Brooke filled a tape with a clear, accurate description of the operation of the Financial Department in the 1950s, 1960s and 1970s.

Edwin H. Seidler
   "Down to earth" and "practical" were the two adjectives I thought of first when Ed worked in the Tower Building. They are still descriptive phrases, and he was a very good source of information on the Construction Department.

Leon L. Nonemaker
   Possibly the most knowledgeable of our interviewees, Lee came to the interview very well-prepared, and he surprised me with the wealth of experiences he had as a a young engineer before he became "Mr. Nonemaker."

Brentwood S. Shunk
   Brent was known to most as "the Lancaster vice president," but his experience ranged back to Pine Grove SES and covered a surprising number of jobs.

George F. Vanderslice
   George has a way of making the financial side of the company understandable.

Norman W. Curtis
   Norm gave us invaluable information about the building of Susquehanna SES.

Lois E. Eaton
   Lois is a second-generation employee who offered a good glimpse into life in the Williamsport area— both in her own time and in that of her father.

James W. Geiling
   Jim had one of the most varied careers in PP&L, holding jobs ranging from Suburban SES to his unusual stint as Susquehanna SES superintendent where there was no Susquehanna SES.

Norman M. Snyder
   "Mo" Snyder is one of those rare people who started working at PP&L before he was 16 years old and still remembers most of what went on during that period.

Grace J.M. Raker
   Grace was a gold mine of information on the life of PP&L's former home economists.

Donald E. Cummings
   Don is a former Air Products employee from whom we sought information and insights on Chas. Oakes.

Kenneth S. Boyer
   An ex-elevator operator, Ken not only offered good insights into everyday life in the Tower, but he also suggested a number of other potential interviewees.

Edward F. Reis
   I talked with Ed on his last day in the office. He surprised me with his detailed recollections of life in the Fuels Department.

Jack W. Thomas
   Jack is the only fourth-generation employee I've ever met. His interview contributed some sobering thoughts about safety in the old days.
Robert R. Fortune
   Norm Curtis and George Vanderslice told me that no story about Susquehanna SES would be complete without a recounting of Bob Fortune's role. They were absolutely right.
Robert T. Schnitzer
   Bob is a recent retiree with a remarkable range of jobs under his belt. He's the only person I know who worked on the reconstruction of the Wallenpaupack flow line.
Alice M. Schumacher and Judith J. Lynch
   Alice and Judy are employees who worked as switchboard operators in the old "wire-board" days.
J. Ford Fritzinger
   Ford is a retiree with a keen memory, who provided an interesting look at life and work at the old Hauto Steam Electric Station.

Barry L. Dorshimer
   Barry is an employee in drafting, with a work history that includes Martins Creek SES and a stint as an elevator operator in the Tower Building.
Fred J. "Fritz" Kemmerer Jr.
   Fritz, a retiree, worked the longest stint as a manual elevator operator in the Tower, but he had a varied work history both before and after that post.
Harley L. Collins
   Harley's wide-ranging experience and detailed recall for events provided an exceptionally interesting interview.
Royal W. Kramer
   A recent retiree, Roy provided an astonishingly detailed recollection of his father's career as a substation operator for PP&L.

Contributions and Such

Literally dozens of people responded to our call for donations of documents, material and memorabilia. It seems proper at this point to single out the following employees and retirees for their exceptional—and voluntary—contributions to the project:

Joseph G. Bauer—photographs and memorabilia
Robert H. Bielecki—photographs
Richard P. Bloch—assistance and memorabilia
Sharon L. Bostic—photographs
AnnaMarie Ehritz—assistance and historical printed materials
Thomas O. Fellin—photographs
Austin Gavin—historical printed material
James W. Geiling—historical printed material
Roger W. Gilbert—historical printed material
Thomas W. Grim—research
Allan J. Holtz—assistance and photographs
Raymond H. Holst—assistance, photographs and historical printed materials
Susan G. Jones—photographs and loan of antique cookie cutter depicting the Tower Building

Andrew P. Kelhart—historical printed materials
Robert F. Lehman—photographs and memorabilia
Wilma H. Lucente—assistance and historical printed materials
Nadine B. Podany—historical printed material
Edward F. Reis—historical printed material
Robert J. Rishel—historical printed material
Dorothy M. Sagat—assistance, recollections and photographs
Charles W. Sandel—photographs
Donald L. Simmons—historical printed material
Anthony N. Tier—photographs
Patricia A. Unser—historical printed materials
Kenneth L. Williams—photographs
Ralph W. Younger—historical printed material

Outside the immediate PP&L family, those notable for contributing more information and assistance than was asked for include: LoisAnn Oakes, daughter of former President Chas. Oakes; Michael Nash, Christopher Baer and Marjorie McNinch of the Hagley Library in Wilmington, Del.; Doug Tarr, archivist at the Edison National Historic Site, West Orange, N.J.; Linda Aston of the James V. Brown Library in Williamsport, Pa.; Mary Orwig in the geneaological section of the Lycoming County Historical Society in Williamsport, Pa.; Susan Lindman and Linda Shopes of the Pennsylvania Historical and Museum Commission in Harrisburg, Pa.; Russell J. Christesen, chairman emeritus of EBASCO, New York City, N.Y.; Frank Whelan and friends from the *Morning Call* in Allentown, Pa.; Michael Kneis and Lance Metz of the Hugh Moore Historical Park and Museums in Easton, Pa.; Maureen Mullin of the Cleveland Public Library in Cleveland, Ohio; John Mies, public relations manager at Mack Trucks, Inc., in Allentown, Pa.; June Griffiths, librarian/archivist at the Lehigh County Historical Society in Allentown, Pa.; Irene Coffey of the Franklin Institute in Philadelphia, Pa.; and many others.

Bill Beck
Indianapolis, Indiana

Bob Compton
Allentown, Pennsylvania

Index